Judah
Israel
Edom
Esau
Jacob
Ishmael
Midian
Nahor
Serug
Peleg
PERSIA
NINEVEH
Elam
Elisa
Tarshish
Chittim
Dodanim
Shem
Japheth
Noah

ANCIENT HISTORY,

ILLUSTRATED BY COLORED

MAPS, AND A CHRONOLOGICAL CHART,

FOR THE USE OF

FAMILIES AND SCHOOLS.

BY C. A. BLOSS.

"Geography and Chronology are the two eyes of History."

REVISED AND IMPROVED BY

JOHN J. ANDERSON, A. M.,

AUTHOR OF A SERIES OF SCHOOL HISTORIES OF THE UNITED STATES.

NEW YORK:

CLARK & MAYNARD, PUBLISHERS,

5 BARCLAY STREET.

1867.

PUBLISHERS' NOTICE.

THE work, of which the present one is a revision, was originally prepared several years since, and was soon used with great satisfaction in some of the best educational institutions in the State of New York. In consequence of the death of its accomplished author, the work (not being stereotyped) passed out of print after two large editions had become exhausted. At the suggestion of several eminent educators, who were anxious to have it for use in the institutions under their own charge, the present edition has been published.

Its preparation was committed to Mr. JOHN J. ANDERSON, whose long experience as a teacher, and whose peculiar fitness for writing history for use in schools, as had been shown by the great favor with which his series of School Histories of the United States had been received, indicated him as eminently qualified for the task. His work has been chiefly confined to dividing the matter into convenient paragraphs, with suitable questions upon each, and the addition of a valuable series of review questions, placed after each principal division. He has left the body of the work as the author wrote it, with very slight exceptions. Indeed, one of its essential characteristics is the author's singular felicity of expression, combined with great brevity and clearness of statement. These and other qualities have rendered it exceedingly attractive—interesting, while instructing the pupil, and making the study of ancient history, usually so dry, pleasant and agreeable to the young.

NEW YORK, *Sept.*, 1867.

PREFACE.

The science of Ancient History, though universally considered essential to a finished education, is still very imperfectly taught in our schools. The difficulty of combining the interest of a consecutive narrative with an intelligent view of cotemporaneous events has proved a serious embarrassment to writers and teachers; while students, lost in the dim regions of the past, confused with a multiplicity of characters, to which they were unable to attach any definite idea, have thrown down their text-books in despair, and turned their attention to some more alluring study.

This state of things must exist so long as teachers attempt to store the minds of their pupils with *facts* unconnected by the two strong associations of *time* and *place*.

The present work has been compiled from standard authors, and submitted to the criticism of distinguished individuals, by whom it has been warmly commended. It combines the features, to a large extent, which have made Anderson's series of United States Histories so successful in the many schools throughout the country in which they are used; and, having already passed the test of experience, the work, it is believed, will prove such a combination of the chronological and ethnographical methods as shall make Ancient History one of the most agreeable and useful branches of education.

TO TEACHERS.

GENERAL PLAN OF THE WORK, AND DIRECTIONS FOR USING THE CHART.

It is the plan of this work to consider the history of the world as divided into periods of one thousand years each, four of which expired before the commencement of the Christian era. These periods are called millenniums.

The book comprises the histories of Assyria, Egypt, Persia, Greece, the four kingdoms formed from the empire of Alexander, and Rome. Assyria, Persia, Greece, and Rome were the four "Universal Monarchies;" but as Egypt, owing to the extraordinary fertility and early civilization, was the parent of the arts and sciences, and the great fountain of heathen mythology, its history is introduced in the order of chronology.

The Sacred Scriptures are the only record from which we derive our knowledge of the events which transpired before the Flood, so that the first two millenniums contain only very brief accounts of the Creation, the fall of man, the expulsion from Eden, the genealogy of the antediluvian patriarchs, their deaths, the wickedness of the world, and its consequent destruction by the deluge, and the various settlements made in Asia, Africa, and Europe by the descendants of Noah.

By consulting the Genealogical Tree, inserted at the beginning of the book, it will be seen that the children of Japheth peopled Europe, and those of Shem and Ham, Asia and Africa. From the plain of the Euphrates, the "Land of Shinar," where the "children of men began to build a city and a tower," were the tribes of the earth scattered abroad; from Nineveh and Babylon, the most ancient cities, the course of empire took its way in a westerly direction, the scepter of universal rule being transferred successively from the Assyrians to the Persians, from the Persians to the Greeks, and from the Greeks to the Romans.

It is certain that no satisfactory knowledge of history can be acquired unless its chronology and geography are well understood. A free and systematic use of the Chronological Chart and Maps is therefore especially recommended. A class consisting of ten pupils might represent a millennium, each pupil naming from the chart the principal events of one century. Let this exercise take place preliminary to the recitation of every lesson. The uniform flow of time will thus be clearly presented, and cotemporaneous events fixed indelibly upon the memory. Beside a systematic use of the chart, such as is here suggested, a variety of questions could be asked, which, in answering from the chart, would convey to the mind of the learner, in the readiest manner, facts of a comprehensive character.

Take these, for example:

How long was it from Adam to Noah? Adam to Abraham? Adam to Solomon? Noah to Abraham? Noah to Solomon? Noah to the Christian era? From the Creation to the Flood? What was the most important event in —— millennium? Which millennium contained the most important events? Why? At what time did the history of Greece commence? What was the duration of the Roman Empire? &c., &c.

An alphabetical list of the names of individuals and places *pronounced* will be found in the closing pages of this work, and it is proposed that the teacher require the scholar, as an exercise in composition, to write a biography of every important character, and a history of every important place.

CONTENTS.

SECTION—		PAGE
I.	ASSYRIA	7
II.	EGYPT	16
III.	PERSIA	32
IV.	GREECE	87
"	(MACEDONIA)	223
V.	THRACE	289
VI.	EGYPT	297
VII.	ROME	314
VIII.	THE CHRISTIAN ERA	404

MAPS.

	PAGE
No. 1. MAP OF EUROPE, ASIA, AND AFRICA AS KNOWN TO THE ANCIENTS	7
" 2. MAP OF GREECE	87
" 3. MAP OF ALEXANDER'S TRAVELS	243
" 4. MAP OF ITALIA	314

☞ INDEX AT THE END OF THE VOLUME.

ASSYRIA.

SECTION I.

1. THE history of the First Assyrian Empire is comprised within a period of 1450 years; that of the Second, within a period of 210 years; so that Assyria, commencing about 2200 B. C., and ending 538 B. C., occupies nearly two Millenniums. In the year of the World, 1656 the Deluge destroyed all the inhabitants of the earth except Noah and his family, and the creatures with them in the ark. The earth lay in its shroud of waters one year, according to our computation, and when the flood subsided, the ark rested upon Mount Ararat, in Armenia; and Noah, with his wife, his three sons, Shem, Ham, and Japheth, and their wives, came forth to take possession of the New World.

2. It is supposed that Noah migrated to the East, and founded the Empire of China, as the Chinese dates agree thereto, and no mention is made of him in Scripture, though he lived 350 years after this event. Nor have we any record of the wanderings of his sons and their descendants till about 100 years after the flood, when we find them engaged in an attempt to settle on the banks of the Euphrates, around a city and a tower which they united in building, of the bituminous earth with which that country abounds. Their design was frustrated by the confusion of tongues, and thence "they were scattered abroad upon the face of all the earth: and they left off to build the city." This city was called Babel; and from this place as a point, the migrations and settlements of the different tribes radiated. "Out of that land went forth Asshur and builded Nineveh;" Misraim, with his adherents, found his way to Egypt; Canaan settled Phenicia, on the eastern coast of the Mediterranean; the descendants of Javan migrated to Greece; and from Ur of the Chaldees, 200 years later, Abram was called to possess the Land of Promise.

Read Gen. vi. 13; also vii. and viii. entire; xi. 1-10. For settlements of Japheth, read x. 5. For Assyria, see Gen. x. 8-10. Egypt, Gen. x. 13.

ASSYRIA.—*Questions.*—1. How many Assyrian empires were there? What was the duration of each? When did the Deluge occur? What did it effect? How long was the earth under the water? Where did the ark then rest? Name those who were saved in the ark. (See Ark, map No. 1; also Armenia, map No. 3.) 2. What further account can you give of Noah? What took place about a hundred years after the flood? Describe the Euphrates. (See map 1.) What further account can you give of the design "to build a city and a tower?" What was the city then called? Where was it located? (See map No. 1.) What can you state of Asshur? Of Misraim? Canaan? Javan's descendants? Abram?

3. B. C. **2200.**—The first kingdom of which we have any account was Assyria, founded by Asshur, son of Shem. Nimrod, the grandson of Ham, not long after, distinguished himself as a "mighty hunter," and from subduing the beasts of the field, came to be leader of a tribe which fixed their head-quarters at Babel. The abandoned city was repeopled, the ancient tower was converted into the fane of Belus, and soon this city, Babylon, rivaled Nineveh in its extent and beauty. (Here occurs a chasm of great length in the history of Assyria.)

Read Gen. x. 11, for Nineveh. Gen. x. 9, 10, for Nimrod and Babylon.

4. B. C. **1300.**—Ninus claimed to be the son of the god Belus; but as such assumptions of divinity were common in those early ages, nothing can be determined as to his parentage. Ninus so much enlarged and beautified Nineveh, that he is styled its founder. This great city, situated upon the Tigris, was an oblong square, 60 miles in circumference; surrounded by walls 100 feet high, and so thick that three chariots might be driven abreast on the top of them. Upon the walls stood 1,500 towers, each 200 feet in height; and the whole was so strong as to bid defiance to all weapons of warfare then known. Ninus is said to have spent 17 years in conquest, and to have extended the bounds of his dominions over the whole of Middle Asia. In Bactria he would have suffered defeat, but for the counsel and conduct of Semiramis, wife of one of his officers. He married her after the death of her husband, but she could not be satisfied to rule the empire by influencing the emperor; she was determined to be absolute sovereign; and the doting Ninus having been persuaded to commit to her hands the government for five days, she contrived to attach the principal lords to her interest, and, procuring the death of her husband, possessed herself of the empire.

5. To immortalize her name, Semiramis employed 2,000,000 men in enlarging, fortifying, and beautifying Babylon. Its walls were not inferior to those of Nineveh; its whole area was divided into 676

Questions.—3. Why was Assyria so named? How extensive was Assyria? *Ans.* It extended from the Armenian mountains to the Persian Gulf, a distance of about 700 miles. What was its first city? Its second? Who transformed Babel into Babylon? *Ans.* Nimrod. How was the tower converted into the fane of Belus? *Ans.* It was used as a temple for idolatrous worship. How large was it? *Ans.* Half a mile in compass at the base, rising, by eight stories, to the height of 600 feet. Where was Nineveh? Babylon? (See map 1.) During the nine centuries which are wanting in the history of Assyria, settlements were being made in Greece and upon the whole seacoast of the Mediterranean and Egean, and the children of Israel were establishing themselves as a nation in Palestine. 4. What can you state of the assumption made by Ninus? What did he do? What can you state of the construction of Nineveh? Of the fate of Ninus? Where is the Tigris? Mention the Middle Asia from map 1. 5. By whom was Babylon improved? What object did Semiramis have in view? In what did the improvements consist?

squares by the streets, which crossed each other at right angles; these streets were terminated at each end by massive gates of brass, overlooked on each side by lofty towers; and the mighty river which rolled through the town, was inclosed with walls as strong as those which encompassed the city.

6. She visited every part of her dominions, and left in every place monuments of her greatness. The country was rough and uncultivated. She hollowed mountains, filled up valleys, built aqueducts, leveled roads, and converted the unbroken wilderness into fertile plains. She extended her dominions beyond Asia even. Ethiopia submitted to her arms, and in Africa she visited the temple of Jupiter Ammon, to inquire of the oracle how long she should live. She was answered, "Till her son conspired against her." On her return she undertook the conquest of India, but was signally defeated. Her son seized upon this occasion to alienate the affections of her people, and this coming to her knowledge, she resigned her dominions, and retired to a private station. The Assyrians worshiped her under the form of the white dove.

7. B. C. **1200.**—Ninyas, son of Ninus and Semiramis, having thus gained possession of the throne, gave himself up to a life of seclusion and pleasure. (Here occurs another chasm in the history of Assyria, during which it is supposed the empire was broken, or of very little consequence.)

B. C. **900.**—According to chronologers, Jonah preached to the inhabitants of Nineveh, 862 B. C., and by historians Pul is supposed to have been the king who averted the threatened judgment by repentance.

Read Jonah iii. entire, and iv. 11.

8. B. C. **800.**—Sardanapalus was the last king of the First Assyrian Empire. His vices and follies alone rescue his name from oblivion. A monument found by Alexander, in Cilicia, proves that he must have made an expedition to Western Asia; but the greatest part of his time was spent in his seraglio, spinning with the women, or imitating their habits of dress and conversation. His effeminate manners rendered him contemptible; and Arbaces, a Median governor, with Belesis, the most distinguished member of the Chaldean sacerdotal college, conspired against him, and collected a numerous force to dethrone him.

Questions.—6. What other improvements did Semiramis make? What conquests did she make? What further can you state of her? Trace Semiramis from Babylon to Ethiopia. To India. 7. Who was Ninyas? What can you state of his life? Of Jonah? Of Pul? 8. Who was the last king of the first Assyrian empire? What was his character? What conspiracy was formed against him? What then followed?

Sardanapalus quitted for a while his voluptuous retreat, and appeared at the head of his armies. He was beaten, and besieged in the city of Ninus two years. At last, finding all was lost, he erected a throne of his treasures, collected his women about him, and, having set fire to the palace, perished with them in the flames. Thus ended the First Assyrian Empire, 1450 years after its founding by Nimrod. The conspirators seized upon the government, and divided it between them, whence arose two kingdoms.

9. B. C. 747. THE ASSYRIANS OF NINEVEH RULED BY ARBACES.—Arbaces took up his residence at Nineveh, and reigned there under the name of Ninus the Younger. He is called in Scripture Tiglath-pileser. He took the city of Damascus, and put an end to the Syrian kingdom, which had long vexed the Jews, and he made Ahaz, king of Judah, pay dearly for being delivered from his troublesome neighbors.

Read 2 Kings xvi. 7–9. Isa. xvii. 1–3. Amos i. 3, 4.

10. THE BABYLONISH ASSYRIANS RULED BY BELESIS.—Belesis took up his residence at Babylon. With his reign began the famous era of Nabonassar, according to Berosus, in this manner: "Nabonassar, having collected the acts of his predecessors, destroyed them, in order that the computation of the reigns of the Chaldean kings might be made from himself." It began the year Feb. 26, 747 B. C.

11. B. C. 728.—THE TWO KINGDOMS REUNITED.—Salmanaser, son of Ninus II., besieged Samaria three years, and after the people had suffered every hardship, took the city and carried the inhabitants captive, 250 years after the revolt of Israel from Judah, 721 B. C.

B. C. 717. Sennacherib exacted a tribute of Hezekiah; and not content with "all the treasures of the house of the Lord, and of the king's house," invaded Judea with a large army. By his emissaries he insulted the already humbled Jews, and blasphemed against the

12. Prince Merodach Baladan sent to congratulate Hezekiah upon his recovery from sickness, and to inquire about the shadow's going back upon the dial of Ahaz, for the Chaldeans were great astronomers. They had records in their city of observations made 1500 years before, or about the time of the confusion of tongues. Of the succeeding kings of Babylon we

Questions.—8. What was his fate? How was the first Assyrian empire brought to a close? 9. What did Arbaces do? By what other names is he known? Where is Damascus? (See map No. 1.) 10. What can you state of Belesis? How did the reign of Nabonassar begin? 11. What did Salmanaser accomplish? What did Sennacherib do?

God of heaven; but Hezekiah spread his impious letter before the Lord, and received assurances of divine protection. That night the destroying angel was sent forth into the camp of the Assyrians, and 185,000 of Sennacherib's host slept the sleep of death. Filled with shame and rage, the impious king returned to Nineveh, where two of his own sons conspired against him and slew him. Then his son, Esarhaddon, reigned in his stead.

Read 2 Kings xviii. 13–20, and xix. 8–37. Also read 2 Kings xvii. 1–7. Lev. xxvi. 32, 33, and Deut. xxviii. 36.

know little, except their names.

Read 2 Kings xx. 11–15. Trace the embassadors from Babylon to Jerusalem.

13. B. C. **700.**—Esarhaddon, perceiving that Babylon was filled with anarchy, took advantage of the times to reduce it to its former subjection. Thus he reunited the Assyrian Empire, B. C. 680. He planted strangers in the land of Israel, who were the progenitors of the Samaritans. In his reign Manasseh was carried to Babylon, where he remained in captivity 12 years. In the days of King Nebuchadnezzar I. several tributary princes revolted, and he was involved in a war with the Medes.

Read 2 Kings xvii. 24, and Ez. iv. 2–10.

14. The monarch Saracus resembled Sardanapalus in his taste and pursuits. The general of his army, Nabopolassar, having the burden of state affairs to sustain, thought himself more worthy of the throne than his effeminate monarch. He accordingly formed an alliance with Cyaxares, king of Media, to dethrone the last of the race of Arbaces. With their joint forces they besieged Saracus in Nineveh, and finally gained possession of the place and slew the monarch. After this the glory of Nineveh faded, and Babylon, its ancient rival, became the most famous city in the world.

Read Nahum, chap. iii.

15. Nabopolassar the Chaldean, having thus acquired sovereign power, commenced a new dynasty, under which Assyria reached its greatest glory, and fell to rise no more. By his warlike exploits he

Questions.—11. How did his invasion of Judea end? What became of Sennacherib? Who was his successor? 12. What is said of the Chaldeans? What act did Merodach Baladan perform? 13. What did Esarhaddon accomplish? What is stated of Manasseh? Trace the strangers from Nineveh to Samaria. Nebuchadnezzar from Nineveh to Media. 14. Give an account of Saracus. When was he slain? *Ans.* 648 B. C. What is said of the subsequent history of Nineveh and Babylon? 15. What is said of Assyria under Nabopolassar?

roused the jealousy of all his neighbors. Necho, king of Egypt, marched to the Euphrates to stop his conquests, Syria and Palestine revolted, and he found himself in his old age surrounded by enemies. In this emergency he thought proper to invest his son Nebuchadnezzar with a share in the government. The young prince proved himself worthy of his father's confidence. He invaded Palestine, took Jehoiakim, and carried him captive to Babylon, with numerous young persons of the royal family, among whom were Daniel and the three children, Shadrach, Meshach, and Abednego. This event took place in the 4th year of Jehoiakim, B. C. 606.

Read 2 Kings xxiv. 47, and 2 Chron. xxxvi. 6, 7. Dan. i. 1, 2. Jer. xlvi. 2, 25, 26.

16. B. C. **600.**—In 599 Nebuchadnezzar fought a great battle with Necho, and entirely defeated him. In the beginning of his reign he had a remarkable dream, which, as interpreted by Daniel, contained the history of all succeeding ages. By his officers Jehoiachin was deposed, and Zedekiah placed upon the throne of David, but he also rebelled against the king of Babylon. Nebuchadnezzar went in person to punish the treachery of Zedekiah. He besieged Jerusalem two years, and when all the bread was spent in the city, the men of war attempted to flee by the way of the plain, but were captured by the hosts of Chaldea. The Holy and Beautiful house built by Solomon perished in the conflagration of the city, and all the precious things of the sanctuary, together with the king and his nobles, were carried to Babylon, B. C. 588.

Read 2 Kings xxiv. 10–20; xxv. 1–8. 2 Chr. xxxvi. 9–21. Jer. lii. 4–12.

17. TAKING OF TYRE.—Four years after, Nebuchadnezzar besieged Tyre, a strongly fortified and opulent city of Phenicia, "the Queen of the sea, whose merchants were princes, and whose nobles were among the honorable of the earth." Here, for thirteen years, his troops suffered incredible hardships, so that "every head was made bald, and every shoulder was peeled;" and when the place finally surrendered, the exhausted besiegers found no treasure within its walls to reward their labors, the inhabitants having removed their principal effects to an island about half a mile distant, where in a short time a new city arose which far eclipsed the glory of the old.

Read Ez. xxix. 18–20 and Is. xxiii. 5–9, 11, 13.

Questions.—15. Whom did he invest with a share in his government? Why did he take this step? What did Nebuchadnezzar accomplish? 16. What occurred in 599 B. C.? What is said of a dream? On what expedition did Nebuchadnezzar go? With what result? Where is Jerusalem? (See map No. 1). 17. When did Nebuchadnezzar besiege Tyre? Give an account of the siege.

18. Conquest of Egypt.—Nebuchadnezzar then turned himself upon Egypt, which was at that time suffering from intestine commotions. Amasis and Apries having divided the people by a contest for the throne, no effectual resistance was offered to the invaders. "The good of all the land of Egypt was before them," and they spared nothing. With the spoil of the splendid temples of Apis, and the wealth of the conquered people, the great king returned to Babylon, having rendered the country tributary, and made Amasis his deputy.

Read Is. xix. 1, 4, 17, 22, 23. Jer. xlvi. 13, 25, 26. Ez. xxx. 10, 13, 24–26.

19. Nebuchadnezzar was now sole monarch of Chaldea, Assyria, Syria, Arabia, Palestine, Egypt, and Ethiopia. He married Amyit, princess of Media, who rivaled Semiramis in the splendid works with which she beautified the city of Babylon. A bridge 5 furlongs in length spanned the Euphrates, and terminated at each end in a palace of vast dimensions. The old palace on the east side of the river was nearly 4 miles in circumference, but the new palace, surrounded with three walls, one within another, was 7 miles in compass. In the last palace were the Hanging *gardens*, built by Amyit to resemble the woody country of Media. Arches were raised on arches till they reached the height of the walls; the ascent was from terrace to terrace by stairs ten feet wide. On the top of the arches were first placed large flat stones, then a layer of reeds, then bricks closely cemented together, and then thick sheets of lead upon which lay the mold of the garden, so deep that trees of the largest size might take root in it; and beneath their shade were plants and flowers of the greatest beauty and most exquisite perfume. An engine at the top drew up the waters of the river and scattered them in showers over the gardens, and in the spaces between the arches magnificent apartments were fitted up, commanding a delightful prospect of artificial hills and forests, streams and fountains.

20. Temple of Belus.—Near the center of the city stood this edifice. It was circular, having eight stories, diminishing upwards to the height of 600 feet. The wealth of this temple, in statues, tables, censers, cups, and other implements of massive gold, was almost incredible. One ancient writer makes it amount to $100,000,000. On the summit was an observatory, from which the Chaldean astrologers watched the motions of the stars, and made those calculations which Calisthenes

---

Questions.—18. What was Nebuchadnezzar's next movement? What rendered the undertaking easy? How was the king rewarded? 19. To what power did Nebuchadnezzar attain? Whom did he marry? How was Babylon beautified? Give a description of the Hanging Gardens. 20. Give a description of the Temple of Belus.

transcribed and sent to Aristotle. Nebuchadnezzar, proud of the mighty realm which owned his sway, and proud of the magnificent city which he had enriched with the spoils of Nineveh, Jerusalem, and Egypt, refused to listen to the warnings of that Daniel who had made him acquainted with the divine will. But in the very hour "when his heart was lifted up, and his mind hardened in pride," he was seized with a kind of madness, and driven from his throne to dwell with the beasts of the field. At the end of seven years his reason returned to him, his kingdom was restored, and excellent majesty was added unto him. He reigned 43 years.

Read Dan. iv. 30-36.

21.—B. C. 562. Evil-Merodach, son of Nebuchadnezzar, was a gentle and weak prince, unfitted to govern the vast empire left to his care. He was dethroned after two years by Nereglissar, his sister's husband.

B. C. 560.—If the success of Nereglissar had equaled his ambition, Assyria would have had little cause to lament the change in administration; but, endeavoring to extend his dominions, he periled all. After making alliance with Crœsus, king of Lydia, he declared war against the Medes, but was slain in the first battle. His son Laborosoarchod, the man with the long name, the wicked life, and short reign, succeeded him. Nine months his subjects bore with his impious cruelty, and then put him to death.

Read 2 Kings xxv. 27-30.

22. B. C. 555.—While the contest with the Medes was still undecided, and the Assyrians were lost in luxury, the sceptre descended to the weak hands of Belshazzar, grandson of Nebuchadnezzar. The war with Cyrus, and the danger of his kingdom, could not draw him away from his pleasures. His armies and allies were defeated, and finally Babylon alone, of all his vast dominions, held out against the conqueror. For two years this city was closely invested; yet such was the strength of its fortifications—such the quantities of provisions stored in its granaries, and afforded by its gardens—that the Assyrians, thinking themselves secure, ridiculed the besiegers from the walls, and defied them from their impregnable towers.

23. Taking of Babylon.—Nebuchadnezzar, in repairing the walls of the Euphrates, had made a great lake to receive the waters of the

Questions.—20. Why did Nebuchadnezzar refuse to listen to the divine warnings? What consequently befell him? What further account can you give of him? Trace the Chaldean armies to Jerusalem; to Tyre; to Egypt. 21. What can you state of Evil-Merodach? Of Nereglissar? Who succeeded him? Give an account of Laborosoarchod. 22. Who was Belshazzar? What was his character? What city was the last of his possessions? By whom was it then invested? Why was it not readily captured? 23. What plan of capture did Cyrus finally decide upon?

river, and had secured its entrance with strong dykes. Cyrus, having learned that on a certain day a grand festival was to be celebrated, sent a party of soldiers to break down the dam, and let the waters flow away from their accustomed channel; then dividing the rest of his army, he stationed one part at the place where the river entered the city, and the other where it came out, with orders to enter the channel as soon as the water was fordable, and approach each other. The dykes were broken down; and the waters filling the lake, and the trench of circumvallation which the Persians had spent the two years in digging, the bed of the mighty stream was left nearly dry. About midnight the army of Cyrus passed under the walls, and proceeded silently along the channel to a point near the center of the great palace; that palace in which Belshazzar, surrounded by his drunken lords, was listening with quaking heart to Daniel's interpretation of the handwriting on the wall.

24.—The brazen gates leading to the river had been left unfastened; the guards, partaking in the negligence and disorder of the night, offered but a feeble resistance, and the city was filled with the enemy before the doomed inhabitants awoke from their fancied security. Belshazzar was slain at the door of his palace, and Babylon fell into the hands of Cyrus, B. C. 538. Thus ended the Second Assyrian Empire, 210 years after its founding by Arbaces. Assyria then became a Persian province.

Read Jer. l. 1, 8, 9, 10, 13, 14, 15, 16, 29, 35, 36, 37, 38, 41, 42, 43, 44; Jer. li. 1–14, 28, 30, 31, 32, 39, 55–58; Dan. v. entire.

The Chaldean Dynasty of Assyria.

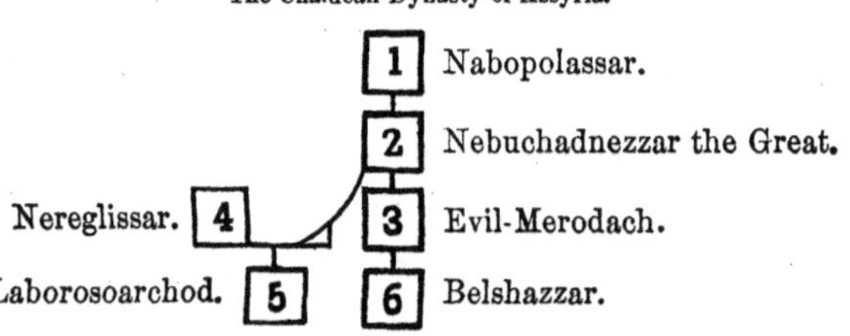

Questions.—24. Give a further account of the success of Cyrus. What was Belshazzar's fate? When did that event occur?

EGYPT.

Egypt, in commencing with Misraim, 2188 B. C., and ending with Psammenitus, 525 B. C., continued 1663 years.

SECTION II.

1. EGYPT, one of the most celebrated spots on the face of the globe, occupies the northeastern corner of Africa, lying between the Mediterranean Sea on the north, and Nubia on the south; and between the Red Sea on the east, and the deserts on the west. It is about 600 miles long, and 350 broad; but its most interesting portion is a vale, varying in width from 15 to 20 miles on each side of the Nile. This majestic river, the source of its wealth and fertility, rises in the mountains of Abyssinia, and, running nearly parallel to the Red Sea, flows into the Mediterranean by seven different mouths.

2. It never rains in Egypt, but the want of showers is abundantly supplied by the annual overflowing of the Nile, which, bringing down the precious mud from the mountains, deposits it upon the earth, and imparts to it a richness greater than is found in the soil of any other country. Ancient Egypt, in fact, unlike every other country on the globe, brought forth its produce independent of the seasons and the skies; and while continued drought in the neighboring countries brought one season of scarcity after another, the granaries of Egypt were always full. Its early settlement and civilization were doubtless owing to these favorable circumstances.

3. No part of ancient history is more obscure and uncertain than that of Egypt. That it was peopled in the earliest ages, its monuments most fully prove; but the traditions and records preserved by its priests are so beclouded with fabulous boasting, that it is impossible to separate the true from the false. According to the religious legends preserved in volumes of papyrus, and shown to Herodotus when he visited Egypt, the deities themselves first ruled the country. To them succeeded a race of demi-gods, of which Osiris was the head. Next followed a dynasty of kings, composed of real flesh and blood, of whom

---

EGYPT.—*Questions.*—1. How is Egypt located? What are its dimensions? What can you state of the Nile? 2. Of its overflowings? Of the fertility of ancient Egypt? What are the boundaries of Egypt? 3. What is said of the early history of Egypt? Why is this so? 3. What is set forth in the religious legends of the country?

Menes was the first. This Menes, they said, completed the work of the gods by perfecting the arts of life, and dictating to men the laws he had received from the skies. Though many new rites were added in after ages, yet to him Egypt owed its peculiar religious institutions, and general plan of animal worship.

4. Osiris the sun, and Isis the moon, were the principal objects of adoration,—Osiris dwelling in the body of the bull Apis, and Isis existing under several mystic forms. Magnificent temples were erected to their honor, and numerous ceremonies were performed before them. If Apis lived 25 years, he was drowned in a sacred fountain; if he died before that period, all Egypt went into mourning, and this mourning continued till a new Apis was found. The deceased animal was embalmed in the most costly manner, and buried with such pomp, that on one occasion the funeral expenses amounted to a sum equal to $55,000.

5. The priests then traversed the whole land in quest of a successor. He must be a calf of a perfectly black color, with a square white spot in the forehead, the figure of an eagle upon the back, a crescent on the side, and a beetle on the tongue. These marks were of course produced by the contrivance of the priests; but the people, supposing them to be indubitable evidences that he contained the soul of Osiris, were filled with the greatest joy when he was brought in triumph to Memphis. Here in his splendid temple, "the walls of which shone with gold and silver, and sparkled with the gems of India and Ethiopia," he was served by a whole college of priests, who fed him from golden dishes, and attended him with the utmost care.

6. The annual festival of Apis began with the rising of the Nile, and presented for seven days a scene of uninterrupted rejoicing. The god was then displayed to the view of the people, covered with embroidered cloths of the finest texture, and surrounded by a whole troop of boys, singing songs in his praise. Many other animals were also esteemed deities. The dog, the wolf, the hawk, the crocodile, and the cat, were popular divinities, and he who killed one of them, even by accident, was punished with death. At the decease of a cat, every inmate of the family cut off his eyebrows; but when a dog died the whole head was shaven. It was customary for Egyptian soldiers to return after

Read Ez. xxxii. 1-6, 18, 19.

Questions.—4. Who were Osiris and Isis? What was done with reference to Apis? 5. What else was done with reference to Apis? 6. Give an account of the festival of Apis. How were other animals also esteemed? Name some that were so esteemed. What penalty was affixed to the killing of them?

long expeditions, bringing with them the bodies of these animals which they had found on their journey, and embalmed with superstitious care.

7. They also worshiped certain portions of the vegetable kingdoms, whence the poet took occasion to satirize them:

> "But should you leeks or onions eat, no time
> Would expiate the sacrilegious crime;
> Religious nations sure, and blest abodes,
> Where every orchard is o'errun with gods!"

Among the institutions of Egypt, none exercised a more important influence on the character of the nation than the division of the people into tribes, or castes. The son was obliged, by the customs of the country, to follow the trade of his father; so that *priests*, *warriors*, *herdsmen*, and *traders*, were always distinct classes.

8. According to the Egyptian doctrine of transmigration, the soul of man was destined to pass through the bodies of different animals, and, at the end of 3000 years, to return and inhabit a human form: but the cycle could not commence till the body began to perish; hence, say many historians, arose the practice of embalming the dead. The greatest attention was bestowed upon this work, which was enforced by severe and sacred laws. Many hands were employed in the ceremony: some drew the brain through the nostrils; others opened the side and took out all the softer parts of the body; others then filled the cavities with spices and drugs. After a certain time the body was wrapped in fine linen, dipped in gum, and impregnated with perfumes; finally it was delivered to the relatives, who put it in an open chest, and placed it upright against the wall of a sepulchre.

9. The chains of rocky mountains which bounded the valley of the Nile were formed into vast catacombs, and fitted up with chambers for the repose of the dead. The tomb was always prepared for the husband and his wife. Whoever died first was deposited there, or kept embalmed in the house till the decease of the other. The upper rooms of the tombs were ornamented with paintings and sculptured figures, representing the Egyptians in all the occupations of every-day life. All the operations of agriculture—plowing, sowing, and reaping; all the employments of the housewife—spinning, weaving, sewing, washing, dressing; all the mechanic arts; all the amusements of the people, even the very balls and dolls with which the children played,

---

Questions.—7. What else did the people worship? What is said of the tribe and caste divisions? What was the son obliged to do? What was the result? 8. What, say historians, gave rise to the practice of embalming the dead? Give a description of the work of embalming. 9. What and where were the Egyptian catacombs? Give a description of them. Where is the Nile? (See map No. 3.)

are still to be seen portrayed with striking fidelity and distinctness in these stupendous palaces of the dead.

10. In one painting is represented the judgment of a wicked soul, condemned to return to the earth in the form of a pig, after having been weighed in the scales before Osiris, and found wanting. It is placed in a boat, and, attended by two monkeys, is dismissed from heaven, and all communication with that delightful place cut off, by a man who hews away the ground behind it with an ax. The sacred rites of sepulture could not be conferred, even upon kings, until the dead had been solemnly judged by a tribunal appointed for the purpose, and declared worthy to enter the abodes of the blessed.

11. All the ancient kings of Egypt are called in Scripture Pharaoh. In the time of the Pharaohs, Egypt was divided into the Thebais, or Upper Egypt; Middle; and Lower Egypt. Lower Egypt extended from the Mediterranean to the place where the Nile began to branch off; and Middle Egypt extended from that place to Thebes, nearly where the Upper portion commenced, and reached to Nubia. The Pyramids are all situated on the west side of the Nile, and extend in a direction nearly parallel to it, for about 70 miles. Their vast antiquity, their amazing magnitude, and the mystery which envelops their history, render them objects of intense interest.

12. Menes or Misraim Founds Egypt, B. C. 2188.—After the confusion of tongues at Babel, the sons of Noah separated into different parts of the world. Ham had four children, three of whom settled in Africa. Misraim, the second son, founded Egypt, and all historians agree in considering him the Menes of the Egyptian priests. He is supposed to have founded Memphis, by digging a new channel for the Nile, and laying the foundations within its ancient bed. Many of its ruins have served as materials for building Cairo, but a sufficient number remain to excite our admiration of the wonderful skill of the Egyptians in architecture. In the 12th century, these ruins extended half a day's journey in every direction, but now there are only scattered fragments of idols, 40 feet high, and blocks of granite inclosed in rubbish, to interest the antiquary.

Read Gen. x. 6.

Questions.—10. What painting is described? What ceremony had to be observed with reference to the dead? 11. What titles were given to the Egyptian kings? How was Egypt divided? Where are the Pyramids? What renders them objects of interest? 12. Whither did the sons of Noah go? Ham's children? Misraim? What supposition is made in connection with Misraim? What can you state of the ruins of Memphis? In which division of Egypt was Memphis?

13. Busiris built Thebes, the city of an hundred gates, from each of which issued, upon state occasions, 200 chariots and 10,000 fighting men. It is now called Said, and lies magnificent in ruins; its fallen columns and moldering temples eminently beautiful even in the midst of decay. The sculptured figures which ornamented gates, and walls, and capitals, show the perfection of Egyptian art; even the colors of the paintings in its deserted palaces are undimmed by the hand of time; so happily did the Egyptians stamp immortality upon their works.

14. OSYMANDIAS.—Diodorus gives a description of many beautiful edifices erected by this king. One was adorned with a sculptured representation of his expedition into Asia. Another temple contained a magnificent library, the oldest mentioned in history. The Egyptians used hieroglyphical writing, and their records were preserved not only by inscription upon monuments, but in books made of the leaves of the papyrus. This library was called "the office or treasury for the diseases of the soul." The life of Osymandias was such as secured to him a distinguished sepulchre. It was encompassed with a circle of gold, 365 cubits in circumference, ornamented with figures showing the rising and setting of the heavenly bodies; for so early as this the Egyptians had divided the year into 12 months of 30 days each, and every year added 5 days to bring the sun to the equinoctial points. Champollion thinks the splendid ruins of the Memnonium in Thebes are the remains of this tomb, as the statue of Osymandias is still to be seen in them, though shattered in a thousand pieces.

15. B. C. **2000.**—Uchoreus raised a very high mole to protect Memphis from the inundations of the Nile, and fortified the city otherwise in so impregnable a manner, that it was ever afterwards the key of that river. Moeris made the famous lake which bears his name. The object of this wonderful excavation was to regulate the inundations of the Nile. It was joined to the river by a canal; in its center were two pyramids upon which the rise of the water was marked; when it rose above the usual point it flowed off into the lake, and when it did not reach so high, the deficiency was supplied from the lake.

16. B. C. **1900.**—Some time in this century Egypt was invaded by people from Arabia, called Shepherd Kings. Every place yielded to

Questions.—13. By whom was Thebes built? How was that city located? (See map No. 1.) What can you say of its ruins? 14. What account do we get of Osymandias? What is hieroglyphical writing? What is papyrus? What is said of Osymandias's sepulchre? Of the division of the year? 15. What work did Uchoreus accomplish? Moeris? Describe the lake. 16. When was Egypt invaded by the Shepherd Kings? What success did they have?

these fierce barbarians, who, having taken Memphis and fortified Pelusium, organized the government to suit themselves, and founded On, or Heliopolis, the city of the Sun. Another race might have reigned at Thebes during the same time, for the state of Egypt was one of anarchy and confusion during this period. 1800 B. C.—It was in the days of the Hyscos, or Shepherd Kings, that Joseph was sold into Egypt. To connect him with the highest tribe or family, and so constitute him a governor, he was married to the daughter of Potiphera, priest of the Sun.

Read Gen. xxxvii. 23-28; xli. 41-46; also l. 22-26.

17. B. C. **1700.**—Among the ruins of Thebes is the statue of Memnon, an image of the Sun-king, cut out of the solid rock. It was said to greet the rising of the god of day with a musical sound resembling the tone of a harp. This work was ascribed to Amenophis II. Ramases Miamun was the king that so cruelly oppressed the Israelites. They built for him the treasure cities of Ramases and Pithom.

Read Ex. i. 8-11.

18. B. C. **1500.**—Amenophis III. is the prince who it is supposed endured the ten plagues, and perished in the Red Sea. Diodorus says: "A tradition has been transmitted through the whole nation, that once an extraordinary ebb dried up the waters of the Red Sea, so that its bottom was seen, and almost immediately after a violent flow brought back the waters to their accustomed channel."

Read Ex. vii. 20, 21; viii. 6, 17, 24; ix. 6, 10, 24, 25; x. 13-15, 22, 23; xii. 29-38, and Ex. xiv. 9-31; xix. 1, 2.

19. Though much dispute prevails among the learned as to the time in which Sesostris flourished, yet the numerous monuments inscribed to him prove him to have been something more than a fabulous personage. In the temples of southern Ipsambul, in the ruins of Thebes and Memphis, his statues appear stamped (Champollion asserts) with the reality of portraiture. In almost every temple up to the confines of Ethiopia, his deeds and triumphs are wrought in relief and painting. The greater part of the celebrated obelisks bear his record; one side of Cleopatra's needle is occupied with his deeds, and his legends clothe with interest the stupendous ruins of Luxor and Carnac. The best authorities make him the son of Amenophis, and date his reign from the Exodus, 1491 B. C.

Questions.—16. What account can you give of Joseph? Trace the Shepherd Kings from Arabia to Egypt. Where is Pelusium? (See map No. 1.) Heliopolis? 17. What is said of the statue of Memnon? What of Ramases Miamun? 18. Of Amenophis III.? What tradition is mentioned? 19. When did Sesostris reign? What can you state of his monuments, statues, &c.?

20. His father, by the authority of an oracle, as the Egyptians say, formed the design of making his son a conqueror. For this purpose, all the male children born on the same day with Sesostris were brought to court and educated with him. Their common exercise was hunting, and they were never suffered to eat till tney had run a race, either on foot or on horseback. The energies of theii bodies were thns developed, and the ambition to excel in courage and skill was constantly cherished.

21. The enmity still prevalent against the Hyscos he turned to his own account, and in the lifetime of his father pursued the remnants of the hated race into Arabia. The success of this expedition stimulated him to still greater efforts. Libya, so celebrated for its burning deserts and fiery serpents, was overrun and subdued by the young prince and his companions. Upon the death of his father he entered upon his great work, the Conquest of the World! Before leaving home, he made it his care to gain the hearts of his people by his justice and generosity, and to attach his soldiers to his person by all the ties of affection and interest.

22. He divided the country into 36 districts, or nomi, and bestowed them upon persons of merit and fidelity. His troops, commanded by 1700 officers (most of whom had been educated with him), when drawn out in battle array, covered a space of more than 200 acres. His chariots and horsemen, issuing from the gates of Thebes, filled all the plain, and, leaving the fertile vale of the Nile, they entered upon the mountainous country of Ethiopia. He conquered even the Southern Ethiopians, and forced them to pay a tribute of ebony, gold, and elephants' teeth. In the Nubian temples, representations of his numerous victories line the walls. One of them shows the conqueror standing among huge logs of ebony and golden ingots, while a vanquished queen and her children stretch out their hands to him as if imploring mercy.

23. With the aid of a fleet which he fitted out, the islands and cities upon the Red Sea were subdued; on the height overlooking the narrow strait of Babelmandel one of his columns was erected. Following the track of ancient commerce, he entered Asia and subdued

---

Questions.—20. What design did the father of Sesostris have? How did he commence to carry out his purpose? 21. What were the first successes of Sesostris? What great work did he then enter upon? What was his first care? 22. What division did he make of the country? What army did he have? What did he accomplish in Ethiopia? What is shown in the Nubian temples? 23. What did he accomplish, aided by his fleet? What other conquests did he make?

the countries even beyond the Ganges. Thence it is supposed he marched in a westerly direction; for history states that he left an Egyptian colony in Colchis, where they were long after known by their swarthy complexions, frizzly hair, and peculiar customs. In every country that he conquered, he set up pillars with this inscription: "Sesostris, king of kings and lord of lords, subdued this country by the power of his arms."

24. Herodotus found in Asia Minor two statues of Sesostris, one near Ephesus, the other on the road between Smyrna and Sardis; they were five palms high, armed with a javelin and bow, after the Egyptian manner. A line drawn from one shoulder to the other bore this inscription: "This region I obtained by these my shoulders." Certain monuments show also that he entered Thrace, and bounded his conquests by the Ganges and the Danube—but we must not forget that conquest was, in those early ages, but little else than a forced march through primitive forests, inhabited by scattered tribes, unacquainted with the stratagems of war, and accustomed to fly with their flocks and herds at the approach of an invading foe. The want of provisions for his army, the difficulty of the passes, and intelligence of treason in Egypt, induced him to return home after he had borne the sword of conquest up and down the world for nine years. He took no pains to preserve his acquisitions. True, he was laden with the spoils of the vanquished, and followed by a countless multitude of mourning captives; but he left the countries he had depopulated and the cities he had pillaged to recover at leisure from those desolations which had covered his name with glory.

25. He rewarded his officers and soldiers with a munificence truly royal, and employed the repose of peace in raising works calculated both to enrich Egypt and immortalize his own name. He raised a number of lofty mounds on which cities were built, where the people might retire with their flocks during the inundations of the Nile. He fortified the whole coast from Pelusium to Heliopolis, to prevent any future invasion of the Hyscos. He erected a temple in every city of Egypt, and raised gigantic statues representing himself, his wife, and his four sons. In all these stupendous works, captives only were employed, and he caused to be inscribed on the temples: "No one native

Questions.—23. What pillars did he set up? What is the Strait of Babelmandel? (See map No. 1.) 24. What discoveries did Herodotus make? Describe the statues. 24. How far did the conquests of Sesostris extend? How do we get at that information? What was a conquest in those days? How many years was he absent from Egypt? Why did he return? Where is Smyrna? 25. What is said of the rewards bestowed by Sesostris? Of the mounds raised by him? Fortifications? Temples?

labored hereon." The kings and chiefs of conquered nations came at stated times to do honor to their victor, and to pay the accustomed tribute. On certain occasions he is said to have unharnessed his horses, and, yoking kings together, made them draw his chariot. At length this mighty monarch lost his sight, and rather than endure the loneliness of old age in darkness, he put an end to his own life.

26. B. C. **1400.**—In this century and a great part of the next, occurs one of those chasms so frequent in Egyptian history. Four years before the close of the thirteenth century, Proteus began to reign in Egypt. From a custom of adorning his head with representations of animals, vegetables, or even burning incense, arose the fable of *Protean forms*, so often quoted among the Greeks. Homer calls him a sea-god, and says that, when caught by Menelaus, he turned into a lion, a serpent, a tree, &c.

27. B. C. **1200.**—Proteus received Paris and Helen when on their way from Sparta to Troy, and erected a temple to Venus the stranger. His numerous forms may signify the duplicity of his character. Cheops, a most wicked and oppressive monarch, built the pyramid which bears his name. Ten years were spent in preparing for the work, and twenty more in erecting it. It stands a little south of Cairo, and lifts its head about 45 feet higher than St. Peter's at Rome. On its side was an inscription which the priests told Herodotus was an account of $1,700,000 expended merely in furnishing the workmen with leeks and onions. Cephrenius was also a monster of wickedness. By his exactions and oppressions he incurred the hatred of his subjects, and filled Egypt with mourning.

28. B. C. **1100.**—Mycerinus, "the peaceful," was as remarkable for his justice and moderation, as his predecessors had been for their extortion and excess. He built the third pyramid. It was smaller than the others, but equally expensive, being faced half way up with Ethiopian marble. The goodness of this monarch did not exempt him from calamity. The death of his only darling daughter clouded his life with sorrow. He ordered extraordinary honors to be paid to her memory; exquisite odors were burned at her tomb by day, and a

Read 1 Kings ix. 16, 24; and 2 Chron. viii. 11.

Questions.—25. What is stated about his chariot? His death? Trace his whole course, and mention the modern names of the countries through which he passed. 26. When did Proteus begin to reign? How did the fable of the Protean form have its origin? What did Homer say of Proteus? 27. What further can you state of Proteus? Give an account of Cheops. Of Cephrenius. Where was Sparta? (See map No. 1.) Troy? Cairo? 28. What was the character of Mycerinus? What event clouded his life with sorrow? Give a further account of him.

lamp illuminated it by night. Having reigned for no great length of time, he was informed by an oracle that he was destined to die in six years. On complaining because he, a pious prince, was not allowed a long reign, while his father and grandfather, who had injured men and despised the gods, had each reigned half a century, he was told that his short life was the direct consequence of his piety; for the fates had decreed that Egypt should be afflicted for the space of 150 years, and as he had not proved a minister of vengeance, he must give place to one less inclined to mildness and lenity.

29. Asychis.—This king, during a scarcity of money, enacted a law permitting any man to borrow money, by giving in pledge the body of his father; but in case he afterwards refused to pay the debt, he should neither be buried in the same place with his father, nor in any other, nor have the liberty of burying the dead bodies of any of his friends, who for want of the sacred rites would not be permitted to enter the peaceful realm of Osiris. One of his immediate successors was the king who gave his daughter in marriage to Solomon.

30. B. C. **1000.**—Shishak was the Pharaoh that reigned in Egypt when Jeroboam fled thither to avoid the wrath of Solomon. In the reign of Rehoboam the same Shishak invaded Palestine, seized upon all the strongest cities of Judah, penetrated as far as Jerusalem, plundered "the treasures of the house of the Lord, and the king's house," and carried away "the shields of gold which Solomon had made."

Zerah, king of Ethiopia and Egypt, made war upon Asa, king of Judah, with an army far superior to the whole number of Jews, women and children inclusive; but he was defeated, and obliged to retire in haste to his own land.

Read 1 Kings xi. 40; and xiv. 15, 16; also 1 Chron. xiv. 9-14.

31. B. C. **800.**—What transpired in Egypt during the ninth century is unknown. The next king of whom we read was Anysis, a blind man. Sabachus, or So, king of Ethiopia, dethroned him, and reigned in his stead. The kingdom thus obtained by violence was nevertheless governed with justice. Instead of putting criminals to death, he employed them in repairing public works, and in other menial offices serviceable to the state. He is thought to be the So mentioned in Scripture as entering into a league with Hoshea, king

---

Questions.—29. What singular law did Asychis enact? What is said of one of his successors? 30. Who was Shishak? When did that event occur? What account can you give of Shishak? Of Zerah? 31. Give an account of Anysis. Of Sabachus's government. What is supposed with reference to So?

of Israel. At the end of 50 years he had a dream, which the priests interpreted as a warning that he could no longer hold the kingdom in safety or happiness, upon which he voluntarily retired to his own country.

Read 1 Kings xvii. 4.

32. Sethon was both king and priest of Vulcan. He gave himself up to religious contemplation, and not only neglected the military class, but deprived them of their lands. At this they were so much incensed that they refused to bear arms under him, and in the midst of the commotion Sennacherib, king of Assyria, arrived before Pelusium with a large army. Sethon attempted to raise a body of troops to oppose him, but none of his soldiers would follow him. In despair he betook himself to his god, and while yet in the temple, praying to be delivered from his enemies, he fell into a deep sleep, during which Vulcan exhorted him to take courage, and assured him of victory.

33. Thus sustained, he assembled about 200 shopkeepers, laborers, &c., and advanced to Pelusium. The next morning he found the Assyrians in great disorder, preparing to fly. A prodigious number of rats had entered their camp during the night, and gnawed to pieces the quivers, bow-strings, and shield-straps. Unable to fight, they endeavored to make good their retreat, but Sethon, falling upon them, made terrible slaughter in their ranks. In memory of this remarkable deliverance, Sethon erected a statue of himself holding a rat in one hand, with these words issuing out of its mouth:

"Whosoever beholdeth me, let him be pious."

This story is no doubt a corruption of that related in 2 Kings xix.

34. B. C. **700.**—The invasion of the Ethiopians and other troubles had reduced Egypt to a deplorable state of anarchy. At length 12 of the principal noblemen seized upon the government, and divided it into 12 absolute sovereignties; and because an oracle had declared that the whole kingdom should fall to the lot of him who should offer his libation to Vulcan in a brazen bowl, they bound themselves by the most solemn oaths to protect each other's rights. For 15 years they reigned together in the utmost harmony, and, to leave a monument of their concord to posterity, united in building a famous labyrinth near Lake Moeris.

Questions.—31. How did his reign end? 32. Who was Sethon? What was Sethon's course of conduct? What danger threatened him? What then occurred? 33. Give an account of Sethon's deliverance. 33. How did he commemorate the event? 34. What was the condition of Egypt seven hundred years before Christ? How had that been produced? What summary act was done by twelve persons? How long did they reign? Why did they build a labyrinth? Where did they build it? Where was Lake Moeris? (See map No. 3.)

35. This remarkable structure consisted of 12 separate palaces, stretched along in a succession of splendid apartments, spacious halls, and lofty terraces; adorned with statues, hieroglyphics, and every other appendage of Egyptian art. A vast number of intricate passages ran around the base of the building, and around these a wall was thrown, leaving only one entrance to the labyrinth; while at the other end stood a pyramid, containing a way leading to 12 subterraneous palaces, exactly corresponding to those above. The whole structure contained 3000 rooms; 1500 above ground and as many below. All the roofs and walls were of stone, adorned with sculptured figures, and all the halls were surrounded with pillars of white marble. Herodotus visited the upper rooms, but was not permitted to enter the subterranean palaces, because the bodies of the sacred crocodiles lay there embalmed.

36. It happened one day, that the twelve kings were sacrificing in the temple of Vulcan at Memphis, and that the high priest, who distributed the golden cups for libations, had brought with him, by some accident, only eleven. Psammetichus, who stood the last in order, took off his brazen helmet, and poured his libation out from that. This incident occasioned great disquiet among his colleagues, and they accordingly banished him to the seacoast. After passing some years in the solitude of exile, Psammetichus secured the aid of a company of Greeks, whom adverse winds had driven on the coast. By their assistance he overcame the eleven, and became sole master of Egypt.

37. B. C. 625.—In gratitude to his Grecian friends, he gave them lands and revenues, and placed children under their care to learn the Greek tongue. These, in process of time, formed a distinct caste, called, in the days of Herodotus, *Interpreters.* The limits of Assyrian conquest had never been clearly defined, and a quarrel now arose about the boundary of that empire, on the southwestern border. The Assyrians had taken Syria and the territory of Israel, and were waiting till a favorable opportunity should occur for seizing Palestine and invading Egypt. Some years before, Tartan had taken Ashdod, or Azotus, and Psammetichus set himself to recover this important post; but owing to the natural strength of the fortifications and the vigorous defense of the garrison, the siege lasted 29 years; the longest of any recorded

---

Questions.—35. Give a description of the labyrinth. What can you state of the visit of Herodotus? 36. What occurred in relation to the eleven cups? How did Psammetichus get to be sole master of Egypt? 37. What is said of the Interpreters? Of a boundary dispute? What successes had the Assyrians gained? Tartan? What can you say of the siege of Ashdod?

in history; nor does it appear that the Egyptians afterward derived any particular benefit from the possession of the place.

Read 1 Samuel v. 1; Is. xx. 1; also, Acts viii. 40.

38. B. C. 616.—Pharaoh Necho, son of Psammetichus, attempted to join the Red Sea to the Mediterranean by a canal through the isthmus of Suez. He persisted till 120,000 men had perished in the work, and then abandoned it. In another enterprise he was more successful. Having taken some Phenician navigators into his service, he instructed them to sail around Africa, and solve the great mystery of the form and termination of that continent. In their small row-galleys, well equipped, they departed, and at the end of three years returned in safety. They stated, that passing down the Red Sea, they entered the Southern Ocean; that at the approach of Autumn they landed on the coast and planted corn; when this was ripe they cut it down, and again departed. In passing the southern point of Africa, they were surprised to observe the sun upon their right hand:* then turning to the north, they continued their course; the third year they doubled the columns of Hercules, and returned to Egypt through the Mediterranean.

39. Nabopolassar, the Chaldean, having usurped the Assyrian throne, became so powerful as to rouse all the ancient enmity of the Egyptians. Necho undertook an expedition against him. Josiah, king of Judah, hearing that he intended to pass through Palestine, assembled all his forces and stationed himself in the vale of Megiddo, to oppose his progress. Necho sent a herald to inform him that he meant the Jews no harm, but was commissioned by God against another nation. Josiah would not listen to this remonstrance; he gave battle, was defeated, and received a wound of which he died. The victorious Necho continued his march to the Euphrates, defeated the Assyrians, and took the city of Carchemish. On his way home he stopped at Jerusalem, levied a tribute upon the Jews, placed Johoiakim upon the throne, and carried Jehoahaz captive into Egypt. Soon after the Babylonians dispossessed the Egyptians of all they had gained, retook Carchemish, and Necho died.

Read 2 Kings xxiii. 29, 30, 33–35; also, 2 Chron. xxxv. 20–24; and xxxvi. 34.

* Herodotus doubted the truth of this story, from the fact of their seeing the sun in the north, but to us this is its greatest confirmation.

Questions.—37. Where was Ashdod? (Map No. 3.) 38. Who was Pharaoh Necho? In what great enterprise did he fail? In what was he successful? Give an account of the successful enterprise. Where are the columns of Hercules? *Ans.* One is at Gibraltar, and the other opposite, on the African coast, at the western extremity of the Mediterranean. 39. Who was Nabopolassar? What expedition did Necho undertake? By whom was he opposed? What followed? What successes did Necho afterward gain? After what events did he die?

40. B. C. **600.**—In the reign of Psammis, son of Necho, the Eleans, having rearranged the Olympic games, sent a splendid embassy into Egypt, to give an account of the regulations they had established; for they were desirous of gaining the approbation of a people then considered the wisest in the world. When the delegation arrived, Psammis assembled the priests and sages to listen to the communication of the distinguished strangers. After mature deliberation, the grave council remarked, that the persons appointed to award the prizes, being Greeks, could scarcely be impartial in their decisions; upon which the deputies returned home, satisfied, no doubt, with going abroad after praise.

41. Apries, the son of Psammis, is called in Scripture Pharaoh Hophrah. In the first years of his reign he invaded Cyprus, took the city of Sidon, and made himself master of Phenicia. Inflated with pride, he boasted that not even the gods could dethrone him. Zedekiah king of Judah, unmoved by the "woe" of Isaiah, made an alliance with Apries, and, relying upon his assistance, broke his oath of allegiance to the king of Babylon. In the war that followed, Zedekiah found that the Egyptian help was "a broken reed;" for though the Chaldeans departed once from Jerusalem for fear of Pharaoh's host, yet in the end the Egyptians abandoned their allies, and left them to meet the wrath of Nebuchadnezzar alone.

42. Some years after, the chastising rod fell heavily upon Apries. A large army which he had sent into Lybia having been destroyed, as was supposed, by his connivance, a great part of his subjects rebelled. Apries sent one Amasis, a particular friend, to bring back his subjects to a sense of their duty; but the moment Amasis began to speak, the rebels fixed a helmet upon his head, and proclaimed him king. Amasis accepted the honor, and became leader of the mutineers. Apries, greatly exasperated at the defection of his favorite, sent a nobleman with orders to bring Amasis, alive or dead, before him. The messenger, unable to seize an individual protected by an infuriated mob, returned without his captive; and his master, in a rage, ordered his nose and ears to be cut off. This piece of wanton cruelty alienated the affections of his people, so that the revolt became general, and he was obliged to abdicate his throne in favor of Amasis. The new king

Questions.—40. Who was Psammis? What embassy was sent by the Eleans during his reign? Give an account of the ceremony that took place. 41. Who was Apries? What is he called in Scripture? What events took place in the first years of his reign? What influence did his success exert upon his character? Who formed an alliance with him? In what manner did he treat his allies? 42. What causes led to the overthrow of Apries? Who then was king? How did Amasis then treat Apries?

confined Apries in one of his palaces, and treated him with great respect; but the people were implacable, and the tyrant, being delivered "into the hands of those who sought his life," was strangled.

Read Ez. xxviii. 21, 22; also Ez. xxix. 3, and xvii. 12–17; Is. xxxi. 1–3, and Jer. xxxvii. 7, 8, and xliv. 30, and Ez. xxix. 2, 3, 4, 7.

43. While these troubles had been going on, Nebuchadnezzar invaded Egypt, and subdued the country as far as Syene. He made horrible devastation wherever he came, killed great numbers of the inhabitants, loaded his army with treasure, and, having made Amasis his deputy, returned to Babylon. During the reign of Amasis, Egypt is said to have been perfectly happy, and to have contained 20,000 populous cities. He espoused a Grecian female, and displayed his attachment to the Greeks by permitting them to settle on his coasts, and by contributing liberally to the rebuilding of the temple at Delphi. Solon visited Egypt during his reign.

44. The prosperity of Amasis was at last disturbed by the preparations which Cambyses, king of Persia, made to attack his kingdom. The Persian monarch had demanded the daughter of Amasis in marriage; but Amasis attempted to deceive him by sending him the daughter of Apries. The lady disclosed the imposition to Cambyses, and he, in great wrath, determined to march against Egypt. Amasis, however, died in season to escape the perils that threatened him, and the whole fury of the storm fell upon his son, Psammenitus.

45. Psammenitus was scarcely seated on the throne when Cambyses arrived before Pelusium, with all his forces. Pelusium was taken, a great battle fought near Memphis, Psammenitus put to death, and Egypt became a Persian province, B. C. 525. Subsequently this country fell under the power of the Macedonians, Romans, Saracens, Mamelukes, and, lastly, of the Turks; thus verifying the words of

---

Questions.—42. What further can you state of Apries? 43. Who invaded Egypt at that time? How far did Nebuchadnezzar subdue the country? Where is Syene? (See map No. 3.) What is said of Nebuchadnezzar's devastation? Whom did he make his deputy? What is said of the condition of Egypt during the reign of Amasis? Whom did he marry? How did he manifest his favor to the Greeks? 44. How was the prosperity of Amasis disturbed? Give the story of the deception. Who was Psammenitus? 45. What battles were fought soon after Psammenitus ascended the throne? What became of him? When did Egypt become a Persian province? Under what powers did it afterward fall? What prophecy was verified?

prophesy, "Egypt shall be the basest of kingdoms," and, "there shall be no more a prince of the land of Egypt."

Read Ez. xxix. 10, 15, and xxx. 6, 13.

1 Psammetichus.

2 Necho.

3 Psammis.

4 Apries.

1 Amasis.

2 Psammenitus.

Egypt becomes a Persian province.

REVIEW QUESTIONS.

		PAGE
1.	What account can you give of Noah?	7
2.	What of the city of Babel and its tower?	7, 8
3.	Of Ninus and the manner of his death?	9
4.	Of Semiramis and the worship accorded her?	9, 10
5.	Of the Assyrian Empire during the next 400 years?	9, 10
6.	Of the reigns of Arbaces and Belesis?	10
7.	State what afterward occurred, till 680 B. C.	10, 11
8.	Name the further events to the conquest of Egypt.	11, 12
9.	What countries were in Nebuchadnezzar's domains?	13
10.	What is said of his next three successors?	14
11.	Give an account of Belshazzar's reign.	14, 15
12.	Of the settlement of Egypt.	19, 20
13.	Of events in Egypt to the time of Sesostris.	20, 21
14.	Give an account of Sesostris.	21, 22, 23, 24
15.	Name the events of the next seven centuries.	24, 25, 26
16.	Give an account of Psammetichus.	26, 27, 28
17.	Name the events of Pharaoh Necho's reign.	28
18.	Also those of Psammis's and Apries's.	29, 30
19.	Give the further history of Egypt.	30, 31

PERSIA.

SECTION III.

1. The monarchical form of government follows most naturally upon that state of society in which a strong-minded, ambitious man, from being head of a family, comes to be chief of his relatives, and leader of a tribe. Accordingly we find that all the early governments were monarchies. Among the Persians the prince was styled, "The great king, the king of kings." The crown was hereditary, but subject to the will of the father rather than to the law of primogeniture.

2. The young heir was never committed entirely to the care of a nurse, but persons of distinguished merit were chosen to take charge of his health and manners. At seven he was put into the hands of competent masters, who taught him to ride on horseback, to draw the bow, throw the lance, and engage in other athletic exercises. At 14, four of the wisest and most virtuous men in the state were appointed his preceptors. They taught him the religion of Zoroaster, the principles of government, the administration of justice, and the bearing of a king. When he ascended the throne, seven counselers, chief lords of the nation, were appointed to assist him by their abilities and experience. Public registers were kept, in which all the edicts of the king were recorded, together with all the privileges granted to the people, or benefits conferred upon individuals, for serving the state.

Read Esther i. 14; and ii. 23; also vi. 1. For king, read Ezra vii. 12.

3. The Persians thought it reasonable to put the good as well as the evil into the scales of justice, so that one single crime should not destroy the reputation of a man habitually just and upright. No person was condemned without being brought face to face with his accuser, and having time allowed him to gain an impartial decision. If the accused proved innocent, the accuser suffered the punishment in his stead. The empire was divided into 127 provinces, the govern-

---

Persia.—*Questions.*—1. Where is Persia? (See map No. 3.) Of what is a monarchical form of government the natural result? What do we accordingly find? What title did the Persians give to their prince? 2. What was the custom with reference to the prince? With reference to the public registers? 3. With reference to persons accused of crime?

ors of which were called satraps, who inflicted capital punishment in the same manner as kings. Of these satraps the king took cognizance in person; and an officer of his household was appointed, to repeat to him every morning when he waked, "Rise, sir, and think of discharging the duties for which Oromasdis has placed you upon the throne."

4. The Medes and Persians were originally a pastoral people, but after the establishment of their monarchy, they paid great attention to agriculture and manufactures. Their fields produced every necessary, and their gardens abounded in the choicest fruits and sweetest flowers. Median vestments, woven of fine wool, and dyed in the gayest colors, were held in the highest esteem, even by the Greeks. In order to receive certain intelligence of the affairs of the provinces, a high road, on which distances were regularly marked, connected the western coast with the seat of government; and along this road couriers, trained to extraordinary speed, traveled without intermission in the king's name.

5. The revenues of the Persian king consisted partly of moneys (chiefly gold raised by taxes), and partly of an annual levy of corn, horses, camels, or whatever the province afforded. In the days of Persian power, the satrap of Armenia sent regularly every year 20,000 young colts to the king. Certain cantons were set apart for furnishing the queen's wardrobe, and were named according to the article they supplied: one being called the queen's girdle; another, the queen's vail, &c. The Persians served in the army from the age of 20 to 50, and it was esteemed a crime to desire exemption from military duty. The king's guard consisted of a body of 10,000 men, called the Immortal Band, because when one died his place was immediately filled by another noble, so that the number should be always complete.

Read Esther vii. 10; and i. 1, 6; and viii. 8, 10.

6. The Persians adored the Sun, and bowed with their faces to the east, with reverential delight, when he appeared above the horizon. A splendid chariot was dedicated to him; and the Steed of the Sun, extravagantly caparisoned, formed an important part of every grand procession. As an emanation from the god of day, or as an emblem of the deity, they paid particular honors to *fire*, always invoking it

---

Questions.—3. Of Satraps? 4. What is said in relation to the early occupations of the Medes and Persians? What method of conveying intelligence was used? 5. Of what did the Persian king's revenues consist? What is said of the composition of the Persian army? Of the king's guard? 6. What is said of the Persians' adoration of the sun? Their adoration of fire?

first in their sacrifices. The Sacred Fire was intrusted to the keeping of the Magi, who were originally one of the seven Median tribes. The priesthood descended from father to son, and no stranger could be instructed in the mysteries of their religion without the king's permission. They erected neither statues, temples, nor altars to their gods, but offered their sacrifices in the open air, on hill-tops, or "in high places."

7. Zoroaster is generally believed to have been the founder of the sect called the Magi, in the time of Cyrus the Great. He first made his appearance at Xis, a town of Media, and improving upon the ancient doctrines of the Magian tribe, brought their religious tenets into a more consistent form. He erected a temple where he kept a fire, which he said came directly from heaven. This was distributed through the kingdom, and maintained by the priests with the greatest care. They watched it day and night, fed it with wood stripped of the bark, and never blowed it with their breath for fear of polluting it. Zoroaster taught that there are two grand principles: the one, the cause of all good; the other, the cause of all evil; the former, represented by light; the latter, by darkness.

8. The good spirit he called Oromasdes, and the evil, Arimanius. When the Persians besought blessings for themselves, they presented their petitions to Oromasdes; when they invoked evil upon their enemies, they addressed Arimanius. Some held that both these gods were eternal; others, that only the benevolent being was eternal, and the malevolent created; but all agreed that there would be a continual strife between the two till the end of time, and then, a final restitution of all things being made, Oromasdes would reign in an elysium with all the good, and Arimanius be confined to a world of darkness, with all the evil who had followed his counsels on earth.

9. Polygamy prevailed among the Persians. The king had a seraglio, and the nobles followed his example. But though the women were guarded with the most jealous care, shut up in separate apartments at home, and never suffered to go abroad without being closely vailed, yet the virtue of chastity was very rare. To recount the intrigues of the Persian court would disgrace the pages of history. They considered the burning of the dead as a great indignity. It was their custom to wrap the body in wax, and lay it in a sepulchre; but

Questions.—6. Of the succession of the priesthood? How were the sacrifices offered? 7. What is believed with reference to Zoroaster? What did he do? What did he teach? 8. What did he call the good spirit? The evil spirit? How did the Persians discriminate in their petitions? What opinions were held in reference to the two spirits or gods? 9. What is said in reference to polygamy? Burning the dead?

Cyrus commanded his children to restore his body to the earth from which it was formed.

10. B. C. **2300.**—Elam, son of Shem, and brother of that Asshur who founded Nineveh, is supposed to have been the progenitor of the Persians, whence they were called Elamites. B. C. **2000**—In the time of Abraham, Chedorlaomer, king of Elam, assisted by three confederate princes, made war upon the kings of Sodom and Gomorrah, subdued them, and made them tributary 12 years. No further mention is made of Persia till it comes into notice as a province of Media, 1400 years after.

Read Gen. x. 22; Is. xxi. 2, and Acts ii. 9; also Gen. xiv. 1-15.

11. B. C. **800.**—It is interesting to trace the progress of a people from a rude and savage state, in which they subsist upon the spontaneous fruits of the ground, through all the various stages of civilization, till they gain a name and a place among the nations of the earth. In the history of Assyria, we have seen that Arbaces, satrap of Media, was one of the conspirators who dismembered the first Assyrian empire. The Medes then existed in separate tribes, and if Arbaces incorporated them with the second Assyrian empire, no mention of it is made in history. Some time after, Dejoces, a judge of great probity, became so distinguished in his own district, that people came from a distance to appeal to his judgment. Encouraged by his popularity, he formed the design of being king, and pretending disgust with the fatigues of office, retired from business.

12. Lawlessness and iniquity thereupon increased, until, an assembly of the Medes being summoned, the friends of Dejoces represented that the only means of curing these disorders would be to elect a king. This opinion was generally approved, and then they unanimously agreed that there was not in all Media a man so capable of holding the reins of government as Dejoces. He was accordingly elected their king, B. C. 710. When Dejoces ascended the throne, he determined to surround himself with all those external marks of dignity calculated to inspire awe and command respect. He obliged his people to build him a magnificent palace, and chose the noblest of his subjects for his body-guard. The city of Ecbatana, of which his palace was the center, and chief ornament, is thus described by Herodotus:

Questions.—10. What is said of Elam? What is known of Persia during the three following centuries? What took place during the time of Abraham? In what century did that take place? When is Persia again noticed? 11. Who was Arbaces? What is said of Dejoces as a judge? 12. How did he manage to be made king? When was he elected? What did he then determine upon? What did he compel his people to do?

13. "The Medes, in obedience to their king's command, built those spacious and massy fortifications now called Ecbatana, circle within circle, according to the following plan: Each inner circle overtops its outer neighbor, by the height of the battlements alone. This was effected partly by the nature of the ground, a conical hill, and partly by the building itself. The number of circles was seven. The circumference of the outermost wall, is nearly the same as that of Athens. The battlements of the first circle are white; of the second, black; of the third, scarlet; of the fourth, azure; of the fifth, orange; all colored with the most brilliant paints. But the battlements of the sixth are silvered over, and the seventh shines with gold."

14. B. C. **700.**—Dejoces spent most of his time in polishing and refining his subjects. He kept himself secluded from public view, and established the most severe etiquette in the palace. No courtier was allowed to laugh or spit in his presence, and all officers of state approached him with the greatest ceremony. He reigned 53 years. B. C. 675.—Phraortes, son of Dejoces, then ascended the throne. He was ambitious of extending his dominions, and succeeded so far as to bring the barbarous tribes of the Persians into subjection, and, having enlisted the vanquished soldiers into his army, pushed his conquests into Upper Asia.

15. The Assyrians still considered the Medians as a tributary people, and Nabuchodonoser, their king, being engaged in a war, summoned Phraortes to assist him with troops. Phraortes treated the demand with contempt; and Nabuchodonoser, greatly enraged, swore "by his throne and his reign," that he would sweep the Medes from the earth with the "besom of destruction." A battle was fought between the Assyrians and Medes, which proved fatal to Phraortes. He sought safety in flight. Nabuchodonoser pursued his course, penetrated into Media, took the beautiful city of Ecbatana, gave it up to pillage, and stripped it of all its ornaments. He then hunted Phraortes like a hart in the mountains, and, having taken him prisoner, caused him to be set up as a target for his bowmen, in which cruel manner he expired.

16. B. C. 653. CYAXARES.—This prince succeeded to the throne of Media, filled with a determination to avenge his father's death, and

---

Questions.—13. Describe Ecbatana. Where was Ecbatana? (See map No. 1.) What is it now called? *Ans.* Hamadan. What is shown there? *Ans.* The tombs of Mordecai and Esther. What city is now near where Ecbatana stood? *Ans.* Ispahan. 14. How long did Dejoces reign? What is said of his course as king? By whom was he succeeded? When did Phraortes become king? Where did he go? 15. What quarrel did he have? With what result? Relate the manner of Phraortes's death. 16. Who was Cyaxares?

repay the injury done to Ecbatana. Accordingly, having made the requisite preparations, he invaded Assyria. He was victorious in the first engagement, and was pressing on to attack Nineveh, when he was called home to repel the Scythians, a nomadic horde, who, pouring down from their native wilds, were now passing through Media. He hastened to meet them, but met them to his cost. The Scythians defeated him; and, preferring Media to their own country, concluded to settle there. For 28 years these barbarians maintained their position, notwithstanding all the efforts of Cyaxares to dislodge them. They still adhered to their predatory habits; but though they wandered to neighboring countries for pasturage or pillage, they always returned to Media as their home.

17. The Medes, at length, worn out with the enormities of their unwelcome guests, resorted to a stratagem to free themselves. A general feast was proclaimed throughout Media, to which each master of a family invited as many Scythians as he could entertain. The evening passed in festivity, and the barbarians were plied with wine till they sunk into the deep and helpless sleep of intoxication. The massacre then commenced, and so faithfully did the Medes carry out the intention of their king, that most of their tormentors never waked again. The few remaining Scythians fled to the king of Lydia, who received them kindly, and espoused their quarrel. This of course gave rise to a war between the Lydians and Medes.

18. After several years spent in mutual hostilities, the affair terminated in a singular manner. Great preparations had been made for a general battle, but just as the two armies closed in the fight, an eclipse of the sun spread darkness over the scene. The furious combatants paused in the heat of the onset, and gazed in mute terror at the heavens. A dark pall seemed to be hung over the sun, to signify the displeasure of the gods. Both Lydians and Medes, ignorant of the true cause of the phenomenon, and trembling at the fear of speedy judgments, hastened to ratify a peace. An alliance was formed between the contending parties, the daughter of the Lydian king was affianced to Astyages, son of Cyaxares, and the two monarchs, to render the contract binding, opened a vein in their arms and licked each other's blood.

Questions.—16. Upon what did he determine? How much did he accomplish? How was he diverted from his purpose? What then occurred? What conclusion did the Scythians then come to? How long did they remain in Media? 17. How did the Medes at last get rid of them? How was a war between the Lydians and Medes caused? 18. How did the moon affect the fortunes of Cyaxares?

19. Cyaxares, thus relieved from his Scythian foes, returned to his favorite project of humbling Nineveh. Nabopolassar, general of the Babylonian army, disgusted with the weak rule of Saracus, joined him in besieging this great city. In this siege were fulfilled the terrible denunciations uttered by Nahum against the "bloody city," whose oppressions had crushed the people of God for so many years. Astyages, son of Cyaxares, was married to the sister of Crœsus, king of Lydia, according to the contract made during the eclipse. As an oracle had declared that his grandson should be greater than he, he married his only child, Mandane, to Cambyses, a needy Persian prince, hoping thereby to defeat the will of the gods.

Read the 2d chapter of Nahum.

20. B. C. **600.**—In the year 600 B. C., Astyages had a son born, whom he named after his father, Cyaxares. Cyrus, son of his daughter Mandane, was born one year after, and the history of these two princes will be given together. The Persians at this time consisted of twelve tribes, numbering about 20,000 men, and inhabiting a small province, in what is now called Persia. By the wisdom and valor of Cyrus, the name and dominion of Persia afterward extended from the Indus to the Tigris, east and west, and from the Caspian Sea to the Ocean, north and south.

21. CYRUS'S YOUTH.—The system of education which we have previously delineated was rigidly adhered to in the youth of Cyrus. The only food allowed him and his companions was bread, cresses, and water. They were sent to school to learn virtue and justice, just as boys go now to learn the sciences. Speaking the truth was strenuously insisted upon, but the crime most severely punished in them was ingratitude. When Cyrus was twelve years old, his mother took him into Media to see his grandfather. The Persians at this time were far inferior to the Medes in refinement, and Cyrus beheld with astonishment the shining battlements of Ecbatana, and the magnificent palace of the king.

22. The ancients, to set off the beauty of the face, used to form

---

Questions.—19. What was his next movement? Who was Nabopolassar? What can you say of the siege of Nineveh? What is ancient Scythia now called? *Ans.* Tartary. How many children did Astyages have? *Ans.* It is supposed he had three—Amyet, wife of Nebuchadnezzar, and mother of Evil-Merodach; Mandane, mother of Cyrus; and Cyaxares II. The story of the oracle is not generally believed. 20. When was Cyaxares II. born? When Cyrus? Of how many tribes did the Persians then consist? How many men? What country did they occupy? How was the name and dominion of Persia afterward extended? 21. What system was adopted in educating Cyrus? How did the Persians then compare with the Medes in refinement? 22. How did the ancients paint themselves?

the eyebrows into perfect arches by coloring them black. They tinged the lashes likewise with a drug of the same hue, which also possessed an astringent quality, and, by drawing up the lid, made the eye appear larger and more brilliant. When Cyrus saw Astyages painted in this manner, with his purple coat, necklaces, and other ornaments, he went up and embraced him; then, looking at him attentively, he exclaimed, "O, mother, how handsome is my grandfather!" Astyages, pleased with the simplicity of the child, spared no pains to interest and amuse him. He was taught to ride, permitted to hunt in the park with the nobles, and magnificent entertainments were prepared for him; but though Cyrus loved his exercises on horseback exceedingly, he looked with contempt upon the luxuries of the table, observing, that "the Persians, instead of going such a round-about way to satisfy their hunger, found that a little bread and cresses would answer the same purpose."

23. Perceiving that Astyages treated his cup-bearer with great favor, Cyrus begged the honor of being permitted to serve the wine. This being granted, he presented the goblet with such dignity and grace, that all present were charmed with his behavior. Astyages inquired why he omitted the important ceremony of tasting (for it was the duty of the cup-bearer to pour some of the liquor into his hand, and taste it before presenting it to the king); "because," said Cyrus, "I thought there was poison in the wine, for not long ago, at an entertainment you gave to the lords of your court, after the guests had drunk a little of it, I perceived that their heads were all turned; they talked they knew not what, then fell to singing very ridiculously, and you yourself seemed to have forgotten that you were a king, and that they were your subjects." History is silent with respect to the effect of this temperance lecture. When Mandane was preparing to return home, Astyages requested that his grandson might stay with him; and Cyrus, expressing a desire to perfect himself in the art of riding, was permitted to remain there several years.

24. B. C. 583. CYRUS'S FIRST EXPEDITION.—When Cyrus was about sixteen years old, Evil-Merodach, prince of Assyria, was married; and, to celebrate his nuptials, made a great hunting match on the borders of Media. All the nobles of his court attended him, together with a body of light-armed foot, to rouse the beasts from their thickets; but

---

Questions.—22. What is said of the meeting between Cyrus and Astyages? 23. Relate the circumstances in relation to the serving of the wine by Cyrus. 24. Who was Evil-Merodach? (See also Assyria, 27th paragraph.)

when he arrived in sight of the Median garrisons, he thought it would be a greater exploit to plunder them, than to carry home the antlers of stags, or the skins of bears and lions. Notice being given to Astyages that the enemy were in the country, he speedily gathered together what forces he could, and marched to meet them.

25. On this occasion, Cyrus, completely clad in a new suit of armor which his grandfather had caused to be made for him, mounted his horse, and followed the troops. Astyages wondered by whose command he came, but permitted him to remain; and Cyrus, perceiving a body of plunderers making off with their booty, spurred upon them with his uncle, Cyaxares, and put them to flight. After the enemy were completely routed, he would not retire with the rest, but galloped round the deserted field, viewing the slain, till he was almost dragged away by those sent for him. His praise was then in every mouth, and to him was ascribed all the glory of the action.

26. B. C. 582.—CYRUS RETURNS HOME.—Cambyses, hearing of his son's exploit, sent for him home, that he might complete his education according to the institutions of Persia. Astyages, having presented him with horses, and whatever else he delighted in, sent him away. Great multitudes attended him part of the way on horseback, boys, youth, and men. They shed many tears at parting, and Cyrus presented to his companions all those little gifts which he had received from Astyages, and at last, taking off his Median robe, he gave it to Araspes, a youth whom he loved most tenderly. Astyages never saw him again, for Cyrus remained in Persia till his grandfather died, and his uncle, Cyaxares, began to reign.

27. B. C. 560.—Nereglissar, king of Assyria, having overthrown many of the neighboring nations, considered the Medes as the only obstacle to his universal dominion. Being of a warlike disposition, he summoned all his subjects to take up arms, and sending messengers to Crœsus, king of Lydia, and other sovereigns, representing the rising power of the Medes in the most odious light, he entreated them to unite with him in overthrowing them. Cyaxares, on his part, sent embassadors to all his friends for speedy help, and entreated his brother-in-law, Cambyses, to dispatch Cyrus to his assistance, with all the forces he could muster.

28. CYRUS'S SECOND EXPEDITION.—Cambyses, having chosen

Questions.—24. How was a battle between him and Astyages brought about? 25. What account can you give of the battle? 26. Give an account of Cyrus's return home. 27. Who was Nereglissar? Why did he wish to overthrow the Medes? What defensive measures did Cyaxares adopt? 28. How did Cambyses respond?

10,000 archers, 10,000 targeteers, and 10,000 slingers, submitted them to the discipline of his son for a time; and, when all was ready, set off with him for the borders of Media. By the way, he discoursed with him upon the business of an officer, the care of supplies, the manner of encampment, and the necessity of inspiring his soldiers with confidence in his abilities. "But what shall a man do," said Cyrus, "to appear more skillful and expert than others?"—"*He must really be so*," replied Cambyses; "and in order to be so, he must apply himself closely, and study diligently what the most able and experienced have said, and, above all, he must have recourse to the protection of the gods, from whom alone we derive all our wisdom and all our success."

29. Discoursing in this manner, they arrived upon the confines of the two kingdoms, where they made their supplications to the gods, and having embraced each other, the father returned to Persia, and Cyrus marched on into Media to Cyaxares. While the two princes were conferring together upon the discipline of their forces, and the probable number of allies they could bring into the field, embassadors arrived from the king of India, to inquire into the cause of the quarrel between the Medes and Assyrians. They said they were commanded to proceed thence to the court of Babylon, and make the same demand of Nereglissar, and that their master had determined to espouse the cause of the injured. Cyaxares then said, "You hear me declare that we have done no injury to the Assyrians, and if he declares that we have, we choose the king of India himself to be our judge." With this answer the embassadors departed.

30. Both parties were employed three years in forming alliances, and making preparations for war. When Cyrus had all things in readiness, he proposed to lead his army into Assyria, telling his uncle that he thought it better for the troops to eat up the enemy's country than their own, and that so bold a step would inspire them with valor. This course was determined upon, and the troops being drawn up in order of march, Cyrus invoked the wisdom and favor of the gods, beseeching them to smile upon the expedition in which they were engaged. When they reached the confines of Assyria, Cyrus again drew up his army, and paid homage to the gods of the country upon which they had entered, and then dividing his forces into different detachments, he sent them out different ways to plunder the villages of the enemy.

Questions.—28. Relate the conversation between him and Cyrus. 29. How did the king of India undertake to interfere? What reply did Cyaxares make? 30. What bold course was determined upon?

31. Cyrus's First Battle.—The next day they came in sight of the enemy, encamped in the open country, and intrenched with a deep ditch. Cyrus, beholding the multitudes which filled the plain, was glad to avail himself of several hills to conceal the small number of his troops. The next morning the Assyrians moved out of their intrenchments, and before the Persians had time to come up, greeted them with a hail-storm of arrows, stones, and javelins; but when the battle was joined, the superiority of Cyrus's men became evident. They broke the Assyrian and Lydian battalions, and the Median cavalry coming up at the same moment, the enemy thought only of making good their retreat. The panic became general, Crœsus retired, the other allies followed his example, and Nereglissar was slain.

32. Cyrus pursues the Fugitives.—Cyrus, perceiving that without the destruction of the allies, the victory would not be complete, thought best to pursue them that night; but to this Cyaxares was exceedingly averse, being desirous to enjoy the victory, and afraid of incurring any further fatigue. However, after much solicitation, he gave Cyrus permission to take as many of the Median cavalry as would be willing to follow him. A sufficient number were found not only willing, but eager to engage in the pursuit, and after hasty refreshments they set off at full speed. Toward morning they overtook the enemy, put them to a final rout, slew the guardians of the camp, and seized upon the treasures of the confederate kings. Here Cyrus took a great number of horses, which enabled him to accomplish one of his favorite desires, the formation of a body of Persian cavalry.

33. The Hyrcanians also came over to the conquering side, and thus the Persian army, instead of losing by the battle, was greatly reenforced. At sunrise, Cyrus called in the Magi, and desired them to choose out of the booty every thing that was most proper to be offered to the gods. The remainder he delivered to the Medes and Hyrcanians, to be distributed to the whole army. When Cyaxares awoke next morning from the fumes of his wine, he was greatly displeased to find most of his army gone with his nephew. He dispatched an officer to him, with orders to reproach him severely, and bring back the Medes. Cyrus, however, wrote him a respectful letter, and the affair passed over.

Questions.—31. In what were the Assyrians superior? In what the army of Cyrus? Give an account of Cyrus's first battle. Trace Cyrus from Persia to Media and Assyria 32. In what particulars did the characters of Cyaxares and Cyrus differ? How was this difference shown? 33. Where was Hyrcania? (See map No. 3.) In which direction from Media? Persia? Assyria? How was the Persian army increased? What disposition of the booty did Cyrus make? What displeasure did Cyaxares evince? How was he appeased?

34. Two Assyrian Noblemen join the Persians.—While Cyrus was making the necessary arrangements to profit by all these successes, a noble Assyrian, somewhat advanced in years, arrived on horseback, attended by a train of servants. He told Cyrus that he commanded a strong fortress, and had furnished the king with 1,000 horse, and that Nereglissar had sought to ally him to the royal family, by marrying his daughter and son to the young prince and princess. "But alas," said he, "my son, being sent for by the king, went out to hunt with the young prince; and having pierced a lion with his spear, which Laborosoarchod had just missed, the impious wretch stuck a javelin into his breast, and took away the life of my dear, my only son! Then I, miserable man, brought him away a corpse instead of a bridegroom. My king joined with me in my affliction, but the prince has never testified any remorse, nor can I ever serve under him, or give my daughter to the murderer of her brother."

35. When Gobryas had finished his melancholy story, Cyrus gave him his hand, and promised, with the help of the gods, to avenge his cause. The other nobleman, Gadates, had been ill-treated, merely because one of the king's wives had called him handsome; and burning with revenge, he joined with Gobryas in a scheme to bring over the Caducians to Cyrus. They were entirely successful, and the Persian army was thus re-enforced by a strong fortress near Babylon, and a body of 30,000 men.

36. Susian Princess.—Among the prisoners which they had taken was Panthea, wife of Abradates, prince of Susiana. As she was exceedingly beautiful, she was placed in a costly tent, found also among the spoils, till Cyrus's pleasure should be known concerning her. Cyrus committed her to Araspes (the person to whom he gave the Median robe when a boy), but Araspes, not so much engaged in war as his master, fell violently in love with the handsome captive; on this, Cyrus sent him away to the enemy, as if he had banished him; but with secret instructions to act as a spy. Panthea, thinking that she had been the cause of trouble to her noble protector, sent Cyrus word not to be distressed at the loss of Araspes, for she could supply his place with one equally brave; and not long after, being sent to her husband, she persuaded him to come over to the side of the Persians, with all his forces.

Questions.—34. Why did Gobryas, an Assyrian nobleman, join Cyrus? 35. Why did Gadates join him? Where did the Caducians live? *Ans.* In Assyria. What aid did the Assyrian noblemen bring to Cyrus? 36. Relate the story of the captive princess Panthea. What is the modern name of Susiana. *Ans.* Kurdistan. Where was Susiana? (See map No. 3.)

37. Cyrus's Meeting with his Uncle.—When Cyaxares heard that Cyrus was returning re-enforced by the Hyrcanians, Caducians, and Susians, he was filled with envy; and when Cyrus, alighting from his horse, came up to embrace him, he turned away his face, and burst into tears. The tender and respectful conduct of his nephew, however, soon softened him; and many presents, with a splendid supper, removed all unkindness. The next day, a general assembly was summoned to take into consideration the propriety of carrying on the war, and the majority of the allies being in favor of pressing Laborosoarchod to the last extremity, it was decided to make all preparations for another campaign. From deserters and prisoners they learned that the king of Assyria had gone to Lydia, taking with him talents of gold and silver, and presents of the most costly kind. The spies, too, brought in intelligence of the most alarming nature.

38. Like the messengers of evil tidings to Job, one courier seemed to tread on the heels of another, with accounts of the formidable alliances making by the Babylonians. The Indian envoys, who had been to inquire the cause of the war, came back with an exact account of those mighty preparations which agitated all Asia. They said the combined forces were assembling in Lydia; that the Thracians had engaged themselves; that 120,000 men were marching from Egypt; and another army was expected from Cyprus; that the Cilicians, the Phrygians, the Paphlagonians, Cappadocians, Arabians, and Phenicians had already reached the rendezvous; that Crœsus had sent over to form a treaty with the Lacedemonians, and it was thought a greater army would be assembled at Thymbra than was ever before brought into the field.

39. Cyrus marches to Lydia.—Cyrus, on his part, spared no pains to perfect the discipline of his troops, and to strengthen himself by powerful alliances. He knew all the officers of his army by name, and was continually among the soldiers, endeavoring to inspire them with the zeal and ardor he himself felt. The king of India, satisfied that the Assyrians were the aggressors, sent him a sum of money, and promised to stand his friend; but beside the allies who had before joined him, he had no powerful princes to assist him. Notwithstanding the comparative inferiority of his forces, he determined again to carry the war into the enemy's country; and, having left a part of the

---

Questions.—37. What effect did the success of Cyrus have upon the mind of Cyaxares? How was the feeling removed? What was done next day? 38. What is said of the messengers of evil tidings? What forces were in combination against Cyrus? 39. What preparations did Cyrus make? What assistance did he receive?

Medes with his uncle, set forward with his army on his *third expedition.*

40. When a short distance from Thymbra they took some prisoners, who informed them that the Assyrians and their confederates, hearing of their approach, had been three days preparing for battle; and that Crœsus, assisted by a Greek and a certain Mede, were busy in drawing up the soldiers with great exactness. At the mention of the Mede, Cyrus was greatly rejoiced; and not long after, Araspes (for it was he) came to him, bringing an exact account of the disposition of the enemy. As this is the first pitched battle of which we have a particular description, a delineation of it will be given at some length.

41. Marshaling of the Forces.—Cyrus's army consisted of 196,000 men; Crœsus's of 420,000. In addition to the regular infantry and cavalry, Cyrus had three hundred chariots, each drawn by four horses abreast. The pole of each chariot was armed with two long pikes, to pierce whatever opposed its advance, and several rows of sharp knives were placed at the back, to prevent the enemy from mounting behind. At each axletree, horizontal scythes, three feet long, were fastened in such a manner as to mow down the ranks of the enemy; and still further to increase their power, short scythes were fixed, point downward, under the chariot, to cut in pieces whatever the impetuous onset should overturn.

42. He had also a great number of towers mounted on wheels, each drawn by sixteen oxen. Each tower held twenty men, whose business it was to discharge stones and javelins upon the enemy. A body of camels, each trained to fight, with two Arabian archers on his back, were stationed opposite the Lydian cavalry, because a horse will fly from the presence of a camel. Crœsus's troops were ranged in order of battle, *thirty* deep. The infantry filled the center, and the cavalry, with which he meant to surround the Persians, was stationed upon the wings. His army, thus drawn out in line, extended nearly five miles. Cyrus, in order to make as broad a front as possible, placed his infantry only *twelve* deep, and his cavalry in the same manner upon the wings, and then his army fell short of that of Crœsus half a mile at each end.

43. First in the line of infantry came the spearmen; next, the archers; and still a third body, to sustain or threaten those who gave

---

Questions.—40. Where was Thymbra? (See map No. 2.) What information did Cyrus get from some prisoners? What caused Cyrus to rejoice? 41. What was the strength of the respective armies? What is said of Cyrus's chariots? 42. Of his towers? How were the troops of the respective armies ranged? 43. How did Cyrus further arrange his forces?

way—to kill traitors, and keep cowards in their places; and behind them came the moving towers, so high that the soldiers in them discharged their slings and javelins above the heads of the advance Persians; and to prevent all possibility of retreat, a row of baggage was placed behind them, and the lines filled up with infantry and camels, so that the enemy would be obliged to take a long circuit to surround them, and then would be impeded by wagons, boxes, tent-poles, and all the paraphernalia of a camp. The scythe-armed chariots were separated into three divisions; the one commanded by Abradates, placed in front of the battle, and the other two upon the flanks:

CAVALRY.	ARCHERS. SLINGERS. SPEARMEN.	Solid battalion of EGYPTIANS; Thirty men each way.	ARCHERS, ten deep. SLINGERS, ten deep. SPEARMEN, ten deep.	CAVALRY.

CAMELS. CAVALRY. 100 CHARIOTS.	SPEARMEN. SLINGERS. ARCHERS.	100 CHARIOTS. SPEARMEN, 3 deep. ARCHERS, 3 deep. 3d BODY.	SPEARMEN. SLINGERS. ARCHERS.	CAVALRY. CAMELS. 100 CHARIOTS.
CAMP FURNITURE.		TOWERS.	CAMP FURNITURE.	

From this imperfect sketch, an idea may be formed of the position of the troops as they were drawn out the day before the engagement.

44. BATTLE OF THYMBRA.—Early in the morning, Cyrus made a sacrifice; and the soldiers, having taken some refreshment, and poured out libations to the gods, arrayed themselves in their armor of burnished brass, and took their places in the ranks. Panthea had made a robe for Abradates, and she put it on him with her own hands. She bound on his golden helmet and arm-pieces, the tears all the while streaming down her cheeks, though she besought him to prove to Cyrus that he was worthy of the confidence reposed in him. Abradates, lifting his eyes to heaven, prayed that he might appear a husband worthy of Panthea, and a friend worthy of Cyrus; then mounting his chariot, he bade her farewell, and never saw her more! The Persian standard was a golden eagle perched upon a pike, with its wings stretched out, and Cyrus warned his soldiers to take care of that, and move forward without breaking their ranks.

45. When Crœsus discovered how much superior his own forces were to those of Cyrus, he ordered his front to remain firm, while the

Questions.—44. What was done early on the morning of the battle? By what name is the battle known? What aid did Panthea give? 45. Give an account of the beginning of the battle.

wings advanced to inclose the Persians, and join the battle on three sides at once. But at this, Cyrus's wings faced round, and stood thus:

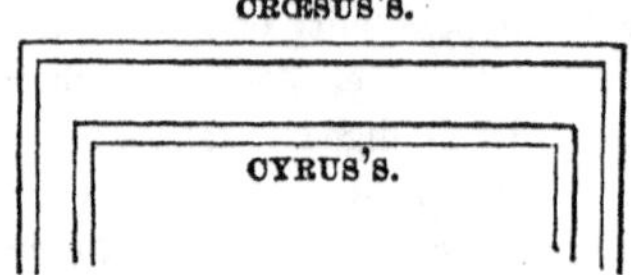

waiting in breathless silence for the event. At once loud and clear rose the voice of their leader, chanting the battle hymn. A responsive shout burst from the soldiers, and with invocations to the god of war they rushed on to the charge. The wings were first engaged; the cavalry of the enemy began to give way before the camels, and the chariots falling furiously into the mêleé, the rout became general.

46. Abradates, who had been waiting for this signal, now commenced the attack in front; but here the Egyptians maintained their ground not only, but overturned the chariots, slew Abradates, and drove the Persian infantry as far back as the fourth line; but there such a tremendous storm of arrows and javelins fell upon their heads from the rolling towers as caused them to waver in their ranks, and at the same instant Cyrus, coming up at the head of his victorious cavalry, attacked them on the rear. Advance or retreat was now impossible; but the Egyptians, turning upon their new assailants, defended themselves with incredible bravery. Cyrus himself was in great danger. His horse having been stabbed by a fallen foe, sank under him, and he was precipitated into the midst of his enemies. Officers and men, equally alarmed at the danger of their leader, rushed headlong into the thick forest of pikes to his rescue. He was quickly remounted, and, his men rallying round him, the battle became more bloody than ever.

47. Concerned at the destruction of so many brave men, Cyrus finally offered them honorable terms of capitulation, and the Egyptians having surrendered, all hope of retrieving the day was gone. The battle lasted till evening. Crœsus retreated as fast as possible to Sardis, and the other kings followed his example, each taking up the line of march for his own country. As soon as the confusion had in some measure subsided, Cyrus inquired of the officers assembled about

---

Questions.—46. Give a further account of the battle. 47. What capitulation was offered and accepted? What allies of the Assyrians fought most bravely? To what place did Crœsus retreat? In which direction is Sardis from Thymbra? (See map No. 2.)

him for Abradates, and one of the servants related his overthrow by the Egyptians. No sooner had Cyrus heard of his death than he leaped to his saddle and set off in search of him.

48. On the bank of the river Patolus sat the wretched Panthea, with the head of her husband on her knees; she was bathing his pale face with her tears, while, with an air of distraction, she watched her servants digging his grave upon a little hill close by: Cyrus came up, with his attendants, bringing sweet odors, ornaments, and every thing proper for the burial; but Panthea seemed incapable of receiving consolation. She sent them all away till she should require their assistance, and then, having exacted a promise from her nurse to wrap her body in the same robe with her husband, she thrust a sword into her bosom, and, laying her head upon his breast, expired. They were wrapped in one mantle, and laid in one grave—the brave Abradates and his loving wife; and Cyrus caused a mound to be raised over them, which continued till the days of Xenophon.

49. Taking of Sardis and Crœsus.—The next day he advanced upon Sardis, and made great preparation for taking it by storm; but a Persian slave betrayed to him a private entrance into the citadel, so that he secured possession of it without bloodshed. He took Crœsus prisoner, and, according to the custom of the times, prepared to burn him. When the pile was lighted, the fallen monarch exclaimed, three times, "O, Solon! Solon! Solon!" Struck with the accent, Cyrus ordered him to be unbound and brought before him. Upon inquiring the cause of this peculiar exclamation, he learned that Solon, an Athenian philosopher, had seen all the monarch's treasures, and yet had refused to call him happy, because he did not know what sad reverses might yet befall him. Thus forcibly reminded of the fickleness of fortune, Cyrus pardoned the king for the sake of the instruction conveyed by the philosopher, and ever after Crœsus was his friend.

50. Cyrus goes to Babylon.—As this war belonged in reality to the Assyrians, Cyrus thought it not terminated so long as Babylon held its supremacy among the nations. So, calling all his troops together, and ranging them in the order of march, he set off for that great city which, since the fall of Nineveh, had been without a rival in Asia. The first measure of Cyrus was to surround Babylon with

---

Questions.—48. Relate the story of Abradates and Panthea. Where is the river Pactolus? (See map No. 2.) 49. Relate the circumstances of the taking of Sardis and Crœsus. Of the escape of Crœsus from execution. What did Cyrus do with Crœsus? *Ans.* He took him back to Persia with him, where he lived to be very old, renowned for his wisdom and piety. 50. In what direction was Babylon from Sardis? (See map No. 3.)

his troops; but so great was the extent of the walls, that his forces seemed weak and contemptible when stretched over so large a space. He therefore called a council of war, and learning from Gobryas and Gadates the position of the palace, and the depth of the river, he entered upon a work every way worthy of his great genius and indomitable perseverance. He drew a line of circumvallation quite round the city with a large deep trench, as though he intended to invest the place and reduce it by famine; but as the besieged had provisions for twenty years, they ridiculed the idea of his taking up his abode there till they were starved into surrender.

51. For two years his troops labored upon the vast excavation, and when it was found capacious enough to drain the Euphrates, together with the artificial lake dug by Nebuchadnezzar, he gave orders, on the night of a grand festival, to break down the dykes, and let the water flow away from its accustomed channel. The bed of the river made the path for his troops, and, once in the city, Gobryas and Gadates conducted them directly to the palace. In the confusion and clamor of killing the guards, Belshazzar seized his sword and ran to the gates, where he was immediately slain, and the two noblemen, amply avenged, took possession of the palace. Cyrus then sent a body of horse up and down the streets, proclaiming safety to those who remained in their houses, and thus, ere the sun again rose on Babylon, "the kingdom of Belshazzar was given to the Medes and Persians."

Read Jer. li. 11; Is. xiii. 15, 22, 17; Is. xlv. 1–4; Is. xxi. 2; and Dan. v.

52. CYRUS'S TRIUMPHAL PROCESSION.—The next morning, those who were shut up in their houses, perceiving that their king was dead, gave up their arms and submitted quietly to the Persian. When Cyrus found himself well established in the kingdom, he prepared to triumph in a manner proportioned to his success. Having called his chief officers together, he gave them each a Median robe, that is, a long garment reaching to the feet, of the brightest colors, and richly embroidered with gold and silver. To the inferior officers he also presented robes of purple or scarlet. The next morning the army assembled before sunrise, clad in the garments which had been prepared for them. Four thousand guards, drawn up four deep, ranged themselves in front of the palace, and 2,000 placed themselves in the same manner on each side. The armed cavalry and gilded chariots were also marshaled, half on one side and half on the other.

Questions.—50. How did Cyrus proceed against Babylon? 51. Give an account of the siege and taking of Babylon. Of the fate of Belshazzar. 52. What took place next morning? What presents did Cyrus make? What display was then made?

53. When all was ready, the gates of the palace were thrown open, and a great number of bulls of peculiar beauty were led out by four and four, to be sacrificed to Jove; next followed splendid horses, to be sacrificed to the sun; then a cavalcade of chariots and horses, followed by men bearing the Sacred Fire in a large hearth; and then Cyrus appeared in his lofty car, with his purple robe flowing gracefully from his shoulders, and a vest of mingled purple and white closely fitted to his noble person. The royal tiara was placed upright upon his head, encircled with the diadem of a conqueror.

54. At sight of him, the people prostrated themselves in adoration; and then the guards, moving forward, made way for the coming of the officers of the king's household, the Immortal Band, the Median cavalry, and the cavalry of the allies. The chariots of war marched in the rear, and closed the procession. Simultaneously, and with beautiful precision, they moved to the fields consecrated to the gods, where the victims were sacrificed in a solemn holocaust to Jupiter and the sun; after which, offerings were made to the earth and to the demi-gods of Assyria. The ceremonies of the day concluded with games and races, and a grand entertainment crowned the evening with mirth. Cyrus then made every one a present, and dismissed the assembly, filled with joy and gratitude.

55. CYRUS MARRIES THE DAUGHTER OF CYAXARES.—When Cyrus had regulated affairs to his mind, he took a journey into Media. Cyaxares was glad to see him, and Cyrus acquainting him with all his arrangements, his uncle was exceedingly rejoiced, and sent his daughter to the conqueror of Asia with a crown of gold, bracelets, a collar, and Median robe. The maid, as she was ordered, put the crown upon his head. Cyaxares then said, "I give you the maid too, as your wife, and all Media as her dowry." Cyrus replied, "I applaud the race, the maid, and the presents, and, with the consent of my father and mother, will marry her." So he continued his journey to Persia, taking with him such magnificent presents as the subjects of his father had never seen, and enough to make them all rejoice in his return.

56. Cambyses greeted him with all the tenderness which a father might feel for so good and dutiful a son, and having constituted him his heir, suffered him to depart again for Media to marry his cousin. The nuptials were performed with all due magnificence, and, accom-

---

Questions.—53 and 54. Describe the ceremonies that followed. 55. Upon the return of Cyrus, how did Cyaxares manifest his pleasure? Why did not Cyrus marry immediately? 56. Was this his first wife? *Ans.* Probably not, for his son Cambyses began to reign nine years after.

panied by his wife and father-in-law, he again returned to Babylon. There Cyaxares reigned two years under the name of Darius the Mede.

DANIEL.—Daniel had now been prime minister to the kings of Babylon sixty-seven years, and such was his reputation for wisdom and integrity, that Darius made him chief of the three superintendents of the kingdom. Darius is supposed to have yielded to the craft of his courtiers in the affair of the lions' den, while Cyrus was absent subduing the countries near the Red Sea.

Read Daniel v. 31; also, Dan. vi. 1-23, and xi. 1.

57. CYRUS KING OF PERSIA, B. C. 536.—By the death of his father and uncle, Cyrus now became sovereign of the Second Universal Monarchy. Every province from the Indus to the Egean acknowledged his authority, and the little territory of which his father had been chief was greatly enlarged. It was twenty-three years since he left Persia, at the head of a small band of soldiers, to engage in war with Nereglissar, the most powerful monarch of the East: his troops, as he now reviewed them, consisted of 600,000 foot, 120,000 horse, and 2,000 armed chariots; and he reigned seven years unquestioned lord of Asia.

58. In the first year of his reign expired the seventieth year of the Babylonish captivity, and Cyrus, true to the prophesy, published the remarkable edict permitting the Jews to return to their own land. "The chosen people," under the conduct of Zorobabel, soon after departed for Jerusalem. Daniel, at whose instigation this favorable turn in their affairs was doubtless effected, must have been at this time more than eighty years old. Josephus says that he was much distinguished for his skill in architecture, and mentions a famous edifice built by him at Susa. It was a common tradition that he died in that city, and was honored with a splendid monument, which remained even to the time of Christ.

59. To return to Cyrus. Historians differ as to the manner of his decease. Herodotus says he died a prisoner, but Xenophon makes him close a long life of enterprise and virtue with a calm and happy

---

Questions.—56. How many years did Cyaxares rule in Babylon under the name of Darius? What individual history in the Scriptures is emphatically connected with that of Darius during his reign in Babylon? Did Daniel remain in Babylon? *Ans.* It is supposed that he died in Susa, in the third year of Cyrus, after having persuaded that monarch to issue the decree to restore and build Jerusalem. 57. When did Cyrus become king of Persia? How extensive was his territory? How large his military force? How long did he reign unquestioned lord of Asia? 58. In the first year of his reign, what edict verified the prophesy in relation to the Jews? Who escorted the Jews to Jerusalem? What is said of Daniel in connection with this circumstance? 59. What difference of opinion is there respecting the death of Cyrus?

death. The minister of God's vengeance upon those nations whose "cup of iniquity was full," he still tempered victory with humanity, and made the dominion of the "Arms of silver" more tolerable than that of the "Head of gold." He fulfilled his peculiar destiny, and effected the purpose for which he was raised up, unconscious that God had chosen him, and called him by name by the mouth of his prophet Isaiah, a century before his birth; but it is thought that his edict for restoring Jerusalem proceeded from a mind instructed in the Divine Oracles; and the Jews say, he acknowledged that he received the empire of the world from the God of Israel.

Read 2 Chron. xxxvi. 22, 23; Ezra i. 1, 2; and vi. 1-5; also, Dan. ii. 38, 39; and vii. 5; also viii. 3, 4, 20.

60. B. C. 529.—CAMBYSES.—Cambyses, son of Cyrus, succeeded to the throne of Persia. The wealth of his kingdom had not failed to affect his morals. As one born to command, he could not bear a refusal of that he desired, even from an equal; so that when Amasis, king of Egypt, sent him another lady for his seraglio, instead of his own daughter, he was filled with rage, and determined to invade that country. His preparations being completed, in the 4th year of his reign he marched to the frontiers of Egypt, where he learned that Amasis was just dead, and that Psammenitus, his son, was gathering all his forces to stop him at Pelusium. This place was very strong, and the siege of it might have detained him some time, had he not resorted to the following stratagem: in front of his army he placed a great number of cats, dogs, sheep, and other animals held sacred by the Egyptians, and then attacked the city by storm. The soldiers of the garrison, not daring to fling a dart or shoot an arrow, for fear of wounding their gods, Cambyses took the place without opposition.

61. Soon after, Psammenitus approached with a large army, and offered battle. A desperate engagement followed, in which the Persians were entirely victorious. Those of the Egyptians who escaped, fled to Memphis. The bodies of the slain were collected, the Persians by themselves and the Egyptians by themselves, and buried in mounds one over against the other. In the days of Herodotus, the bones of the Egyptians and Persians were still moldering in the places where they were buried. The skulls of the former were so hard, that a vio-

---

Questions.—59. What is said of his character? Of his destiny? 60. Who succeeded Cyrus to the throne of Persia? When did that event take place? What influence had the wealth of the kingdom upon the character of Cambyses? In what year did he wage war upon Egypt? Who was the king of Egypt at that time? By what stratagem did he overcome the forces of Psammenitus? 61. Describe the battle that followed. Relate the story of the skulls.

lent blow from a stone could scarcely break them; while those of the latter were so soft, that a man might pierce them with a common walking-stick. The reason of this may be found in the different habits of the two nations. The Egyptians shaved their heads, and went always uncovered, while the Persians wore the turban, both at home and abroad.

62. Cambyses pursued the fugitives to Memphis, and sent a herald to summon them to surrender. Contrary to the laws of war, the Egyptians fell upon him and his attendants, and slew them. Cambyses, doubly enraged, attacked the place without loss of time. His efforts were successful, and as soon as he had made himself master of the city, he selected ten times the number of his slaughtered embassadors from the principal nobility, and caused them to be publicly executed. Among these was the eldest son of Psammenitus. As for Psammenitus himself, Cambyses seemed disposed to treat him with lenity. He spared his life, and appointed him an honorable maintenance; but subsequently, finding him engaged in a conspiracy, he ordered him also to execution. Egypt was thus added to the Persian dominions, B. C. 525. From Memphis, Cambyses proceeded to Sais, where he ordered the dead body of Amasis to be dragged from its tomb, and burned, thinking that the greatest indignity he could offer it.

63. B. C. 524.—THE ETHIOPIAN EXPEDITION.—The next year, Cambyses determined to make war in three different countries, viz.: against the Carthaginians, the Ammonians, and the Ethiopians. The first of these projects he was obliged to abandon, because his Phenician sailors would not assist against the Tyrian colony, Carthage; and the other two served but to show the madness of a man drunk with power. He sent embassadors into Ethiopia, carrying presents of purple cloths, golden bracelets, and perfumes, with secret orders to act as spies, and bring back an exact account of the state and strength of the country.

64. The Ethiopians despised the presents, and with their natural shrewdness concluded the embassadors to be what they really were, enemies in disguise; but to return the courtesy of Cambyses, the Ethiopian king took a bow in his hand, which a Persian could hardly lift, and, drawing it with the utmost ease, said to the messengers, "This is

---

Questions.—61. How long had they been there when Herodotus saw them? *Ans.* About 70 years. 62. Relate the story of the ambassadors. When was Egypt then added to the Persian dominions? What did Cambyses do at Sais? Where was Sais? (See map No. 1.) 63. What project did Cambyses contemplate for the next year? In what year was that? Which of the projects did he abandon? Why? How did he commence against the Ethiopians? 64. How did the Ethiopians act in the matter?

the present, and this the counsel, which the king of Ethiopia gives to the king of Persia. When the Persians shall be able to bend a bow of this bigness and strength, with as much ease as I have now done, then let him come to attack the Ethiopians, and bid him bring more forces than Cambyses is master of. Till then, let him thank the gods for not having put it into the hearts of the Ethiopians to extend their dominions beyond their own country."

65. Upon the receipt of this answer, Cambyses determined to set off immediately, and he made such injudicious haste, that his army was not half supplied with provisions. He pushed on, however, without stopping, till he reached Thebes. There he separated a chosen detachment of 50,000 men, and sent them into Ammonia, with orders to ravage the country, and destroy the famous temple of Jupiter Ammon. The devoted band, strangers to the perils of their journey, set off to obey the mandate of their king. For several days, nothing occurred to hinder their progress, save the hunger and thirst of a desert; but finally a strong wind came up from the south, and lifting the sands like waves of the sea, moved them forward with irresistible power. The terror-stricken Persians struggled manfully with their fate, but the simoom of the desert was stronger than they, and, far from hope or help, they sank down, and were buried beneath the drifting sands.

66. In the mean time, Cambyses pursued his journey. The barrenness of the country increased at every step. For the luxuries of Egypt, the army substituted herbs, roots, and leaves; but these failing, they began to devour their beasts of burden, and finally they were reduced to the horrible alternative of starving or eating one another. The lot was cast, and every tenth man was doomed to become food for his companions. Cambyses, in sight of all this misery, had feasted daily, according to his custom; till at last, so many of his forces died, and discontent became so general, that, fearing a mutiny, he gave orders to return. With the remains of his army he reached Thebes, where he thought proper to vent his mortification upon the temple of the gods. The pillage amounted to 300 talents of gold, and 2,300 of silver; a sum greater than 2,000,000 of our dollars. He also took away the circle of gold from the tomb of Osymandias.

67. CAMBYSES'S TYRANNY.—From Thebes, Cambyses proceeded to

Questions.—65. How did their conduct influence Cambyses? Relate what befell the chosen detachment. Where was the temple of Jupiter Ammon? (See map No. 1.) 66. How did the army of Cambyses suffer? How did Cambyses vent his mortification upon his return to Thebes. Where was Carthage? (See map No. 1.) In which direction was it from Babylon. Ethiopia from Babylon? 67. Tell the story of Cambyses's tyranny to the Egyptians.

Memphis. As he approached the city, the sound of mirth and festivity greeted his ears. Supposing that the people were rejoicing at the ill success of his expedition, he fell into a violent passion, and, sending for the magistrates, demanded of them the cause of these unwonted demonstrations of joy. They told him that their god Apis, recently deceased, had reappeared, and all the people were welcoming his arrival. Considering this as an evasion, he sent them to instant execution. He then called for the priests, of whom he made the same inquiry. Receiving the same answer, he ordered the god himself before him; but when the deity appeared, and he found it was nothing but a calf, he ran up to it, and thrust his sword into its thigh, and upbraiding the priests for worshiping a beast, ordered them to be scourged. The poor calf was carried back to its temple, where it died of its wound. The Egyptians said, that after this impious act Cambyses went mad, but, judging from his conduct, he was bereft of reason long before.

68. Cambyses's only brother, Smerdis, accompanied him into Ethiopia; but as he was the only man who could draw the bow brought back by the embassadors, Cambyses became jealous of him, and sent him home. Afterward he dreamed that Smerdis was king, which so wrought upon his imagination, that he sent Prexaspes, one of his chief favorites, to put him to death. However, Prexaspes was most cruelly punished for his crime by the same jealous tyrant. Cambyses had caused several of his principal noblemen to be buried alive, and so many of his friends had suffered from his fury, that he began to fear for his life. In one of his jealous moods he obliged Prexaspes to tell him what his subjects said of him.

69. Prexaspes spoke with the utmost caution. "They admire a great many excellent qualities they see in you, but they are somewhat mortified at your immoderate love of wine."—"I understand you," replied the king, "they pretend that wine deprives me of my reason: you shall be judge of that immediately." Then calling for the son of Prexaspes, who was his cup-bearer, to bring the goblets, he drank a greater quantity of wine than ever before, and ordering the youth to stand at the farther end of a long hall, with his left hand upon his head, he took his bow, and declaring he aimed at the boy's trembling heart, discharged the arrow. To complete the cruel scene, he commanded Prexaspes to open his son's side, and see if wine had impaired the steadiness of his hand! The wretched father, trembling for his own life, replied, "Apollo could not have shot better."

Questions.—68. Of his tyranny to his brother. 69. Of his tyranny to Prexaspes.

70. CAMBYSES'S DEATH.—In the eighth year of his reign, Cambyses left Egypt for Persia. When he came into Syria, he found a herald there, sent from Susa to proclaim Smerdis, son of Cyrus, king, and to command the army to transfer their allegiance to him. Cambyses, to know the facts in the case, had the herald brought into his presence, and cross-questioned with Prexaspes. From this examination it appeared that the true Smerdis was really dead, and that the usurper could be no other than Smerdis the magian, who bore a strong resemblance to the murdered prince.

71. Upon this, Cambyses made loud and public lamentations, declaring that his dear and only brother had been put to death by mistake, and, ordering all his army to prepare to take vengeance upon the man who had assumed his name, he prepared to march against him. But just as he was mounting his horse, his sword slipped from its scabbard and wounded him in the thigh. The Egyptians looked upon this as a judgment, for the indignity offered their god Apis. When Cambyses saw that he must die, he sent for the chief Persians, and, making them acquainted with all the circumstances concerning Smerdis, besought them not to suffer the sceptre to pass into the hands of a Median tribe, but to elect a king from their own number. He reigned seven years and five months.

72. B.C. 522.—CONCERNING SMERDIS'S EARS.—The Persians, thinking Cambyses had forged the story he told them, out of hatred to his brother, paid no attention to it, and at his death quietly submitted to the magian. To continue the imposture by which he had gained the throne, Smerdis shut himself up in the palace, and admitted only his chief officers to his presence; and to strengthen himself in the kingdom, he married all his predecessor's wives, among whom was Atossa, daughter of Cyrus (for Cambyses had married two of his own sisters), and Phedyma, daughter of Otanes, a noble Persian.

73. This nobleman, suspecting the imposition, sent a messenger to his daughter, to know whether the king was the real Smerdis or some other man. She answered, that never having seen Smerdis, the son of Cyrus, she could not tell. He sent again, bidding her ask Atossa, who would, of course, know her own brother. She replied that the king kept his wives in separate apartments, and she was not permitted

Questions.—70. When did Cambyses leave Egypt for Persia? What danger threatened him in Syria? What facts did he ascertain? 71. What course of duplicity did he pursue? Tell the story of his death. In going from Memphis to Syria, in what direction did Cambyses march? (See map No. 1.) 72. Who was the successor of Cambyses? In what year did the magian gain the throne? By what means did he endeavor to continue the imposition? 73. How was the imposture discovered?

to see Atossa. Otanes sent a third time, telling her that Cambyses had cut off the ears of Smerdis the magian, and bade her watch her opportunity when the king was asleep, and see whether he had any ears or not. She did so, and putting her hands carefully under his turban, found that he was in reality earless.

74. Conspiracy and Confession.—When Otanes learned that his suspicions were correct, he entered into a conspiracy with Darius Hystaspes and five other noblemen, to dethrone the usurper. Every thing was kept secret till the very day fixed for the execution of the plot. On that day a strange circumstance prepared the minds of the people for the event. The magians, constantly uneasy lest their artifice should be unveiled, had extorted a promise from Prexaspes, that he would declare, before an assembly of the people, Smerdis the king to be the son of Cyrus. Prexaspes, at the appointed time, mounted to the top of a tower, and, to the astonishment of the assembled multitude, confessed that he had murdered the true Smerdis with his own hand. He begged pardon of the gods for the crime he had been compelled to commit, and, leaping from the tower, was instantly killed by the fall.

75. Death of Smerdis and Election of Darius.—This unlooked-for event filled the magians with consternation. Smerdis retired to an inner chamber in the palace; thither the conspirators pursued him, and having slain his guards, cut off his head and brought it out to the people. The mob, infuriated at being imposed upon, fell upon the magi, and destroyed so many of them that the day was ever after called "The slaughter of the magi." When the tumult had in some measure subsided, the lords entered into a consultation about the form of government which should be adopted. Otanes declared for an aristocracy, but Darius gave so many good reasons in favor of a monarchy, that he brought the other lords into his opinion, and a monarchy was decided upon.

76. The next inquiry was, who should be king; and this being referred to the gods, the lot fell upon Darius, and he was accordingly anointed sovereign of Persia. The lords who had placed him on the throne were his privy counselors, and in all public affairs were the first to deliver their opinions. They wore their tiaras bent forward, to distinguish them from the king, who wore his upright, and from

Questions.—74. What measures did Otanes take? What did Prexaspes do? 75. Give an account of the death of the impostor Smerdis. How were the magi made to suffer? What consultation was held? With what result? 76. How was Darius elected king? What is said of the wearing of the tiaras?

the other nobles, who wore theirs bent back. 521. B. C.—Darius was the son of Hystaspes, of the royal family of Persia. In his youth he had served under Cyrus, and been rewarded for his valor by the hand of the daughter of Gobryas. After his accession to the throne, he took his predecessor's wives, and Aristona, another daughter of Cyrus. He was the greatest and most powerful king that ever filled the throne of Persia.

77. Cyrus and Cambyses had conquered nations, but Darius was the true founder of the Persian state; the various countries which *they* had brought into subjection, *he* organized into an empire, where every member felt its place and knew its functions. His realm stretched from the Egean to the Indus, from the steppes of Scythia to the cataracts of the Nile. This vast tract he divided into twenty districts, and settled how much each portion was to contribute to the royal treasury; but though the sum required was much less than the inhabitants were able to pay without inconvenience, they murmured at it. They called Cyrus father; Cambyses, master; but Darius they styled "the merchant." The annual revenue in his days amounted to $9,600,000.

78. The building of the temple, and the rearing up of the walls of Jerusalem, had been interrupted in the preceding reigns; but in the second year of this prince, Haggai the prophet, and Zechariah the son of Iddo, stirred up the people to the work. The ancient enemies of the Jews strove to hinder them, and even sent a letter to Darius to advertise him of what was going on in the province of Judea. The records of Cyrus being searched, his decree was found at Acmetha or Ecbatana, and Darius gave orders that the builders should not only be tolerated, but assisted in their pious work.

Read Esther i. 1, 2, and Ezra iv. 4; and v. entire; also vi. 1, 2, 6, and Hag. i. 1.

79. TAKING OF BABYLON.—In the beginning of his reign, Darius meditated an invasion of Scythia; but this expedition was delayed by the revolt of Babylon. During the troubles about Smerdis, and the election of Darius, the inhabitants had been engaged in laying up provisions, and preparing for war: they now boldly threw off the yoke. The Jews, warned by the exhortation of Zechariah, "Thou Zion that

---

Questions.—76. When did Darius become king? What is said of the power and greatness of Darius? 77. What is said of him as a founder and organizer? What was the extent of his realm? Compare it with the realm of Cyrus. Where was the Egean Sea? (See map No. 3.) What is the Egean Sea now called? *Ans.* The Archipelago. Where is the Indus river? (See map of Asia.) Where was Scythia? (See map No. 1.) What are the steppes of Scythia? 78. What is said of the building of the temple and walls of Jerusalem? 79. What invasion did Darius meditate? Why was it delayed?

dwellest with the daughter of Babylon, flee from the country and save thyself," had probably availed themselves of the king's permission, and returned to Jerusalem. To make their provisions last as long as possible, the Babylonians determined to destroy all the unserviceable persons in the place. They assembled their wives and children together and strangled them, only permitting each man to retain his best beloved wife, and one maid-servant to do the work of the family. The capitulation of the city by famine seemed as hopeless as in the days of Cyrus. The Persians tried the old stratagem of draining the Euphrates in vain; the battering-rams made no impression on the massive walls, and at the end of eighteen months victory seemed as far off as ever.

80. But assistance came to Darius in an unlooked-for manner. Megabyses, one of the seven conspirators against Smerdis, had a son Zopyrus whom Darius tenderly loved. What was the king's astonishment to see this young nobleman appear before him one day with his ears and nose cut off, and his whole body mangled in the most shocking manner. Starting up from his throne, he cried out, "Who is it, Zopyrus, that has dared to treat you thus?"—"Yourself, O king," replied Zopyrus; "the desire that I had of rendering you service has brought me into this condition. As I was fully persuaded that you would never have consented to this method, I consulted only the zeal I have for your service." He then unfolded his design to the king, and with him concerted a plan to insure its success. All wounded and bleeding as he was, Zopyrus made his way to Babylon, and begged admittance. The guards took him in, and carried him before the governor.

81. To him Zopyrus represented that Darius had thus mutilated his body, because he tried to dissuade him from continuing the siege, and he added that his only feeling now was a desire of revenge. His name and person were well known at Babylon, his wounds testified to the truth of his story, and the governor fell at once into the snare. Zopyrus was most active in the garrison. He sallied out with the Babylonians, and defeated the Persians in so many engagements, that the whole city rang with his praise. Finally, he was appointed generalissimo of the army, and intrusted with the keeping of the walls. At the time agreed upon, Darius came up with his forces, and Zopyrus opened the gates to his master. The king then ordered the hundred gates to be pulled down, and the massive walls to be demolished, that

Questions.—79. What preparations did the Babylonians make for resistance? 80. What unexpected assistance came to Darius? 81. How was Babylon taken by Cyrus?

the city might never again defy the Persian arms. Three thousand of the principal rebels were impaled, and the remainder received a free pardon.

82. THE SCYTHIAN EXPEDITION.—This inconvenient insurrection being thus terminated, Darius set out for the Scythian war. The whole military force of the empire was put in motion, and the numbers of the army amounted to 700,000 men. His fleet, manned chiefly by Ionian mariners, was directed to sail up the Egean, through the Hellespont and Bosphorus into the Euxine; thence up the Danube to a certain point, where he would join it with his land forces. At the head of his army he moved through Asia Minor, crossed the Bosphorus on a bridge of boats, and proceeded through Thrace to the place of rendezvous. In several places he erected magnificent pillars, with high-sounding inscriptions. On one was carved, "This pillar was erected by Darius, the best and handsomest of all men living."

83. To cross the Danube, he made another bridge of boats, the keeping of which he committed to the Ionians, telling them, if he did not return in two months, they might retire. The Scythians, hearing of this formidable invasion, sent their wives and children, their flocks and herds, into those impenetrable fastnesses, known only to themselves. They also filled up the wells, stopped the springs, and consumed all the forage of those places through which the Persians were to pass. Thus secure, they slowly retreated before the advancing hosts, drawing them on, deeper and deeper, into the forests of Europe. Darius, weary of the tedious pursuit, sent a herald to the king of the Scythians, inquiring why he did not stop and give battle; or, if he feared him, why he did not acknowledge his master, by sending earth and water. The Scythian replied, that he had neither cities nor lands to defend, and that he acknowledged no other master than Jupiter.

84. The farther Darius advanced into the country, the greater were the hardships to which his army were exposed. Just when it was reduced to the last extremity, there came a herald to him from the Scythian prince, bringing a bird, a mouse, a frog, and five arrows, as a present. Darius was sorely puzzled to know what these typified; but one of his seven lords explained the enigma in this manner:

Questions.—81. How did he punish the Babylonians for their revolt? 82. After the insurrection, on what expedition did Darius set out? What direction did he give to the fleet? How did he proceed with the army? Trace the course of the fleet from the Archipelago into the Danube. Trace his land army from Susa to the Pruth, where it joined the fleet. 83. Who were the Ionians? (See map No. 2.) What is said of the bridge of boats across the Danube? What plan of action did the Scythians adopt? What message did Darius send? What reply was made? 84. What was sent to Darius by the Scythian prince?

"Know," said he, "that unless you can *fly* away in the air like a bird, or *hide* in the earth like a mouse, or *swim* in the water like a frog, you shall not be able to escape the *arrows* of the Scythians." The Persians had now come upon a barren country, and were in danger of perishing for want of water, so that Darius found himself under an absolute necessity of abandoning his imprudent enterprise.

85. Therefore, as soon as night came on, the Persians built their camp fires as usual, and leaving the infirm and sick behind them, marched away as fast as possible towards the Danube. The Scythians, discovering their retreat, sent an express by a shorter path, to persuade the Ionians to destroy the bridge, and thus throw the Persian king into their power. Miltiades, then tyrant of Chersonesus, perceiving that this would break the yoke from the neck of the Ionian colonies, strongly advocated the measure; but Histiæus, governor of Miletus, represented that, as they held their power of Darius, to turn against him would be to destroy themselves. The Persians were therefore permitted to pass the bridge in safety, and Darius finally reached Sardis, where he spent almost a year in recruiting his army.

86. CONQUEST OF INDIA.—B. C. 508.—To wipe away the disgrace of this unfortunate enterprise, the Persian monarch shortly after undertook an expedition against India. He caused a fleet to be fitted out upon the Indus, which, under the command of Scylax, passed down through the Southern Ocean, and up the Red Sea. By the conquest of India, an immense revenue was added to the Persian treasury. 502. B. C.—This year, to attach the Phenicians to his interest, Darius restored independence to Tyre, seventy years after it was taken by Nebuchadnezzar.

Read Is. xxiii. 15.

87. B. C. **500.**—This century is filled with the most important events to Persia and Greece. The Persian invasions introduce so complete and interesting a comparison of these rival powers, that the attention of the historian is especially directed to them, and the student is requested to make himself particularly familiar with all the causes which contributed to the overthrow of the hosts of Asia by the Grecian states. Histiæus, tyrant of Miletus, who had preserved the bridge of boats

---

Questions.—84. How was the riddle explained? 85. By what stratagem did Darius escape? By whose policy was he suffered to repass the bridge committed to the care of the Ionians? Trace Darius from the Pruth to the Volga, and back to Sardis. 86. What expedition did Darius next undertake? Why did he do so? What course did his fleet take? How did he attach the Tyrians to his interests? 87. Who was Histiæus? Where was Miletus? (See map No. 2.) What can you say of Miletus? *Ans.* It was reckoned next to Carthage and Tyre for its commerce. What invitation was extended to Histiæus? Where was Susa? (See map No. 1.) In what direction was Susa from Miletus?

over the Danube, was invited to Susa by Darius. Before setting out for court, he committed the government of Miletus to Aristagoras, his son-in-law. About the same time, Darius made his own brother, Artaphernes, governor of Sardis. A quarrel arose between Aristagoras and Artaphernes. Histiæus, who knew the character and temper of the Greeks, and was at the same time anxious to return home, sent a messenger to Aristagoras, telling him that his wisest course would be, to revolt from the Persians entirely, and to engage all the Ionian colonies to do the same.

88. Aristagoras complied with his father's desire, and soon all the states of Grecian descent in Asia Minor were engaged in a common league against Persia. Still further to strengthen his arm, Aristagoras made a voyage across to the Egean, to persuade the Greeks, by their ties of kindred, and their ancient freedom, to assist their brethren of Ionia in regaining their liberties. An insult which the Athenians had themselves received from Persian pride, induced them to listen to his representations. About ten years before, they had banished Hippias, for usurping authority over the state. Artaphernes had received the exile, and listened to his complaints. The Athenians sent to justify their conduct to the Persian governor, and received for answer, if they wished to be safe, they must take Hippias for their king. When Aristagoras therefore told them of the oppressive rule of Artaphernes over the Ionian colonies, and entreated their help to break the yoke, they entered readily into his feelings, and agreed to assist the league with twenty ships.

89. Burning of Sardis.—The Eretrians, inhabitants of a little city in Eubœa, added five more; and with this slight re-enforcement, Aristagoras returned to Ephesus, where he landed with his confederates, and marched to Sardis. The governor retired to the citadel; the Greeks had free plunder; and a soldier, perceiving that most of the buildings were roofed with reeds, set one of them on fire. The flames spread from house to house, and soon the whole city was on fire. This burn-

---

Questions.—87. Who was made governor of Sardis? Between whom did a quarrel begin? What advice was given to Aristagoras? How had the Ionian colonies been settled? *Ans.* Asia Minor was originally settled by the descendants of Javan, who therefore were of the same family as the Ionians; but the term Ionians embraces only the colonies settled by the Grecians driven from Peloponnesus, after the Trojan war, by the Dorians. Eolia had eleven cities and Ionia twelve. They were subjugated by Crœsus, and of course, fell with Lydia under the dominion of Persia. 88. With what success were the efforts of Aristagoras attended? Why did the Athenians listen to him? Where is Athens? (See map No. 2.) 89. Who were the Eretrians? Where was the island of Eubœa? (See map No. 2.) What is it called now? *Ans.* Negropont. Give an account of the burning of Sardis.

ing of Sardis by Aristagoras and the Athenians was the torch which lighted the flame of war in Asia Minor, and kindled in the breast of Darius an inextinguishable desire for revenge. When the intelligence was brought to him, he called for a bow, put an arrow into it, and shot it into the air, with these words: "Grant, O Jupiter, that I may be able to revenge myself upon the Athenians." After he had thus spoken, he commanded one of his attendants to exclaim thrice every time dinner was set before him, "Master! remember the Athenians."

90. DEATH OF ARISTAGORAS AND HISTIÆUS.—During all these commotions, Histiæus had remained in Susa; but perceiving that Darius suspected that his relative had acted by his directions, he begged permission to go and quell the revolt. His request was finally granted; but before he arrived at Miletus, Aristagoras was slain in battle. Histiæus offered himself at once to the Ionians, and used every means in his power to become head of the league; but they all feared him, and at last, his intrigues being discovered, he was crucified by Artaphernes.

91. EXPEDITION OF MARDONIUS, B. C. 494.—In the 28th year of his reign, Darius, having fitted out a fleet, committed it to the command of Mardonius, his son-in-law, with orders to punish the Greeks for the burning of Sardis. Mardonius was a young man, and not over skillful in the art of war; and though more entitled to consideration for being the king's son-in-law, was not perhaps the more gifted on that account. In doubling Mount Athos, his fleet encountered a violent storm, in which three hundred ships were wrecked, and about 20,000 men drowned. His land army shared a similar fate. The Thracians attacked the camp by night, made a great slaughter, and wounded Mardonius himself. Thus the first army fitted out against Athens did not succeed in reaching Greece at all!

92. EXPEDITION OF DATIS AND ARTAPHERNES.—The losses of Mardonius only animated Darius to greater exertions. He caused another army to be assembled, appointed Datis and Artaphernes, two generals of tried abilities, to command it, and engaged the banished Hippias to conduct them to Athens by the shortest route. However, to leave no stain upon his clemency, he first sent heralds into Greece, demanding

---

Questions.—89. What was the consequence? Where was Sardis? (See map No. 2.) 90. What became of Aristagoras? What did Histiæus do? 91. Who was Mardonius? What command was given to him? In what year did that occur? Where is Mount Athos? (See map No. 2.) What disaster occurred there? What further is said of the expedition? 92. What effect did the losses of Mardonius have upon the mind of Darius? How did he undertake to relieve himself against a charge touching his "clemency?"

"earth and water." Some of the States, intimidated by the mighty preparations making in Asia, yielded the required tokens of submission; but the heralds sent to Athens and Sparta were thrown, one into a ditch, and the other into a well, and tauntingly told to help themselves to "earth and water."

93. When every thing was ready, Darius sent away his generals, telling them to give up Athens and Eretria to be plundered, to burn all the houses and temples, and to bring all the inhabitants to Persia, bound in chains, which he provided for that purpose. This time the Persians passed directly across the Egean, and landed without any accident upon the island of Eubœa. They took and burned the city of Eretria, according to the commandment, and sent home a company of chained captives as an earnest of future victories. Thence conducted by Hippias, they departed, crossed the strait of Euripus, and landed on the plains of Marathon. A description of this battle will be given in the history of Greece. Let it suffice to say, that the Persians were totally defeated, that they made a rapid retreat, and that Hippias was slain. Thus ended the second attempt upon Greece.

94. Further Preparations of Darius.—The anger of Darius was doubly inflamed against Athens by the event of Marathon, and he resolved that the insolent people who had invaded his territories, burned his city, abused his heralds, and driven his generals to a shameful flight, should feel the full weight of his arm. The preparations he now set on foot, were on a vast scale, and demanded a longer time. For three years all Asia was kept in a continual stir; in the fourth, his attention was distracted by a quarrel between his sons respecting the succession, and by an insurrection in Egypt. The crown he settled upon Xerxes, his eldest son by Atossa, daughter of Cyrus; but he died before he had finished his preparations against Egypt and Athens. He reigned thirty-six years. On his tomb was inscribed, "We were able to drink much wine, and to bear it well."

95. Xerxes the Great, B. C. 485.—By the death of Darius, and the accession of Xerxes the Persian, the scepter passed from the hands of a prince reared among the privations of a camp, to one born in a palace,

---

Questions.—92. How were the heralds treated who were sent to Athens and Sparta? 93. What directions followed from Darius to his generals? What did the Persians accomplish? Where did they meet total defeat? What course did the fleet take in sailing from Ephesus to the island of Eubœa? (See map No. 2.) From Eubœa to Marathon? 94. How did the disaster at Marathon affect Darius? What quarrel distracted his attention from military preparations? Who was Xerxes? How and when did he become king? How long had Darius reigned? What was inscribed upon his tomb? 95. What is said of the early life of Xerxes in contrast with that of Darius?

the favorite son of a favorite queen, who had been nurtured in luxury, and taught to look upon the kingdom as an inheritance to which the blood of Cyrus gave him a pre-eminent claim. Xerxes was not naturally ambitious, but his flatterers persuaded him that it was absolutely necessary for him to carry out the great projects which his father had left unfinished. The Egyptians were first punished. He invaded the country in person, and purposely made the yoke of the inhabitants more galling than before. Stimulated by this success, he resolved on the invasion of Greece.

96. A council was called of the most illustrious persons in the empire, before whom he laid his plans. The speech put into his mouth by Herodotus, will best display the character and extent of his views. "I desire," said he, "to imitate the example of my predecessors, who all distinguished their reigns by noble enterprises. I ought to revenge the insolence of the Athenians, who presumed to fall upon Sardis and burn it to ashes. I ought also to revenge the disgrace which my country received at the battle of Marathon. I anticipate great advantages from a war which may lead to the conquest of Europe, the most fertile country in the universe." After thus expressing his desires, and adding various arguments in favor of their being carried out, he waited till the others should express their opinions.

97. Mardonius spoke first, and gave his voice for war, as necessary to wipe out the foul blots from the Persian name, and to teach the cowardly Greeks the danger of offending the great king. The rest of the assembly, seeing how well Xerxes received his brother-in-law's adulation, dared not contradict it, with the exception of Artabanus, the king's uncle, who endeavored to divert the course of deliberation to more serious considerations than the *glory* of the expedition. But Xerxes, who could not bear contradiction, gave his faithful adviser a severe rebuke, and told him that he should be punished by being left among the women, whom he resembled in cowardice. The war was therefore resolved upon.

98. Preparations for War.—Xerxes's aim was not merely to collect a force sufficient to overcome all opposition, but to set his whole power in magnificent array, that he might enjoy the sight of it himself, and display it to the admiration of the world. For four years longer

---

Questions.—95. How was his ambition first aroused? What successful enterprise influenced him to invade Greece? 96. How, according to Herodotus, did he express his desires? 97. For what purpose did Mardonius second the wishes of Xerxes? Who was Artabanus? What did he do? What rebuke did he consequently receive? 98. What warlike preparations were made during the next four years?

Asia was kept in restless turmoil: less time would not suffice to provide subsistence for the countless host about to be poured upon Europe. Besides the stores to be carried by the fleet, magazines were to be formed along the whole line of march as far as the confines of Greece. The most skillful engineers of Phenicia and Egypt were sent forward to build a bridge of boats across the Hellespont, and a multitude of men were dispatched to the Chalcidice to excavate a canal through the isthmus which joined Mount Athos to the continent. Nay, the "great king" himself honored the mountain with a letter couched in these terms: "Athos, thou proud aspiring mountain, that liftest thy head to the heavens, be not so audacious as to put rocks and stones in my way. If thou opposest my servants, I will cut thee down, and throw thee headlong into the sea."

99. When these preparations were drawing to a close, Xerxes set forth for Sardis, where he designed to spend the winter, and gather the multitudes together, who were assembling in all the provinces of his vast empire. During his stay in this place, a violent storm drove the boats from their moorings, and destroyed the bridge over the Hellespont. Xerxes, enraged at the loss of so much time and labor, put the architects to death, and caused chains to be thrown into the sea to teach it submission. Another bridge was speedily commenced of double rows of boats; one for the army, and the other for the baggage. This bridge was made by chaining together 674 vessels, and fastening them at each end by cables thrown over strong piles driven into the earth. Massive anchors were dropped from the sides to hold them in their places; flat-bottomed boats, lashed firmly together, formed a floor above, and battlements were erected on each side to prevent the cattle from being frightened by the violence of the waves. The length of the bridge was not far short of a mile.

100. XERXES'S MARCH.—Early in the spring (B. C. 480), Xerxes began his march from Sardis with the mighty armament which had been collected from Media, Persia, and all the tributary nations, a motley crowd, including many strange varieties of complexion, dress, and language, each tribe retaining its national armor and mode of fighting. There were recruits from all the different people who were allied with Crœsus against Cyrus the Great. There was the Immortal Band; there the Median cavalry; there the Persian lancers, with

Questions.—98. What letter is mentioned? 99. To what place did Xerxes then go to spend the winter? What misfortune took place while he was there? What did Xerxes thereupon do? Describe the second bridge. 100. Give a description of the great army of Xerxes.

spears knobbed with gold; there the sacred horses richly caparisoned; and there the royal chariot where Xerxes sat in state, except when, fatigued with riding, he sheltered himself from the heat of the sun in an easier carriage. The fleet coasted along the Egean, and the army moved forward to Abydos, a city of Bithynia, near the straits.

101. Here Xerxes, desirous to witness a mock sea-fight, ascended a lofty throne and beheld, as far as the eye could reach, the bosom of the Hellespont crowded with his ships, and the plains and mountains of ancient Ilium covered with his troops. A feeling of pride and satisfaction spread through his heart as he surveyed the glittering array, and reflected that, at the head of the largest army ever brought into the field, he was about to subjugate the fairest portion of the earth. But a sudden shade passed over his countenance: for a moment the pomp and pageantry of the mustered hosts faded from his view: "In one hundred years' time," said he, "not one living soul will remain of all the thousands who now surround me;" and the monarch, throned in power and pride, wept at the thought.

102. Passing the Bridge.—As soon as the sun's first rays appeared upon the horizon, the bridge was strown with myrtle, and sprinkled abundantly with sweet odors. Then Xerxes poured out libations into the sea, and, turning his face to the rising sun, implored the protection and guidance of the great god Mithras, till he should complete the conquest of Europe. After golden vessels and a sword had been thrown into the sea, the ten thousand Immortals, crowned with chaplets, advanced upon the bridge. The army followed as rapidly as possible, the officers lashing the poor soldiers all the way to quicken their speed; yet so vast was the multitude that the living tide flowed without interruption seven days and seven nights before the last man, Xerxes himself, the tallest and most majestic person in all that host, had arrived upon the European shore.

103. In the great plain of Doriscus, on the banks of the Hebrus, an attempt was made to number the army. Ten thousand men were formed in as small a space as possible. A fence was then raised around them; they were dismissed, the inclosure filled again and again, till all had passed within the circle; and according to this muster the infantry alone amounted to 1,700,000. The cavalry was counted by

---

Questions.—100. How did the fleet and army proceed? Where was Abydos? (See map No. 2.) 101. What took place near Abydos? What feeling pervaded his mind in view of his greatness? What moral sentiment even then subdued the haughty monarch to tears? What waters did the Hellespont connect? (See map No. 2.) 102. Describe the crossing of the Hellespont. 103. Of how many persons did the army of Xerxes consist? What method was adopted to number them?

divisions, and the mariners by the number which each ship carried, and the whole exceeded two millions and a half of fighting men. The women and servants who always attended the Persian camp could not be less than as many more, so that the whole body was estimated at five millions.

104. To feed this multitude with only the scanty portion allowed to slaves, required 662,000 bushels of flour per day; yet such preparations had been made that, with the provisions laid up in the magazines and those carried by the vessels of burden, there was no lack of any thing in the camp. Avant, couriers had been sent out to prepare for the coming of the lord of Asia. Wherever the royal train halted a superb pavilion was erected, adorned with the most costly furniture. Many cities of Europe, anxious to propitiate the mighty power moving through their territories, provided even vessels of gold and silver for the table. The rapacious attendants of the Persian court spared nothing; in the morning, when the army marched, all was carried off. In this manner Xerxes continued his course till he reached the spot where Demaratus, a banished Lacedemonian king, had told him he would find his whole army stopped by a handful of men.

105. THERMOPYLÆ.—Thermopylæ is a narrow pass of Mount Œta, about fifty paces broad. On one side roared the sea; on the other rose the precipitous mountain. Through this narrow defile lay the path of the Persians, and an army could scarcely reach Attica by any other route. When Xerxes came to this place, he found the truth of Demaratus's words. A band of heroes were stationed here, determined to give such an impression of Grecian valor as should teach the haughty Persians the character of the men they had come to enslave. Xerxes waited four days, hoping to frighten them away, or bribe Leonidas, their leader, to betray his country. He waited in vain, and Leonidas rejected his offers with scorn.

106. On the fifth day he ordered a body of Median cavalry to fall upon the rash and insolent enemy, and lead them all captive into his presence. A throne was erected for him, from which he could survey the narrow entrance of the pass, and the prowess of his soldiers. Their numbers served only to impede their efforts; the foremost fell, the hinder advanced over their bodies to the charge; their repeated onsets

Questions.—103. How many women and servants were along? How many persons, then, were there in all? 104. What is said of provisions for the camp? Of occurrences during the march of the army? From whom had erxes received a warning? What was the warning? 105. What is Thermopylæ? Describe it. Where was it located? (See map No. 2.) What did Xerxes find there? For what did Xerxes wait in vain? 106. What occurred on the fifth day?

broke upon the Greeks idly as waves upon the rock. The day wore on; and, spent with fatigue, and greatly thinned in their ranks, they were recalled from the contest. The despised Greeks were now thought worthy to cope with the Immortals, and all the next day the impatient monarch saw with grief and rage the slaughter of his own body-guard. Three times he started from his throne, as though about to chastise the intrepid Spartans with his own hand for the havoc they were making in his chosen band.

107. The day following, the attack was renewed with no better success, and the confidence of Xerxes was changed to gloom and despondency, when an inhabitant of the country revealed to him a secret path over the mountain. A party was immediately sent out with the traitor, and by daybreak the next morning the Grecians learned that the Persians were coming over the brow of the mountain, and before noon the devoted band of Spartans were attacked in front and rear by the whole power of Xerxes. They fought desperately to the last, and were finally overwhelmed by the arrows, javelins, and stones of the enemy. Where they fell they were buried; their tomb, as the poet sang, was an altar; a sanctuary, in which Greece revered the memory of her second founders. Xerxes lost 20,000 men in this engagement, and his fleet also suffered the same day a severe defeat off Cape Artemisium.

108. Detachment sent to Delphi.—Xerxes had heard so much of the wealth of Delphos, that he thought to enrich himself by the plunder of its treasures. A detachment was accordingly sent across the Parnassian mountains, to bring away the vessels of gold and silver deposited there. The Delphians, hearing of its approach, asked counsel of the oracle. The Pythia responded, "The arms of Apollo will be sufficient for the defense of his shrine." Thus encouraged, no preparations were made to resist the enemy. As the Persians were marching through the dark and deep defiles of the mountains, a violent storm arose, the wind prostrated huge trees across their path, the mountain torrents loosened rocks and stones, and poured them down upon them with a mingled tide of earth and water; the Delphians added their wild cries to the howling of the storm; and the thunder, repeated by a thousand echoes, completed their consternation. They

---

Questions.—106. On the sixth? 107. On the seventh? What treason occurred? Describe what followed. How many men did Xerxes lose? What other loss did he sustain? Where was Cape Artemisium? (See map No. 2.) 108. By what means did Xerxes expect to enrich himself at Delphi? Where was Delphi? (See map No. 2.) Give an account of the march and overthrow of the detachment.

fled, or fell, overcome with terror; they trampled one upon another; they became entangled in the forest or were thrown down precipices; and but few of them ever returned to tell the tale of their disaster.

109. Burning of Athens.—Meantime, the rest of the Persians advanced through Beotia to Attica. No troops came out to dispute their passage. Xerxes thought he had not calculated in vain upon the cowardice of the Grecians. When he reached Athens, the streets were deserted. With the exception of a few old people, devotees and priests, who had taken shelter in the citadel, every person had escaped to the islands of Egina and Salamis. Xerxes plundered the temples, stormed the citadel, and reduced the city to ashes. The pictures and statues which the refined Athenians had spent years in executing, he sent to his uncle Artabanus, with the glad tidings *that Athens had shared the fate of Sardis.*

110. Battle of Salamis.—In the narrow strait between Attica and Salamis, the little fleet of the Greeks awaited the storm of war which was slowly rolling round the promontory of Sunium. The Persians advanced with their numerous vessels, and filled up the port of Phalereum. In the consternation and agony of seeing their city burned, and their bay crowded with hostile ships, many of the Greeks advocated the propriety of moving down to the vicinity of Corinth, and awaiting the enemy there; but Themistocles induced them to give battle there, and thus the engagement took place in a strait so narrow that the Persians could scarcely turn their ships, but were forced to fight hand to hand. From a lofty eminence, Xerxes again beheld his troops repulsed by the hardy Greeks; many of his ships were entangled and sunk, and his disheartened soldiers retired in the greatest disorder.

111. That night the whole fleet abandoned the coast of Attica, and sailed away for the Hellespont. Mardonius, who perceived that Xerxes was desirous of escaping from the dangers and mortifications which surrounded him, proposed that the king should return to Asia with the body of the army, leaving himself, with 300,000 of the best troops, to complete the conquest of Greece. To this proposal the monarch gladly assented. Xerxes, having passed into Thessaly, permitted Mar-

---

Questions.—109. In what direction was Beotia from Thermopylæ? (See map No. 2.) How is Athens situated? What did Xerxes find on reaching Athens? What acts did he commit at Athens? What tidings did he send to his uncle? 110. In which direction was the island of Salamis from Attica? (See map No. 2.) What account can you give of the disaster to the Persian navy? By what name is that battle known? 111. What then was done by the fleet? What proposition was made to Xerxes? What prompted Mardonius to make it? To what place did Xerxes then retreat? Where is Thessaly? (See map No. 2.)

donius to select his soldiers, and leaving them to winter there, pursued his march toward Asia. "Widely different from the appearance of the glittering host which a few months before had advanced over the plains of Macedonia and Thrace to the conquest of Greece, was the aspect of the crowd which was now hurrying back along the same road. The splendor, the pomp, and the luxury and ease were exchanged for disaster and distress, want and disease." The contents of the magazines had been destroyed or purloined by those who had the charge of them; comfortable food was not to be obtained; and as the retreating multitude passed those places, impoverished by their recent visit, they were forced to subsist upon the bark and leaves of trees.

112. Sickness came with famine; great numbers were left to the charity of their enemies; and when they reached the river Strymon, numbers still greater were drowned in attempting to pass upon the ice, which the sun was fast melting away. In forty-five days after he left Mardonius, Xerxes reached the Hellespont. The rebellious sea had torn his vessels from their anchors, and dashed in pieces the bridge which it had cost so much time and labor to construct; but the fleet (or what remained of it) was there, to transport the poor fragment of his army to Abydos. The exploits of Mardonius will be recounted in the history of Greece. The life of Xerxes, after this inglorious campaign, may be told in a few words. He gave himself up to a round of pleasures, and was slain by Artabanus, captain of his guards, B. C. 474.

113. Artaxerxes Ascends the Throne.—Xerxes had four sons: Darius, Hystaspes, Artaxerxes, and Achæmenes. When Artabanus left the chamber of the murdered monarch, he went directly to that of Artaxerxes, and, awakening him from sleep, told him that his brother Darius had assassinated his father. The youth immediately arose, and without waiting to inquire into the affair, hastened to his brother's bed and killed him. Artabanus having thus got rid of Xerxes and Darius, proclaimed Artaxerxes king, thinking he would prove a convenient tool, till a faction could be formed strong enough to place the crown upon his own head; but the young prince, suspecting the game his pretended friend was playing, ordered him to execution. By this time, intelligence of his father's death had reached Hystaspes, governor

Questions.—111. What comparison is made? What is said of the destitution that existed? 112. Of sickness? Numbers left? Of what occurred at the Strymon? Where was the Strymon? (See map No. 2.) What had occurred at the Hellespont? How, then, did Xerxes get to Abydos? What further account can you give of Xerxes? 113. How many sons did Xerxes have? Give their names. By what means did Artaxerxes obtain the throne?

of Bactria, who consequently prepared to assert his right to the crown. Two battles were fought by the rival brothers; in the last of which Hystaspes was slain. Artaxerxes thus gained quiet possession of the throne of Persia, B. C. 473. He was called Artaxerxes Longimanus, from the length of his arms.

114. THE EGYPTIAN REVOLT.—B. C. 466.—The Egyptians always wore the yoke of Persia uneasily; and in this year, having made Inarus, prince of the Lybians, their king, they revolted. Artaxerxes sent his brother Achæmenes, with 300,000 men, to reduce them to obedience. It fared ill with the Persians at first. The Athenians made alliance with the Egyptians, and Achæmenes was slain with one-third of his army. The other 200,000 Persians made their escape to Memphis, where they entrenched themselves in a part of a city called the White Wall. There the Egyptians besieged them three years. As soon as practicable, Artaxerxes fitted out another army to go to the relief of his unfortunate subjects. While Artabasus sailed up the Nile, with a part of the troops, Megabysus (son of Zopyrus, who gained Babylon) advanced with his division by land to Memphis.

115. The tables were now turned. Defeat followed Inarus and his allies, while victory crowned the efforts of the Persians. The besiegers were in their turn besieged in Biblos, a city built between two arms of the Nile. For a year and a half the Persians maintained the blockade; and finally, by draining one of the encircling arms, opened a passage to the city. Inarus then surrendered, with fifty of his Athenian friends, on the solemn promise of Megabysus that their lives should be spared. The rest of the Grecians had free permission to leave the country, and the Egyptians were again reduced to servitude. Artaxerxes kept Inarus and the Athenians five years as prisoners of war, during which time his mother importuned him daily to deliver them into her hands, that she might sacrifice them to the manes of her son Achæmenes. Overcome by her entreaties, the king finally yielded, and the inhuman princess put them all to a cruel death.

116. Megabysus felt this contempt of his solemn oath most keenly. He left the court, retired to his government of Syria, and finally openly revolted. After overcoming the armies sent against him, and in all things showing himself superior to his sovereign, he was at last per-

---

Questions.—113 Why was he called Artaxerxes Longimanus? 114. Why did the Egyptians revolt from Persia? Who was their king? Who were sent against the Egyptians? What became of them? Where was Memphis? (See map No. 1.) 115. In what manner were the tables turned upon the Egyptians? Upon what condition did Inarus surrender? Was the condition faithfully complied with? State how it was not. 116. Why was Megabysus displeased? What course did he pursue?

suaded to return to his allegiance by his wife Amytis, sister of Artaxerxes. But in hunting with the king one day, like the son of Gobryas, he killed a wild beast, which the monarch had roused from the thicket. Though by this act he saved the life of his royal master, yet he was condemned to die for a breach of court etiquette. His wife again interposed, and prevailed upon her brother to commute his punishment into banishment. After remaining five years in lonely exile, he disguised himself as a leper, and repaired to Susa, where his wife recognized him, and by entreaties again restored him to royal favor, which he enjoyed till his death. He was a man of the greatest abilities, and the ablest general in all Persia.

117. HISTORIANS.—In the reign of Artaxerxes, Esdras, Nehemiah, and Ezra were sent to Jerusalem. They arranged the books of Scripture in their present order, composed the books of Chronicles, and those bearing their own names. While engaged in this important business, Herodotus commenced his works, so that profane history took the seal of authenticity about the time that the sacred writers closed their labors. Herodotus was followed by Xenophon, Diodorus, Livy, Tacitus, and others whose works still exist in the original Greek and Latin. This Artaxerxes is supposed to have been the husband of Esther.

Read Neh. i. entire; and ii. 1–8; also xiii. 6, 7. Ezra vii. 1, 6, 7, 8, 11, 12–26; and viii. 31, 32; also Esther x. entire.

118. XERXES II. B. C. 425.—Xerxes was the only legitimate son of Artaxerxes; but it was his misfortune to have seventeen half-brothers, one of whom, Sogdianus, followed the newly elected monarch to his apartment, and killed him while overcome with wine. He reigned 45 days. Sogdianus then, B. C. 424. assumed the royal tiara, to wear it only about six months. All his brothers envied him, and *he* feared all his brothers. Ochus, governor of Hyrcania, to escape the death which Sogdianus threatened him, openly declared himself the avenger of Xerxes's blood. The nobility joined him; Sogdianus was taken prisoner, and thrown into a cylinder filled with ashes, which was made to revolve till he was suffocated. He reigned 195 days.

119. OCHUS, OR DARIUS NOTHUS.—B. C. 424.—As soon as Ochus ascended the throne, he took the name of Darius, to which the Greeks

---

Questions.—116. Give a further account of him. 117. What historians were sent to Jerusalem during the reign of Artaxerxes? What did they accomplish while there? Who commenced writing profane history at that time? By whom was Herodotus followed? Whose husband was Artaxerxes supposed to have been? 118. Give a sketch of the life of Xerxes II. Of Sogdianus. What was there peculiar in Persian punishments? 119. When did Ochus ascend the throne? What name did he assume; and what was added?

added Nothus—illigitimate. Troubles in Asia Minor, Egypt, Arabia, and Media would have kept Darius in a constant state of anxiety, had not Parysatis, the queen, contrived to engage him in a continual round of pleasures, while wars were carried on in all these places by the Persian generals. Tissaphernes, satrap of Sardis, and Pharnabaces, governor of Bithynia, intermeddled constantly with the affairs of the Greeks, and vast sums were expended to foment the dissensions of Athens and Sparta.

120. At the instigation of Parysatis, Darius finally gave the dominion of all Asia Minor to his son Cyrus, a youth of sixteen. Here the young prince, to secure the alliance of the Lacedemonians, then esteemed the best soldiers in the world, assisted them with money and supplies, and assured Lysander, their general, that rather than see them want any necessary for carrying on the war with the Athenians, he would melt down the throne of gold and silver on which he sat, and coin it into money for them. He had an object in this liberality, much dearer to him than his friendship for the Lacedemonians. Parysitas, not content with seeing her favorite son governor of this extensive province, besought Darius to declare him heir to the throne instead of Arsaces, their oldest child; but to this Darius would not consent. He reigned twenty years.

121. ARTAXERXES MNEMON.—B. C. 404.—As soon as Arsaces ascended the throne, he changed his name to Artaxerxes—Mnemon was afterward added, on account of his astonishing memory. The new king, as the custom was, set out for Psargardae, to be crowned in a temple of the goddess of war. The prince to be consecrated must enter that temple, put off his own robe, and clothe himself in the one worn by Cyrus the Great, before he was king. This garment had been preserved with superstitious reverence more than 150 years Before the crown was put upon his head, the sovereign must eat a cake of figs, chew some turpentine, and drink a cup of mingled vinegar and milk.

122. Young Cyrus, driven to desperation at seeing the scepter to which his mother had taught him to aspire, transferred to the hands of his brother, determined to assassinate him in the temple itself, in the presence of the whole court, just as he took off his own to put on

---

Questions.—119. What troubles agitated Persia at that time? 120. What was done at the instigation of Parysatis? To whom did Cyrus render assistance? What assurance did Cyrus give? What was his object? What proposition did Darius reject? How long was he king? 121. When did Arsaces ascend the throne? To what did he change his name? By what name is he known? Relate the particulars of the coronation custom. 122. What deed of assassination did young Cyrus determine upon?

the robe of Cyrus. Tissaphernes, having gained intelligence of this design, revealed it to Artaxerxes. The rash youth was in consequence seized in the temple and condemned to death; when Parysatis, almost out of her senses, flew to the place, clasped him in her arms, bound the tresses of her hair about him, and by her tears and entreaties prevailed on Artaxerxes to pardon him, and send him back to Sardis. Cyrus, instead of appreciating the magnanimity of his brother in sparing his life, and continuing his government, remembered only the indignity of his chains, and, in resentment, strengthened himself in the determination to overthrow the king.

123. WHAT CYRUS DID IN ASIA MINOR.—The haughtiness and pride which had led him, when but a youth, to condemn two persons of royal blood for wearing their hands uncovered in his presence, were exchanged for the most winning affability. His emissaries at court constantly magnified his merits as a statesman and a warrior, and many turbulent noblemen stood ready to espouse his cause. It was now his turn to solicit favors from the Lacedemonians. He wrote to them, promising that "to the foot he would give horses, and to the horsemen, chariots; that on those who had farms he would bestow villages, and on those who had villages, cities. Their pay, he said, should not be *counted*, but *measured* out to them. He told them he had a greater and more princely heart than his brother; that he was better instructed in philosophy, and that he could drink more wine than Artaxerxes without disordering his senses!"

124. The Lacedemonians, moved by gratitude or avarice, sent a scytale to Clearchus, commander of their forces in Asia Minor, with orders to obey Cyrus ine very thing he demanded; but they wisely affected ignorance of the enterprise in which he was engaged. A company of Beotians also joined him, and some Athenians, among whom was Xenophon. The better to conceal his design, Cyrus gave out that his expedition was directed against the Pisidians. Tissaphernes, rightly judging that several hundred thousand men would not be collected for so slight an occasion, set out post from Miletus to inform Artaxerxes of what was going forward.

125. This news occasioned great trouble at court. Parysatis and all her favorites were looked upon as holding intercourse with the rebel. Statira, the queen, continually loaded her with reproaches.

Questions.—122. How was it prevented? What followed? Was Cyrus grateful to his brother? 123. What policy did Cyrus pursue? What promises did he make? What information did he add? 124. Of whom was the army of Cyrus composed? How did Artaxerxes get information of Cyrus's design? 125. What suspicions rested upon Parysatis?

"Where is now," said she, "that faith which you have so often pledged for your son's behavior? Your unhappy fondness has kindled this war, and plunged us into an abyss of misfortunes." Parysatis replied with equal warmth, and their hatred finally became so great that they could not dwell together in one palace.

126. Meantime, Cyrus set out from Sardis with an army amounting to nearly 300,000 men. When they reached Tarsus, the Greek soldiers, suspecting their destination, refused to go farther; but the persuasions of Clearchus, and the powerful eloquence of an extra gold piece, added by Cyrus to their pay, finally induced them to proceed in search of the enemy, which Cyrus said he expected to meet near Babylon. From Cilicia they passed on through Syria, forded the river Euphrates at Thapsacus, meeting with no opposition till they reached the plain of Cunaxa.

127. Battle of Cunaxa.—All the country through which they marched was so quiet, that Cyrus supposed his brother feared to meet him in the field. Under this impression, he traveled leisurely along, armed only with a saber, and attended by a small guard. When about 75 miles from Babylon, a horseman came up at full speed, crying out that the enemy were approaching. In an instant all was hurry and confusion; Cyrus leaped from his chariot, buckled on his armor with the greatest dispatch, and, without giving his army time for refreshment, arrayed them for the conflict. Clearchus with his Greeks occupied the right wing, the barbarian mercenaries the left, and Cyrus, with a band of six hundred horse, took his position in the center. All things were ready about noon, and the soldiers stood there in battle array three hours.

128. At length, when both their patience and strength were nearly exhausted, a great cloud of dust appeared like a white cloud, and soon spread itself densely over the whole plain; the steady tramp of soldiers, and the clattering of horses' hoofs were heard, and, not long after, the glittering of helmets, lances, and standards, proclaimed the approach of the royal forces. Tissaphernes led up the left wing opposite Clearchus; and Artaxerxes, supported by the flower of his army, took his post almost in front of his brother. When the two

---

Questions.—125. In what words did the queen address her? What was the consequence? 126. With how large an army did Cyrus march? From what place did he start? Where was that place? (See map No. 2.) How did Cyrus persuade the Greeks to follow him? Where was Tarsus? (15, map 3.) Where was Thapsacus? (29, same map.) Cunaxa? (Map No. 3.) 127. How far was Cunaxa from Babylon? What battle occurred there? How did Cyrus behave on the morning of the battle? 128. How was the battle commenced?

armies had approached near enough, the Greeks moved forward singing their loud pæan; and then, striking their darts upon their shields to frighten the horses, rushed upon the Persians with all their force. The enemy scarcely waited for the charge; the horses, maddened by the din, wheeled, and pranced with ungovernable fury; the riders, equally frightened, sought safety in flight; and Tissaphernes, with a small body of troops, alone maintained his ground.

129. The attendants of Cyrus, seeing the flight of the Persians, proclaimed him king upon the spot; but while the main body remained unbroken and his brother lived, Cyrus thought the kingdom still in dispute. Keeping his 600 horse in a body, he observed the motion of the king, and perceiving him wheeling to the left, charged his guards with great impetuosity. The Persians gave way, and the attendants of Cyrus dispersed in the pursuit, but with a few nobles he maintained his position. At length, discovering the king, he spurred on, crying out, "I see the man," and gave him a wound in the breast, at the same time that he himself received a blow in the eye from a javelin. The two brothers then fought hand to hand, and those about them engaged furiously in the defense of each, till Cyrus was slain, and eight of his principal friends lay dead upon his body. Artaxerxes gave his eunuch, Mesabates, charge to cut off the head and right hand of Cyrus, while he collected his followers and plundered his brother's camp.

130. The Greeks returned about dark from the pursuit of the fugitives, and, supposing they had gained the victory, put off their armor, wondering much that no messenger came from Cyrus to compliment them upon their valor. The refreshments provided by the prince had been carried off by the plunderers, and they were forced to retire supperless to rest. In the morning they learned the extent of their misfortune. By the messenger who brought them news of Cyrus's death they sent word to Ariæus, next in command, that being victors, they would make him king; and while waiting for his answer, they killed the oxen of the baggage wagons, and, collecting the broken weapons from the field of battle, roasted the flesh and made their breakfast. Not long after there came heralds from the king, summoning them to deliver up their arms. They replied that they would die before they would part with them; that if Artaxerxes would

---

Questions.—129. Give a further account of the battle. What orders did Artaxerxes give to Mesabates? 130. What did the Greeks learn on the morning after the battle? To whom did they then send word? What word did they send? How did they prepare their breakfast? What summons came to them? What was their reply?

receive them into the number of his allies, they would serve him with fidelity and valor; but if he endeavored to reduce them to slavery, he would find them determined to lose their lives and liberty together.

131. In the mean time the messenger returned from Ariæus, saying that that general declined the honor intended him, for there were so many noblemen in Persia superior to himself, that if Artaxerxes were dethroned, he could not expect to reign unmolested. He afterward engaged, by the most solemn oaths, to conduct them to their own country without fraud, and the bond was ratified by dipping their spears in the blood of animals slain for the purpose. It was also agreed to return home by a more northern route, to avoid the king's army and gain provisions. They accordingly withdrew from that place, and rested three days in some little villages, where they were visited by Tissaphernes and several of the Persian grandees.

132. TREACHERY OF TISSAPHERNES.—Tissaphernes began his story by telling them that, being a neighbor of Greece, and seeing them surrounded with dangers, he had used his good offices with the king to obtain permission to conduct them to their own country; that the king had not granted his request directly, but had sent him to inquire why they had taken up arms against him. "We call the gods to witness," replied Clearchus, "that we did not enlist ourselves to make war with the king. Cyrus, under different pretexts, brought us almost hither without explaining himself, and when we found him surrounded with dangers, we thought it infamous to abandon him after all the favors he had bestowed upon us. As he is dead, we are released from our engagement, and have no desire to contest the crown with Artaxerxes, nor to ravage his country, if he does not oppose our return."

133. Tissaphernes said he would acquaint the king with their reply, and bring them his answer. He was gone three days, and when he came back he told them that the king, after much solicitation, had appointed *him* to the government of Sardis, and had given *them* permission to depart under his safe conduct, and if they would wait till he had settled his affairs at court, they would set out together. These arrangements were confirmed by an oath on both sides. The Greeks waited very impatiently twenty days, every day

---

Questions.—131. What was the reply of Ariæus? What agreement did Ariæus enter into? By whom were the Greeks visited? 132. What story did Tissaphernes tell? Who replied on the part of the Greeks? What reply did he make? 133. What did Tissaphernes say to this? How long was he gone? What message did he bring? How long did the Greeks then wait?

becoming more distrustful of his intentions, and more suspicious of Ariæus, who had been freely pardoned by the king. Finally, Tissaphernes arrived with a body of troops, and they all marched on together; but they had too good reasons for being enemies to confide entirely in each other's truth. Occasions of distrust occurred daily as they advanced to the head waters of the Tigris, and at last Tissaphernes, having invited the Greek officers to a conference, put them all to death. Soon after, Ariæus rode up to the Greeks, and demanded their arms in the king's name.

134. B. C. **400.**—Nothing could exceed the consternation of the Greeks at this tragical turn in their affairs. In the words of another, "All gave themselves up to despair. They felt that they were still 2,000 miles from the nearest part of Greece, close to the vast armies of the king, and surrounded on all sides by tribes of hostile barbarians, who would supply them with nothing but at the expense of blows and blood; they had no guide acquainted with the country, no knowledge of the deep and rapid rivers which intersected it, and no cavalry to explore the road or cover their rear on the march. As if discipline and hope had ended together, the roll-call was scarcely attended to; the watch-fires were scantily, or not at all supplied; and even their principal meal was neglected; where chance led, they threw themselves down to rest, but not to sleep—for sleep was banished by thoughts of that country and those friends whom they no longer expected to behold again."

135. XENOPHON.—But there was among them a man, Xenophon, hitherto distinguished only by his love of the instructions he had received in the school of Socrates, who now felt the native energies of his mind roused to meet the critical emergency into which they were thrown. After a vain endeavor to sleep, he rose at midnight, awaked some of the principal men, and, representing to them the ignominious death which would certainly follow submission, exhorted them to elect new officers, and pursue their route. This measure was resolved upon. Five generals were chosen, of whom Xenophon was one; the army was assembled, and encouraged by all the cheering suggestions which the desperateness of their circumstances would admit, and by break of day they were ready to set off.

Questions.—133. What is said of Ariæus? What treacherous act did Tissaphernes commit? What Ariæus? 134. What is said of the consequent consternation of the Greeks? How did they reason about their condition? How did they act? 135. Who at last inspired them with new courage? In what way did he do so? What was consequently done?

136. Retreat of the Ten Thousand.—It were long to tell how often these determined veterans were forced to turn back, when a deep and rapid river rolled across their path; how many times they were obliged to make a long and tedious circuit around the base of some huge mountain; how many skirmishes they fought with the barbarians, through whose territories they passed; how often they were compelled to halt and form in battle-line to repel the assaults of the treacherous Tissaphernes, who, with the forces of Artaxerxes, hung upon their rear; how much they suffered from cold and hunger; what murmurings, discontents, and jealousies arose; how many died of hardship and fatigue; and how many, in utter despair of again seeing their native land, yielded to their hard fate, and were left unburied upon the plains of Asia.

137. In passing through Armenia, they encountered vast snowbanks, into which they sunk at every step; they also suffered intensely from a violent north wind; many lost their sight by the painful glare of the snow; and numbers perished with the cold. Sometimes, however, they came to little villages, where the inhabitants treated them kindly, supplied them with provisions, and suffered them to rest after their fatigues. Marching on thus, through dangers by flood and field, for many a long and weary month, they ascended at length a very high mountain, and turning their eyes to the west, beheld, far in the distant horizon, the dark waters of the Euxine. At once a glad shout burst from every lip: "The sea! the sea!" was repeated by a thousand voices; the soldiers embraced their officers with tears of joy, and then running to the top of the hill, and piling up a great heap of stones, raised a trophy of broken armor taken from the different enemies they had overthrown in their long and toilsome march.

138. The remaining perils of their journey were encountered with buoyant spirits; and when they reached Trebizond, they encamped thirty days to perform the vows they had made in the hours of distress, and to celebrate the Olympic games. In this place they separated, a part embarking by sea, and a part continuing their journey by land; they reunited, however, at the Thracian Bosphorus, and crossing over to Byzantium, found themselves once more upon European

---

Questions.—136. The retreat that followed is called what? What difficulties did "the ten thousand" encounter? 137. What did they encounter in Armenia? How were they treated at villages? Relate the events that took place on the mountain. Where was the Euxine Sea? (See map No. 3.) What is the Euxine called now? *Ans.* The Black Sea. 138. Where is Trebizond? (Map No. 3.) Where was Byzanium? (No. 2.) What is Byzantium now called. *Ans.* Constantinople. What was Trebizond once called? *Ans.* Trapezus.

soil. Xenophon computes, that from Ephesus, where they enlisted, to Cunaxa, where the battle was fought, was ninety-three days' march; from Cunaxa to Byzantium was something more; and the time taken by the Greeks, going and returning, was fifteen months. This retreat of "The Ten Thousand" has never had a parallel in the annals of war, and to this day it stands upon the pages of history as the most perfect model of an enterprise formed with valor, conducted with prudence, and executed with success.

139. VENGEANCE OF PARYSATIS.—To return to the affairs of the Persian court. Artaxerxes claimed the honor of having given Cyrus his death-wound; but a Carian soldier insisted that he himself had dispatched the pretender, as he was feebly attempting to rise after being unhorsed. Artaxerxes, having tried various ways in vain to stop his boasting, delivered him over to Parysatis as the murderer of her son. She caused him to be tortured ten days, and put to death by having melted brass poured into his ears. Mithridates, an officer of distinction, who also had a share in the death of the young prince, was next marked out as an object of the queen's vengeance. He was sentenced to the punishment of *the troughs*, a species of torture too horrid for description; and lingered out seventeen days in inexpressible agony.

140. The eunuch Mesabates, at the command of his king, had cut off the head and right hand of Cyrus; but as he stood high in the favor of Artaxerxes, Parysatis knew not how to accomplish his destruction. Nevertheless, what she could not effect by open accusation, she brought about by patient ingenuity. She made use of every art to win the confidence of her son, humored all his whims, ministered to his pleasures, and spent hours with him in playing dice. One day she allowed him to win a large sum of money from her, and then, pretending to be very much chagrined at her loss, offered to play with him for a eunuch. Artaxerxes assented, and Parysatis, exerting all her skill, won the game. She seized upon Mesabates as the forfeit, and before the king learned her purpose, caused him to be flayed alive.

141. DEATH OF STATIRA.—But Parysatis was not satisfied. She had her eye upon a more beautiful and more illustrious victim, who was so intrenched in the affections of Artaxerxes, that she could not hope to supplant her. This was Statira, whose charms she had always envied,

---

Questions.—138. What computation did Xenophon make? What is said of the famous retreat? 139. What claim did Artaxerxes make? Was his claim disputed? How was the offender disposed of? Give the account of Mithridates. 140. Give the account of Mesabates. 141. Was Parysatis then satisfied? Who was selected to be the next victim?

and whose influence over her son had long before excited her hatred. To cloak her design the more effectually, she feigned a reconciliation with her daughter-in-law, exchanged visits with her, and often invited her to sup in her apartment. The two queens appeared to be on the most friendly terms, but the fear of poison kept them constantly uneasy, and they would never eat except from the same dishes. But Parysatis could not be foiled. One day at table, she took a nicely dressed bird, cut it in two, and giving one-half to Statira, eat the other herself.

142. Immediately after, Statira was seized with the most excruciating pain, and sending for Artaxerxes, accused Parysatis of having poisoned her. Convinced by the dreadful convulsions in which his beloved queen expired, Artaxerxes put all the servants of his mother to the torture, when Giges confessed that she had poisoned one side of the knife with which Parysatis had divided the bird. She was punished by having her head crushed between two stones: the wicked queen was banished to Babylon.

143. Peace with Greece.—Meanwhile Tissaphernes, by intermeddling in the affairs of Sparta and Athens, kept up a continual war in Asia Minor, which was finally productive of great honor to Persia. The two rival states became so much weakened by their own dissensions that the Persians gained the advantage of them; and, in compelling them to sign the treaty of Antalcidas, wiped out the stain of their former defeats, B. C. 387.

144. Troubles at Home.—B. C. 361.—The end of Artaxerxes's reign was filled with troubles and cabals. He was of a sweet and amiable disposition, but indolent, and enslaved by the luxuries of the court. The satraps of the provinces, abusing his good-nature and infirmities, loaded the people with taxes, and made the Persian yoke intolerable. Many of the tributary provinces, in consequence, revolted; but as they acted without concert, quarreled among themselves, and betrayed one another to the king, the troubles excited by them expired of themselves. Artaxerxes had three sons by his wife, and 150 by his concubines. The rival interests of so many princes filled the whole court with factions. To prevent these disorders, Artaxerxes declared

---

Questions.—141. What course of conduct did Parysatis then pursue? How at last did she accomplish her purpose? 142. What measures did Artaxerxes adopt in order to learn the cause of his queen's death? What confession was made? What was the consequence? 143. What is said of Tissaphernes? What was the result to Sparta and Athens? 144. What was the general character of Artaxerxes? How many sons did he have? Why did he declare Darius his successor?

Darius his successor, and permitted him to wear the royal tiara, and assume the name of king.

145. Darius, not satisfied with these marks of favor, formed a design against his father's life, in which he engaged fifty of his brothers. A day was fixed by these unnatural children for the completion of their scheme, but the thing having been related to the old king, he caused them to be arrested as they entered his chamber with the instruments of death in their hands. They were all executed as they deserved. Ochus, the third legitimate son, then began to entertain ambitious thoughts for himself. By assassinating one brother, and threatening another into suicide, he removed the obstacles which stood between him and the throne, and broke his father's heart. Artaxerxes sunk to the tomb overwhelmed by repeated afflictions. He reigned 44 years.

146. OCHUS, B. C. 360.—Ochus desired distinction, and he gained it. Of all the monarchs that had ever disgraced a throne by violence and cruelty, he takes the pre-eminence. The vices of his predecessors shrank into insignificance when compared with the absolute deformities of his character, so that it might be said of him in the words of Scripture, "There was none like unto *Ochus* who sold himself to work wickedness." To rid himself at once of all fear of his family, he put every member to death, without regard to age, sex, or tender entreaty. He caused his own sister, Ocha, to be buried alive, though her daughter was his queen. He shut up an uncle with one hundred children and grand-children in a court of the palace, and ordered them to be shot to death with arrows, merely because the young princes were held in high estimation. He treated all who gave him cause for uneasiness throughout the empire with the same barbarity, and filled every province of Persia with lamentation.

147. His only expedition of importance was against Egypt, which he invaded with complete success. After his return he abandoned himself to his pleasures, leaving the affairs of his kingdom to be administered by Mentor the Rhodian, and Bagoas his eunuch, an Egyptian. Not contented with having dismantled the cities, pillaged the houses and temples of Egypt, he carried away the archives of the nation, which the priests had so long preserved with pious veneration.

Questions.—145. What plot did Darius form? How was it defeated? Who was Ochus? What baseness was he guilty of? How long had Artaxerxes been king? 146. Who succeeded Artaxerxes on the throne? What was the character of Ochus? Name some of his barbarous acts. 147. What success attended his arms? To whom did he then leave the affairs of his kingdom?

In addition to his impiety, he had caused the god Apis to be served up at dinner for his household, and had even gone so far as to compel Bagoas to eat of it. This the outraged Egyptian never forgave, and it is said that Ochus died by poison administered by his hand. Nor did this satisfy his revenge. He caused another body to be interred instead of the king's, and, cutting up the flesh of Ochus in small pieces, fed it to cats, and fashioned his bones into handles for knives and swords, the proper emblems of cruelty, B. C. 338.

148. When Bagoas had thus disposed of Ochus, he placed Arses, the youngest son of the king, upon the throne; but not finding him so convenient a tool as he had anticipated, he caused him to be assassinated, and bestowed the crown upon Darius Codomanus, one of the surviving descendants of that uncle whom Ochus had massacred. The Persian empire was now tottering to its fall. The "arms of silver" had become enervated by luxury, and their strength had departed; "the ram" had ceased "to push westward and northward and southward," and quietly reposed "beside the river," while the "he-goat" was preparing to attack him.

149. FALL OF PERSIA, B. C. 336.—It was two hundred years from the time when the whole eastern world bowed to the yoke of Cyrus the Great, that Darius Codomanus clothed himself in the robe of that mighty conqueror, and attempted to sway the imperial scepter over revolted provinces and effeminate subjects. In the same year *Darius* and *Alexander* began to reign, the one in the East, the other in the West. Darius had scarcely time to discover that Bagoas was plotting against his life, and to bring that wicked person to punishment, when news was brought to him that Alexander had invaded his dominions. It was not till after the battle of *Granicus* had been fought, that the ill-disciplined forces of the empire were collected to attend their monarch in his march to repulse the Greek.

150. In the battle of *Issus*, Darius was first defeated, and compelled to flee with great precipitation. Two years after, in a second battle at *Arbela*, he was again utterly defeated. His intention then was to pass through Media, laying waste the country as he went, till he found refuge the other side of the Oxus. There he supposed the conqueror would leave him unmolested; but his plan was defeated by one of his

---

Questions.—147. What indignity did he force upon Bagoas? How was Bagoas avenged? When did that occur? 148. Who was Arses? Give the account of him. Who was Darius Codomanus? To what position did he attain? 149. How many years had passed since the reign of Cyrus the Great? What feeble imitation was attempted by Darius Codomanus? 150. How many battles did Darius fight in person?

own satraps, who dethroned him, and carried him off a close prisoner to Bactria. Alexander pursued him, and finding escape impossible, the treacherous satraps stabbed their king in several places, and left him by the road-side weltering in his blood. He was indebted to a Macedonian soldier for the last draught of water, and expired, committing his body to the conqueror, B. C. 330.

By the subjugation of all the eastern world to Alexander, Persia became a Grecian province.

Read Dan. viii. 2–7, 20, 21.

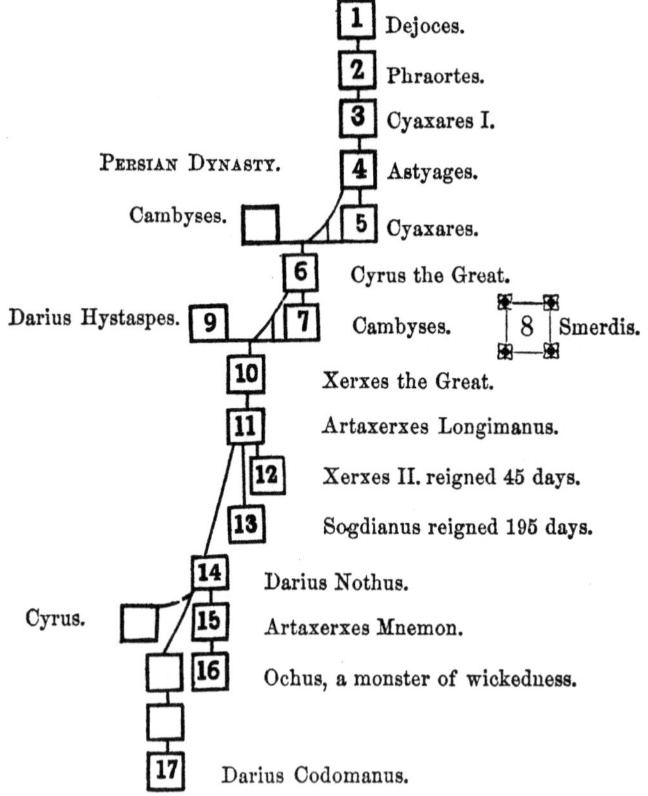

Persia becomes a Grecian province.

Question. 150. Relate the story of his death. When did that event take place? What did Persia then become?

REVIEW QUESTIONS.

PAGE
1. What can you state of the early history of Persia?.............. 35
2. Give an account of Dejoces.................................... 35, 36
3. Of Phraortes.. 36
4. Of Cyaxares...36, 37, 38
5. Give, as far as you can, the history of Media up to the time of Cyrus..................................13, 33, 34, 35, 36, 37, 38
6. Give an account of Cyrus till his 16th year..................... 38, 39
7. Of Cyrus's first expedition and return home.................... 39, 40
8. What led to Cyrus's second expedition?........................ 40
9. Give an outline of that expedition.......................41, 42, 43, 44
10. Describe the preparations for the battle of Thymbra.............. 44–46
11. Give an account of the battle, and of Panthea's fate............. 44–48
12. Give an account of Crœsus, king of Lydia................40, 42, 44–48
13. Why did Cyrus wish to capture Babylon?......................... 48
14. Give an account of his operations and success.................. 48, 49
15. Give his further history till he became king.................... 50, 51
16. Give his further history till his death........................... 51, 52
17. Why did Cambyses make war upon Egypt?....................... 52
18. Give an account of Cambyses's success......................... 52, 53
19. Of his expedition against the Ethiopians........................ 53, 54
20. Of his tyranny and cruelty at Memphis......................... 55
21. Of his cruelty toward Smerdis and Prexaspes.................... 55, 56
22. Give an account of the true and false Smerdis............... 55, 56, 57
23. Describe the taking of Babylon by Darius....................... 58, 59
24. Give an account of the Scythian expedition...................... 60, 61
25. Name the important succeeding events.......................... 61, 62
26. What is stated in connection with the burning of Sardis?......... 62, 63
27. Name the events till the battle of Marathon..................... 63, 64
28. The further events, till the death of Darius..................... 64
29. What preparations were made against Greece?.................. 65, 66
30. Give an account of Xerxes's march......................... 66, 67, 68
31. Of the battle of Thermopylæ................................... 68, 69
32. Of the further movements of Xerxes............................ 69, 70
33. Of the battle of Salamis and consequences...................... 70, 71
34. Name the events of the next seven years....................... 71, 72
35. Give the account of the Egyptian revolt........................ 72, 73
36. Name the important events succeeding the revolt.............73, 74, 75
37. Name the events connected with young Cyrus............74, 75, 76, 77
38. Describe the Retreat of the Ten Thousand...................... 77–81
39. Give an account of Ochus...................................... 83, 84
40. What further can you state of Persia?.......................... 84, 85

GREECE.

SECTION IV.

Greece, commencing with its settlement by the children of Javan, about 2000 B. C., and ending with its subjugation by the Romans, 146 B. C., continued nearly two millenniums.

1. We have contemplated the "Head of gold" and "Arms of silver," described in Nebuchadnezzar's image; we come now to the "Body of brass," which comprises a far more interesting and instructive portion of history. Assyria and Persia were empires ruled by despots, and dependent in a great measure for their prosperity upon the individual character of the king; consequently the history of the monarch became the history of the nation. A striking deviation from this order will be observed in the following pages. Greece was a republic. It was settled at different times, in different places, by adventurers from different countries. The laws of the different states were not the same; yet a common bond of brotherhood, and a common hatred of tyranny, led them to unite in repelling every foreign invader, and gave them at one time the dominion of the world.

2. Though Greece at first possessed only a very small extent of territory, yet the advantages of its natural position were very great. It was in the center of the most cultivated portions of three quarters of the world; its extensive coasts were indented with numerous bays, and furnished with commodious harbors; it was watered in every direction by an infinite number of small streams, which, rising in the lofty hills, flowed through fertile vales, and imparted a delicious coolness to a climate naturally warmer than that of any other part of Europe. Its superficial content was 29,600 square miles; not half as large as the territory of New England; yet within this limited space were twenty rival states, which for a long period bade defiance to the world, and perished only when they turned their arms upon one another.

GREECE.—Section IV.—*Questions.*—1. What is said of Nebuchadnezzar's image? Why is the history of Greece considered more interesting than that of Assyria and Persia? What was Greece? What is said of its settlement? Of its laws? Why did the Grecian states unite? What was the consequence? 2. What is said of the natural advantages of Greece? How large was its territory? Of how many states did it consist? What is said of their power? Why did they perish?

3. A dime, laid upon the southern part of Turkey, in Europe, as delineated upon the common maps, would cover all the territory of Greece proper, and Macedonia beside; yet here stood the beautiful city of Athens; here were the vales and groves of Arcadia; here the bloody fields of Marathon and Platea; here was "High Olympus," with his neighboring eminences, Pelion and Ossa; here was lofty Parnassus, sheltering the famous temple of Delphi; here were the classic waters of Helicon, and the Castalian fount; here all those woods, and vales, and streams made sacred by the visits of the gods themselves. Here too lived and flourished the wisest philosophers, the mightiest heroes, and the most renowned statesmen the world ever saw; and to this comparatively insignificant spot, sculpture, painting, poetry, and music lent their magic powers to such a degree, that to this day the models of the Grecian school are imitated, but not surpassed.

4. GEOGRAPHY.—We will consider Greece under four divisions.

I.—Illyria, Macedonia, and Thrace were not reckoned a part of Greece until about the time of Alexander.

II.—*Northern Greece* had Thessaly on the east and Epirus on the west.

1. Thessaly, afterwards so celebrated for its cavalry, contained Mts. Ossa and Olympus, separated by the delicious vale of Tempe, through which flowed the magnificent river Peneus. Here also was the plain of Pharsalia, where three very important battles were fought.

2. Epirus contained the oracle of Jupiter at Dodona.

5. III.—*Of Central Greece* or *Hellas*, 3, 4, 5, 6, were very little celebrated. 7. Phocis contained the oracle of Delphi, the city of Crissa, and Mt. Parnassus. 8. East Locris contained Thermopylæ, which is thus described: "At Thermopylæ a steep and inaccessible mountain rises on the west, and on the east side are the sea and the

---

Questions.—3. What is the illustration in connection with the dime? What city was there? Vales and groves? Bloody fields? Eminences? Mountain? Temple? Waters? Fount? Woods, vales, and streams? Philosophers, heroes, and statesmen? What is said of the sculpture, painting, poetry, and music of Greece? [The importance of a "geographical knowledge of history" cannot be too deeply impressed upon the mind of the student; it is, therefore, *earnestly requested* that every pupil become perfectly familiar with the situation of the different states upon map No. 2, and also with the relative position of Greece on the maps in general use.] 4. What three states are first mentioned? What is said of them? Which of them was farthest east? (See map.) Of what two states was Northern Greece composed? (See, also, map.) For what did Thessaly become celebrated? What did it contain? Epirus? 5. By what name was Central Greece best known? Name the states of Central Greece. (See, also, map.) Give the names of those bordering on Northern Greece. What did Phocis contain? East Locris?

marshes. The road is fifty feet wide, but in the narrowest part there is room only for one carriage." 9. Eubœa, separated from Beotia by the narrow strait of Euripus, had one city, Eretria, which took an active part in the Persian wars. 10. Beotia was a large plain shut in by mountains. Beside Thebes, the capital, it contained Platea, Leuctra, and Cheroneia, places which will often be mentioned in the course of this history. 11. Attica was sixty-three miles long and twenty-five broad. Its only city was Athens: Marathon, Eleusis, &c., were only villages. 12. Megara was a Dorian colony, subject to Attica.

6. IV. *Peloponnesus.*—13. Corinth was in everybody's way. It was the key of Southern Greece, and the hostile armies which passed from Hellas into the Peloponnesus frequently laid it waste. The citadel of Corinth, Acro-Corinthus, was a lofty rock, clearly visible from Athens, a distance of forty miles. 14. Sicyon, the capital of Sicyonia, was the oldest settled town in Greece. 15. Achaia was never much distinguished till after the death of Alexander, when its twelve cities united to resist the power of Macedon, and were for a time the sole defenders of Grecian liberty.

7. 16. Elis was the *Holy Land* of Greece. No wars were allowed to violate this sacred soil; armies in passing through it were deprived of their weapons. Here was the temple of Olympian Jove, and here all the descendants of Hellen met once in four years to celebrate the Olympic games. 17. Arcadia was the country of hills and valleys, of flocks and herds. The Arcadians were equally ready to fight for freedom and for money, and generally enlisted on the side which furnished the best pay. 18. Argolis took the lead of all the states in the Trojan war, and never after. 19. Laconia was the ancient name of Lacedemonia, the capital of which was Sparta. The Spartans laid waste and subdued (20.) Messenia, very early in the history of Greece.

8. MYTHOLOGY.—The religious beliefs and observances of the Greeks, constituting their mythology, are intimately connected with the fabulous and poetical portion of their history. The origin of Grecian religion has been differently stated by different historians; some asserting that it came from Egypt; others that Phenicia was its parent; while others bid us search in Crete and Samothracia for the authors of those

---

Questions.—5. Eubœa? Beotia? Attica? What is said of Megara? 6. By what name was Southern Greece most known? Why was Corinth in everybody's way? What is said of Acro-Corinthus? Of Sicyon? Of Achaia? 7. What is said of Elis? Of Arcadia? Of Argolis? Of Laconia? Of Messenia? [The teacher is requested to give out the numbers, and permit the pupil, with his eyes fixed upon the map, to describe the states.] 8. What constituted the mythology of the Greeks? What is stated in relation to the origin of Grecian religion?

fables which peopled "Old Olympus" with all the deities of the Pantheon. These fables, whether invented by the natives or introduced by foreigners, were spread throughout Greece in the form of traditions, till the poets collected and arranged them into one uniform system, which the beauty of their verses caused to be universally adopted.

9. According to this system, the beginning of all things was Chaos —a heterogeneous mass, containing all the seeds of nature. Hesiod says, "Chaos was first;" then came into being "broad-breasted Earth, the gloomy Tartarus, and *Love*." The progeny of Chaos were Nox, Erebus, Day, and Ether. Cœlum, Heaven, and Terra, the Earth, were the parents of Saturn, the oldest of the gods, but he, having the Titans for brothers, obtained the kingdom only by an agreement to destroy all his offspring. This promise he fulfilled till Rhea, his wife, contrived to hide Jupiter, Neptune, and Pluto, which becoming known to the Titans, they cast Saturn into prison. Jupiter, meanwhile, was reared in the isle of Crete, rocked by Adrastea in a golden cradle, fed with ambrosia brought by pigeons from the streams of Ocean, and nectar, which an eagle drew each day with his beak from a rock.

10. When Jupiter had grown up to manhood he overcame the Titans and restored Saturn to his throne; but he afterwards quarreled with his father and chased him into Italy, where the banished god spent his time in civilizing the rude inhabitants. He brought them into such a state of blessedness, that this period was ever afterwards called the Golden Age. He was represented in pictures as an old man, with a scythe in one hand, and a child, which he was about to devour, in the other. According to a more rational account, Saturn is but another name for time. Days, Months, and Years are the children of Time, which he continually devours and produces anew, even as Saturn is fabled to have destroyed his own offspring.

11. After Saturn had been driven into exile, his three sons divided the universe among themselves. Jupiter became sovereign of the heavens and earth. Neptune obtained the empire of the sea, and Pluto received the scepter of the infernal regions. Jupiter, however, was soon disturbed in his dominions by the offspring of Titan, a race of terrible giants, who by piling Pelion upon Ossa attempted to ascend

---

Questions.—8. What is intimately connected with the poetical portion of Grecian history? 9. What did they style the beginning of all things? Who were the parents of Saturn? Who were the Titans? How many children had Saturn? What is said of the youth of Jupiter? 10. What further account can you give of Jupiter? How was Saturn represented? What more rational account do we have of Saturn? 11. Who ruled over the three empires? By whom was Jupiter disturbed? In what way?

to heaven and pluck him from his throne. The gods, in great alarm, fled from Mt. Olympus to Egypt, where they sheltered themselves under the forms of various animals.

12. Jupiter finally overcame his enemies, including the huge Typhon, whom he buried beneath Etna, where he heaves the lofty mountain with his groaning sides, and vomits flames to this day. Jupiter was always represented as sitting on a throne of ivory and gold, holding the thunderbolts in his right hand, and a scepter of cyprus in the other, with an eagle standing by his side. He took in marriage his sister *Juno*, a beautiful, but ill-tempered goddess, who kept the "father of gods and king of men" a little in awe of her tongue, which did not always deal in the gentlest epithets. She was delineated as riding in a chariot drawn by peacocks, with a scepter in her hand, and a crown of roses and lilies upon her head.

13. Nine of the principal deities were considered as the children of Jupiter. Apollo was the god of music, poetry, painting, and medicine. He was represented as a beautiful young man, with a bow in his hand and a quiver of arrows at his back. At the banquet of the gods on Olympus, Apollo played on his lyre while the Muses sang. When he resolved to choose the site of his first temple, he traversed Greece till he came to Crissa, a quiet, sequestered spot, sheltered by Mt. Parnassus, where he slew the monstrous serpent Python, and set about erecting a temple; whence the place was called Pytho. Mars, the god of war, was represented as driving furiously along in a chariot drawn by Fear and Terror, in the form of foaming steeds, with Discord running before him, in tattered garments, and Anger and Clamor following close behind.

14. Bacchus, the god of revels and revelers, is too well known, with his red eyes and bloated face, to need a description here. Mercury was the messenger of the gods, and of Jupiter especially. He was the god of speech, of eloquence; the patron of merchants and of dishonest men, particularly thieves. He presided over highways and crossways, guided travelers through by-ways, and conducted the souls of the dead to the world below. In token of his office he was painted with wings upon his hat and upon his heels, with a rod called Caduceus in his hand, which Apollo gave him in exchange for the Lyre. Square blocks of granite surmounted with his head, standing at the crossing of streets, were called statues of Hermæ.

Questions.—12. What success did Jupiter have? How was he represented? Who was his wife? What was Juno's character? How was she represented? 13. How many children had Jupiter? Describe Apollo. Mars. 14. Describe Bacchus. Mercury.

15. Minerva was the goddess both of wisdom and of war, and was fabled to have sprung, all armed and equipped, from the head of Jupiter. The spindle and the distaff were her invention, and the solemn owl her emblem. She superintended the building of the ship Argo, and taught Epeus how to frame the wooden horse. Athena, her Greek name, was given to Athens. Another name of hers was Pallas. The Palladium, her image, fell down from heaven into the city of Troy. When the Grecians besieged that place, they found it could never be taken while the Palladium remained in it. Ulysses and Diomedes crept into the city, through the sewers, and stole the precious protection, after which Troy was captured.

16. Venus was the goddess of beauty and of love. The three graces danced around her, and the mischievous little Cupid played at her feet. She sprang from the froth of the sea, and was laid, like a pearl, in a shell instead of a cradle. The rose-colored shallop, with its precious freight, was wafted by Zephyrus to the island of Cyprus, where the gold-filleted Seasons received her, clothed her in immortal garments, adorned her with every ornament which could add to her beauty, and took her to the abode of the gods, every one of whom admired and loved her, and desired to espouse her. She finally fell to the lot of Vulcan.

17. Vulcan, attended by his grisly one-eyed Cyclops, was represented as a blacksmith, forging thunderbolts for Jupiter. It was said that the first woman was fashioned by his hammer, and that every god gave her some present, whence she was called Pandora; and that Jupiter, to be revenged upon Prometheus, who stole fire from heaven to animate the man he had formed, sent Pandora to him with a sealed box. When the precious casket was opened, all sorts of evils and diseases flew out of it, and nothing but Hope was left at the bottom. Aurora, the goddess of the morning, was represented clothed in a saffron-colored robe, coming out of a golden palace, and throwing back a flowing vail, as she opened with rosy fingers the gates of day for the fiery steeds of Apollo. She was the mother of the winds, and wept the dew from her eyes in liquid pearls. The Muses were nine beautiful goddesses, who presided over musicians, orators, historians, poets, &c.

18. Neptune, the god of the ocean, was drawn by dolphins, in his scallop-shell chariot, over the foaming waves. His hair was black

---

Questions.—15. Describe Minerva. 16. Venus. 17. Vulcan. Aurora. The Muses. 18. Neptune

as the midnight storm, and his eyes as blue as the peaceful sea. An azure mantle floated from his shoulders; in one hand he held his trident, and with the other clasped his wife, Amphitrite. Triton, his son and trumpeter, attended his father.

Frowning, he seemed his crooked shell to sound,
And at the blast the billows danced around.

19. Beside the *celestial* and *terrestrial* deities, of which not a tithe have been enumerated, the *infernal* gods were often quoted. According to Grecian fables, the passage which led to the infernal regions was a wide and dark cave, opening upon a stagnant lake called Avernus. Four rivers were to be passed by the dead, the most celebrated of which was the Styx. Charon, the ferryman of hell, received the souls of the buried dead (those of the unburied being compelled to wander one hundred years about those gloomy shores), and rowed them over to the palace of Pluto. The gate of this palace was guarded by a three-headed dog, Cerberus, whose body was covered with snakes instead of hair. After bribing this ferocious keeper by the present of a cake, they entered to the presence of the sovereign of the infernal regions.

20. This was Pluto, the brother of Jupiter, who sat upon an ebon throne, holding in his hand the key of "death and Hades." By his side sat Proserpine, the daughter of Ceres, who became his wife in the following manner: When all the goddesses had refused to marry Pluto, he seated himself in his chariot of darkness, which rendered him invisible, and suddenly emerged from a cave in Sicily, near which some beautiful nymphs were gathering white daffodils. He seized Proserpine, and sank with her into the earth. Ceres, alarmed at the absence of her daughter, lighted a torch at the flames of Etna, and wandered up and down the earth in search of her. She found her at last in the infernal regions, the bride of Pluto.

21. THE TRIBUNAL OF THE DEAD.—All persons received their deaths impartially from the Fates. Then their condemnation impartially from the three Judges. And afterwards their punishment impartially from the three Furies. The Fates, three sisters, who ordered the Past, the Present, and the Future, were constantly employed in spinning the thread of life. Lachesis turned the wheel, Clotho drew out the thread, and Atropos cut it off with the fatal scissors. The three

---

Questions.—19. What is said of the infernal regions? 20. Who had charge of the infernal regions? Who was his wife? In what manner did he get his wife? 21. What is said of the tribunal of the dead?

judges, Minos, Rhadamanthus, and Eacus, were the sons of Jupiter. The three tormenting Furies were monsters, with the faces of women. Grief, Terror, and Madness were their inseparable followers; in one hand they held a lighted torch, while with the other they scourged the souls of the lost throughout all the gloomy caverns of hell. Beside the furies, these melancholy regions were peopled with Harpies, Sphinxes, Gorgons, "and chimeras dire," presenting every disgusting appearance, and every terrible form of punishment.

22. Elysian Fields.—There was a place in the province of Pluto called Elysium, where all the souls of the good, after being purged from their light offenses, were permitted to take up their abode.

"The few who're cleansed, to those abodes repair,
And breathe in ample fields the soft Elysian air;
From holy rites performed, they take their way,
Where long extended plains of pleasure lay.
The fields are verdant, and with heaven may vie,
With ether vested, and a purple sky:
The blissful seats of happy souls below,
Stars of their own, and their own sun they know."

After years spent in these delightful retreats, the souls of the blessed were instructed to drink of the river Lethe, which washed away all remembrance of the past, and then they returned to earth again, to inhabit other bodies.

23. The Greeks had also a class of demi-gods, who had human bodies, sacred minds, and celestial souls, and were sent into the world for the benefit of mankind. Among these were Hercules, who performed several mighty exploits; one of which was the rending asunder of Spain and Africa, thus permitting the strait of Gibraltar to flow between two rocks, called the pillars of Hercules; Jason, who headed the Argonautic expedition; Esculapius, the god of medicine; Orpheus, Achilles, Ulysses, and many others, which it would be impossible to notice in the limits of this work.

24. Beside all these gods, a species of imaginary beings filled every corner both of the earth and sea. Every mountain had its Oreads, the woods and vales were peopled with Dryads, the sea was furnished with Tritons and Nereids, and every fountain rejoiced in its guardian Naiad. To the Greeks, the thunder was the voice of Jupiter; the soft breeze of summer, was the wing of Eolus; the echo of the forest was the pensive whisper of a goddess and the murmur of the streamlet

Questions.—22. What is said of the Elysian fields? 23. Of the demi-gods? 24. Of imaginary beings? Of thunder? Soft breeze? Echo of the forest? Murmur of the streamlet?

was the tone of a presiding deity. In short, whatever sound or sight charmed their fancy was ascribed to the agency of unseen, but beautiful and immortal beings.

25. Effect of Grecian Mythology.—It will readily be inferred, that a religion so interwoven with all that was lovely in nature, and all that was poetic in imagination, must have exercised a powerful influence upon the character of the people. The Greek honored his deity as his friend; and to defend *his* temple, was a more sacred duty than to protect his own fireside. To paint the ideal beauty of Venus, to make the marble personate the lofty purity of Minerva, or the dread majesty of Jupiter, employed all the genius of the painter and the sculptor. To sing the combat of the gods with the giants; to charm the listeners at the Olympic games with the loves of Olympian Jove; to recount the exploits of the heroes before the walls of Troy; to magnify the strength of Hercules, and the address of Theseus; awakened the imagination, and gave wings to the genius of the poet and historian; hence it is that Greece stands proudly pre-eminent as the birth-place of the sciences, and the cradle of the fine arts.

26. Till the time of Homer, the Greeks, like other savages, worshiped in the open air, in sacred groves, or in temples rudely constructed for the purpose. The priesthood was limited to no particular family or class; and oftentimes distinguished generals or magistrates assisted in the most solemn rites. In the marriage ceremony, the bride was conducted in the evening from her father's house to her husband's, seated in a chariot, between the bridegroom and her most intimate friend. Torches were carried before them, and a nuptial song was chanted by the way. Before the door of the dwelling, the axletree of the carriage was broken, to signify that she was never to return to her father's house.

27. At the death of friends, the Greeks abstained from all banquets and entertainments; they tore or cut off their hair, they rolled in the dust, and covered their heads with ashes. Before the interment, a piece of money was put into the mouth of the deceased, which was considered as Charon's fare for wafting the soul over the infernal river. The corpse was likewise furnished with a cake of honey and flour, designed to appease the fury of Cerberus, and procure the ghost a safe and easy entrance to the realms of Pluto. In the early ages, it was customary to lay the dead in the ground, but burning afterward

---

Questions.—25. What was the effect of Grecian Mythology? 26. Where did the Greek. conduct their worship? Describe their nuptial ceremonies. 27. Describe their funera' ceremonies. What was esteemed a great disgrace?

became the common practice. The pile was lighted by the nearest relative, and, while it was consuming, the friends stood by, pouring out libations, and calling upon the departed soul. Then followed feasts, at which all the guests appeared crowned, and employed the time in lauding the deceased, so far as was consistent with truth; for it was esteemed a great disgrace to *lie* upon such an occasion.

28. The most powerful engines of Grecian polity were the mysteries and oracles. In every state of the Republic there were certain ceremonies of a secret religion, over which the solemn veil of mystery was thrown. The sacred rites of Ceres, and the oracular responses from the dismal cave of Trophonius, the venerable oak of Dodona, and the inspiring vapor of Delphi, exercised over the enthusiastic minds of the inhabitants a power which designing men seized upon to further their own ambitious views.

29. DESCRIPTION OF DELPHI.—The oracle that gained the highest reputation was that of Delphi. On the southern side of Mount Parnassus, not far from Crissa, the mountain crags formed a natural amphitheater, in the midst of which a deep cavern discharged from a narrow orifice, a vapor powerfully affecting the brain of those who came within its influence. This, we are told, was first brought into notice by a goatherd, whose goats, browsing upon the brink, were thrown into convulsions; upon which, the man, going to the spot and endeavoring to look into the chasm, became agitated like one frantic.

30. The spot which produced such marvelous effects, became the object of universal curiosity; people came from all quarters to inhale the inspiring fluid, and the incoherent words uttered in the intoxication were considered prophecy. But the function of the prophet became not a little dangerous, for many through giddiness fell into the cave and were lost. An assembly of the neighboring inhabitants was therefore convened, a priestess was appointed by public authority; a frame, resting upon three feet, called a tripod, was prepared, seated upon which the Pythoness inhaled the maddening vapor, and uttered incoherent sentences, which her attendants wrote down as the responses of Apollo. A rude temple was built over the cavern, priests were elected, ceremonies were prescribed, and sacrifices were performed. Delphi, which was really near the center of Greece, was reported to be the center of the world.

31. No enterprise of importance was undertaken, without first con-

Questions.—28. What is said of the mysteries and oracles? 29, 30, 31. Describe Delphi. Where was it located? (See map No. 3.) What is it now? *Ans.* A small village called Castri. How did Delphi become a "national bank?"

sulting this oracle; to do which, it was necessary to propitiate the god by presents; and, as the priests had it always in their power to deny answers, to delay answers, or to give answers direct, dubious, and unintelligible, the applicants soon came to understand the philosophy of magnificent donations. In addition to these incentives to munificence, the names of those who presented valuable gifts were registered, and the articles exhibited to visitors; and thus interest and vanity combined to adorn the temple, till it became "one of the seven wonders of the world." These treasures were carefully guarded; the wealthy deposited their gold and jewels there for safe keeping, and, in this manner, Delphi finally became, also, the great National Bank of Greece.

32. B. C. **2100.**—GREECE SETTLED BY THE SONS OF ION OR JAVAN. —Javan the son of Japheth was, according to historians, the progenitor of the Grecians. His four sons, Elisa, Tarsis, Chittim, and Dodanim, were supposed to have settled the country, and in them we recognize the heads of those tribes which afterward became so renowned for arts and arms. Elis, Elysian fields, and the river Elissus derived their names from Elisa; Chittim was the father of the Macedonians; and Dodona was but a change of Dodanim. In amalgamations, revolutions, and migrations, the distinctive features of these tribes were finally lost, and they came to be known under the general appellation of "The Pelasgi," who were first noticed as a race of savages, living in caves, and clothing themselves in the skins of wild beasts. They founded Sicyon, B. C. 2089.

33. A rude and massive style of building, of which many specimens were found in Southern Greece, was ascribed to the Pelasgi. Inachus, a Pelasgic leader, founded the city of Argos about the middle of the nineteenth century. At an uncertain, but very early date, an Asiatic people, named "Hellenes," migrated to Greece, and intermingled with, or expelled, the Pelasgi. In 1616, Corinth was founded by Sisyphus. In 1550, Cecrops, at the head of a colony from Egypt, founded Athens, and introduced the rudiments of civilization into

---

Questions.—32. From which of Noah's sons were the Grecians descended? Name four sons of Javan. What derivatives came from the name Elisa? Who were "The Pelasgi?" In what direction did Javan's sons travel from Babel? Where was Sicyon? (See map No. 2.) 33. What was the Cyclopic style of architecture? Where was it found? To whom was it ascribed? In what part of Greece was Argos? (See map No. 2.) By whom was it founded? When? Who were the Hellenes? By whom was Corinth founded? In what year? When was Athens founded? By whom? From what place did he emigrate? How much older was Athens than Sparta? How did they become incorporated with the native inhabitants? Give the location of Athens and Sparta. (See map No. 2.)

Greece. In 1516, Sparta was founded by Lelex, also an Egyptian. These colonists, however, united with the original inhabitants, and became so incorporated with them as to seem one race.

34. B. C. **1500.**—The genealogy of the principal tribes may be understood from the following diagram:

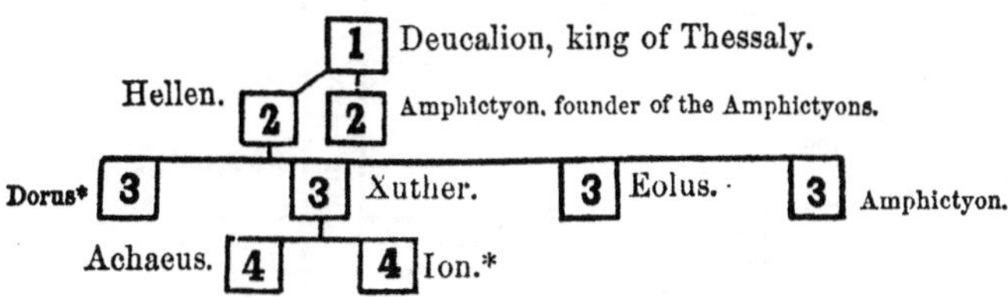

In very early times an assembly of deputies from the provinces had been in the habit of meeting to consult upon the common interests of the confederacy, in the temple of Ceres, near the pass of Thermopylæ. Their constitution is not accurately known, but they seemed the guardians of religion, rather than the representatives of a general government. The code of laws by which their motions were governed was drawn up by Amphictyon, son of Deucalion. During this century the assembly began to meet semi-annually: at Delphi in the spring, and at Thermopylæ in the autumn. They bound themselves by an oath to protect an Amphictyonic city, and to *defend the territories of the god;* invoking curses upon their land and their children, defeat and distress in all enterprises and judicial controversies, in case they failed to perform their oath. In 1455, Cadmus, with a company of Phenicians, landed in Beotia and founded Cadmeia, the citadel of Thebes. He is said to have brought with him sixteen letters of the Greek alphabet.

35. B. C. **1400.**—About 1350 B. C., Pelops, a Phrygian prince, settled in Southern Greece, married the daughter of one of the native potentates, and became a man of so much consequence that the coun-

* Mark the relations of the Dorians and Ionians.

Questions.—34. What council was instituted in this century? When was Thebes founded? By whom? Trace the genealogy of the tribes. What were the early usages of the provinces? Where did the assembly meet? What is known of their constitution? What city did Cadmus found in 1455? How many of the Greek letters did he introduce? 35. Who was Pelops? Where did he settle? In what year? Which way did he travel? How did Peloponnesus come by its name? Trace the line of genealogy.

try was named from him, Peloponnesus. Here follows the genealogy of his descendants:

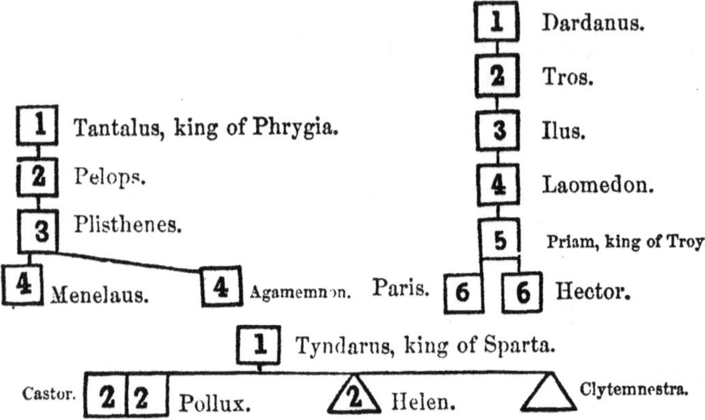

The genealogy of Helen, wife of Menelaus, and of Paris, prince of Troy, may also be traced above.

36. B. C. **1300.**—THE ARGONAUTIC EXPEDITION.—According to the mythic legends so often quoted, Phryxus and Helle, two children of a Beotian king, to avoid the persecutions of their step-mother, escaped upon a winged ram, which had a fleece of gold. They intended to land in Colchis, where their uncle lived; but, as they were passing the narrow strait that divides Asia from Europe, Helle fell into the sea, which was named from her, Hellespont.* Phryxus arrived in safety at Colchis. The ram died there; and to recover his fleece, Jason, a relative of Phryxus, with fifty of the most renowned warriors of the age, among whom were Castor and Pollux, Hercules, Theseus and Laertes, undertook the Argonautic expedition. That a company sailed from the shores of Greece to the eastern borders of the Euxine, during this century, is no doubt a fact; but what real purpose was veiled under the symbol of the *golden fleece* it is impossible to determine.

37. B. C. **1200.**—TROJAN WAR.—Castor and Pollux having died in youth, and Clytemnestra being married to Agamemnon, king of Argos, Tyndarus, king of Sparta, looked for a successor in the husband of his

* The Hellespont was the strait through which the tides of the Euxine flowed into the Egean. It was 60 miles long, and, in some places, 3 miles broad.

Questions.—36. Relate the mythic legend connected with the thirteenth century. What expedition is said to owe its origin to this fable? 37, 38, 39. How did the Trojan war originate? Relate the story.

Helen.* The beauty of this princess, together with the throne, drew numerous suitors from all parts of Greece, and Tyndarus began to fear that, in selecting a husband for his daughter, he should surround her with enemies in the persons of her rejected lovers; he therefore compelled them all to take an oath to protect her in possession of the object of her choice. Menelaus, brother of Agamemnon, was so fortunate as to win her regard, and to him Tyndarus consigned his daughter and his throne.

38. Not long after, Paris, son of Priam, king of Troy, hearing of the charms of Helen, made a voyage across the Egean to see her. He was kindly received, and hospitably entertained by Menelaus, who, during his stay, having occasion to visit Crete, left his wife to amuse his guest. Paris, who was the most beautiful man of his time, seized the opportunity to persuade the fickle queen of the superior happiness to be enjoyed in his father's court. When Menelaus returned, he found his home deserted and pillaged of all its treasures; the perfidious guest who carried away his wife having also loaded the ship with the precious things of Sparta.

39. Burning with the desire of revenge, Menelaus summoned the former suitors of his treacherous queen to fulfill their vow, and assist him in burying the dishonor of Greece beneath the ashes of Troy. Agamemnon, the most powerful prince of the age, was appointed to head the expedition. Under this leader, all the chieftains, with their followers, from the end of Peloponnesus to the end of Thessaly, together with Idomeneus from Crete, Ulysses from Ithaca, and other potentates from the islands, assembled in Beotia to embark in their enterprise of vengeance. The fleet, consisting of 1200 open vessels, each carrying from 50 to 120 men, had a prosperous voyage. The Greeks landed upon the coast, and soon compelled all the descendants of Dardanus to take refuge within the walls of Troy.

40. How Troy Fell.—The siege became a blockade, and famine began to threaten the Trojans; but the besiegers were themselves in little better condition. Supplies came slowly from the far-off shores of Greece, and finally they were obliged to disperse in different directions to seek for sustenance. A band was sent over the Hellespont to cultivate the Chersonesus, and Achilles is said to have plundered twenty-three towns in marauding expeditions. The besieged also made

* See page 99.

Questions.—37, 38, 39. Who was the leader in the expedition against the Trojans? Who assisted Menelaus as allies? Where did the army assemble? What movement was then made? 40. Give a description of the siege that followed.

frequent sorties; Hector performed prodigies of valor, and Homer represents the gods themselves as mingling in the strife, and urging on the combatants. Thus the war was protracted during ten years.

41. The Greeks at last had recourse to stratagem. Pretending to abandon the siege, they formed a wooden horse of vast size, as a present for Minerva; and, making all preparations for returning home, embarked in their ships and set sail, leaving a band of their bravest heroes within the body of the horse. The Trojans, overjoyed to be rid of their foes, tore down a part of the walls, and dragged the offering for Minerva within their city. That night was spent in festivity through Troy. The guards were withdrawn, the weary soldiers threw aside their arms, and wine, amusement, and repose ruled the hour. Meantime the Grecian fleet drew back to the shore; the warriors disembarked, and silently approached the devoted city; the heroes in the wooden horse sallied forth, opened the gates, and the Greeks entered. The night, which was begun in feasting and carousal, ended in conflagration and blood. The destruction of Troy took place B. C. 1184. Independence and sovereignty never returned to the "land of Priam;" it became a part of the kingdom of Lydia, and followed the fortunes of the great empires.

42. CONSEQUENCES OF THIS EXPEDITION.—But though the Greeks had extinguished the flames of their resentment in the best blood of Troy, they had little reason to glory in their revenge. Their fleets were dispersed, and their vessels were wrecked on dangerous coasts. Many of their chiefs wandered through long voyages, and settled in foreign parts; some became pirates, and made their homes among the islands of the Egean; and of the few who were so fortunate as to reach the shores of Greece, but a very small number were able to wrest their thrones from the usurpers who had filled them during their absence. Clytemnestra, following the example of her sister, had bestowed her affections upon another, and Agamemnon, on his return to Argos, was assassinated.

43. DORIAN INVASION.—The remainder of this century was darkened by clouds of domestic strife. The descendants of Hercules, having been driven from Southern Greece by the Pelopid race, had dwelt in the mountainous region of Doris, now, profiting by these commotions, they crossed the Corinthian Gulf, and seized upon their former inherit-

Questions.—41. By what stratagem was Troy at last taken? In what year did it fall? What did it become? Trace the Greeks from Beotia to Troy. (See map No. 2.) 42. What were the consequences of the expedition to the Greeks themselves? What became of Agamemnon? 43. Who was Hercules? *Ans.* One of the demi-gods, whose children, returning from Doris, overran and settled all Southern Greece. In what direction did they move?

ance. In consequence of this revolution, Elis, Messenia, Laconia, and many other states of the Peloponnesus became Dorian; the former inhabitants escaping to Asia Minor, or being reduced to a state of vassalage.

44. B. C. **1100.**—The Heraclidæ, encouraged by their success in Southern Greece, advanced up through the isthmus and fell upon Attica. Codrus, at that time king, having been told that "either the state or the king must perish," disguised himself as a peasant, went into the camp of the enemy, insulted one of the soldiers, and was slain, thus nobly devoting himself for his country. The Heracleids were driven back into the Peloponnesus, and Medon, son of Codrus, was made *Archon* instead of *King* of Athens. B. C. **1000.**—Homer is accounted the most ancient writer, except Scripture historians. He was a blind old man, who lived in one of the Ionian colonies of Asia Minor. Hesiod is supposed to have been a shepherd, who fed his flocks by the side of Mt. Helicon.

45. B. C. **900.**—OLYMPIC GAMES INSTITUTED BY IPHITUS. LYCURGUS'S LAWS.—Homer mentions certain games which were celebrated in his time, but it seems they were only occasional meetings; and during the long troubles arising from the Dorian conquest, the customs and institutions of the Peloponnesians were so altered and overthrown, that even the *memory* of the ancient games was nearly lost. In this season of turbulence, Iphitus ascended the throne of Elis. Active and enterprising, but not by inclination a warrior, he was anxious to find a remedy for the disorderly situation of his country. For this purpose he sent a solemn embassy to Delphi, to inquire "How the anger of the gods, which threatened the total destruction of Peloponnesus, through endless hostilities among its people, might be averted." The answer was, "The Olympic festival must be restored; for the neglect of that solemnity has brought on the Greeks the indignation of the god Jupiter, to whom it was dedicated, and of the hero Hercules, by whom it was instituted; and a cessation of arms must immediately be proclaimed for all cities desirous of partaking in it."

46. This reply of the god was promulgated throughout all Greece,

---

Questions.—What places were settled by the expelled Pelopids? *Ans.* Eolia and Ionia? For what were the inhabitants afterward distinguished? *Ans.* For elegance of taste and love of the arts and sciences. They were the teachers and examples of the other Greeks. Homer, Pythagoras, Parhasius, and Sappho, were natives of these colonies. Trace the Heracleids from Thessaly and Doris to Peloponnesus. 44. Where did the Heraclidæ next go? Relate the story of Codrus. Trace the Heraclidæ from Laconia to Attica. Who was Homer? What did he write? Who was Hesiod? What did he write? *Ans.* The stories of the gods. 45. By whom were the national games revived? What led to their revival? Relate the story.

and Iphitus caused the armistice to be published. With the approbation of the other Peloponnesians, it was ordained that a festival, open to the whole Greek nation, should be held at the temple of Jupiter, in the spacious plain of Olympia; that it should be repeated at the termination of every fourth year; that it should consist of solemn sacrifices and games: and that, whatever war might be in progress, a cessation of arms should take place before and continue long enough after the festival to allow all the Hellenic race to leave their homes, attend the games, and return again in peace. Thus *Elis became the Holy Land of Greece*, and a reputation of sacredness attached itself to the whole Eleian people. In the time of Iphitus the foot-race was the only game exhibited.

47. Afterward, at different periods, wrestling, boxing, chariot-racing, and horse-racing were added; and when sculpture, painting, poetry, and music, began to give refinement to pleasure, it was at the Olympic games that the artist exhibited specimens of his skill, and the poet gained his proudest laurels. A mart, or fair, was a natural consequence of a periodical assembly of multitudes in one place. He, who had any thing to sell, could find purchasers in this vast concourse; he, who had any thing splendid to exhibit in dress or equipage, could attract admiring eyes in a place where every thing that augmented the glory of the Greeks was applauded; and thus it happened, that all the wealth, skill, and beauty of the nation passed in general review once in four years. This meeting supplied the want of a common capital; matters of general interest were here promulgated, treaties were signed, and expeditions planned, which the strong national feeling, awakened by this display of strength, tended greatly to facilitate.

48. Other Games.—The advantages and gratifications of the Olympic games excited the Greeks to establish similar festivals in their own states. Three of these only, the Delphian, Isthmian, and Nemean, ever rose to any importance; and they never equaled the Olympic in celebrity and splendor. The Delphian were celebrated at Delphi, in honor of Apollo; the Isthmian upon the Corinthian Isthmus, in honor of Neptune, whose temple there commanded a view of the sea; and the Nemean in Argos, in honor of Juno. They were held at intervals

---

Questions.—46. Of what did the Olympic festival consist? What is said of Elis? Where was Olympia? (Map No. 2.) 47. Which were the only games during the time of Iphitus? What other games were afterward added? What is said of the artist and the poet? What good resulted to the people in business transactions? 48. To what did the Olympic games excite the Greeks? What other festivals rose to importance? What can you state of the Delphian? Isthmian? Nemean? Where was Delphi? (See map No. 2.) Argos? Corinthian Isthmus? (13, map No. 2.)

of four years, each taking its year between the Olympic meetings, so that every summer there was a festival common to all the Greek nation, with an armistice enabling all, who desired, to attend.

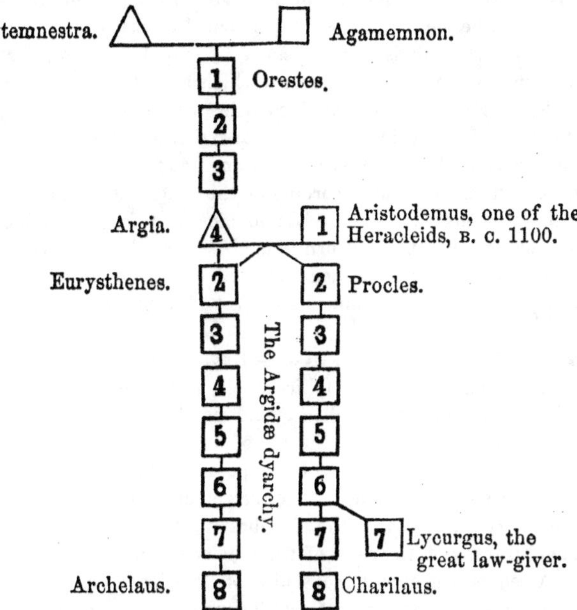

49. The race of Orestes terminating in a daughter, Argia, she was married to Aristodemus, one of the Heracleids, to whose share Laconia fell in the general division of the Peloponnesus. Aristodemus died soon after, and his twin sons, Eurysthenes and Procles, shared the kingdom jointly. The government thus formed a dyarchy. For seven generations the crown descended in each line from father to son in unbroken succession. Each king naturally had his own partisans, and hence it is no matter of surprise that, after the lapse of two centuries, faction and anarchy should have obtained possession of the state.

50. Order and peace had long been banished from Lacedemon when Lycurgus, by the death of his brother, was put in possession of the authority held by the line of Procles. He, however, resigned his newly-

---

Questions—49. Who was Aristodemus? How was his kingdom governed after his death? How does a dynasty differ from a dyarchy? What troubles originated in the dyarchy form of government? 50. To what position did Lycurgus attain?

acquired dignity in favor of his infant nephew Charilaus, and, to fit himself for a law-giver, took what in those days was esteemed a long and perilous journey into Crete, Egypt, and Asia. In Crete he studied the laws of Minos, and formed an intimacy with a poet of that island, whom, when he left for Egypt, he persuaded to pass over into Sparta, and prepare the minds of the people, by popular poems, for those changes in government and manners which he intended to introduce.

51. From Egypt he journeyed to Asia, where he found the poems of Homer, and observing in them many moral sentences and much political wisdom, he collected them in one body and transcribed them with his own hand. The disorders of the state, meantime, increased to such an extent, that the Lacedemonians sent frequent messengers to entreat their regent to return home. When all things were ready, he accepted the invitation, and, entering the city of Sparta amid the rejoicings of the people, immediately set himself to alter the whole frame of the constitution.

52. B. C. 884.—Lycurgus's Laws.—Having strengthened his authority by the sanction of the Delphic oracle, which declared that "The constitution he should establish would be the most excellent in the world," and having secured the aid of a numerous party among the leading men who took up arms to support him, he procured the enactment of a series of ordinances affecting the civil and military constitution of the commonwealth, the distribution of property, the education of the citizens, and the rules of their daily intercourse and domestic life. A senate was chosen, consisting of experienced individuals, who gave to the government a just equilibrium: "The twenty-eight senators adhering to the kings, whenever they saw the people too encroaching; and, on the other hand, supporting the people, when the kings attempted to make themselves absolute."

53. The city was overstocked with indigent, indolent persons. Lycurgus, to give them employment, and at the same time a motive for exertion, caused the whole territory of Laconia to be divided in thirty-nine thousand parts, which were portioned out to the inhabitants. After this, he attempted to divide the movables,* but here he found great difficulty; the people strongly objecting to the sacrifice of their goods. He therefore adopted another method, counter-working their

* Furniture.

Questions.—50. Why did he take the long journey? What did he do in Crete? 51. What did he do in Asia? How were state affairs in Laconia during his absence? 52. How did he strengthen his authority? What is said of the Senate? 53. What "Land Reform" did Lycurgus introduce?

avarice by a stratagem. He stopped the currency of gold and silver, and substituted iron money in its stead; at the same time, fixing the rate of this new coin so low, that, to remove a sum equal to one hundred dollars, a cart and oxen would be required. This iron was good for nothing else, having been deprived of malleability, by being heated and plunged into vinegar. Neither would it pass among the other states, so that the Spartans had no means of purchasing any foreign or curious wares; nor did any merchant-ship unlade in their harbors. No sophists, wandering fortune-tellers, or dealers in gold and silver trinkets, were found in that country, there being no money to tempt them that way. Hence luxury, losing by degrees the means which supported it, died away of itself.

54. Another regulation was the institution of public tables, where all the men were to eat in common of the same meat, and of such kinds of it as were appointed by law. They were not permitted to eat at home on any occasion, and they made it a point to observe and reproach any one, that seemed to lack appetite, as effeminate, and weary of the common diet. About fifteen persons formed *the mess* of one table, and each was required to bring, monthly, one bushel of meal, eight gallons of wine, five pounds of cheese, and a little money to buy flesh and fish; but the food held in highest esteem was "black broth," a kind of soup made of lentils. Children were introduced at these tables, that they might learn sobriety, and listen to discourses upon government. They were taught to joke without scurrility, to sustain raillery with equanimity, for, "It was reckoned worthy a Lacedemonian to bear a jest." When they first entered the hall, the oldest man present pointed to the door, saying, "Not a word spoken in this company goes out there."

55. Discipline of the Young.—To render his institutions permanent, Lycurgus caused them to be inwoven with the whole fabric of society. From the earliest period of life, the discipline of youth was stern and severe. Feeble and defective children were thrown into a cave, and left to perish; such as, upon a public examination, were deemed sound and healthy, were adopted as children of the state, and committed to their mothers for the period of infancy. At the age of seven, they were taken from their parents and educated at public expense. They were enrolled in companies, and kept under the same order and discipline as a military band.

Questions.—53. What currency alteration? What was the effect? 54. What regulation was introduced in relation to public tables? "The Mess" of one table? Children at the tables? 55, 56. What was the discipline of the youth? What is said of theft?

56. The youth who showed most courage was made captain; and frequent skirmishes took place between rival parties, which the old men encouraged by commendations. As they advanced in age, their hair was cut very close, they were forced to go bare-foot, and play, for the most part, quite naked. They slept on beds of reeds, gathered with their own hands, and were allowed but a spare diet, that their ingenuity might be cultivated to supply their wants. One of the ablest men in the city was appointed inspector of the youth; he gave the command of each company to a young man who had been two years out of the class of boys, and was therefore called an Iren. This Iren, when twenty years old, gave orders to his inferiors, with all the dignity of a colonel. He called upon them to serve him at his house; some he sent to get wood, others to gather herbs, or to steal any eatable from the common tables. Ingenuity in these little thefts was highly honored, but detection insured disgrace.

57. A boy, having stolen a fox, and hidden it under his garment, suffered the creature to tear out his vitals, rather than encounter the sneers of his companions. The Iren, reposing himself after supper, used to order one of the boys to sing a song; to another, he put some question, such as "Who is the best man in the city?" If the respondent hesitated in his answer, he was considered a boy of slow parts, and he who gave a wrong answer had his thumb bitten by the Iren. The magistrates often attended these little trials, and if the Iren were guilty of too much severity or remissness, he himself suffered punishment after the boys were gone.

58. Short and pithy sentences became the style of Laconia. Lycurgus himself adopted and encouraged this manner of discourse. The Spartans cultivated poetry and music, as every thing else, in subserviency to a martial spirit. There were three choirs in their festivals. The old men began,

"Once in battle bold we shone;"

the young men responded,

"Try us; our vigor is not gone;"

and the boys concluded,

"The palm remains for us alone."

In war the severity of their discipline was relaxed; the men were permitted to comb their hair gracefully, and to study elegance in their

---

Questions.—57. Relate the story of the boy and fox. What further discipline were the youth subjected to? 58. What style of expression did the people adopt? What arts did they cultivate? Where was the severity of their discipline relaxed?

arms and apparel; but at home, the city was like one great camp, where all had their stated allowance, and knew their public charge, "Each man concluding that he was born, not for himself, but for his country."

59. *They were expressly forbidden to exercise any mechanic art or agricultural employment.* The Helots, inhabitants of a small sea-port town in Laconia, had been reduced to a state of servitude some years before, and upon them fell the burden of all the labor. These slaves were treated with the greatest inhumanity. They wore dog-skin bonnets, and sheep-skin vests; they were forbidden to learn any liberal art, and once a day they received a certain number of stripes, lest they should forget their condition. Sometimes they were intoxicated and exposed in the public halls, to the ridicule of the children, and when there was danger of their becoming too numerous, the Spartan youth were instructed to sally out in the night and kill all the Helots they met.

60. END OF LYCURGUS.—The last act of Lycurgus was to sacrifice himself for the perpetuity of his work. Having assembled all the Spartans, he told them that it was necessary to consult the oracle upon an important subject; then, taking an oath of the kings, and senators, and people, to obey his laws till his return, he bade farewell to his beloved Sparta, and bent his steps toward the Delphi. When the last seal had been set to his institutions by the oracle, which foretold that Sparta should flourish as long as she adhered to them, he transmitted the prediction to his fellow-citizens, and, that they might never be freed from their oath, determined to die in a foreign land. The place and manner of his death are veiled in obscurity. Both Delphi and Elis claimed his tomb. Sparta, faithful to her oath, adhered to his institutions five centuries, and each year honored the lawgiver as a god, with solemn sacrifices.

61. B. C. **800.**—THE FIRST OLYMPIAD.—In the year 776, B. C., Corœbus, having won the prize in the Olympic games, had his name inscribed in the gymnasium, and this period began the first Olympiad. The prizes in these games were at first of some intrinsic value, but from the 7th Olympiad, or twenty-eight years after the victory of Corœbus, the only prize given was a garland of wild olive, cut from a

---

Questions.—58. What was the conclusion of each man? 59. What prohibition was imposed upon the people? Who were the Helots? What did they become? How were they treated? 60. What was the last act of Lycurgus? Relate the circumstances attending it. What was the tendency of the laws Lycurgus established? Trace him through his travels. 61. In what year began the first Olympiad? After the victory of Corœbus, what became the prize in the games? How were the victors honored?

tree in the sacred grove at Olympia, which was said to have been brought by Hercules from the land of the Hyperboreans. Palm leaves were at the same time placed in the hands of the victors, and their names were proclaimed by a herald. A victory at Olympia, being the highest honor a Greek could obtain, conferred such glory on the republic to which he belonged, that he was permitted to enter his native city in triumph through a breach made in the walls for his reception; banquets were given to him by his friends, and often an annuity was settled upon him by the State.

62. In this century the office of Ephori was instituted at Sparta. This court consisted of five members only, chosen annually from among the people. "They were empowered to fine whom they pleased, and exact immediate payment of the fine." They could suspend the functions of any other magistrates, and arrest and bring to trial even the kings. The archonship of Athens, which had hitherto been hereditary in the family of Codrus, was in this century made decennial.

63. B. C. 743.—First Messenian War.—The first trial the Lacedemonians had occasion to make of their military discipline was in a war with the Messenians, their western neighbors. A rich Messenian put out some cattle under the care of herdsmen (his own slaves) to pasture, by agreement, on the lands of a Lacedemonian. The Lacedemonian sold both cattle and herdsmen, pocketed the reward of his iniquity, and pretended to the owner that they had been carried off by pirates. One of the slaves, however, escaped from his purchaser, returned to his master, and related the whole affair. The injured Messenian sent his son to demand the money of the perfidious Lacedemonian, who added to his enormities by murdering the youth. The father, full of grief and indignation, went himself to Sparta and laid his complaint before the kings and people. Finding no disposition in them to grant him redress, he returned to his own country, and avenged himself by murdering all the Lacedemonians he could meet. These outrages resulted in a war, disastrous to Lacedemon, and almost fatal to Messenia.

64. Without any of those formal declarations of war which the law of nations even then required, the Lacedemonians prepared secretly for hostilities, and so extreme was their enmity that an oath was taken, "That no length of time should weary them, and no misfortune deter

---

Questions.—In what manner was victory estimated? How long was one Olympiad? *Ans.* Four years. 62. What office in Sparta was instituted during this century? What change was made in the archonship of Athens? 63. What caused the first Messenian war?

them, but they would prosecute the war, and on no account return to their families till they had subdued Messenia." For nineteen long years the conflict raged with doubtful success; if Messenia was depopulated, Sparta was in no better situation, for all the men capable of bearing arms were exiles by their oath, and Lacedemon was inhabited only by women. But Spartan discipline and Spartan perseverance at length prevailed. Ithome, the last stronghold of the wretched Messenians, was beseiged and taken, the garrison fled by sea, the miserable multitude scattered in various directions about the country, and the Lacedemonians reduced them to a state of servitude little better than that of the Helots, B. C. 724.

65. B. C. **700.**—SECOND MESSENIAN WAR. DRACO'S LAWS.—During forty years, Messenia remained in quiet subjection. Another race were by this time grown up, ignorant of the comparative strength of themselves and their conquerors, and filled with that irresistible spirit of liberty which animated every Grecian breast. Aristomenes, a noble youth, who traced his origin to Hercules through a long line of kings, was the instigator and leader of the revolt. Supported by allies from Argos and Arcadia, he attacked a body of Lacedemonians, and showed such skill and courage that the Messenians saluted him king on the field of battle, a name which he, however, declined in favor of that of *general*. To practice upon the superstitious fears of the enemy, he entered Sparta, which had neither walls nor watch, and hung against the Brazen House (the temple of Minerva) a shield, with an inscription declaring that Aristomenes, from the spoils of Sparta, made that offering to the goddess. Alarmed lest their enemy should win the favor of their protecting deity, the Spartans sent to consult the oracle, and were directed to take an Athenian adviser.

66. The *Spartans* were little pleased with this response, the jealousy between the Dorians and Ionians being already rife, and the *Athenians* were little disposed to aid in the subjugation of the brave Messenians; but the embassy was sent for the required leader, and the Athenians, fearing to offend the god, complied in such a manner as they thought would render compliance useless. They sent to the Spartans Tyrtæus, a lame schoolmaster and poet, who, notwithstanding his disabilities, proved more serviceable than they designed. By his poetry he roused the drooping spirits of the Spartans, and persuaded them to enlist a

---

Questions.—64. How long did it continue? What was the result? 65. Who was Aristomenes? What is said of him? What allies did he have? Could they have reached Messenia without going through Laconia? 66. Who was Tyrtæus? On what mission was he sent? What success did he meet with.

band of Helots among their soldiers. Though Aristomenes continually harassed them with incursions, yet it was not till the third year of the war that the contending parties came to any decisive engagement.

67. In the great battle of the Trenches, the Messenians were betrayed by the king of the Arcadians, and Aristomenes, escaping with a scanty remnant of his forces, was obliged to give up the defense of his country and concentrate his remaining strength at Ira, a stronghold near the sea. Making this place his headquarters, he sallied out upon the enemy and carried off prey or prisoners, till at last, falling in with a body of Lacedemonians under both their kings, he was taken with about fifty of his band.

68. How Aristomenes Escaped.—They were tried as rebels, and sentenced to be thrown into a deep and dark cave, used for the punishment of the worst criminals. Aristomenes was saved as if by a miracle. His shield, which he had been allowed to retain in compliment to his valor, striking against the sides of the cave, broke the violence of his fall, so that he tumbled alive upon the dead bodies of his companions. After the first feeling of gratitude for deliverance had subsided, his heart sank at the prospect of a lingering death in this horrid charnel, peopled with the skeletons and putrid carcasses of former criminals. He retreated to the farthest corner, and, covering his head with his cloak, laid down to wait for death. On the third day of this dreadful imprisonment he was startled by a rustling noise. Rising and uncovering his eyes, he perceived by the glimmering light a fox devouring the carcasses.

69. It immediately occurred to him that this animal must have entered the cavern by another way than that by which he had himself descended. Acting upon this suggestion, he seized the fox with one hand, while with his cloak in the other he prevented its biting him, and in this way followed it through a narrow bury till the passage became too strait for his body. But here a peep of daylight renewed his courage, and setting vigorously to work with his hands, he soon made an opening large enough to creep through, and thus found himself once more at liberty. His friends at Ira received him as one risen from the dead. The Spartans affected to disbelieve the story of his reappearance, but Aristomenes soon proved to them that he had lost none of his valor by his sojourn in the cavern.

70. Fate of Ira and the Messenians.—Through his untiring ingenuity and perseverance, the siege of Ira was protracted during eleven

---

Questions.—67. Give an account of the first battle. What misfortune befell Aristomenes? 68, 69. Relate the circumstances of his escape. 70, 71. How long did the siege of Ira last?

years, and at last was taken only by treason. A Spartan deserter, learning that an outpost of Ira had been abandoned one stormy night, re-deserted to his countrymen with the intelligence. Guided by the double-dyed traitor, the Lacedemonians silently carried ladders to the defenseless point and mounted unresisted. The barking of dogs awakened Aristomenes. Hastily summoning his men, he rushed to the rescue, and all that night the clash of arms and the shout of combatants mingled with the howling of the storm; the women assisting by throwing tiles from the house-tops, or bearing arms in the fight.

71. But the numbers of the Lacedemonians enabled them constantly to bring up fresh troops, while every Messenian was obliged to stand at his post, without rest or refreshment, under the peltings of the pitiless storm. Cold, wet, sleepless, jaded, and hungry, they kept up the struggle for three nights and two days, and then resolved upon the last effort of despair. The men were drawn up in a hollow square, with the women and children in the center, and a passage demanded, sword in hand. The Spartans gave way on every side, and this miserable remnant of a heroic people advanced unharmed. The Arcadians came to meet them on the frontiers of their country, bringing food and clothing, and saluting them with words of kindness and sympathy. The aged and infirm Messenians remained in Arcadia, but the young and vigorous determined to seek independence in a foreign land.

72. While they yet deliberated on the choice of a country, a messenger arrived from Rhegium, sent by the king of that place, to offer the exiles an asylum in his dominions. This refuge was joyfully accepted, but scarcely were they comfortably located with their hospitable entertainers, when they were harassed by the piratical incursions of the Zancleans across the strait. Here seemed an opportunity to reward their benefactors and provide a home for themselves; therefore, assisted by the Rhegians, they besieged Zancle, both by sea and land, conquered the inhabitants, united with them, and founded the city of Messina, which remains to this day a witness of the valor of the Messenians.

73. WHAT BECAME OF ARISTOMENES.—Aristomenes sent his son with the colony to Zancle, but for himself, he said, he would never

---

Questions.—How was Ira finally taken? What was the fate of the Messenians? 72. Where did the Messenians take refuge? Where did they finally settle? What is said of the city of Messina? Where is that city? (See map No. 4.) What is its present population? *Ans.* About 100,000 inhabitants. Trace the Messenian exiles from Ira to Arcadia, thence to Rhegium, and thence to Sicily. 73. What account can you give of the son of Aristomenes? What exertions did Aristomenes make?

cease to war with Lacedemon. He vainly sought the means of farther hostilities. He passed over into Asia, hoping to get assistance there; and finally spent some years with a Rhodian king, who, being told to marry the daughter of the most illustrious Greek, unhesitatingly chose the child of Aristomenes. He lived universally respected by the most powerful princes of his time, and died at Sardis, deeply lamented by all who knew him. His actions dwelt in the memories of his countrymen, and cheered their wanderings and sufferings; and in their legendary songs, his character was represented as combining all the elements of goodness and greatness, in a degree almost unparalleled among Grecian heroes.

74. From the death of Codrus, 1070, to the year B. C. 624, nothing of particular interest occurred in the history of Athens. The Archonship descended from father to son, in the family of Medon, son of Codrus, till the thirteenth generation, when, by a change in the constitution, upon the death of Alcmæon, the office was laid open to the ambition of all the nobles, and the Archons were *elected* once in ten years. The children of Alcmæon, as descended from a king, and from *that Alcmæon* who first settled in Attica, looked upon themselves as *the* aristocracy, and assumed airs little pleasing to the other citizens. There was then in Athens a young man named Cylon, who had distinguished himself at the Olympic games, and married a daughter of the king of Megara. Fully persuaded that he was equal, if not superior to the proud Alcmæonids, he determined to set the matter beyond all doubt by making himself master of the republic.

75. With a band of troops which he obtained from his father-in-law, he seized the citadel of Athens. Megacles, the head of the Alcmæonid family, being at that time Archon, summoned the citizens to arms, and, surrounding the Acropolis, cut off every resource from the young aspirant and his followers. Cylon saved himself by a disgraceful flight; his deserted adherents fled for protection to the altars. Not caring to stain these sacred places with their blood, Megacles lured them forth by a promise of pardon; but no sooner were they in his power, than he caused them all to be put to death as traitors! The *sacrilege*, thus wantonly committed under color of the law, alienated the minds of the Athenians from the Alcmæonidæn, and proved a fruitful source of trouble in later times. Megacles and his adherents

---

Questions.—What became of Aristomenes? Trace the course of Aristomenes? 74. In what year does Athenian history resume its interest? What is said of the Archonship? Of the children of Alcmæon? Who was Cylon? Upon what did he determine? 75. Give an account of the attempt made by him. Who was Megacles? What can you state of him?

were banished, but still tranquillity was not restored. The existing laws were insufficient to quell the disorders which daily arose; and, finally, the Athenians appointed Draco, an old man of acknowledged probity, to fill the office of legislator.

76. DRACO'S LAWS.—Draco brought forward his code of laws, B. C. 621. They were peculiar only for the penalties annexed to them. The *slightest theft* was punished capitally, as well as the most *atrocious murder;* and one remarked of them that "they were written with blood, and not with ink." His own words, "small crimes deserve *death*, and I know of no heavier punishment for greater," serve to illustrate the severity of his disposition. The laws, of course, fell into disuse; the penalties were too severe to be executed, and the law-giver himself was obliged by the anarchy that ensued to retire to Egina, where he was suffocated by the number of cloaks and garments thrown upon him in the theater—a method which the inhabitants took to express *their* esteem for him.

77. B. C. **600.**—RECAPTURE OF SALAMIS.—The island of Salamis, wearied of the weak and uncertain government of Athens, threw off its allegiance, and set up for independence. Many unsuccessful attempts were made to reduce it to its former state of dependency; and, finally, the people met in general assembly, and decreed capital punishment to any private or magistrate who should propose to lead them again to the conquest of Salamis. The nobles, unable to administer the government, and the people, incapable of acting in any public capacity, were equally dissatisfied with the posture of affairs, but none dared to propose any change.

78. In these circumstances, came forth one of the greatest characters Greece ever produced. Solon, a young poet, descended from Codrus, though a native of Salamis, had resided for some time at Athens. Perceiving that the people regretted their foolish resolution, he gave out that he was subject to occasional fits of insanity, and shut himself up in his house, while he composed a poem on the loss of the *lovely island.* Having every thing prepared, one day, during an assembly of the people, he ran into the market place, like one frantic, mounted the herald's stone, and recited his poem to the crowd. Some of his friends stood ready to raise the shout of admiration; the people caught the phrensy, the odious law was repealed by acclamation, a

---

Questions.—Who was Draco? 76. When did he offer his code of laws? What can you state of the laws? What became of Draco? Trace Draco to Egina. 77. Where was the island of Salamis? (See map No. 2.) What political change took place? What attempts were made? What decree was made? What, then, was the condition of affairs at Athens? 78. Who was Solon? In what manner did he distinguish himself?

new expedition was ordered, and Solon was appointed to command the troops. Under his guidance, the Athenians were successful, and Salamis again acknowledged the authority of the parent state. In the general joy, the exiles were restored; Megacles returned, and the Alcmæonids again ruled the city.

79. FACTIONS.—But the discords of Athens, having their origin in a defective constitution, were not removed. The mountaineers and common people sighed for a complete *democracy;* the rich landed-proprietors aimed to establish an exclusive *oligarchy ;* and the mercantile men were anxious to see the different orders harmonized in a *mixed government:* hence, *Highlanders, Lowlanders, and Coastmen,* became the distinguishing names of the factions which long divided the Attic people. While matters were growing worse and worse, and many were looking to a despotism for relief, the superior abilities of Solon drew the attention of all parties. Though one of the nobles, he had never oppressed the poor; though the favorite of the people, he had never excited their clamors against the rich: his wisdom had been proved, his integrity was above question; and he was accordingly, with unanimous consent, elected Archon, with peculiar powers for reforming the laws and constitution.

80. B. C. 594.—SOLON'S LAWS.—In the inquiry, what the Athenian constitution was, it will be necessary to take a view of the COMPONENT MEMBERS of the Athenian State. Athens was inhabited by three distinct classes: I. A *citizen,* born of free Athenian parents, or admitted to the freedom of the state, was one of the people, and eligible to any office. II. *Strangers,* who came to settle at Athens, for the sake of commerce, or any other reason, had *no* share in the government, no votes in the assembly of the people, and could not be admitted to any office. III. *Servants,* were those taken in war, and bought and sold as parts of their master's estate. They were treated with great kindness, and could ransom themselves, even without their master's consent, when they had laid up sufficient money for the purpose.

81. It was the object of Solon's laws to equalize, as much as possible, the privileges and authority of the citizens. He repealed all the laws of Draco, except those against murder. But the distinguishing feature of the new constitution was the substitution of *property* for *birth,* as a title to the honors and offices of the state. Solon divided

---

Questions.—79. How many factions were there? Name them. Why was Solon elected Archon? 80. How many classes were there in Athens? What privilege belonged to the free born citizen? What is said of strangers? Of servants? 81. What was the object of Solon's laws? What was the distinguishing feature of the new constitution?

the people into four ranks; the FIRST consisted of those whose income amounted to five hundred measures yearly; the SECOND, of those whose revenues came up to three hundred, who, being able to keep a war-horse, were called *knights;* the THIRD were called by a name and filled a rank similar to that of *yeomen;* and the FOURTH consisted of hired laborers in husbandry. Out of the first class *only*, nine Archons were chosen *yearly*. The *first*, called *the* Archon, took care of legacies and wills provided for orphans, and punished drunkenness; the *second* had the charge of religious ceremonies, and enjoyed the title of *king;* the *third* had the care of strangers; and to each of the others separate offices were assigned.

82. COURTS, COUNCILS, AND ASSEMBLY.—Every Archon on laying down his office became a member of the COURT OF AREOPAGUS. This court consisted entirely of ex-archons, who held their offices for life, unless they were expelled for immoral conduct. It was the *first* court that ever decided upon life and death; it was the only court from which there was no appeal to the people. The members held their meetings on "Mars-hill," a small eminence at a little distance from the Acropolis. They sat in the open air in the night, around an altar dedicated to Minerva, near which were rude seats of stone for the defendant and his accuser. No eloquent pleadings nor moving representations were allowed before this court, lest the minds of the judges should be warped by them. The Areopagites took cognizance of murders, impiety, immoral behavior, and particularly of *idleness*, which they deemed the cause of all vice. They guarded the laws and managed the public treasury; they had the superintendence of youth, and provided that all should be educated according to their rank and fortune.

83. The institution of the council of *Four Hundred* was uniformly ascribed to Solon; but the judicial power which he relied upon most for the correcting of all abuses was a body of 6000 citizens, called the *General Assembly*, chosen by lot yearly to form a kind of *supreme court*. There were also *ten courts of judicature* in Athens, and, to save the inhabitants of Attica the trouble of coming to the city for justice, itinerant judges, called *the Forty*, were appointed to go through the boroughs and decide cases of inferior consequence. Solon ordered that all those who took no part in public affairs should be punished; for,

---

Questions.—81. How did Solon divide the people? 82. How was the court of Areopagus formed? What is said of this court in particular? What else is said of the court? 83. What is said of the Council of Four Hundred? Of the General Assembly? Of the courts of judicature? Of itinerant judges?

said he, "That is (in my opinion) the most perfect government where an injury to any *one* is the concern of *all.*"

84. As many of the citizens had sold themselves for debt, the law-giver caused a general cancellation to take place, and lessened the rate of interest, that the poor might be able to recover from the oppression under which they had so long groaned. No son was compelled to support his father in old age, unless the father had taken care to bring him up to some trade or profession. These enactments, in which Solon was supported by the nobles as well as by the people, were inscribed upon blocks of wood made to turn upon an axis. They were kept at first in the Acropolis, but afterward in the Prytaneum or place of the General Assembly. They formed the basis of the Roman Twelve Tables, and thence became incorporated in the institutions of Alfred the Great; so that we may trace our trial by jury and representative government to the laws of Solon.

85. First Sacred War.—The territory of Crissa, situated upon a gulf of the same name, contained three cities whose harbors were crowded with vessels from every quarter, bringing pilgrims to the neighboring temple of Delphi. The commerce thus created filled the coffers of the Crisseans with the gold of Asia, Africa, and the islands of the Egean. Not content with these honest gains, the rapacious inhabitants levied a tax upon every foreigner, and a few individuals, more impious still, filled up the measure of their iniquities by forcing the gates of the temple and plundering its treasures. This sacrilegious act affecting, as it did, the *pecuniary* interests of all Greece, could not be forgiven. Solon represented to the Amphictyonic council the necessity of punishing the offense with the greatest rigor. A messenger was accordingly sent to Crissa, to require the surrender of the criminals. The Crisseans made common cause with their guilty fellow-citizens, and an insulting answer was returned to the venerable guardians of the holy shrine.

86. War was in consequence declared against the sacrilegious rebels, and Solon was appointed to command the armies which assembled from all parts of Greece, to avenge the injury done to the god. The Amphictyonic forces besieged the city of Crissa nine years

---

Questions.—84. What general bankrupt law went into effect? What view had Solon of indolence? How were filial duties regulated? Upon what were the laws inscribed? What did they eventually become? What regulations in our own government can be traced to the laws of Solon? 85. In what division was Crissa? *Ans.* Phocis. What is said of the three cities? Of the rapacity of the inhabitants? Give the primary causes of the war that followed. 86. What appointment did Solon receive? What city was then besieged? How long did the siege continue? Where was the Gulf of Crissa? (Map No. 2.)

without gaining any decisive advantage. The length of the war dampened their zeal, and a pestilence which broke out in the camp threatened it with a final extinction. Deputies, sent to the oracle for counsel, returned with the singular answer, "Send to Cos for the *fawn of gold.*" What this was, or how it could help them, was more than they could tell; but in those days it was deemed proper to obey the commands of the gods, even though they seemed hard to be understood; and messengers were dispatched upon the mysterious errand.

87. When the envoys made known their business in the Coan assembly, a dead silence ensued; for the magistrates *there* knew no more of the article in question than did the Amphictyons themselves. After an embarrassing pause, an old man arose and said—"My name is Nebros, which in our language signifies *fawn*, and my son's name is Chrysos, which signifies *gold.* Chrysos, my son, therefore, must be the 'fawn of gold' intended by the gods, and he shall go with you." Strengthened and animated by the success of their mission, the ambassadors returned, and great was the joy in the Amphictyonic camp, when Chrysos, by means of his medical knowledge, restored the sick to health, and raised the drooping spirits of the soldiers. By accident, he also discovered a pipe which conducted water into the city, and found means to poison the fountain. The garrison was thus conquered by an unseen foe, and Crissa fell into the hands of the Amphictyons.

88. But Cirrha and Anti-Cirrha, two powerful cities, still remained, and threatened to stand a siege as long as had already detained the forces of Apollo. Again the oracle was consulted, and again the response plunged them all into perplexity. "The Amphictyons," said the Pythia, "will never be successful till the waves of the sea wash the sacred precincts of Delphi." While all the deputies were speculating on the possibility of getting the sea over the Parnassian mountains, Solon relieved their embarrassment by suggesting that, as they could not bring the *sea to the sacred bounds*, they might take "the converse of the proposition" and *bring the sacred bounds to the sea.*

89. This plan struck the Amphictyons favorably. With various imposing rites and ceremonies, they consecrated all the territory of Crissa to Apollo, and called on him to aid in the punishment of its sacrilegious possessors. Superstitious hopes and fears now aided in the contest. The Amphictyons were filled with courage, the Cir-

Questions.—86. Why were deputies sent to Delphi? What answer did they get? 87. What further can you state of the *fawn of gold?* What did Chrysos accomplish? 88. What two cities still held out? What course was adopted? What was the response? What did Solon suggest? 89. What effect did it produce upon the enemy? To what purpose were the spoils of the captured cities consecrated?

rhœans with dismay; nor was it long before victory declared in favor of the assailants. The doomed inhabitants were put to the sword or banished; and the lands, which had been enriched by long and skillful culture, were left desolate. From the spoils of the captured cities, a fund was created to reward victors at the Olympic games.

90. SOLON GOES TO ASIA.—But Solon, with all the wisdom of his institutions, and all the popularity he had acquired as a general and a statesman, could not prevent a new ebullition of faction in his beloved city. The parties of the Highlands, the Lowlands, and the Coast, still contended for superiority; and what one class approved in his laws, another desired to see amended. Anxious for the success of his great work of legislation, Solon finally assembled the people; and after acknowledging that his own mind was not perfectly satisfied as to the utility of all his measures, he obtained from them a pledge to obey his laws ten years, while he visited those countries most distinguished for the excellence of their government, and revised the constitution he had framed for Athens. Having thus secured to his institutions a fair trial, he sailed for Egypt and abode some time, as he himself relates,—

"On the Canopian shore, by Nile's deep mouth."

From Egypt he went to Cyprus, and from Cyprus passed, by request of Crœsus, king of Lydia, to Sardis.*

* The interview of Solon with Crœsus is very justly celebrated. That monarch, who was considered the richest in the world, attempted to dazzle the eyes of the philosopher with a display of magnificent furniture and jewelry. Solon, though a plain republican, gazed upon the splendor of royalty without the least surprise; and Crœsus, chagrined at the indifference of the humble Grecian, demanded, "*If he had ever seen a happier man?*" Solon replied, "*He had; and that person was one Tellus, a worthy citizen of Athens, who, having been above want all his life, died, gloriously fighting for his country.*" Crœsus again inquired, "*Whether, after Tellus, he knew* ANOTHER *happier man in the world?*" Solon replied, "*Yes; Cleobis and Biton, famed for their dutiful behavior to their mother; for, the oxen not being ready, they put themselves into the harness and drew their mother to Juno's temple, who was extremely happy in having such sons, and moved forward amidst the blessings of the people. After the sacrifice, they laid down to rest, but rose no more, for they died that night without sorrow or pain, in the midst of so much glory.*" "*Well,*" said Crœsus, highly displeased, "*and do you not then rank* US *in the number of happy men?*" "*King of Lydia,*" said the philosopher, "*the vicissitudes of life suffer us not to be elated by any present good fortune, or to admire that felicity which is liable to change. Futurity carries for every man various and uncertain events in its bosom. He, therefore, whom heaven blesses with success to the last, is, in our estimation,* THE HAPPY MAN. *But the happiness of him who still lives, and has the dangers of life to encounter, appears to us no better than that of a champion before the combat is determined, and while the crown is uncertain.*"

Though Crœsus dismissed the stern law-giver with contempt, yet, when his city was

Questions.—90. What factions continued to agitate Athens? By what means did Solon endeavor to perpetuate his laws? What was the object of his journey? What places did he visit? Recite the anecdote in the note. Where is Cyprus? (Map No. 8.)

91. THE PISISTRATIDÆ.—Of the three parties in Athens, Lycurgus, leader of the Lowlanders, belonged to the "Old Aristocracy," the ancient Eupatridæ. Megacles, distinguished for being the head of the Alcmæonidæ, for numerous victories in the Olympic games, for the wealth and splendor of his house, and for having married the heiress of the throne of Sicyon, was leader of the Coast party. But the most powerful man in Athens was *Pisistratus*, cousin of Solon, whose engaging manners, agreeable person, and persuasive eloquence gained for him the pre-eminence among the democratic Highlanders. Each party was wedded to its own opinions, and contention seemed to increase, without any prospect of termination, till one day Pisistratus came into the agora with several marks of violence upon his person.

92. The people gathered round him with looks of curiosity and concern. He told them that "as he was going into the country he was waylaid by his political opponents, and with difficulty had escaped, wounded as might be seen, hence they could judge whether it would be safe for any man longer to be a friend to the poor. It was obvious," he said, "that *he* could no longer live in Attica, unless they would take him under that protection which he implored." Immediately one of his partisans proposed to grant this injured friend of the people a guard of fifty men for the security of his person. The vote was passed, and Pisistratus, taking advantage of the terror inspired by his armed followers, seized upon the citadel. Lycurgus and his party submitted quietly for a time, and *the Alcmæonidæ left the city.*

93. Though Pisistratus thus became *a tyrant*, yet he changed nothing in the Athenian constitution. All the laws, courts of justice, and magistracies remained the same, and he himself once obeyed a citation from the Areopagus on charge of murder. He courted the friendship of Solon, and often availed himself of his relative's wisdom, but the philosopher died the year following these events, at the age of 80.

taken, himself made prisoner, and laid bound upon the pile to be burned, the truth of this discourse wrung from him the passionate exclamation, "O, Solon! Solon! Solon!" Upon the inquiry of Cyrus, "What god or man he invoked in so great a calamity," he related the conversation he had with one of the *seven wise men of Greece*, and the conqueror was so struck with it that he released the prisoner and made him his friend. Thus Solon saved the life of one king, and improved the character of another.

Questions.—91, 92. Who was Lycurgus? What party did he lead? What is known of Megacles? What particularly distinguished Pisistratus? By what means did he increase his power? How was the citadel of Athens built? *Ans.* The Acropolis, or citadel of Athens, was built upon a rock, three-fourths of a mile in circuit. It commanded the town, and was accessible only from one side. 93. What did Pisistratus thus become? Did he effect any changes in the fundamental laws? Whose friendship did he seek? At what age did Solon die?

94. B. C. 559.—"UPS AND DOWNS." A WEDDING AND A QUARREL.—Pisistratus not long after lost all the power he had usurped. The rival factions of Megacles and Lycurgus united to overthrow him; but no sooner had they effected their object, than they quarreled among themselves. At the end of five years, Megacles sought out the retired Pisistratus, and offered to give him his daughter in marriage, and assist in restoring him to his former station. Pisistratus returned to Athens, amidst the acclamations of the people, and received his young bride at the hand of her father with apparent joy; but, looking upon her as descended from a race struck with an everlasting curse, he treated her with entire neglect. The Alcmæonidæ, indignant at the affront, again made common cause with the party of Lycurgus, and Pisistratus was again driven from Athens. He resided ten years in Eubœa. Hearing then that the government of his rivals had become unpopular, he landed upon the plain of Marathon with a considerable force, and marched toward Athens. He was everywhere successful; the disaffected flocked to his standard, and he soon saw himself possessed of greater power than ever before.

95. What he had twice lost, and now so hardly regained, he determined henceforth to hold with a firmer grasp. No longer relying upon the affections of the fickle multitude, he took a body of foreign mercenaries into pay, and by their aid inspired awe, where he could not command respect. His refined and elegant taste, however, led him to employ his power for the benefit of Athens. He took every method to promote agriculture; he beautified and adorned the city;* he gave liberally of his private property to relieve the distressed, and enacted a law making public provision for those wounded in the service of their country. He is said to have founded the first *public* library in the known world, and to have made the first *complete* edition of Homer's poems. He continued to direct the administration of government to an advanced age, and died in the city which he had robbed of liberty, and crowned with prosperity.

* He commenced a temple to Olympian Jove, more vast than any the ancient world ever saw, but lived to complete only the foundations. He formed the Lyceum, a beautiful garden furnished with stately buildings, and watered by a fountain which flowed in *nine* artificial channels through delightful groves, by the side of shaded walks.

Questions.—94. When did Pisistratus lose the power which he had usurped? How was his overthrow accomplished? How was he restored to his former station? Why was he again driven from Athens? How did he afterward gain greater power than he had before? 95. How did Pisistratus secure his power? How did he use it? In what respects? What is said of him as a "founder?" As a compiler? What further can you say of him?

96. HIPPIAS AND HIPPARCHUS.—The sons of Pisistratus succeeded to his power, and for some years trod in his steps. Hipparchus, who seemed to inherit all his father's literary taste, devoted himself to the improvement of the moral and civil condition of the people. He invited learned men to the city, and cultivated letters and the arts, under their guidance. He caused marble statues of Hermæ, with moral sentences engraved upon the sides, to be erected in the principal streets; he relieved the people of a heavy tax; called in and recoined the money; and for eighteen years contributed not a little to the flourishing condition of the country. This period was called the "Golden age of Greece;" and Thucydides, in speaking of the Pisistratidæ, remarks, "Those tyrants singularly cultivated wisdom and virtue." A rule so tranquil, so beneficent, and so popular, seemed likely to be lasting; when an event occurred, which, though simple in itself, brought a train of complicated miseries upon Athens.

97. Hipparchus, acting in his public capacity, as director of the holy rites, dismissed the sister of Harmodious (against whom he had a private pique), from bearing the sacred vessels at a public festival. This insult stung Harmodius to the quick, and kindled the indignation of his friend, Aristogiton. They resolved, in their prosecution of revenge, to overthrow the ruling dynasty. At an assembly in which the citizens bore arms, they rushed upon Hipparchus and slew him; but his guards, coming up immediately, killed Harmodius, and, not long after, Aristogiton was taken and put to death. B. C. 512. Now it was that tyranny properly began. Grief, anger, and excitement rendered Hippias revengeful and suspicious; he increased his enemies by putting several distinguished individuals to death, and began to look *abroad* for the support he had hitherto found among his *own people.*

98. The Alcmæonids and their party found means to profit by the failing popularity of Hippias. They had employed the years of their exile in a work which made all Greece their debtors. The temple of Apollo, at Delphi, having been consumed by fire, the Amphictyons engaged to give three hundred talents for its rebuilding. The Alcmæonids undertook the job, and finished it in the most superb style, exceeding their contract in the expense they put upon the structure, and completing the beauty of the edifice by carrying up the whole

---

Questions.—96. By whom was Pisistratus succeeded? What was the character of Hipparchus? Name some of his acts? How long did the country thus flourish? What was the period called? What remark is quoted? 97. What event occurred to disturb the general harmony? Who were the principal actors in the tragedy that followed? What became of them? Why did Hippias become revengeful and suspicious? How did he manifest these feelings? 98. By whom was advantage taken of the failing popularity of Hippias?

front with Parian marble. The god proved not ungrateful; for, whenever the Spartans applied to the oracle for counsel, in addition to the regular response, they were admonished *to give liberty to Athens.* Now, when Athens was all commotion, the people of Sparta determined to obey the injunction of Apollo. They sent out Cleomenes, their king, with a band of men to aid in overthrowing the Pisistratid party. Hippias was defeated in the field, and the Athenians, fearing a siege, consented to deliver up the city in five days. In this time the most obnoxious escaped, and Hippias made good his retreat to the Hellespont.

99. Exile and Return.—Clisthenes, son of that Megacles who contended with Pisistratus, being thus restored to his country, enjoyed a brief period of power. To please the people, he changed the number of tribes from *four* to *ten*, and enacted that fifty persons should be chosen from each to constitute a *senate;* which was from this time called the *Council of Five Hundred.* His Eupatrid opponents appealed to the Spartans, and Cleomenes was in consequence sent with another army up from the Peloponnesus, to destroy the dominion he had so recently established. A herald preceded him, demanding the banishment of the Alcmæonidæ, as the descendants of sacrilegious parents. Not daring to bring the matter before the people, Clisthenes and his party retired; and Cleomenes, emboldened by this success, banished 700 families from Athens. He was proceeding to remodel the constitution, and arrange affairs to suit the aristocracy, when he was interrupted in his labor of love, by a refusal on the part of the Athenians to be so governed. The indignant people ran to arms; and Cleomenes, after being besieged in the citadel two days, was permitted to return home and take his partisans with him. *The Alcmæonidæ again returned to Athens.*

100. The Athenians, concerned at a breach with the warlike Spartans, and at a loss for allies, sent over to Sardis to form a connection with Artaphernes, the governor of that place. The satrap received the deputies of the little unheard-of republic with that haughtiness so becoming in a viceroy. When they were admitted into his presence, he demanded who they were, and why they desired an alliance with the Persians? These questions having been answered with all due respect, he condescended to say, "That if they would

---

Questions.—98. How did they take such advantage? To what place did Hippias retreat? Trace the Alcmæonids from Delphi to Sparta, to Athens; and Hippias to the Hellespont. 99. Who was Clisthenes? What was the *Council of Five Hundred?* State what was done by Cleomenes? In what proceeding was he interrupted? What followed? 100. What was the first public transaction between Greece and Persia?

give *earth and water* to Darius, they might be received into alliance, otherwise they must depart." The ambassadors, considering only the immediate danger of their country, consented to these humiliating terms. *Such was the first public transaction between Greece and Persia.* When the ambassadors returned home, they were severely censured by the people for the craven spirit they had manifested, and nothing further was done about the alliance with Persia.

101. The Clouds Gather.—Yet the danger which hung over Athens was not yet averted. Cleomenes could not forget that he had effected a disgraceful retreat from the Acropolis. He left no means untried to excite a league against the Athenians. In the Spartan senate he asserted, that, while shut up in the citadel, he discovered, among the archives of the republic, a record of the means by which the Alcmæonids bribed the Pythia, and gained the command to *give liberty to Athens.* He urged, therefore, that the Spartan government had acted unjustly, irreligiously, and imprudently, in expelling Hippias; and that they could not do their duty to gods nor men otherwise than by restoring him. By the influence of this speech, Hippias was invited to Sparta; but, as the other states refused to enter into a league to restore the banished tyrant, he soon after retired to the court of Artaphernes, where he was kindly received, and treated with the greatest attention.

102. The Athenians sent to request that Artaphernes would not countenance their banished citizens. The satrap returned for answer, "If the Athenians wish to be safe, they must receive Hippias for their king." This haughty reply threw all Attica into a ferment. Every man was aroused by indignation or alarm. At this critical moment, Aristagoras, governor of Miletus, arrived at Athens. He had come to persuade the Athenians to assist their brethren of Ionia in a rebellion against Persia. Being introduced into an assembly of the people, he used every argument in his power to point their vengeance against the Persian rulers of Asia Minor. And he succeeded. Twenty ships were voted, to aid the Ionians in their projected revolt; and "these ships," adds the historian, "were the beginning of evils to Greeks and barbarians."

Note.—*Pythagoras*, a famous Grecian philosopher, flourished in this century. He was a native of Samos, and a great traveler. He is said to have been carried from Egypt, in the

Questions.—100. How were the ambassadors treated upon their return? Trace them to Sardis and back. 101. What could not Cleomenes forget? What assertion did he make? What did he urge? What influence did the speech have? To what place did Hippias afterward retire? 102. What message was sent to Artaphernes? What was his reply? What was the effect? Who, just then, arrived at Athens? What was his object? How far did he succeed? What says the historian about the ships?

army of Cambyses, to Persia, where he compared what he had learned from the Egyptian priests with the doctrines of the magi. From Persia he passed into other countries, collecting everywhere materials for his great system He finally took up his abode in Crotona, in Italy. He established a school there, into which he admitted those whom he thought capable of becoming true philosophers. The candidates were first put upon trial by being subjected to rigorous exercise, severe abstinence, and strict silence. During these years they neither saw nor heard their master, but were instructed by some inferior preceptor, who settled every doubt by "*ipse dixit*," "he," that is Pythagoras, "said so." If any one, wearied of this rigid discipline, chose to withdraw, he was dismissed with double the share that he had advanced to the common stock: a tomb was erected for him as for a dead man; and he was forgotten as soon as possible. Having passed the severe ordeal, the candidates were permitted to hear Pythagoras lecture from behind a curtain. His doctrines they committed to memory, that the wisdom of their master need not pass to the vulgar through the medium of books.

He taught by numbers; the Divine mind being considered the *Monad*, from which nature emanates and recedes, as numbers depart from unity.

The Diatonic scale was discovered by Pythagoras. In passing a smith's forge, he observed that *three* of the sounds made by the four workmen were harmonious, while the *fourth* was discordant. He found the difference to be in the weight of the hammers. Acting upon this hint, he went home, and preparing four strings exactly alike, hung upon them four weights corresponding to the weights of the hammers. Thus he formed a musical scale, and proceded to construct stringed instruments. He conceived that the spheres in which the planets move, striking upon ether, must produce a sound, and that, all their motions being harmonious, their sounds must be harmonious also; and his scholars, ambitious to increase their master's fame, declared that he had been permitted by the gods to "listen to the celestial music of the spheres."

His theory taught that fire holds the middle place in the universe, and that the earth is one of the planets which make their revolutions about the sphere of fire.

Pythagoras believed in the transmigration of souls, and declared that he could remember what passed while he inhabited the bodies of different animals. He lived to an advanced age, venerated by the credulous, and loved by the good. He had such a command over his countenance that it never expressed either grief, joy, or anger.

103. B. C. **500.**—THE PERSIAN INVASIONS. THE PELOPONNESIAN WAR.—The Athenians, who went over to Ionia in the ships, landed at Ephesus, and marched immediately to Sardis, which they took and burnt; but, as some dissatisfaction arose between them and the Ionians, they returned without any other act of hostility. But this invasion of his territories was enough to rouse the resentment of Darius, and induce him to set in array the whole force of his kingdom against the republics of Greece. Cleomenes, meantime, opposed Demaratus, his brother sovereign, in every thing; and, by procuring a decision against him from the Delphic oracle, effected his banishment. Demaratus, like Hippias, retired to Persia. Cleomenes having committed suicide, his nephew, Leonidas, succeeded to the throne, in the line of Eurysthenes, about the same time that Leotychidas, nephew of Demaratus, received the power vested in the house of Procles.

Questions.—103. What did the Athenians do in Ionia? How did the invasion affect Darius? What became of Cleomenes? Of Demaratus? By whom was Cleomenes succeeded? What power did Leotychidas receive?

104. The line of Spartan succession continued.

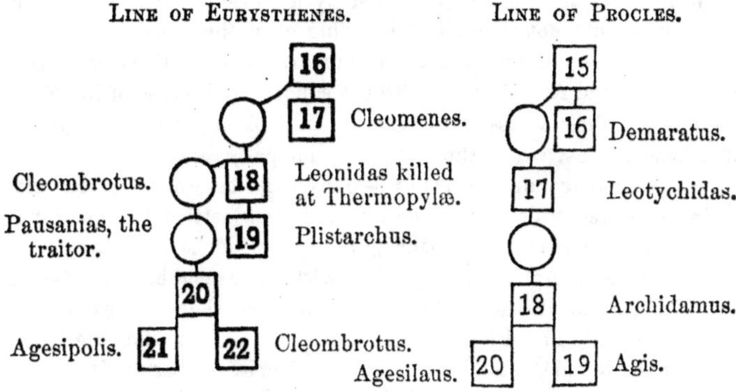

105. SITUATION OF THE GRECIAN STATES.—And now, while the hosts of Persia are gathering to pour their full tide of vengeance upon the offending Greeks, let us look at the condition of these little states, and inquire into their means for resisting the tremendous shock. The *Thessalians*, who should have guarded the northern frontier, were so at uariance among themselves, that they could not agree, even against a common enemy. The *Thebans*, and with them almost all Beotia, had sent *earth and water* to the Persians. *Argos* had been almost depopulated by Sparta, and *Athens* had not yet forgotten the injuries she had received from Cleomenes.

106. Beside these divisions between the different republics, each state was divided in its own counsels; the aristocracy could not brook the measures of the people, and the people would not support the measures of the aristocracy; and what was far worse, Hippias and Demaratus, the banished princes of Athens and Lacedemon, were residents of the Persian court, and instigators of the war. And yet, even at these fearful odds, in this distracted state of the country, neither Athens nor Sparta could tolerate the idea of submission to a foreign power; and when the heralds arrived, demanding "earth and water," in the name of Darius, king of kings, they dared to exasperate the already maddened sovereign, by throwing one of the messengers into a ditch, and the other into a well, as the places where they could best find the required tokens of submission.

Questions.—105. In what condition were the Thessalians to resist invasion? The Thebans? Argos? Athens? 106. What was the general condition among the states? What made matters worse? What was the spirit of Athens and Sparta? By what acts was this spirit manifested?

107. B. C. 493.—The first armament sent out by Darius, under his son-in-law, Mardonius, was shattered by a storm, off Mt. Athos, and consequently did not succeed in reaching even the shores of Greece. The next three years were spent in preparation on both sides. And while Datis and Artaphernes, with the congregated forces of the East, are slowly sailing across the Egean, let us look at the military power of Athens, against whom the attack is principally directed.

108. GENEALOGY OF MILTIADES.—Many years before this period, the peninsula called "The Chersonesus" had been settled by the Athenians in a singular manner. During the time of Pisistratus, the native inhabitants of the place, being at war with their neighbors, sent some chiefs to consult the god. The oracle directed them to invite into their country, to found a colony there, the first person who, after their quitting the temple, should invite them to the rites of hospitality. The chiefs started on their journey homeward. Turning into Attica, their way led them past the country-house of Miltiades, a descendant of a wealthy and honorable Athenian family. Miltiades, happening to be in his portico, and seeing men pass in a foreign dress, accosted them, and offered them refreshment. They entered his house, and soon acquainted their hospitable entertainer with the purpose of their journey, and the oracular response they had received.

109. Miltiades readily accepted the divine direction. A number of Athenians, whom Pisistratus very willingly dismissed, joined in the enterprise, and Miltiades, with the followers he had collected, departed with the strangers. The colony thus planted acknowledged him as their head; and he became, without a struggle, the tyrant of Chersonesus. He died childless, and his estate and authority passed to the son of his brother Cimon. This youth, also named Miltiades, was at that time in high favor with Hippias and Hipparchus. These politic tyrants, anxious to preserve the authority of the mother country over the colony, sent young Miltiades to collect his inheritance, and take upon himself the administration of affairs.

110. When Darius marched against the Scythians, Miltiades followed in his train, and was left, with the other Ionian chiefs, to guard the

Questions.—107. When did Darius send out his first armament? Who commanded it? What is said of the expedition? Where was Mt. Athos? (See map No. 2.) How were the next three years employed? What is said of Datis and Artaphernes? 108. Who was Miltiades? Who entered his house? Why did they do so? Where had the chiefs been? What direction did the oracle give? What information did the oracle impart to Miltiades? 109. How did Miltiades act in reference to the divine direction? Who joined in the enterprise? What colony was thus planted? Who was Cimon? To what distinction did his son attain? What was the name of that son? What is said of Hippias and Hipparchus? 110. What charge was assigned to Miltiades?

bridge of boats across the Danube. It was this Miltiades who proposed to break up the bridge, and free Ionia from the yoke of Persia, by leaving Darius to perish among the Scythians; a measure which was prevented by that very Histiæus who instigated the Ionian colonies to revolt, and thus commenced the war which now threatened Athens. It does not appear that Miltiades took any active part in the revolt; but, finding himself obnoxious to the Persians, he put his effects on board five triremes, and sailed for Athens, where he soon gained great popularity, and was made one of the generals.

111. Such was the man who, while the Persians were subduing the islands of the Egean and storming Eretria, was employing all his energies to raise a force sufficient to meet them, when they should make their descent upon Attica. No measures had yet been taken for the general security. The Ionian colonies that began the war had been conquered; all the islands had submitted: Eubœa, the guardian of the eastern coast, had wasted her best blood in a fruitless resistance; and the Persian army had even passed the narrow strait of Euripus, before any league for common defense had been proposed. On the capture of Eretria, a messenger was sent from Athens to Sparta, to communicate the alarming intelligence, and entreat assistance. The Lacedemonians promised their utmost help, but their laws and their religion, they said, forbade them to march before the full moon, of which it wanted five days. *In five days the Persians might ravage all Attica.*

112. The Athenians were thus left to meet the storm alone. Their forces were commanded by ten generals of equal authority, and among *them* a question arose, involving the issue of the war, and the fate of all Greece. Should they sustain the horrors of a siege within their city, or should they advance into the open plain to meet the enemy? It was at this crisis that the genius and experience of Miltiades saved his country. He knew the character of the Persians, he knew the valor of his countrymen, and he left no means untried till he had prevailed upon the archon to give the casting vote in favor of marching out of the city. Aristides, reflecting that a command which changed every day could not be uniform or efficient, resigned in favor of Miltiades; and, the other generals following his example, this chief was

---

Questions.—110. What proposition did he make? Why was not the proposition carried out? Why did Miltiades go to Athens? What success did he gain there? Trace his movements. 111. What successes did the Persians gain? How was Miltiades meanwhile employed? What is said of Eubœa? Where was the strait of Euripus? (See map No. 2.) Eretria? What messenger was sent? What was the reply? 112. Did the Spartans assist the Athenians? By what process was Miltiades invested with sole authority?

invested with sole authority. As the Persians possessed the command of the sea, Miltiades was forced to wait for intelligence as to the point of debarkation: they had therefore landed their whole force without molestation, upon the eastern coast of Attica, and were in quiet possession of the plain of Marathon, when the Athenian army appeared on the hills above.

113. B. C. 490.—BATTLE OF MARATHON.—Let us take a view of the rival armies, as they lay encamped the night before the battle. The barbarian host numbers six-and-forty different nations. They are surrounded with all the pomp and panoply of war: 100,000 foot-soldiers, wearing stockings and turbans, and carrying bows and short spears, the successors of those troops who under the great Cyrus conquered all Asia, flushed with the hopes inspired by recent victory, wait for the morrow to earn new laurels: 10,000 horses, richly caparisoned, each carrying a short spear on the forehead, and another upon the breast, with 10,000 riders armed with spears and javelins, are prepared to pursue the fugitives to the very gates of Athens. The fleet appears in the distance, carrying provisions and baggage for the soldiers, chains for the captives, and marble for monuments; and even the servants which are left to guard it are more in number than all the inhabitants of Attica, men, women, and children, included.

114. Sheltered by the hills, the 10,000 Athenians, with a few volunteers from Platea, and attending slaves to act as light armed infantry, invoke the aid of their protecting gods and heroes in the approaching conflict. Who can prophesy aught but victory to the Persians? Who can predict aught but destruction to the Greeks. When Miltiades viewed the narrow valley, bounded by rocky and difficult heights, in which the Persians were inclosed, he determined to commence the attack. Finding his troops animated as he wished, he issued an order to lay aside missile weapons, to advance, running down the hill, and engage in close fight. This command was obeyed with the utmost alacrity. The Persians beheld the mad onset, at first, with ridicule, but the shock they sustained soon turned their attention to self-defense. The horse, incumbered by the narrowness of the ground, could not move without throwing their own ranks into disorder; and

---

Questions.—112. Which party had command of the sea? Where did the Persians land their army? Of what place did they take quiet possession? Where was Marathon? (See map. No. 2.) 113. What battle is described? How large was the army opposed to the Athenians? How were the foot-soldiers attired? What is said of the horses and riders? By whom was the army commanded? (See paragraph 107.) 114. How large was the Athenian army? By whom was the battle commenced? Why did not Miltiades wait to be attacked? How was the battle commenced? How did the Persians regard the onset?

the infantry, having no use for their bows and slings, threw them away, and engaged hand to hand with the Greeks. The center of the Persian army maintained its ground till the wings gave way, and then all fled for protection to their ships. The Athenians pursued them, and, in the confusion of embarkation, made great slaughter. They took seven galleys, with all their contents. The Persians lost 6,400 men, the Athenians only 192.

115. Immediately after the battle, an Athenian soldier, still reeking with the blood of the enemy, quitted the army and ran with the glad news to Athens. He reached the gates, and, shouting to the anxious multitude, "Rejoice, rejoice; the victory is ours," fell down exhausted and expired. The Persian commander, Datis, was killed in the battle, and the aged tyrant, Hippias, met an inglorious death. The Persian armament, however, was still very formidable; nor was Athens, by the glorious victory of Marathon, delivered from the danger that threatened her. Miltiades, suspecting that an attempt might be made upon the city, marched rapidly across the country with his forces, and arrived upon the hill, Cynosarges, before the Persian fleet succeeded in doubling Cape Sunium, and coming to anchor in the port of Phalereum. Perceiving the warlike disposition of the Athenian troops, the Persian commander, without attempting any thing further, weighed anchor, and steered for Asia.

116 Two days after, a body of Lacedemonians arrived. They had marched instantly after the full moon, and reached Athens in three days, a distance of not less than one hundred and twenty miles. Finding themselves too late to share in the glorious action, they visited the battle-field, and, after having bestowed many encomiums upon the valor of the Athenians, returned home! In the plain a lofty mound was erected over the bodies of those Athenians who fell in the conflict, their names being inscribed upon pillars sculptured from that very marble brought over by the Persians to commemorate their anticipated victory. This tumulus is still to be seen, and some remains of the marble monuments are yet visible. *Thus ended the first Persian invasion.*

117. Death of Miltiades.—The popularity and influence of Mil-

---

Questions.—114. Give a further account of the battle. 115. What is related of an Athenian soldier? What was the next movement of Miltiades? Where was Cape Sunium? (See map No. 2) Where did the Persian fleet anchor? What was the next movement of the fleet? 116. What help came for the Athenians? Why had not the Lacedemonians arrived in time to take part at Marathon? What, then, did they do? What celebrated mound was erected? Is it still to be seen? 117. What is said of the popularity and influence of Miltiades? Where was the island of Paros? (See map No. 2.)

tiades were now unbounded. To punish a personal affront of the Parians, he requested a fleet of seventy ships to be employed in a manner which would bring great riches to the republic. The people granted them without requiring him to tell how he meant to use them. With this force he attacked the isle of Paros, under pretense of punishing the people for assisting the Persian fleet. The Parians resisted him bravely; he was dangerously wounded, and obliged to return home in disgrace. The glory of Miltiades had roused the slumbering envy of the Alcmæonidæ, and his failure at Paros furnished the desired occasion for destroying him.

118. Xanthippus, who had married a niece of *Megacles*, accused him of leaving Paros because he was bribed by the commanders of the Persian fleet, then stationed at a little distance on the continent. The gallant Miltiades, too ill to leave his house, was brought in his bed before the general assembly of that people he had so recently delivered from destruction. He attempted no defense, but lay there a melancholy spectacle, while his brother recounted his services, and endeavored to excite the compassion of his judges. A fine of fifty talents was, nevertheless, laid upon him, and, being unable to raise this sum, he was thrown into prison, where he died of his wounds. The fine was afterward paid by Cimon, his son.

119. The Persian Court.—On the return of his generals from this disastrous expedition, Darius determined to invade Greece in person; but troubles in Egypt and at home prevented the execution of his design, and, five years after, death closed all his schemes of revenge. But the Persians continued to retain the character of a warlike and conquering people, which their fathers had bequeathed to them. They were not accustomed to insults within their dominion, like the burning of Sardis, still less to defeats in the field like that of Marathon. Xerxes, therefore, instigated by his courtiers to undertake a war which would extend his dominions to the western ocean, began to make arrangements for carrying out the design, both by sea and land.

120. Four years were employed in preparation. An army was collected, greater than the world ever saw, either before or since. Every sea-port, in the whole winding length of coast from Macedonia to the

---

Questions.—117. What naval expedition did he undertake? Give an account of it. What misfortune at home followed? 118. What accusation was brought against him? What scene occurred? What judgment was pronounced? What further can you state of Miltiades? 119. Upon what did Darius determine? What prevented him from so doing? By whom was Darius succeeded as king? What arrangements did Xerxes begin? By whom was he influenced so to do? What had the Athenians done? 120. How long was Xerxes busy in making preparations? What army was collected?

present Gulf of Sidra, was ordered to prepare ships and impress mariners. To prevent all risk of future disasters like that which attended the fleet of Mardonius, a ship canal was excavated, at immense expense, across the isthmus which joins Mt. Athos to the main-land; and when we consider that Xerxes expected to add Europe to his dominions, and that the passage across the Egean was very dangerous, and the doubling of Mt. Athos especially so, this canal appears to have been a very wise preparation.

121. At length, the levies being completed, the forces from all the eastern, southern, and western provinces of Persia assembled at Sardis. Thither the monarch went himself, to take the command. Thence heralds were sent to all the states of Greece (Athens and Sparta excepted), demanding *earth and water;* and, according to Oriental custom, ordering entertainment to be prepared for the king. Every thing was ready before the vernal equinox. And now leaving Xerxes to prosecute his pompous march toward Thermopylæ, where a signal defeat awaits him, let us look again at the state of the Grecian republics.

122. It was now ten years since the battle of Marathon. The Greeks had long had intelligence of the immense preparations making in Asia, yet still no measures had been concerted for general defense: on the contrary, many of the smaller states had sent earth and water to the invaders. The Argives, still weak from the slaughter under Cleomenes, declared to the deputies sent to beg assistance, that "The Spartan arrogance was intolerable, and that they would rather be subject to the barbarians than to Lacedemon;" and they ended their indignant refusal by commanding the ministers to leave the territory before sunset, on pain of being treated as enemies.

123. The Spartan kings were Leonidas, and Leotychidas who had defeated the Persian fleet in the battle of Mycale. The Athenian counsels were governed by Themistocles and Aristides. Both of these distinguished men had proved their valor in the battle of Marathon. Of the ten Athenian generals, Aristides was the only one that agreed with Miltiades upon the propriety of meeting the enemy in the field; and he it was who, renouncing his day of command in favor of the superior skill of Miltiades, induced the other generals to do the same. Yet, such was the power of faction at Athens, that through the

---

Questions.—120. What canal was made? Where was Mount Athos? (See map No. 2.) Why was the canal made? 121. At what place did the forces of Xerxes assemble? Where was Sardis? (See map No. 2.) At what place did Xerxes take formal command? What demands and orders did he issue? 122. When did the battle of Marathon take place? *Ans.* 490 years B. C. When did Xerxes march against Sparta? 123. Who were the Spartan kings? Who the leading Athenian counselors? What is said of Aristides?

intrigues of Themistocles, this great and good man had been in banishment six years, and was now only recalled when his country felt the need of his services.*

124. Themistocles, with the natural penetration of an ambitious mind, saw in the approaching struggle an occasion for Athens to rise to a new rank in Greece; and to gain for her this exalted position, and at the same time to take the lead in her counsels, had developed his energies, and called into exercise all the powers of his great intellect. Egina, though a small island, possessed the largest fleet in Greece. To make Athens a maritime power, he had roused her envy of Egina, and by his eloquence had persuaded the people to devote the proceeds of a silver mine to the building and equipping of triremes. Thus, by his foresight, Athens was furnished in this emergency with a fleet of two hundred ships; and now, while the storm of Persian invasion was slowly approaching, he was busied in allaying animosities, and silencing disputes among the Grecian cities, and in devising every stratagem to secure a victory which he hoped would make Athens supreme in Greece, and Themistocles supreme in Athens.

125. THE RESPONSE.—He hoped almost alone. The courage of the mass was the stern resolution of despair. Many were dismayed by the overwhelming force collecting in Asia, and more were disheartened by the fearful response of Apollo; for, persons deputed by public authority, having performed the prescribed ceremonies, entered the temple, and as they sat by the shrine, the Pythia exclaimed, "Wretches,

* The Athenians had a mild way of gratifying envy, which they called a method of humbling those who possessed too much power. Every citizen took a shell, and, writing upon it the name of the person he considered most obnoxious, threw it into a spot inclosed for the purpose with wooden rails. The magistrates then counted the shells, and, if they amounted to six thousand, the *ostracism* was declared complete, and the individual whose name was found upon the greatest number of shells was banished ten years. Aristides had been commissioned to take charge of the spoils after the battle of Marathon. He discharged his trust with the most perfect fidelity. He was also distinguished for his inflexible justice in every transaction. Themistocles, envying the love and respect with which he was treated, insinuated that he was insensibly gaining the sovereign power, though without the ensigns of it. By this means the people were induced to banish the most virtuous man in the state. While the shells were getting inscribed at the assembly that passed the sentence of ostracism upon him, a peasant approached, and begged him to write the name of Aristides upon the shell. The good man, surprised at the adventure, asked him "Whether Aristides had ever injured him?" "No," said he, "nor do I even know him, but it vexes me to hear him everywhere called *the Just*." Aristides made no reply, but wrote his name upon the shell, and returned it to his envious countryman.

Questions.—124. What did Themistocles see in the approaching struggle? Was he selfish in his efforts? What is said of Egina? How was it situated? (See map No. 2.) What had Themistocles induced the Athenians to do? What is a trireme? *Ans.* A galley or vessel with three benches or ranks of oars on each side. How large was the Athenian fleet? 125. Why were the people disheartened? What was the response.

why sit ye there? Leave your houses and the lofty ramparts of your city, and fly to the furthest part of the earth. For not the head shall remain firm, nor the body, nor the extreme feet, not therefore the hands, nor shall aught of the middle remain, but all shall pass unregarded. For fire and keen Mars, urging the Syrian chariot, shall destroy. Nor yours alone, but many other strong towers shall he overthrow. Many temples of the immortal gods shall he give to the consuming fire. Even now they stand dropping sweat, and shaking with terror. Black blood flows over their highest roofs, foreseeing the necessities of wretchedness. Depart, therefore, from the sanctuary, and diffuse the mind in evils."

126. The Athenian deputies were thrown into the deepest consternation. In their anxiety, they consulted with one of the principal Delphian citizens; he advised them to take the symbols of suppliants, and go again to the oracle. They did so, and addressed the shrine thus: "O sovereign power, prophesy unto us more propitiously for our country, regarding these suppliant tokens which we bear, or we will not depart from the sanctuary, but will remain here till we die."

127. The prophetess answered, "Minerva is unable to appease Olympian Jupiter, though entreating with many words and deep wisdom. Again, therefore, I speak in adamantine terms. All else within Cecropian bounds, and the recesses of divine Cithæron shall fall. THE WOODEN WALL alone great Jupiter grants to Minerva, to remain inexpugnable, a refuge to you and your children. Wait not, therefore, the approach of horse or foot, an immense army coming from the continent, but retreat, turning the back, even though they be close upon you. *O divine Salamis!* thou shalt lose the sons of women, whether Ceres be scattered or gathered."

128. Writing down this answer, which appeared milder than the former, the deputies returned to Athens. When the matter came to be discussed, various opinions were advanced upon the meaning of the words which interested them so deeply. Some thought they directed the defense of the citadel, the ancient palisade of which was intended by the *wooden wall.* Others insisted that the wooden wall could mean nothing but the fleet, on which the oracle encouraged them to depend, but they concluded from the last sentence that, if the fleet came to an engagement, it would be defeated off Salamis. They

---

Questions.—126. How did the deputies then act? What address did they make? 127. What answer did the prophetess make? 128. To what place did the deputies then return? What opinions were advanced? What advice given?

advised, therefore, to make use of the fleet for quitting, with their families and effects, a country which they could no longer defend.

129. But Themistocles was eloquent, determined, and popular. He had procured the building and appointment of the fleet, in view of this very emergency; he was supposed to have instructed the Pythia as to the *wooden walls*, and he now ascended the herald's stand to give the finishing touch to his deep-laid scheme, by bringing the people into his views. "There was one emphatic word," he said, "which clearly proved the late construction wrong. For if the last sentence had been meant unfavorably to Salamis, the oracle would scarcely have said, O, *divine* Salamis, but rather, O, *wretched* Salamis. Defeat at sea was therefore portended not to them but to their enemies; the wooden wall unquestionably meant their fleet, and a naval engagement must save the country."

130. The Athenian people felt at once the force of his reasoning; Athens was hallowed by the blood of heroes, and by the presence of Minerva, the guardian deity. It was determined to remove the women and children, for a brief period, to Salamis and Egina; to put the whole strength of the commonwealth into the navy; to increase the number of ships as fast as possible; and to meet the enemy at sea. Then it was, after Xerxes had assembled his army at Sardis, that "the busy note of preparation" began to sound in Greece.

131. The Congress.—A national congress was formed by each state sending deputies to Corinth to consult upon the conduct of the war. None were more forward to join the confederacy than the Thessalians. When intelligence arrived that the Persian army had crossed the Hellespont and was advancing toward the frontiers, the Thessalians begged that forces might be sent to guard the passes of their country. All the soldiers, therefore, that could be assembled were sent up to take possession of the vale of Tempe, between Ossa and Olympus; but hearing that the Persians could still enter Greece by going further west, they abandoned the pass, and returned to Corinth. The Thessalians, thus deserted, submitted to the Persian monarch, and many

---

Questions.—129. What had Themistocles already procured? What supposition was made in reference to him? What argument did he use to bring the people into his views? 130. What effect did the reasoning of Themistocles have? When did Greece begin to prepare for defense? 131. At what place did a congress meet? Of whom was the congress formed? What was the object of the congress? Who were among the earliest to join the confederation? What request did the Thessalians afterward make? What response was consequently made? What were Ossa and Olympus? *Ans.* Mountains. Where were they situated? (See map No. 2.) How did the forces sent afterward act? What was the consequence as regards the Thessalians?

enlisted zealously in his service. The Grecian confederacy, which remained to resist the whole force of the Persian empire, now consisted of a few little states, not equal in territory to the state of Massachusetts, and whose population would not equal that of a single county of England.

132 STATIONING THE TROOPS.—The whole strength of Athens went to the naval armament. It was the season for celebrating the Olympic games, and it was deemed unnecessary to divert the attention of all Greece from these sacred rites; but, to secure the fidelity of the states, which still belonged to the confederacy, the congress thought best to give a pledge of their interest in the general welfare, by sending a small force to garrison Thermopylæ. Leonidas, king of Sparta, foreseeing that they should be called to sell their lives for their country, selected from his subjects three hundred men who had sons to bear up their names; and Plutarch states that he and his little band solemnized their own obsequies by funeral games before their departure.

133. Each Spartan was attended by one or more Helots; Arcadia furnished 2120 men, Corinth armed 400, Phlius* 200, and Mycenæ† 80. Messengers were sent to Phocis and Locris to summon their whole force. "They were reminded that the invader was not a god, but a mortal, liable as all human greatness, to a fall; and they were bidden to take courage, for the sea was guarded by Athens and Egina, and the troops now sent were only forerunners of the Peloponnesian army, which would speedily follow. The Phocians immediately sent forward 1000 men, and the Locrians were equally prompt; the Thespians‡ volunteered to the amount of 700, and Leonidas compelled the Thebans to furnish 400 more. Thus, with an army of about 6000 men, Leonidas marched to defend Thermopylæ against all the forces of the east.

134. While the Spartans were thus advancing to their fatal station, the fleet was moving round to the adjoining strait of Euripus. The Delphians, unable to do any thing for the defense of their country, had recourse to the oracle, and were told "to pray to the winds, for these might be powerful assistants to Greece." The summer was far

* A city of Arcadia. † A city of Argolis. ‡ From Thespis, a city of Beotia.

Questions.—131. How much of the confederacy remained? 132. In what preparations did the Athenians invest their strength? What was deemed unnecessary? Why was a force sent to Thermopylæ? How many Spartans did Leonidas select for the purpose? What event did he foresee? What statement is made by Plutarch? 133. What additions were made to the Spartan army? How large was the entire force of Leonidas? 134. What did the oracle tell the Delphians?

advanced when Leonidas and his forces came in sight of Mount Eta, and the fleet came to anchor near the adjacent shore. Suddenly the heavens began to blacken with clouds. The Athenians, filled with joy at sight of the rising tempest, redoubled their cries to the god of the Thracian wind. They besought the deity to vindicate Attica, and bring destruction on the barbarian fleet, as he had formerly done at Athos.

135. "Whether this really induced Boreas to fall upon the barbarians," says Herodotus, "I cannot undertake to say, but the Athenians assert it, and have therefore built him a temple." The storm lasted several days. Four hundred Persian galleys were sunk, with all their crews, besides the loss of coasting vessels. Fifteen galleys, which had been dispersed, some days after fell in with the Grecian fleet, and were captured. The prospect of Grecian affairs was now brightening a little. If their fleet could meet that of Persia with success, and Leonidas defend Thermopylæ, Xerxes could never reach Athens.

136. THE FIGHT.—Nor was it long before the day of trial came. The first sight of the Persian host, covering the Trachinian plains, struck some of Leonidas's followers with dismay, and many were for retreating and making a final stand at the isthmus of Corinth; but Leonidas, having set a body of Phocians to guard the only mountain path by which they could be surrounded, and having sent off for a reinforcement, prepared to give such an example at Thermopylæ as should rouse all Greece to action. Day after day the haughty monarch waited, expecting that the grand display of his forces would frighten away the opposing Greeks. A horseman, sent out to reconnoiter, returned with the answer that he found the Spartans out of their intrenchments; some quietly seated combing their flowing hair, others employed in exercise. At length, despairing of their voluntary retreat, he sent out his Median cavalry, and finally the *Immortal band*, to repulse them, but the Grecians held the pass against their utmost efforts.

137. How long the contest might have lasted, had not treachery revealed a secret path to the Persians, it is impossible to tell. This

---

Questions.—134. What encouragement did the Greeks receive from the elements? 135. Who was Boreas? Did the prayers of the Athenians induce Boreas to act in their behalf? What effect did the storm have? How did Grecian affairs then appear? 136. What was Thermopylæ? *Ans.* A celebrated defile between Thessaly and Locris. (See map No. 2.) How did the first appearance of the Persians affect the men of Leonidas? What preparations had Leonidas made? For what did Xerxes look day after day? What information did he receive? How did the battle of Thermopylæ commence? 137. What treachery occurred?

path, neglected as it had been, was not unknown to the Grecians, and Leonidas set a company of Phocians to guard it. A Thessalian betrayed the secret to Xerxes, and for a considerable bribe offered to conduct a body of forces over the mountain to the rear of the Grecian camp. They started about dusk, and, marching rapidly all night, reached by daybreak the spot where the Phocian guard was posted. The oaks, with which the mountain was covered, concealed their approach. The Phocians were first alarmed by the noise of a multitude of men treading among the fallen leaves. They sprang to their arms, and, retreating to the side of the path, prepared to sell their lives as dearly as possible; but the Persians, having another purpose in view, left them unharmed, and made all speed for the plains below.

138. The Immortal 300 and their King.—When Leonidas learned that the Persians were advancing in his rear, he called a council of war. Opinions were divided; some thinking it best to maintain their post, and others contending that this would be a useless waste of lives. The debate ended in a general resolution to retreat with all speed to their respective homes, with the exception of Leonidas and his three hundred Spartans, and the gallant Thespians, who determined to remain, and give such a specimen of Grecian valor as should forever strike terror into the hearts of the Persians; and they retained the Thebans as hostages. As the oracle had declared that either Lacedemon or her king must perish, Leonidas resolved at once to be himself the sacrifice.

139. The whole Persian army was under arms before the sun rose, the king himself attending in solemn pomp to wait the appearance of the luminary, for beginning the devotional ceremonies prescribed by the Persian religion. The Spartans, having given up all thoughts either of conquering or escaping, looked upon Thermopylæ as their burying-place, and prepared to leave their bodies a monument to after ages, of their obedience to that law of Sparta, which forbade a soldier to fly from an enemy. When their frugal breakfast was prepared, Leonidas exhorted his men to take some nourishment, telling them that they should sup that night with old Pluto, upon which they set up a shout as if they had been invited to a banquet. About the middle of the forenoon, the Persians advanced to the attack in front and

---

Questions.—137. What is said of the Phocians? 138. Why did Leonidas call a council of war? What opinions were offered? What resolution was formed? What declaration had the oracle previously made? 139. What preparations were made by the Persians early on the following morning? What, by the Spartans?

rear; but Leonidas, nothing daunted, collected his little band before a wall which had been built in former times, and awaited the charge.

140. The first shock was exceedingly violent. Leonidas gave loose to the fury of men prepared for death. Advancing a little, he attacked the Persians in the widest part of the valley, made great slaughter among them, and caused such confusion, that, through want of room, numbers of the ill-disciplined multitude were forced into the sea, and many were trodden to death by their own people. The Spartan king fell early in the engagement, and the contention for his body animated the combatants to new fury. But when the Persian band came up in the rear, and the Spartans saw on every side the bristling ranks of steel, they retreated again to the narrow wall, and, placing their backs against it, fought till every man was slain;* and never was field of glory strewed with braver dead. This is that battle of Thermopylæ to which allusion is so often made; and this is that Leonidas whose name still takes the highest rank in the list of heroes.

141. The Naval Engagement.—During the memorable scene at Thermopylæ, the hostile fleets met in the neighboring channel. The business of the Grecian fleet, like that of the army, was to *defend the strait.* A sharp skirmish resulted in favor of the Greeks, and the capture of 30 galleys. Scarcely had the rival ships cast anchor, when Boreas again excited the elements to anger. The sea heaved in tumultuous waves toward the frowning skies, and the skies in turn poured down their torrents upon the troubled sea. The drift of the storm carried the wrecks of the late engagement among the Persian ships. Their cables were entangled, their oars impeded; repeated flashes of lightning seemed to discover the horrors of the scene, while the thunder, resounding among the summits of Pelion, struck the Ionian seamen in Persian pay with the idea that the gods were thus declaring their displeasure, because they were bearing arms against their mother country. Superstitious terror weakened their strength, and embarrassed their efforts. A squadron also, which had been sent around Eubœ to attack the Grecians in the rear, was driven upon the rocks of that dangerous coast, and all perished. "Thus the deity to whom

* Aristodemus and Pantites were absent at the time, but as it appeared that they might have been there had they made the necessary exertion, no one would keep company or converse with them. Pantites, in despair, strangled himself, but Aristodemus lived to redeem his character at the battle of Platea.

Questions.—139. What movement was then made by Leonidas? 140. Give a further account of the battle. What is said of Thermopylæ? Of Leonidas? 141. Where, meanwhile, did the hostile fleets meet? What was the business of the Grecian fleet? What encouragement did the Greeks receive from the elements?

they had prayed again interposed to reduce the Persian force more nearly to an equality with the Grecian."

142. THE PERSIANS ADVANCE.—The Persians were thus prevented from making any advance, but when intelligence came that Leonidas and his men were slain, and that the rest of the army had retreated, the commanders of the Grecian fleet weighed anchor and sailed for the Saronic Gulf. Xerxes and his army proceeded south from Thermopylæ, guided by the Thessalians. They spared the places which had formerly submitted, but they burned thirteen cities, whose gallant people refused to join their enemy's ranks. Some were reduced to slavery, and others fled beyond Parnassus. The Peloponnesian land army determined to abandon Attica to its fate; they therefore retired to Corinth, built a wall across the isthmus, and set Cleombrotus, brother of Leonidas, to guard it. In Athens, the alarm was extreme. All their frontier lay exposed to the advancing enemy; all their men of war were on board the fleet; and the only resource left for the deserted inhabitants was to seek a refuge in the islands, which would doubtless be in their turn attacked.

143. At the awful moment of abandoning their country, all hearts were filled with the deepest anguish; the women and children mingled their cries together, and the whole shore resounded with lamentations. Some old persons, too infirm to move, and some individuals, who sought the citadel *wooden walls*, remained behind. Themistocles, to facilitate the embarkation, had recourse to popular superstition. It was believed from ancient times in Athens, that a large serpent was a divine guard to the temple of Minerva; and it was customary to place cakes as an offering to this reptile, every new moon. The chief-priest of the temple declared, that the cakes which had hitherto always been eaten by the divine serpent now remained untouched; an incontrovertible proof that the goddess had forsaken the citadel.

144. This induced the citizens readily and quietly to quit their city; nay, so far were they moved by it, that they stoned to death an orator who tried to persuade them to remain and submit to the king; and the women, equally excited, inflicted the same punishment upon his

---

Questions.—142. Why did the Grecian fleet sail? For what waters did it sail? Where was that gulf? *Ans.* Between Attica and Argolis. (See map No. 2.) In what direction did Xerxes and his army move? What places did they spare? How many cities did they burn? What became of the inhabitants of the destroyed cities? What decision was made as regards Attica? What defensive measures were then adopted? What was the prospect for Athens? 143. How did the people behave on leaving Athens? Why did Themistocles resort to superstition? What belief prevailed? What declaration did the chief-priest make? 144. With what effect?

wife. The city was finally evacuated, and the inhabitants, bidding a sorrowful farewell to their houses and temples, sailed away to the neighboring islands of Salamis, Egina, and Troesene. They were kindly received, and hospitably entertained. The Persian army, advancing meanwhile, found no obstacle till they reached Athens. After a longer resistance from the devotees than could have been expected, the place was taken, the temples pillaged, and the houses burned.

145. Themistocles gains his Point.—Intelligence of this event came to the fleet, while a council of war was sitting. It occasioned such alarm, that some of the commanders left the debate, hastened on board their galleys, and prepared for instant flight. Night came on, and all was confusion. Themistocles, firm in his former opinion, persuaded Eurybiades* to summon another council immediately. There, in the course of debate, he urged the necessity of protecting the islands, and concluded with declaring, "That if so little regard was shown to the Athenian people, who had risked every thing in the Grecian cause, their fleet would either make terms with the enemy, or seek some distant settlement for a people so unworthily treated."

146. Eurybiades, alarmed, bent to this argument, and it was decided to meet the enemy in the bay of Salamis. Themistocles, fearful still of defection, sent a trusty messenger to Xerxes, to say that the Athenians thought of deserting to the Persians, and that the other confederates had determined to fly. The great king, alarmed at the idea of his prey's escaping from his grasp, caused his fleet to form a semicircle, and cut off all retreat from the Greeks. Thus Themistocles saw the Grecian fleet confined in the very place he wished, and the ships of the enemy so closely wedged in, that their numbers proved a serious embarrassment.

147. Battle of Salamis.—In the sea-fights of the ancients, the principal advantage was gained by driving the beak of the vessel into the enemy's galley; and the skill of the Grecians in turning and rowing was much greater than that of the Persians. By daybreak, on the 20th of October, B. C. 480, the two fleets were drawn out in order

* The Spartan admiral of the fleet.

Questions.—144. Where did the Athenians seek shelter? What then befell Athens? 145. What intelligence reached the fleet? What was the effect? Who was the Spartan admiral? To what did Themistocles persuade Eurybiades? What then did Themistocles urge and declare? 146. What decision was arrived at? Why did Themistocles send to Xerxes? What word did he send? What measures did Xerxes then adopt? What did Themistocles then see? 147. How was the principal advantage among the ancients gained in sea-fights? In what did the Grecians excel the Persians? When did the battle of Salamis occur?

of battle. The shores, the heights, the fields of the neighboring coast, were crowded with anxious spectators. Xerxes, enthroned upon a lofty promontory, overlooked the scene. As the sun rose, the Persian trumpets sounded; the Greeks lifted up their loud pæan; the harbors of Phalereum, Peiræus, and Munychia* sent forth their vulture-beaked triremes, and every man prepared himself for the conflict.

148. The onset was vigorous on both sides. But space did not suffice for the Persians to bring their whole fleet regularly into action; zeal to distinguish themselves in the presence of their sovereign hurried them confusedly forward; damage, loss of oars, and wounds in the hull from the beaks of their own ships, followed; the Athenians bore down every thing before them; "shortly the sea itself became scarcely visible, from the quantity of wreck and floating bodies." Such is the expression of the poet, who fought himself in the Athenian squadron. The Lacedemonians sustained their part with invincible bravery; some of the Ionians revolted to their parent country; the confusion increased, and the rout became general. All the Persian galleys, that could disengage themselves from the fatal straits, fled; some were taken, many were sunk, and a few escaped.† Forty Grecian triremes were destroyed; but most of their crews saved themselves on board other vessels.

149. The Joyful Morning.—The defeat of this fleet deranged the measures of the Persian commander. No port was near, capable of protecting its shattered remains. A hasty order was that night given to sail for the Hellespont. Day broke, and the Greeks, who expected a renewal of the action, looked in vain for an enemy. The bay of Salamis, the Saronic gulf, lay calm and peaceful in the morning light, unconscious of the bloody tragedy which had been acted upon their surface. Xerxes hastily decamped with his land forces, and Themistocles, to give wings to their speed, gave them intimation that a project was on foot to destroy the bridge over the Hellespont, a measure which he himself proposed, but which Eurybiades prevented, on the ground of the danger of reducing so powerful an enemy to despair.

* The three harbors of Athens.

† Artemisia, queen of Halicarnassus, had joined Xerxes fleet with five ships. She displayed so much courage and skill in this battle, that the monarch remarked, "His men had acted like women in the fight, and his women, like men." Had Xerxes listened to her advice, he would not have attacked the Grecians in the narrow strait of Salamis.

Questions.—147. How was it commenced? 148. Give a full account of the battle? 149. How did the results of the battle affect the measures of Xerxes? What hasty order was given? What was the state of affairs on the joyful morning? What is said of the retreat of Xerxes?

Xerxes, however, lost no time upon his backward journey; and with the exception of Mardonius and 300,000 men, who went into quarters in Thessaly, Greece was in one month freed from its invaders.

150. THE ATHENIANS RETURN.—The effect of so glorious, so important, and so unexpected a victory as that of Salamis can be imagined, but cannot be described. The Athenians returned to their desolate homes; and the sound of the axe and the hammer mingled with the happy voices of those who engaged in rebuilding their houses and temples. Winter approached, and with it came a political calm, very unusual among the factious states. Gratitude to the gods, for the signal deliverance they had granted, seemed to swallow up all feelings of ancient enmity. The most valuable portions of the spoil were publicly dedicated to the gods; honors were decreed to the first and second for merit in war.

151. All Greece now resounded with the fame of Themistocles; and when the Grecian commanders met in the Temple of Neptune, to award the palm of individual merit, every man gave the *first* vote for himself, and nearly every one the *second* for Themistocles. The Spartans invited him to their city; and though they gave to their own general, Eurybiades, a crown of olive leaves for superior bravery, they conferred a similar distinction upon Themistocles for wisdom and maritime skill. They added a chariot, the best the city possessed; and when he returned, an escort of three hundred knights attended him to the borders of the country.

152. THREATS OF WAR AND PROPOSALS OF PEACE.—Spring, and the recollection that Mardonius was still in Thessaly, awakened the Greeks from their happy repose. Before making any warlike demonstrations, Mardonius sent Alexander, king of Macedon, to Athens, with offers of peace; and this important news, quickly spreading through the country, the Spartans also sent ambassadors to exhort the Athenians to prove faithful to Greece. By the judicious directions of Aristides, the Lacedemonian deputies and Alexander were admitted to an audience of the people, at the same time. Silence was proclaimed. Alexander rose and addressed the assembly in this simple and antiquated style:

153. "Athenians! thus saith Mardonius:—The commands of the

Questions.—149. Did Xerxes take all his men with him? 150. Describe the events subsequent to the battle. 151. Who was declared first in war? How was Themistocles honored? 152. Who was sent on an important mission? By whom was he sent? On what mission was Alexander sent? What was done to counteract this mission? How did Aristides arrange the audience? 153. Give the speech which Alexander made?

king are come unto me, saying, '*I forgive the Athenians all their offenses against me. Now, t'erefore, Mardonius thus do; restore to them their territory, and add to it whatsoever themselves shall choose, leaving them to their own laws; and if they will make alliance with me, rebuild all the temples which have been burnt.*' Such being the king's commandment to me, so I must necessarily do, unless you prevent. For myself, I say to you thus: Why would you persevere in making war against the king? You cannot overcome him. You know how numerous his armies are, and what they have effected. As a friend, I recommend to you, not in a vain contest to lose your own country, but to seize the honorable opportunity of this offer, from the king himself, for making peace. Be free: and let there be an alliance between us without fraud or deceit."

154. Alexander added a few words of his own, in which he urged the Athenians to accept the offers of the king, because they would thus secure, not the safety of their city only, but the sovereignty of Greece. The king of Macedonia concluded, and the chief of the Spartan ministers rose. "The Lacedemonians," he said, "have sent to request that you will admit nothing to the prejudice of Greece, nor receive any proposal from the Persians. We grieve for your sufferings, that now, for two seasons, you have lost the produce of your lands; and that the public calamity should so long press so heavily on individuals. We will engage to maintain your families while the war shall last. Let not, therefore, Alexander persuade you to accept Mardonius's offers; prudence forbids it, for you well know that among barbarians there is neither faith nor truth."

155. In the name of the Athenian people, Aristides made the following answer to Alexander: "We know that the power of the Persian empire is many times greater than ours, but, independency being our object, we are determined to defend ourselves to the utmost. You may therefore tell Mardonius that the Athenians say, 'While the sun holds his course, we will never make alliance with Xerxes, but, trusting in our gods and heroes, whose temples and images he, setting at naught, has burnt, we will persevere in resisting him.'" Then, turning to the Lacedemonian ministers, the orator thus continued his discourse:

156. "After the proofs you have had of the resolution of the Athenians, your fear that they would accept the terms of the barbarian

---

Questions.—154. What reply was made by the chief of the Spartan ministers? 155. What was the reply of Aristides to Alexander? 156. In what words did he address the Lacedemonians?

becomes dishonorable apprehension. No riches, nor the offer of the finest country on earth, could bribe us to connect ourselves with the Persians to the enslaving of Greece. The images and temples of our gods, burnt and reduced to ashes, prevent it; our connection as a Grecian people in blood and language, our common dedications to the gods, our common sacrifices, and our similar customs and manners, forbid it. Know then this, if before ye knew it not, that while one Athenian survives, we will never ally ourselves with Xerxes. We acknowledge your kind attention, in proposing to maintain our families; we will not, however, be burdensome to you. These, then, being *our* resolutions, let there be no delay on *your* side. Your army must march immediately, for Mardonius will move instantly upon learning that we have rejected his proposals. Before, therefore, he can arrive in Attica, it will behoove us to meet him in Beotia."

157. ATHENS BURNED.—With these answers, the king of Macedonia and the Spartan ambassadors departed. The Athenians had conjectured rightly. Upon the failure of his negotiation, Mardonius broke up his camp, and advanced immediately, by nearly the same road that Xerxes had taken, toward Athens. The Spartans hesitated and delayed as before; the Persian army was already in Beotia; and the Athenians, left defenseless once more, retired to Salamis, and witnessed from its shores the conflagration of the houses they had rebuilt. Finally, the Peloponnesians put themselves in motion, and Mardonius, afraid to meet them in the hill-country of Attica, withdrew to Beotia. He chose his station on the border of the Platean lands, where he fortified a space of about a square mile, and fixed his camp.

158. Thither the confederated Greeks, amounting to 70,000 regular soldiers, with attendant slaves and Helots, headed by Pausanias,* pursued him, and pitched their camp over against the camp of the Persians, the little river Asopus flowing tranquilly between them. As the diviners on both sides declared that the attacking party should be defeated, the commanders made their dispositions to act upon the defensive; and, with the exception of some skirmishing among the cavalry, ten days were passed in inaction, each party waiting in the vain hope that the other would begin the engagement. At length Mardonius, seeing but a few days' provision left, and that fresh troops

* Pausanias, son of Cleombrotus, was cousin and guardian of Plistonax, the young son of Leonidas.

Questions.—157. What movement was made by Mardonius? What destruction did the Athenians witness? To what place did Mardonius retire? 158. How many Greeks rallied to meet the enemy? Why was an encounter mutually delayed? What decided Mardonius to make an attack? What plan of attack did he decide upon?

daily arrived to the Grecians, resolved to pass the Asopus next morning, and fall upon his enemies before they had time to prepare for the conflict.

159. At midnight, however, a man on horseback softly approached the Grecian camp, and begged to speak with Aristides. The watchful general came immediately, and the unknown person said to him, "I am Alexander, king of Macedon, who, from the friendship I bear to you, have exposed myself to the greatest dangers, to prevent your fighting under the disadvantage of a surprise; for Mardonius, impelled by the scarcity of provision, has determined to attack you to-morrow, by daybreak." The king of Macedon, having thus testified his interest in the welfare of his country, departed as secretly as he came; and Aristides repaired immediately to the tent of Pausanias with the important intelligence he had received. With all possible dispatch the other officers were summoned, and sent throughout the camp, with directions to put the troops under arms; an arrangement which was scarce completed before the gray mists of morning began to roll up the sides of Cithæron,* and skim along the margin of the river.

160. To place the Athenians opposite the Persians, Pausanias ordered them to change places with the Spartans, wheeling from the left wing to the right; which they did, exhorting one another, by the way, to act with bravery. "The enemy," said they, "bring neither better arms nor bolder hearts than they had at Marathon; they come with the same bows, the same embroidered vests, and profusion of gold; the same effeminate bodies, and the same unmanly souls. We fight, not like them, for a tract of land, or a single city, but for the trophies of Marathon and Salamis, and that Athens may have the glory of them." Mardonius, seeing this change in the position of his enemies, moved his Persians to bring them opposite the Spartans; upon which, Pausanias again changed his wings, and brought the Athenians face to face with the Persians.

161. Thus the day passed without any action at all. In the evening, the Greeks held a council of war, in which they determined to decamp, and take possession of a place better supplied with water, because the springs of the present camp were spoiled by the enemy's horse. When night was come, the Greeks struck their tents, the

* A mountain ridge, at the foot of which the Greeks were encamped.

Questions.—159. Give an account of Alexander's visitation? What action was consequently taken? 160. What army changes did Pausanias make? How did the Athenian soldiers reason? What changes did Pausanias again make? 161. Upon what did the Greeks determine? Give an account of the movement.

Athenians leading the way by the plain, toward the little city of Platea; the allies following confusedly; and the Spartans reluctantly bringing up the rear, over the foot of Cithæron, many of them so indignant at the idea of retreat that they could scarcely be made to keep their ranks. The day was dawning, when Mardonius, seeing the Greeks, as he thought, retreating, summoned his men to pursue and secure the easy victory. The barbarians, thinking they had only to plunder the fugitives, rushed on, uttering loud shouts, and clanking their arms, as if to increase the fright of the Grecians. Pausanias, seeing this, ordered his men to stop and fall into their ranks; yet, through the confusion that reigned, they did not engage readily, but continued scattered in small parties, even after the fight had begun.

162. In the mean time, Pausanias offered sacrifice, but, as no auspicious token appeared, he commanded his men to lay down their shields at their feet, and wait his orders. The steadiness and patience of the Spartans now appeared in a wonderful manner. While the enemy were bearing down upon them with insulting shouts, and arrows were flying thick and fast around them, they stood defenseless, waiting the time of heaven and their general; and, without lifting a shield, or hurling a spear, suffered themselves to be slain in their ranks. Pausanias, with tears trickling from his eyes, turned with uplifted hands toward the temple of Juno, and besought the goddess that "they might at least be permitted to show the enemy that they had brave men to deal with."

163. The very moment that he uttered this prayer, the diviners discovered the desired tokens, and Pausanias gave the signal for action. At once, the soldiers, who a moment before had stood passive and silent as targets for the arrows of the enemy, grasped their shields, and, heaving their bristling pikes, rushed in solid phalanx, like an infuriated animal, upon their assailants. The barbarians perceived at once that they had to do with men ready to spill the last drop of their blood for their country. They fell back and rallied, they sent forth storms of arrows, they betook themselves to their swords, and, grappling close with the Greeks, made a long and obstinate resistance.

164. The Athenians all this while stood still, expecting the Lacedemonians; when the clash of armor reached their ears, they hastened toward the place where the noise was heard, but were intercepted by the Thebans and other allies of the Persians. The battle was thus

---

Questions.—161. How, at last, did the encounter begin? 162. For what did Pausanias wait? How did the Spartans manifest steadiness and patience? How did Pausanias then act? 163. Give an account of what followed? 164. Give a further account of the battle.

divided into two parts; the Spartans contending fiercely with the Persians, and the Athenians and other allies being equally engaged with the treacherous Greeks. Mardonius, who had thought himself pursuing an enemy that dared not resist him, was filled with the deepest anguish when he saw the tide of victory turning against him. He rushed into the thickest of the battle; he encouraged his men; he fought with desperation; but he fell, mortally wounded, and the hopes of the Persians fell with him. His death was the signal for instant flight; and the rout and pursuit once commenced, the slaughter became dreadful.

165. The Athenians, who had just broken the ranks of the Thebans, hearing that the barbarians had retreated to the wooden fortifications of their camp, permitted their treacherous brethren to escape, while they pressed on to assist in destroying the last hope of the enemy. The passions of the Greeks were inflamed by long distress and danger, and now that the day of vengeance had arrived, they showed no mercy. Of the 300,000 men who had been left with Mardonius, 40,000 horse made good their retreat with Artabazus, but of the others, not 3,000 escaped alive from the ruins of the camp.

166. The Supper.—Sated with slaughter, the conquerors turned their attention to plunder. The appendages of the royal household were found in the tent of Mardonius, and most of the domestic slaves had escaped the massacre. Pausanias, after surveying the richness of the scene, ordered the slaves to prepare a supper exactly as they had been accustomed to do for Mardonius. His orders were diligently executed; the splendid furniture was arranged; the side-boards displayed a profusion of gold and silver plate; and the table was covered with the most exquisite elegance. Pausanias then directed his usual Spartan supper to be placed by the side of this sumptuous entertainment, and summoning the principal Grecian officers, "I have desired your company here," he said, "to show you the folly of the Persian general. Living luxuriously as you see at home, he came thus far to take from us such a miserable pittance as ours."

167. Disposition of the Spoil.—The Helots attending upon the Lacedemonian camp were ordered to collect the spoil. Tents and their furniture, collars, bracelets, hilts of cimeters, cups of gold, and other utensils of the same precious metal, together with horses, camels,

---

Questions.—164. What is said of the conduct of Mardonius? What followed his death? 165. What did the Athenians permit? How many men belonging to the army of Mardonius were slain? By what name is that battle known? *Ans.* Platea. 166. Give an account of the supper. 167. What were the principal spoils of the victors?

slaves, and women, were the principal booty. A tenth was first set apart as an offering to the gods. The historian says, "from this tenth the golden tripod, which stands upon the three-headed brazen serpent next to the altar, was dedicated to the god at Delphi." The brazen statue of Jupiter, fifteen feet high, at Olympia, and the brazen statue of Neptune, at Corinth, were derived from the same source. The Tegeans found a brazen manger of very curious workmanship, which they were allowed to place in the temple of Minerva, with this inscription: "To that divine *Wisdom* which directs what human ignorance calls *Chance*."

168. CONSUMMATION OF THE VICTORIES.—Meanwhile, Artabazus and his followers pursued their journey with all speed. They passed the mountains of Thessaly and crossed the greater part of Macedonia without loss. But at the passage of the river Strymon, those Greeks who had submitted to the Persians turned against them; slew great multitudes; and took prisoners enough to enrich themselves greatly by the sums paid for their ransom; so that this battle of Strymon had lasting fame, as the consummation of misfortune and disgrace to Persia, and of safety and glory to Greece.

169. While the arms of the confederate Greeks were thus wonderfully crowned with success against the immediate invaders of their country, the fleet, which had lain all summer inactive at Delos, was at length excited to enterprise. The commanders, Xanthippus and Leotychidas, received secret messengers from the Ionian colonies, with the intelligence that they were ready to revolt, and only waited the appearance of the Grecian galleys off the coast to rise to action. The very next day the whole fleet sailed for Samos.

170. The Phenicians, the best navigators in Persian pay, seeing no prospect of any further business, had requested permission to depart before the equinoctial storms, and had by this time reached home. The Persians, greatly alarmed at the appearance of the Grecians, steered for the promontory of Mycale, where, drawing up their galleys upon the beach in the form of a fort, they raised a wall of stones around them. It was not without surprise that the Grecians found

Questions.—167. What disposition was made of them? 168. What command did Artabazus have? How far did he get without loss? Where was the river Strymon? (See map No. 2.) What is its present name? *Ans.* Karasou, or Black River. Give an account of the battle of Strymon. 169. Where was the island of Delos? (See map No. 2.) Samos? (Same map.) Who commanded the fleet of the confederate Greeks? What secret intelligence did they receive? What move did they then make? 170. Why had the Phenicians gone home? What are equinoctial storms? Where was Mycale? (See map No. 2.) What occurred there? Give an account of it.

the sea yielded to them; and, encouraged by such evident signs of fear, they agreed to disembark and attack the Persians in their intrenchments. They did so; the Ionians turned to the side of their countrymen, and never was rout more complete, or ruin more dreadful. Almost all the Persians were slain. The Greeks carried off every valuable of easy removal, then set fire to the rest, and the whole Persian fleet was consumed. This took place the very day of the battle of Platea, September 22d, B. C. 479.

171. The season was too far advanced for any other attempts upon Ionia. The Grecian commanders therefore sailed for the Hellespont, to break up the bridges there, but the storms raised by the Thracian wind had done the work for them; the few Persians in the neighborhood fled at their approach, and the Grecian fleet, having cleared the Egean of every foe, crowded all sail for their own delightful harbors. The Persian monarch remained in Sardis, to see the sad relics of his forces that found means to fly from Mycale, and to receive the overwhelming intelligence of the still greater loss of his army in Greece. Shortly after, he moved to his distant capital of Susa. "Such was the conclusion of the expedition of Xerxes, after two campaigns wonderfully glorious to Greece, and both in themselves, and for their

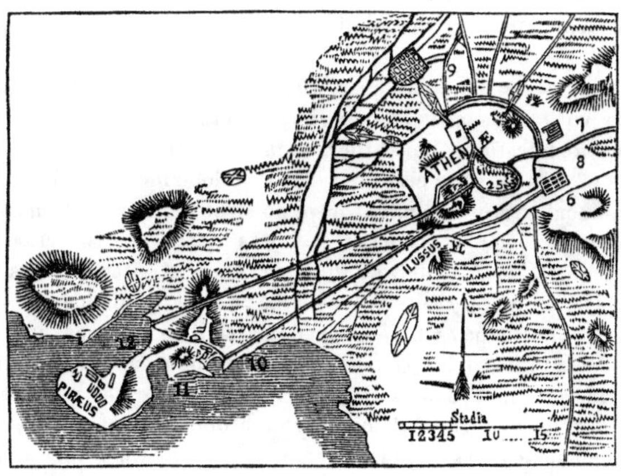

1. Acropolis.
2. Propylæ.
3. Theater.
6. Lycæum.
7. Cynosarges.
8. Agora.
9. Academia.
10. Phalereum.
11. Munychia.
12. Port of Piræus.

Questions.—170. When did the event occur? 171. What further was accomplished by the Grecian fleet? What is said of the conclusion of the expedition of Xerxes?

known consequences, perhaps the most remarkable and important in the annals of mankind."

172. MONUMENTS.—The usual piety of the Greeks then exerted itself in dedications to the gods and honors to the dead. Eighty talents of silver were allotted to the little city of Platea, with which a temple was erected to Minerva. Means had hitherto been wanting to pay due honors to those who had fallen in the extraordinary action under Leonidas, but now the care of their obsequies was committed to the Amphictyonic council. Two structures of marble were reared on the spot of the engagement, with inscriptions which may be thus translated: "Here 4000 men from Peloponnesus fought 3,000,000," and "Stranger, tell the Lacedemonians that here we lie in obedience to their laws."

173. THE STRATAGEMS OF THEMISTOCLES.—The Athenians, in retaking possession of their city, found only a small part of the wall standing, with a few houses which had been reserved for the residence of the Persian officers. A jealousy which had been excited by the honors shown him at Sparta, and a boastful display of his own glory, had shut out Themistocles from any public employment in the last campaign; when, however, the rebuilding of the city came into consideration, he again stepped forth upon the political stage, and, by his skillful management, regained popular favor.

174. The Spartans, having heard that the Athenians were inclosing their city with walls, sent embassadors to urge them "not to go on with their fortifications, but rather, as far as in them lay, to demolish the walls of all the other cities out of the Peloponnesus, that the enemy, if he again returned, might have no strong place to fix his headquarters, as recently in Thebes." It was dangerous to *refuse* this modest request, for Athens was in no situation to enter the lists with Sparta; but to *comply* with it would be to give up all idea of independence. Themistocles here showed his skill in intrigue, and with great address relieved his countrymen from their painful embarrassment. He told the Spartans they must be misinformed with regard to the intentions of the Athenians, and promised that embassadors should immediately be sent to Lacedemon, to give a satisfactory account of their proceedings. Having caused himself to be elected one of the envoys, he departed alone, leaving directions for his associates to fol-

Questions.—172. Recite the article, Monuments. 173. In what condition did the Athenians find their city? What is said of Themistocles? 174. What message did the Spartans send to the Athenians? Why did not the Athenians comply? What course did Themistocles pursue?

low him as soon as the walls were of sufficient height to give security to a garrison.

175. Having arrived at Sparta, he delayed the promised explanations from day to day. When the Ephori inquired his reasons, he told them he waited for his colleagues, and wondered they were not arrived. The people, meanwhile, sustained the policy of their leader. The work was prosecuted by night and by day; freemen did not scruple to toil among slaves; the women and children exerted all their strength in waiting upon the workmen, and every kind of material was used in carrying up the walls, even to the remains of buildings and tombs. Those who had occasion to pass between the two countries continually brought intelligence of the progress of the walls, and the king of Egina came express to confer upon the subject. Themistocles, nevertheless, constantly asserted that they were misinformed, and upbraided them for believing unfounded reports. "Let men of rank," said he, "be sent to Athens, to inquire into the affair, and I will remain a hostage in your hands to insure the proper conduct of the Athenian people."

176. This proposition completely outwitted the Spartans. Three persons of eminence were sent to Athens, and Themistocles managed to intimate to his countrymen the propriety of detaining them till his own safe return. Not till the walls of Athens were advanced to the height that was necessary did Aristides and his other colleague join Themistocles in Sparta. The author of the plot then threw off the mask, and boldly declared that, "by the last intelligence received, he had the satisfaction to learn that Athens was now sufficiently fortified for its security." Whatever the Lacedemonians might have felt, upon perceiving the trick put upon them, their steady wisdom showed itself in the suppression of all resentment. No reproaches were vented; on the contrary, a civil apology was made, and the embassadors from both states returned home.

177. This important and difficult negotiation thus successfully terminated, the ambitious views of Themistocles were more fully opened. Amid all her sufferings from the Persian wars, Athens, through the superior abilities of her leaders, had been gradually assuming a *rank* far above that which she had formerly held in the Grecian states. By her naval power, Themistocles now thought to lead her to *empire.* The greater part of her citizens were already *seamen;* it was necessary in the

---

Questions.—175. Give a further account of the stratagems of Themistocles. 176. How did he bring them to a successful issue? How was the whole affair closed? 177. What is said of the growing importance of Athens? What ambition did Themistocles have for her?

next place to have a *port*. For this purpose he gained the co-operation of Aristides and Xanthippus, and soon fortifications more complete than those of Athens rose round the harbor of Piræus, which was joined to the city by long walls of such height and thickness as to be capable of sustaining a siege for a great length of time.

178. Though Themistocles planned and executed these great works, yet to carry them on required such vast sums of money, that he was forced to disoblige the allies by sailing round the islands and extorting money from them. He had likewise the misfortune to offend the people of Athens by recounting the many services he had rendered the state, and by erecting a temple near his house, inscribed "to the goddess of the best counsel," intimating that to him his country owed its present prosperity. At last the Athenians, thinking he had risen above the equality which a commonwealth requires, subjected him to the ordeal of ostracism, by which he was banished for ten years. In the time of his exile he took up his abode at Argos. He never returned; for circumstances entirely beyond his control soon put a final close to the schemes he had laid for the glory of Athens.

179. End of Pausanias.—As the Persians still possessed Asia Minor, it was necessary for the Greeks to maintain a fleet in the Egean to protect the islands. Pausanias, who had led the Greeks to victory in the battle of Platea, was sent in the capacity of commander-in-chief of the confederates to the island of Cyprus, which he freed from all fear of Persia with very little trouble. The upright Aristides and the brave Cimon, son of Miltiades, were admirals of the Athenian squadron, and far more popular than the imperious Pausanias. From Cyprus they sailed to the Hellespont and Propontis. The city of Byzantium* was then, as now, an important place. It was the depository of Persian arms, the key of Europe, and the residence of many distinguished individuals. After a long siege it was taken, and several persons of royal blood made prisoners.

180. This good fortune proved the ruin of Pausanias. The luxury he had affected to despise at Platea now surrounded him in the most attractive form; the luster of his own glory blinded him to the dangers which beset the path of the ambitious; and the thought that he soon must resign his command to his young relative, and sink into the in-

* Constantinople.

Questions.—177. How did he commence operations? 178. Why was he ostracised? To what place did he go? What further is said of him? 179. Why did the Greeks maintain a fleet in the Egean? What success did Pausanias gain? What third success? 180. What weakness of character did Pausanias at last exhibit?

significance of private life, filled him with repining. He saw his kinsman, the banished Demaratus, living in ease and splendor, more a sovereign than when king of Sparta; and he began to covet the refinements of dress, the luxuries of the table and the bath, and the arbitrary power of a despot, for himself. As a preliminary step, he permitted his prisoners to escape, and then dispatched a trusty messenger to the Persian court, with proposals in which *Pausanias, the commander of the Lacedemonians*, agreed to place all Greece under the dominion of Persia, if Xerxes would give him his daughter in marriage, with those advantages of rank and fortune essential to such lofty alliance.

181. His proposal was very favorably received. No sooner did he learn this fact than his pride and arrogance burst all bounds. As if already son-in-law of the great king, he assumed the airs and manners of a Persian satrap. He never spoke to the officers of the allies but with sharpness and anger; and he inflicted punishment upon the soldiers in the most arbitrary manner. The sea captains and land officers of the Greeks, contrasting his conduct with the steady justice of Aristides, quitted the Spartan banners and ranged themselves under those of the Athenians. These things being told at Sparta, Pausanias was recalled and tried upon several charges. He was deposed from his command, but joined the army as a volunteer, that, being near Asia Minor, he might communicate more easily with the king. When his plans were nearly ripe, he returned to Sparta and began to tamper with the Helots, promising them liberty in the insurrection he meant to raise.

182. A boy whom Pausanias had brought up was sent with a letter to the Persian satrap. Remembering that no former messenger had ever returned, he opened the letter and read, besides the particulars of the treason, an order to put the bearer to death. Alarmed at his danger, he carried it immediately to the Ephori. Still the evidence was thought insufficient. The boy was directed to go as a suppliant to the temple of Neptune; while the Ephori hid themselves in a place where they could overhear all that might be said to him, Pausanias, as had been anticipated, repaired to the spot, and promised the boy great rewards if he would not betray him. The magistrates, having thus heard the particulars from his own mouth, were about to apprehend him, when he escaped and took refuge in the temple of

---

Questions.—180. What proposal did he make? 181. How was his proposal received? How did this affect him? What further account can you give of him? 182. Give a further and closing account of him.

Minerva. As it would have been sacrilege to drag him from the altar, the entrance was blocked up with stones, and he was left to perish of cold and hunger.*

183. End of Themistocles.—After the death of Pausanias, the Spartans pretended that they had found papers which fully proved that Themistocles had been a participator in his crimes; and orders were in consequence sent to bring him to trial before the Amphictyons. Themistocles heard of his danger in time to escape to Corcyra, but finding the people there unable to shelter him, he crossed over to the opposite coast of Epirus. Admetus, king of Molossus, had been his enemy, but he determined to throw himself upon his generosity. Themistocles entered his palace in his absence, and, being instructed by the queen in the most solemn form of supplication, took the young prince in his arms and kneeled down before the household gods. In this position Admetus found him upon his return, and, moved by his distress, undertook to assist him. He sent an escort with him across the mountains to Pydna, where the fugitive embarked, in disguise, on a merchant-ship bound for Asia.

184. He was landed in safety at Ephesus. But here also the most dreadful dangers awaited him. The Grecian officers of justice were in pursuit of him, and the king of Persia had offered two hundred talents for his apprehension. He lay concealed in the house of a friend some days, and was then sent off in a close carriage to Susa; his attendants being instructed to tell those they met, that they were carrying a lady from Ionia to a nobleman at court. Having with some difficulty obtained an audience with Artaxerxes Longimanus, he prostrated himself before the throne, and on the interpreter's inquiring who he was, replied, "The man who is now come to address himself to you, O king, is *Themistocles the Athenian*, an exile, persecuted by the Greeks. If you save me, you save your suppliant; if you destroy me, you destroy the enemy of Greece."

185. Artaxerxes received him with the greatest joy, assured him of his protection, and prayed to Arimanius that his enemies might always be so infatuated as to banish their ablest men: nay, so great a treasure did he consider his distinguished guest, that he exclaimed three times in his sleep, "I have got Themistocles the Athenian."

* His aged mother placed the first stone at the door of the temple.

Questions.—183. In what manner was Themistocles involved in his disgrace? To what place did he first flee? Then where? How did he get Admetus to help him? 184. Give an account of his flight to Susa. Of his interview with Artaxerxes Longimanus. 185. How was he received? What exclamation is reported of Artaxerxes?

The honors that were paid the exile were far superior to those that other strangers received. The king took him out to hunt, admitted him familiarly to the palace, introduced him to his mother, and permitted him to be instructed in the doctrines of the magi. He gave him three cities in Asia Minor for his support, and paid to him the *two hundred talents* offered for his head.

186. But when Athens assisted Egypt to revolt, and Cimon rode triumphant over the seas, the king of Persia called upon Themistocles to perform the many promises he had made, and assist in humbling the power of Greece. Whether his noble heart broke in the conflict between love for his country and gratitude to his royal benefactor; or whether, despairing of being able to effect his purpose, he put an end to his life by poison, cannot now be determined. It is certain, however, that he never bore arms against his beloved Athens; but, dying in a foreign land, gave orders that his bones should be secretly conveyed to Attica; and long after, a tomb within the harbor of Piræus, on the seaside, was pointed out as the humble grave of the illustrious Themistocles.

187. End of Aristides.—Aristides, meantime, continued to deserve and receive the favor of his country and her dependents. He settled the articles of alliance between Athens and the other states; he apportioned the sum to be paid yearly for the current expenses of the commonwealth; he took charge of the public treasury; and in all these offices acquitted himself with such integrity and justice, that envy itself could find nothing against him. While Cimon and Xanthippus were busy in procuring the banishment of Themistocles, Aristides alone did nothing against him; for as he had never envied his rival's prosperity, he did not now rejoice in his misfortunes. We are not acquainted with the time and manner of his death, but his monument was erected at the public expense; and he left his family so poor that his daughters were portioned from the city treasury.

188. Cimon.—When Artaxerxes, by the death of his father, succeeded to the Persian throne, he was so much engaged in settling affairs at home, that he had little leisure for carrying on the war with Greece. However, to preserve the Ionian colonies, he ordered a

---

Questions.—185. What treatment did Themistocles afterward receive at the hands of the king? 186. What closing account can you give of Themistocles? Where did he die? *Ans.* At Magnesia, a town on the Meander river, a little west of Sardis. Trace the course of Themistocles from his residence in Argos to the place of his death. 187. What can you state of the end of Aristides? 188. What colonies did Artaxerxes undertake to preserve? In what way?

numerous fleet to move round the river Eurymedon, and sent out a land army to act in conjunction upon its banks. Meanwhile, Cimon, son of Miltiades, under the judicious management of Aristides, had become one of the leading men in the Athenian state. The treason of Pausanias and the banishment of Themistocles had made him the commander-in-chief of the Grecian fleet, which was anchored at Cnidus.

189. As soon as intelligence of the movements in Pamphylia was conveyed to him, he embarked some of his best troops, and sailed for the mouth of the river. The Persians, counting upon their superior numbers, advanced boldly to meet him. A fierce engagement ensued, in which the Persians were defeated; many of their ships were sunk, and about three hundred fell into the hands of the victors. The number of prisoners amounted to 20,000; and this circumstance, together with the brief duration of the contest, suggested to the active mind of Cimon a stratagem, which made the victory complete.

190. Having dressed his best soldiers in the robes of the captives, he embarked with them in the Persian galleys, and sailed up the Eurymedon to the place where the land army awaited the arrival of their friends. The unsuspecting Persians hailed their return, and went out to meet them with every demonstration of joy. They were fatally undeceived when their supposed brethren, brandishing the Grecian spear and battle-ax, fell upon them with resistless fury. Unarmed and surprised, they made but a feeble resistance. A few of them escaped in the darkness, but most of them were taken prisoners; so that Cimon acquired the singular glory of gaining two victories and erecting two trophies in one day.

191. By this great success the Persian power was so broken that offensive operations were totally intermitted; and it became the boast of the Greeks that no armed ship of Persia was to be seen west of the coast of Pamphylia; and that no Persian troops dared show themselves within a day's journey of the Grecian seas. The plunder of the camp amounted to an immense sum, one-tenth of which was devoted to Apollo. A large portion fell to the share of Cimon. This money he employed in beautifying Athens. In his youth he had

Questions.—188. How did Cimon get to be commander of the Grecian fleet? 189. To what river did he sail? Where is that river? *Ans.* In Pisidia. (See fig. 9 on map No. 3.) Give an account of the naval engagement. 190. Also of Cimon's second victory. What glory did he thus acquire? 191. How did the success of the Greeks affect the Persians? What is said of the plunder which the Greeks took? What change took place in the manners of Cimon? Where were Cnidus, Pamphylia, and Eurymedon? (Map No. 2.)

affected a roughness of manners, and a contempt for the refinement of life; but in his riper years he became a model of politeness.

192. He patronized every liberal art, and studied to procure elegant as well as useful gratifications for the people. By his munificence were raised those lofty porticos, under whose magnificent shelter the Athenians delighted to assemble and pass their time in conversation. In a wood, before rude and without water, he formed commodious and elegant walks, whose sides were adorned with running fountains; and this became the widely celebrated *grove of Academia.** He planted the agora† of Athens with the *oriental plane;* and, ages after, these beautiful trees sheltered the buyers and sellers who came thither to grow rich by traffic.

193. Not satisfied with these public benefactions, he threw down the fences of his *own* gardens and orchards, that all might eat freely of the fruit; a table was spread at his house for the poorer citizens; and every day he invited from the agora some indigent persons to a sumptuous repast. He was commonly attended by a large retinue, handsomely clothed; and if he met an elderly citizen ill clad, he directed one of his followers to change cloaks with him. He was equally attentive to lending and giving money; and such was the estimation in which he was held, that he was considered as brave as Miltiades, as wise as Themistocles, and second to none but Aristides in justice.

194. B. C. 469.—THE EARTHQUAKE AND ITS CONSEQUENCES.—The Lacedemonians had looked on with envious eyes while Athens, under these able statesmen and skillful generals, was acquiring riches and dominion; but just as they were upon the point of adopting measures to humble her pride, their attention was recalled to personal affairs. One day, while the sons of the principal families were exercising in the gymnasium, a terrible earthquake laid waste all Laconia. The building in which the youth were assembled fell, burying them in its ruins; the shocks were repeated; multitudes were crushed by the falling houses; the earth opened in several places; vast fragments tumbled down the sides of Mt. Taygetus; and, in the end, only five houses were left standing in Sparta. The Helots in the fields suffered less than the citizens; and, witnessing the terror and confusion of their masters,

* See map of Athens, page 150. † Market-place.

Questions.—192. What did he do for the comfort and gratification of the Athenians? 193. What else did he do? In what estimation was he held? 194. What had the Lacedemonians meditated with reference to the Athenians? Give an account of the earthquake. What then did the Helots determine upon?

rapidly assembled to complete the work of destruction, and regain their liberty.

195. Archidamus, the king, perceiving the imminent danger of Sparta, ordered the trumpets to sound to arms, upon which the flying multitudes instinctively rallied around their respective standards. The Helots, awed by the appearance of a regular army, dispersed around the country, and incited their brethren to revolt. The greater part of these miserable men were descendants of those Messenians who had fought so bravely for liberty ages before. They remembered the heroism of their ancestors; they recalled the exploits of Aristomenes; and, determined to strike once more for freedom, they seized and fortified Ithome, the spot rendered sacred by the blood of their fathers. They outnumbered the Spartans by many thousands, and they had become so familiar with the art of war, in attending upon their masters, that their revolt seemed more formidable to Sparta than the hosts of Persia.

196. Nor was this the worst feature in this distressing calamity. The Lacedemonians were completely helpless in any kind of business. Deprived of their slaves, they were in danger of starving; agriculture stopped; the mechanic arts ceased. The Spartans were thus reduced to the mortifying necessity of applying to their allies for succor. There was found in Athens a strong disposition to refuse the required aid; but Cimon, who had always been a favorite with the aristocratic powers of Greece, silenced all opposition; and a considerable body of forces under his command marched into the Peloponnesus. This measure, though intended to keep the peace between the rival states, had a contrary effect.

197. It was in the leisure and inactivity of the siege of Ithome that those heart-burnings arose, which first occasioned an avowed aversion between the Lacedemonians and Athenians, and led, not *immediately*, but *consequently*, to the fatal Peloponnesian war. Here Athenian vanity had full opportunity for display, and Spartan pride full leisure to take offense. The Spartans remembered that these Athenians were Ionians, whom the Dorians considered an alien race: suspicion arose that they might join the enemy, and upon some trifling pretext they were civilly dismissed.

198. The Athenians returned home so exasperated by the treat-

---

Questions.—195. Give an account of the preparation made by the Helots. 196. What condition of things soon followed? What aid went to the Spartans? 197. What was the remote cause of the Peloponnesian war? What did the Spartans remember? Why were the Athenians sent home?

ment they had received, that a decree was immediately passed, renouncing the confederacy of Lacedemon. Cimon's popularity had been for some time on the decline; not that he was less brave, or less generous, than formerly; but that the *Alcmæonidæ* were again struggling for power, and that the present commotion offered a favorable opportunity to crush him. He had always professed himself an admirer of the Spartan institutions; and now, insulted as he had been, he did not join in the hue and cry against Lacedemon. All these circumstances were cited against him; and when the public mind was sufficiently aroused, the ostracism was called for, and he was banished.

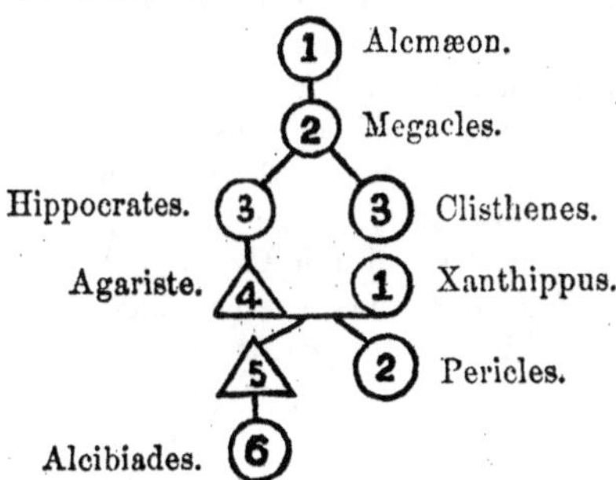

199. Xanthippus, who conducted the accusation against Miltiades, was married to Agariste, niece of that Clisthenes who gained so much favor by rebuilding the temple at Delphi, and procuring the banishment of the Pisistratidæ. Their son, Pericles, was now the head of the Alcmæonidæ, and the rival of Cimon. He had been the pupil of Anaxagoras, and attracted public notice soon after the banishment of Themistocles. He had an agreeable person* and popular manners; and in the art of speaking so far surpassed other orators, that he received the surname of *Olympius;* for they said that in his harangues he thundered and lightened.

200. As he had never been an archon, he could not sit in the court of Areopagus; he therefore entered into a scheme with the leading men to contract the powers of this august court; a measure which gratified the people, and added not a little to his popularity. Still further to strengthen his power, he provided the most elegant amusements for the multitude; the dramas of Eschylus, Sophocles, and Euripides, and the satires of the comic poets, were exhibited in the magnificent theaters; the religious festivals were celebrated with new

* His head was so disproportionately long that he was styled the "Onion-headed," from its similarity to the sea-onion.

Questions.—198. What decree did the Athenians pass? Why was Cimon banished? 199. Who was Pericles? Can you describe him? 200. What efforts did he make to gain the applause of the people?

splendor; and every thing was done to keep the people pleased with the change of administration.

201. But to maintain these increased expenses, new supplies were necessary. The common treasury, located at the sacred island of Delos, for the support of the navy, was moved to Athens, and the assessment which Aristides had apportioned to the allies was converted into a direct and burdensome tax. To obviate the unpleasant feelings which these measures were calculated to excite, the people were employed in the fleet which watched the Persian and Phenician navies. In the confusion which followed the death of Xerxes, Inarus aroused the greater part of Egypt to rebellion. Finding, in the war that followed, the necessity of engaging a maritime power in his interest, Inarus sent proposals of alliance to Athens. Pericles hoped that in this expedition a revenue of wealth and fame would accrue to his native city, equal to that gained by Cimon on the coast of Asia Minor; and the alliance with Inarus was accordingly formed.

202. DISASTERS IN EGYPT.—The fleet sailed from Cyprus to Egypt, where Grecian valor and Grecian discipline at first overbore all opposition; but a turn in the tide of Athenian fortunes was at hand. Megabysus, an able Persian general, succeeded in shutting up his foes on an island in the Nile, where he cut off their supplies, and reduced them to the brink of destruction. Inarus was betrayed to the Persians, and most of the Greeks perished. The few that remained were carried prisoners to Persia. Nor was this all. Fifty trireme galleys going to Egypt entered the mouth of the Nile, ignorant of what had happened. The Phenician fleet attacked them in the river, while the Persian army assisted from the shore; a few ships forced their way to sea, and escaped; but the greater part were destroyed or taken. Such was the conclusion of the Athenian enterprise against Egypt, after it had been carried on six years.

203. FIGHTING AMONG FRIENDS.—Meanwhile, the Athenians had not been idle at home. They had taken part with Megara against Corinth, subdued Egina, which Pericles styled "the eye-sore of the Piræus," and made several campaigns in Beotia. The Spartans, having carried on the siege of Ithome ten years, finally granted the rebels liberty to depart unharmed, with their wives and children, goods and chattels. The Athenian fleet took them on board, sailed with them into the

---

Questions.—201. How were means to meet the increased expenses raised? Who was Inarus? What proposition did he make? Why did Pericles form the alliance? 202. To what place did the fleet sail? What is said of its first successes? Who was Megabysus? What did he succeed in doing? Give a further account of the Athenian enterprise against Egypt. 203. What, meanwhile, had the Athenians done at home?

Corinthian gulf, and settled them in Naupactus, a maritime town of Locris. There, retaking the name of Messenians, they formed themselves into a free republic, and were once more numbered among the Grecian people.

204. All parties were now tired of a war in which they gained nothing, and lost much. The Athenians especially, fearing the united vengeance of Sparta and Corinth, were particularly desirous of peace; and Pericles, as a preparatory step, exerted himself to procure the recall of Cimon. This banished noble was at that time living on his lordship in Chersonesus; but he did not refuse the call of his factious countrymen. Through his influence a truce was obtained for five years, which time was actively employed by Pericles in completing the *long wall* begun by Themistocles.

205. Expedition to Cyprus, and Death of Cimon, b. c. 449.—But such had become the state of things at home, that even Cimon concurred in the purpose of turning the spirit of enterprise once more toward foreign conquest, in the hope of scattering the elements of faction, which were already brooding war in Greece. A fleet of two hundred galleys was equipped for an expedition against Cyprus, of which Cimon took the command. He reached the place of his destination in safety, but received a wound in the siege of Citium, of which he died. His spirit seemed still to hover over the fleet; for the galleys which were conveying his remains to Attica, encountered the Phenician fleet, and gained a great victory. His bones were interred in Attica, and a magnificent monument erected to his memory.

206. After the death of Cimon, the nobility, perceiving that Pericles possessed far too great authority, set up Thucydides* as his opponent;

* Thucydides was descended in the female line from Miltiades. He was born in Attica, B. C. 471. The first circumstance related by his biographers, is an account of his attending the Olympic games with his father, when about fifteen years of age. Herodotus at that time recited his history, and the young Thucydides was so much affected with the work, and the applause it received, that he shed tears. On observing this, Herodotus exclaimed to his father, "Your son burns with ardor for learning." Of his early manhood we have no account, but he doubtless served the usual time in the militia; for after the death of Cimon he was set up as the opponent of Pericles. In his 47th year, he was appointed to the command of the Athenian fleet off the coast of Thrace, but being too late by half a day to relieve Amphipolis, then besieged by the Spartans, he was banished. He continued an exile twenty years, during which he wrote the history of the Peloponnesian war, in eight books. He returned to his native state the year after Athens was taken by Lysander, and died there.

Questions.—203. What became of the Messenians? 204. Why did the Athenians desire peace? What preparatory step was taken? What course did Cimon pursue after his recall? 205. What object had he in recommending foreign conquest? What expedition did he command? In what engagement did he perish? What victory followed? 206. Who was Thucydides? Give his history contained in the note.

and such was the effect of the eloquence of these two rival statesmen that the city was quite broken in two, one part being called the *nobility*, the other the *people*. Pericles addressed himself particularly to please the people, and his success was so great that Thucydides said, "When I wrestle with Pericles, if I throw him ever so decidedly, he can persuade the spectators that he threw me." Pericles also gained a decree for sending out sixty galleys every year, manned with citizens, who not only improved themselves in maritime skill, but were paid for their time; and when they returned he contrived all kinds of shows, games, plays, and processions, to amuse them. In addition to this, carpenters, masons, brasiers, goldsmiths, painters, turners, and artificers of every kind, were employed upon those splendid buildings which were erected by his recommendation.

207. The Odeum, designed for musical performances and the rehearsal of new tragedies, was built almost entirely of the masts of Persian vessels, and was so constructed as to imitate the form of Xerxes's tent. The Parthenon, or temple of Minerva, situated on the summit of the Acropolis, in beauty and grandeur surpassed all other buildings of the kind. In this edifice was the statue of the goddess sculptured in ivory. It was thirty-nine feet high, and forty talents of gold were employed in ornamenting it. The orators of Thucydides's party raised a clamor against Pericles, insisting that he had brought the greatest disgrace upon Athens by removing the public treasures from Delos, and taking them into his own custody. The works were notwithstanding carried steadily forward, and finished in an incredibly short time, with an elegance combining the freshness of youth and the sublimity of antiquity.

208. B. C. 445.—GRANDMOTHER CORINTH, MOTHER CORCYRA, AND LITTLE EPIDAMNUS.—Ambition, pride, and jealousy, had strown Greece with combustible materials; and from a fatal spark, which kindled a flame in the corner of the country, the blaze spread finally over the whole; insomuch that the remainder of its history is but a tale of domestic calamity and suffering. In very early times, the republic of Corinth established a colony upon the island of Corcyra. The colony flourished exceedingly; her people were rich and powerful, and her fleet ranked next to that of Athens. She also sent out colonies, one of which settled in Epidamnus. Epidamnus likewise

Questions.—206. What amusements procured popularity for Pericles? 207. What remarkable buildings were erected? Give a description of the Odeum. Of the Parthenon. 208. What is said of the remaining history of Greece? The early history of Corcyra? Of Epidamnus?

increased in goods and pride, and threw off all allegiance to the parent state. The barbarous tribes in the neighborhood of Epidamnus, not long after, invaded her territories, and reduced her to the brink of destruction.

209. In this state of distress, she applied to Corcyra for help; but the mother, thinking the present troubles only a salutary correction of her child, turned a deaf ear to her petitions. The Epidamnians then turned their eyes to grandmother Corinth, and, being encouraged by the oracle, dispatched a solemn embassy thither, acknowledging that city as their metropolis, and imploring assistance. The Corinthians readily listened to the appeal, and, sending out a fleet, took military possession of the colony. Corcyra had thus her mother enraged on one side, and her daughter incensed on the other; she, however, determined to carry out her intentions, and steadfastly resist all interference in her government.

210. The Corinthians, alarmed by the preparations Corcyra was making for war, called on the allies for aid; and Corcyra, taking alarm also at the number of confederates who responded to the call, sent to make alliance with Athens. This was a delicate point for the Athenians to decide. If they assisted Corcyra, they in effect declared war against Corinth; if, on the contrary, they permitted her to be overcome, the Peloponnesians would be strengthened by the fall of the greatest naval power of Greece. After much hesitation, they dispatched a fleet of thirty galleys to defend the Corcyreans. The war was, however, productive of little gain or glory to either side, and might have passed unnoticed but for its political effect, in leaving upon the mind of Corinth such a sense of the supremacy of Athens as led her to enlist on the side of Sparta in the Peloponnesian war.

211. The ostracism being called for about this time, Thucydides was banished, and thus Pericles became sole master of Athens and all its dependencies. The revenue, the army, the navy, the friendship of kings, and the alliance of princes, were all at his command. But, though possessed of such unlimited power, he kept the public good in his eye, and pursued the straight path of honor. According to the representation of Thucydides, his rival, he was a man of popularity

---

Questions.—209. Where was Corcyra? (See map No. 2.) What is it called now? *Ans.* Corfu. What is said of the colony of Corcyra? 210. What produced alarm among the Corinthians? What aid did they consequently invoke? Why was Corcyra alarmed? What alliance was sought? State the delicate points. What assistance was sent to Corcyra? What effect had the Corcyrean war upon Athens, politically? 211. How did Pericles become master of Athens and its dependencies? What was his character?

and unblemished reputation;* money could not bribe him, and he was so much above the desire of it, that, though intrusted with so many offices, he added not one *drachma* to his personal estate.

212. Potidæa, a Corinthian colony on the coast of Macedonia, had been brought under the dominion of Athens. In this time of commotion, the Potidæans received a body of troops from Corinth, and declared themselves free! The Athenians immediately ordered their fleet around that way, and blocked up Potidæa by sea and land. The Corinthians, therefore, sent deputies to Sparta, to complain that in so doing they had broken the truce,† and the Spartans readily invoked a general assembly of the states, to listen to complaints against Athens. When the deputies had arrived, proclamation was made, giving permission for those to speak who had any thing to advance. The Eginetans first occupied the attention of the meeting, with a complaint of the destruction of their fleet by Pericles, and of the dependency in which they were held; and the Megarensians urged, that, contrary to the existing treaty, they were prohibited all intercourse with Attica.

213. The Corinthians then opened their grievances in the following form: "Often have we warned you, O Lacedemonians, of the wrongs which the Athenians were preparing for us; but not till we had already suffered, and hostilities were commenced, would you summon this assembly of our confederacy, in which we have, perhaps, more cause than others to come forward, injured as we have been by the Athenians, and neglected by you. Not that we alone are interested; all Greece is concerned; many states being already reduced

* He was, it is true, greatly influenced by the courtesan Aspasia; but she owed her power to her great abilities, rather than to her personal charms. At a time when the education of Grecian females was little superior to that of slaves, when their minds were uninformed, and their manners unpolished, Aspasia, the Milesian, appeared in Athens. She was endowed with accomplishments rare even among men; and by the combined attractions of her beauty, manners, and conversation, completely won the affection and esteem of Pericles, so that he put away his wife, and bound himself to her by the most intimate relation which the laws permitted him to contract with a foreign woman. Nor was he alone sensible of her charms. Her private circles were frequented by the most enlightened and accomplished men of the State, who often brought their wives to be instructed by her conversation. Socrates said he learned eloquence of her; and Plato did not hesitate to assert, that the funeral oration pronounced by Pericles, one of the most eloquent compositions extant, was written by the gifted Milesian.

† A truce for thirty years had been concluded between Sparta and Athens.

Questions.—212. Where was Potidæa? (See map No. 2.) Why did the Athenians besiege Potidæa? By whom was a general assembly of the states called? Why was it called? Of what did the Eginetans complain? The Megarensians? 213. Who were the third to complain? With what did they open their grievances?

to subjection, and others notoriously threatened. Corcyra, capable of furnishing a fleet superior to that of any republic in our confederacy, is already taken from us, and Potidæa, our most important post for carrying on commerce in Thrace, is at this time besieged. These injuries are in a great measure to be imputed to you.

214. "After the Persian war, you permitted the Athenians to fortify their city; then to build their long walls; and still you have continued to look on (though boasting to be vindicators of the freedom of Greece), while they *have deprived* of freedom not only their own, but our confederates. Is this a time to inquire whether we have been injured? No; rather, how we shall repel the injury. The Persians, we know, came from the farthest parts of the earth before you had made any adequate preparations for defense; and now you are equally remiss against the Athenians, in your own neighborhood. Let this, then, be the term of your dilatoriness; give at length that assistance to your allies which you owe them, and relieve the Potidæans. This can be done only by an invasion of Attica. Consult then your own interest, and do not diminish that supremacy in Peloponnesus which your fathers transmitted to you."

215. The Corinthians ceased; and when all others had expressed their opinions, they were requested to withdraw, that the Spartans, who claimed the dignified station of sovereign arbiters, might decide upon the question. WAR was resolved upon; but to gain time, and sow the seeds of dissension in Athens, an embassy was sent thither, requiring that all *execrable** persons should be banished, lest some general calamity should fall upon Greece.

216. THE EMBASSIES.—The embassadors were received at Athens, and discharged their commission with all due gravity; but Pericles, against whom this blow was aimed, as a descendant of that Megacles who murdered the followers of Cylon, recollected that the principal families of Sparta had also been guilty of sacrilege, in the case of Pausanias, and in the murder of some Helots who had been dragged from the sanctuary of Neptune. The great earthquake had been attributed to this last act of impiety. Pericles, therefore, proposed that the Lacedemonians should set the first example of regard for the wel-

* Those guilty of sacrilege.

Questions.—214. What did they charge upon the Lacedemonians? With what advice did they close? 215. What then was resolved upon? Why was an embassy sent to Athens? What was the embassy instructed to require? 216. What answer was given to the embassy?

fare of Greece, by banishing their own sacrilegious citizens. With this answer the deputies departed.

217. A second embassy arrived soon after, with very different instructions. These envoys urged that the siege of Potidæa ought to be raised, Egina restored to independence, and the decree against Megara revoked. The two first propositions were scarcely noticed; upon the third, the Athenians condescended to explain, that the Megarensians had been guilty of plowing up a spot of ground consecrated to the Eleusinian goddess, and of receiving runaway Athenian slaves. With this answer, the second embassy returned to Sparta; and soon after came a *third*, men of eminence and influence, who said nothing of sacrilege, Potidæa, Egina, or Megara, but simply put forward the modest requisition, "That *all* the Grecian states held in subjection by Athens should be restored to independency."

218. An assembly was convened to determine on a final answer. Many spoke in favor of peace on these conditions, and many urged the necessity of war. Finally, Pericles ascended the bema. He showed that what the Lacedemonians wished was not the independence of Megara or Egina, but the submission of Athens; that they were determined to assert their own supremacy; and if one point were granted, another would immediately be put forward, till Athens must finally fight or be shorn of all her glory, allies and dependencies. He drew a lively picture of the progress and results of the coming war, and closed by recommending a compliance with the demands of Sparta, as soon as she would herself set the example, by giving liberty to her allies. This answer was conveyed to the embassadors nearly in the words of Pericles; and all hopes of peace being thus destroyed, both sides began vigorously to prepare for war.

219. B. C. 431.—THE PELOPONNESIAN WAR.—The spark which had fallen in Corcyra, and been kindled into a flame in Potidæa, now blazed forth in Beotia. The Thebans had longed to subject the little city of Platea, but feared the power of Athens, who protected it. As soon, therefore, as war was considered certain, they seized upon this place, and succeeded at first in getting possession of it. "At this time," says Thucydides (who, having expiated his crime of being a great man by ten years' banishment, had returned to the fleet), "Greece abounded with youth, who, filled with admiration for the wonders wrought by their fathers in the Persian wars, were anxious to win

Questions.—217. What was urged by the second embassy? What answer was given to the envoys? What was required by the third embassy? 218. What course did Athens then take? What were the arguments of Pericles? What was the result? 219. What befell the city of Platea? What is stated as having been said by Thucydides?

for themselves a place in the records of fame." Oracular responses were also reported; many prodigies were seen; an earthquake shook the sacred island of Delos; and Greece abounded with portents, which each party interpreted *for* themselves and *against* their enemies.

220. The two confederacies, now upon the point of engaging in long and deadly strife, were very differently composed; but the forces of Greece were very equally divided between them. Sparta had for allies 4,* 5, 6, 7, 8, 12, 13, 14, 16, 17, and a part of 2 and 10; 20 had been destroyed, and 18 remained neuter. Athens had 3, 1, a part of 10, and the little settlement of Naupactus; but most of the islands in the Ionian sea had been brought into her interest by Corcyra; her fleet commanded the Egean, and brought efficient aid from the colonies of Asia Minor. Athens was the head of the Ionic race; Sparta of the Doric. Athens was regarded as a democracy, and the advocate of the rights of the people; Sparta, as an aristocracy, and a defender of the privileges claimed by the nobility. Athens demanded *tribute* from her allies, while Sparta was contented with *supremacy* alone. In every island, therefore, which owned the dominion of *Athens*, a strong party was found favorable to the success of Sparta.

221. FIRST INVASION OF ATTICA.—Archidamus, the good old Spartan king, the friend of Pericles, was made commander-in-chief of the Peloponnesian forces. They marched 60,000 strong up toward the Corinthian isthmus; but as their leader was opposed to the war, and tried every measure to intimidate the Athenians before taking any decisive step, an interval occurred, which was well employed by the Athenians in making preparations against the invaders. Pericles, foreseeing from the beginning the consequences of his course, had not been remiss in providing for them. Knowing the superior force of the Spartans by land, he persuaded the Athenians not to venture a battle; but to lay waste their fields and retire into their city, depending upon their fleet for supplies.

222. He told them that for these there were abundant resources in the commonwealth. The annual tribute amounted to $600,000: there were in the treasury $60,000,000, and the uncoined gold and silver

* Let the pupil name them from the Map.

Questions.—219. What is said of the portents? 220. Who were the allies of Sparta? (See map No. 2.) Who of Athens? What political feature distinguished Athens from Sparta? 221. Who was constituted commander-in-chief of the Peloponnesian forces? To what course did Pericles persuade the Athenians? Why did he do so? 222. What representations did he make?

which might be employed was not less than $500,000 more. There was besides *one ton's weight* of pure gold upon the statue of Minerva, which could be taken off without injury, and replaced when deemed expedient. Sheltered by the walls of their city, they would be able to look on in security while the Peloponnesians *ravaged their country;* and embarking on board their fleet, they might take ample vengeance by *ravaging the coast of the Peloponnesus.*

223. But, though these representations encouraged the people to trust for the final result, yet they were far from being contented. It was very inconvenient for the free denizens of the mountainous regions to be cooped up in a space where no one could move without intruding upon his neighbor; the inhabitants of the plains were not pleased with the prospect of seeing the elegant houses they had built burned to the ground, and the gardens and vineyards they had planted laid waste by the hand of the destroyer. They lingered wistfully about their homes, and it was not till the confederates had actually laid siege to a frontier town that they sought refuge within the city.

224. Archidamus reached Attica with his army just as the corn began to ripen, and, laying waste the whole country in his path, used every effort to provoke his enemies to battle. Pericles, notwithstanding, remained firm; he would call no assembly of the people; nor would he quit the city when the fleet went to ravage the Peloponnesus, lest some misfortune should happen in his absence. However, when the enemy retired he led out all the citizens to plunder Megara, and having by the fleet expelled the Eginetans from their island, he settled an Athenian colony there.

225. The Funeral Ceremonies.—When winter set in, and hostilities were suspended, Pericles employed his fertile genius in devising means to animate the people, and to convert even their calamities into an occasion of triumph. The funeral rites of those who had fallen in defense of their country were publicly solemnized. Three days before the burial, the bones of the bodies previously burned were collected and laid in state under an ample awning. There their relatives visited them, and strewed them with evergreens and spices, as affection or superstition dictated. On the appointed day, the bones were laid in ten chests of cyprus wood, and conveyed on carriages to a public tomb in the most beautiful suburb of the city, the people following in a long, mournful procession, and the female relations filling

---

Questions.—223. How did the representations affect the people? Why were the denizens of the mountains dissatisfied? Why, the inhabitants of the plains? 224. What did Archidamus effect? What course did Pericles pursue? 225. Describe the funeral obsequies.

the air with lamentations. After the ceremony of entombing was over, Pericles passed through the crowd to a lofty stand prepared for the purpose, and delivered an oration, which, as transcribed by Thucydides, is considered the most remarkable of all ancient compositions, and a finished model of beautiful conceptions, chastened and elevated by a noble severity.

226. SECOND INVASION OF ATTICA.—THE PLAGUE.—The next spring the confederate army met again upon the isthmus, to decide the fate of Athens. In this second invasion, Archidamus laid aside the forbearance he had practiced the year before, and left scarce a corner of the land unravaged. But a greater calamity than their offended brethren could inflict, now fell upon the Athenians. A dreadful plague, which, commencing in Ethiopia, had passed through Lybia and crossed the Mediterranean, burst at once upon Athens. Persons apparently in perfect health were seized with extreme heat in the head and redness of the eyes. The tongue and throat then assumed a bloody appearance, a violent cough came on, with hiccoughs and spasms; inflammation ensued, and the body was rapidly covered with loathsome ulcers. As it began in the head, it proceeded through all parts of the body, and finally fixed itself in the extremities; so that those who survived lost their hands, or feet, or eyes. The patients were afflicted with intolerable thirst; many dragged themselves to the fountains and there fell down dead, with none to bury them.

227. It was midsummer, and not only every house was fully occupied, but many families were crowded together in stifling huts, where they died in heaps. The very temples were filled with dead bodies, and every part of the city exhibited a dreadful scene of mortality and mourning. Beasts of prey, though perishing with hunger, refused to touch the carcasses of those who died of it; and birds of ill-omen flew about, and by their dismal croakings excited fearful forebodings. The Peloponnesian army had wasted the vale of Attica, and were rapidly proceeding toward the seacoast, when, becoming alarmed by accounts of the plague, they hastened homeward, after occupying the country forty days.

228. MISFORTUNES OF PERICLES.—The firm mind of Pericles was not to be depressed by the sword without, nor by the pestilence within, nor even by the irritation and despair of the Athenians, who accused him of being the author of their calamities, by drawing such multi-

---

Questions.—225. What afterward took place? 226, 227. What is said of the second invasion by Archidamus? Give an account of the Plague. 228, 229. Relate the story of the misfortunes of Pericles.

tudes into the city as to poison the very air. In the anguish of their feelings, they forgot all he had done and suffered for them; and by a public decree deposed him from his military command, and fined him an immense sum. Nor was this his only misfortune. His advisers fell victims to the pestilence, and the greater part of his family friends died of the same dreadful disease. Still he neither wept nor performed any funeral rites, nor was he seen at the grave of any of his relatives until the death of Paralus, his last legitimate son.

229. He attempted, indeed, then to keep up his usual calm behavior and serenity of mind, but in putting the garland upon the head of the deceased his firmness forsook him; he broke out into loud lamentations, and shed a torrent of tears. Athens made trial, in the course of a year, of the rest of her generals and orators, and finding none capable of extricating her from the difficulties in which she was involved, once more invited Pericles to take again the direction of affairs. He had shut himself up at home to indulge his sorrow, and it was with difficulty that Alcibiades and his other friends persuaded him to reassume the reins of government. During the following winter, the Potidæans, after suffering most intensely from famine, surrendered; and thus Athens gained at least one disputed point.

230. But anxiety and care had done their work for Pericles. He was attacked by the plague in a modified form, and sunk by slow degrees to his rest. When he was at the point of death, his friends, sitting about his bed, began to discourse upon his extraordinary virtue and great exploits; for while he was commander-in-chief, he had erected no less than nine trophies to the honor of Athens. They said these things, supposing his senses were gone; how great, then, was their astonishment when he suddenly aroused, and observed, "I am surprised that while you extol these acts of mine, in which fortune had her share, you take no notice of the most honorable part of my character: *that no Athenian, through my means, ever put on a mourning robe.*" Thus died Pericles, who had held the pre-eminence for the space of forty years among some of the most distinguished men Greece ever produced; who had managed the finances of the republic without the least taint of avarice; and who, though all the power of the magistrates centered in himself, had so preserved his popularity, that he was the first great man, after Solon, that escaped banishment.

231. In the former war with Corcyra, the Corinthians, having taken some prisoners, treated them with the greatest kindness, and sent them

Questions.—230. Give an account of his death. What is stated of his acts and character? 231. What is related of prisoners taken by the Corinthians?

home devoted to the aristocratic interest. No sooner had they arrived than they created a sedition in the republic. The nobles were assassinated in the senate-house, and the people were massacred in the general assembly. These civil commotions lasted two years, and finally the Athenians were compelled to send out an armed force to decide the cause in favor of the democracy.

232. As the fleet, on its return, sailed along the coast of the Peloponnesus, a storm compelled the commanders to cast anchor in the harbor of Pylos, the ancient seat of old Nestor's kingdom. Foul weather prevented their departure; and the sailors, for amusement, assisted the Messenians in their company to erect a fort; and in six days Pylos was strong enough to sustain a siege. It was not long before the transactions at Pylos were known in Sparta, and the alarm occasioned by a Messenian garrison being established within fifty miles was very great. To prevent a union between the garrison and the Lacedemonian slaves, an army was sent to invest the place by *land*, and the confederate fleet was manned with adventurers who went out to take possession of the little island of Sphacteriæ, lying between the fort and the *sea*.

233. Meanwhile, the Athenian fleet had moved to Zacynthus, and Demosthenes,* who commanded Pylos, found himself blockaded both by sea and land. He, however, managed to send a messenger to Eurymedon, commander at Zacynthus. The admiral, hearing of the critical situation of the little garrison, sailed to its relief, and, driving away the Spartan fleet, spread his ships around Sphacteriæ, so that there was a double blockade: Pylos blockaded by Sphacteriæ, and Sphacteriæ blockaded by the Athenian fleet. Under these circumstances, the Spartans made proposals of peace, which Cleon persuaded the Athenians to refuse. "If *he* were a general," he said, "Sphacteriæ should soon be compelled to surrender; and then they might dictate their own terms." Nicias† at once offered to resign the command to him; but Cleon, who was a notorious coward, declined the honor. The people, glad to enjoy a joke, even at their favorite's expense, insisted upon his accepting the office; till finally, thinking it best to put a bold face upon the affair, he came forward, and declared that

* An ancestor of the celebrated orator.

† A man of birth and fortune, commander of the Athenian army.

Questions.—232. Where did the Athenian fleet stop on their return from Corcyra? What was done at Pylos? Where was Pylos situated? (See map No. 2.) What was done by Sparta? 233. Where was Zacynthus? (See map No. 2.) How did the double blockade occur? What then did the Spartans propose? Why was not the proposal accepted?

"within twenty days he would bring all the Lacedemonians in Sphacteriæ captives to Sparta."

234. This impudent boast was received with shouts of laughter; but events over which he had no control enabled him to fulfill his promise. At the head of a band of adventurers, he reached Pylos in safety; and a fire happening to break out in the woody parts of Sphacteriæ, the Lacedemonians were driven from their defenses. Assisted by Demosthenes, of whose skill he had the good sense to avail himself, Cleon led his men to the attack, killed one hundred and twenty-eight of the enemy, and, true enough, took all the rest prisoners and carried them to Athens. Nothing occurred, during the whole course of the war, so contrary to the general opinion as this event; and as the prisoners were of the first rank, it was decided to keep them in chains till terms of peace were settled; or, if the Spartans again invaded Attica, to put them to death.

235. B. C. 424.—REVOLT OF OLYNTHUS.—In this year the Athenians, under Nicias, made the important conquest of the island of Cythera. A general dejection prevailed in Sparta. During seven campaigns, not an individual among the confederates had distinguished himself except Brasidas, and he was yet a young man. As the Spartans had undertaken the war without an adequate fleet, he saw the policy of commencing hostilities in a quarter which would withdraw the Athenian ships from the coast of the Peloponnesus; but his countrymen, though most courageous in the field, were exceedingly timid in the cabinet. Even when Olynthus and other maritime states of Macedon entered into a combination to humble the naval power of Athens, it was with difficulty that Brasidas persuaded them to send with him an army to the north. The Lacedemonians were afraid to diminish their force at home, for Pylos was garrisoned by Messenians, and their slaves stood ready to revolt.

236. Proclamation was therefore made, that any Helots, who thought they could merit the dignity of citizens by feats of arms, should present themselves before the magistrates to undergo the honorable trial. The most warlike and ambitious assembled, of course, and two thousand being chosen and crowned with chaplets, were marched in solemn procession around the temple, as an initiatory ceremony to freedom. Soon after they disappeared, and the massacre was

---

Questions.—234. How did Cleon rise to importance? 235. Where was the island of Cythera? (See map No. 2.) When did the Athenians capture it? Why were the Spartans dejected? What did Brasidas recommend? Why were the Lacedemonians afraid to diminish their forces at home? 236. What hurried preparations did the Spartans make for leaving home? Where was Amphipolis? (See map No. 2.)

managed with such careful secrecy, that in what manner they perished never was known. After this shocking precaution, Brasidas was permitted to set out without loss of time. When the Athenians heard that Brasidas had marched to Macedon with a large army, they ordered Thucydides to move westward with the fleet, and defend Amphipolis. He did so; but, being too late by half a day, the place surrendered, and Brasidas went into winter quarters there. This loss affected the Athenians most sensibly; they banished Thucydides for twenty years, and finally agreed upon a truce of one year with the Spartans.

237. B. C. 421.—BATTLE OF AMPHIPOLIS.—Cleon, emboldened by his accidental success at Sphacteriæ, gave the Athenians no rest till they sent him with a large army to recover Amphipolis. This time, however, fortune did not smile upon him. He led his troops to battle in a disadvantageous position, and was defeated. Both generals were also slain. The two parties were then about even; for the death of Cleon was better than victory to the Athenians; and the loss of Brasidas, worse than defeat to the Spartans.

238. The war had now been in progress ten years, during which both sides had suffered severely. They had alternately ravaged each other's lands; they had slaughtered their brethren in battle, and executed them as prisoners; they had endured famine and pestilence; they had lost their houses, and wasted their revenue; and now, tired of hostilities, and ready to let their weapons drop out of their hands, they listened to the counsels of the peaceful Nicias, and concluded a truce for fifty years, on condition that all the towns and prisoners taken should be restored, and the different states placed in the position which they occupied before the war!

239. But though the rival powers had concluded upon a peace, there was nothing like quiet in the country. The other states thought *they* had something to say upon the subject; and Corinth, in particular, could not consent to give up Potidæa. The people of Amphipolis refused to exchange the supremacy of Sparta for that of Athens, and Sparta contended that she could not compel them to do so; and thus the contest went on, between recriminations and negotiations, affronts and reprisals, for the next six years.

Questions.—236. Why was Thucydides banished? Where was Amphipolis? (See map No. 2.) What is it called now? *Ans.* Iamboli. 237. On what expedition was Cleon sent? When did that occur? What was the result? What made the two parties about even? 238. How had both parties suffered during the war? What counsels did Nicias give? What was the result? 239. Why did not the truce concluded upon bring peace? How were the next six years then spent? Where was Potidæa? (See map No. 2.)

240. B. C. 415.—EXPEDITION TO SICILY.—There was at this time in Athens a young man so eminent for all his qualifications of person, mind, and fortune; so ambitious of distinction; and so gifted with eloquence and dissimulation, as to mark him at once for a leader of that giddy multitude which ruled the city. This was Alcibiades, descended in the paternal line from Ajax, and in the maternal from the *Alcmæonidæ.* He was extravagant, but with an air of nobility; he was dissolute, but engaging and graceful; he had been the pupil of Socrates, and had thrice won the olive at the Olympic games; he was the nephew of Pericles, and the favorite of Aspasia.

241. After the death of Cleon, Alcibiades came forward to set aside the policy of the cautious Nicias, and rekindle a war in which he might have full scope to display his abilities. The factions ran so high that the ostracism was again called for. Both parties were greatly alarmed at their danger, for the struggle was between the *young*, who wanted war, and the *old*, who desired peace. Finally, the leaders agreed to join their influence against Hyperbolus, a friend of Cleon, who had been instrumental in calling up the ostracism at this time. The plan was entirely successful, and Hyperbolus was banished. Though the Athenians laughed at first at the turn things had taken, yet when they came to reflect that they had honored the low-born Hyperbolus by ranking him with Aristides, Themistocles, and Cimon, they were so chagrined that they never resorted to the ostracism again.

242. It was just about this time that embassadors arrived from Egesta, an Ionian colony of Sicily, praying for assistance against the people of Syracuse, who had endeavored to bring them into subjection. Alcibiades was for espousing the cause of Egesta at once, but Nicias, who knew that to quarrel with a Dorian colony* was, in effect, to declare war against the Peloponnesian confederacy, strenuously opposed the rash undertaking. The multitude, however, listened to the glowing representations of Alcibiades,† and after some trifling precautions the expedition was determined upon, Nicias, Alcibiades, and Lamachus being appointed commanders.

243. The prudent Nicias still sought to cool the ardor of the people,

* Syracuse was a Corinthian colony.

† When Timon the man-hater saw Alcibiades, after gaining his point, conducted home in great honor from the assembly, he went up to him, and shaking his hand, exclaimed, "Go on, my brave boy, and prosper, for your prosperity will bring on the ruin of all this crowd."

Questions.—240. In what year was the expedition sent to Sicily? Who was Alcibiades? What is stated about him? 241. What circumstance put an end to ostracism? 242. What causes produced the Sicilian war? What reasons were given for and against it?

by representing the number of obstacles it would be necessary to surmount. He said the fleet not being sufficient, a land army must be provided at immense expense, and he doubted the ability of the Egestans to pay and feed the soldiers. He reminded them that the Syracusans would be at home, among friends who could assist them with men, money, horses, and provisions; while the Athenians would be in an enemy's country, so far from Greece that it would take four months to receive supplies in winter; that if they were successful they should gain nothing; but if they were unsuccessful it would reflect eternal disgrace upon the Athenian name; and for his part, he was determined not to go, unless he were supplied with every thing requisite for carrying on the war.

244. This sensible remonstrance, so far from having the desired effect, only furnished the partisans of Alcibiades with a pretext for making more magnificent preparations, and a decree was in consequence obtained for raising as many troops and fitting out as many galleys as the generals thought necessary. Indeed, so sanguine were the people upon the subject, that young men in their places of exercise, and old men in their shops, drew maps of Sicily, and planned the passage thence to Africa; for in the splendid conquests of which they dreamed, they comprised Carthage, Italy, and the sea, to the pillars of Hercules.

245. THE EMBARKATION.—The levies being completed, the generals resolved to set sail immediately for Sicily, by way of Corcyra and Rhegium. On the morning appointed for embarkation, the citizens enrolled for the expedition appeared on the parade by daybreak. The whole city accompanied their march to the Piræus. In that assembly there were no uninterested spectators. No city had ever fitted out so numerous and gallant a fleet as the present; and not even the Athenians, skilled as they were in naval affairs, had ever undertaken so grand or distant an expedition; and no family mingled in the vast procession, but felt the honor and the pain of contributing its most promising member to this hazardous enterprise.

246. When the last adieus had been said, and the troops were embarked, the trumpets sounded as a signal for silence, and prayers were put up with the greatest solemnity, the whole assembly uniting their voices in one grand petition for success. Goblets of wine were then produced, from which officers and soldiers together poured out liba-

---

Questions.—243. What representations did Nicias make? 244. What effect did the representations produce? Draw a map of Sicily and the principal conquests of Athens. 245, 246. Describe the embarkation. Where was Corcyra? (Map No. 2.) Rhegium? (No. 4.)

tions, and drank to the prosperity of the commonwealth and the armament. Then, far above the roar of the sea and the voice of the wind, rose the loud pæan of the Greeks; and amid the waving of banners, and fluttering of pennons, the fleet moved majestically out of the harbor, the inhabitants of the city following it with their eyes till it seemed to be lost between the sea and the sky. At Corcyra the Athenian squadron was joined by the ships of the allies, and, the winds and waves proving favorable, the combined fleet had a prosperous journey thence to Sicily. They landed without opposition, and took up their station at Catana.

247. Alcibiades.—This advantageous debarkation of the troops was all that Alcibiades effected in the enterprise from which he had anticipated so much glory; suspicions, which had well-nigh detained him in Athens, soon occasioning his recall. Some time before the fleet sailed, the statues of Hermæ were all mutilated in one night, and it was generally believed that Alcibiades and his companions had been guilty of the sacrilege during a drunken revel. Taking advantage of his absence, his enemies magnified his follies into a plot to subvert the government, and many persons were apprehended as being privy to the affair. All Athens was in alarm; the conspirators were thought to be in league with Sparta, and one whole night the people watched under arms. At last, one of the prisoners told his fellows that it would be better to confess something than to submit to torture. They accordingly disclosed the pretended plot, and received their liberty as a reward for their villainy.

248. All those whom they accused were immediately condemned and executed; but Alcibiades, whose name figured largely in the *awful disclosures*, being in Sicily, they knew not how to effect his destruction. If they put him under arrest there, it might occasion a sedition in the army. It was therefore resolved to send the Paralus* after him, with a simple command to return to Athens. Immediate obedience was paid to this order. Alcibiades followed the sacred trireme in his own ship, as the humblest individual in the commonwealth, but when they stopped to take in provisions on the coast of Italy he absconded. The heralds, having searched for him in vain for several days, returned without him. The Athenian people, however, pronounced sentence of death against him, in what was called "deserted judgment;" his

* The sacred trireme.

Questions.—246. What occurred at Corcyra? Catana? 247. Of what was Alcibiades accused? 248. Why was he not put under arrest in Sicily? What plan was resolved upon instead? What is stated in relation to his absconding? The judgment against Alcibiades?

whole estate was confiscated, and all orders of religion were commanded to curse him.

249. When Alcibiades heard of this severe sentence, he exclaimed, "I hope one day to make them sensible that I am still alive." From Italy he made his way to Sparta, where he found persons very willing to assist his designs against his country.* He told them that the Athenians did not mean to bound their conquests by the shores of Sicily, but that, after subjecting that island, together with Italy, Carthage, and Spain, they intended, by the aid of numerous fleets and allies, to bring all Greece under their dominion; and he counseled the Lacedemonians, if they would avoid abject dependence, to send an army into Sicily, and nip the growing power of Athens in the bud. His advice was taken. The Lacedemonians decided to assist the Syracusans and renew the war.

250. Measures of Nicias.—Nicias, meantime, having fortified his camp, put off an attack upon Syracuse week after week, and month after month, till finally the buoyant spirits of his troops were all evaporated, and they strolled about in search of amusement rather than conquest. The Syracusans, too, having recovered from the fright which so grand an armament had occasioned, came up to his intrenchments, and scoffingly asked "if he had come to settle at Catana." Roused by this taunt, he determined to *settle* at Syracuse if anywhere, and, with his usual caution, set about making arrangements for that purpose. He bribed a Sicilian to go to Syracuse with a story, that the Athenians lay in the town every night without their arms, and that on a certain morning, which he named, the Syracusans might unite with the disaffected persons in the neighborhood, burn the Athenian camp and fleet, and free the island at once of its invaders.

251. The enemy, pleased with the idea of terminating the war in so summary a manner, fell readily into the snare. At the very time, however, that the Syracusans set out for Catana, Nicias left Catana for Syracuse, and, landing there in the absence of the garrison, fortified himself in the outskirts of the town. The Syracusans, on arriving at Catana, and finding only an empty camp, were so provoked at the trick put upon them, that they marched back to their city with all speed, and presented themselves without the walls in order of battle.

* He gained the confidence of the Spartans by conforming strictly to all the laws of Lycurgus. He bathed in cold water, took the most violent exercise, and dined on *black broth*, with great relish.

Questions.—249. What exclamation is reported of Alcibiades? What evils did he seek for his country? 250. Did Nicias act with energy? What was the result? To what stratagem did Nicias resort? 251. Give an account of what followed. Where was Catana? (4.)

Nicias immediately attacked and beat them. Not, however, having courage to commence the siege of the place, he returned with all his forces, and went into winter quarters at Catana.

252. B. C. 414.—SIEGE OF SYRACUSE.—The next spring, having received a supply of horse from Athens, Nicias resolved to block up Syracuse both by sea and land. He conducted all his movements with so much prudence, that he gained possession of a hill that overlooked the town, before the Syracusans knew of his approach. By diligent exertions, his soldiers inclosed the city with a wall, to cut off its communication with the country; and, during the time the work was in progress, came off victorious in eight different engagements with the enemy. Several Sicilian cities, attracted by the prosperous state of Athenian affairs, came over to their interest, and supplied them with provisions; so that, naturally desponding and cautious as he was, Nicias began to conceive high hopes of success.

253. The Syracusans, on their part, seeing nothing before them but famine or the sword, began already to think of surrender, when the fleet which the Spartans had fitted out, at the instigation of Alcibiades, appeared off the coast! As Nicias disbelieved the report of Gylippus's arrival, he placed no regular guard to prevent his landing, and therefore was not a little surprised and alarmed to see that officer drawing up the Syracusans, and marshaling his own forces in order of battle. His alarm was changed to anger soon after, when a herald came to him, saying, that "Gylippus would allow the Athenians five days to quit Sicily." He prepared for battle with unwonted animation, and was victorious in the first engagement; but afterward fortune forsook him, so that, giving up all thoughts of *conquest*, he sought only *safety*.

254. Enfeebled by a long and distressing illness, and discouraged by the turn of affairs, he transmitted to the Athenians a most melancholy account of his situation. He told them that instead of besieging Syracuse he was himself besieged, and in danger of capture. He said that his fleet had gone to decay, that many of the ships were leaky, and the crews diminished; that they were forced to go so far for wood and water, that they were always fatigued with constant duty; that the slaves deserted, and many of the allies went home without leave; that the temper of the Athenian people being averse to subordination,

---

Questions.—251. Did Nicias then lay siege to Syracuse? What did he do? 252. When did Nicias finally conclude to lay siege to Syracuse? What advantages and successes did he gain? 253. What turned the tables in favor of the Syracusans? Give an account of what followed. 254. What did Nicias write home?

he found it impossible to control the perverse disposition of some under his command; and that it was absolutely necessary for the Athenians either to recall the armament, or to send out another, not inferior in numbers and equipments, and furnished with more money. He closed by begging to be superseded in the command, on account of his ill-health, and as a reward for his past services.

255. It was midwinter when this letter reached the Athenians, but immediate preparations were made to retrieve their affairs. Eurymedon was sent off with a small squadron, and money to pay the soldiers, while all hands at home were busily employed in fitting out substantial re-enforcements for the spring. As for the request of Nicias, they would not listen to it, but they appointed two officers to assist him in his charge. The intelligence brought by Eurymedon roused all the energies of Gylippus. He attacked the Athenians by sea, and was completely victorious; and wrested from them the fort which protected their naval stores, so that they could receive no supplies without making their way through the fleet of Syracuse.

256. B. C. 413.—ARRIVAL OF DEMOSTHENES.—Nicias, almost overcome with the difficulties of his situation, and the gloom of his prospects, turned his eyes involuntarily towards his native country, when a sight the most animating and cheering burst upon his view. Seventy-three Athenian galleys, richly decorated, adorned with costly streamers, and manned with eight hundred men, were steering for the harbor of Syracuse. As they approached the shore, the sound of trumpets and the shouts of the sailors made the whole city resound. The Syracusans, struck with terror, did not attempt to prevent the disembarkation. The joyful greetings and fresh hopes of the adventurers diffused new life through the camp; but Nicias soon began to tremble at the rash measures which Demosthenes advocated. He had private intelligence that many of the Syracusans, tired of the imperious manner of Gylippus, were making preparations to surrender; but as he was not at liberty to speak openly upon the subject, he advised the other commanders to wait a certain time. This, however, only subjected him to taunts about his timidity, and he was at last forced to give up his point.

257. Demosthenes put himself at the head of the land forces, and attacked Epipolæ* by night. As he came upon the guards by surprise,

* A strong fort upon an eminence overlooking Syracuse.

Questions.—255. How was his request answered? What disaster befell the Athenians? 256. What then was their condition? Describe the arrival of Demosthenes. How did his arrival affect the troops of Nicias? What advice did Nicias give? Was his advice acceptrd?

he killed many of them, and routed those who stood upon the defense. But when he reached the spot where the Beotians were posted, his men were driven back. As they turned to fly, they encountered another band of Athenians coming down the hill, who, mistaking them for enemies, fell upon them. In striving to rally, they repeated their watchword so often that the enemy learned it, and used it to lead them astray. At last the rout was complete. Some fell headlong from the rocks or walls. Some escaped, and wandered through fields and woods till they were found next day, and cut to pieces by the enemy's horse. Thus, at once, were blasted all the hopes which had sprung up in the hearts of the Athenians upon the arrival of Demosthenes.

258. THE SEA-FIGHT.—There remained now only the sad alternatives of returning in disgrace to Athens with the remnant of the splendid armament which sailed from Piræus under such happy auspices; or of remaining to die of pestilence, famine, or the sword, in Sicily. Demosthenes advocated the former course; but Nicias, who understood the Athenian method of rewarding generals, declared that "he would rather die by the hands of the enemy than by those of his fellow-citizens." Thus the favorable opportunity for *escape* was lost, and the sickly season found the Athenians dispirited and doubting in their quarters before Syracuse. At last, Nicias, overcome by the general calamity, gave orders to strike the tents and prepare to move. With the greatest secrecy and dispatch, every thing was put in readiness; but just as the troops were on the point of embarking, the moon was shrouded in an eclipse.

259. This natural phenomenon struck the whole armament with terror; and Nicias, who, according to the superstition of the times, had always delayed an enterprise three days after such an event, now, by advice of his soothsayers, determined to wait *nine times three days.* Quitting every other care, he sat still, observing his sacrifices, and praying for favorable tokens, while the Syracusans shut up the mouth of the great harbor with galleys anchored firmly with iron chains; nor would he take any measures for repelling the insults of the enemy, or effecting a retreat, till the Athenians, with great indignation, called upon him to lead them off by land. Unwilling, however, to comply with their demand, he made an effort to break through the encircling fleet.

Questions.—257. Give an account of the attack made by Demosthenes, and of its immediate result. 258. What alternatives remained for Nicias? What course did Demosthenes advocate? Why did not Nicias adopt it then? Why did he afterward change his mind? What occurred as the troops were about to embark? 259. What was the effect upon the troops? Upon Nicias? What effort to escape did he at last make?

260. Then it was that the great sea-fight began, remarkable not only for the vigor and bravery of the combatants, but for the agitation and despair of the spectators. The Syracusans came out on the walls of their city to behold the sight, and the Athenians thronged the Epipolæ to gaze upon the last effort of those gallant seamen who had so long been accustomed to conquer, and had so reluctantly learned to bear defeat. After suffering incredibly from repeated attacks, the Athenian fleet was driven on shore, and the soldiers were so dispirited that they neither opposed the enemy who were seizing their vessels, nor demanded their dead. Escape by sea was now impossible. It was therefore resolved to move to Catana.

261. THE RETREAT.—Nothing could be more affecting than the commencement of this retreat. The dead were left unburied, though thus their souls were condemned to wander in darkness upon the dismal shores of the Styx; the dying, abandoned to wild beasts, with gloomy presentiment of the same fate, lifted up their last cries in curses upon their departing countrymen; the wounded dragged themselves along after the army, entreating assistance; and such a scene of lamentation and mourning was presented as might have moved even Spartan hearts to pity. The enemy had seized all the difficult passes, broken down the bridges, and stationed cavalry all along their route, so that the Athenians could not move one step without fighting.

262. Nicias, though oppressed with sickness and worn out with privations, did all in his power to cheer and encourage his men; but when they remembered his well-grounded objections to the war, and saw that so religious a man as he had no better fortune than the most profligate soldier in the army, even their trust in heaven abandoned them, and nothing but tears and sad presages were seen and heard on every side. During a march of eight days, though attacked and harassed by the enemy all the way, Nicias preserved his division tolerably entire; but the remainder of the army under Demosthenes, having lost their way in the night, were surrounded and taken captive.

263. The next day, Nicias and his band were overtaken at the ford of the river Asinarus. The most terrible havoc was made in the ranks of the Athenians; and finally Nicias, to stop the slaughter, surrendered on the single condition that Gylippus should spare his men; yet even then the number of the saved was greatly inferior to the number of the slain. When the Syracusans had collected all the

Questions.—260. Give an account of the sea-fight. What then was impossible? What resolution was consequently made? 261, 262. Give an account of the retreat. Of the condition of the Athenians. Disaster to Demosthenes. 263. Give an account of the next day's occurrences. Where is Syracuse? (Map No. 4.)

prisoners they could find into one body, they dressed up some of the tallest and straightest trees by the river with the arms they had taken from them, which they left as trophies of the most complete victory ever gained on their island. Then, having shorn the horses of the Atheuians, and ornamented their own in the most splendid manner, they marched home with garlands on their heads, and were welcomed to their city with every demonstration of joy.

264. It would have been a singular triumph for Gylippus to have carried Nicias and Demosthenes prisoners to Sparta, but the jealous and cruel temper of the Syracusans deprived him of this glory. A decree was passed that the generals should be put to death; and they were accordingly scourged with rods, and then stoned. The miserable remnants of their once flourishing army were reserved for a still severer fate. A vast quarry, whence stone had been taken for building the city, was judged the safest place of confinement for such a number of skillful warriors. Food was given in quantities barely sufficient to support life; no shelter was afforded from the inclemency of the weather; and Thucydides summed up their miseries by saying, "That no suffering could possibly result from so wretched a situation, which was not experienced by the Athenian prisoners." A few of them, who were sold as slaves to individuals, gained their liberty by repeating passages from the tragedies of Euripides, and lived to thank their benefactor in Athens for the obligations they owed to his pen.

265. The Story told in Athens.—Rumor carried the news of this total shipwreck of their power and glory to the Athenians, long before an official notice of it could reach them. The first man who disseminated the evil tidings, however, being only a poor barber, was subjected to the torture, till the whole city was thrown into agony by the confirmation of the report. How changed was the morning which rose upon Athens, destitute of horse, foot, money, ships, or mariners, from that morning when the Piræus was crowded with a gallant fleet, departing as was supposed to certain conquest! Then the excited multitude, with hearts full of hope, stood gazing upon the joyous flutter of gay streamers and waving pennons; now, bereaved and desponding, they looked wistfully across the sea, as if expecting, yet dreading to behold, Gylippus with his victorious fleet approaching to commence the siege of their city.

266. But amidst the general gloom they were not idle. As day

Questions.—263. Give an acconnt of the proceedings of the Syracusans. 264. What would have been a singular triumph to Gylippus? Why were they not carried there? What was their fate? Of their army? How did a few escape? 265. How were the evil tidings received in Greece? What comparison was made?

wore on after day, and no enemy appeared, they began to take courage. They levied money for building new ships and raising fresh troops; they retrenched all superfluous expenses; and, to avoid the embarrassment of factions, established a council of old men to examine every matter before it was brought before the people. Meanwhile, the attention of all Greece was excited, and the politics of every republic put in motion, by the blow Athens had received in Sicily. Those who had yielded her an unwilling homage now prepared to revolt; those who feared the vengeance of Sparta were impelled to do the same; her friends became cold; her enemies impudent; and, bleeding as she was from the loss of those members of the commonwealth which were her eyes to see, and hands to execute, she felt that this severe rebuke was but "the beginning of sorrows."

267. The Lacedemonians, encouraged by the success of Gylippus, also undertook the building of a fleet; and thus, at the close of the nineteenth year of the war, preparations were making on both sides, as if hostilities were just then commenced. The people of Chios, Lesbos, and Cyzicum sent to treat with the Spartans about leaving the Athenians to join the Peloponnesian confederacy; Alcibiades had gone to Asia Minor some time before, and was now forming a treaty with Tissaphernes, satrap of Sardis, for furnishing the Spartans with money and ships; and Pharnabazus, satrap of Bithynia, was also anxious to gain the friendship of Athens's enemies.

268. Before, however, the Spartans formed all these alliances, they held a congress of the confederates. There they concluded to haul their ships, which were in the Corinthian Gulf, across the isthmus; to man them in the Saronic Gulf, and send them to Chios and Lesbos with the articles of treaty, and dispatch them thence to the Hellespont to act with Pharnabazus. This purpose was so far carried into execution, that twenty-one triremes had been dragged over the isthmus with great labor and difficulty, and prepared for departure; but it happened that some Athenians, who were there attending the Isthmian games, penetrated the design, and returned home with the startling intelligence. A company of adventurers immediately set out from the Piræus and attacked the little fleet; killed the admiral, and compelled the crews to draw the ships again upon shore.

269. Measures of Alcibiades.—This event occasioned great alarm

---

Questions.—266. What preparations did the Athenians again make? What effect did the misfortunes of the Athenians have in Greece? 267. What preparations did the Lacedemonians make? What help came to the Spartans? What was Alcibiades about? 268. What purpose did the Spartans form in relation to their ships? How far was it executed? How was it foiled? Where was the Saronic Gulf? (See Map No. 2.)

at Corinth, the Spartans too were discouraged, and determined not to engage in any enterprise on the other side of the Egean. Thus the whole matter would have fallen through, had not Alcibiades undertaken the affair. He sailed from Miletus to Chios, confirmed the revolt, and brought the Chians into the Lacedemonian confederacy. But the glory of Alcibiades was already on the wane: Agis, the Spartan king, hated him for his private vices; among the confederates many envied him; all feared him, and but few loved him. In his transactions with Tissaphernes, he managed to gain favor for himself, rather than for the people who sent him to ask it; and now, examining the doubtful and dangerous position which he occupied, he determined by a master stroke of policy "to restore himself to his country, before that country was reduced so low as to be not worth returning to."

270. Yet, urgent as were his reasons for a reconciliation, he still feared the giddy multitude by whom he had been condemned. Fully convinced that he could never rule in the hearts of the people, as Pericles had done, he set about changing the government of Athens from a democracy to an oligarchy, with his characteristic zeal. Having strengthened his interest with the satrap by the most subtle flattery, he managed to communicate with the commanders of the Athenian fleet at Samos, signifying to them *his power to bring Tissaphernes into their interest*, and through him to lead Darius himself into their alliance. But this he would not do, unless the power were taken from the *Many* and given to the *Few*. The generals of the army, being in reality the leading men in the commonwealth, immediately sent a messenger to the nobility at Athens, with a request that they would assume the government, and deprive the people of the power they had hitherto enjoyed.

271. The nobility joyfully set about the performance of a work so congenial to their feelings; nevertheless, up to the last hour of the DEMOCRACY, every thing was conducted in a truly *democratic* manner. A general assembly was summoned. A resolution was passed, permitting any one to make any proposal without fear. Then it was decided that a *new council* should be formed, having full power to administer public affairs. This council consisted of four hundred members, but, to amuse the people, it was added, that they would call in the aid of five thousand citizens in cases of emergency. Thus the

Questions.—269. What did Alcibiades then do? Where was Miletus? (See map No. 2.) Chios? (Same map.) Why was Alcibiades losing favor with the Spartans? Upon what did he consequently determine? 270. What did he fear among the Athenians? Why did he wish the government changed? What communication did he send? 271. By what process was the government changed?

people of Athens voted away their beloved democracy, after having enjoyed it about one hundred years after the banishment of the Pisistratidæ.

272. THE TYRANNY OF THE FOUR HUNDRED.—When the assembly broke up, the Four Hundred, vested with their new powers, and followed by one hundred and twenty young men, who acted as attendants or assassins, as the case might require, entered the senate-house, paid the council of Five Hundred the arrears in their salaries, and commanded them instantly to retire; an order which they prudently obeyed. Having now all power in their hands, they put to death those who disputed their authority; and feeling fully competent to order affairs in the best possible manner, *they determined not to recall Alcibiades*, lest he might interfere in some of their plans. Anxious, however, to secure the favor of the army at Samos, they sent out ten commissioners to explain their measures, and soothe the feelings of the soldiers. This the pacificators found no easy task; there was no disguising the facts in the case; the people were deprived of power, and Athens was ruled by four hundred tyrants! The soldiers sent immediately for Alcibiades, and, having appointed him their general, begged him to sail at once for Athens, and destroy the enslavers of their country.

273. This measure, which would have saved Sparta any further trouble with Athens, Alcibiades prevented; using arguments and entreaties with some, and force with others. The commissioners were, however, sent back with a message from himself, requiring the immediate abolition of the self-constituted council, and the restoration of the senate. When the commissioners delivered their message, and reported the state of things in Samos, the Four Hundred determined to submit to Sparta rather than fall into the hands of their infuriated brethren. They opened negotiations for this purpose; but before they were able to effect any thing, the people rose against them, and they were glad to escape with their lives. Alcibiades was then earnestly solicited to make all possible haste to the relief of Athens; but, proud as he was, he wished to return under happier auspices than from a mutinying army to a seditious city. Parting, therefore, from Samos with a few ships, he cruised along the Egean, in search of some adventure which should enable him to strike a blow for his country.

274. Had the Spartans been on the alert during these times of trial,

---

Questions.—272. What is stated of the tyranny of the Four Hundred? What action did the soldiers take? 273. What course did Alcibiades then pursue? What became of the Four Hundred? Why did not Alcibiades then go to the relief of Athens?

they might have conquered Attica while the people were hesitating between the orders received from the Athenian commonwealth at Samos, and the Athenian commonwealth at Athens; but, with their usual tardiness, they lost the time in embarrassing negotiations with the vacillating Tissaphernes. The false satrap was seeking to play off the Athenians against the Spartans, by keeping them in perpetual hostility; so that soon after he promised Alcibiades to make an alliance with the Athenians, he engaged to pay the Lacedemonians for protecting the coasts of the Egean.

275. BATTLE OF ABYDOS.—Myndarus, the Spartan admiral, having intelligence from Pharnabazus that the Athenians were in his neighborhood, directed his course that way; and Alcibiades, hearing of the intended fight, followed. The two fleets met near Abydos, and a battle ensued which lasted till night, without decisive advantage to either side, when several foreign galleys were seen approaching. The Spartans, recognizing Alcibiades, felt sure of timely assistance; but when they saw the Athenian flag hung out, and perceived that he bore down upon them with hostile intentions, they thought only of making good their retreat. The Athenians having, by the assistance of Alcibiades, captured thirty galleys, and recovered their own, erected a trophy.

276. THE VISIT.—After this glorious success, Alcibiades prepared presents, and went to wait upon Tissaphernes with a princely train. The treacherous satrap, however, to throw the balance again upon the side of the Spartans, seized him, and sent him prisoner to Sardis. From this place he contrived to escape to Clazomenæ, and, finding six ships there, embarked immediately and sailed for the Hellespont. The troops received him with joy; and learning that Myndarus and Pharnabazus were together at Cyzicus, he convinced his men that it was necessary to pursue them, and strike a decisive blow. Had the Spartans known the number of his fleet, they would not have ventured a battle; but Alcibiades, coming up in a tremendous storm of rain, showed only a part of his ships, and when they were engaged poured in the others, till the Spartans were completely routed. Pharnabazus fled; Myndarus was slain; and the Athenians took every ship of the squadron.

277. The soldiers were rewarded with an abundance of spoil; Cyzicus surrendered, and the Athenians not only secured the Hellespont,

---

Questions.—274. What opportunity did the Spartans lose? Which side did Tissaphernes take? 275. Who decided the battle of Abydos? Give an account of the battle. Where was Abydos? (See map No. 2.) 276. Of what treachery was Tissaphernes guilty? How was Alcibiades fortunate? Give an account of the battle that took place. Where was Cyzicus? (See map No. 2.) Clazomene? (Same map.)

but entirely cleared the sea of Lacedemonians. A letter was also intercepted, which, in the Laconic style, was to give the Ephori an account of the condition of the Spartans. "Our glory is faded. Myndarus is slain. Our soldiers are starving; and we know not what step to take." Success began to bring back the "summer friends" of the Athenians. When the islands saw the whole fleet of the Peloponnesus annihilated at a blow, and knew that Alcibiades stood at the helm of state, they began to think the commonwealth would outride the storm; they talked no more of revolt, or of alliance with Sparta, but furnished regularly and cheerfully their stipulated quota of money, men, and ships.

278. Alcibiades, understanding the embarrassments arising from an exhausted treasury, determined to bring the towns of Chalcedon and Byzantium (which commanded the lucrative trade of the Euxine) again under Athenian jurisdiction. Thus fortified, he might treat with Pharnabazus, awe Tissaphernes, stop the Spartan supplies from Persia, and establish the superiority of Athens beyond question. It was a comprehensive and feasible plan, but it came too late. The sun of Athens was already in its evening declination, and the dark clouds of faction were gathering like a pall around her glory. Alcibiades, combining in himself the address of Themistocles and the talents of Pericles, prolonged, for a little, her brief day; but perished himself in the ruin of his native city.

279. In the twenty-fourth year of the war, he led his whole force to the siege of Chalcedon. He inclosed it with a wall which reached from sea to sea. The Lacedemonian commander of the garrison sent to Pharnabazus for assistance, but that prince began to grow tired of an alliance which brought frequent battles and no victories, and made constant demands upon his purse, without bringing him in either dominion or glory. He therefore sent proposals of accommodation to the Athenians, and a treaty was finally concluded in the following terms: "That Pharnabazus should pay $20,000 for the ransom of Chalcedon; that all arrears should be paid up, and the Chalcedonians pay tribute to Athens as formerly; and that Pharnabazus should conduct embassadors to the king from the Athenians." On these conditions the siege of Chalcedon was raised. Pharnabazus, thus secure in

Questions.—277. What is said of the intercepted letter? What effect did success have? 278. Why were Chalcedon and Byzantium so important? *Ans.* Vast quantities of wheat were formerly, as now, raised upon the shores of the Black Sea, and the commerce in breadstuffs was regulated by these ports. Where were the two ports? (See map No. 2.) What is the present name of Byzantium? *Ans.* Constantinople. What plan did Alcibiades determine upon? 279. Give an account of his success as regards Chalcedon.

his own satrapy, left Alcibiades at liberty to proceed with the siege of Byzantium.

280. B. C. 407.—CAPTURE OF BYZANTIUM, AND RETURN OF ALCIBIADES.—This place he undertook to reduce by drawing a line of circumvallation about it. But the Byzantines, warned by the fate of Chalcedon, made overtures to him, which he accepted. A gate was in consequence opened to his troops in the night, and after a sharp struggle with the Spartan garrison the place was taken, and the flag of Athens once more commanded the Bosphorus. The services which Alcibiades had thus rendered his country were perhaps greater than any Greek had ever before performed. When he first joined the fleet at Samos, Athens commanded little more territory than her walls inclosed; she had no revenue; no regular pay for soldiers; and they were consequently dispirited and mutinous. Under his auspices, her dominion had been restored; her fleet again rode triumphant over the seas; and the allies again proudly ranged themselves under her banners.

281. His heart now yearned after his native country. He sighed to be the acknowledged benefactor of Athens; to walk from the Piræus to the city saved by his efforts, with a prouder step than when he quitted it eight years before, the commander of the Sicilian expedition. He longed to stand upon the bema, and sway the most enlightened audience in the world by the breath of his eloquence; and to hear his praises shouted by the voices which had been loudest to condemn him unheard, as the multilator of the Hermæ. Having settled affairs in Byzantium as rapidly as possible, he led the armament to Samos. There, selecting twenty ships of his convoy, he sent the others on to Athens, following himself at a distance, agitated alternately with hopes and fears as to the reception he should meet.

282. He cruised along the coast of Laconia until informed by his friends that he had been elected general of the commonwealth, with two colleagues, when he sailed directly for Attica. Having covered his galleys with bucklers and spoils of all sorts, in the manner of trophies, and made an imposing display of ships, with their arms and ensigns, he entered the harbor of Piræus. When his approach was announced, a vast crowd assembled about the port, each vying with the other in extolling the merits of Alcibiades, praising his abilities,

---

Questions.—280. Give an account of his success as regards Byzantium. What is stated of the services of Alcibiades to Athens? What were those services? 281. What was the great desire of Alcibiades? For what did he sigh and long? What arrangements did he make to return to Athens? 282. When did he sail for Attica? Give an account of the reception he met with.

his liberality, and his patriotism. A few, indeed, ventured to whisper that he had been the cause of all their misfortunes, by advising the Sicilian expedition, and concerting plans for the Spartans; but their voices were drowned in the acclamations of the multitude.

283. His friends gathered round him as he leaped on shore; such as could approach him, crowned him with garlands; while those who could not get near for the crowd, viewed him from a distance, shedding tears of joy. The greetings being over, he proceeded to the city, and went into the assembly of the people, where he very modestly complained of *their* treatment, and excusingly ascribed it to the influence of some envious demon. He then opened before them the hopes and designs he had formed, and they were so much pleased with his harangue that they crowned him with crowns of gold, and gave him the *absolute command* of their forces. Thus armed with authority and established in favor, he proceeded to direct the enrollment of fresh troops, and the equipment of a fleet, with which he proposed again to cross the Egean.

284. Lysander's Policy.—Meanwhile Pharnabazus, with the Athenian embassadors whom he had undertaken to conduct to Susa, was met in Phrygia by Cyrus,* who had come into the western provinces clothed with royal authority. The young prince had, however, been commanded by his father to assist the Spartans, and the Athenians were consequently repulsed. A general now entered the arena fully equal in dissimulation and intrigue to Alcibiades. This was Lysander, the Spartan admiral, who, though educated in the laws of Lycurgus, and accustomed to the heavy sound of iron money all his life, understood at once the superior weight of gold and silver. He had been sent out in the winter, to take command of the army in Asia Minor; and, collecting the scattered forces of Lacedemon at Ephesus, had diligently employed the time in building ships and furnishing a fleet.

285. As soon as he heard that Cyrus had arrived at Sardis, he hastened to pay his court to him, and to acquaint him with the conduct of Tissaphernes. Cyrus was very glad to hear the satrap accused, because he knew him to be his enemy; and as Lysander conformed to all his requests, and flattered him continually, he soon granted him whatever he desired. When the crafty Lacedemonian was about to take his leave, Cyrus provided a grand entertainment for him, and after drinking to him according to the Persian manner, inquired,

* Brother of Artaxerxes. See article "Cyrus Revolts," in Persia.

Questions.—283. Of the occurrences in the assembly of the people. 284. What is said of Cyrus? Of Lysander? 285. What did Lysander accomplish at Sardis?

"What can I do for you that will give you the most satisfaction?" Lysander replied, "Nothing would gratify me so much as the addition of a single obolus* to the seamen's daily wages."

286. Cyrus was so pleased with this answer, that he made him a present of ten thousand pieces of gold. Lysander employed the money to increase the wages of his men, a measure which worked like magic upon the two fleets. There were, both among the Lacedemonians and Athenians, multitudes of Beotians, Phocians, Argives, Arcadians, and others, who cared neither for the right or the wrong of the matter, but attached themselves to the side which offered the best pay. The gold of Persia decided them in favor of the Lacedemonians; so that this stroke of policy almost unmanned the Athenian galleys.

287. The Fatal Skirmish.—The news of the alliance between Cyrus and Lysander had not reached Athens when Alcibiades, in the third month after his return, sailed again for the theater of war. He stopped first at Andros, which had revolted. He was in part successful, but seeing that the walls of the principal city were strong enough to sustain a long siege, he erected a trophy, and proceeded to Samos. Disappointed in his expectations of gaining the favor of Cyrus, he did not yet yield to despair. He anchored his fleet at a convenient distance from Ephesus, and left it there in charge of Antiochus, the pilot, giving him strict orders not to engage with the Spartans, while he went to the Hellespont to raise supplies. Antiochus disobeyed this command, went out, and by insulting language provoked Lysander to an engagement, was defeated, and slain. Fifteen Athenian ships were taken; the remainder escaped to Samos. When Alcibiades heard of what had been done, he hastened back, and, drawing out his whole force, offered battle; but Lysander refused to engage, and the Athenians were compelled to bear the disgrace.

288. The Fall of Alcibiades.—The people of Athens bore the intelligence that Andros had been abandoned very well; for they expected to hear that Chios and Ionia were conquered; but when the report came that their fleet had fled before an inferior force, and that an alliance had been consummated between Lacedemon and Persia, all Athens was in an uproar. They had thought Alcibiades invincible,

* About two cents.

Questions.—285. What inquiry did Cyrus make? 286. What response was made to the request? How was the money used? 287. Where was Andros? (See map No. 2.) Ephesus? (Same map.) What was done by Alcibiades at Andros? To what place did he next proceed? Give an account of the skirmish there. Of Lysander's offer. 288. What news reached Athens?

and their first feeling upon discovering their mistake was one of indignation and distrust. They suspected that it was not from want of ability, but from lack of inclination, that he had not fulfilled his promises; and, excited by the startling dangers that lay before them, urged on by artful and interested orators, without waiting to understand the facts in the case, they proceeded to pass the fatal decree which sealed the ruin of Athens.

289. Alcibiades and his associate, Thrasybulus, the two persons who, by experience and the gifts of nature, were beyond all others the best qualified to save the commonwealth, were dismissed from their employments. Ten generals were appointed in their room, of whom Conon was chief. Thrasybulus remained with the fleet, but Alcibiades retired to his estate in Chersonesus.

290. B. C. 406.—BATTLE OF ARGINUSÆ.—At the time of his appointment, Conon was employed in the siege of Andros. A decree of the people directed him to go immediately, with the twenty ships under his orders, and take command of the fleet at Samos. It was already late in the year, and on his arrival he found a general dejection pervading the army. His first measure was precisely that for which Alcibiades had been condemned. He selected seventy triremes, and sent them out in various directions, to collect revenue from such islands and towns as had not already revolted.

291. The term of Lysander's command having expired, he was superseded by Callicratidas, his equal in courage, but not in cunning. There was too much of the true Spartan in him to stand all day about the doors of Cyrus, waiting till he had done drinking, and was ready to admit strangers; so, after being laughed at by the porters as an ignorant rustic, he went back without any money to pay his soldiers. However, he took one of the principal towns of Lesbos by storm, and having pursued Conon into the harbor of Mitylene, captured thirty of his ships, and besieged him there. Then, hearing that the other generals were returning, and making all sail for the relief of Mitylene, he advanced to meet them over against Arginusæ. His pilot advised him to retreat, because the Athenians had the greater number of ships; but he replied, "My death would be a small loss to Sparta; my flight would be a disgrace."

Questions.—288. How did it affect the Athenians? Why did they pass the fatal decree? 289. What was the fatal decree? What appointments were made instead? 290. Where was Samos? In what direction from Andros? (See map No. 2.) To what place did Conon sail? What was his first measure? 291. Why was Lysander superseded in command? Who was his successor? What did Callicratidas accomplish at Mitylene? What advice did his pilot give? How did he reply? Where was Lesbos? Mitylene? (Map No. 2.)

292. The hostile fleets met, and a bloody action ensued. Callicratidas, in attempting to break the Athenian line, was precipitated into the sea, and drowned. The Spartans soon after fled. The Athenian generals brought up their galleys alongside of each other, and held a council of war. It was decided to leave Theramenes with forty ships, to collect the dead for burial and the wounded from the wrecks; while they proceeded, as was first intended, to liberate Conon. But neither of these plans was carried into effect. A violent storm came on, which compelled all to seek shelter, and thus the unfortunate crews of the disabled ships were left to perish.

293. Reward of the Victors of Arginusæ.—This sudden turn of affairs might have retrieved the fallen fortunes of Athens, had she not been equally incapable of bearing defeat with fortitude, or success with composure. Hence this splendid victory was followed by one of the most extraordinary, most disgraceful, and most fatal strokes of faction recorded in history. Of the eight generals who commanded at Arginusæ, six went home, dreaming, perhaps, of garlands and crowns which the grateful populace would bestow upon them; but scarcely had they arrived, when they were taken into safe custody till they could give an account of their transactions. When the assembly of the people met, Theramenes came forward and accused the prisoners of neglecting to save the lives of the wounded, after the battle.

294. The generals were scarcely permitted to speak a word in their own defense. They were hurried through a mockery of a trial, and condemned to death. Socrates, who was that day the presiding officer of the Senate of Five Hundred, unintimidated by the clamors of the people, inveighed against the sentence, as illegal and unjust; the voice of the majority, however, prevailed, and they were led off to execution! Many followed them with tears to the place of death, and felt in that melancholy hour the weight of guilt which had fallen upon their country.

295. Battle of Ægos Potamos.—The Spartans, ignorant of the steps Athens had thus taken to accelerate her own downfall, were greatly troubled by the defeat at Arginusæ, and the death of Callicratidas. There was not a man that could relieve their embarrassments like Lysander; and the law forbade his re-election to the same office. To evade this regulation, they sent out another admiral, with Lysander for lieutenant. On reaching his station, Lysander immediately waited

Questions.—292. Give an account of the battle of Arginusæ. What did the Athenian generals then do? 293, 294. How were the victors rewarded? Who tried to save them 295. How did the Spartans evade a certain regulation? What measures did Lysander promptly take? Where was the battle of Arginusæ fought? (Map No. 2.)

upon Cyrus and obtained supplies, which enabled him to pay up all arrears, and proceed with his arrangements for opening the campaign in the spring, with a fleet equal to that of Athens. Soon after the vernal equinox he moved from Ephesus to Abydos, and thence to Lampsacus,* where he anchored his fleet.

296. Conon, hearing that Lysander had gone to the Hellespont, pursued him with all speed, trembling for the important cities in that region. He stopped at Sestos for refreshment, and that night landed at Ægos Potamos, or Goat's River. As the strait there was only about two miles wide, the arrival of the Athenians was instantly known to Lysander, and he took his measures accordingly. By daybreak next morning his galleys were ranged in order of battle. The Athenians, equally prompt, rowed out to meet them; but the Lacedemonians rested upon their oars, and gazed upon them in stern silence. These movements were repeated three days in succession.

297. From the top of his castle Alcibiades could see the manœuvers of the two fleets, and he was shrewd enough to guess at the purpose of Lysander. In the hour of her danger, his love for his country revived; and though at the peril of his life, he went to the Athenian camp and told the commanders, that, as Ægos Potamos contained no harbor, and they were obliged to go every day two miles to market, it would be better to move the fleet down to Sestos, and await the attack of Lysander there. This advice, so politic and so seasonable, was treated with contempt; and one of the generals was so insolent as to bid him begone, for that they, and not he, were now to give orders. Alcibiades told his friends who conducted him out of the camp, that if he had not been insulted by the generals he would have soon brought the Lacedemonians to battle by attacking them with his Thracian archers.

298. It was not long before the wisdom of his counsels was seen, for on the fifth day Lysander moved across the strait with his whole fleet. Conon alone, of all the Athenian generals, was in any state of preparation. When he saw the enemy in motion, he sounded the call to arms; but the soldiers and seamen were too far away to hear it, and the Peloponnesians were upon them before they were ready for action. Conon's trireme, with seven others of his division, and the

* A city on the southern shore of the Hellespont, where Themistocles died.

Questions.—296. What pursuit took place? Where did Conon make a landing? Give an account of the events of the three days. 297. By what act did Alcibiades manifest his love for his country? How was his advice treated? 298. Give an account of the battle of Ægos Potamos? What did Conon do after the battle? Where was Ægos Potamos? (Map No. 2.)

sacred ship Paralus, having their crews aboard, put off from the shore. All the rest were seized at anchor. Finding he could effect nothing, Conon fled while the enemy were intent upon the capture, and, having cleared the mouth of the Hellespont, hoisted all sail. Afraid to go home with the evil tidings, he sent an account of the affair by the Paralus, and directed his course to Cyprus, where Evagoras kindly received him.

299. CONSEQUENCES OF THE BATTLE OF ÆGOS POTAMOS.—Lysander, having taken possession of the Athenian ships to the number of one hundred and seventy, began the pursuit of the scattered troops. The greater part of them, together with all the generals, were made prisoners. They were carried to Lampsacus, where a council of war decided that *every Athenian citizen among them should be put to death;* and Lysander commenced the work by slaying one of the commanders with his own hand. The Athenian marine being thus entirely destroyed, Lysander had only to sail around the Egean, and take possession of the islands and towns upon the coast. As soon as he appeared in the strait between Byzantium and Chalcedon, messengers came to him from those places with terms of surrender. He sent every Athenian directly home, that the city, having many mouths to feed, might be the sooner reduced by famine.

300. The Paralus, meantime, protected by its sacred character, had reached its destination, with that intelligence which no other ship had dared to convey. In the words of another, "Alarm and lamentation, beginning immediately about the harbor, were rapidly communicated through the town of Piræus, and then, passing from mouth to mouth by the long walls up to the city, the consternation became universal, and that night no person slept in Athens." Grief for the numerous slain, the flower of Athenian youth, among whom every one had some relative or friend, was not all. They feared for themselves; they had abused the day of power, and they trembled at the approach of the day of retribution. Athens was not yet without men capable of guiding her through any ordinary difficulty, but she was now in a strait from which there was no egress.

301. On one side howled the waves of faction, decreeing death to the proposer of an unsuccessful measure; on the other frowned the power of Lacedemon, stern and immovable as the pillars of Hercules. None knew what course to take; the orators dared not advise; the

---

Questions.—299. What became of the captured Athenians? What then did Lysander do? 300. What news did the Paralus take to Attica? How did the news affect the Athenians? 301. What strait was Athens then in?

democracy dared not decree; the aristocracy dared not command. To raise another fleet would be impossible; to venture a battle with the Spartans by land would be madness; and, exhausted by the efforts of despair, all ranks sullenly prepared to sustain a siege, both by sea and land. Lysander, having cruised leisurely along the Hellespont, and received the submission of the cities, sent off a part of his fleet to secure the islands, and dispatched a messenger to the Spartans, telling them that he was ready to sail to the Piræus with two hundred triremes.

302. SIEGE OF ATHENS.—No sooner was this intelligence received, than the Peloponnesians summoned their allies to assist in putting a final period to a war, which had lasted, with little intermission, twenty-six years. All the states except Argos sent out their troops; the whole force of Laconia was mustered for the important occasion. Effecting a union upon the borders of Attica, they marched fearlessly up to the walls of Athens, and fixed their head-quarters in "Academus's sacred shade." Lysander arrived at the appointed time, and cast anchor in the harbor, and thus all supplies were cut off from the devoted city. No assault was attempted; famine did its work with fearful certainty; and the Lacedemonians looked on with perfect composure while their long-hated rival wasted away.

303. Yet it was not till many had died of hunger that any even proposed to capitulate; and then it was three long and weary months before the terms were fixed upon. The Corinthian and Theban allies, indeed, contended that no terms should be granted; they said that the people ought to be sold into slavery, and the site of the city made a sheep-walk, like the Cirrhæan plain. The Spartans, more merciful, settled the following conditions: "That all ships of war should be surrendered, except twelve; that the long walls and the fortifications of the Piræus should be destroyed; that all the exiles should be restored to the rights of the city; that the Athenians should hold for friends or enemies all other people, as they were friends or enemies of Lacedemon; and that the Athenian forces should go wherever Lacedemon might command, by land or sea."

304. When these proposals were received, food had become so scarce that it was impossible to hold out many days; yet it was not without much debate that the vote was gained to accept the conditions. The Spartan king, Agis, and Lysander, with their troops, then

---

Questions.—301. What movements did Lysander make? 302. How long had the war lasted? What united efforts were made to bring it to a close? How was Athens proceeded against? 303. What conditions were the Athenians finally compelled to submit to?

began the demolition of those walls which had so long made Athens impregnable. A band of musicians was employed, to animate them in the work of destruction by the sound of their instruments; while the confederates, crowned with flowers, danced for joy, and hailed the day as the first of their liberty.

305.—B. C. 404.—The Spartans next proceeded to give laws to Athens. Notices were sent to the exiles and fugitives to return and take possession of their estates. The assembly of the people was abolished, and the supreme authority committed to a council of thirty, among whom was that Theramenes who procured the death of the six generals. Affairs being thus settled, Agis led away his forces, and Lysander sailed to Samos, conquered the island, and banished all who resisted his power. Having secured the Egean, he dismissed the ships of the allies, and, with his Lacedemonian squadron, returned home. "So ended the Peloponnesian war, in its twenty-seventh year; and so Lacedemon, now in alliance with Persia, became again the leading power of Greece; and the aristocracy triumphed over the democracy in almost every commonwealth of the nation."

306. THE THIRTY TYRANTS.—Though the Spartans would not, as they said, "be guilty of putting out one of the eyes of Greece," by the entire destruction of Athens, yet, wishing to destroy entirely her political importance, they chose men for her tyrants who had nothing to recommend them but a hatred of democracy. These men, instead of giving to the republic a more perfect body of laws, merely chose 3,000 citizens to confirm their decrees, and help them bear the odium which repeated executions brought upon them. The chairman of the Thirty was Critias, a man who, having been banished, had resided for some time at Sparta, where he published a treatise upon the institutions and laws of that country, which probably recommended him to Lysander. This man determined to be lord of Athens. The others became passive subjects of his will; the 3,000 sanctioned his acts; and the whole city was soon filled with fines, imprisonments, confiscations, and executions.

307. Fearing, however, the revenge their tyranny was calculated to excite, the Thirty obtained a guard from Sparta, and by their assistance put to death all who opposed them. But though Athens was thus fallen and enslaved, she still retained the empire of mind. So-

Questions.—304, 305. How were the conditions carried out? What then did Agis and Lysander do? In what year did the war close? By what name is the war known? What position did Lacedemon then hold? What is said of the aristocracy? 306. What is said of the Thirty Tyrants? Of Critias? 307. What fears had the *Thirty*? How did they quiet their fears? What did Athens still retain?

crates, Xenophon, and Plato still resided within her dismantled walls; Alcibiades, Thrasybulus, and Conon, though in exile, possessed such abilities as few men could boast; and amid all their misery, the people flattered themselves that while *they* lived Athens could not be wholly undone. Their hopes were disappointed in Alcibiades, but more than realized in Thrasybulus and Conon.

308. The Tyrants also feared Alcibiades, and sought his ruin. When the Lacedemonians gained the empire of the sea, he left his home in the Chersonesus and took refuge in Bithynia; intending, like Themistocles, to visit the Persian court, and gain that protection from a foreign power which his own country could not afford him. He was residing in a small village in Phrygia when Lysander, having received a scytale from Sparta to get Alcibiades dispatched, sent to desire Pharnabazus to put the decree in force. The persons intrusted with the execution of this dastardly order surrounded the house of the illustrious Athenian, and set it on fire. Alcibiades forced his way through the flames and drove back the barbarians, who, retreating to a distance, overwhelmed him with a shower of darts and stones. He sunk down under a multitude of wounds, and expired. Timandra, his mistress, took up his body, dressed it in the finest robes she had, and performed over it those ceremonies necessary to secure the soul an entrance into the kingdom of Pluto.

309. Successful so far, the Thirty proceeded to still greater lengths in wickedness. To support their riotous expenses, and pay their Spartan guard, they concluded to select every one his man; accuse him of some crime; cause him to be put to death; and seize upon his estate. Theramenes was struck with horror at this proposal. He inveighed against it in the strongest terms, but he only brought destruction upon himself. Critias denounced him, and, by bringing his guards with drawn swords about the place of trial, awed the judges into a sentence of condemnation. He sprang to the altar, and claimed protection from its sanctity; but the Thirty had lost all fear of the crime of sacrilege; he was dragged to prison, and compelled to drink the hemlock; a fate which would have commanded more of our commiseration, had he not himself brought about a similar tragedy in the case of the victors at Arginusæ.

310. Thrasybulus.—Meanwhile, Thrasybulus, who had been living

Questions.—307. In whom? What hopes did the Athenians still have? In whom were the hopes disappointed? In whom realized? 308. Give an account of the death of Alcibiades. What ceremony did Timandra perform? 309. What wickedness did the *Thirty* next plan? Give an account of the death of Theramenes. 310. Where had Thrasybulus been living in the mean time?

at Thebes, felt the miseries of his country, and longed to relieve them. He conversed with those who fled thither from Athens, and gradually collected a party of followers, not formidable indeed from their numbers, but all determined in the cause of freedom. Without exciting the suspicions of the Thirty, he made the necessary arrangements, and with his little band seized on the strong fortress of Phyle, about twelve miles from Athens. The Thirty, their guard, and the assistant 3,000 marched out to dispossess them, and sat down before the town in the form of a regular siege; but a great snow-storm coming on, they were obliged to march back to the city. Thrasybulus, being re-enforced by other citizens, pursued his course, and took possession of Piræus. The Thirty, and all the followers they could muster, attacked them there, but were defeated, and Critias was slain. As the rest were flying, Thrasybulus cried out, "Wherefore do you fly from me as a victor, rather than assist me as the avenger of your liberty? We are not enemies, but fellow-citizens; neither have we declared against the city, but against the Thirty Tyrants."

311. The attacking army listened and were convinced. Thrasybulus, at the head of his associates, and the volunteers who came over to his side, marched into the city in triumph, expelled the Thirty, and appointed ten magistrates in their room. The Tyrants met the death they so richly merited, and Athens resumed her ancient laws. The Spartans ratified the acts of Thrasybulus;* a general amnesty was proclaimed: it was decreed that all past actions should be buried in oblivion; and as these things took place in the archonship of the Euclides, all events beyond the time of legal memory were said to be "Before Euclides." The laws of Solon were transcribed and put in force, and quiet once more reigned in the city.

312. DEATH OF SOCRATES.—At this time, when the greatest zeal was professed for the revival of the ancient institutions, all who had uttered any thing against the old laws and usages of the state were looked upon as dangerous persons. In this number was found the wise and virtuous Socrates.† Amid the darkness of paganism he had

* Pausanias, the king, secretly favored Thrasybulus, and obtained peace for Athens.

† Socrates, the son of a statuary, was born B. C. 470. He was exceedingly homely, and very ungraceful in his manners; and being deprived of his little property by the dishonesty of a relation, his prospects for rising in the world were very small; but a wealthy Athenian, observing his love of study and wonderful abilities, took him into his house, and gave him the care of his children. Here he had the privilege of attending the lectures of the most

Questions.—310. Upon what did he determine? What was his first successful step? Give an account of the attack upon him. 311. Who restored liberty to Athens? What followed? 312. For what was great zeal in Athens professed at that time? In what number was Socrates included?

attained the idea of ONE SUPREME BEING, whom he acknowledged as the framer and preserver of the universe; and he consequently treated many of the superstitions of the times with contempt. Having also been eye-witness to the inconstant, uncertain, and even *cruel* government of the democracy, he had expressed some aristocratic sentiments; and having been the tutor of Alcibiades and Critias, their follies and vices were in some measure imputed to him.

313. These circumstances constituted "the head and front of his offending;" but as the Athenians had been too much engaged with other affairs to do more than to listen to the ridicule which the comic poets heaped upon him, no notice had been taken of his atheism; now, when the revolution of Thrasybulus had placed them again at ease, it seems to us quite natural that they should seal the dark scroll of a century, peculiar for instances of ingratitude, with the blood of the purest and wisest of their citizens.

314. Instigated by the rhetoricians and sophists, whom Socrates had irritated by his cutting sarcasms, a young man went to the king-archon, and impeached him in the following form: "Melitus, son of Melitus, declares these upon oath, against Socrates, son of Sophroniscus. Socrates is guilty of reviling the gods whom the city acknowledges; and of preaching other new gods; moreover, he is guilty of corrupting the youth of Athens. Penalty,—death." Before the case was tried, one of his friends composed a speech, and brought it to Socrates for his defense; but he refused to use it, or to resort to any of those methods by which criminals are accustomed to move the hearts of their judges to mercy. He looked upon death with pleasure,

eminent philosophers; and applied himself to the study of nature, with a diligence that made him "wiser than all his teachers." He served the regular term in the militia, and signalized himself at the siege of Potidæa, both by his valor and the hardihood with which he endured fatigue. But though he did not refuse his country's call to the field, he had no taste for the excitements of a military life. He loved better to walk through the Academia, attended by the youth of Athens, giving instruction by asking such questions as exposed the absurdities of error. Indeed, he looked upon the whole city as his school, and neglected no occasion of communicating moral wisdom to his fellow-citizens. It was his custom, in the morning, to visit those places set apart for gymnastic exercises; at noon, to mingle with the crowds in the market-places; and to spend the rest of the day where he could instruct the greatest number of persons. *In the evening, he generally took a lecture from his wife.* This woman, whose name was Xantippe, exercised her tongue upon the failings of the patient philosopher without any mercy. Sometimes she would become so enraged as to tear his cloak upon his shoulders in the open street. Socrates, instead of attempting to control her temper, consoled himself with the idea that if he could bear *her* insults. no other circumstance would have power to annoy him. While he was in prison, his friends came to see him and enjoy his conversation. One of them lamenting that he should die innocent,—" What," said Socrates, " would you have me die guilty?"

Questions.—312. What is said of the religious views of Socrates? Of his political views? 313. Why had not the Athenians taken notice of the offenses of Socrates before? 314. What formal charge was brought against Socrates? What refusal did he make? How did he look upon death?

as a relief from the joyless period of old age. He however declared his innocence in the strongest terms, and contended that he deserved rewards and honors, rather than the punishment of the malefactor.

315. After his condemnation, he addressed his judges in a speech of some length, and in conclusion said: "But it is time for me to depart—I to die, you to live; but which for the greater good, God only knows." It was customary to execute on the day following trial, but as the sacred galley had just been crowned and sent to Delos, it was not lawful to put any one to death till its return. Thus for thirty days Socrates lived in the prison, conversing freely with his friends, and unfolding his doctrines with the greatest force and power. When the fatal cup was brought to him, he took it with a serene air, and drank its contents with the most perfect composure. He walked about till he felt the poison begin to work, and then lay down and expired, B. C. 400. He was seventy years of age.

316. B. C. **400.**—RETREAT OF THE TEN THOUSAND.—In the first year of the former century, Cyrus betrayed the secret of the favor with which he had treated the Lacedemonians. Looking upon them as the bravest soldiers of Greece, he had sought to attach them to his person, that they might assist him in a revolt against his brother, Artaxerxes Mnemon. The Grecians who were led by him in this enterprise to the plains of the Euphrates, consisted of a body of Spartans under Clearchus, a body of Athenians under Proxenus, and volunteers from the other states, amounting in all to thirteen thousand men. Cyrus having been slain in the battle of Cunaxa, the Greeks were left without a leader or guide in a strange land.

317. By the chances of war, the length of the way, and the inclemencies of the season, they had lost three thousand of their number; but in the beginning of this century, the famous Ten Thousand reached Byzantium in safety. Opinions were then divided as to what course it was best to pursue. Some proposed to seize upon several cities of the Chersonesus, and plant a colony there; others were for returning directly home. The states which owned the adventurers were little pleased with the prospect of being visited by ten thousand armed men, who had subsisted by plunder more than a year; they began,

---

Questions.—314. What did he declare? What claim? 315. Give an account of his death. In what year did he die? How old was he then? 316. How did Cyrus regard the Lacedemonians? What did he seek as regards them? How large an army of Grecians did Cyrus lead to the plains of the Euphrates? Of whom were they composed? How came the Greeks to be left without a leader? 317. How many of the thirteen thousand reached Byzantium? What had become of the others? Upon what were opinions divided? What prospect did not please certain states?

therefore, to plan a war which should engage the attention of the returning soldiers. The Ionian colonies of Asia Minor, having contributed money and men to the unfortunate expedition of Cyrus, began now to fear the vengeance of their king, whose satrap, Tissaphernes, had returned, clothed with new powers, to Sardis.

318. Messengers from the Ionians arrived in Lacedemon, imploring protection, just about the time that the Spartans were inquiring where a war could be kindled to the best advantage. It was immediately determined to grant the required aid, and the forces sent out from home were directed to enlist the forces just returning from the east. Xenophon, with a body of six thousand, accordingly entered the army of Agesilaus, and from his pen we have an account of those exploits of the Spartans, which made the monarch tremble in his distant capital at Susa. Convinced by the victories of Marathon, Thermopylæ, Salamis, and Platea, of the immense superiority of the Grecian soldiers over the common hirelings of the day; and now stimulated by the glorious "retreat of the Ten Thousand," Agesilaus formed the bold and grand design of dismembering the Persian Empire, and giving to each satrapy its freedom, as freedom was understood among the Greeks.

319. Agesilaus.—The good old king, Archidamus, who led the confederates in the beginning of the Peloponnesian war, at his death left two sons, Agis, who succeeded him, and Agesilaus, who was at that time quite young. As the crown belonged in the family of Agis, Agesilaus had nothing before him but a private station, and therefore was educated according to the institutions of Lycurgus; but he always showed such an ambition to excel, and at the same time such a sense of honor and justice, as made him the peculiar favorite of his companions. When his brother refused to acknowledge Leotychidas, considering him the son of Alcibiades, Agesilaus began to entertain hopes of the crown; and no sooner was Agis dead, than Lysander, by various intrigues, raised him to the throne of Sparta. This being accomplished about the time that the Ionian colonies sent to Sparta for assistance, Lysander persuaded Agesilaus to undertake the affair, and went himself in the capacity of counselor.

320. The Campaigns of B. C. 396, 395, and 394.—When Agesilaus

Questions.—317. What is said of certain Ionian colonies? 318. What request did the Ionians make? How was the request met? Who formed the plan of dismembering the Persian empire? What circumstances gave rise to the project? 319. How was Agesilaus educated? What is said of his character? By what circumstances was he made king of Sparta? What events took place about that time? To what was Agesilaus persuaded? Who persuaded him? In what capacity did Lysander go? Who commanded the expedition?

arrived at Ephesus, Tissaphernes sent to inquire what induced him to take up arms in Asia. Agesilaus replied, that he had come to aid the Greeks established there, and to restore to them their ancient liberty. The satrap assured him that his master would give the Greek cities their freedom; and finally engaged him to enter into a truce, while couriers could go to Susa and return with the commands of the great king himself. Agesilaus spent this interval in making suitable regulations, and learning the exact force of the cities; but Tissaphernes, false as ever, privately assembled troops on all sides. Having every thing prepared, he sent heralds to Agesilaus, commanding him to withdraw immediately from Asia, and declaring war against him in case of refusal. To be revenged upon Tissaphernes, Agesilaus gave out that he was going to plunder the province of Caria, but, when the barbarians were drawn to that quarter, he turned suddenly into Phrygia, took many cities, and enriched himself with immense spoil.

321.—B. C. 395.—The next spring, he intimated that he should visit Lydia. The satrap did not believe him; and Agesilaus had established himself upon the plains of Sardis before Tissaphernes could get there with his forces, and when the armies met, the Greeks routed the barbarians with great slaughter. This campaign finished the race of Tissaphernes. The treacherous satrap, who had deceived the Spartans and the Athenians; who had acted the part of informer twice by young Cyrus, and stained his hands with the blood of the Grecian generals; now, being thought guilty of treason to his sovereign, was beheaded.

322. From Lydia, Agesilaus marched into the province of Pharnabazus, where he pitched his camp, and not only lived in plenty, but collected large subsidies. Pharnabazus, instead of attempting to drive him away, collected his furniture, and moved about from place to place. At last, becoming wearied with this manner of life, he sent to desire a conference with his enemy. Agesilaus assented, and coming first to the place appointed with his friends, sat down upon the long grass in the shade. The Persian grandee came up, and his servants, as their custom was, began to spread soft skins for him to recline upon, but he had the grace to be ashamed of this luxury, and carelessly threw himself upon the ground beside the Spartan.

323. He opened the negotiation by complaining of the Spartans for

---

Questions.—320. When he arrived at Ephesus, what question was put to him? What was his reply? Of what treachery was Tissaphernes guilty? How did Agesilaus extricate himself? Where was Phrygia? (See map No. 2.) 321. In what year did Agesilaus gain a victory on the plains of Sardis? Give an account of the battle. Give a closing account of Tissaphernes. 322, 323. What is stated of Agesilaus and Pharnabazus?

ravaging his country, when he had always been their friend, and had assisted them so much against the Athenians. Agesilaus was a little embarrassed by this just rebuke, but excused himself by inviting Pharnabazus to join the league against the king; telling him that from the moment he threw off his vassalage, the Grecian arms, ships, and battalions should become the guardians of his liberty. Pharnabazus replied, "If the king sends another lieutenant in my room, I will be with you; but while he continues me in the government, I will to the best of my power repel force with force, and make reprisals upon you for him." Agesilaus, charmed with this reply, took his hand, and parted with him in the most friendly manner.

324. All Asia was now ready to revolt from the Persians. Agesilaus settled the police of the cities, and brought them into excellent order, without banishing or putting to death a single subject. Encouraged by the success which had crowned his efforts, he determined to remove the seat of war from the coasts of the Egean to the heart of Persia, that the king might be called upon to fight for Ecbatana and Susa instead of sitting there at his ease, and hiring the states of Greece to destroy each other. In the midst of these splendid schemes, a messenger came to him from Greece, to tell him that Sparta was involved in a war with the other states, and that the Ephori had sent him orders to come home and defend his own country. To explain the reasons of this command, which stopped the conquests of Agesilaus, and left Asia unconquered for Alexander, it will be necessary to examine the position of the different republics after the fall of Athens.

325. SPARTA AND THEBES.—When the Peloponnesian war closed, the Spartans considered themselves undisputed masters of Greece. Those states, however, that had been so anxious to exchange the supremacy of Athens for that of Lacedemon, found they were no great gainers by the bargain. Spartan pride was quite as intolerable as Athenian arrogance. Corinth, in particular, who had felt herself a very important character during the war, disliked to assume the position of an humble ally; and Thebes also, having gradually risen to eminence, began to aim at independence. The result was, Corinth, Thebes, Athens, and several other cities entered into a league against Sparta. Instead of allowing, as formerly, supremacy to one republic, the new confederates formed a congress, composed of deputies from the different states, who should be empowered to regulate the affairs

Questions.—324. Upon what change did Agesilaus then determine? How were his schemes frustrated? 325. Give some account of the internal commotions of Greece. What league was formed against Sparta? What is said of it as regards its congress?

of the Greek nation. This league was devised and carried into effect by orators whom Tithraustes, successor to Tissaphernes, had hired* to excite a war in Greece, thinking that such an event would occasion the recall of Agesilaus.

326. The Spartans sent an army into Beotia under Pausanias, and directed Lysander to draw down with his forces from the Hellespont. He did so, but, failing to effect a junction with his king, he was defeated and slain. Pausanias, not thinking it prudent to hazard another engagement, merely begged a truce to perform the funeral rites of the slain. The Ephori cited him to give an account of his measures, but, fearing punishment for his unskillful conduct, he fled to another city. In this embarrassing position of their affairs, the Spartans were compelled to send for Agesilaus from Asia, at the very time when he seemed likely to humble the Persian empire in the dust. Unwelcome as was this call to Agesilaus, still he hesitated not to obey it. Hastily arranging his affairs, in such a manner that they might be in readiness for his return, he marched to the Hellespont, crossed Thrace and Macedonia, and entered Thessaly by nearly the same route that Xerxes had traveled about a century before.

327. As he was passing through this country, he heard that a great battle had been fought near Corinth, in which the Spartans were victorious; but instead of being elated by the intelligence, he exclaimed, with a deep sigh, "Unhappy Greece! why hast thou destroyed with thy own hands so many brave men, who, had they lived, might have conquered all the barbarians in the world." Having passed the straits of Thermopylæ, and traversed Phocis, he entered Beotia, and encamped upon the plains of Cheronæa. Here the army of the allies met him, and a battle was fought which Xenophon says was the most furious one of his time. Agesilaus was pierced through his armor with spears and swords in many places. He was, however, victorious. Though much weakened by his wounds, he would not retire to his tent till he had been carried through all his battalions, and seen the dead borne off upon their shields. This splendid victory, however, could not relieve his mind from the anxiety occasioned by the distressing intelligence which he received a few days before the battle.

* He hired them with 30,000 pieces of money impressed with the figure of an archer; which gave Agesilaus occasion to say, "that 30,000 of the king's *archers* drove him out of Asia."

Questions.—325. By whom was it devised and carried into effect? 326. What befell Lysander? What is said of Pausanias? Now state why Agesilaus was recalled to Greece. What route did he take to Greece? 327. When in Thessaly, what news did he hear? How did it affect him? Mention the particulars of the battle of Cheronæa. Where was Cheronæa? (See map No. 2.)

328. Conon defeats the Spartans at Sea.—That Conon who fled with nine ships from the disastrous action at Ægos Potamos, had not been unmindful of his country in her fallen state. When Evagoras first received him, Conon entered readily into his service, doing all in his power to improve the Cyprian fleet; and no sooner had Agesilaus left Asia, than he brought about an alliance between his friend and Pharnabazus. He even visited the court of Artaxerxes, and convinced that monarch of his own ability to drive the Spartans out of the Egean, if he had but a fleet. Thus, before Agesilaus had reached Beotia, Conon, Evagoras, and Pharnabazus were furnished with ships, money, and men, to revenge the injuries of their several countries upon the Spartans. Agesilaus had left the Spartan fleet under the command of his brother-in-law, a brave but inexperienced officer. Conon, with his confederates, attacked, defeated, and slew him, and took fifty ships. This was the news which reached Agesilaus in Beotia, and destroyed at once the hopes he had formed of subverting the Persian Empire. Though victorious in every engagement on his route from Beotia to Sparta, he could not escape the painful reflection that his parent state had already lost the command of the sea, and that the armies which should have conquered her most distant foes were only able to protect her at home.

329. Two Expeditions.—Athens Rebuilt.—The next spring, Conon and Pharnabazus undertook the work of revolution, and from the shore of Ionia to the oft-conquered Melos, every island threw off the yoke of Sparta. Thence proceeding to the coast of Laconia, they effected a landing in various places, plundered and ravaged the country, and sailed away before the inhabitants had time to rally in self-defense. They took the island of Cythera, and placed it under an Athenian garrison. Then directing their course to the Corinthian isthmus, where the congress of the confederacy was assembled, they visited the leading men, concerted measures with them for prosecuting the war with Sparta, and, having furnished them with a sum of money, sailed again for Asia.

330. Encouraged by the joy of Pharnabazus at this successful expedition, Conon now revealed the design he had meditated from the beginning. He represented the expense and inconvenience to Persia of maintaining the fleet, and he proposed that the satrap should transfer this burden to Athens, after having first put her in a situation to

Questions.—328. How had Conon been employed meantime? What news reached Agesilaus in Beotia? What hopes did the news destroy? What reflection was painful to Agesilaus? 329. What did Conon and Pharnabazus accomplish? 330. What design did Conon reveal?

exact tribute from the islands as formerly, and secured her against the attacks of Lacedemon. The liberality of Pharnabazus granted all that Conon desired. He permitted him to re-establish *Athenian* supremacy in the Egean, and to rebuild his native city.

331. Thus the unfortunate commander at Ægos Potamos, after thirteen years' voluntary exile, returned with the present of a fleet, fortifications, money, timber, masons, mechanics, and dominion in his hand, to restore his ruined country. The states of the confederacy lent their aid to the city which they had formerly hated and humbled: every person wrought with diligence, and Athens soon "rose like a Phœnix from her ashes." The *long walls* which Lysander had demolished, with insulting triumphs of music, were rebuilt; and the city looked again from the harbor of Piræus over a sea of which she was undisputed queen. B. C. 393.

332. Death of Thrasybulus.—Thrasybulus was honored with the command of the new fleet which Athens had thus most unexpectedly received. He sailed first to the Hellespont to re-establish Athenian dominion, and, having fortified the several towns upon the Thracian coast, proceeded to Byzantium, where he restored the collection of toll from the trade of the Euxine. He had similar success at Chalcedon, and, moving thence to Lesbos, reconquered the island, and passed the winter there in a safe and commodious harbor. In the spring he coasted along among the islands and maritime towns till he came to the river Eurymedon, the scene of the double victory of Cimon, to demand tribute of the Aspendians. They paid the tax, for they were unable to make effectual resistance; but, exasperated by some excesses of the soldiers, they attacked the Athenian camp by night, and killed Thrasybulus in his tent. Such was the end of Thrasybulus, a man of the highest estimation, and worthy to rank with Aristides and Cimon.

333. The Peace of Antalcidas.—Meantime the Lacedemonians, humbled and distressed, turned their thoughts to a reconciliation with Persia. For this purpose they sent Antalcidas, a man who had lived long in Asia Minor, to Tiribazus, satrap of Sardis, with proposals of peace; and also directed him to state that Conon had defrauded the great king of the money given him to rebuild Athens; and that he had formed the design of driving the Persians out of Eolia and Ionia. The other states of Greece, hearing of the negotiation contemplated by Sparta, sent each a deputy to secure an equitable adjustment of

Questions.—330. How did Pharnabazus respond? 331 How long had Conon been in exile? With what did he return to Athens? Who rebuilt Athens? 332. Who commanded the new fleet? What did he accomplish? What became of Thrasybulus? 333. What stratagems were used to effect the peace of Antalcidas?

affairs. Conon was the minister from Athens, but no sooner had he arrived than Tiribazus, regardless of his sacred character, threw him into prison. The other embassadors objected to every article in the proposed treaty, and were consequently dismissed without having effected any thing, while the crafty satrap, having secured the only man he feared, visited Susa to learn the pleasure of the great king. Conon, in the absence of his only friend,* pined to death in prison, or was privately executed.

334. Thus deprived of her generals, Athens was not averse to peace; and when Tiribazus, upon his return, summoned a congress of deputies from all the belligerent states, her ministers were sent with the others to listen to proposals for a general pacification. The congress being duly opened, Tiribazus produced a writing sealed with the king's signet, and read the arbitration, or rather the command, of the Persian monarch, in the following words:—"Artaxerxes the king holds it just, That all cities on the continent of Asia belong to his dominion, together with the islands of Clazomenæ and Cyprus; and that all other Grecian cities, little and great, be independent, except that the islands of Lemnos, Imbros, and Sciros remain as of old, under the dominion of Athens. If any refuse these terms, *against* such I will join in war *with* those who accept them, and give my assistance, by land and by sea, with ships and with money."

335. These terms, which destroyed at once all the schemes of conquest which Agesilaus had formed, which wrested from Athens her most valuable dependencies, and gave to Persia almost all she had ever claimed, were acceded to, either willingly or unwillingly, by all the states. Thus peace was established throughout Greece and Asia Minor, the fleets were laid up, or employed in friendly commerce, the soldiers were dismissed to their homes, and "the land had rest from war."

336. OLYNTHIAN WAR.—The universal quiet which reigned for some time after the ratification of this treaty, was interrupted by the arrival of persons at Lacedemon, who came to complain that Olynthus, having engaged most of the towns of the Chalcidice in a confederacy, had nearly expelled Amyntas, king of Macedon, from his government. Ministers had passed between Olynthus, and Athens, and Thebes; and the complainants represented to the Spartans that a powerful coalition

* Pharnabazus, who, having married the king's daughter, had removed to Susa.

Questions.—333. What became of Conon? 334. Why was not Athens averse to peace? What was done by Tiribazus? What terms did the Persian monarch dictate? 335. What is said of the terms? Was the peace honorable to any Grecian state? 336. Where was Olynthus? (See map No. 2.) What complaint was made against Olynthus?

was forming in that quarter, which would overthrow the supremacy of Lacedemon, and destroy the liberties of Greece. A congress of the Peloponnesian allies was immediately summoned; the subject laid before them in all its political bearings; and a resolution taken to send ten thousand men into Macedonia. Such forces as could readily be collected, set out immediately. They lost no time in traversing the frequented route through Corinth, Megara, Beotia, and Thessaly; and as Potidæa gladly opened its gates to them, they found comfortable quarters to await the other troops.

337. THEBES SEIZED BY PHŒBIDAS.—The remaining division was sent off under the command of Phœbidas, who, quitting the line of his instructions, set on fire a train of evils which kindled another Peloponnesian war, and destroyed forever the supremacy of Lacedemon. In his march northward, he encamped for the night under the walls of Thebes. The leader of the aristocratic party in the city found his way to the tent of Phœbidas, and invited him to enter the city, seize the Cadmeia,* and change the government. This temptation was too strong for the virtue of the Spartan. He entered the town by night, and took possession by force of arms. The leaders of the democratic party were thrown into prison, many of the citizens fled to different places, and a band of about four hundred found refuge in Athens.

338. When an account of this affair was carried to Sparta, the ephors fined Phœbidas for turning aside from his duty; but they sent Archias to govern Thebes, and appointed officers as they would for a conquered city. The war in Olynthus still went on with various success. No permanent advantage was gained till Agesipolis, the young colleague of Agesilaus, was sent thither to take the command. He wasted the Olynthian territory; he took Torone by storm; but in the midst of his success he was seized with a fever, which soon terminated his life. His body was preserved in honey, and carried the long and difficult journey to Sparta, to be interred with the usual ceremonies in the tombs of the Spartan kings. Cleombrotus, his brother, succeeded him.

339. But though the Olynthians were thus delivered from their most active foe, they were in extreme distress. In resisting the power of Lacedemon, they had counted on assistance from Beotia and Attica. The unexpected revolution in Thebes had, however, cut off all

* The citadel of Thebes, named from Cadmus.

Questions.—336. What resolution was passed? What route did the forces take? 337. What is said of Phœbidas? How was he tempted? 338. What is said of Agesipolis? By whom was he succeeded? 339. What is said of the condition of the Olynthians?

aid from these sources, and, without losing any decisive battle, they were compelled to surrender, B. C. 379; but the new government of their city was any thing but grateful to the body of the Theban people.

340. THE COUNTER-REVOLUTION IN THEBES.—It happened soon after the surrender of Olynthus, that Phyllidas, the secretary of Archias, was sent to Athens on business. While there, he fell into conversation with a Theban exile, an old friend, and having explained the state of things in his native city, began to deplore the miseries which Spartan treachery had brought upon his fellow-citizens. The conversation resulted in a plot to overthrow the tyranny which Sparta had established in Thebes, and restore again the democratic form of government. It was carried into execution in the following manner: A select band of exiles set out from Athens, and, without exciting suspicion, quartered themselves in a little town not far from Thebes. Pelopidas and Melon, the leaders, then choosing ten associates, dressed themselves like hunters, and beat about the woods with poles and hounds, as if in search of game. About night-fall they entered the city at different gates, where they were met by their accomplices, and conducted to the house of one Charon, a patriot of great wealth and respectability.

341. Phyllidas had performed his part with equal success. He had invited Archias and Philip, with the principal Spartan rulers, to his house, under promise of introducing them to some of the most beautiful women in Thebes. Scarcely, however, had the entertainment commenced, when a rumor reached them that the exiles were concealed somewhere in the city, and they sent immediately for Charon. The conspirators looked upon themselves as lost; but the intrepid Charon obeyed the summons with alacrity. He replied to the questions of the polemarchs in such a manner as entirely lulled their suspicions, and departed with their authority to inquire into the affair. Phyllidas then led his guests back to their wine, when a new danger threw him into the utmost consternation. A horseman, sent from Athens by those who had learned the particulars of the plot, riding in hot haste, came up to the door, and dismounting, forced his way into the banqueting-room. "My lord," said he, out of breath with the speed he had made, "here are letters from a friend of yours, who begs you will read them immediately, being serious affairs."—"Serious

Questions.—339. When did they surrender? How did they like their new government? 340. How was the counter-revolution in Thebes commenced? What plot was formed? How was it carried into execution? 341. How had Phyllidas performed his part? Give the particulars of his movements.

affairs to-morrow," replied Archias, laughing, and thrusting the letters under his pillow.

342. Phyllidas now entered to say that the women were arrived, and the tyrants commanding them to be introduced, Charon and his friends came in, clothed in female attire, and crowned with garlands. The drunken lords received them with shouts of joy; but the pretended women, having each selected his man, drew their swords, and rushed upon them with the greatest fury. They made but a feeble resistance, and the conspirators soon issued from the house in triumph. Messengers were then sent to bring up their fellows left on the way; the prison doors were thrown open, and five hundred Thebans issued from their dungeons to join the ranks of freemen. Criers went up and down the streets, calling upon the people to resume their liberties; and arms were taken from the shops and distributed to all who joined in the cry against Sparta. Epaminondas,* with a few chosen followers, joined the conspirators; the houses were filled with torches; the streets were thronged with a multitude who hardly knew what had happened, or which side to take; and never was there such a night of confusion, anxiety, and hope, in Thebes.

343. The Lacedemonian garrison in the citadel, though one thousand five hundred strong, knew not the limited extent of the conspiracy, but, seeing the tumult, set a guard at all the gates of the Cadmea, and dispatched a messenger to Sparta for assistance. The next day the revolutionists were re-enforced by the arrival of numerous exiles and armed cavalry from Athens. An assembly of the people was summoned, and addressed by Epaminondas, who exhorted all to aid in the restoration of the ancient freedom of their city. His appeal was answered by loud acclamations and clapping of hands; and Pelopidas, Melon, and Charon were unanimously chosen magistrates. The courier arrived at Sparta, and told his news. A band of soldiers was immediately sent off, but did not reach Thebes in time to interrupt the progress of the revolution. The garrison, pressed by famine, had already capitulated; and the city of Cadmus was free. Such was the commencement of the second Peloponnesian war, which ended in the humiliation of Sparta, as the first did in that of Athens.

* An intimate friend of Pelopidas, who delighted in philosophical studies and the practice of every virtue. He was never known to tell a lie, even in jest. When the Spartans seized upon Thebes, Pelopidas fled to Athens; but Epaminondas, being looked upon as a mere philosopher, remained in the city, and did all in his power to inspire the youth with sentiments of bravery.

Questions.—342. Give further particulars. Who was Epaminondas? 343. How strong was the Lacedemonian garrison in the citadel? What precaution did they take? Did they succeed? What war was thus commenced?

344. SECOND PELOPONNESIAN WAR.—It remained now for the Lacedemonian government to punish the rebellion at Thebes, or resign at once the supremacy of Greece. The latter thought was not to be tolerated; the former was therefore resolved upon, and though mid-winter, the army was ordered to march into Beotia. The grand purpose of Agesilaus being to unite the Grecian states in an attack upon the power of Persia, he was extremely averse to this war. The command of the army was consequently committed to Cleombrotus, his brother sovereign.

345. Athens, still unrecovered from the wounds which Sparta had inflicted upon herself, and seeing the great preparations making against Thebes, scarcely knew which side to take. While she continued thus irresolute, Sphodrias, a Spartan general, made an unsuccessful attempt to seize upon the Piræus. This furnished a fine argument for the orators in the Beotian interest. They declared that the Lacedemonians meant to subvert the liberties of the Athenians, as they had done of the Thebans; and such a storm of invective was raised, that all in favor of moderate measures were obliged to hide their heads, while *war*, offensive and defensive, became the popular care. Ships were built, soldiers were levied, and every thing prepared to assist Thebes in the approaching contest. Meanwhile, the Beotian lands were ravaged by the Peloponnesian forces, and Thebes suffered almost famine from the repeated destruction of her harvests.

346. It would require too much space to detail all the petty skirmishes, political intrigues, and short-lived factions, which occurred during the seven years that followed the attack of Sphodrias upon the Piræus. Athens, intimidated by the mighty army which passed through her borders to Beotia, renounced the alliance of Thebes, and assumed as nearly as possible a neutral position. But during all this time the Thebans had been learning the art of war, inuring their bodies to labor, and acquiring both experience and courage in their various encounters with the Spartans. The Sacred Theban Band, or *band of lovers*, consisting of three hundred youths, bound together by the ties of friendship, and all sworn to die side by side rather than fly before an enemy, had been trained by Pelopidas, and inspired with an ardent desire to establish the liberty of their country. Pelopidas, indeed, was never idle. From the day that he was chosen general to the day of his death, he was always engaged in some public employ-

---

Questions.—344. What remained for the Lacedemonian government? Why was Agesilaus averse to the war? To whom was given the command of the army? Why? 345. About what was Athens irresolute? How was a decision at last made? 346. Why was the decision altered? What had the Thebans been about? Who instituted the Sacred Theban Band? What was the Band? What is said of Pelopidas?

ment, either as captain of the Sacred Band, or as governor of Thebes.

347. B. C. 371.—BATTLE OF LEUCTRA.—The Lacedemonians, having made peace with all the other Grecian states, determined to strike a decisive blow in Beotia. Cleombrotus was therefore sent thither, with 10,000 foot and 1,000 horse, and other troops joined them on the way, till his army swelled to 20,000. Epaminondas, who was at that time commander-in-chief of the Theban forces, could bring only 6,000 men into the field; but as universal terror of the Spartans forbade the hope of gaining any allies, he and his friend Pelopidas decided to join battle with their enemies. Having taken their resolution, they strengthened the hopes of their army with all the favorable omens and prognostications they could put in circulation; and thus, strong in the confidence that the fates were propitious, the troops advanced joyfully to Leuctra.

348. Epaminondas, being unable to oppose front to front and man to man in the battle, placed his men in the shape of a wedge, and made his attack directly upon the point where Cleombrotus was stationed. The enemy, perceiving this, began to extend the right wing to surround the Thebans; but Pelopidas coming up just at the moment, with his three hundred invincibles, threw them into disorder, and completely frustrated their design. The consequence was, such a rout and slaughter as never had been known before. Cleombrotus was carried from the field mortally wounded. The Lacedemonians lost 4,000 men, and then fled to their intrenchments. The Thebans had only 300 men killed. They erected a trophy upon the spot, which was esteemed the most glorious and most important ever won in a battle of Greeks with Greeks. When Epaminondas was congratulated upon his most unparalleled victory, he replied, "I think only of the happiness it will give my mother."

349. The news of this defeat reached Sparta while the people were engaged in the celebration of public games. The ephors, to whom the dispatches were delivered, without interrupting the entertainment, communicated the names of the slain to their relatives, but forbade the women to make the clamorous lamentations common on such occasions. Next day the parents of those who had fallen in the battle went to the temples to thank the gods for the glory their sons had acquired, while those whose children still survived were overwhelmed with the deepest affliction. The law also augmented their misery.

Questions.—347. When was the battle of Leuctra fought? How many men did Cleombrotus command? How many Epaminondas? 348. Give an account of the battle. What reply did Epaminondas make to those who congratulated him? 349. How did the Spartans receive the news of this defeat? Where was Leuctra? (See map No. 2.)

Those who fled from the field were to be degraded, so that it would be a disgrace to intermarry with them; they were compelled to wear patched and party-colored mean and dirty garments, to go half shaved, and suffer every insult and abuse. Such numbers had incurred these severe penalties that a public commotion was feared; besides, these soldiers could ill be spared at a time when it was necessary to recruit the army. In this distressing emergency, the whole power was placed in the hands of Agesilaus. He made a decree that the law should lie dormant for one day, and thus the citizens were saved from infamy.

350. Invasion of Peloponnesus.—Nor was it long before Sparta needed all her soldiers to protect her own territory. Numbers of Greek cities, before neutral, made alliance with Thebes, and Epaminondas soon saw himself at the head of 70,000 men. With this overwhelming force he invaded Peloponnesus. It was 700 years since the Dorians established themselves in Laconia, and in all that time their country had never been invaded by a hostile army. Agesilaus had often boasted that "no woman of Sparta had ever seen the smoke of an enemy's camp;" how deep, then, was his mortification when 70,000 men crossed the Eurotas, captured several Lacedemonian towns, and ravaged all the lands to the sea; pitching their tents in whatever spot they chose, and spreading themselves over the country "like grasshoppers for multitude."

351. Nor was this all. The Thebans published a decree recalling the Messenians to their ancient inheritance. They came from Rhegium, from Sicily, from Naupactus, and from all places where they had taken refuge in the dark day of adversity. The Thebans and their allies exerted themselves with such zeal in the rebuilding and fortifying of Ithome, that the city was completed in eighty-five days. The entrance of the Messenians to the home of their fathers was attended with pomp and ceremony, and solemn sacrifices. Amid all their wanderings and desolations, they had retained their laws, religion, and language; and now, regaining their place among the nations of the earth, they took possession of the lands from which their forefathers had been banished two hundred and eighty-seven years before, with the proud consciousness that they were able to defend them even against the power of Sparta. Thus the province of Messenia, amounting to half her territory, was lost to Lacedemon forever.

Questions.—349. What power was given to Agesilaus? How did he use it? Trace Cleombrotus from Sparta to Leuctra. 350. Who invaded Peloponnesus? What boast had Agesilaus made? How then was he mortified? 351. What people were recalled to their ancient inheritance? Give an account of their returning. What loss did Lacedemon thus sustain? Where was Ithome? (See map No. 2.)

352. On their return from this expedition, Epaminondas and Pelopidas were brought to trial for having retained their authority four months beyond the time prescribed by law. Pelopidas condescended to beg his life of the people, but Epaminondas boldly defended the course he had taken, and made such an eloquent appeal to the feelings of his judges that he returned from the place of trial with more glory than from the field of Leuctra.

353. Political Affairs.—During the next five years, these two illustrious generals passed through great varieties of fortune. In the year B. C. 368, Epaminondas again invaded Peloponnesus, but not being so successful as before, he was degraded to the rank of a private soldier, in which capacity he marched with the army into Thessaly. Here the Thebans were reduced to the greatest distress, and again had recourse to the wisdom of Epaminondas, who, being made general, effected their retreat in safety. Two years after, he led an army into Achaia, and brought the whole confederation into the Theban alliance. Pelopidas was sent over to Asia Minor to contract an alliance with the great king. Artaxerxes rejoiced to see him, and loaded him with honors; confirmed the restoration of Messenia, and reckoned the Thebans among his hereditary friends.

354. Upon his return, Pelopidas, being sent against Alexander, a Thessalian tyrant, was slain in battle, and Epaminondas was left alone to guide the helm of the Theban state. It was an arduous task. The Grecian states began to perceive that Thebes was merely endeavoring to wrest from Sparta that supremacy which Sparta had wrested from Athens. It was at best but a change of masters that they had gained, and, disappointed of liberty, they began to incline again to aristocracy. Athens on her part became jealous of the rising glory of Thebes. If she must have a rival, she preferred that that rival should be in Peloponnesus rather than in Hellas; accordingly, she forsook the alliance of the city she had helped to elevate, and gave her friendship to her ancient enemy, Sparta.

355. The Arcadians invaded Elis and plundered Olympia, which sacrilegious act tore open again the unhealed wounds of civil discord. As Sparta seemed to take the part of the plunderers, they made proposals for a renewal of the former alliance, upon which the Theban

---

Questions.—352. What charge was brought against Epaminondas and Pelopidas? How were they saved? 353. When did Epaminondas again invade Peloponnesus? With what success? What was the consequence to him? How did he regain position? What successes attended the exertions of Pelopidas in Asia Minor? 354. What further can you state of him? What did the Grecian states soon perceive? Why did Athens forsake Thebes? 355. Which state did the Arcadians invade? Give an account of what followed. How was Elis situated? (See map No. 2.) Olympia?

minister at Mantinea imprisoned some of the principal citizens for treason. Messengers were immediately sent to Thebes to complain of his conduct. Epaminondas told the deputies that the Theban minister had done well when he seized the Arcadians, for the Thebans invaded Peloponnesus the first time only to benefit Arcadia, and that any proposal of peace on their part *was* treason to Thebes. "Be assured, therefore," he added, "we will march into Arcadia, and with our numerous friends there prosecute the war."

356. The return of the embassadors with this answer put all Peloponnesus in a ferment. Each state felt indignant for itself in particular, and for Peloponnesus in general, that Thebes, a power just risen, should *presume* to command war for them in their own peninsula when they desired peace; and, what was worse, should *dare* to march an army into their territory to enforce such a command. Arcadia, Elis, and Achaia composed their difficulties as soon as possible; made alliance with Lacedemon in the common cause, and messengers were sent to Athens for aid in resisting the growing power of Thebes.

357. BATTLE OF MANTINEA.—To overthrow this confederacy, and punish the defection of his former allies, Epaminondas invaded the Peloponnesus for the fourth time, B. C. 366. He had under his command the effective force of all the Beotian towns, and numerous auxiliaries from Thessaly and Locris. On his entrance into the Peloponnesus, all the disaffected joined his army; and the Messenians, who looked upon him as the restorer and champion of their country, flocked to his standard, so that his troops greatly outnumbered those of the enemy.

358. The combined forces of Peloponnesus were encamped at Mantinea, and Epaminondas, hearing that Sparta had been left unprotected, directed his march thither; and, but for intelligence conveyed to Agesilaus by a Cretan, the city would have been taken, says the historian, "like a bird's nest destitute of defenders." Agesilaus, upon hearing that the Thebans were coming down the mountain road, put himself at the head of his troops, and, marching with great rapidity, reached the place before them. They now felt the truth of Lycurgus's declaration, that "that city is well defended which has a wall of men instead of brick." It was impossible to take a place where every man fought for his own hearthstone; and Epaminondas reluctantly gave orders to withdraw after a severe skirmish, in which numbers were slain.

Questions.—356. What consequences followed the invasion? 357. For what purpose did Epaminondas invade Peloponnesus a fourth time? In what year was this invasion? What army did Epaminondas then have? 358. How was Mantinea situated? (See map No. 2.) How was Sparta saved by Agesilaus? What remark of Lycurgus is quoted?

359. Failing in this project, he immediately conceived another of equal importance. It was summer, and thinking the Mantineans would be engaged in gathering in their harvest, he sent his cavalry forward to intercept the convoys and capture the laborers. This plan, too, failed by an unexpected occurrence. The cavalry traversed the lofty mountain barrier of Lacedemon without accident, and found, as they anticipated, the slaves, cattle, and citizens of Mantinea at work in their fields. A body of Athenian horse had just arrived, and were waiting for refreshment after a forced march of two days. When the Mantineans saw the Thebans approaching, they quitted their labor in the utmost alarm, and besought the Athenians to remount, weary as they were, and fly to the rescue. They immediately complied, and, jealous for the glory of their country, spurred their jaded steeds to the scene of pillage, and engaged, at fearful odds, with the renowned Thessalian and Theban cavalry. Brave men fell on both sides; but the enemy were finally repulsed, and the Athenians brought off their allies in safety, with all their property.

360. Epaminondas now found it necessary to give battle. With the aid of a skillful general, he ranged his troops in the order in which he intended to fight, and caused them to march in a column upon the hills, until within about a mile of Mantinea, where they halted and laid down their arms, as if preparing to encamp. Deceived by this movement, the enemy quitted their ranks and dispersed themselves about the camp, wherever interest or curiosity led them. Suddenly the Thebans resumed their arms, and marched directly towards Mantinea. Their approach threw the Peloponnesians into the utmost confusion. Some were running here, and some there; some buckling on their breastplates, and some bridling their horses; and they were hardly in their places when the Thebans commenced the action. The battle began with the cavalry. The troops fought on both sides with the greatest bravery. Epaminondas, at the head of his chosen soldiers, charged the Lacedemonian phalanx. They commenced with spears, but these being soon broken, they drew their swords and fought hand to hand, trampling alike on the prostrate bodies of friends and foes.

361. The Theban cavalry had put the Athenians to flight, but still the Lacedemonians had not yielded an inch of ground. Seeing the necessity of deciding the battle before the enemy could rally, Epaminondas formed a little troop of his bravest soldiers, and charged the

Questions.—359. In what second project did Epaminondas fail? Give an account of it. 360, 361. Give an account of the battle of Mantinea.

center of the enemy's line. He wounded the Lacedemonian general with the first javelin he threw, and finally broke the phalanx; but as he pressed on to the victory, he received a wound in his breast.* The wood of the javelin broke off, and the iron head remaining in the wound, he sank down in mortal agony. The contest around him was frightful; but the Thebans finally prevailed, and carried their wounded general off the field. Both sides then rested upon their arms, and the trumpets, as if by common consent, sounded a retreat at the same moment. Both parties claimed the victory, and erected a trophy; but the Lacedemonians finally begged permission to bury the dead, which was in effect confessing a defeat.

362. Epaminondas was carried into the camp. The surgeons examined his wound, and declared that his death would immediately follow the extraction of the dart. These words filled all about him with the deepest distress. His friends lamenting that he left no posterity, he said, "Yes, I have left two fair daughters, the victory of Leuctra and this of Mantinea, to perpetuate my memory." Soon after, the javelin was extracted, and he expired, exclaiming, "All is well."

363. Xenophon remarks upon this victory: "Universal expectation was strangely deceived in the event of this battle. Almost all Greece being met in arms, there was nobody who did not suppose that the victors would in future command, and the defeated must obey. But God decided otherwise. Each party claimed the victory, and neither gained any advantage; territory or dominion was acquired by neither; but indecision, and trouble, and confusion, more than ever before that battle, pervaded Greece." Wearied, then, with the sad history of his country's woes, which from youth to age he had chronicled, he thus concludes his narrative: "Thus far suffice it for me to have related. The following events, perhaps, will interest some other writer."†

* The fatal dart was thrown by the hand of Gryllus, son of Xenophon.

† "It is impossible," remarks a distinguished historian, "for the *compiler* of Grecian history not to feel a peculiar interest in the fortunes of the soldier-philosopher-author, who has been his conductor through a period of half a century, amid transactions in which he was himself an actor;" and it is hoped that the *student* also will be interested in reading a short account of the life of Xenophon. His father was an Athenian of rank and affluence. In early life, he was the pupil and friend of the great Socrates. At the solicitation of Proxenus, and by the advice of the oracle, he enlisted in the army of young Cyrus. He was present at the battle of Cunaxa, and was the chief instrument in effecting the retreat of the famous "Ten Thousand." During his absence. Socrates was executed; and upon his return, he found that the same party had procured a decree of banishment for himself. Thus prevented from visiting his native city, he joined the army of Agesilaus in Asia Minor, and

---

Questions.—361. What befell Epaminondas? 362. Give an account of the death of Epaminondas. 363. What are the remarks of Xenophon upon this victory?

364. After the death of Epaminondas, with which Xenophon's narrative closes, no regular historian took up the tangled thread of Grecian affairs; we are therefore indebted to a class resembling modern news-writers for the documents which enabled Diodorus Siculus to compile his history, and Plutarch to write his "Lives." From them, it appears that the battle of Mantinea was followed by a general peace, during which the armies on both sides were disbanded, and the troops permitted to return quietly to their homes.

365. AGESILAUS.—Agesilaus, who began to reign when Sparta was in her glory, and who had indulged the ambitious hope of humbling the power of Persia, could not be pleased with the posture of affairs. Within his memory, Lacedemon had lost the alliance of the Greek cities in Asia Minor and the Egean; the friendship and money of the Persian king; the fertile province of Messenia; and, what he valued still more, the lofty position of supreme lord of *the confederated Greek nation.* He could not rest upon his humiliated throne. It was with joy, therefore, that he accepted the invitation of an Egyptian prince to assist him in throwing off the yoke of Persia. Upon his arrival in Egypt, all the officers of the kingdom came to pay their court to him; but what was their surprise, to find in the person of the *great* Agesilaus only a little lame old man, in a plain Spartan cloak, seated on the grass, amid a company of rude soldiers. When, however, he changed his politics, and instead of assisting Tachos, who had invited him thither, joined the standard of Nectanabis, they learned to fear rather than deride him. Having placed Nectanabis upon the throne, and received immense rewards for his services, he sailed for home in midwinter, determined to use his money in recovering the lost Messenia, B. C. 361. He died on the voyage; and his body, embalmed in wax,

acquired considerable wealth in those campaigns. He returned with this king to Lacedemon, and exchanged his military life for more peaceful occupations. The Lacedemonians gave him the little town of Scillus, on the borders of Elis, to hold under their supervision as a lordship; and there he settled with his family, consisting of a wife and two sons. With the money he had saved, he purchased an extensive tract of land, upon which he erected a temple to Diana. This place, about twenty-five miles from Olympia, where every four years he might see such friends as he chose, formed an appropriate residence for the illustrious Athenian refugee. Here he wrote the Life of Cyrus, the Memorables of Socrates, and a continuation of Thucydides' great history. When the Arcadians made Sacred Olympia the seat of war, finding his residence at Scillus unsafe, he removed to Corinth. Though a decree had been passed inviting his return to Athens, yet an absence of thirty years had so weakened his attachment to his native country that he chose to remain upon the isthmus, where he passed in dignified ease the remainder of a life protracted beyond his ninetieth year. His son Gryllus was killed in the battle of Mantinea; and of the other, no further mention is made.

Questions.—364. What condition of things followed the battle of Mantinea? 365. What is said of Agesilaus? What invitation did he accept? At what were the Egyptians surprised. Why did they afterward fear? When did Agesilaus die? Where was he then?

was taken to Sparta for burial. He lived eighty-four years, of which he reigned forty-one. He was succeeded by his son, Archidamus.

366. THEBES AND ATHENS.—The glorious victory of Mantinea, won by Thebans, proved to no other state so disastrous as to Thebes herself. The loss of Epaminondas could not be repaired; the sun of his country's glory set when he expired; and though Thebes did not become lost in obscurity, she ruled no more. Athens might have held the balance of power for the Grecian republic, but she could not bear prosperity. Long before, Solon's laws for encouraging industry and punishing idleness had ceased to be regarded. "A sovereign multitude, who could vote the rich into banishment and appropriate their estates to the good of the public, would not work." To them it was far more agreeable to live upon the sacrifices provided by the treasury of the state; to feast at the tables of the demagogues who courted their favor; to spend their time in bathing, or walking in the sacred groves; in listening to the discourse of philosophers, applauding the eloquence of orators, or in witnessing those theatrical entertainments with which Athens was so well supplied, and of which every Athenian was so immoderately fond.

367. The fleet of Athens still rode triumphant over the Egean; the islands were her tributaries, and she had vast possessions in Thrace; but these appearances of prosperity were like the *mistletoe* which crowns with parasitic greenness the decaying monarch of the forest. Athens was dead at heart. The unnatural pulsations which had put forward one great man after another to meet the exigencies of her circumstances, had weakened her energies and destroyed her vitality. The measures of her government were fluctuating and uncertain; the public voice became the organ of tyranny; and the decrees of one day were rendered powerless by the decisions of the next. But her *glory* could not die. That very freedom which made her the prey of faction awakened every latent spark of genius in her people; the very defects of her government roused every slumbering energy of the gifted and ambitious; hence it was, that the brightest galaxy of philosophers and orators illumined the night of her political degradation.

368. Plato, the most celebrated philosopher of Athens, a descendant of Solon, was born at Ægina, B. C. 428. He was called Plato, "broad," from the shape of his forehead. He had a lively fancy, and when quite young composed several dramatic pieces; but happening to hear Socrates in conversation, he abandoned poetry, and turned his atten-

Questions.—What else can you say of him? 366. What is said of Thebes? Of Athens? 367. Of the fleet of Athens? Of the condition of Athens? Of her glory? 368. When was Plato born? What was he called? Why? Give an account of his early life.

tion to philosophy. He was twenty years of age when this occurred, and he continued the disciple of that philosopher till Socrates fell a victim to the violence of the times. Plato attempted to plead for the life of his master, but was prevented by the judges; he then presented him with money sufficient to redeem his life, which Socrates refused to accept; but he enjoyed the melancholy satisfaction of attending him in prison, where he gathered from the conversation of his beloved instructor the substance of his most admired composition, Phædo—"Concerning the Soul." In this dialogue, Socrates is represented as proving the immortality of the soul by its spirituality, the objects to which it naturally adheres being spiritual and incorruptible.

369. After the death of his master, Plato spent some years in traveling through Italy, Cyrenaica, and Egypt. In Sicily he worsted Dionysius the tyrant in an argument, and was in consequence sold into slavery. His friends and scholars raised money for his ransom, but his noble-minded master gave him his liberty, and with the sum contributed, purchased for him a garden in the groves of Academus. Here the philosopher founded the celebrated Academy, where he taught the gifted and high-born youth, who came from all parts of Greece to listen to his instructions. He lived to a good old age, enriching his country and the world with numerous philosophical works, adorned with the chaste beauties of the Attic tongue, and enlivened with all the graces of a brilliant imagination. The grove and garden which had been the scene of his labors at last afforded him a sepulchre. Statues and altars were erected to his memory, and his portrait was preserved in gems; but the *living image* of his mind may be seen in his writings, stamped with the impress of immortality.

NOTE.—Isocrates was born at Athens, B. C. 436. He was the companion of Plato in the school of Socrates; and after the execution of his master, was the only person who had courage to put on mourning. He was teacher of an oratorical school, and charged about $180 for a complete course of instruction. He was a friend of peace, and kept up a correspondence with Philip, urging upon him the policy and propriety of bringing all Greece into a confederacy against Persia. After the battle of Cheroneia, he refused to take food for several days, and thus closed his long and honorable career. at the age of 98.

Only twenty-one of his orations are now extant. One of these is said to have occupied him ten years.

Questions.—369. What further can you say of him? Of the honors paid to his memory?

REVIEW QUESTIONS.

		PAGE
1.	Give the early history of Greece	97, 98
2.	Give an account of the Trojan war	99, 100, 101
3.	Of the Olympic and other games	102, 103, 104, 108
4.	Of Lycurgus and his laws	104–108
5.	Of the first and second Messenian wars	109–112
6.	Of Solon and his laws	115–119, 199, 220, 339
7.	Of the Pisistratidæ	120–124
8.	Of the battle of Marathon and its consequences	129, 130
9.	Of affairs till the invasion by Xerxes	130–137
10.	Of Leonidas and the battle of Thermopylæ	136–139
11.	Of the battle of Salamis and its consequences	141–143
12.	Of Mardonius's operations and death	143–148
13.	What success did Xanthippus and Leotychidas have?	149, 150
14.	What success did Themistocles have?	132–143, 151–156
15.	Give an account of Pausanias	126, 145–155
16.	Give an account of Cimon's operations	156–162
17.	Of the contest between Pericles and Thucydides	162–174
18.	Of the first Peloponnesian war	167–174
19.	Of the battle of Amphipolis and its consequences	174
20.	Of Alcibiades and his operations	175–198
21.	Give the closing account of the Peloponnesian war	195–197
22.	Give an account of Nicias and his operations	172–183
23.	Give the history of the "Four Hundred"	185, 186
24.	Give the early account of Lysander	74, 190–192
25.	Give the subsequent account of him	193–205
26.	Give an account of Conon	192–208
27.	Of the battle of Arginusæ and consequences	192, 193
28.	Of the battle of Ægos Potamos and consequences	193–196
29.	Of the siege of Athens and results	196, 197
30.	Give the history of the "Thirty Tyrants"	197–199
31.	Give an account of Socrates	79, 175, 193–201, 220, 221
32.	Of the "Retreat of the Ten Thousand"	78–81, 201, 202
33.	Give an account of Agesilaus	126, 202–219
34.	Of Thrasybulus and his operations	192–207
35.	Of the Olynthian war	208–210
36.	Name the events in the second Peloponnesian war	212–219
37.	Give an account of Epaminondas's successes	211–220
38.	Give the biography of Plato	198–221
39.	Describe the battle of Mantinea	216
40.	What was the condition of Greece then?	218–220

MACEDONIA.

1. THUS leaving Sparta, Thebes, and Athens, to act the inferior part to which their own factions condemned them, let us turn to greet with becoming attention a new hero of the Grecian drama.

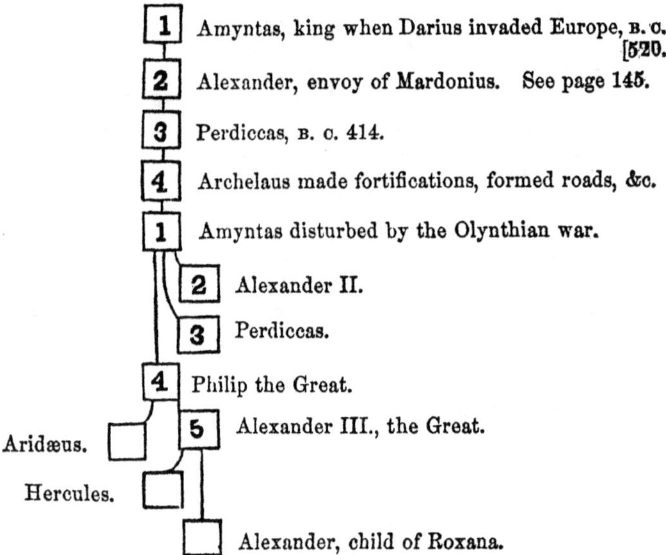

The Macedonians claimed their descent from Hercules, and therefore had a kindred feeling with all the Dorian brotherhood; but as they were far inferior to the other states in civilization, they made little figure in history until the year B. C. 360, when the crown devolved upon *Philip*, only surviving son of Amyntas.

2. This youth, in the troubles arising from a disputed succession,

---

Questions.—MACEDONIA.—1. When did Macedonia come into political notice? Who wa Philip?

had been taken by Pelopidas as a hostage to Thebes, where he received a military and philosophical education in the house of Epaminondas, and no doubt witnessed a refinement unknown in his brother's court. Upon ascending the throne, Philip found himself in the most perilous circumstances. The Illyrians, who had slain his brother Perdiccas, were plundering his country on the *west;* the Pæonians were engaged in the same enterprise on the *north;* Pausanias, a Lacedemonian, putting forward a claim to the throne, united with the Thracians, and invaded Macedonia from the *east;* the Athenians sent out a fleet to vindicate their right to Amphipolis, on the *south;* and Argæus, a rival of his brother's, raised a party among the nobles, and assailed him in his *very court.*

3. Fortunately, he was well qualified by nature and education to meet the exigencies in which he was placed. He was eloquent, shrewd, and courageous; but choosing to negotiate rather than fight, he permitted the Illyrian savages to carry off their plunder unmolested, knowing that the enjoyment of it would prevent another immediate incursion. He bought off the Pæonian chiefs; and by the powerful eloquence of *gold*, convinced the Thracian king of the injustice of Pausanias's claims. He withdrew his troops from Amphipolis, and sent home the Athenian prisoners he had taken, with proposals of peace; and, attacking Argæus, killed him in battle, and quelled the insurrection of his rude nobles.

4. The Athenians, won by his generous policy, concluded a treaty of peace and alliance with Macedonia; and "thus," says the historian, "this young prince, called to a throne nearly overwhelmed by *two* foreign enemies, attacked by a *third*, threatened by a *fourth*, and contested by *two* pretenders, before the end of the third summer, had overcome these threatening evils not only, but had acquired new dominion and new security."

5. Athenian Policy.—After the battle of Leuctra, Olynthus again asserted her independence, and now joining with Amphipolis, who had thrown off the yoke of Athens, threatened Macedon itself. Philip of course united with the Athenians, to put down the rising powers. A Macedonian army besieged Potidæa by land, while an Athenian fleet blocked it up by sea. The city, thus closely invested, soon surrendered, and received an Athenian garrison. Torone shared the same

Questions.—2. Where was Philip educated? What difficulties surrounded him as the king of Macedon? 3. What were his three principal characteristics? What did he gain by means of gold? What else did he gain? 4. By what policy did he make friends of hostile enemies? 5. Where was Olynthus? (See map No. 2.) Amphipolis? Potidæa? Torone? Methone? Pydna? What convulsions agitated Athens and Macedon?

fate shortly after, and Methone acknowledged the sovereignty of Athens; but this grasping power, emboldened by success, seized also upon Pydna, the only remaining seaport in Macedonia. Philip sent deputies to Athens to complain of this violation of the public faith, but his remonstrance was unheeded. Demosthenes,* who saw a mighty rival in the Macedonian king, advocated every measure calculated to cripple his power, and extend the supremacy of Athens.

6. As the Athenians, after the seizure of Pydna, could expect no further assistance from Philip, they withdrew their forces from Olynthus, and laid siege to Amphipolis upon their own behalf. By the dexterous management of Charidemus, a native of Eubœa, in Athenian pay, Amphipolis was induced to surrender, and thus Athens possessed *all* the maritime towns of Macedonia and Thrace. Demosthenes did not overrate the importance of this conquest when he said, "While the Athenians hold Potidæa and Amphipolis, the king of Macedon cannot be safe in his own house."

7. PHILIP'S ALLIANCE WITH OLYNTHUS.—But Philip knew his own interest far too well to leave the Athenians in quiet possession of

* This illustrious orator and statesman was born at Athens, B. C. 385. He was left an orphan heir to a large estate at the age of seven. His first appearance as a public speaker was in the prosecution of his guardians for embezzling his estate. The justice of his cause, rather than the eloquence of his diction, gave him success. Indeed, it was only by the most untiring industry and perseverance that he acquired the art of oratory. He had a stammering in his speech, which he remedied by declaiming with pebbles in his mouth. He had a weak and effeminate voice, which he strengthened by pronouncing orations upon the sea-shore. He had also an awkward habit of shrugging one shoulder, which he corrected by suspending a sword over it; and he practiced before a looking-glass to overcome the grimaces which accompanied his utterance. He constructed a closet under ground, where he studied for months together, shaving one side of his head, that shame might prevent a wish to go abroad. In this solitary retreat, by the light of a lamp, he copied and re-copied ten times all the orations recorded in Thucydides's great history, and acquired a style so pure and forcible, that mankind have by common consent yielded to him the palm of unrivaled excellence in oratory. The *theme*, the *time*, and the *theater* of his orations contributed not a little to his success. Liberty, or the ascendency of Athenian democracy, awakened for him a sustaining and cheering response in every Athenian breast; hope and fear lent him their powerful interest in those thrilling moments when Athens seemed about to gain every thing, or to lose all; and never was orator surrounded with scenes so rich in imagery, and so capable of furnishing him with all that was heart-stirring and exciting in appeal, as was Demosthenes, when with one hand he could direct the eye to every spot made sacred by trophies of Athenian valor, and with the other point to the rising glory of Macedon, before which the city of Minerva was destined to suffer a final eclipse. His Olynthian orations, his four Philippics, viewed as pictures of the political state of Greece, or as specimens of oratory, are incomparably interesting and beautiful. The whole Athenian people were swayed by the breath of his eloquence, and Philip used to say that he feared him more than all the fleets and armies of Athens, and that "he had no enemy but Demosthenes."

Questions.—5. Who was Demosthenes? 6. State how Athens acquired possession of all the maritime towns of Macedonia and Thrace. How did Demosthenes estimate the importance of the Athenian conquest?

Methone, Pydna, Amphipolis, and Potidæa. *He* also changed his ground, and formed an alliance with the Olynthians, for the express purpose of driving the Athenians entirely from the shores of Macedonia. The Athenians were taken by surprise. They had counted on the ancient enmity between Olynthus and Macedon, to prevent a coalition of this kind. They found they had counted in vain. They made overtures of peace, which were rejected, and in spite of all their efforts the combined forces of their enemies laid siege to Amphipolis. The city was taken by assault; and Philip, entering it sword in hand, displayed his mercy as a conqueror, and his merit as a statesman. He banished only the most factious citizens, dismissed all prisoners of war without ransom, and treated with particular attention all those who had espoused his cause. After securing quiet possession of this important post, the allied armies marched to Pydna. There was a strong Macedonian party in the town, and no sooner did Philip appear in arms before it, than the gates were opened to receive him.

8. Potidæa stood next upon the list. The town's people, consisting of Macedonians and Olynthians, hearing of the approach of their friends, rose against the Athenian garrison, forced them to retire into the citadel, and threw open the gates with every demonstration of joy. Philip released the Athenian prisoners, and furnished them with means of returning home (that being the most direct method of opposing Demosthenes), and then turned his attention to the improvement of his revenue. Not far from Amphipolis were the gold mines of Crenidæ. They had been wrought by the neighboring inhabitants till the subterranean waters had filled up the veins, and rendered them nearly useless. With great labor and expense, Philip constructed machines for draining these mines, and finally succeeded in gaining from them about $1,000,000, yearly. He provided for the protection of the people against their barbarian neighbors, and, in pledge of future attention, named the place *Philippi.*

9. Alliance with Thessaly and Epirus.—The next spring, Philip was called to settle affairs in Thessaly. His father had owed his throne to the attachment of the Thessalians, and his brother had also been in alliance with the nobles of that country. Now, when two tyrant brothers had seized upon their liberties, the people looked to Philip as the person who might deliver them from their oppressors,

---

Questions.—7. What four cities did Athens and Macedon quarrel for? What alliance did Philip make? For what purpose did he make it? Why were the Athenians then surprised? Give an account of Philip's success at Amphipolis. At Pydna. 8. At Potidæa. Relate the origin of Philippi. 9. Give some account of Philip's alliance with Thessaly and Epirus. Whom did Philip marry

without subjecting them to a severer yoke. The result of this embassy is given in the following words: "Philip, marching into Thessaly, defeated the tyrants, and acquiring thus freedom for the cities, he showed a liberality which so attached the Thessalians, that in all his following wars and political contests they were his zealous assistants, and continued such afterward to his son." After his return from this successful expedition, he married Olympia, a princess of Epirus, descended from the hero Achilles. The magnificence with which their nuptials were celebrated, formed the theme of many ancient writers. From that time, the Macedonian court became distinguished for its elegance and splendor, and the greatest resort of refined society in the world.

10. SECOND SACRED WAR.—B. C. 359.—While the Athenians had been thus fruitlessly contending with Macedon, Thebes had renewed her hostility with Sparta in another form. Unable to punish her rival as she desired for the treachery of Phœbidas, she complained of the act to the Amphictyonic council. The council listened to the story of Theban wrongs, and fined the Lacedemonians an immense sum. They refused to pay it; and after a specified time the fine was *doubled.* They still made no exertions to meet the demand; and after another period it was made *three-fold.*

11. The Phocians were always enemies of the Thebans, and for that, if for no other reason, friends of the Spartans. The Thebans, therefore, accused them of having plowed up the *Cirrhæan plain*, which the council had so solemnly consecrated to the god. This accusation was responded to by a decree, "That the Cirrhæan land had been devoted, and the Phocians must immediately cease to use it, and pay a fine." It was so long since the Amphictyons had interfered in Grecian affairs, that many contended they had no right to do so: the subject was "taken up in the lips of talkers," and much uneasiness was excited; but the land, meantime, was cultivated as before, and the fine remained unpaid.

12. When the appointed time had expired, this fine, like the one imposed upon Lacedemon, was doubled, and a new decree of the council declared, that "All states guilty of such contempt for Amphictyonic law, as, after the duplication of the fine, to let the limited time pass without taking any measures for payment, forfeited all their lands to the god; and that accordingly *all the lands of the Lacedemonians*

Questions.—9. For what did the Macedonian court become distinguished? 10. What complaint did Thebes bring against Sparta? What action did the council take? 11, 12. What complaint did Thebes make against the Phenicians? What was the result?

and Phocians were forfeited." This was followed by a proclamation to the Greeks, that it behooved every man and every state, as they hoped for divine favor, or feared divine wrath, to do their utmost toward carrying the decree into execution. The Amphictyons having thus sounded the trumpet of war, consternation and dismay pervaded the valleys of Phocis.

13. Alliance between Phocis and Lacedemon.—Though the Phocians had never meddled in Grecian politics, they were not destitute of courage, nor insensible to the charms of liberty. One man was found among them, the oldest of three brothers, who might have vied with Pericles, had he lived to perfect all the great qualities which the present exigency called into action. A congress of the Phocian cities having been called, to deliberate upon the state of the country, this man, Philomelus, represented to them that the Cirrhæan land had belonged to the Phocians from time immemorial; that they also had a right to the presidency of the Delphic oracle, of which the Amphictyons had unjustly deprived them; and that as they were now struggling against their oppressors, they might reasonably hope for the divine blessing upon their endeavors.

14. The assembly felt the force of his reasonings, and committed to him the direction of affairs, with the title of general-autocrator. He proceeded at once to Sparta to concert measures for withstanding the Thebans, who were preparing to show their piety by enforcing the Amphictyonic decree. He was well received by the Ephori; and Archidamus, the king, did all in his power to further his plans. It was agreed that the Delphian treasury was unsafe in the hands of the Amphictyons, and ought immediately to be reduced to a dependence upon Phocian virtue; but how to bring about so desirable a change was an important question.

15. Sparta had no money to hire mercenaries, and her own troops could not reach Delphi without fighting their way through hostile Arcadia. With money supplied by private liberality, Philomelus, however, succeeded in hiring those soldiers who, since the battle of Mantinea, had been roving about in idleness; and, watching his opportunity, got them conveyed across the Corinthian Gulf. With all possible dispatch he marched to Delphi, and putting the guard to flight, gained possession of the place. His first act was to destroy the decrees against Phocis and Lacedemon, by defacing the marble upon which

Questions.—13. What alliance was formed in consequence? Who was Philomelus? What representation did he make? 14. What power was committed to him? Give an account of his movements. 15. Give a further account of his movements.

they were engraved. Then, publishing a declaration that he had taken charge of the temple and its treasures, by command of the Phocians, to whom the holy shrine belonged, he requested all the states of Greece to assist his countrymen in maintaining their ancient right.

16. Athens entered at once into a confederacy with Phocis. Most of the Grecian states engaged in the quarrel, and many bloody but indecisive battles were fought. The Thebans, having taken several prisoners, caused them all to be put to death as sacrilegious wretches; and the Phocians retaliated this cruelty upon some Theban captives. Finally, having been defeated in a great battle, Philomelus was driven to an eminence whence there was no retreat; and, rather than fall into the hands of his enemies, threw himself headlong from the rock, and was dashed in pieces. The command then devolved upon his brother, Onomarchus.

17. PHILIP ENTERS THE LISTS.—Philip was at this time engaged in the siege of Methone, which Athens had stirred up to make incursions upon his territory. The siege lasted through the winter, nor did he withdraw his troops from the place till it was dismantled and added to the Macedonian territory. Then, hearing that Onomarchus was supporting a revolt in Thessaly, he engaged in the *Sacred War*. He lost two battles and was obliged to retreat to his own country; but, raising another army, he advanced again to Thermopylæ, where he met the Phocians and defeated them with great slaughter. Upwards of 6,000 were slain upon the spot; and the prisoners, amounting to 3,000, were thrown into the sea, as the professed enemies of religion. Onomarchus was slain, and the command devolved upon his brother, Phayllus.

18. By this great victory, *all* Thessaly came under the dominion of Philip; nor was it in the power even of Demosthenes to diminish the credit which Philip had gained by destroying those who had usurped the guardianship of the oracle, and used its treasures in hiring soldiers to resist the decrees of the Amphictyons. "It is incredible," says an ancient historian, "what glory the victory over Onomarchus earned to Philip among all nations. He was the avenger of sacrilege; he was the protector of the religion of Greece. Next to the immortal gods is he, by whom the majesty of the gods is vindicated."

Questions.—16. What confederacy was formed? What is said of other states engaging in the quarrel? What cruelties and retaliations were perpetrated? Give an account of the death of Philomelus. Who then commanded? 17. Where was Philip at this time? What success did he meet with there? How came he to be engaged in the *Sacred War?* How did his first battles result? At what place did he gain a great victory? Give some ac count of it. 18. What condition of things followed the victory? What is reported as having been said by an ancient historian?

19. Phayllus was victorious in several battles with the Thebans, but died soon after, of consumption. Faction, that curse of the Grecian republics, then fixed its venomous fangs upon the Phocians. There arose two pretenders to the office of autocrator-general, and while they were intent upon settling this affair, Philip, at the head of his forces, joined the Thebans in an attack upon Phocis. The distracted Phocians, unable to defend themselves, appealed to his generosity to escape the vengeance of the Thebans. They requested only that they might have permission to abandon their houses and lands, and seek safety in flight. This request was granted. The principal Phocians emigrated; and thus, after many bloody struggles during ten years, the Sacred War quietly ended.

20. THE DOUBLE VOTE.—To settle the points now agitating Greece, Philip invited a congress of all the states to meet at Thermopylæ. This grave assembly, in commencing their difficult and complicated business, referred the affair of the Phocians to the Amphictyonic council. By their decree all the Amphictyonic rights of the Phocians were said to be forfeited, and all their principal cities were given over to be dismantled; it was ordered that no village should contain more than fifty houses, and that a yearly rent of $4,800 should be paid from the Phocian lands till the debt of the god was liquidated. The *double vote* in the Amphictyonic council which the Phocians had heretofore enjoyed was bestowed upon Philip, in consideration of the benefits he had conferred upon the Greek nation. A general peace was then concluded; and throughout Greece, with the exception of the war party in Athens, all voices were joined in extolling Philip as their friend, and benefactor, and preserver.

21. MACEDONIAN WAR.—While the Sacred War was in progress, the Athenians commenced hostile demonstrations in Thrace, for the recovery of the lost Chersonese and the recapture of Byzantium. This attack, which resulted in the *Macedonian War*, proceeded step by step with the *Sacred War;* so that while the Athenians were allies of the Phocians in that fatal struggle, they were at the same time "parties of the first part" in a war of their own seeking. Philip, on his side, had to contend with all the enemies the Athenians could stir up against him. The Illyrians again commenced hostilities upon the west, the Pæonians on the north, and the Thracians on the east.

Questions.—19. What success did Phayllus have? What occurred soon after? By what means was the war terminated? 20. By whom was a congress called? At what place? For what purpose? What decree was made? How was Philip rewarded? With whom had he been fighting during the war? 21. What was the cause of the *Macedonian War*? What opposition confronted Philip?

But he was never unready for business. He sent Parmenio with an army against his troublesome neighbors, and marched himself into Thrace, where his good fortune was so great, that, according to Demosthenes, "he made and unmade there what kings he chose."

22. Birth of Alexander.—Philip had just returned from this successful expedition, when a messenger came to him with the welcome intelligence of a great victory which Parmenio had gained over the Illyrians. The same day another courier brought him word that his horse had won the palm in the Olympic games. Scarcely had he been congratulated upon these successes, when a third messenger arrived with the information of the birth of a son. "O, fortune," exclaimed the happy monarch, "send some little evil to temper all this good." Not long after, he wrote the following letter to Aristotle, inviting him to take charge of the young prince. "Philip to Aristotle, greeting. I desire you should know I have a son born. Greatly I thank the gods for it, and yet less for the mere circumstance that I have a son, than because it happens in the age wherein you are living. I trust that, being put under your care and instruction, he will become worthy of his birth, and of the inheritance awaiting him."

23. Olynthus and Athens.—It was just after these events that Philip engaged with Methone and the Phocians. Demosthenes, disappointed in the result, brought about a confederacy with Olynthus. Since the alliance of that republic with Macedon, it had prospered wonderfully; but, becoming jealous of its neighbor, it entered into a treaty with Athens, contrary to its existing engagements with Macedon, and prepared for war with a zeal which showed a sense of the just indignation of Philip. The war party of Athens were now "in the full tide of successful experiment." "Now was the favorable moment, they said, to engage all Greece in a league against the threatening ambition of the Macedonian king." Philip was represented as the most false and cruel of tyrants, who had a certain design upon the liberties of Greece.

24. Demosthenes commenced his Olynthiac orations, and undertook the difficult and dangerous experiment of persuading the Athenians to divert the theoric revenue (the sum appropriated to the support of theaters) from its legitimate object, to the purposes of war. This

---

Questions.—21. On what expedition did he send Parmenio? To what place did Philip march? What did Demosthenes say of Philip's good fortune? 22. What three pieces of good news did Philip receive? What exclamation did he make? What was the language of his letter to Aristotle? 23. Why did Olynthus turn against Philip? What was the object of Demosthenes? How was Philip represented? 24. What dangerous task did Demosthenes undertake?

attempt to rob the amusement-loving Athenians of their greatest pleasure, would have cost the life of a less popular man than the renowned orator; but he had so fixed the attention of the populace upon the great *actor*, Philip, that they consented to give up their customary entertainment, to assist in the grand tragedy going on in Olynthus. Indeed, the representations of the orator produced such a zeal in the Athenian people, that a force was fitted out to assist Olynthus, such as had never, since the fatal Sicilian expedition, been sent upon foreign service.

25. Philip was not prepared for this new war. His country was open on the Olynthiac side, and his enemies had overrun and plundered his territories before he had time to make any effectual opposition. In the winter, the Athenian general, Chares, returned to Athens. The people assembled as usual to hear his report. He gave a thrilling account of a glorious battle and uninterrupted success, and, to complete the gratification of his fellow-citizens, he made a great feast for all the people, which cost at least $50,000. This money was not furnished from his private purse, nor from the profits of his command, but from the Delphian treasury, having been extorted from their allies, the Phocians. While these rejoicings were going on in Athens, the Olynthians were very uneasy. Philip was making grand preparations for the spring campaign, and when Chares returned to the theater of war, he found a force far superior to his own assembled upon the Olynthian border. He ventured a battle, and was defeated; a second, with no better success. The Olynthians were then obliged to take shelter behind their walls.

26. The other towns of the confederacy submitted at once to the conqueror, and Philip approached within five miles of Olynthus, and fortified his camp. The wretched inhabitants then desired to enter into a treaty. He answered, "That it was too late; he had before abundantly and repeatedly expressed his disposition to treat, but now it was become too evident that there was but one alternative; *they* must quit Olynthus, or *he* Macedonia." The surrender of the place occurred not long after, and the victor carried out his determination of compelling them to leave the peninsula. It seemed advisable now, even to Demosthenes, to make peace; and Philip having manifested

Questions.—24. Why would it not have been safe for any other person to have made the attempt? Why was Demosthenes successful? 25. Why was not Philip prepared for this new war? What account did Chares give to the Athenians? What is said of his feast? Of his first two battles thereafter? 26. How near to Olynthus did Philip approach? How was Olynthus situated? (See map No. 2.) What desire did the Olynthians express? What was Philip's reply? What followed? How did this war terminate?

the same disposition, it was soon concluded. The Macedonian court became the focus of negotiation for the Grecian republics, and at the very time and place of the settlement of the disputes arising out of the Sacred War, the difficulties of Macedon and Athens were finally adjusted, and a general peace brought repose to the country.

27. PHILIP'S EXPEDITION.—B. C. 343.—Three years after, Philip turned his attention to the barbarians who had inhabited his north-eastern frontier. They fled before him, and he pursued till winter overtook him upon the banks of the Danube, and his way was entirely hedged in. Reports of various kinds were spread in Greece. It was said he was sick. It was rumored that he was dead; and, depending upon the truth of these stories, or counting more certainly upon the dangers with which he was surrounded, the war party* in Athens, of which the great orator was the life and soul, began again to lift its head. By making war in Thrace, it was contended that "Philip had broken the peace, and that it was evidently his design to destroy Athens and overthrow democracy." Acting under this persuasion, the Athenians instructed the commanders of their fleet to stop all the ships bound to Macedonia, and, condemning the crews as enemies to Athens, to sell them into slavery.

28. Philip remonstrated in vain. Demosthenes had in effect exalted himself to the station of prime-minister of the republic; viceroy of that sovereign assembly which met to decide upon the fate of thousands; and *his* voice "was still for war." To discharge the duties of his arduous office, he applied himself to every kind of business with untiring vigilance, and watched an opportunity to bring all the states of Greece into a confederacy to overthrow Macedonian supremacy. For this purpose, he did not scruple to receive money from the Persian king, nor to exert his influence in healing the breach between Athens and Thebes. Though these cities had fought on opposite sides at the battle of Mantinea and in the Sacred War, yet Demosthenes having shown them the advantage of being friends, they readily consented to bury private animosities in the grave they were digging for the power of Macedon.

29. The coalition was for a time successful. Chares had been sent

* The war party opposed every measure of Philip's; but Phocion and the venerable Isocrates sought only for the pacification of Greece.

Questions.—27. Give an account of Philip's expedition. What charge did the Athenian war party make against Philip? What instructions were given to commanders of Athenian vessels? 28. To what position had Demosthenes risen? To what did he apply himself? Of whom did he receive money? For what purpose? What reconciliation did he effect?

with succors to Byzantium, which was attacked by the Macedonian king; but, failing in his commission, was recalled in disgrace. Phocion then undertook to preserve that city for Athens. The virtue and moderation of this general were well known; and a man of eminence in Byzantium, who had been his intimate friend at the Academy,* pledged his honor to the city in his behalf. The Byzantines then threw open their gates, admitted the Athenians, and joined them against Macedon. By these means Philip lost all the towns on the Chersonese, and suffered not a little in his military reputation. He was now, as ever, very desirous of peace, and particularly anxious to gain the friendship of the Athenians, for reasons of his own; but Demosthenes opposed the terms which Phocion† advised them to accept, and the war went on with mutual attacks and reprisals four years longer, without any decisive advantage to either side.

30. Third Sacred War.—But a new leaven was at work in the great loaf of Grecian discomfort, which soon produced a fermentation throughout the whole mass. Amphissa, a town not seven miles from Delphi, bordered on that devoted Cirrhæan plain forbidden to the use of man. The Amphissæans, unwarned by the fate of the Phocians, used the land for pasturage, and ventured to repair the long-deserted harbor. These acts Æschines, an orator in the interest of Macedon, represented as a repetition of the former sacrilege, and the Amphictyons, of which he was a member, declared war against the Amphissæans, and invited Philip to command the armies of the god. This brought the crafty Macedonian at once into the midst of Grecian affairs. Demosthenes immediately sounded the alarm for the Grecian states. Even Corinth, the old enemy of Athens, joined the war party. All was bustle and confusion; fortifications were repaired, arms made and burnished, and every man was on the alert. Diogenes, the famous

* The school of Plato.

† Though Phocion had engaged in hostility with Philip, and driven him out of the Hellespont, he was still in favor of peace; but he was not a gifted orator, and therefore failed to carry his point. The perils of his country alone induced him to mount the bema. He excelled in readiness of reply, and exposed with cutting sarcasm any fallacy in argument. Demosthenes, who had often felt the keenness of his wit, styled him the *Hatchet.*

Questions.—29. Where did the Athenian troops meet Philip? What did Phocion effect? What then was Philip's condition? Why was not the war then brought to a close? 30. What causes produced the third Sacred War? What course did Demosthenes take? What were the consequences? What did Diogenes do? Who was Diogenes? *Ans.* A famous Cynic philosopher, born in Pontus: he lived in the summer at Corinth, and in the winter at Athens. He taught that a man, to be happy, must despise honor, power, and all the enjoyments of life. He walked the streets barefooted and without any coat. At night he slept in a tub. He exposed the follies of the age by the keenest sarcasms. Being asked, "What is the most dangerous animal?" he replied: "Among wild animals, the slanderer; among tame the flatterer."

Cynic philosopher, at that time in the city, began to roll his *tub* about in a remarkable manner. Being asked why he did so, he said "he did not wish to be the only man in Corinth not absurdly employed."

31. But all their preparations were in vain. Philip easily punished the Amphissæans; and then, as if afraid of Athens and her confederates, seized upon Elatea, the principal city of Phocis. It was late in the evening when a courier arrived at Athens with the news of the fall of Elatea. The Prytanes were at supper, but, instantly rising from the table, some of them went to the agora, dismissed the ware-sellers, and burned their stalls; others sent to call the trumpeter, and the whole city was filled with tumult. Next morning the people were called together, and a herald proclaimed that any one who would advise the assembly might speak. A dead silence ensued. Finally, Demosthenes mounted the bema, and, having clearly demonstrated to the people that Philip meant to enter Attica, and reduce them all to slavery, he so wrought upon the passions of his audience, that it was decreed to send the whole force of Attica to oppose the Macedonian, and defend the liberty of the Greeks.

32. Battle of Cheroneia.—B. C. 338.—It was upon the plain of Cheroneia, about sixteen miles from Elatea, that the allied forces of Thebes and Athens led the "forlorn hope" of Grecian democracy against the overwhelming power of the Macedonian monarchy. The particulars of the battle it is not necessary to relate. Philip was victorious. Alexander, at the head of the Macedonian youth, cut down the *Sacred Theban Band.* They neither turned nor wavered in the fight, but fell upon the spot where they were stationed, each by the side of his darling friend, like the three hundred Spartans, leaving their bodies a monument of their constancy to the cause of liberty. The news of the defeat at Cheroneia produced terror and consternation among the Athenians. They looked for nothing less than a second Lysander in the king they had so often provoked. Demosthenes, who fought in the battle, made his escape in the general flight, and, embarking in a trireme, sailed from the Piræus, saying that he was going to collect tribute. Philip, however, did not pursue the fugitives: he even sent the prisoners home without ransom, determined, if possible, to attach the Athenians to his interests.

33. From the field of battle the victorious army marched to Thebes.

Questions.—31. What city fell into the hands of Philip? Where was Elatea? (See map No. 2.) What effect did the news of the fall of Elatea have at Athens? What was done by Demosthenes? 32. Where was the plain of Cheroneia? When was the battle of Cheroneia fought? Give an account of it. What is said of Demosthenes? Of Philip's generosity? 33. To what place did the victors then march?

No opposition was made to their entrance. The government passed quietly into the hands of the Macedonian party, and Beotia rejoiced in the change of masters. As soon as it was known that the conqueror was disposed to peace, an embassy was sent from the Athenians to negotiate in their favor. Philip made no hard conditions, and Phocion had the satisfaction of contributing to the welfare of his country in the peace which was ratified. The great purpose of the monarch's soul was now unvailed. Diodorus says, "Philip, encouraged by his victory at Cheroneia, was ambitious of becoming military commander of the Greek nation. He declared therefore his intention of *carrying war in the common cause of the Greeks against the Persians.*" By the national congress which he summoned at Corinth, he was elected general-autocrator of Greece, and the proportion of troops which every state should furnish for the Persian war was settled.

34. DEATH OF PHILIP.—B. C. 336.—Thus crowned with honor, he returned to Macedon, to prepare for the great enterprise which had so long occupied his thoughts; but the dagger of the assassin cut short his schemes, and left Asia unconquered for his son. Philip loved conviviality, and was often intoxicated. Olympias was proud and imperious. The other princesses, whom policy or a more tender motive led her husband to introduce into his palace, excited her contempt, and aroused her resentment; and, after many quarrels, she retired to her brother's court. Alexander espoused his mother's cause, and took up his abode in Illyria. This breach was apparently healed; and the mother and son had returned to Macedon. Cleopatra, Alexander's sister, was to be married to her uncle, the king of Epirus, and great preparations were made for the wedding. Philip, having summoned the states of Greece to furnish their soldiers, and having received a satisfactory response from the oracle,* intended on this occasion to secure the peace of his dominions by every possible friendly alliance before setting out for Asia.

35. Guests were bidden from all parts of Greece. The most celebrated actors and musicians were engaged to entertain the goodly company. Deputies came to offer congratulations, and to present him with golden crowns. The day following the nuptials, a grand exhibition was to take place in the theater. Philip, clothed in white robes,

* The response was this: "*Crowned is the victim, the altar is ready, the stroke is impending.*"

Questions.—33. What followed? What is said of Phocion? What ambitious views had Philip? To what position was he elected? 34. What is stated as against Philip? What quarrel occurred? What marriage was arranged? What preparations therefor did Philip make? 35. How far were the preparations carried out? Give an account of Philip's death.

advanced at the head of the procession; but just as the shouts of the admiring multitude announced *the king*, a young man ran out from the crowd, and, drawing a sword, stabbed him to the heart. Philip fell dead. The assassin fled, but was pursued and killed as he was mounting his horse. It was said to be a matter of private revenge; but Olympias was suspected of having instigated the crime, and Alexander did not escape the horrid imputation.*

36. Alexander the Great was born at Pella, B. C. 356, on the very day that the temple of Diana at Ephesus was burned to the ground. All the magi who were at Ephesus, looked upon the *fire* as an emblem of a much greater misfortune, and ran about the town beating their breasts, and crying out, "This day has brought forth the scourge and destroyer of Asia." Whether the forebodings of the magi were real or feigned, Asia had good reason to tremble when he who was destined to subdue her ancient lords, and water her plains with the blood of her sons, entered upon the stage of life. Leonatus, an austere man, was his governor till eight years of age, when Lysimachus, an Acarnanian, became his instructor. As the family of Olympia claimed their descent from the renowned Achilles, Lysimachus ingratiated himself into their favor by dignifying his pupil with the name of that warrior—a circumstance which doubtless contributed to foster the ambitious feelings which had been observed in him from his infancy.

37. In his fifteenth year, Alexander was placed under the immediate tuition of the celebrated Aristotle,† and continued to receive instruc-

* No sooner did Demosthenes hear of the death of his great enemy, than he assembled the Athenian people, and persuaded them to offer a sacrifice as upon news of a splendid victory; and though he was at that time in mourning for his only child, he put on a festal robe, and attended the ceremony crowned with flowers.

"Thus fell the greatest potentate of his time in Europe. With very small resources in the outset, he acquired the most powerful monarchy that had ever existed among the Greeks; but his great success arose less from the force of his arms, than from his obliging disposition and conduct."

† ARISTOTLE was born at Stagira, an island on the Macedonian coast, B. C. 384. At the age of seventeen he went to Athens, and devoted himself to philosophy in the school of Plato. His uncommon acuteness and indefatigable industry gained for him so high a rank, that Plato used to call him the "Mind of the School," and to say, when he was absent, "*Intellect* is not here." He lived in Athens twenty years, during which he wrote many works; thence he passed to Macedonia, where he remained in quality of tutor to Alexander eight more, and then returned to Athens. He kept up, however, a correspondence with the young king, and persuaded him to use his power and wealth in the service of philosophy. Alexander employed several thousand persons in different parts of Europe and Asia to collect animals of various kinds, birds, beasts, and fishes, to send to Aristotle, who, from the information thus afforded, wrote fifty volumes on the history of

Questions.—36. Where was Alexander the Great born? When? What memorable event took place the same day? Where was Pella? (Map No. 2.) Who were the first instructors of Alexander? 37. What is said of his subsequent training? Who was Aristotle?

tion from that philosopher in all the branches of human knowledge, until he came to the throne. For him Aristotle wrote a work on Government, and revised the Iliad, that he might present to his royal pupil an accurate copy of his favorite poem. This volume Alexander preserved with the greatest care, placing it every night with his sword under his pillow. His tutor too he held in the highest esteem, and believed himself bound to love him as much as his father, declaring, "That he was indebted to the one for *living*, and to the other for living *well*."

38. While Alexander was yet a boy, there was sent from Thessaly to Philip a noble war-horse, called Bucephalus, which, upon trial, proved so strong and fiery that no one dared to mount him. Philip gave orders that the unmanageable creature should be sent back again, when Alexander interposed, and besought permission to try his skill. It was granted. Alexander went up to the horse, spoke kindly to him, and, perceiving that he was frightened at his own shadow, turned him about, vaulted upon his back, and rode him round the circle of admiring courtiers with the greatest ease and address. When he alighted his father embraced him, exclaiming, "My son, seek a kingdom more worthy of thee, for Macedon is below thy merits." Bucephalus was ever after the favorite horse of Alexander, and the animal became so attached to his master that he would permit no one else to mount him.

39. At the age of sixteen, Alexander received the embassadors of Persia in the absence of his father, and, instead of inquiring about the palace and court, with a curiosity natural to his years, engaged with them in conversation upon the subjects of government, battles, and sieges, displaying such intelligence and discernment as quite surprised his visitors. At the age of eighteen, he commanded the Macedonian youth in the battle of Cheroneia, and cut down the Sacred Theban Band. *At the age of twenty, by the death of his father, he became monarch of Macedon, and generalissimo of the Greek forces.*

40. First Arrangements of Alexander.—Macedon had been

animated nature. He differed with Plato in philosophy, and established a school at Athens, in the grove called Lyceum, in opposition to the Academy. He delivered his lectures while walking about, and his followers were in consequence called *Peripatetics*. He continued his labors there thirteen years, and then retired to Chalcis, in Eubœa, to escape a fate similar to that of Socrates. He died there at the age of sixty-three. He was buried at Stagira, where his memory was honored with an altar and a tomb.

Questions.—37. How did Alexander regard Aristotle? 38. Give the account of Alexander and the horse Bucephalus. 39. What is related of Alexander at the age of sixteen? Of him at the age of eighteen? Of him at the age of twenty? 40. What changes had Philip effected in Macedon?

greatly changed by the energetic and beneficent policy of Philip. The inhabitants, from rude, uncultivated herdsmen at war with neighboring states, had been transformed into agriculturists, mechanics, or soldiers, who knew how to maintain a respectable position among the nations of Greece. But though Macedon was thus improved in its internal state, and comfortably allied with its neighbors, yet the death of Philip again roused the spirit of faction throughout Greece. The young king, however, showed himself fully capable of meeting his enemies, either in the field or cabinet. "The king's name is indeed changed," said he to the Macedonian assembly, "but the *king*, you shall find, remains the same." He retained the able ministers and generals who had assisted his father, and by their counsel and aid succeeded in quelling a rebellion already excited in his own dominions, and in securing the friendship of Thessaly, his most powerful ally.

41. Thus fortified, he proceeded to Thermopylæ, and took his inherited seat in the Amphictyonic council. Notwithstanding the efforts of Demosthenes, embassadors were sent from Athens as from the other states, to congratulate him upon his accession to the throne, and to desire *a continuation of the friendship formed with his father.* From Thermopylæ Alexander proceeded to Corinth, where, a congress of the states being assembled, the question of his election to the station of autocrator-general to carry the war into Persia was warmly discussed. He was elected by a great majority, though the Lacedemonians sternly opposed the measure. While in this region he determined to consult the oracle, but, as he happened to go upon an unlucky day, the priestess refused to officiate. The impetuous prince, however, seized her by the arm and dragged her into the temple, when she cried out, "My son, thou art invincible." Alexander, hearing this, said, "He wanted no other answer, for he had the very oracle he desired."

42. Wars in the North, East, and West.—Upon his return home, he began to make preparations for his great enterprise, but was prevented from setting off immediately by his troublesome neighbors. The Triballians and Thracians formed a league against him on the northeast, and the Illyrians again commenced incursions on the west. Parmenio, the general who had so faithfully served his father, was

---

Questions.—40. What caused the spirit of faction to break out again in Macedon? What did Alexander say to the Macedonian assembly? 41. What inherited seat did Alexander take? What efforts did Demosthenes make in vain? To what place did Alexander next proceed? What was done at Corinth? Give the account of Alexander with the oracle. Trace Alexander on the map, from Pella through his journey. 42. What troubles threatened Alexander on the northeast and west? On what expedition was Parmenio sent?

sent against the latter, and Alexander himself marched against the barbarians. He pursued them to the mountains, and overcame every obstacle with ease, till he reached the rugged chain of Hæmus, whose defiles Count Diebitsch so gallantly forced in the late war between Russia and Turkey. The mountaineers, unpracticed in regular warfare, established themselves upon the summits overlooking the only practicable pass, and, loading wagons with stones, prepared to roll them down upon the invaders.

43. The shields of the Macedonians were of a rectangular form, and large enough to protect the whole body. Alexander accordingly directed his soldiers to open their ranks, and let the wagons pass, and, where this was impracticable, to fall upon the ground, and cover themselves with their compacted shields. This plan succeeded. The wagons were wasted in vain; not a man was killed by their impetuous descent; and the phalanx, rapidly forming, advanced up the hill with loud shouts. The barbarians were routed, and their women and children falling into the hands of the Macedonians were sold for slaves. Alexander, determined in the beginning to make sure work, had ordered vessels from Byzantium to proceed up the Danube. After three days' journey through cultivated plains, he reached the banks of that mighty stream, and beheld upon the other side the country of the Getæ, or Goths, covered with wheat, already white to the harvest. Here, meeting his vessels, he transported his army across in the night, and the next day advanced towards the capital of the barbarians.

44. The Goths had assembled to give battle, but when they saw the phalanx approaching, with spears presented and burnished shields, hardly admitting a sight of what bore them, together with the cavalry moving with miraculous regularity, they fled in the greatest dismay. Their city fell into the hands of the Macedonians, and this bloodless victory was rewarded with great booty. Returning from this expedition before the Illyrians were subdued, he marched against them, and, falling upon them when they thought him still at a distance, gained so complete a victory that they never attempted rebellion again in his reign.

45. CONFEDERACY AGAINST MACEDON.—Scarcely were these enemies reduced, when new ones required his attention. Demosthenes, who

---

Questions.—42. On what expedition did Alexander march? How did the mountaineers prepare to encounter Alexander? 43. How did Alexander meet this kind of warfare? What was the result? What direction had Alexander given to vessels? Why? Give a further account of Alexander's movements. 44. How did the Goths behave? What was the consequence? What rapid movement did Alexander then make? Trace Alexander's route. 45. What did Demosthenes do while Alexander was absent?

hated and feared the son as sincerely as he had the father, and who used unsparingly the eloquence with which nature had so richly endowed him, and the gold with which the king of Persia so liberally furnished him, had succeeded in forming another confederacy against Macedon. After the battle of Cheroneia, a Macedonian garrison had been left in Thebes. The commanders of this garrison were both murdered in one night, and a report was at the same time circulated that Alexander was dead. A revolution immediately took place in Thebes, the Macedonian alliance was removed, and the city declared independent. The Thessalians, knowing whence the storm arose, declared war against *Athens and Thebes;* and Greece was again all commotion.

46. When these circumstances were reported to Alexander, in his camp in Illyria, he lost no time in deliberation. Taking the shortest route over a country of rocky, wooded mountains, in twelve days he arrived before the walls of Thebes with a chosen band. He hoped by the uncalculated rapidity of his march to intimidate his enemies, and compose matters without bloodshed; but though the Thebans were struck with dismay when they heard of his approach, they still determined to make an effort; and though the *Athenians* were not yet in arms, nor the *Arcadians* ready to march, they shut themselves up in their city, and, relying upon the strength of their walls, obstinately refused all offers of peace.

47. Ruin of Thebes.—The horrors perpetrated at the storming of Thebes have been rarely paralleled in the annals of war. Many brave men fell upon both sides before the gates were forced, but when once the multitudes of Phocians, Thespians, and Plateans (who had suffered so much from Theban cruelty, and were now found ranged under the banner of Alexander) came to settle their long account of blood, the city of Cadmus fell beneath the fearful retribution. The conquering army ravaged the town, careless of commands, and slaughtered alike the submissive and resisting. The altars, to which many fled for protection, flowed with the blood of the slain; even the slaves of the Thebans turned against their masters, and joined in the work of vengeance.

48. It does not appear that Alexander had power to mitigate these horrors, but, unwilling to bear the odium of destroying a Grecian city,

Questions.—45. What took place in Thebes? Why did the Thessalians declare war against Athens as well as Thebes? 46. Where was Alexander at the time? What rapid movement did he make? What did he expect to gain? Did the Thebans yield at once? What did they do? 47. Give an account of the fall of Thebes. 48. What measures were adopted preliminary to the destruction of Thebes? Where was Thebes? (See Map No. 2.)

he summoned a congress of the states to decide upon her fate. By this assembly the same measure which the Thebans had meted out to the Phocians, at the conclusion of the Sacred War, was now measured out to her. It was decreed that the Theban state should be annihilated, the town utterly destroyed, the surviving inhabitants sold into slavery, and the territory given to the conquering allies. Alexander succeeded in saving the house of the poet Pindar from the flames, and all his descendants from slavery, B. C. 335. Thus ended the city founded by Cadmus, after having been one of the heads of Greece seven hundred and ten years.

49. WHAT PASSED IN ATHENS.—A part of the Theban cavalry escaped to Athens, and the consternation which pervaded that city at the news they brought can scarcely be imagined. Not even Demosthenes dared to mount the bema and harangue the people. The counsels of Phocion consequently prevailed, and an embassy was sent to the victors, to apologize for the part Athens had taken, and beg for peace. Alexander received the deputies with favor, but insisted that the Athenians should deliver up ten of their most factious citizens to be tried, as the common enemies of Greece. In this number were Demosthenes and Charidemus. By the fable of the sheep who gave up their guardian dogs, the *great orator* dissuaded his countrymen from complying with the demand. Another embassy was therefore sent, to solicit better terms; and Alexander finally granted them, insisting only on the banishment of Charidemus, whom he suspected of having been an accomplice in his father's murder. We shall hear of him again in Persia.

50. The domestic troubles of Greece being thus once more quieted, the autocrator returned home, to prepare for that expedition which had so long occupied his ambitious thoughts. He intrusted the government of Macedon to Antipater, with a body of twenty thousand soldiers, to keep the states of Greece in awe. For the conquest of Asia, in which he was now setting out, he had only thirty thousand foot and five thousand horse, one month's provisions, and about forty thousand dollars in money. With this comparatively insignificant force, Alexander marched to attack that power which had swallowed up

---

Questions.—48. Give an account of the destruction of the city. What exception was made in the work of destruction? 49. To what place did a part of the Theban cavalry escape? What was the effect of the news there? What action did the Athenians take? Upon what did Alexander insist? How was he induced to change his exaction? What terms were finally agreed upon? 50. What was the next movement of Alexander? To whom did he intrust the government of Macedon? What was Alexander's great object? What preparations did he set out with?

Assyria, Chaldea, Egypt, and all the countries from the Egean on the west to India on the east, and which, one hundred and fifty years before, had sent a host of five millions of persons, to overwhelm that very Greece which was now prepared to roll back the tide of war upon the shores of Asia.

51. FIRST CAMPAIGN IN ASIA.—B. C. 334.—(1.*) AMPHIPOLIS.—Assembling his troops at this place in the spring of the year, Alexander marched at their head to (2.) THE HELLESPONT. With Homer's Iliad for his guide, he embarked from the spot where Agamemnon's fleet had weighed anchor eight hundred and fifty years before, and, taking the tiller in his hand, acted the part of steersman in the passage. Midway he lay on his oars, while a bull was sacrificed to Neptune and the Nereids, and then, pouring libations upon the waves from a golden vessel, resumed his course, and landed in the Achaian port, in imitation of his great predecessor.

52. Here he raised altars to Minerva and Hercules, and then proceeded to (3.) TROY. On this classic spot there was only a small village, still retaining the ancient name of Ilion. In a temple of Minerva were consecrated suits of armor, preserved since the Trojan war. He took down one of these, and hung up his own in its stead; and having performed sacrifices in honor of the Homeric heroes, and crowned the tomb of his ancestor Achilles, he proceeded on his way. No army attempted to stop his progress till he reached (4.) THE FORD OF THE GRANICUS, a river which flowed from Mount Ida into the Propontis.

53. BATTLE OF GRANICUS.—Darius, hearing of the expedition of Alexander, had sent a commission to his satraps in this quarter, to seize the "Mad Boy;" to whip him severely; to clothe him in mock purple, and bring him bound to Susa; to sink the ships in which he had crossed the Hellespont, and send his army in chains to the farther shore of the Red Sea. The Persian lords, in compliance with these gentle orders, assembled a large force on the banks of the Granicus; but the Macedonians forded the river, and ascended the steep bank in the face of their opposition, fought a tremendous battle, and gained a

* Let the pupil now look upon map No. 3, as Alexander's course is marked out.

Questions.—51. Where was Amphipolis? (See map No. 2, also number 1, Map No. 3.) [NOTE.—In reciting the campaigns of Alexander, take this method: Let the teacher say, "No. 1," and the pupil answer, "Amphipolis, a town in Macedonia, now Turkey in Europe. Here Alexander assembled his troops in the spring of 334 B. C., and marched," &c. "No. 2."—"The Hellespont, a strait leading from the Egean to the Propontis, now called Dardanelles." Here Alexander," &c.] 52. "No. 3."—"Troy: the exact spot where it stood cannot now be determined. Here Alexander," &c. Did Paul ever visit this spot? (See 2 Tim iv. 13.) 53, 54. "No. 4."—"Granicus, a small river which falls into the Sea of Marmora. Here Alexander," &c.

glorious victory. The Persians lost one-tenth of their army, and nine officers of distinction.

54. Alexander was first in the fight, and besides distinguishing himself for his bravery, was rendered conspicuous by his buckler and his crest, on both sides of which he wore a beautiful white plume. Two Persian officers made him their object of attack. One of them gave him a blow with a battle-ax which clove his helmet, and penetrated to the hair. As the barbarian raised his arm to repeat the stroke, Clitus, his foster-brother, ran him through with a spear. Alexander had now passed the *gates of Asia*, and made good his entrance into the dominion of the enemy. Twenty-five of his personal friends had been killed, to each of whom he erected a statue of brass; and upon the arms taken he caused to be inscribed, "Won by Alexander, of the barbarians of Asia." Most of the plate and furniture he sent home to his mother.

55. (5.) SARDIS.—The victory of Granicus intimidated the Persians and encouraged the Grecians. After marching through a great extent of country with the quiet and comfort of peace, Alexander was met, about seven miles from Sardis, by the principal men of the city, who came to throw themselves upon his mercy. He received them kindly, and, entering the place with them, took possession of the citadel. Here he ordered a temple to be erected to Jupiter, on the spot where the palace of Crœsus had stood.

56. He remained at Sardis only three days, regulating the government and tribute of the province, and then, by one day's march, arrived at (6.) EPHESUS, just as the Grecian party had overpowered the Persian, and were ready to hail him with joy at their gates. He gave orders that the tribute formerly paid to the Persians should be employed in rebuilding the temple of Diana; and having attended a magnificent sacrifice to this goddess, with all his troops, he moved forward to (7.) MILETUS. His fleet entered the bay at the same time his forces appeared before the town, and the Milesians, yielding to the powerful motives furnished by the battering-rams, surrendered.

57. (8.) HALICARNASSUS.—The fertile province of Caria, of which

---

Questions.—54. Who commanded the Persians in the battle? *Ans.* Memnon, the Rhodian: his widow was the mother of Hercules. (See page 272.) 55. "Sardis, now called Sait, a small village. Here Alexander, &c." What was written to the church of Sardis in Rev. iii. 1–5? How long before Alexander did Crœsus live? 56. Where was Ephesus? (See map No. 2, also number 6, map No. 3.) "Ephesus. Here Alexander gave orders," &c. Who founded Ephesus? *Ans.* Androchus, son of Codrus. Who laid the foundation of its greatness? *Ans.* Lysander, when he built a fleet there. (See page 190.) What is written to the church of Ephesus? (See Rev. ii. 1–5. "Miletus. Here," &c. When was the temple of Diana burned? 57. Give the location of Halicarnassus. What distinguished man was born there? (See page 163.)

Halicarnassus was the capital, was ruled by Ada, a descendant of that famous Artemisia who fought in the fleet of Xerxes, and sister of that still more famous Artemisia, who erected in honor of her deceased husband, Mausolus, the sepulchral monument reckoned among the "seven wonders of the world." An insurrection had been raised against Ada by her brother, and she was now deprived of a great part of her possessions. To this disputed point Alexander directed his course. Ada went out to meet him, adopted him for her son with great ceremony, gave him the keys of her strongest fortress, and so managed affairs that his march across Caria, of nearly one hundred miles, should be as through a friendly country. Halicarnassus submitted for the same reasons that had influenced Miletus.

58. Winter now approaching, he permitted a part of his army to return home, with authority to engage recruits; but he himself determined that the season should not pass in inactivity. Committing the government of Caria to his good mother, Ada, he went forward through Lycia and Pamphylia with his chosen troops, every town submitting upon his approach, and sending presents. At (9.) ASPENDUS, on the river Eurymedon, the people made considerable resistance. As a punishment, Alexander obliged them to furnish double the quantity of horses and money that he required of the other vanquished states.

59. (10.) GORDIUM.—In this place he visited the castle where was preserved with superstitious care the *Gordian knot.* The story of the knot was this: In those early ages when remarkable events were so common, a Phrygian peasant named Gordius, being engaged in plowing, an eagle perched upon the yoke of his oxen, and quietly rode up and down the field. Interested in the phenomenon, he left his work and went to seek some one to explain the mystery. He wandered on till, approaching a village, he saw a girl drawing water from a spring, and finding upon inquiry that she belonged to a race of seers, he told her his business. She advised him to return, and sacrifice immediately to Jupiter. This led to a multitude of inquiries as to the manner in which the ceremony was to be performed; and finally he persuaded the girl to marry him and accompany him home. Nothing important occurred till a son of this match, named Midas, attained manhood.

60. The Phrygians were then debating upon a change in their form of government, and while in assembly, were told that "A cart would bring them a king to relieve their troubles." Soon after, Gordius and

---

Questions.—57, 58. Who was Ada? By what process had she been deprived of part of her possessions? State what took place at Halicarnassus. At Aspendus. Where was Aspendus? What happened to Cymon and Thrasybulus at the river Eurymedon? 59, 60. Where was Gordium? (See map.) Relate the story of the *Gordian knot.*

Midas came in a cart to the convention, and the people, believing the oracle to be thus answered, elected Midas king of Phrygia. In commemoration of this event, Midas dedicated the cart and its appendages to the gods. The yoke was tied to the pole with a piece of the bark of the cornel-tree, in such a knot as no one could unloose. A tradition arose, that *whoever should untie that knot should be Lord of Asia;* and the failure of many ambitious men who had attempted it gave great importance to Alexander's visit. Some say that he cut the knot with his sword. Arrian asserts that he wrested the pin from the beam, and so took off the yoke. The means are of no consequence. He was believed to have accomplished the oracle, and to be the "destined lord of Asia." Here the troops that had been home rejoined the army.

61. Second Campaign.—B. C. 333.—(11.) Ancyra.—At this place an embassy met the king of Macedonia, bringing offers of submission from (12.) Paphlagonia. Thence he marched southward through (13.) Cappadocia, every town of which surrendered, till he reached the lofty ridge of Taurus, which separates Asia Minor from Syria. (14.) The Pass of Mount Taurus, called the Gate. The Persians thought to defend this important point, but the troops took flight at the approach of the Grecians, and Alexander encamped without molestation upon the plains of Cilicia. (15.) Tarsus.—The Persian forces stopped here, and Alexander hastened on to meet them. They fled again, but his exertion had so heated his blood, that the sight of the Cydnus, rolling its cool waters from the snow-clad summits of the mountains, was perfectly irresistible. He plunged in and amused himself some time in swimming, but he paid a severe penalty for his imprudence. A violent fever seized upon him and brought him down to the brink of the grave.

62. (16.) Anchialus.—As soon as he was sufficiently recovered, Alexander sent Parmenio to secure the passes into Syria, while he engaged in the more active business of reducing that part of the country west of Tarsus. At Anchialus a monument was found, bearing this inscription: "Sardanapalus, son of Anacyndaraxes, in one day founded Anchilaus and Tarsus. Eat, drink, and play: all other human

Questions.—61. Where was Ancyra? What took place there? What at the Pass of Mount Taurus? Where was Tarsus? What took place at Tarsus? Why was Tarsus a free city? *Ans.* The inhabitants took part with Cæsar in the civil wars, and were exempted from tribute when he became master of the world. It still remains, though only the shadow of its former self. What beautiful light was once seen on the Cydnus? (See page 303.)
62. On what expedition did Alexander send Parmenio? In what business did Alexander engage? What was found at Anchialus? Has previous reference been made to the Sardanapalus monument in this book?

joys are not worth a fillip." Darius, alarmed by the rapid advances of the Greeks, determined at last to take the field and meet the "mad boy" in person. He drew up his troops near Babylon, with a pomp little inferior to that displayed by Xerxes. The magi, carrying the Sacred Fire on altars of massy silver, led the van, chanting a solemn hymn. Three hundred and sixty-five youths vailed in Tyrian purple followed; then came the splendid chariot of Jove, drawn by white horses; and then the magnificent *steed of the sun*. Then followed ten chariots richly embossed with silver and gold; and the cavalry of the twelve nations, displaying arms and ensigns of the most curious workmanship.

63. The Immortal Band took the next rank, and 15,000 men dressed in the costliest apparel, called the king's relations, followed. Then came the king himself, seated in a lofty chariot, so richly ornamented that it can hardly be described, with the images of Ninus and Belus, and a golden eagle fixed upon the sides. Ten thousand men, armed with spears of silver and darts of glittering gold, followed, and 30,000 infantry inclosed him as a body-guard. His mother, wife, and children also, surrounded by chosen attendants, traveled with the army and king, according to the custom of the Persians; and a multitude of nations brought up the rear.

64. With this vast cavalcade of near a million of souls, resembling more a triumphal procession than a host armed for battle, Darius moved from the plains of the Euphrates northward toward the mountains of Syria, in quest of a handful of Greeks, who had already wrested from him the fertile territory of Asia Minor. As Darius I. had his Hippias, and Xerxes his Demaratus, so this king had also his attendant Grecian exile, Charidemus. While reviewing his immense army, Darius turned to Charidemus, and inquired if even the sight of such a multitude would not be sufficient to frighten Alexander. The Grecian, proud of the superiority of his countrymen, replied with such a cutting comparions between troops nurtured in the lap of luxury and those taught by necessity to meet danger in the most appalling forms, as displeased his royal patron. Darius, naturally mild and gentle, was now so agitated by jealousy and fear that he ordered his faithful monitor to instant execution.

65. (17.) Issus.—The mighty host commanded by Darius here came to an engagement with the Grecians, and was entirely defeated. The

Questions.—62, 63, 64. Upon what did Darius at last determine? Give an account of the number and kind of forces Darius had. Relate the circumstances of Charidemus's death. How long had he been in Persia? 65. Give an account of the battle of Issus. [NOTE.—Remember that this is the first battle where the two monarchs fought in person.]

moment Darius saw his troops giving way he retreated with the greatest precipitation, and getting into difficult places, where his chariot could not pass, he threw down his bow, shield, and royal mantle, and fled on horseback. Some of his army struck into the high road to Persia; some ran into the woods, or wandered among the mountains; 100,000 of his men were left dead upon the field; and his mother, queen, and children were taken prisoners in the camp.

66. The royal tent, furnished with vessels of gold and every species of eastern luxury, was a curiosity to the hardy Macedonian king. After having surveyed the silken drapery, tasted the delicious wines, and inhaled the luscious perfumes, he exclaimed contemptuously, "This, then, it is to be a king!" One beautiful casket he appropriated to himself. The manuscript of Homer's Iliad, prepared for him by Aristotle, was placed into it, and ever afterward styled the Casket copy. From the tent of Darius he proceeded to that of the princesses. The kindness and generosity with which he treated them forms one of the most beautiful traits in his history. The child of Darius, seing a man in armor, stretched out his hands to the conqueror, and Alexander, taking him in his arms, caressed him with the utmost tenderness.* To the ladies the victor granted every privilege demanded by Persian custom.

67. (18.) Damascus.—This was a treasure city of Darius, and Alexander sent Parmenio to take it. The governor surrendered at once, and such vast quantities of spoils fell into the hands of the victors as loaded 7,000 beasts, besides heaps of valuable jewelry. (19.) Sidon.—The inhabitants of this city gave up their keys with joy to the conqueror. While in Syria, he received a letter from Darius, in which that monarch offered any sum of money for the ransom of his family, and desired conditions of peace. The king of Macedonia replied by alluding to the invasions of Greece by the Persians. He charged Darius with stirring up the Greeks against Macedonia, and procuring the death of his father.

68. (20.) Tyre.—As he proceeded along the coast of Phenicia, a deputation met him from Tyre, bringing offers of *friendship*, but not

* The boy could not have mistaken him for his father, for Darius was of a tall, elegant form, while Alexander was rather short, and ungraceful in his person.

Questions.—66. What is said of the royal tent? Of Alexander's conduct after the battle? Of that of Darius's child? 67. How is Damascus situated? State how it was taken. What took place there? State how Sidon was taken. Why were the Sidonians so willing to surrender? *Ans.* They hated the Persians for having miserably destroyed their city. So much gold was melted in its conflagration that Ochus sold the ashes for large sums of money. What letter is spoken of? What was Alexander's reply? 68. Where was Tyre? What negotiations took place?

of *submission.* He thanked them for their amicable professions, and expressed his intention of visiting the city to worship the Tyrian Hercules. The gates were closed when he arrived, and he received a polite intimation that the Tyrians did not wish to admit him. Thereupon, he resolved to besiege the place. Old Tyre had been destroyed by Nebuchadnezzar 240 years before; but New Tyre, standing on an island half a mile from the shore, was at this time the strongest maritime town in the world. Its walls were 100 feet high and 18 miles in circuit. With a fleet obtained from Sidon and Cyprus, Alexander blockaded it by sea; while by land he undertook the carrying out a mole from Old Tyre to the rocky ramparts of the new city.

69. The Tyrians defended themselves with the most determined bravery. They destroyed the mole several times; they caught the workmen with grappling-irons, and dragged them within the walls; they sent out fire-ships, and burnt many galleys, and poured down showers of heated sand upon the besiegers, which, penetrating through the chinks of the armor, burned to the very bone. For six months this dreadful siege lasted, and then Tyre was "taken but not rendered." From house to house, and from street to street, every inch of ground was disputed; mercy was neither asked nor given, until a great part of the garrison had fallen. Eight thousand Tyrians fell in the onslaught, and thirty thousand captives were sold into slavery. While the siege of Tyre was in progress, Alexander received another letter from Darius, in which the monarch offered him his daughter in marriage, and the whole country from the Euphrates to the Mediterranean as her dowry. "If I were Alexander," said Parmenio, "I would accept it."—"So would I, were I Parmenio," said the king.

70. (21.) JERUSALEM.—From Phenicia, Alexander marched to Palestine. The Jews, whose city and temple had been rebuilt by the Persians, loved their benefactors, and faithfully adhered to their cause. It was therefore not without terror that they heard of the approach of the victorious commander at Issus. Josephus says that Jaddua, the high priest, clothed in his sacred robes, went out to meet Alexander,

Questions.—68, 69. By whom and when had Old Tyre been destroyed? What was the condition of New Tyre? How did Alexander proceed against the place? How did the Tyrians defend themselves? How long did the siege last? Describe the taking of the city. When was it taken? *Ans.* On the 20th of August, B. C. 332. When did Alexander receive a second letter from Darius? What was the purport of the letter? What conversation took place between Alexander and Parmenio? Read Is. xxiii. 10, 11; Ezek. xxvii. 10–13, 16, 18, 19, 23–25, 34, 35; and xxviii. 7, 8; Zech. ix. 3–5, 12, 13, 16. 70. Why were the Jews faithful to the Persians? What is related of Jaddua? What privilege did Alexander grant the Jews? *Ans.* He exempted them from paying tribute every seventh year, for in that year they neither sowed nor reaped. Read Daniel viii. 20–22.

and no sooner did the Macedonian monarch behold him than he prostrated himself, and worshiped the holy name inscribed upon his miter. When the astonished nobles inquired the reason of this strange reverence, he told them that such a person had appeared to him in a vision, and invited him to undertake the conquest of Asia. Jaddua pointed out to him those passages in the book of Daniel where his rapid conquests were foretold, and, after some more conversation, was dismissed in a friendly manner.

71. (22.) GAZA was situated two miles from the sea, on a lofty rock, surrounded by a territory of deep sand. The governor refused to surrender, and Alexander would not leave an unconquered place behind him. Timber and earth were brought from a distance, a mound formed as high as the walls, and battering-rams erected. After a great expense of time, money, and lives, the place fell into the hands of the Greeks. Every man of the garrison died fighting. The governor was taken alive, and put to death in the most horrid manner. (23.) PELUSIUM.—In seven days' march from Gaza, Alexander arrived with his army before this place, at the same time that his fleet sailed into the harbor. The Egyptians, haters of the Persians since the days of Cambyses, received him with joy, and thus he became the acknowledged lord of this fertile and wealthy country without striking a blow.

72. (24.) HELIOPOLIS, the city of the Sun. To know the country, and arrange the government of the people who had become his peaceful subjects, he advanced up the right bank of the Nile to Heliopolis, where he crossed the river and proceeded to (25.) MEMPHIS, the place of the tombs and treasures of the Egyptian kings. (26.) ALEXANDRIA. Learning that Egypt had no convenient seaport, he explored the coast of the Mediterranean till he reached a suitable point, where he founded the city which still bears his name.* Far within that vast tract of sand known as the Lybian Desert, lay the beautiful oasis containing the temple of Jupiter Ammon. An insatiable desire to be considered rather a god than a man, had, by the conversation of his mother, been instilled into the mind of Alexander. Stimulated by this foolish vanity, he marched with a small escort along the seacoast about 200 miles, to (27.) PARETONIUM.

* It was marked out in the shape of a Macedonian cloak.

Questions.—71. How was Gaza situated? How was the place taken? How was Pelusium situated? How was it taken? 72. What took place at Heliopolis? What is said of Memphis? By whom was the city of Alexandria founded? What led to the act? When was the city founded? *Ans.* B. C. 332. Where was the temple of Jupiter Ammon? What great desire did Alexander have? How did he contract the desire?

73. Thence he turned south, and traversing those fields which a tropical sun renders ever arid and sterile, he arrived safely at (28.) THE TEMPLE OF JUPITER AMMON.—The island of delightful green, which greeted his eyes on emerging from the vast ocean of sand, was only about five miles across, each way. The air was pleasantly cool; springs of the finest water were plentiful; and beneath the shade of lofty trees, whose spreading branches shut out the scorching rays of the sun, the weary band reposed after their perilous and fatiguing journey. The priest confirmed the monarch's pretensions, and he left the temple *the acknowledged son of the god!* Thence he returned again to (25.) MEMPHIS, where embassadors from the states of Greece were waiting to congratulate him on his success.

74. THIRD CAMPAIGN.—B. C. 331.—While Alexander wintered in Egypt a re-enforcement from Greece arrived, and upon the opening of spring he moved again to (20.) TYRE, the place appointed for the meeting of the fleet, army, and embassies. Thither the Athenian ship Paralus conveyed ministers from the different republics, who acquainted him with the state of affairs in his own country. After having made arrangements for the security of Greece he went on his way, and about the beginning of June reached (29.) THAPSACUS, the place where young Cyrus crossed the Euphrates with his Grecian troops. The bridges were broken down, and a body of Persians stood ready to dispute his passage; but their hearts failed at his approach, and, taking flight, they left the Greeks to repair the bridges and continue their route unmolested. It was Alexander's intention to march immediately to Babylon; but learning that Darius had assembled a larger force than he commanded at Issus, and was waiting his approach on the eastern bank of the Tigris, he directed his course thither, and without obstruction crossed that rapid river at a ford.

75. (30.) ARBELA.—Here Darius deposited his heavy baggage and military stores; and very judiciously chose his station about six miles from the town, in a place suitable for the action of his cavalry and scythe-armed chariots. Alexander approached, and prepared for battle. That night he slept soundly, though Darius reviewed his troops by torch-light, and the murmur of the immense multitude seemed like the roaring of the sea when the waters are agitated by the violence of the wind. Two years after the victory at Issus, Alexander again

---

Questions.—73. By what route did he reach the temple of Jupiter Ammon? Describe the island. What did the priest do? To what place did Alexander then go? Where was Memphis? 74. What arrangement did Alexander make to get information from Greece? What took place at Thapsacus? Where was Thapsacus? Why did not Alexander proceed direct to Babylon? 75. Where was Arbela? What took place there? *Ans.* A battle.

mounted Bucephalus, as a signal for battle with the monarch of Asia. He wore a short coat closely girt about him; over that, a breastplate of linen strongly quilted, which had been found among the spoils of Issus. His helmet of polished iron shone like silver. A superb belt, given him by the Rhodians, encircled his waist, from which was suspended a sword of the finest temper. Aristander the soothsayer rode by his side, clothed in a white robe and a golden crown.

76. Just as they were advancing, an eagle appeared above their heads and slowly sailed toward the enemy. As soon as the army caught sight of the noble bird, they rushed on like a torrent to the fight. Alexander, following the example of Epaminondas, directed his efforts to one point, and selected for that point the spot where Darius rode upon his lofty chariot in the midst of his royal forces. The king of Asia sustained himself much better than on the former occasion; but the onset of the Macedonians was so terrible, that his body-guard were seized with consternation and fled. A few of the bravest of them indeed lost their lives in defending their sovereign; and falling in heaps, one upon another, strove to stop the pursuit by clinging in the pangs of death to the Macedonians, and catching hold of the legs of the horses, as they pranced over their prostrate bodies.

77. Darius had now the most dreadful dangers about him. His defenders were driven back upon him; the wheels of his chariot became entangled among the dead bodies, so that it was almost impossible to turn it; and the horses, plunging among heaps of slain, bounded up and down, and no longer obeyed the charioteer. Again he quitted his chariot, and, throwing away his arms, fled on horseback. At first, Alexander pushed on after him; but at dark abandoned the pursuit, and returned to the camp. About midnight, with a band of chosen troops, he rode off to Arbela, and, surprising the town, gained possession of it without bloodshed. The Persian empire appearing to be entirely destroyed by the defeat at Arbela, Alexander was acknowledged *king of Asia.* Without waiting for the formal abdication or destruction of Darius, he turned to secure the treasures which the fugitive monarch had left in his grasp.

78. (31.) Babylon.—As the conqueror approached this city he was met by the whole population, following in solemn procession the nobles and priests, who brought him presents, and surrendered the

Questions.—75, 76, 77. How was Alexander attired for the battle? What is said of Aristander? Of an eagle? Give an account of the battle. What is said of the dangers which beset Darius during the battle? Of his escape? What were the occurrences after the battle? 78. Where was Babylon? How did Alexander get possession of Babylon?

citadel, treasury, and town into his hands. The ready submission of his new subjects so pleased Alexander, that he ordered the former temples to be restored, and assisted himself at a sacrifice of Belus. (32.) SUSA was the common winter residence of the Persian court. Before Alexander reached this place the son of the governor met him, assuring him that the gates were open to receive him, and a treasury, containing a sum equal to $45,000,000, waiting his disposal.

79. The spoils found in Susa were such as no other city ever presented to a conqueror. There were stuffs of such exquisite purple, that though treasured 190 years, they still retained their freshness and beauty; splendid vases containing the waters of the Nile and Danube, which the Persians kept among their precious things, to show the extent of their dominions; and, what Alexander valued more than all, the brazen statues of Harmodius and Aristogiton,* which Xerxes had stolen from Greece, and which the autocrator-general now sent back as a peace-offering to the Athenians. Here he reinstated the family of Darius in the palace where they had passed the happy years of power; and, having committed the administration of affairs to a Persian, went on his way.

80. The passage from Susa to Persepolis was rough and difficult, leading over mountains inhabited by savage tribes, to whom even the kings of Persia had paid toll; but the rapidity of Alexander's movements disconcerted their plans of defense, and the Greeks took possession of their strongholds. The officers of Darius fled from the city at his approach, not even stopping to plunder the treasury of Cyrus, in which Alexander found as much coin as he did at Susa, and such quantities of rich movables as loaded 20,000 mules and 5,000 camels. He stayed in this place four months, that his troops might rest after their fatigues, and prepare for the spring campaign. The first time he sat down on the throne of the Persian kings, under a golden canopy, an old Corinthian exclaimed, while the tears streamed from his eyes, "What a pleasure have those Greeks missed who died without seeing Alexander seated on the throne of Darius!"

81. Before breaking up his winter quarters he made a great enter-

* After the banishment of the Pisistratidæ, Harmodius and Aristogiton received almost heroic honors. Statues of the finest brass were erected to their memory, and their names were held in the highest veneration.

Questions.—78. Where was Susa? How did Alexander get possession of Susa? 79. What spoils were found in Susa? What is said of Alexander's treatment of the family of Darius? 80. Where was Persepolis? (33.) What rapid movements did Alexander make? What is said in connection with his sitting on the throne of the Persian kings? 81. What is said of the entertainment provided by Alexander?

tainment, at which all the guests drank to excess. An Athenian courtesan, Thais, having studiously praised the lord of the feast during the whole evening, suggested the idea of closing the banquet by a conflagration of the royal palace, in revenge for the burning of Athens by Xerxes; and she desired to light the flame with her own hands, that it might be said, the *women* had taken better vengeance upon the Persians than all the generals of Greece. The whim struck the conqueror favorably; and the guests, heated with wine, received the proposition with acclamations. Immediately they rose from the table, and following Thais, with lighted tapers in their hands, proceeded to set fire to every part of the grand palace, accompanying the exploit with loud peals of mirth and music.

82. B. C. 330. FOURTH CAMPAIGN.—From the fatal overthrow at Arbela, Darius had proceeded to Ecbatana, hoping to raise an army there of sufficient force to preserve to him the ancient kingdom of Media, with Bactria and Sogdiana; but finding that a universal panic had seized his soldiers, he gave up all hopes of regaining his lost kingdom, and sought only to escape with the relics of his treasure to some distant province. Five days before Alexander reached (34.) ECBATANA, the defeated monarch left that city, and retreated through the passes of the mountains that skirt the Caspian Sea. Alexander stopped long enough to reorganize his army, to reward his soldiers with princely munificence, to re-engage those who wished still to push their fortunes in his service, to dismiss those weary of campaigns and victories, and to settle the affairs of the province.

83. Then, with a chosen band, he resumed the pursuit of Darius. After marching eleven days so rapidly that many horses died of fatigue, he received tidings, tending rather to increase than retard his speed. He learned from two of Darius's servants that Bessus, governor of Bactria, and another satrap, had seized their sovereign, and carried him off a close prisoner; that it was their intention, if Alexander overtook them, to deliver him up, and so gain favor for themselves; or, if they succeeded in escaping, to depose him, and usurp the government of the northern provinces. This news roused every energy of Alexander. He traveled day and night without intermission till he came up with

Questions.—81. Of the conflagration? What can you state of the ruins of the palace? *Ans.* The ruins called Chilminar, or Forty Columns, near Sclinaz, are supposed to be the remains of the palace burned by Thais. [NOTE.—Now let the pupil trace Alexander's course on a map] 82. Why had Darius gone to Ecbatana? Why was he not successful in this? How near did Alexander come to capturing Darius in Ecbatana? How long did Alexander stop there? 83. Give an account of Alexander's further pursuit of Darius. Who was Bessus? Upon what did Bessus determine? How was he foiled?

the traitors (or rather with their prisoner), for Bessus, finding himself unable to push on with the chariot as fast as necessary, had given Darius several severe wounds, and left him weltering in his blood.

84. Only about sixty of the Macedonians were able to keep pace with Alexander till he reached the enemy's camp. There they rode over scattered garments, and furniture, and golden vessels; and, passing a number of carriages filled with deserted women and children, came to the chariot where Darius lay in the agonies of death. He called for a drink of water, and after having quenched his thirst with the cooling draught, stretched out his hand to the soldier that brought it, saying, "Friend, this fills up the measure of my misfortunes, to think I am not able to reward thee for this act of kindness. But Alexander will not let *thee* go without a recompense, and the gods will reward *him* for his humanity to my mother, my wife, and my children. Tell him I gave thee my hand in his stead, and convey to him the only pledge I am able to give of my gratitude and affection." When Alexander came up, Darius was already dead. The conqueror was greatly afflicted at the tragical end of his rival. He threw his own robe over the bleeding body, and with generous care caused it to be conveyed to Susa, where the queen, Sisygambis, interred it with funeral honors.

85. Meanwhile, the conspirators betook themselves to the lofty wooded mountains of (35.) HYRCANIA, where Bessus, adopting the name of Artaxerxes, prepared to vindicate his title to the throne of Persia. Alexander continued the pursuit, and conquered the province; but Bessus made his escape with a body of 600 horse. Thus successful in all his enterprises against the barbarians, Alexander was wounded by a domestic affliction, for which the most brilliant victory could not compensate. Parmenio had been the "one general" whom *Philip* loved and trusted; the able counselor and guide of Alexander in his youth, and his companion in all his toilsome campaigns. Philotas, the son of Parmenio, had been one of the monarch's most intimate and favored friends from childhood. This Philotas was accused of treason, and being put upon the rack, confessed the crime, and named his father as one of the accomplices.

86. An assembly of the Macedonians was called, and the father and son were both condemned to die. Philotas was stoned to death, and

Questions.—84. Give an account of Alexander's final pursuit. Give an account of the death of Darius. Of Alexander's care for the body of Darius. 85, 86. Where was Hyrcania? What name did Bessus adopt? What is said of him? Who was Parmenio? Who Philotas? What accusation was brought against Philotas? What confession did he make? What sentence was passed? How was the sentence carried out?

a particular friend of Parmenio's was sent into Media, where that venerable general was stationed, to execute the sentence upon *him*. Parmenio was walking in his park, and, seeing his friend approaching, ran to embrace him, inquiring after his son and his king with the greatest tenderness. The assassin gave him a letter from Alexander, and, while he was reading it, stabbed him in the side, repeating his blows till assured he was dead. Thus fell this great man, illustrious both in peace and war. He was seventy years of age, and had served his sovereign with fidelity and zeal in numberless campaigns; two of his sons had died in battle, and with the third and last he himself fell a victim to the suspicions which an infamous boy had aroused, and vicious favorites had fostered in the mind of the king, for whom he had so often hazarded his life.

87. The lust of power and the pride of dominion had already taken deep root in the mind of Alexander. He was surrounded by flatterers, and his foolish ambition to be considered *a god* exposed the weak points in his character. Philotas ridiculed this pretension, and thus plucked down ruin upon his own head; for his guilt, to say the least, was not fully proved. Knowing that the execution of these distinguished individuals might create discontent, Alexander again marshaled his forces and set out after Bessus, who had retreated to Northern India, laying waste the country behind him. He met with no particular adventure till he reached the head waters of the Indus. Winter overtaking him there, he employed his troops in building a city, which he named (36.) ALEXANDRIA. It is still a flourishing place on the great route of Candahar, by which caravans go through Affghanistan and Northern India to Agra and Lahore.

88. B. C. 329.—FIFTH CAMPAIGN.—Observing the hardiness and vigor of the natives of these climates, he enrolled 30,000 boys among his followers, and caused them to be trained in the Macedonian discipline. Meanwhile, Bessus had established himself in Bactria, and Alexander, anxious to come upon him before he was prepared, moved early in the spring to the north. The soldiers, tired of marches and countermarches, and thinking the object of their expedition already accomplished by the subjection of Persia and the death of Darius,

Questions.—86. What further is said of Parmenio? What observation has been made about Alexander's successes? *Ans.* It has been stated that "Parmenio obtained many victories without Alexander, but Alexander not one without Parmenio." 87. What was the foolish ambition of Alexander? To what did it lead? Why did Alexander soon marshal his forces again? What place did he reach by winter? What is said of the place? How is it located? (See map No. 1.) 88. How did Alexander add 30,000 troops to his army? Where had Bessus established himself? Where was Bactria? (See map No. 1, number 37.) What caused murmurings in the camp of Alexander?

were so little pleased with the idea of traveling to the north while the snow was yet upon the ground, that nothing but murmurings and repinings was heard within the camp. Alexander called them all together, and addressed them as his friends and supporters, so mixing the tender with the animating in his speech, that he excited their sympathies, and raised their drooping spirits; and they declared themselves willing to follow wherever he should lead. Profiting by this favorable disposition, he made all speed into Bactriana.

89. (37.) Bactria and (38.) Aorni, the two principal cities of the province, were taken by assault, and all the rest quietly submitted. After crossing the river Oxus on skins stuffed with straw, he received tidings of Bessus. Two of the traitor's servants, imitating his example, had treated him in the same manner that he treated his royal master. They seized his person, forced the diadem from his head, tore the royal robe of Darius from his shoulders, set him on horseback, and brought him bound to Alexander. The miserable Bessus was sent to the mother of Darius to receive his doom. She ordered four trees to be bent down, and the limbs of the criminal to be fastened to them; the trees were then permitted to fly back, each bearing away its portion of his body. (39.) Sogdiana.—Here Alexander rested with his army, while horses and other recruits were collected for the invasion of Scythia.

90. Nothing of importance occurred till he reached (40.) The Jaxarthes. Scythia in Europe and Scythia in Asia, the great fountains from which issued, in later times, the fierce warriors of Ghengis-Khan and Timurlane, from which came forth Huns and Turks upon their work of destruction, were at this time inhabited by wandering tribes, which Alexander could have no motive to molest. Nevertheless, to fortify his empire against their incursions, he built upon the Jaxarthes a city, and called it Alexandria, which is the last one we shall notice, though in his travels he founded no less than twenty cities of this name. The "Speech of the Scythian embassadors to Alexander," so justly celebrated, is too long for insertion here; nor will it be necessary to detail the particulars of the hostilities in which he soon after engaged with this barbarous people.

91. He spent the winter in Bactria, and the historian, in speaking of him here, mentions that he had changed the Macedonian for the Per-

Questions.—88. How did he quiet the murmurs? 89. What was Alexander's success in Bactriana? How did he cross the Oxus? By what name is the Oxus now known? *Ans.* Jihoon or Gihon. How was Bessus at last taken? What was his fate? Where was Sogdiana located? (See map No. 1.) What is it now called? *Ans.* Samarcand. 90. What is the Jaxarthes now called? *Ans.* The Sihon. What city did Alexander build on that river? Why did he build it? What other cities did he found? 91. What is said of Alexander's change of costume and manners?

sian costume. Indeed, Alexander's conformity to the luxurious habits of the East had weakened his virtues, and rendered him odious to many of his most faithful friends. It was five years since he left Macedonia, with a comparatively small army; he was now surrounded by numbers, among whom there were as many *Asiatics* as *Greeks*, and the adoption of the manners and customs of the nations he had subjugated seemed to *him* the dictate of profound policy; while, to the veterans who had retained the native simplicity of Grecian manners, it seemed but another manifestation of that vanity which claimed the worship rendered only to the gods.

92. B. C. 328. SIXTH CAMPAIGN.—The summer of 328 was spent in quelling a revolt among the Sogdians, of which no particulars of interest are recorded, except that Spitamenes, the leader of it, was the individual who betrayed Bessus. He perished, like his predecessors, by the hands of false friends, who cut off his head, and carried it as a valuable present to Alexander.

93. B. C. 327. SEVENTH CAMPAIGN.—"Winter still lingered in the lap of spring," when Alexander moved to the destruction of (41.) THE SOGDIAN ROCK, the last stronghold which resisted his power. It was a mountain fortress, built upon a rock so lofty that its head was crowned with perpetual snows. When summoned to surrender, Oxyartes, the governor, looked proudly down upon the herald, and inquired "if Alexander had provided himself with winged soldiers." The conqueror could not bear this taunt. He offered immense sums to those who would scale the cliff. A band of the bravest youths undertook the perilous adventure, and succeeded by driving iron pins into the congealed snow, and suspending scaling-ladders upon them. The barbarians, thinking they must have been assisted by invisible beings, surrendered immediately upon their summons; and Roxana, the beautiful daughter of the governor, so captivated the conqueror that he made her the partner of his throne.

94. DEATH OF CLITUS.—Persia and its environs were now subdued, and Alexander projected the conquest of India. Before leaving these provinces, he regulated the government and committed it to Clitus, a valued friend, who had saved his life at the Granicus. As usual, the Macedonians prefaced the expedition with sacrifices and feasts. While they sat drinking, the conversation turned upon the history of Castor

Questions.—92. How was the summer of 328 spent? What is said of Spitamenes? 93. What was the Sogdian Rock? Where was it situated? Who, in 327, was the governor? What inquiry did he make of Alexander? State how the place was taken. Who was Roxana? What is said of her? 94. What conquests had Alexander completed in 327? What charge was committed to Clitus?

and Pollux, said to be the sons of Jupiter. This, by association, brought up Alexander's pretensions to the same high birth. The king, indeed, boasted not a little of his exploits, and the courtiers about him chimed in with the grossest flattery.

95. Clitus, heated with wine, took upon himself the office of reprover, contending that Philip was a greater man than his son, and that Alexander owed his victories not so much to his own prowess, as to the brave men by whom he had been supported. Alexander retorted; and Clitus, far from giving up the dispute at the instigation of the more temperate part of the company, called upon his king "To speak out what he had to say, or not invite freemen to his table, who would speak out their sentiments without reserve. But perhaps," continued he, "it were better to pass your life with barbarians and slaves, who will worship your Persian girdle and white robe without scruple." Alexander, no longer able to restrain his anger, threw an apple in his face, and then looked about for his sword. The company interposed, and forced Clitus from the room; but he soon returned by another door, singing, in a bold and insolent tone, these lines from Euripides:—

> "Are these your customs? Is it thus that Greece
> Rewards her combatants? Shall one man claim
> The trophies won by thousands?"

96. Alexander's fury knew no bounds. He sprang from the table, snatched a spear from one of the guards, and laid his foster brother dead at his feet, exclaiming, "Go now to Philip and Parmenio." The blood of his friend sobered him in a moment; he threw himself upon his body, forced out the javelin, and would have dispatched himself with it, had not the guards carried him by force to his apartment. He passed that night and all the next day in the deepest anguish, and it was some time before his philosopher-courtiers could comfort him. Not long after, a conspiracy was discovered among the royal pages. Calisthenes, nephew of Aristotle, who had accompanied Alexander partly as a philosopher, and partly to collect valuable materials for scientific research, was implicated.* All the conspirators were put to death except Calisthenes. He was mutilated, and carried about with the army in an iron cage, until he terminated his life by poison.

* Some authors say Calisthenes was put to death because he promised to adore Alexander, and broke his word. This was the man who transcribed the Chaldean records found in the fane of Belus.

Questions.—95. Relate the controversy that took place. 96. What was the sequel of the dispute? Did Alexander regret his rashness? How did he manifest his regret? What is said of a conspiracy that afterward occurred?

97. B. C. 326. EIGHTH CAMPAIGN.—CONQUEST OF INDIA.—Alexander having set out for the conquest of Asia with a land force of less than 40,000 men, and with a revenue too scanty for their support, now, with the income of the Persian Empire, too vast for computation, commanded an army which could scarcely be numbered. He had read in the Grecian fables that Hercules and Bacchus, both sons of Jupiter, had marched as far as India, and he determined to outdo his brothers, and go still farther. Late in the spring of the year 326, he broke up his camp in Bactria, and proceeded with rapid march to his new field of glory. It will not be necessary to specify all his adventures. Nothing was found capable of resisting his power. He took eight towns by storm, fought many battles, crossed the Indus, and went on to meet an Indian king beyond the Hydaspes, whom fame reported to be worthy of his arms. Between these two rivers he took up his winter quarters.

98. B. C. 325. NINTH CAMPAIGN.—(49.) THE HYDASPES was swollen with the melting of the snows and the spring rains, when the Grecians began to make preparations for crossing. Porus (the Indian king), aware of Alexander's intention, assembled his army on the banks, determined to dispute his passage; but our hero had ingenuity as well as courage. Every night he sent out bodies of cavalry, with orders to sound their trumpets and raise their war-cry, as if preparing to force their way across the river. Porus at first drew out his men at every fresh alarm; but, finding it amounted to nothing, he suffered his troops to enjoy their repose, and neglected watching the fords altogether. Every thing fell out as Alexander had calculated. One dark night, when a dreadful thunder-storm shook the surrounding hills, and drowned the noise of the embarkation, the Macedonians crossed an arm of the river to a small island densely wooded, and before morning were far advanced in preparation for passing the other branch of the stream.

99. The Indian outposts sent immediate notice of the enemy's approach to Porus; but as his attention was engaged with a body of horse, which appeared about to attempt the fords opposite the place where he had stationed himself, he considered the alarm up the stream as a feint, and merely sent his son thither with a small band. Alexander effected a landing in safety, attacked the Indian cavalry, and slew the son of Porus. Both sides then prepared for a decisive battle.

Questions.—97. When did Alexander break up his camp in Bactria? What great object did he have in view? Why was he so actuated? What were his successes? Between what two rivers did he quarter during the winter? 98, 99, 100. Who was Porus? What ingenuity did Alexander manifest? Give an account of the battle.

Porus placed his cavalry and war-chariots upon the wings, drew up his elephants in front of his line, and his infantry in a solid mass in the rear. The charge was violent and bloody; the elephants threw the Greeks into confusion just as the left wing of the Indians was put to flight; but as the Macedonian light troops came up and immediately slew their guides, these unwieldy animals, not knowing which way to go, and irritated by wounds, ran round the field and increased the general tumult.

100. Porus, who was easily distinguished from all others by his stature, bravery, and the size of the elephant on which he rode, fought with the most determined courage. Even after the fortune of the day was lost he remained upon the field, striving to rally his forces and retrieve his honor. The noble beast on which he was mounted took the greatest care of his person; and when he perceived him ready to sink under the multitude of weapons showered upon him, he kneeled down in the softest manner, and with his proboscis gently drew every dart from his body.

101. Porus was taken prisoner and brought before Alexander, who inquired of the fallen monarch how he would like to be treated. "Like a king," was the proud reply. Delighted at finding in another sentiments so congenial to his own, Alexander distinguished Porus with unusual favors; for he not only restored to him all his own dominions, but added very extensive territories to them, so that though he subdued him as *king* of one nation, he left him acting as *emperor* of a country which contained *fifteen nations*, 37 populous cities, and numerous flourishing villages. On the field of battle the Macedonians threw up the walls of Victory-town, in commemoration of their success, and, at the point where they crossed the Hydaspes, Alexander built a city which he called Bucephalia, in honor of his favorite horse, which died there of old age. Here he stationed a part of his army to build a fleet, with which to explore the Indus.

102. The Soldiers refuse to go Farther.—Curiosity and love of conquest had now become so settled in the mind of Alexander, that he could not be satisfied with the vast extent of country south and east of Porus's dominions, which his soldiers subdued with almost incredible rapidity. A great sovereign was said to reside far to the eastward, governing a populous and wealthy continent, so extensive that its utmost limits were entirely unknown. To reach this continent, and overthrow this empire, became the object of his solicitude; and

Questions.—101. What misfortune befell Porus himself? What question and reply are noted? What was the consequence to Porus? What city did Alexander then build?

orders were accordingly given to prepare for advancing to the Ganges, a river which was reported to be thirty-two furlongs wide and one hundred fathoms deep. The Macedonians, who had traveled through so many lands, and wasted the best part of their lives in fatiguing campaigns, were now incessantly turning their eyes to their dear native country, and longing to revisit it. For two months they had been exposed to violent storms; and now, when new wars and new dangers were proposed, neither the severity of military discipline, nor their love for their young sovereign, could prevent their feelings from breaking forth in loud lamentations. Some bewailed their calamities in the most plaintive terms, while others resolutely declared they would go no farther. The dissatisfaction spread among all ranks, and included even Alexander's most confidential friends.

103. Still bent upon his expedition, the conqueror assembled his army, rehearsed in a moving manner all the victories and spoils they had won, and the perils they had encountered together, and set before them in glowing colors the new laurels they should gain if they continued their route to the ocean. But all in vain. The soldiers, with eyes fixed upon the ground, maintained a resolute silence, until a venerable man, more bold than the rest, took up the reply. He stated in the most respectful tone, that of the Macedonians who left Greece with their general, eight years before, some had fallen in battle; some, disabled with wounds, had been left in different places, far from their families and friends; many had died of sickness, fatigue, and forced marches; and of the few that remained, the bodily energies were weakened, and the minds impaired. He reminded his sovereign that his own family had a right to expect him; that the Grecian republics, of which he was the chosen head, had been troubled by divisions in consequence of his absence; and that every principle of honor and moderation required his return home.

104. The soldiers received this statement of their grievances and desires with enthusiastic applause, and the king, greatly chagrined, dismissed the assembly, and retired silently to his tent. Here he shut himself up, and refused for two days to see even his friends; but finding that his affliction wrought no change in the minds of his soldiers, he ordered a sacrifice to be performed, by which the matter was referred to the gods. Then, assembling his officers, he told them that as the divine powers were favorable to the desires of the army, he

Questions.—102. What orders for advancing were given? What object did Alexander then have before him? Why did the soldiers refuse to go farther? 103. State how Alexander endeavored to change their purpose. Give the points of the speech made to Alexander. 104. What course did Alexander then take?

would cheerfully give up his own wishes, and they might communicate his intentions to move homeward. The joy of the heroic Ten Thousand when "the sea" burst upon their longing gaze, could scarcely have equaled the emotions of the sorrowing Grecians when these glad tidings were communicated to them. The whole camp echoed with praises and blessings of Alexander, and hardy veterans wept tears of joy, as imagination presented the distant shores of Greece to their delighted view.

105. THE OCEAN.—Before he set out on his return, Alexander caused twelve altars, seventy-five feet high, to be erected in honor of the twelve victories he had achieved in India; and, marking out an immense camp, left in it mangers for horses of twice the usual size, and every thing else in proportion, to convey the impression that his followers were nearer gods than mortals. Having constituted Porus viceroy of all the conquered countries, he returned to the Hydaspes, where a fleet of 800 galleys, besides vessels of burden and boats, had been provided by the party left there for the purpose. In these the army took its departure (except a detachment which marched each side of the river), about the time of the setting of the Pleiades, that was in October.

106. It took them nine months to move down the river, and conquer all the various tribes upon its banks. When they were first greeted by the sea-breeze, Alexander leaped with joy, and besought the soldiers to row with all their might, for now they were come to the end of their toils, and without fighting any more battles, or spilling any more blood, were masters of the universe. With feelings of mingled delight and awe, the army gazed upon the heavy swell of the ocean, a scene quite new to them; nor was their astonishment less, when, six hours after, the roaring waves retired in a regular ebb, and exposed the sandy beach to their curious eyes; but Alexander, thinking that the boundaries of the earth had been reached, and a limit set to his ambition, "wept because there were no more worlds to conquer."

107. B. C. 324. RETURN FROM INDIA.—After having besought

Questions.—104. What caused joy to his troops? How did they behave? 105. What was done by Alexander in honor of victories? Whom did he leave as viceroy of the conquered countries? What is the modern name of the Hydaspes? *Ans.* Behut or Jhylum. Of what river is it a tributary? *Ans.* The Indus. How large was the fleet prepared for the return of Alexander's army? *Ans.* 2,000 vessels. What materials must they have had in order to build them? What do you infer from this concerning the state of the arts in that place? 106. Give an account of the further progress of Alexander's army. Of what took place at the sea. What sea? *Ans.* The Erythræan, now called the Arabian. What mistaken idea did Alexander have? Why did he weep? 107. In what year did Alexander return from India? What petition did he make?

heaven "That no man might ever reach beyond the bounds of this expedition," he prepared to traverse the tract now known as Beloochistan, on his way to Persia. He sent his fleet out under the admiral Nearchus, with orders to coast along the unknown sea, and join the land army in the Euphrates. In (50.) THE DESERT his troops suffered incredibly from want of provisions and wholesome water; and such mortality prevailed, that he brought back from India only about one-fourth of his army. After they had eaten all the palm-tree roots they could find, they fed upon their beasts of burden, and finally upon the horses, so that, having no means of transporting those rich spoils which they had gone to the ends of the earth to collect, they were obliged to throw them away. At last the miserable remains of that gallant army reached (51.) CARMANIA, where plenty once more smiled upon them.

108. The governors of the provinces, hearing of the conqueror's approach, sent all kinds of provisions, arms, and presents; and the remainder of his route to (33.) PERSEPOLIS was one triumphal procession. His chariot was drawn by eight horses. Upon it was placed a lofty platform, where he and his principal friends reveled day and night. Other carriages followed, covered with rich tapestry, or paper hangings, or shaded with branches of trees, fresh gathered and flourishing. In these were the rest of the king's generals and friends, crowned with flowers and exhilarated with wine. In this whole company was not to be seen a buckler, a helmet, or spear; but instead of them cups, flagons, and goblets. These the soldiers filled from huge vessels of wine placed by the wayside, and drank till intoxication drowned the remembrance of the friends they had lost in the expedition.

109. Nearchus, having made the port with his fleet, left it anchored at the isle of Ormus, while he went across the country to report progress to his sovereign. His account of the voyage excited in Alexander a great desire to go upon the ocean. He proposed to sail round Africa, as Necho's fleet had done; to enter the Mediterranean by the Pillars of Hercules; to humble the pride of Carthage, which he hated for the assistance it had given the Tyrians; then to cross into Spain, and, having subdued every thing there, to coast along Italy to Epirus,

Questions.—107. By what route did his fleet proceed? Who commanded the fleet? In what desert did the troops suffer? *Ans.* Sandy Desert, now Kerman. What is said of the sufferings of the troops? At what place did they get relief? 108. Give an account of Alexander's march from Carmania to Persepolis. 109. Where did Nearchus anchor his fleet? Where is the isle of Ormus? (See map No. 8 again.) Then where did Nearchus go? How did his account of the voyage affect Alexander? What grand scheme did Alexander thereupon propose?

and thence return over land to Macedonia. For this purpose he sent orders to the viceroys of Mesopotamia and Syria to build ships upon the banks of the Euphrates; and commissioned Nearchus to bring his fleet up the Persian Gulf, to the general rendezvous at Babylon.

110. The tomb of Cyrus, at Persepolis, had been violated during his absence. It was a dome of stone, consisting of one chamber, in which stood a bed with golden feet, covered with Babylonian tapestry. On the bed was a coffin of gold, containing the embalmed body of Cyrus. The inscription on the wall seemed expressly intended for Alexander. It reads thus: "O MAN! WHOSOEVER THOU ART, AND WHENSOEVER THOU COMEST (FOR COME I KNOW THOU WILT), I AM CYRUS, SON OF CAMBYSES, WHO ACQUIRED EMPIRE FOR THE PERSIANS, AND REIGNED OVER ASIA: ENVY ME NOT THIS MONUMENT." The lid of the coffin was gone, and all the furniture of the chamber had been carried away. Alexander punished those concerned in the theft with the greatest severity.

111. From Persepolis he proceeded to (32.) SUSA, where he set himself about the regulation of his vast empire. To cement the union of the conquered and the conquerors, he married Statira, daughter of Darius, and gave her sister to Hephæstion, his dearest friend. His chief officers he also united to distinguished Persian ladies. When about 10,000 such matches had been made, the weddings were celebrated in the Persian fashion; but after supper, according to the Grecian custom, the ladies were introduced. Each, as she entered, was received by her husband, who took her by her right hand, gave her a kiss, and seated her by his side. To prevent any ill-humor from arising among the lower ranks of the Grecians, these nuptial ceremonies were made the occasion of a grand festival. All the debts of the soldiers were paid from the royal treasury, and tables loaded with every luxury were spread throughout the camp, that none might be excluded from partaking of the munificence of their sovereign. To those who had distinguished themselves, magnificent presents were given; and the king himself placed a crown upon the head of the most eminent.

112. Here, again, he was joined by Nearchus, and feeling still a desire to see the ocean, he went on board the admiral's galley, and

---

Questions.—109. What preliminary orders did he give? 110. What is said in relation to the tomb of Cyrus? What was the inscription? What action did Alexander take? 111. Where was the city of Susa? By what acts did Alexander undertake to cement the union of the conquered and the conquerors? Give an account of the ceremonies that followed. 112. Where did Nearchus again join Alexander? On what river was Susa? *Ans.* The Ulai, a tributary of the Euphrates. What sail did Alexander take?

sailed down to (52.) THE PERSIAN GULF, and then up to (53.) THE MOUTH OF THE TIGRIS, where the main body of his army lay encamped. Here he published a declaration that all those Macedonians who by reason of age, wounds, or infirmities were unable to endure longer the fatigues of service, might return home. The suspicion (which had long been lingering in their minds) that their king had transferred his affections from them to the Persians was thus changed to certainty. Voices were heard through the camp, exclaiming, "He no longer cares for the Macedonians; all his favor is for barbarians;" and some went so far as to vociferate, "Dismiss us all, and for your associate in future campaigns take your father Ammon."

113. Alexander, upon hearing this insolent taunt, leaped from his seat, and, pointing out thirteen of the ringleaders, ordered his men to take them to immediate execution; then, again ascending the tribunal, he addressed the astonished multitude as follows: "I do not address you now to divert you from your eagerness to return home; all are welcome to go; but I desire first to remind you of what you were when you left home, and to what circumstances you are now advanced. In doing this, I begin with acknowledging that not only my obligations, but yours, to my father are incalculably great. The Macedonians were poor and wandering herdsmen, clothed in skins, and living among mountains, when my father began to reign. Philip introduced civil and military order.

114. "Towns then arose, garments of leather were exchanged for cloth, and wholesome laws and improved manners made the people respectable; so that the barbarians, whom they had been accustomed to fear, were compelled to acknowledge their dominion. Those who obtained command in Thessaly had often been their terror; Philip so altered things that the Macedonians and Thessalians became nearly one people. Communication with southern Greece was commonly difficult; success in the war with Phocis made it sure and easy. The Athenians and Thebans had aimed at the conquest of Macedonia. Philip humbled both, so that those states owed their safety to Macedonian generosity. Finally, settling the affairs of Peloponnesus, and establishing peace throughout Greece, he was elected general of the whole nation, for war against Persia—not more to his own honor than that of the Macedonian people.

115. "Succeeding my father, I found in the treasury 60 talents, and

---

Questions.—112. What declaration did he publish? What effect did the declaration have? What exclamations and vociferations were heard? 113, 114, 115, 116. What hasty revenge did Alexander take? What statements did he make in his address? Let the pupil commit the enumeration of Alexander's victories to memory.

borrowed 800 more. Such was the fund with which, together with you, I left Macedonia. Soon, through our success in arms, Ionia, Eolia, Phrygia, and Lydia became tributary. Syria and Palestine soon became yours; and in the same campaign the wealth of Egypt and Cyrenaica followed without contest. Mesopotamia, Babylon, Susa, Bactria, the Persian treasure, the wealth of India, and the command of the ocean beyond, are now yours." He then went on to state that he had borne hunger, thirst, and fatigue with the meanest soldier, and could show scar for scar with the bravest officer in the ranks; that he had appropriated none of the treasures to himself, and was distinguished by nothing but a purple robe and diadem.

116. "For your glory and your wealth," continued he, "have I led you conquerors over plains and mountains, lands and seas. It was my intention to have sent home all those less qualified for further service, the envy of mankind; but as it is the desire of all to go, *go all*, and tell those at home that your king, Alexander, who has led you over Caucasus, and through the Caspian gates, across the river Oxus, and beyond the Indus, who at your head braved the perils of the Gedrosian desert, and the unknown dangers of the ocean, so that fleet and army have hailed him conqueror at Susa, has been deserted by you, and turned over to the care of barbarians, whom with you he had conquered."

117. Having thus spoken, he descended hastily from the tribunal, went to his palace, and did not appear again for three days. Then he sent for the various bodies of infantry which he had formed from the youth of conquered nations, and, surrounding himself with these, permitted none to salute him with a kiss but such as were connected with him by marriage. The Macedonians, overwhelmed with shame and confusion at this severe rebuke, besieged his palace with tears and lamentations, till finally, overcome with their sorrow, he ordered the gate to be opened, and presented himself to his humbled army. A general cry of joy arose; the king mingled his tears with those of his repentant people; all were permitted to approach him, and none were forbidden to take the valued kiss, for he evaded his interdict by calling them *all his kinsmen*. The reconciliation complete, they once more put on their armor, and, lifting up the loud pæan, returned singing to the camp.

118. From the mouth of the Tigris Alexander proceeded to (34.) ECBATANA. Here he celebrated a magnificent thanksgiving for his

Questions.—117. Relate what occurred after the speech. 118. What celebration took place at Ecbatana? Where was Ecbatana?

various and extraordinary successes. There had come to him from Greece 3,000 persons, skilled in various diversions; and these were employed to fill up the intervals of eating and drinking with dramatic entertainments. But in the midst of these festivities Hephæstion fell sick of a fever, and as he could not bear to be kept upon a low diet, he took the opportunity, while his physician was gone to the theater, to eat a roasted fowl and drink a bottle of wine; in consequence of which he grew worse, and died in a few days. Alexander's grief on the death of his friend exceeded all bounds. The sounds of music and mirth were instantly hushed, the poor physician was crucified, and the horses and mules were shorn, that they might appear to share in the general mourning. Sacrifices were offered to Hephæstion as to a demi-god, and the first relief which Alexander seemed to feel was in conquering a barbarous tribe near Ecbatana, and sacrificing the youths to the *manes* of his departed friend.

119. After settling affairs in this province, the conqueror directed his course to the place which he designed to make the capital of his empire. (31.) BABYLON. As he was advancing toward this city, Nearchus came up the Euphrates, to tell him that the Chaldean priests were of the opinion that Alexander should not enter Babylon. But he slighted the warning, and went into the city through the very gate which they had predicted would be fatal to him. However, the unfavorable omens affected his mind considerably, so that he lived mostly in his pavilion without the walls, and amused himself by sailing up and down the Euphrates, and in talking about his grand expedition. From the miasmatic exhalations of the marshes, or, as some say, from excessive drinking, he was seized with a fever, but he made an effort to rise every day, and when not able to do so was carried on a couch to the sacrifices, and received his officers in his tent. His mind was constantly busied upon his projected enterprise; he continued to give orders concerning it till the eighth day of his malady, when he was carried back to his palace. He bestowed his ring upon Perdiccas, and when one inquired to whom the kingdom should be

---

Questions.—118. Whom did Alexander regard as his dearest friend? Give an account of his sickness and death. Of the consequent acts and ceremonies. 119. What improvements did Alexander attempt at Babylon? *Ans.* He began to repair the dykes broken down by Cyrus; for ever since that time the water had flooded the country and rendered it uninhabitable. He also set himself to rebuild the fane of Belus, which Xerxes destroyed after his return from Greece. Some idea of its greatness may be formed from the fact that 10,000 men labored every day upon it for six months, and still the rubbish was not removed at the time of his death. Is there any structure upon the earth now equal in size and height to this celebrated tower? What advice and warning did the Chaldean priests give? Give an account of the sickness and death of Alexander.

given, he answered, "To the most worthy." On the ninth day he was speechless, and on the eleventh day he died, B. C. 323. He lived almost thirty-three years, twelve of which he had reigned, and nearly ten of which he had passed in Asia.

120. INTERMENT OF ALEXANDER.—The moment that Alexander's death was known, the whole palace echoed with cries and groans. The vanquished Persians and the victorious Greeks bewailed alike the man who had established order and peace among the nations, and all exclaimed against the gods for having taken him away in the flower of his age, and the plenitude of his glory. Nor was this great mourning confined to Babylon; it spread over the provinces; it affected every governor; it caused the wounds of Sisygambis, mother of Darius, to bleed afresh. "She who had survived the massacre of her eighty brothers (who had been put to death in one day by Ochus); the loss of all her children, and the entire downfall of her house, now, on the decease of the enemy and conqueror of her line, seated herself upon the ground, covered her head with a vail, and, notwithstanding the entreaties of Statira and her sister, refused all nourishment, until, on the fifth day after, she expired."

121. When the first impressions of grief had subsided, each one began to calculate the consequences of the event to himself. The Greeks were far from home, and without a leader; the empire which they had hoped to see established by their valor had lost its head, and, uncertain what to do, they waited in painful anxiety for the arrangements which those in power would make. Those in power were equally at a stand. Seven days were spent in confusion and disputes, and all that time the body of the mighty conqueror lay unembalmed, waiting till some authority should be constituted to give orders concerning its burial. Finally, all the principal commanders were summoned to a general assembly. The chair of Alexander was brought and placed in the midst; and Perdiccas laid upon it the insignia of royalty, and the ring which Alexander had given him. He then declared that it was indispensably requisite for some person to be elected head of the government, and that the child of Roxana should be acknowledged monarch of the Macedonian empire.

122. To the first proposition all assented; to the last many objected. To commit the scepter of the world to the hands of a guardian in trust for an infant yet unborn, alarmed the prudent and awakened the

Questions.—119. When did he die? How old was he at the time of his death? How long had he reigned? 120. Who mourned for Alexander? Why? What is said of the mourning and death of Darius's mother? 121. How were the first seven days after Alexander's death spent? What was finally done?

jealousy of the ambitious, and a long debate arose as to the propriety and consequences of such a step. Aridæus, the half-brother of Alexander, a man whose energy of body and mind had been destroyed by poisonous draughts, administered by Olympias, was finally chosen monarch, to reign conjointly with the child of Roxana, should it prove a son. They therefore arrayed Aridæus in the royal robes, buckled him with the armor of Alexander, and saluted him by the name of Philip, monarch of Macedon, Perdiccas taking care to secure to himself the office of regent of the kingdom and guardian of the future prince. After this important affair was settled, the body of Alexander was delivered to the Egyptians, who embalmed it after their manner, and then a special officer was appointed to convey it to the temple of Jupiter Ammon. Two whole years were spent in preparing for this magnificent funeral, which made Olympias bewail the fate of her son; who, although the son of a god, was compelled to wander so long on the gloomy shores of the Styx.

123. The Lamian War.—While these important affairs were transacting in Asia, the Greeks at home were not idle. No sooner did the news of Alexander's death reach Athens, than the people determined to overthrow the hated supremacy of Macedon. Demosthenes, who had been banished, was recalled; and his active spirit soon united all the states of Greece against Antipater, who had been left viceroy in Alexander's absence. All the citizens capable of bearing arms were drawn out for the land army; and a numerous fleet was speedily equipped and put to sea. Antipater was defeated in battle, and shut up in Lamia, a city of Thessaly. Being, however, re-enforced by troops from Asia Minor, he charged his enemies in turn, and gained a great victory. Then, offering to treat with the states separately, he roused all their ancient animosities; and finally poor Athens was left to meet his resentment alone. In the treaty formed, Demosthenes was to be given up, the democracy abolished, and a Macedonian garrison to be received into the city. To such humiliating conditions was Athens reduced—she who had been the glory of the world!

124. The Funeral.—Not long after, the funeral obsequies of Alexander were celebrated. A particular description of this august pageant may be found in the 15th book of Rollin. It will only be necessary to say here, that the body of the deceased monarch was laid in a coffin of beaten gold, half filled with spices and perfumes, and

Questions.—122. Who was elected monarch in Alexander's place? What care did Perdiccas have? How long were preparations in progress for Alexander's funeral? 123. What war next occurred? How did it occur? Give an account of it. 124. Give an account of the funeral obsequies of Alexander.

covered with a richly embroidered purple pall. A splendid chariot, drawn by 64 mules, was the hearse on which it was conveyed to Alexandria, where Ptolemy raised a magnificent temple to his memory, and rendered him all the honors usually paid to the demigods of antiquity. The mighty fabric of empire which Alexander had reared was dissolved by his death. His hopes and purposes died with him. There lived no man capable of carrying out the sublime design of uniting the nations by one common bond, and extending civilization from one end of the earth to the other. His remark, that "his death would be followed by strange funeral games," was the language of prophecy. Scarcely was he laid in his tomb when all whom he had loved and trusted engaged in a bloody struggle to wrest from his heirs the scepter of universal dominion.

125. Olympias, the mother of Alexander, was still living in Epirus. His sister Cleopatra resided in Sardis; and his half-sister Thessalonica, in Macedon. His half-brother, Philip Aridæus, lately elected king, was in Babylon. His widow, Roxana, presented the Macedonians with an heir to the throne three months after her husband's death. Statira, daughter of Darius, soon after fell a victim to her jealous cruelty. Alexander had also an illegitimate son in Asia Minor, who was at this time four years old. These persons constituted THE ROYAL FAMILY OF MACEDON. Situated as they were between the pretenders and the crown, they were exposed to attacks from every side, and all fell victims to the ambition of those who should have been their protectors: so that before the close of half a century there was left to the founder of a dynasty for the world "neither name nor remnant, neither root nor branch."

126. Many hands were stretched forth to grasp the crown:

(1.) PERDICCAS, as commander of the household troops, was in reality lord of the empire. He assigned provinces to the government of the other generals, as if by authority of the weak king whom he guarded, or rather governed; and assisted Roxana to silence forever the claims of Statira. Ptolemy, Antigonus, and Antipater, thinking themselves equally entitled to sovereign authority, formed a confederacy against him. Perdiccas declared them rebels; and, taking with him the imbecile Philip and the infant Alexander, advanced into Egypt to give them battle. He lost a part of his forces in passing the Nile; the rest mutinied, and murdered him in his tent. He survived Alexander two years.

Questions.—124. What condition of things existed after Alexander's death? 125. What persons were there in the royal family? What account is given of them? 126. How long did Perdiccas live? Where did he die?

NOTE.—The figures inclosed between parentheses refer to the number of years which these individuals survived Alexander. Those names marked thus * were confederates at the battle of Ipsus. Those marked thus † were opponents of the confederates in that battle.

127. (2.) ANTIPATER, regent of Macedon, then took charge of the kings, and ruled in their names all the empire lying west of the Hellespont. His ability and fidelity commanded the respect of his contemporaries, and while *he* lived Greece was comparatively quiet. He however survived his royal master but four years. On his death-bed he bequeathed his trust to Polysperchon, the eldest of Alexander's generals, to the exclusion of his own son, Cassander, whose ambition had already begun to develop dangerous traits in his character.

128. (3.) EUMENES was appointed by Polysperchon to guard the dominions of the crown in Asia Minor against the rapacity of Antigonus. Of all the self-constituted guardians of the royal family, he alone seemed actuated by a sincere desire to serve them. For several years he maintained a war in which he displayed great abilities and untiring energy, often putting Antigonus to flight, and counteracting all his schemes. He was at last betrayed into the hands of an enemy with whom he had formerly been upon terms of the most intimate friendship. Antigonus dared not trust himself to look his noble prisoner in the face, but, giving orders that he should be kept like an elephant or a lion, relieved him from the weight of his chains, and shut him up in prison: finally, he put him to death.

Questions.—127. What became of Demosthenes? *Ans.* Having been condemned to death by the minions of Antipater, he put an end to his own life. Give an account of Antipater's reign. 128. Of Eumenes's reign.

129. (4.) Polysperchon.—No sooner had this general assumed the charge left him by Antipater, than Cassander began to form a party against him, in which he engaged Ptolemy and Antigonus. To counteract the movements of Cassander's confederates in Asia, Polysperchon commissioned Eumenes to carry on war against them in the name of the kings. To counteract his movements at home, he recalled Olympias from Epirus; and to prevent the Grecian states from favoring the cause of his antagonist, he published an edict for restoring democracy throughout Peloponnesus and Hellas. The disastrous consequences of these measures were felt throughout the empire. Eumenes, as we have before seen, lost his life in the war with Antigonus; Olympias put to death Philip Aridæus and his wife Eurydice; the brother of Cassander and one hundred young noblemen also fell victims to her vengeance; and, to escape the fury which these atrocities excited, she herself fled to Pydna, taking with her Thessalonica, Roxana, and the young Alexander.

130. The edict for restoring democracy in the Grecian states produced revolution upon revolution. Almost every person of rank or merit was stripped of his property or banished. Demetrius Phalereus, governor of Athens, was driven into exile, and the venerable Phocion was sentenced to death. The last message of this excellent man was a command to his son to "forget the injustice of the Athenians." So bitter were his enemies against him, that a decree was passed forbidding his bones to be buried in Attica. The last sad offices were paid him in Megara. A lady of that country collected his bones in her robe, conveyed them to her house by night, and buried them under the hearthstone, praying that they might be faithfully preserved "till the Athenians should become wiser." Her prayer was answered. Cassander made war upon Polysperchon, and drove him into Etolia. Then, marching with an army to Athens, he restored the aristocracy and recalled Demetrius. The remains of Phocion were brought home, and a monument of brass erected to his memory.

131. Cassander soon after commenced the siege of Pydna. He prevented the reception of supplies by sea, and cut off all prospect of relief by land. The condition of the besieged was deplorable in the extreme. The royal family fed on the flesh of horses; the soldiers, upon the dead bodies of their companions; and the elephants, upon sawdust. Famine finally compelled them to surrender. Olympias was immediately put to death, and the widow and son of Alexander

Questions.—129. Of Polysperchon's. 130. To what did Polysperchon's edict lead? Give the account of Phocion. 131. Where was Pydna? (See map No. 2.) Give an account of the siege of that city.

kept close prisoners in Amphipolis. Thessalonica was subjected to an imprisonment still more irksome by being married to her captor. Cassander soon after marched down into Beotia, where he began to rebuild the city of Thebes. The place had lain desolate twenty years, and the inhabitants had lingered round the spot, finding a miserable shelter in the ruins of their former habitations. With the assistance of neighboring towns its walls were again reared up, comfortable dwellings erected, and the grateful Thebans owned Cassander their second Cadmus.

132. Cassander, asserting his claim to the throne of Macedon in right of his wife, Thessalonica, soon perceived that a rival was growing up in the child of Roxana. When the young prince was about fourteen, the Macedonians began to exclaim that it was time for him to slip his leading-strings and take the head of the government. There remained then no alternative for the usurper. He must either give up his power or sacrifice Alexander. He chose the latter. *Roxana and her son were assassinated by order of Cassander.* Polysperchon, who had been quietly waiting the turn of times, now proclaimed *Hercules* king, and raised an army of 20,000 men to support his right to the throne. Cassander had recourse to negotiation. He told Polysperchon that if he would destroy Hercules, and yield him Macedon, an army should be ready to establish Polysperchon's supremacy in Peloponnesus. The cruel old man listened and consented. Hercules was slain by his pretended friend, and the troops were withdrawn. Cassander, however, instead of fulfilling his promise, chased Polysperchon into Locris, where he lingered out his miserable life, a monument of blasted ambition.

133. (5.) ANTIGONUS, having destroyed the faithful Eumenes, and assisted Cassander to usurp the throne of Macedon, assumed the title of *king*, in which he was followed by all the other generals of Alexander. While he lived, Asia was the scene of constant war. He fought against the four confederates in the battle of Ipsus, was defeated, and died of his wounds at the age of 84. (6.) PTOLEMY, the founder of the Lagidæ, was supposed to be the son of Philip. He was educated in the Macedonian court, and became one of the personal friends of Alexander. He led the "winged soldiers" up the Sogdian rock, and killed one of the Indian monarchs in single combat. He will appear

---

Questions.—131. What good did Cassander do? What city did Cassander afterward build? *Ans.* Thessalonica, in honor of his wife. Where was that city? (See map No. 2.) 132. Whom did Cassander sacrifice? Why did he do so? What was the fate of Hercules? What was the fate of Polysperchon? In what direction was Locris from Pydna? 133. Give an account of Antigonus. Of Ptolemy

again as king of Egypt. (7.) LYSIMACHUS received from Perdiccas the government of Thrace, which he maintained by force of arms till the battle of Ipsus, when his title to the sovereign power was confirmed by the confederate princes. (8.) SELEUCUS, the founder of the Seleucidæ, outlived all those who began with him the race for the crown left by Alexander. He was one of the conquerors in the battle of Ipsus, and his kingdom of Syria was one of the *four horns* mentioned by Daniel.

134. We close this chapter by remarking that Antigonus put to death Cleopatra, the sister of Alexander; and that Thessalonica, wife of Cassander, was murdered some years after by her own son. Farewell to the royal family of Macedon. How heavily the hand of the Almighty fell upon them. A fatal curse seemed to pursue them till they were all cut off from the face of the earth. BATTLE OF IPSUS. B. C. 301. In the last year of this century, Cassander, Lysimachus, Seleucus, and Ptolemy united against Antigonus and his son Demetrius. A great battle was fought upon the plain of Ipsus, in Phrygia. The confederates were successful, and immediately proceeded to divide the world among themselves. Cassander had MACEDON and GREECE; Lysimachus, THRACE; Seleucus, SYRIA; and Ptolemy, EGYPT.

135. B. C. **300.** ACHÆAN LEAGUE.—WAR WITH ROME.—After the battle of Ipsus, Cassander, by consent of his confederates, took his seat upon the throne of Macedon, as the supreme head of the Greek nation. He died B. C. 298, leaving Thessalonica with three sons, Philip, Antipater, and Alexander. Philip died within the same year, and the other two fell to quarreling for the vacant throne. Thessalonica espoused the cause of Alexander, and Antipater murdered her with his own hand. Alexander appealed to Demetrius,* who had by this time recovered from the defeat of Ipsus. Demetrius gladly under-

* This singular man, the founder of the last dynasty of Macedon, deserves a more particular description. In his youth he possessed such uncommon beauty that no painter could do justice to him in a likeness; his address was enchanting, and his energy and courage were equaled only by his love of pleasure. He was distinguished for his filial love, in an age when parents and children were often rendered bitter enemies by political troubles; and he was no less celebrated for the ingenuity and promptness with which he extricated himself from difficulty and recovered from misfortune. He was surnamed Poliorcetes, "*besieger of cities*," from the number of machines he invented for capturing walled towns. In the siege of Rhodes he employed the "*Heliopolis* or *Town-taker*," which was an immense tower, supported on eight enormous wheels, and propelled by the labor of 3,400 men.

Questions.—133. Of Lysimachus. Of Seleucus. 134. Where was Ipsus? (See map No. 8.) Give an account of the battle fought there. What division was made of the empire? Did this include any part of Europe? Read Dan. viii. 4–9, 20–22. 135. How long did Cassander's family possess the throne of Macedon? State how the royal family of Macedon became extinct. Who was the founder of the last dynasty of Macedon?

took the affair, but finding that Alexander, having become reconciled to his brother, had no further occasion for his services, and was plotting his destruction, he gained possession of his person and put him to death. Antipater fled into Thrace, where he was assassinated by his father-in-law, Lysimachus; and thus the royal family of Macedon became extinct!

136. Demetrius then ascended the throne, and reigned unmolested seven years. He might have enjoyed the supremacy much longer, had he not embarked in an unfortunate attempt to recover the former dominions of his father in Asia Minor. Seleucus, who was his son-in-law, claimed the territory himself, and steadfastly resisted all the efforts of Demetrius. The poor aspirant was finally taken prisoner by Seleucus, who held him in honorable captivity many years, permitting him to indulge in the pleasures of the chase, and depriving him of none of his accustomed luxuries. Finally, Demetrius lost his relish for active exercises; he became melancholy, grew corpulent, stupefied himself with wine, and chased away thought with dice. At the end of three years he died of chagrin and intemperance, aged 54. At one time he had worn a *double diadem* and purple robes; at another, he had escaped from the battle-field in the disguise of a beggar; he had been honored, nay, almost worshiped, in Athens and Macedon; and he died a poor, disappointed, broken-hearted old man, within the narrow limits of the Chersonesus. His ashes were conveyed to his son, Antigonus, in a golden urn, who celebrated his funeral with great magnificence. This Antigonus became king of Macedon, B. C. 277. As the most remarkable events of his reign were his wars with his uncle, Pyrrhus, for the supremacy of Greece, we will pay a little attention to the history of that monarch.

137. PYRRHUS, KING OF EPIRUS.—Epirus began now, for the first time, to take the lead in Grecian affairs. The monarch, Pyrrhus, was second-cousin to Olympias, and the fifth in the dynasty, of which he was the only person of importance. He married the sister of Demetrius while that distinguished individual was looked upon as the heir-expectant to a great portion of Alexander's dominions; he fought on his brother-in-law's side in the battle of Ipsus, and did not desert him in the day of his misfortunes. He even went as a hostage for him to the court of Ptolemy, king of Egypt. He gained the favor of that monarch, and received a heart-satisfying testimony of it, in being allowed to take his best beloved daughter, Antigona, to Epirus as his

---

Questions.—136. What was the end of Demetrius? Give an account of him. What is said of Antigonus? 137. Who was Pyrrhus? Give some account of him.

bride. When Demetrius embarked in his last fatal attempt to regain Asia Minor, Pyrrhus, at the request of Ptolemy, invaded Macedonia from the west, and was acknowledged king of that country; but the anarchy and confusion that ensued soon after compelled him to return to Epirus.

138. Pyrrhus goes to Italy.—A request which flattered his vanity and excited his ambition, tempted him again to interfere in foreign affairs. The Tarentines, being engaged in an unequal contest with the Romans, sent to Pyrrhus for assistance. Pyrrhus was delighted with the application; for all the great conquerors before him had neglected to crush the rising power of the west. Having prepared a vast number of flat bottomed boats, he set sail from the harbors of Epirus, and after a stormy passage arrived at Tarentum. He fought two battles with the Romans and was victorious, though he suffered a loss almost as discouraging as defeat. Being then invited to Sicily, he went thither, and spent two years in a war with the Carthaginians; being, however, neither able to overcome his enemies nor retain his friends, he returned to Italy. He recommenced hostilities with the Romans, but, having been defeated in a great battle, he thought it both safe and wise to sail again for Epirus.

139. To repair his military reputation, he made war upon Antigonus, drove him from the throne of Macedon, and followed him into the Peloponnesus with a large army. He found it impossible to take the unwalled capital of Laconia, and, after many fruitless efforts to retrieve his fortunes, turned aside to drive Antigonus away from Argos. The Argives had no desire to be subjected either to Pyrrhus or Antigonus, and the latter retired; but Pyrrhus entered the place in the night, and commenced a furious attack upon the inhabitants. The combat was obstinate and bloody. Pyrrhus, who possessed a commanding figure and the greatest personal courage, engaged eagerly in the fight. An Argive singled out the king as an object of attack, and Pyrrhus, crowding his antagonist against the wall, was about to dispatch him, when the mother of the youth threw a tile from the top of the house upon the head of the monarch, and broke his skull. A more particular account of his six years in Italy will be given in the history of Rome. Antigonus Gonatus, having cut off the head of his rival, Pyrrhus, and burned his body with funeral honors, returned to Macedon. The remainder of his life was passed in tolerable tran-

Questions.—138. Of his first expedition to Italy. Of his second expedition to Italy. 139. Of his subsequent career. How was he killed?

quillity; though Peloponnesus and Hellas, which he reckoned among his dependencies, were constantly disturbed by wars.

140. The Achæan League.—The republic of Achaia consisted of twelve small cities, all the inhabitants of which would scarcely people one of our modern towns. The Achæans had lived independent of all other governments, taking very little interest in the affairs of Greece till Philip, in preparing to subjugate Asia, compelled them to acknowledge his authority, and furnish their quota of soldiers for the expedition. In common with their sister states, they took sides in the struggles of the great generals for the empire of Alexander, and alternately enjoyed victory and suffered defeat. When Pyrrhus returned from Italy, and overthrew the power of Antigonus, the Achæans looked up, and resumed their ancient laws. The chief agent in bringing about this happy event was Aratus, a native of Sicyon, who, having succeeded in expelling the tyrants from his own city, formed a design of uniting all the Peloponnesus in a league against Macedon. As general of the Achæans, he was able to raise an army and drive out the enemies of liberty; but the Macedonians having established themselves in Corinth, he could do nothing further while they retained possession of "the fetters of Greece."

141. Corinth Freed.—Many and various were the schemes he devised for regaining this important post; they all proved abortive till accident or *Providence* sent to him a Corinthian, who, for a certain sum, engaged to conduct a band of soldiers to a vulnerable point in the wall of the citadel. Aratus pledged his plate and all his wife's jewels for the stipulated sum, and about nightfall set off with four hundred chosen men on the hazardous enterprise. Their armor glittered in the moonbeams, and had the Macedonian sentinel been watching from the temple of Juno they must inevitably have been discovered. Fortunately, a thick fog at length arose, and wrapped a mantle of deep gloom over the city. They sat down just without the wall, took off their shoes, and silently planted their scaling-ladders. Aratus ascended first with one hundred men, commanding the rest to follow as soon as possible. Scarcely had the little band descended into the city, when they saw a guard of four men approaching with lights. They shrunk back into the shade of some ruins, and when the men were nearly past, sprang upon them. Three were instantly killed;

Questions.—140. How large was Achaia? How had the Achæans lived? Give a further account of them. Who was Aratus? What did he do for Achaia? Where was Sicyon? (Map 2.) How was Aratus foiled by the Macedonians? 141. By what act was Aratus favored? How did he gain the services of the Corinthian?

the fourth escaped with a deep wound in his head, crying out, "The enemy! the enemy!"

142. The trumpets immediately sounded the alarm; the streets were filled with people; torches were carried to and fro; the ramparts of the castle were lit up; and confused cries were heard in every quarter. In this tumult Aratus lost his way, and clambered round among the rocks, uncertain what course to take. The moon, so fortunately vailed before, now looked out from beneath a cloud, and revealed all the intricacies of the path. Aratus and his men mounted the rampart, and were soon engaged in close combat with the guard. The three hundred, having cleared the wall, drew up in a close body under the shadow of a bending rock, and waited there in the utmost anxiety and distress. They could distinctly hear the sound of blows and the shouts of combatants; but these were repeated by so many echoes that it was impossible to tell in what part of the city the fight was going on, or to what point they should direct their steps. Meantime the Macedonian troops came round to attack Aratus in the rear. When they mounted the ascent, the three hundred, guided by their voices, followed them, and, as if issuing from an ambuscade, mingled in the fight.

143. The enemy fled in dismay. The three hundred shouted *victory* to Aratus, and Aratus shouted *liberty* in return. The Corinthians, roused by a sound so delightful to every Grecian ear, joined the Achæans; and by break of day the Macedonians were all either taken prisoners or expelled from the city. As soon as practicable Aratus entered the theater, and the Corinthians crowded in to hear him speak. He stood leaning on his lance, with an air of solemn joy, till a profound silence reigned through the vast concourse—then, having recounted to them the history and principles of the Achæan league, and having exhorted them to join it, and assist in overthrowing the supremacy of Macedon, he delivered the keys of the city to the magistrates, and pronounced *Corinth once more free!* This bold and successful action gained many friends for the League. Several important cities joined the Achæans, and Aratus would doubtless have been successful in giving liberty to the Peloponnesus had not the Spartans become jealous for their own rights and turned against him..

144. The following is the line of Spartan succession, continued from page 126.

Questions.—142. 143. Give an account of his success at Corinth. What course did he afterward pursue? What was the effect? Where was Corinth? (See map No. 2.) 144 Give the line of Spartan succession.

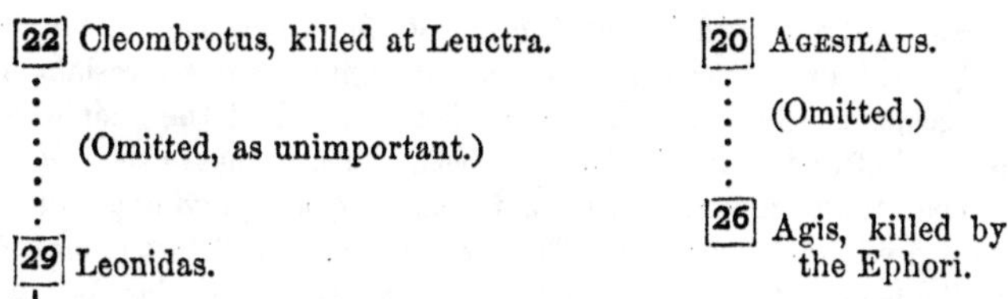

30 Cleomenes marries the widow of Agis, is driven from his throne by Antigonus, king of Macedon, and dies in Egypt, B. C. 214. With him ended the race of Heraclidæ, which had so long occupied the throne of Laconia. Sparta was afterward governed by tyrants.

145. SPARTA.—During all the revolutions which had taken place since the day of Epaminondas, Sparta had been gradually declining in virtue and military renown. Agis ascended the throne of Sparta B. C. 243. While Aratus was using every effort to overthrow the power of Macedon, Agis was planning the destruction of two more dreadful tyrants—Vice and Luxury; but, living as they did in a servile and degenerate age, both these distinguished men fell victims to the hatred which their zeal in the cause of reform inspired. Agis attempted to revive the laws of Lycurgus, which had fallen into disuse, to redivide the lands, which had by degrees passed into the hands of a few individuals, and to cancel those obligations which made the poor slaves to the rich. His brother sovereign, Leonidas, opposed all his measures, and gained the Ephori to his side. Agis was thrown into prison as the instigator of a revolution, and strangled. Leonidas then compelled the widowed queen to marry his own son, Cleomenes, because she was the richest and most beautiful woman in Sparta.

146. Cleomenes, however, was very unlike his father. He respected the feelings of the woman who had so reluctantly become his bride, and listened with the greatest attention while she recounted the virtues and misfortunes of her former husband. He began to admire the character so constantly presented before him, and insensibly formed his own upon the same model. As soon as he was freed from restraint by the death of his father, he made arrangements for carrying out the design which had cost Agis his life. The Ephori being in reality "the power behind the throne, greater than the throne," he determined first to destroy them. One evening while the Ephori were at supper,

Questions.—144. By whom, after Cleomenes, was Sparta governed? 145. When did Agis become king of Sparta? What was the character of Agis? Give an account of him. Who was Leonidas? Who Cleomenes? Whom did Cleomenes marry? Why? 146. What was the character of Cleomenes? How did he come to admire the character of Agis? What determination did he form? How was it carried out?

a small party, headed by the brother of Cleomenes, rushed into the hall with drawn swords, and fell upon them. Four were slain, and one escaped. Cleomenes, now indeed a king, called the people together, and after justifying what had been done, proposed the re-establishment of the government upon its ancient basis, giving up his own estate first for distribution. The people acquiesced in the measure, and the laws of Lycurgus were formally restored.

147. The spirits of Cleomenes rose with success. He began to indulge the hope of making Sparta again the head of the Greek nation. Having gained several victories over the forces of the League, he proposed that the Achæans and Spartans should unite, and make him captain-general of the allied forces. Aratus, who had been thirty-three years possessed of chief authority, could not bear the thought of being supplanted by a youth, and that youth a Spartan. Finding, however, that his friends were inclined to accept Cleomenes' offer, he *sent to the king of Macedon for assistance;* thus voluntarily submitting to a power which he had spent all his life in striving to overthrow. Antigonus Doson, guardian of the young Philip, immediately marched into the Peloponnesus with an army; totally defeated Cleomenes, and made himself master of that renowned Sparta, which had never before surrendered to its enemies. Cleomenes fled to Egypt, where he died by his own hand. Antigonus, having abolished all that Cleomenes had done to re-establish the supremacy of Sparta, committed the unfinished work of destruction to the factions and corruptions with which the city was filled, and returned to Macedon, where he died, B. C. 222, leaving the crown to its lawful possessor, Philip.

148. WAR WITH ROME.—The Etolians, who had been gradually gaining a name among the Greeks, now entered the lists as competitors with the Achæans for supremacy. The Achæans, unable to carry on a war with the Etolians, sent for help to Philip; and the Etolians, unable to carry on a war with the combined forces of Macedon and Achaia, sent to the Romans! Though the Romans were at this time sore pressed by the Second Punic War, yet they sent a consul and a body of troops against Philip. The war between Philip and the Romans went on for several years, Philip changing gradually for the worse, as victory or defeat excited his passions. Aratus, by whose counsels Antigonus had been guided, was at first the friend of the Macedonian king; but, finding that every new situation seemed to

Questions.—146. What change did he then carry out? 147. What hope did he begin to have? What proposition did he make with that view? How was he baffled in his designs? Give an account of Antigonus Doson. 148. What is said of the Etolians? What combinations were formed? Give the account of Aratus.

develop some new trait of tyranny in his character, he withdrew entirely from his retinue. Philip felt the implied reproach; and, resolving to be rid of his silent censor, employed one of his creatures to administer slow poison to the venerable general. Aratus saw his body wasting away by degrees, and understood the cause; but it was useless to complain; once he said, when a friend had observed him spitting blood, "Such, Cephalon, are the fruits of royal friendship."

149. The head of the Achæan league, after the death of Aratus, was *Philopœmen*, called by historians, "The last of the Greeks." He fought with Antigonus against Cleomenes, and ever afterward watched the Spartans with jealous eye. When Machanidas the tyrant attempted to subject the Peloponnesus Philopœmen, resisted him, and slew him with his own hand. As master of the Achæan horse, he distinguished himself above all his predecessors, and commanded the respect equally of enemies and friends. The restless spirit of Philip about this time embroiled him in a war with the Rhodians and Athenians, who also had recourse to Rome.

150. B. C. **200.** GREECE BECOMES A ROMAN PROVINCE.—The senate and people of Rome were deliberating upon the propriety of sending succors to the Rhodians and Athenians, when embassadors came from Athens to implore immediate help, because Philip was preparing to besiege the city. The Romans, upon the receipt of this information, declared war against Philip. The contest lasted four years, and Philip found that, like the dog in the fable, he had lost his own possessions by attempting to grasp another's. He was defeated in the battle of Cynocephale, and compelled to sue for peace. The consul obliged him to pay an enormous tribute, and to give up his son Demetrius as a hostage. The determination of the Romans with regard to the fate of Greece was to be made known at the solemnization of the Isthmian games. Crowds came from the farthest limits of the country to hear what the sovereign arbiters would decree concerning the government of the states. When the vast multitude were assembled, a herald came forward, and proclaimed with a loud voice: "The senate and people of Rome, and Titus Quintius, their general, having overcome Philip and the Macedonians, ease and deliver from all garrisons, taxes, and imposts, the Corinthians, Athenians, Achæans, &c. &c., declare them free, and ordain that they shall be governed by their respective laws and usages."

Questions.—149. Who was Philopœmen? Give an account of him. What new war is spoken of? 150. Why did Athens appeal to Rome? What was the immediate consequence? What were the further consequences? Where was Cynocephale? (See map No. 2.) What did the herald proclaim?

151. At first, a low murmur prevented the people from hearing the glad tidings distinctly, but when the herald repeated the proclamation, their joy broke forth in such loud and repeated acclamations* that the sea resounded on either side, and the hills and valleys of Corinth rang with the echoes again and again. The games could not call off their attention; they ran in crowds to the Roman general to kiss his hand, to throw crowns of flowers upon him, and to salute him as their deliverer. It was a proud day for Titus Quintius Flaminius, when to the trophies of the bodies and lands of the Grecians, won by force of arms, he added their hearts also, won by clemency and virtue. In the following year, B. C. 195, Flaminius was intrusted with a war against Nabis, tyrant of Lacedæmon, who had seized upon Argos. This Nabis was a monster of wickedness. From the very first, he established his power by rapine and bloodshed; those who possessed either rank or fortune were marked as victims to his envy or avarice.†

152. Philip assisted Nabis in his attempt upon Argos; and Philopœmen, with the Achæan forces, assisted the Romans. Flaminius, with his allies, marched into Laconia, and laid siege to Sparta. This city, since the rule of the tyrants, had been surrounded with walls, and was now prepared to stand a desperate attack. Flaminius finally made peace with Nabis, because his term of office had nearly expired, and he wished to leave the country ungarrisoned and free. When Flaminius was about to depart, he assembled deputies from the different states at Corinth, and made his farewell address. After rehearsing the particulars of his administration, and urging them to preserve inviolate the alliance with the Romans, he told them that he was preparing to withdraw his army from Greece, and that within ten days from the time he set sail, every garrison would be disbanded, the citadel of Corinth given up to the Achæans, and every city left to enjoy its own laws and liberties. The whole assembly wept for joy; each one exhorted his neighbor to receive the words of the Roman general

* Plutarch says, the shouts had such an effect upon the air, that several crows, which were flying over the place, fell dead; and so great was the crowd around Flaminius, that he was obliged to retreat for fear of being suffocated.

† To carry out his schemes of extortion, he constructed an automaton resembling his wife, and when any opulent citizen refused to furnish him with money, "perhaps," Nabis would say, "the persuasions of my wife will prove more successful." The individual was then introduced into a private apartment, where the horrid machine was made to clasp him in its arms, and pierce him with sharp iron points, till the torture compelled him to grant the tyrant's demands.

Questions.—151. How did the people receive the tidings? What is said of Flaminius? Who was Nabis? What was his character? 152. What war combinations were made? Relate the doings of Flaminius. What "assembly wept for joy?" What was the cause of the weeping?

as oracles, and lay them up as decrees of fate. As a testimony of their gratitude, the Achæans purchased all the Roman slaves in Greece, and sent them home with Flaminius.

153. But Greece could not be quiet. It was her fortune to come within the limits of that vast whirlpool, which all nations were involuntarily forming around the empire of Rome. The Etolians had been allies of the Romans in the late contest. In the unbounded applause bestowed upon Flaminius, they felt themselves overlooked. Their general projected a mighty league, the head of which was to be a person of no less consequence than Antiochus, king of Syria. Nabis, tyrant of Lacedemon, was to manage the south; Philip of Macedon, the north; Antiochus was to come with a great army from the east; the Etolians were to march from the west; Greece was to be subjected not only, but war was to be declared against Rome, and the *spoils* were to be divided when the conquest was won.

154. B. C. 191. HOW THE LEAGUE PROSPERED.—The Romans, hearing the mighty preparations making against them, immediately took measures to meet the shock. Philopœmen, general of the Achæans, was appointed to settle the account with Nabis, who, by the aid of his *wife*, was raising funds with great rapidity. Philopœmen ravaged Laconia, fought a battle with Nabis, and destroyed three-fourths of his army. Antiochus, in pursuance of the part assigned to him, made a descent upon Eubœa, summoned the town of Chalcis to open its gates, and, with a great flourish of trumpets, promised to deliver all Greece. To this the Chalcidians replied, that they could not guess what people it was that Antiochus came to deliver; that they knew of no city garrisoned by foreign soldiers, or tributary to the Romans; that they had no occasion for a deliverer, being already free; nor for a defender, as they enjoyed the blessings of peace in amity with the Romans; and therefore they should not permit him to enter their city. Antiochus was thus compelled to pass on without effecting any thing.

155. The course of Philip was not exactly such as had been hoped. Instead of assisting the *League*, he sent to the Romans, offering to stand on their behalf, and furnish money and men according to his ability. Antiochus, in conjunction with the Etolians, fortified the pass of Thermopylæ, and there waited the approach of the consul. When the Romans reached the place they were stopped, of course;

Questions.—153. What had made the Etolians dissatisfied? What did their general do? How many persons were engaged in the league? What was the object of the league? 154. What did Philopœmen accomplish? How was Antiochus foiled? Where was Chalcis? (Map No. 2.) 155. What course did Philip pursue?

but Cato, who was a lieutenant in the army, having read of the manner by which the band of Leonidas was surrounded, proposed to lead a select party over the mountain path. He set out with a proper detachment, but, having lost his way, the soldiers passed the greater part of the night in scrambling over rocks, and wandering round in the woods.

156. About daylight they heard the sound of human voices, and perceived at a little distance a body of Etolians. Immediately drawing their swords, they rushed upon the enemy, and put them to flight. The terror of the Etolians created a universal panic. At the same moment the Roman consul, hearing the shouts, commenced an attack upon the main body. A stone struck Antiochus in the face, and shattered his teeth. Excessive *pain* forced him to quit the field—excessive *fright* forced most of his men to follow his example. Many lost their lives in the sea; some were trodden to death in the rout; some perished in dreadful morasses; some fell down craggy precipices; and Antiochus had only about 500 men left of the army with which he meant to subjugate all Greece. Etolia surrendered not long after, and Philip sent embassadors to Rome to congratulate the senate upon their glorious victory. His messengers were kindly received, and his son Demetrius returned home with the highest marks of distinction.

157. Philopœmen had humbled Sparta, demolished its walls, *abolished the laws of Lycurgus*, and subjected the city to the customs and usages of the Achæans. Messenia now drew off from the League. Philopœmen, though sick, set out with his chosen cavalry to bring it back to its allegiance. He was surrounded in a narrow defile by his enemies, and thrown from his horse. The Messenians took him captive while he lay insensible, and cast him into a dungeon. At night the executioner was sent to him with a cup of poison. He was 70 years of age. Polybius, the historian, who carried his ashes in a silver urn to Megalopolis, his native city, sums up his eulogy by saying, "that in forty years, during which he played a distinguished part in a *democracy*, he never incurred the enmity of the people, though he acted with the greatest freedom and independence."

158. End of the Macedonian Dynasty.—When Demetrius, son of Philip, returned from Rome, the marks of distinction with which the senate had honored him created for him both enemies and friends. Fully persuaded of the invincible power of the Romans, he opposed a

Questions.—155, 156. Give an account of the defeat of Antiochus. What then did Philip do? With what result? 157. What had Philopœmen done? Give the further and closing account of him. 158. Who was Demetrius? What caused him to have enemies as well as friends?

war which his father was projecting. Perseus, his brother, by constantly representing that all those who attached themselves to Demetrius were enemies of Macedon, succeeded in turning away his father's heart from his virtuous and upright son. The friends of peace rallied round the youth who had been so much complimented by the Romans, and this made his position still more trying. The infirmities of Philip's disposition daily increased, and the artful Perseus having persuaded him that Demetrius entertained treasonable designs, orders were given for his assassination. Two years after, Philip discovered his mistake, and remorse soon hurried him to his grave. He expired in the most horrid agony, bewailing the fate of his dutiful and loving Demetrius, and calling down curses upon the head of the infamous Perseus. He had reigned forty years.

159. Perseus ascended the throne B. C. 179. His hatred of the Romans had been cultivated from early youth, but from motives of policy he vailed his feelings, while he used every method to strengthen his kingdom, and retrieve the losses sustained in the previous reign. The Romans, however, were not inactive. They crowded him from one humiliating concession to another, till there remained no alternative but war or slavery. We pass over all treaties, negotiations, and embassies, with which such affairs are generally politely prefaced, to come at once to the decisive battle, which was fought near Pydna, B. C. 168. This conflict was very brief and very bloody. The parties were engaged in close fight but an hour, yet when the Romans passed the river the next day, the waters were still stained with blood. Perseus was taken prisoner and carried to Rome, to adorn the triumph of Paulus Emilius, his conqueror.

160. *Achaia* at length became involved in a war with the Romans. Diæus, the last captain-general of the League, took up his station in Corinth. The consul Mummius led a Roman army to the isthmus, and encamped before the city. The besieged made a sortie, and were driven back with great loss. Diæus, abandoning himself to despair, killed his wife with his own hands; set fire to his own house; drank poison, and ended an inglorious life by a shameful death. The following night, every one that could possibly escape left Corinth. The consul abandoned the city to the fury of the soldiers. All the men were put to the sword, the women and children were enslaved; and

---

Questions.—158. Who was Perseus? How did the two brothers get in opposition? What was the result to Demetrius? Also to Philip? 159. How long had Philip reigned? When did Perseus succeed him? How did Perseus regard the Romans? What decisive battle is mentioned? Give an account of it. Where was Pydna? 160. What is said of Achaia? Who was Diæus? Give an account of him. Of the destruction of Corinth.

after the statues and paintings had been removed, the houses and temples were set on fire. The whole city continued in flames several days. The walls were then razed to their foundations, and a blackened mass of ruins alone remained to tell where once proud Corinth stood, B. C. 147.

161. Greece was divided by the Romans into two provinces, Macedonia and Achaia, and governed by annual prætors, sent over from Italy. The rival states, whose contentions for supremacy had so long made an "Aceldama" of the "land of song," sank at once into political insignificance. Athens, however, still retained the supremacy of mind. The sciences and arts proved less perishable than civil and military institutions. In her classic groves the youth of Rome were educated; and that *empire* which Themistocles had failed to gain from the favor of Neptune, was laid as a tribute at her feet by those distinguished individuals who had learned wisdom in the city of Minerva.*

* In the mythic legends of Athens, Neptune and Minerva were represented as contending for the guardianship of the city.

Questions.—161. What supremacy did Athens maintain in spite of political insignificance? What makes a nation great?

REVIEW QUESTIONS.

		PAGE
1.	Give the early account of Philip the Great	223, 224
2.	Name the important events in his life	224–237
3.	Give an account of his contest with the Athenians	225–236
4.	Of Demosthenes, and the part he took	225–270
5.	What events brought Philomelus into notice?	227, 228
6.	Give the full account of him	227–229
7.	How did Thessaly come under Philip's dominion?	226–229
8.	State what you can of Phayllus	229, 230
9.	What account is given of the "Double Vote"?	230
10.	How was the "Macedonian War" brought about?	230, 231
11.	What part did Demosthenės take in the matter?	231, 232
12.	What part did Chares take?	232
13.	What was Philip's success against the Olynthians?	232
14.	What was his success in the region toward the Danube?	233
15.	How was Philip's absence taken advantage of?	233
16.	Give an account of Philip's failure at Byzantium	233, 234
17.	How was Philip brought into the midst of Grecian affairs?	234
18.	State the events preliminary to the battle of Cheroneia	234, 235
19.	Describe the battle and state its consequences	235, 236
20.	What can you state of Olympias?	227, 236, 271–273
21.	Give the particulars of the death of Philip	236, 237

PAGE
22. When and where was Alexander the Great born?.............. 237
23. Give an account of Aristotle........................231, 237, 238, 258
24. What is said of Bucephalus?..........................238, 252, 261
25. How did Alexander establish his authority in Greece?......... 239
26. Give an account of his success against the Goths............. 239, 240
27. Of Demosthenes's success against him...................... 240, 241
28. What course did Demosthenes then take?.................... 241
29. Give an account of the destruction of Thebes................ 241, 242
30. How was Athens saved from destruction?.................... 242
31. What was Alexander's ruling object?....................... 242
32. Name the events of his first campaign..................... 243–246
33. Name the events of his second campaign.................... 246–251
34. What is said in connection with the taking of Tyre?.......... 248, 249
35. Name the events in Alexander's third campaign.............. 251–254
36. Name the events in his fourth campaign..................... 254–256
37. Name the events in his fifth campaign...................... 256–258
38. What occurred in the next campaign?....................... 258
39. Give the events connected with the death of Clitus........... 258, 259
40. What did Alexander accomplish in his eighth campaign?....... 260
41. What was his success against Porus?....................... 260, 261
42. Relate the events preceding Alexander's homeward move...... 261–263
43. Give an account of the homeward move..................... 263–268
44. Of Alexander's death and burial..........................268, 269, 270
45. What events followed?.................................. 269, 270
46. What hands stretched forth to grasp the crown?............. 271, 272
47. What is said of Perdiccas?............................... 271
48. Antipater?... 272
49. Eumenes?.. 272
50. Polysperchon?.. 273
51. Antigonus?.. 274
52. Ptolemy?.. 274
53. Lysimachus?... 275
54. Seleucus?... 275
55. Give an account of Cassander............................. 272–275
56. Of Pyrrhus and his doings................................ 276, 277
57. Of the Achæan League.................................. 278–285
58. Of Cleomenes and his doings.............................. 280, 281
59. Give an account of the war with Rome...................... 281–287
60. State the particulars of Flaminius's success................. 283
61. What is said of Demetrius, son of Philip?................... 282–286
62. Of Antiochus and his career?............................. 284, 285
63. Of Perseus?.. 286
64. How was Greece divided?................................ 287

THRACE.

SECTION V.

1. LYSIMACHUS.—B. C. **300.**—In the general division of the empire of Alexander, after the battle of Ipsus, Thrace fell to Lysimachus, a Macedonian noble. He married Arsinoë, sister of Ptolemy, king of Egypt, though his son, Agathocles, had already united himself to Lysandra, half sister of Arsinoë. Nothing of particular importance occurred in the domestic history of Thrace, until the children of the two Egyptian sisters were grown to manhood. Arsinoë, fearing that the death of Lysimachus would leave her sons in the power of Agathocles, began to poison the mind of the old king against his first-born. Fully persuaded that Agathocles was engaged in a conspiracy, Lysimachus ordered him to be put to death. Lysandra, with her children, fled to the court of Seleucus. This prince, though 77 years of age, was not deaf to the voice of ambition, nor insensible to the claims of the unfortunate. He declared war against Lysimachus, and with a large army marched into Asia Minor.

2. Lysimachus immediately crossed the Hellespont, and advanced to meet his rival in Phrygia, upon a plain called the Field of Cyrus. It was a spectacle over which humanity might weep, to see these two gray-haired old men, the last survivors of those distinguished generals who won such glory in the campaigns of Alexander, now meeting to engage in deadly strife for a dominion which must necessarily be so very brief. Lysimachus was defeated and slain. Seleucus passed over to take possession of Macedonia and Thrace, but was murdered by Ptolemy Ceraunus, brother of Arsinoë, B. C. 280.

3. The friends and followers of Lysimachus at first regarded Ceraunus as the avenger of his blood; but when the cruel Egyptian married his own sister, Arsinoë, and assassinated the two young princes in her arms, they looked upon him with horror and detestation. His career was short. Providence commissioned a distant and barbarous people to do the work of vengeance. The Gauls, finding their own country too populous, sent out a numerous army in quest of more fertile

THRACE.—Section V.—*Questions.*—1. In the division of Alexander's empire, to whose share did Thrace fall? What led to a battle between him and Seleucus? 2. Give an account of the battle. The closing account of Seleucus. Where was Phrygia? (See map No. 2.) 3. How then was Ceraunus at first regarded? What change took place?

regions. Following the valley of the Danube, they arrived in Thrace. While all other princes through whose territory they passed were purchasing safety with money and jewels, Ceraunus prepared for war. A battle was fought, in which he was defeated and taken prisoner, covered with wounds. The Gauls cut off his head, fixed it on a lance, and held it up for derision. Thrace, being thus left without a king, fell under the power of Macedonia, and continued subject to the descendants of Demetrius till Greece was conquered by the Romans.

SYRIA.

4. THE DYNASTY OF THE SELEUCIDÆ, B. C. 311.

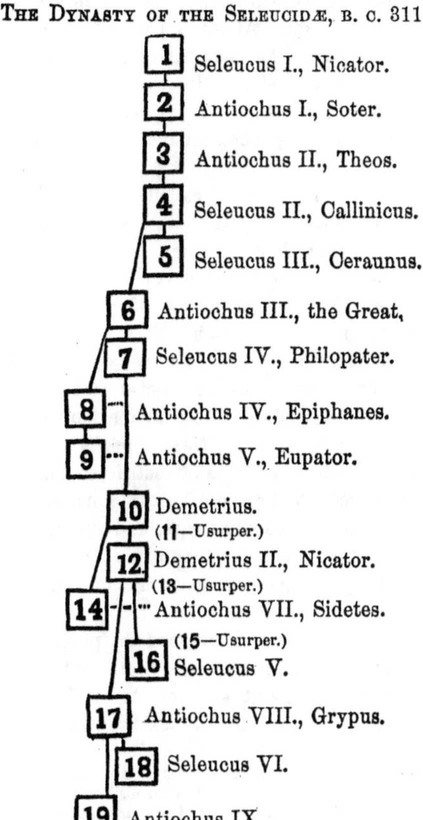

Questions.—3. Give an account of Ceraunus's career.

The era of the Seleucidæ is dated from B. C. 311, when Seleucus alone gained a victory over Antigonus, and entered Babylon in triumph, though some chronologers date the commencement of the Syrian kingdom at the victory of Ipsus, 301.

5. SELEUCUS I., surnamed *Nicator*, or the "Conqueror," received in the general division Syria, Armenia, Mesopotamia, and a part of Asia Minor. He was the greatest and most powerful monarch of the four who divided the empire of Alexander. He built the city of Seleucia, about 45 miles north of Babylon, and gave it the privilege of being a free Grecian city. He built also Antioch, the third city in the world for beauty, greatness, and population. About a year after the death of his friend Ptolemy, king of Egypt, he engaged in a war with Lysimachus, in which that monarch was slain. He was assassinated the following year, B. C. 280. ANTIOCHUS I., *Soter*, "Saviour," succeeded to his father's throne. He was distinguished for his victories over the Macedonians and Galatians.

6. ANTIOCHUS II., *Theos*, "God," was so called by the Milesians, because he delivered them from a tyrant. He engaged in a war with Ptolemy Philadelphus, but, being defeated, was compelled to sue for peace; a boon which he obtained on condition of divorcing his wife, Laodice, and marrying Berenice, daughter of Ptolemy. The happiness of this match was of short duration. As soon as the king of Egypt died, Berenice was repudiated, and Laodice recalled. This wicked queen, fearing another reverse of fortune, poisoned Antiochus, and, pretending that he was sick, sent for the principal noblemen to hear the last commands of their sovereign. Meantime she put a person who much resembled him into his bed, and instructed him what to say. When the nobles arrived, the pretended Antiochus, in a faint voice, recommended his *dear Laodice* to their care, and appointed her oldest son, Seleucus, his successor. The death of Antiochus was soon after made public, and Laodice, having placed her son upon the throne, dispatched Berenice and her son, B. C. 246.

7. SELEUCUS II., *Callinicus*, had scarcely assumed the purple, when Ptolemy Euergetes invaded Syria to avenge the death of his sister, Berenice. The Syrians revolted in great numbers to the Egyptians, and Seleucus was compelled to see his dominions ravaged, without

---

Questions.—4. After the death of Ceraunus, what became of Thrace? 5. At what period commenced the era of the Seleucidæ? Who was Seleucus I.? Give his history. Where is Antioch? *Ans.* Just half way between Constantinople and Alexandria, being 700 miles from each. Here the disciples were first called Christians. For what was Antiochus Soter distinguished? 6. Why was Antiochus II. called Antiochus Theos? Give his history. Relate the crimes of Laodice. 7. Give the history of Seleucus Callinicus.

power to protect them. During these commotions, Arsaces, the governor of Parthia, revolted; and, being victorious in a battle, took Seleucus prisoner. This Arsaces was the founder of the Parthian dynasty, Arsacidæ, a race of tyrants as impious as the world ever saw. Seleucus died after a ten years' captivity, by a fall from his horse.

8. SELEUCUS III., *Ceraunus*, "the Thunderer," reigned ingloriously three years. He was succeeded by his brother, ANTIOCHUS III., the Great. This prince engaged in a long and distressing war with Ptolemy Philopater, and was at last compelled to give up a great part of Syria to purchase peace. He then commenced hostilities with the Parthians to recover Media. This province was very valuable from its producing the finest horses then known. Antiochus took the city of Ecbatana. The royal palace, though built of cedar and cypress, had not the least particle of wood visible. The joists, beams, ceilings, columns, and piazzas, were all covered with gold and silver plates. Alexander, Antigonus, and Seleucus had successively plundered the place, yet Antiochus collected enough of the precious metals to amount to $3,000,000. After a war of seven years, Antiochus made a treaty with Arsaces, and returned to Antioch,

9. TEN KINGS REIGN IN THIS CENTURY.—B. C. **200.**—This was that Antiochus who entered into the famous league with the Etolians to overthrow the Romans, and suffered so much from the *extraction of his teeth at Thermopylæ*. From Greece he removed back to Ephesus, where, in the company of a young woman whom he had found in his travels and married, he passed his time as merrily as possible. He did not awake to a full sense of his danger till his troops had suffered defeat after defeat, and the Romans had actually brought the war into Asia. Then he gave battle, was vanquished, and fled with all speed to Antioch. Thence he sent his nephew to desire peace. It was granted on condition that he should surrender all Asia Minor, pay an immense sum of money, give twenty hostages, and deliver up Hannibal, who had taken refuge at his court. Antiochus agreed to comply with these terms. To obtain the money, he took a plundering tour through his dominions. The inhabitants of Susiana slew him because he robbed their temple. SELEUCUS IV., *Philopater*. To raise the tribute imposed on his kingdom by the Romans employed all the time and

---

Questions.—7. What do you know of the Parthians? *Ans.* They were a tribe of Scythians who lived in the northeast part of Persia. Arsaces drove out the Syrians, founded a new empire, conquered Persia and several neighboring states. The Romans had frequent contests with the Parthians, but never subdued them. 8. What is said of Seleucus Ceraunus? Give the account of Antiochus the Great. What is said of the royal palace at Ecbatana? 9. Give an account of the Antiochus who was at Thermopylæ. Of Seleucus Philopater.

ingenuity of this prince. In his reign occurred the incident of "Heliodorus in the temple," related in the book of Maccabees.

10. Antiochus IV., *Epiphanes*, "Illustrious," ascended the throne left vacant by the death of his brother, B. C. 175. He engaged in a war with his nephew, Ptolemy, and conquered all Egypt except Alexandria. He took the young king prisoner, affected to act as his guardian, and to treat him with the greatest attention. The Egyptians, however, applied to the Romans, who, as arbiters, compelled Epiphanes to set the young king at liberty, and restore the cities he had taken from him. The Jews having revolted, the Syrian monarch marched into Judea. He besieged Jerusalem, and took it by storm. During the three days that the city was abandoned to the fury of the soldiers, 80,000 Jews were put to death, and 40,000 taken prisoners. To his other crimes he added sacrilege. He forced his way into the temple, and ventured to enter the Holy of Holies. He carried away the altar of perfumes, the table for shew-bread, the seven-branched golden candlestick, and other precious things of the sanctuary.

11. Some time after, Antiochus published a decree, requiring all the nations of his dominions to lay aside their ancient forms and ceremonies, and worship the gods he worshiped, after the same form and manner he had adopted. The Jews refused to comply with this command, and such a horrid persecution arose as no pen can portray. At this time happened the martyrdom of Eleazar, and the seven Maccabean brethren. "Tidings out of the east and out of the north" now troubled Antiochus. He divided his forces into two bodies; committed one part to the command of Lysias, with orders to exterminate the Jews, while he led the other detachment against the Armenians. The army of Lysias met the little band of Jews, commanded by Judas Maccabeus, upon the plains of Mizpah. The Syrians were defeated, with dreadful slaughter. Two more battles gave the Jews such decided superiority that they marched to Jerusalem, recovered the sanctuary, re-dedicated it to the service of the true God, and devoted the week to thanksgiving and praise.

12. Antiochus, hearing of the defeat of Lysias, set out himself for Judea. On his way, fresh expresses met him, saying that the Jews had thrown down his idols, overturned his altars, and re-established their ancient worship. At this intelligence he ordered his coachman to drive with the utmost speed, that he might satiate his vengeance by

Questions.—10. When did Antiochus Epiphanes ascend the throne? Who was his nephew? What is said of the young king of Egypt? What misfortune befell the Jews? 11, 12. What decree did Antiochus publish? What followed? What reverse happened to Antiochus? How were the Jews benefited?

making Jerusalem the burying-place of the whole Jewish nation. Scarcely had he uttered the impious words, when he was seized with the most excruciating pain; and as the horses were running at their greatest speed, he fell from his chariot. The agony of his bruises, added to the torment of his disease, drove him frantic. He imagined that specters hovered round, reproaching him with his crimes. Recognizing the hand of Divine justice in the anguish he suffered, he exclaimed, "It is meet to be subject unto God, and man who is mortal should not think of himself as if he were a god." He promised if his life were spared to do magnificent things for Jerusalem; but his sands were run. "He died a miserable death, in a strange country, in the mountains."

13. ANTIOCHUS V., *Eupator*, a youth of nineteen, succeeded his father, but was soon dethroned by his cousin, Demetrius, who had been a hostage in Rome many years. Demetrius freed the Babylonians from a petty tyrant, and made war upon the Jews. Judas Maccabeus was dead, but by this time the Romans had extended their powerful protection to the Jews, and Demetrius, having made peace with them, proceeded to act the king in a more comic manner. He erected a castle in Antioch, flanked by four towers, where he shut himself up to follow the directions of Sardanapalus, "eat, drink, and sleep." This delightful life was disturbed by a young man, who, pretending to be the son of Epiphanes, had been acknowledged king by the Romans. Demetrius quitted the castle of Indolence, and buckled on the panoply of war. In the first battle he was defeated and slain. ALEXANDER THE USURPER then made himself master of Syria. Ptolemy gave him his daughter, Cleopatra, in marriage; and Alexander, thinking his fortune made, determined to give himself no further trouble with public affairs. We do not know whether he chose the castle of Demetrius for the scene of his pleasures, but he followed exactly his course of life, and came to an end precisely similar.

14. DEMETRIUS II., *Nicator*, son of the former king, put forward his claim to the throne. Alexander called on his father-in-law for assistance. Ptolemy Philometer accordingly marched into Palestine with a large army, but finding that a plot was on foot in Alexander's camp to poison him, he took his daughter away from her husband, gave her to the young Demetrius, and engaged to assist him with all his forces. Alexander was defeated and slain. Demetrius, now acknowledged king of

---

Questions.—12. Give the closing account of Antiochus. 13, 14. Who succeeded Antiochus IV.? What can you say of him? Give the history of Demetrius. Of Alexander the Usurper. In what way did Ptolemy Philometer aid the young Demetrius?

Syria, followed the example of his two immediate predecessors, till a revolution in favor of Alexander's son drove him from the throne. In his wanderings and fightings he was taken prisoner by the Parthians, and detained in captivity many years. Cleopatra shut herself up in a strong city with her children, and continued faithful to the memory of Demetrius, till, hearing that he had married a Parthian lady, all her vindictive passions were aroused.

15. She sent to Antiochus VII., *Sidetes*, brother of her perfidious husband, offering to set aside the claims of her children, marry him, and be once more queen. The offer was accepted, the nuptials speedily solemnized, and the usurper not long after slain. Demetrius, meanwhile, was making every effort to escape from his keepers and return to Syria. Antiochus, apprehensive that he would be successful, marched into Parthia, determined to destroy this rival brother, and conquer the country at one blow. He was, however, slain in battle, and Demetrius returned to Syria. The inconstant queen forgave his marriage with the Parthian lady, and acknowledged him Syria's king and Cleopatra's lord. This second honeymoon was very short. The king of Egypt made war upon Demetrius, and defeated him in a pitched battle. The unfortunate monarch fled to the city of his queen, but the gates were shut against him. He fell into the hands of his enemies, and was put to death.

16. Seleucus V., the eldest son of Demetrius and Cleopatra, now ascended the throne; but as he did not admit his mother to a share of power, she stabbed him with her own hand. She then sent to Athens for her second son, and caused him to be declared king immediately upon his return. Antiochus VIII. had the surname of *Grypus*, from his great nose. His mother presented him a cup of poisoned wine, but he compelled her to drink it herself. Syria was thus delivered from a monster that had so long disgraced the names of wife, mother, and queen. Grypus lived after this 27 years. His reign was disturbed by the intrigues of his brothers, both of whom contended for the crown.

17. Syria becomes a Roman Province.—B. C. **100.**—Grypus left five sons, all of whom were kings, or at least pretenders to the throne. Seleucus VI., the eldest, was killed in a mutiny of the citizens, in which his house was set on fire. Antiochus and Philip, the next two brothers, were twins. One was drowned in attempting to swim across

Questions.—14. What misfortunes happened to the latter? 15. What part did the wife of Demetrius take? Give the history of Antiochus Sidetes. Of Demetrius Nicator. 16. Of Seleucus V. Of Antiochus VIII. 17. How many sons did he leave? Give their history. What further can you say of the race of Seleucus? Of Syria?

a river, and the other spent the rest of his reign in fighting with the two younger boys. The kingdom of Syria was torn in pieces by the factions of the royal family, or by usurpers who established themselves for a little time as kings in various cities and districts. Finally, Pompey reduced Syria to a Roman province. The race of Seleucus thus became extinct, or was lost in the common tide of human life.

REVIEW QUESTIONS.

		PAGE
1.	Who was Lysimachus?	289
2.	What account can you give of him?	272, 275, 289
3.	Who was Ceraunus?	289
4.	Give an account of him	289, 290
5.	Who was Seleucus?	275, 291
6.	Give an account of him	275, 291
7.	What is said of Antiochus I.?	291
8.	Of Antiochus II.?	291
9.	Seleucus II.?	292
10.	Seleucus III.?	292
11.	Antiochus?	292
12.	Seleucus IV.?	292
13.	Antiochus IV.?	293
14.	Antiochus V.?	294
15.	Demetrius?	294
16.	What is said of Alexander the Usurper?	294
17.	Who was Demetrius II.?	294
18.	Give an account of his successes and failures	294, 295
19.	What is said of Antiochus Sidetes?	295
20.	Who was Seleucus V.?	295
21.	Give the account of him	295
22.	What can you state of Antiochus Grypus?	295
23.	Of Grypus's sons?	295, 296
24.	When did Syria become a Roman province?	296

EGYPT.

SECTION VI.

1. B. C. **300.** The Three Good Ptolemies.—Dynasty of the Lagidæ.

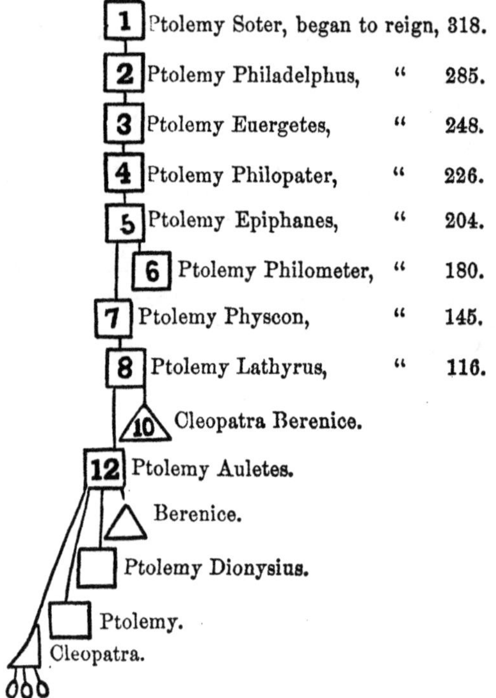

Egypt becomes a Roman Province.

13*

When the empire of Alexander was dismembered, each general taking a limb, Ptolemy secured the "lion's share;" not indeed in extent of country, but in the wealth and submissive disposition of his subjects. He was the reputed son of Lagus, and the dynasty founded by him was called the Lagidæ. The era is reckoned from B. C. 318, though he did not assume the title of king till after the battle of Ipsus, 301.

2. Ptolemy I., *Soter*, was distinguished not only as a warrior but as a ruler; he was accessible to all his subjects, simple in his manners, and a lover of learning. He wrote a life of Alexander, and founded an academy at Alexandria, to which he gave the greatest library in the world. It was his two daughters who were married to Lysimachus and Agathocles; and it was his eldest son, Ceraunus, who, exasperated because his brother Philadelphus was preferred before him, fled to Thrace, and, to gain the throne of that country, murdered the aged Seleucus and the two sons of his sister, Arsinoë. Two years before the death of Ceraunus, Ptolemy Soter associated Philadelphus, his second son, in the government; and the coronation of the young prince was attended with a grand display of all the wealth and splendor Egypt could boast.

3. Ptolemy II. was called *Philadelphus*, "Lover of his Brother," perhaps ironically, because he had supplanted Ceraunus. He might properly have been called *Philemon*, "Lover of Learning," for all the wars and tumults which prevailed thoughout the world could not turn away his attention from the great work of completing the library which his father had founded. Every book brought into Egypt was seized and copied; the copies were handed back to the proprietors, and the originals laid up in the library. The price he paid for the Scriptures will illustrate the sacrifices he made to gratify his ruling passion. Hearing that the Jews possessed a remarkable book containing the laws of Moses, he determined to possess it. He collected all the Hebrew slaves in his dominions, amounting to 120,000, and sent them home, accompanied by embassadors bearing presents and letters, and making a request for the holy volume.

4. The ransomed Jews and the deputies were received at Jerusalem with the greatest joy. An authentic copy of the Scriptures, written in letters of gold, was given to the Egyptians by the high-priest him-

---

Egypt.—Section VI.—*Questions.*—1. Who was the founder of the Lagidæ? What was his origin? In what way did he gain Egypt? When did he begin to reign? 2. For what was Ptolemy Soter distinguished? Was he an author? What did he write? What else did he do? Who was his eldest son? Who his second son? What can you state of the second son? 3. What is said of the library? Of the means taken to get the Scriptures?

self, and six elders from each tribe were sent home with them to translate the Hebrew into a Greek version. The elders were conducted to the island of Pharos, lodged in a house prepared for their reception, and plentifully supplied with every thing necessary for their comfort. When their work was complete it was read before the king, who dismissed the faithful scribes with magnificent presents. This version was called the *Septuagint* translation, from seventy elders having been employed upon it.

5. The famous watch-tower of Alexandria was completed in his reign. This tower, which was called Pharos, and passed for one of the *seven wonders of the world*, was built of white marble, story above story, adorned with columns and galleries of exquisite workmanship. On the top, fires were kept burning to guide mariners into the bay. Philadelphus also kept two powerful fleets, one in the Mediterranean, and the other in the Red Sea, by which means he made Egypt the mart of the world. Though he expended such vast sums in strengthening his kingdom, and constructing public works, yet Egypt was never richer or happier than during his reign. In his old age, he accompanied his daughter, Berenice, into Syria, and assisted at the solemnization of her nuptials with Antiochus II., husband of the repudiated Laodice.

6. Ptolemy III., *Euergetes*, ascended the throne of Egypt B. C. 285. After Antiochus had banished his sister, Berenice, and recalled Laodice, Euergetes engaged in a war with the Syrians, and overran their country as far as Bactria. Among the plunder of the cities, he found those idols which Cambyses stole from Egypt, and, carrying them home, recommitted them to the care of the priests. For this pious act he was surnamed *Euergetes*, "Benefactor." When he set out on this expedition, his wife, Berenice, made a vow to consecrate her hair to the gods if they would bring her husband home in safety. Immediately upon his return she caused her head to be shorn, and her beautiful locks to be hung up in the temple of Venus. The consecrated hair was stolen not long after, and when the priests were called to account, they gravely affirmed that it had been taken to heaven, and gazing fixedly into the sky, declared they could see the light of the golden locks. Some astronomers, equally sharp-sighted, were enabled also to discern a constellation never before noted, to which they gave

---

Questions.—4. What great benefit did Ptolemy confer upon the world? Give the particulars. 5. What is said of the watch-tower? Of the two fleets? Of the richness and happiness of Egypt? What did the king do in his old age? 6. Who was the next king of Egypt? When did he ascend the throne? In what war did he become engaged? What did he accomplish? Why was he called Euergetes? Why is he mentioned in astronomy?

the name of "Berenice's hair." This beautiful cluster of stars is situated in the diamond of Virgo. Euergetes did not forget to enrich his library with all the books and paintings which could be obtained in any part of the world. He was the third and last good Ptolemy.

7. Ptolemy IV. was called *Philopater*, "Lover of Father," from a suspicion that he hastened his father's death. He commenced his reign by the murder of his mother, Berenice, and his brother, Magus. The character which he thus acquired for violence and cruelty was sustained by all the succeeding acts of his life. This was the prince who engaged in a war with Antiochus the Great, and wrested from him a great part of Syria. Satisfied with conquest, Philopater gave himself up to every species of vice. Women, and those women not his wives, governed every thing at court, and conferred all honors and employments throughout the kingdom. His wife shared the fate of his mother and brother, and many distinguished individuals fell victims to the corruption of the times.

8. At last, worn out with dissipation, his constitution gave way. No one that deserved the appellation of friend was present when he died. Two or three of his creatures saw him breathe his last, but instead of committing his body to the proper officers, and ordering a general mourning, they concealed his death till they had carried off all the gold and jewels from the palace. When, however, his decease became publicly known, and the people reflected upon the probable fate of the young prince left to the care of these vile usurpers of power, they assembled and put them all to the sword. Their dead bodies were dragged through the streets, and torn in pieces by the multitude.

9. Four wicked Ptolemies Reign.—B. C. **200.** Ptolemy V., *Epiphanes*. No sooner did Antiochus, king of Syria, and Philip, king of Macedon, learn that the scepter of Egypt had fallen into the hands of a child, than they determined to seize upon the cities which had been so long in dispute, and settle the boundaries of the countries to suit themselves. Antiochus carried out his designs by conquering Cœlo-Syria and Palestine, but Philip had so much to do in Greece that his plans failed. When Antiochus embarked in his great enterprise of the league against Rome, he made peace with Ptolemy Epiphanes, and gave him his daughter in marriage. The young queen was

Questions.—6. What is said of the library? 7, 8. Who next became king? Why was he called Philopater? How did he commence his reign? What further can you say of him? What is said of his death? 9. By whom was he succeeded? What two kings formed a league against Ptolemy V.? How did his wife manifest her attachment?

expected to act as a spy in the Egyptian court, but her attachment to her husband overcame her reverence for her father, and she even joined in the embassy which went to congratulate the Romans on the victory they gained over Antiochus at Thermopylæ.

10. After the death of his father-in-law, Epiphanes determined to wrest from his successor, Seleucus, those cities which had been taken from Egypt in the commencement of his reign. His courtiers inquired where he expected to obtain money for furnishing his army. "My people are my treasure," replied the king. Inferring from this answer that he intended to take unwarrantable liberties with their purses, his parasites caused him to be poisoned. He had reigned twenty-four years.

11. PTOLEMY VI., *Philometer*, "Lover of his Mother," was proclaimed king at the age of six years, and his mother declared regent. As soon as he was old enough to understand war to be the game of kings, he commenced hostilities with Antiochus Epiphanes for the recovery of those cities which had passed from one government to another so many times. He was taken prisoner and kept in confinement, while his brother, Physcon, administered the affairs of the kingdom. Philometer escaped from the too-loving watch of his guardian, and united his fortunes with his brother. This brought Antiochus on his third expedition into Egypt. Philometer sent for help to the Romans. The embassadors deputed by this people to settle the affair landed in Egypt, and came up with Antiochus about a mile from Alexandria. They handed him dispatches, and waited in silence while he read them. Antiochus, wishing to gain time, told the envoys he would consult with his friends, and give them an answer soon. The consul drew a line about him as he stood in the sand, and, raising his voice, "Answer," said he, "the senate of Rome before you stir out of that circle." The king, quite confounded, submissively replied, that he would do as the Romans desired. Accordingly, he left Egypt at the stipulated time, and restored the cities of Cyprus.

12. Some commentators think Antiochus and Philometer the "two kings who spoke lies at one table," and recognize the intervention of the Romans in the passage, "the ships of Chittim shall come against him," &c. The two brothers could not live in peace. Physcon expelled Philometer, who fled to Rome. The senate settled the dispute by a partition of the kingdom between the brothers. Physcon,

Questions.—10. Relate the circumstances of his death. 11. Who succeeded him? When was Ptolemy Philometer declared king? Why did he engage in war? What misfortune befell him? Who was Physcon? What did the Romans do? Antiochus? 12. Read Dan. xi. 30. What disagreement took place

who was dissatisfied with his portion, thought proper to try the effect of *his* person in Rome. The senate received him favorably, and added Cyprus to his dominions; but when he came to ask the hand of Cornelia, the mother of the Gracchi, in marriage, he learned that the daughter of Scipio could despise a crown. Physcon returned to Cyprus, but Philometer made war upon him, and took him prisoner. This Philometer was the king who took his daughter Cleopatra from Alexander, and gave her to Demetrius; and this Cleopatra was the wicked queen who was the wife of three kings, and the mother of four.

13. PTOLEMY VII., *Physcon*, "the Corpulent," ascended the throne of Egypt after the death of Philometer, B. C. 145. He married Philometer's widow, and murdered her son, the heir apparent, in her arms; and he put so many of the friends of his brother to death, that Alexandria was almost depopulated. Philosophers, mathematicians, physicians, and men of science and letters, who had been called together by the generous policy which founded the school and libraries of the city, sought a more congenial atmosphere than the court of a corrupt king. Thus the cruelty of this tyrant scattered the seeds of learning in all the neighboring countries. To re-people his city, Physcon offered the deserted houses rent free to those who would come from foreign parts and take up their abode in them.

14. In this manner the inhabitants of Alexandria became a mixture of every people, tribe, and tongue; but the new settlers soon perceived that they had gained nothing by subjecting themselves to the will of a tyrant. Physcon, fearing the just indignation of his subjects, caused the young men of Alexandria to be assembled in a public place, and ordered his foreign troops to put them to death. All Egypt then revolted, and the wicked king was forced to flee to Cyprus, while Cleopatra, his divorced queen, ascended the throne. Her reign was, however, short, for Physcon collected an army, reinstated himself by force of arms, and reigned for some time, feared by his enemies, and hated by his subjects (he had no friends); his own wife sought his destruction, and he murdered his own son.

15. CLEOPATRA.—EGYPT SUBDUED.—B. C. **100.** PTOLEMY VIII., surnamed *Lathyrus*, from the mark of a pea on his nose, succeeded his father, after many quarrels with his mother and brother. Lathyrus reigned 36 years, during which Egypt was constantly distracted by the

Questions.—12. What did Philometer gain by going to Rome? What did Physcon gain by going? What did he not gain? What further is said of Philometer? What is said of Cleopatra? 13, 14. When did Ptolemy Physcon become king? Of what cruelties was he guilty? What then was he forced to do? What further can you state of him? 15. Who next ascended the throne? What troubles did Lathyrus have?

dissensions of the royal family. BERENICE, his only legitimate child, succeeded him, but as, according to the custom of the country, all the sons took the name of Ptolemy, and all the daughters that of Cleopatra, she was called Cleopatra Berenice. Sylla, at that time dictator of Rome, sent her cousin, Alexander, to claim the throne. He concluded to take Berenice in marriage, and permit her to retain the title of queen; but subsequently repented of his lenity, and put her to death. The fifteen years of Alexander's reign were spent in violence and cruelty; and finally the Alexandrians expelled him, and called Ptolemy Auletes, an illegitimate son of Lathyrus, to assume the reins of their government.

16. Ptolemy Auletes, to purchase the protection of the Romans, entered into an agreement to pay Julius Cæsar, the consul, a sum equal to $90,000. The taxes which he levied to meet this engagement exasperated his subjects, and he was obliged to fly for his life. The Egyptians proclaimed his daughter, Berenice, queen. Auletes, meantime, made his way to Rome. Cæsar was absent in Gaul, but Pompey received the exile kindly, gave him an apartment in his house, and omitted no occasion of serving him. His business in Rome detained him long. The senate had no army to send into Egypt, and he was forced to wait till a change in the consulship was effected. While the Romans hesitated, the Egyptians acted. The government of a woman could not satisfy them. They therefore sent to Seleucus, one of the last princes of Syria, offering him the hand of Berenice and the sovereignty of Egypt.

17. Seleucus came immediately to Alexandria, married his queen, and put on his crown; but avarice made him deaf alike to the call of love and ambition. His first care was to cause the body of Alexander the Great to be put into a coffin of glass, while he melted the golden one into a more convenient form for transportation. Berenice, disgusted with his meanness, employed some of her creatures to strangle him. Auletes returned not long after, supported by Mark Antony and a Roman army. The people were forced to acknowledge him for their sovereign, and with a Roman body-guard he was enabled to take vengeance upon his enemies. His daughter, Berenice, was the first victim; then followed those whose great wealth tempted his cupidity.

Questions.—15. Who succeeded him? What was her fate? What is said of Alexander's reign? Who was Ptolemy Auletes? To what position did he attain? State how. 16. What agreement did Auletes enter into? What were the consequences? Who then became queen? Who became her husband? In what way was the marriage brought about? 17. What was the first care of Seleucus? What became of him? What further is stated of Auletes?

The Egyptians suffered these violences without a murmur; but when a Roman soldier killed a *cat*, the whole authority of Ptolemy could not prevent their tearing him to pieces.

18. Ptolemy Auletes died B. C. 51, leaving two sons and two daughters. By his will he directed that Cleopatra, the eldest daughter, should marry PTOLEMY DIONYSIUS, the eldest son, and reign jointly with him, under the guardianship of Pompey the Great. These directions were followed; but three years after, the ministers of Ptolemy having deprived Cleopatra of her share in the government, she escaped to Syria. It was precisely at this juncture that Pompey, having fled from the plains of Pharsalia, arrived in Egypt to claim an asylum from his enemies. But Egypt was not the place to seek friends in the day of adversity. The fear of Cæsar had arrived there before him. The artful ministers of the young king dared not counsel to receive the unfortunate Roman, lest Cæsar should call them to account; they dared not send him away, lest he should retrieve his affairs, and return to punish their ingratitude. The proverb, "Dead men do not bite," urged by the tutor of the king, decided the fate of the illustrious fugitive. Ptolemy, with his parasites, went down to the shore, as if to welcome the arrival of his guardian; and looked on with the greatest unconcern, while those appointed to do the bloody deed assassinated the noble Roman, cut off his head as a present for Cæsar, and threw his body naked on the strand.

19. When Cæsar, in pursuit of Pompey, landed in Alexandria, he found every thing in confusion. Referring to the will of the late king, he ordered Cleopatra and Dionysius to appear before him, declaring that, as Roman consul, it was necessary for him to settle the differences between the brother and sister, alias, the husband and wife. Cleopatra, conscious of the power of her beauty, determined to use it in furthering her ambitious projects. With only one attendant, she was rowed to the walls of the citadel of Alexandria in the night. There her servant wrapped her up in a bundle of clothes, put a thong carefully around her, and carried her as a bale of goods into Cæsar's apartment. The first apparition of this lovely creature decided the heart of the conqueror in her favor. The next day he decreed that Cleopatra and her brother should reign jointly, according to the *will*, and that the younger brother and sister should have Cyprus.

Questions.—18. When did he die? Can you name any provision of his will? Why did Cleopatra escape to Syria? What happened at this juncture? How did the Egyptians reason about the reception of Pompey? What was the sequel? 19. Whom did Cæsar pursue into Egypt? What persons did Cæsar order to appear before him? How did Cleopatra effect her purpose? What decree did Cæsar make?

20. Ptolemy was dissatisfied with this decision. He stirred up the people to make an attempt upon the Roman fleet. To prevent his galleys from falling into the enemy's hands, Cæsar set them on fire. Some of them were driven by the wind so near the quay, that the flames caught the neighboring houses, and spread throughout the quarter called Bruchion, consuming a part of the books in the famous library. A series of similar attacks and reprisals went on between Cæsar and the Egyptians while he stayed in Alexandria. Finally, a decisive battle was fought, and Ptolemy, attempting to escape in a little boat, was drowned. All Egypt then submitted. Cæsar gave the crown to Cleopatra, in conjunction with her younger brother, PTOLEMY XI., then eleven years of age. He took Arsinoë, the other sister, with him to Rome, where she walked in his triumph in chains of gold, but immediately after he permitted her to retire to Asia.

21. B. C. 41. At the age of fourteen, the young king demanded his share in the government. Cleopatra therefore poisoned him, and remained sole possessor of the regal authority. After the battle of Philippi, when Mark Antony passed over into Asia to establish the authority of the triumvirate, all the kings, princes, and governors of the provinces were cited to appear before him. Among others, Cleopatra was summoned. This princess, then twenty-five years old, had added to her unrivaled attractions all the fascinations which a cultivated mind and a graceful address can give to beauty of face and elegance of person. She was a proficient in music; she could converse with Ethiopians, Jews, Syrians, Medes, Greeks, and Italians, without an interpreter; and she understood every blandishment which a voluptuous court had devised to give effect to female charms. Providing herself with rich presents, large sums of money, and the most magnificent robes and ornaments, she set off for Tarsus, where Antony waited to receive her.

22. She sailed up the Cydnus in a barge with sails of purple silk, and oars flashing with silver. A pavilion of cloth of gold was raised upon the deck, under which she reclined, habited like Venus, with beautiful damsels representing the Nereids and Graces worshiping around her. Flutes, hautboys, harps, and the softest instruments of music, filled the air with harmony, to which the gentle dip of the oars

---

Questions.—20. Who was dissatisfied with the decision? What misfortune to the world of letters occurred? Give the final account of Ptolemy. Who then were appointed to rule Egypt? What is said of Arsinoë? 21. What became of Ptolemy XI.? When did that occur? What accomplishments of mind did Cleopatra possess? What is said of her other acquirements? What summons did she heed? With what did she provide herself for the occasion? 22. Give a description of her pageant.

kept regular time, while the perfume of costly incense regaled the senses of the multitudes who crowded the banks to gaze upon the lovely pageant. A rumor was spread that the goddess Venus had come to visit the god Bacchus, and if Cleopatra so well personated the *queen of beauty*, Antony, on his part, sustained his character of the *prince of revelers*, in all its essentials. As soon as the mimic fleet had come to anchor, Antony sent to invite her to supper. She replied, that she had already ordered an entertainment upon the banks of the river, where she would receive him as her guest. Antony went; and that interview sealed his fate.

23. His love of glory, wealth, and power was lost in his absorbing passion for the fascinating princess; and while his wife, Fulvia, was supporting his interest at home against Octavius Cæsar, and his lieutenants in the east were preparing for war in Syria, he was led off like a captive in the train of Cleopatra to Alexandria. There the veteran warrior fell into every idle excess of puerile amusement, and offered at the shrine of luxury what one has called the greatest of all sacrifices—*the sacrifice of time.* There was no end to their feasts and entertainments; each vied with the other in magnificence and expense. On one occasion Cleopatra laid a wager that she would expend a million (a sum equal to $250,000) upon one supper. Antony took up the bet; and Plaucus, a mutual friend, was to decide it. The banquet was prepared; Antony inquired the price of every dish, and after calculating the expense, said, "You are still far short of a million." The table was cleared, and a single cup of vinegar placed before the queen. "Now," said she, with an air of triumph, "I will see if I cannot spend a million upon myself alone." She took the cup, and, unclasping one of the pearls from her ear, threw it into the vinegar, and, when it was dissolved, swallowed it at a single draught! She was preparing to do the same by the other,* when Plaucus stopped her, declaring she had won the bet.

24. In the midst of these scenes of dissipation Antony received intelligence that his wife, Fulvia, had been overpowered, and driven out of Italy by Octavius Cæsar; and that the Parthians had subjugated Asia, from the Euphrates to Ionia. Waking literally from a fit of intoxication, he set sail with a fleet of 200 ships to meet his wife

* This pearl was afterwards carried to Rome by Augustus, cut in two, and hung in the ears of the statue of Venus.

Questions.—22. What rumor was spread? What invitation did Antony extend? What was the reply? 23. What followed? Give an account of the celebrated bet and banquet. 24. What intelligence did Antony receive? What then did he do?

in Greece. He found her at Sicyon, sick. After reproaching her for being the cause of a war with Cæsar, he left her to die among strangers, and proceeded toward Italy. Cæsar, not being prepared for hostilities, threw all the blame of the late commotions upon Fulvia, and offered to accommodate matters by dividing the empire, giving Antony that portion east of the Adriatic, while he took the west. His sister, Octavia, a woman of great beauty and merit, was, by decree of the senate, excused from mourning for her husband, just deceased, that she might cement the union by giving her hand to Antony.

25. The nuptials were celebrated at Rome, and Antony seemed for a time to forget, in the society of this charming woman, the wrongs of the dead Fulvia, and the love of the forsaken Cleopatra. He even took Octavia back with him to Greece, and lived with her some time at Athens; but when the Parthian war called him to Syria, the fascinations of Cleopatra resumed their full power over his soul. He sent for her to meet him again in Tarsus, and, upon her arrival, made her a present of several kingdoms. His attachment to her proved the ruin of the Parthian expedition. He was furnished with a fine army and plentiful supplies, but his desire to return and spend the winter with her in Alexandria, caused him to set off too early in the spring, and to travel so fast that the engines of war were left behind and seized by the enemy. Having penetrated into Media, and engaged in a long and fruitless siege of a city in which the Parthian king kept his wives he was glad to accept of permission to retreat in safety before the autumnal equinox.

26. In the backward march the Romans suffered every privation. Such was the famine, that a barley loaf sold for its weight in silver; and at one time great numbers of the soldiers partook of a root which brought on madness and death. Thus, while his army was perishing around him, Antony frequently exclaimed, "O the Ten Thousand," alluding to the famous "retreat" which Xenophon had effected through the same dangers which now beset himself. The severity of winter was such that he lost 8,000 men before he reached Sidon. Accompanied by a small party, he went down to a little fort called White Hair, and looked across the sea for the vessels of Cleopatra. They were not in sight, and he had recourse to intoxication to drown his impatience. Sometimes he would start from the table and run leaping and dancing to look out for her approach. She came at length,

---

Questions.—24. How did he treat his wife, Fulvia? What arrangement did he make with Cæsar? Whom did he then marry? 25. Did he live with Octavia long? How did he fall again into the society of Cleopatra? What was the consequence of his attachment to Cleopatra? 26. Give an account of the sufferings of Antony's army. Of Antony's conduct.

bringing large quantities of money and clothing for the troops. Octavia, too, had collected soldiers, beasts of burden, money, and presents for the officers, and set out to meet Antony. The infatuated general, nevertheless, sent her word to remain at Athens, saying that he was about to make another campaign against the Parthians. Cleopatra, however, appeared so afflicted at his leaving her again, that he put off his expedition and accompanied her to Egypt.

27. There he acted a farce more ridiculous than all his preceding follies. He called a public assembly of the Egyptians, and ordering two golden chairs to be placed on a tribunal of silver, one for himself, and the other for Cleopatra, he crowned her queen of Egypt, Cyprus, Africa, and Cœlo-Syria, nominating Cesario, her son by Julius Cæsar, as her colleague. His own two sons, Alexander and Ptolemy, then took their seats on two thrones prepared at the feet of their mother. Alexander, clothed in a Median dress, with the turban and tiara, was proclaimed king of Media, Armenia, and *Parthia, when it should be conquered.* Ptolemy wore the Macedonian long cloak and slippers, with a bonnet encircled by a diadem. He was made king of Phenicia, Syria, and Cilicia. Cleopatra wore, on this occasion, the sacred robe of Isis,* and gave audience to the people under the name of the "New Isis." Antony put the finishing touch to these absurdities by sending a minute account of his measures to Rome.

28. When the injured Octavia returned to Athens, her brother ordered her to quit Antony's house, but she refused, and still continued to take care of Fulvia's children, and her own, with all the tenderness which the most devoted wife could feel for her husband's offspring. Her conduct, however, only injured Antony's cause; for when the people saw the neglect with which such a woman was treated, their indignation was aroused, and they were ready to listen to all Cæsar's insinuations against his colleague. The report of what Antony had done in Egypt added fuel to the flame, so that when he began to make preparations for renewing the civil war, and sent to turn Octavia out of his house, they readily concurred in the decree of war against Cleopatra.

29. Antony had 500 armed vessels, 100,000 foot, 10,000 horse, and a great many auxiliaries. Cæsar had half as many vessels, three-fourths as many foot, and an equal number of horse. Cleopatra would

* This robe was of all colors, to signify the universality of the goddess's influence.

Questions.—26. What relief came? What is said of Octavia's exertions? What word did Antony send to his wife? Did he do so? 27. What farce did he act? 28. How did Antony's treatment of Cleopatra affect his popularity at home? 29. Describe his preparations to meet Augustus.

go in person to this war (because she feared a reconciliation between Antony and Octavia), and, what was worse, she insisted that the first engagements should be fought at sea, though Antony's land forces were complete, and his ships had not half their complement of men. The officers were in consequence obliged to pick up in Greece vagrants, mule-drivers, reapers, and boys. The other preparations showed equally the temerity and folly which governed the counsels of Antony. While one ship brought soldiers, another arrived filled with players and buffoons; one messenger came with news of the arrival of men and provisions, while another announced the advent of a long-expected theatrical apparatus. At last, in spite of all delays from adverse winds, and Cleopatra's caprices, Antony reached Actium with his fleet, while that of Augustus was anchored not far off upon the coast of Epirus.

30. Battle of Actium.—This engagement was fought in the bay of Actium. The prows of the vessels were armed with brazen points, which it was the object of the sailors to drive against the sides of the enemy's galleys; but as Antony's ships were very large, he could not turn them readily, and one was often surrounded by two or three of Cæsar's, the men of which threw firebrands, pikes, and javelins at the crew, as though they were storming a town. While the fight was going on, Cleopatra's sixty galleys hoisted their sails, and took to flight through the midst of the combatants. No sooner did Antony see her vessel under way, than, forgetting the brave men who were shedding their blood in his cause, he took a couple of friends with him, and rowed after her with all his might. Having overtaken her, he went on board her galley, but for three days, either through shame or resentment, did not speak to her. At last the attendants effected a reconciliation, and they proceeded together to Lydia, after Antony had stopped long enough in Greece to recommend his followers to be reconciled to Cæsar. Having sent Cleopatra forward to Alexandria, he shut himself up on a desert island and affected to act the part of Timon, the man-hater; but the strong attraction of the Egyptian siren drew him from his retreat, and, once again embarked upon the sea of dissipation, his guilty love knew neither pause nor stop till it reached its proper end—destruction.

31. Cleopatra and Antony had before established a society called *The Inimitable Livers;* they now instituted another, called *The Companions in Death!* Though the Egyptian queen had destroyed all

---

Questions.—30. Where was Actium? (See map No. 2.) Give an account of the battle. Of Cleopatra's conduct. Of Antony's subsequent conduct. 31. What is said of the two societies?

whom she suspected of being friendly to Cæsar, yet, fearful still of falling into his hands, she formed the design of drawing her galleys over the isthmus of Suez, and sailing in them down the Red Sea, in search of some remote country where she might see no more war. This plan was frustrated by the Arabians, who set her ships on fire. Knowing that Cæsar would sooner or later arrive in Egypt, and that her fatal beauty would prove but an ornament for his triumph, Cleopatra began to look to death for a refuge from disgrace. She collected all kinds of poisons, and tried them upon criminals in the prisons, and examined, also, the effect of venom upon the human system. By these experiments she found that the bite of the asp produced death with the least pain of body or contortion of visage, persons affected by it sinking away as in a gentle sleep.

32. Meanwhile, Antony sent to beg his life of Cæsar; and Egypt for Cleopatra and her children. The conqueror rejected Antony's petition, but said that Cleopatra might expect every favor if she would banish or poison the man she had so long held in her chains. The queen had caused a magnificent monument to be erected near the temple of Isis, into which she removed her treasures and a large quantity of flax, with a great number of torches. She gave orders to her governors to submit to Cæsar, so that when he came round by way of Syria and Pelusium he found no obstacle till he reached Alexandria, where Antony, in the last effort of expiring valor, determined to give battle, by sea and land. Drawing up his army upon an eminence, he sent out his galleys to the attack; but what was his despair and rage when he saw Cleopatra's admiral advance, and surrender the whole fleet to the Romans.

33. He grew desperate, and sent to challenge Cæsar to single combat. Cæsar replied, "If Antony is weary of life, there are ways enough to die." Ridiculed by Augustus and betrayed by Cleopatra, he returned to the city only to be abandoned by his cavalry, which went over in a body to the conqueror. He flew to the palace, determined to wreak his vengeance upon the enchantress who had wrought his ruin. It was deserted—and word was brought him that, preferring honorable death to shameful captivity, she had closed her life in the tombs of her ancestors. The idea of her death completed his frenzy. He passed from the excess of rage to the most violent transports of

---

Questions.—31. What plan of escape did Cleopatra form? How was it frustrated? To what did Cleopatra next turn her attention? 32. For what did Antony beg? What was the reply? What is said of the temple built by Cleopatra? Of the orders given to Cleopatra's governors? What then did Antony do? What followed? 33. What is said about the challenge?

grief, and thought only of following her to the grave. Retiring to his chamber, and unclasping his coat of mail, he called upon his faithful servant, Eros, to strike the fatal blow. Eros drew his sword as if he designed to kill him; but, suddenly turning about, slew himself, and fell at his master's feet. Antony took up the sword, and plunging it into his own body, fell back upon his couch, mortally wounded.

34. At that moment a messenger came to tell him that the queen was yet alive. When the name of Cleopatra was mentioned, he opened his eyes, and requested to be carried to her apartment. His servants conveyed him in their arms to the monument. Cleopatra would not suffer the door to be unbarred, but threw down cords from a lofty window, and assisted her women to draw him up. "Never was there a more moving sight. Antony, all bathed in blood, with death painted in his face, was drawn up in the air; turning his dying eyes, and extending his feeble hands to Cleopatra, as if to conjure her to receive his last breath; whilst she, with features distorted, and arms strained, pulled the cords with her whole strength, the people below encouraging her with cries." She laid him on her bed, rent her clothes, beat her breast, tore her hair, and, wiping the blood from his wounds, called him her lord, her emperor, her husband, seeming to forget, in her sympathy for him, that she had any miseries of her own. Antony strove to comfort her, telling her that "he had conquered like a Roman, and it was only by a Roman that he had been conquered."

35. Scarcely had he breathed his last, when a messenger arrived from Cæsar, who had been informed of Antony's rash deed. She begged permission to bury Antony according to the customs of Egypt, which was not refused. A short time after, learning that Cæsar designed to send her away in three days, she requested the melancholy satisfaction of visiting the grave of Antony once more. It was granted. "Alas! my Antony," said she, kneeling down by his tomb, "it is not long since with these hands I buried thee; they were then free; but thy Cleopatra is now a prisoner, reserved to adorn the triumph over thee. These are the last offerings, the last honors she can pay thee; for she is now to be conveyed to a distant country. Nothing could part us while we lived; but in death we are to be divided. Thou, though a Roman, liest buried in Egypt; and I, an Egyptian, must be interred in Italy, the only favor I shall receive from thy country. Yet if the gods of Rome have power or mercy left (for surely those of

---

Questions.—34, 35, 36. Give an account of Antony's subsequent conduct and death. Of Cleopatra's. When did Cleopatra die? *Ans.* B. C. 30. How old was she at the time of her death? *Ans.* 39 years.

Egypt have forsaken us), let them not suffer me to be led in living triumph to thy disgrace! No! hide me, hide me with thee in the grave; for life, since thou hast left it, has been misery to me." The unhappy queen, having thus bewailed her misfortunes, returned to her monument, bathed, and sat down to a magnificent supper. Then, having called for a basket of figs which a peasant had lately brought, she wrote a letter to Cæsar, and, ordering every one out of the monument except her two women, made fast the door.

36. When Cæsar opened the letter, and read "her last request to be buried with Antony," he suspected her intention, and sent his servants to prevent her carrying it into effect. The messengers ran all the way, and, having broken open the door, entered. There lay the last of the royal race of the Ptolemies, on a golden couch, arrayed even in death with the greatest splendor. Iras, one of her maids, lay dead at her feet; and Charmion, hardly able to stand, was fixing the diadem upon the brow of her beloved queen. "Charmion," said the messengers of Cæsar, "was this well done?"—"Perfectly well," said she, "and worthy a descendant of the kings of Egypt." Saying this, she also sunk down and expired. No mark of violence could be discovered upon the person of Cleopatra; and as the track of a reptile was discerned on the sea-sands opposite her window, it was supposed that the basket of figs contained an *asp*, which, having stung her and her maids, was permitted to escape. In the tomb of Cleopatra was deposited the last sovereign of the Græco-Egyptian dynasty of Lagidæ, a race that had ruled Egypt 294 years.

REVIEW QUESTIONS.

		PAGE
1.	Whose son was Ptolemy said to be?	298
2.	What name was consequently given to his dynasty?	298
3.	When did he assume the title of king?	298
4.	What account can you give of the battle of Ipsus?	275
5.	What account can you give of Ptolemy I.?	298
6.	Why was Ptolemy II. surnamed Philadelphus?	298
7.	Why might he better have been called Philemon?	298
8.	What additions did he make to the great library?	298
9.	What is said of the translation of the Bible?	298, 299
10.	Of the watch-towers called Pharos?	299

PAGE

11. Why was the next Ptolemy surnamed Euergetes?............. 299
12. What is stated of the constellation Berenice's Hair............ 299, 300
13. Why was the fourth Ptolemy surnamed as he was?........... 300
14. Name the guilty acts of his reign.......................... 300
15. What scene followed his death?............................ 300
16. What territory did Egypt afterward lose?.................... 300, 301
17. What account can you give of Ptolemy VI.?................. 301, 302
18. Of Ptolemy VII.?.. 302
19. Of Physcon?.. 297–302
20. Who was Ptolemy Lathyrus?.............................. 302
21. What followed after his reign?............................. 303
22. Give an account of Ptolemy Auletes........................ 303, 304
23. What children did he leave?............................... 304, 305
24. Give an account of the early life of Cleopatra.............. 304, 305
25. Of the fate of Pompey..............................304, 393, 394
26. Of Cæsar in Egypt....................................... 304, 305
27. By what means did Cleopatra gain power?.................. 304, 305
28. What accomplishments did she possess?.................... 305
29. Why did she make a visit to Tarsus?...................... 305, 401
30. Give an account of that visit.............................. 305, 306
31. What was the consequence to Antony?..................... 306
32. Give an account of the costly supper....................... 306
33. Of Fulvia and her doings.............................306, 307, 402
34. Who was Octavius Cæsar?................................ 306, 399
35. Give the names of Antony's three wives.................306, 307, 402
36. Give an account of his Parthian expedition.................. 307, 308
37. Of his crowning of Cleopatra, &c.......................... 308
38. Of the cause and preliminaries of the battle of Actium......... 308, 309
39. Give an account of that battle............................ 309, 402
40. Of Cleopatra's attempt to escape to a remote country.......... 309, 310
41. Of her experiments with poisons.......................... 310, 312
42. Of Antony's final failure, and his death.................... 310, 311
43. What is said of the monument erected by Cleopatra?.......... 310, 312
44. Give an account of Cleopatra's death....................... 311, 312
45. What was the conduct of Cleopatra at the battle of Actium?... 309
46. How did Antony then behave himself?...................... 309
47. What account can you give of their subsequent course?....... 309
48. When did the death of Cleopatra occur?................*Ans.* B. C. 30.
49. How many years had she reigned?..........................*Ans.* 22.
50. How old was she at the time of her death?.............*Ans.* 39 years.
51. How many persons named Cleopatra have played a considerable part in mythology or history?..................*Ans.* No less than 9.
52. Which was the most notorious?.....*Ans.* The one who married Antony.

ROME.

SECTION VII.

1. Rome, commencing B. C. 753, and continuing till the year A. D. 476, occupies a period of 1229 years. Rome, in Nebuchadnezzar's Image, was the "iron kingdom;" and in Daniel's Vision, the "fourth beast, dreadful and terrible, with great iron teeth." By historians it is considered the last of "the four universal monarchies" which bore rule in the earth before the Christian era.

2. Buildings.—Rome was built by Romulus, upon the Palatine hill, but, in the days of its power, embraced also within its limits the Capitoline, Quirinal, Aventine, Cœlian, Viminal, and Esquiline hills. On the top of the Capitoline hill was the capitol, or citadel of Rome. It was the highest part of the city, strongly fortified, and magnificently ornamented. A descent of one hundred steps led to the *forum*, a large open space where the people held their assemblies. It was surrounded with arched porticoes, inclosing spacious markets where various commodities were sold. All the military roads terminated in this place, at a point in which was set up a gilded pillar called *millarium aureum.* Twenty *aqueducts* supplied the city with water, and eight bridges, supported on lofty arches, spanned the "yellow Tiber." The dwellings of the Romans were at first simple cottages thatched with straw. After the city was burned by the Gauls it was rebuilt in a more solid and commodious manner, and, after its second destruction by Nero, the houses were constructed with great attention to elegance and splendor, each dwelling having a portico in front, and an empty court, called a vestibule, before the gate. The gate was reached by ascending several steps. A slave in chains, armed with a staff, and attended by a large dog, performed the office of porter, and kept a fire, round which the images were placed, always burning.

Rome.—Section VII.—*Questions.*—1, 2. When was Rome founded? Who was its founder? What period of time does its history embrace? When end? In what light is Rome viewed by historians? What relation does it bear to Nebuchadnezzar's Image? Give a description of the building of Rome. 3. Of the dwellings and furniture.

3. They had no chimneys, and were in consequence much annoyed with smoke. At first, they made openings to admit the light; as civilization increased, they used paper, linen cloth, and horn, to shut out the wind and rain; and in the fourth century they arrived at the luxury of *glass* windows. A nobleman's *villa*, or country-seat, was a magnificent affair. The building was laid out in dining-rooms, parlors, bed-chambers, tennis-courts, baths, &c.; and the grounds were tastefully arranged with walks, terraces, parks, fish-ponds, garden, and all kinds of delightful groves. The furniture also followed the law of gradual improvement, from the simple four-legged square table, to the circular board inlaid with ivory, gold, and precious stones, till we read of one that cost a sum equal to $35,000.

4. Inhabitants.—Without stopping to discuss any disputed points, it will only be necessary to say here, that the Roman citizens were separated into two great classes—Patricians and Plebeians, whose relative positions will be more clearly defined in the following pages. Among the original population of the city, every man that could show a noble or free ancestry belonged to the patrician order, and had a share in the government of the state. Of the rest of the people, each man was attached, under the appellation of "client," to the head of some patrician family, whom he was obliged to serve, and who, in return, was bound to protect him. There was also the order of knights, consisting of young men chosen for cavalry, either from the patricians or plebeians. They must be eighteen years of age, and possessed of a sum of money equal to $14,000. Their badges of distinction were a gold ring, and a strip of purple sewed on the breast of the tunic.

5. The Roman matrons themselves took charge of the children in their infantile years. Both boys and girls wore a loose robe, bordered with purple, called *toga pretexta.* They were sent to public schools, where the greatest care was bestowed upon their style of reading and speaking. Children of rank were attended to school by a slave, who carried their books, writing materials, &c. Books were written on parchment, or on paper prepared from the leaves of the papyrus. Pens were made of a reed sharpened at the point. Ink was the black liquid emitted by the cuttle-fish. They wrote upon one side of the paper, and then rolled it round a staff, whence it was called a *volume.* Children learned to write with a metal pencil, *stylus*, upon tablets spread with wax.

Questions.—4. Into how many and what classes were the citizens separated? Who belonged to the patrician order? Who the plebeian? 5. What is said of the early education of the children? How were books written?

6. At the age of seventeen, the boy exchanged the *toga prctexta* for the *toga virilis*, or "manly gown," a loose, flowing robe, which covered the whole body. To wear this garment gracefully was a subject of intense study to the dandies of those days; and even persons of a graver temperament made it a matter of serious consideration. A *tunic* was often worn under the toga, and in cold weather a cloak was added. In early times all persons went bare-headed, but when luxury increased, a woman's toilet was called "her world." Every lady of fashion had at least one hair-dresser. The hair was anointed with the richest perfumery, curled with hot irons, adorned with gold and pearls, or bound with gay ribbons.

7. Religion.—The religion of the Romans was idolatry in the grossest extreme. All the gods of the Greeks and Egyptians were duly worshiped; and the virtues and affections of the mind, such as Faith, Hope, Concord, &c., were honored with altars and temples. The Romans also regarded with superstitious reverence the *Penates*, or powers of nature personified, and the *Lares*, or disembodied spirits of their ancestors. If the soul of the dead, in passing from the body, became a pure spirit, and hovered with the wing of love over the friends it had left behind, it was called "*Lar;*" but if, by reason of crimes committed in life, it found in the grave no resting-place, it appeared to men as a phantom; and its name, in that case, was *Larva;* but, as there was no way of ascertaining precisely the lot of the deceased, departed souls received the general appellation of *Manes*. Every household, however, claimed its protecting lares, and victims were sacrificed to them upon the domestic hearth.

8. The priests were chosen from the most honorable men in the state. There were four pontiffs, called together the *Collegium*, whose business it was to see that the inferior priests did their duty. The *Pontifex Maximus* was the supreme judge in religious matters. Every year he drew up a short account of all public transactions; and these *Annals* were exposed in an open place, for the inspection of the people. The *Augurs*, or soothsayers, made observations upon the heavens in the dead of night, explained omens, foretold future events, and exercised wonderful power over the superstitious by means of atmospheric phenomena. The *Septemviri* prepared the games, processions, and public feasts. The *Quindecemviri* had charge of the Sibylline books. The pontiffs, augurs, septemvirs, and quindecemvirs, were called "the four Colleges of Priests." The Sacred Fire, renewed

Questions.—6 What is said of the garments worn? 7. Of the religion of the Romans? 8. Of the pontiffs?

every year on the first of March from the rays of the sun, was watched by the *Vestal Virgins*, and whoever permitted it to go out was scourged by the pontifex maximus. If any vestal violated her vow she was buried alive.

9. MARRIAGE.—No young woman could marry without consent of her parents or guardians. When this was obtained, the auspices were taken, and a sacrifice offered, from which the gall of the victim was carefully removed. The bride was dressed in a long white robe, bordered with a purple fringe; her hair was parted with a spear, and her head covered with a vail. In the house of the lady's father or nearest relative, in the presence of at least ten witnesses, the pontifex maximus joined the pair in marriage, by causing them to repeat a set form of words, and taste a cake made of salt, water, and flour. In the evening the bride was taken, apparently by force, from the arms of her mother, and carried to the house of the bridegroom. Her maidservants followed her with a distaff, a spindle, and wool. As she reached the door, her husband demanded who she was, to which she always answered, "Where thou art Caius, there shall I be Caia." After binding the door-posts with woolen fillets, she gently stepped over the threshold, upon which she was presented with the keys of the house.

10. After the parties had both touched fire and water, the bridegroom proceeded to give the feast. Nuptial songs were sung till midnight, and the guests were dismissed with small presents. At supper the men reclined upon couches, and took their food without forks, the boys sitting at the feet of their elders. The table was consecrated by setting upon it the images of the Lares and salt-cellars. The feast was opened by pouring out libations to the gods, and throwing a portion of every article of food into the fire, as an offering to the guardians of the domestic hearth. The guests were entertained with music and dancing, plays and pantomimes, but the graver portion of the community preferred reading.

11. THE SENATE.—Senators were chosen from the patricians or knights, by the kings, the consuls, the military tribunes, and by the censors. The stated meetings of the senate were on the *kalends*, the beginning, and the *ides*, the middle, of every month. The power of this body varied with the varying politics of the republic. Under the regal government, the senators were the mere counselors of the king; during the palmy days of the Roman Commonwealth, they had the

---

Questions.—9, 10. Of the marriage customs? 11. How were the senators chosen? What is said of their meetings? Of their powers and rights?

supreme authority; and in the times of the emperors, being made the tools of power, they sunk into complete insignificance. Their constitutional rights gave them the direction of the treasury, the nomination of envoys, and the receiving of embassadors from foreign nations; also the power of declaring war and decreeing peace, together with the granting of triumphs to victorious generals.

12. Magistrates.—There were three classes of magistrates in Rome: 1. The *Quæstors*, whose business it was to take care of the public revenue, to exact fines, to keep the military standards, and order the public funerals. 2. The *Ædiles*, whose duty it was to inspect markets, taverns, and all things sold in the forum; to throw nuisances into the Tiber, and to examine the strength and structure of public buildings. 3. The *Prætors*, whose powers were expressed by *do*, *dico*, and *addico*. By "do," they gave the form of any writ; by "dico," they pronounced sentence; and by "addico," they adjudged the goods of the debtor to the creditor. When a cause was to be tried, the prætor took his seat in the forum, on a tribunal or stage, in a chair called *curule*, with a sword and spear placed upright before him. The jury sat on lower seats, as did also the witnesses; clerks were employed to record the proceedings, and criers, to proclaim the hour. On court days, at nine o'clock in the morning, the prætor went to the forum, and there, being seated on the tribunal, ordered the crier to notify the people that it was the third hour, and whoever had any cause might bring it before him.

13. Trials were much like those in our courts of law. In criminal cases *judices* were chosen, and after the cause had been heard, the prætor gave to each judex three tablets; on one was written C., *condemno;* on another A. *absolvo;* and on the third N. L. *non liquet*, "I am not clear." Each judex threw which of these he thought proper into an urn. The prætor took them out, counted them, and decided the case according to this verdict. While the judices were putting the ballots into the urn, the prisoner and his friends fell at their feet, wept, prayed, and used every method to excite compassion. Criminals were punished with *fines*, *bonds*, *blows*, *banishment*, *slavery*, and *death*. None but the whole Roman people could pass sentence upon the life of a Roman. "I am a Roman citizen," stopped at once the proceedings of any tyrannical magistrate, and threw the accused upon the mercy of his fellow-citizens. The body of a malefactor was exposed for a time to public execration, and then thrown into the Tiber.

Questions.—12. How many classes of magistrates were there? Give their names and duties. 13. How were criminals sentenced and punished with them?

14. Occupations.—Agriculture was the principal occupation of the Romans, and was held in the highest esteem; but the constant wars in which the commonwealth was engaged made such large drafts upon the time of the citizens, that useful employments finally fell to the lot of slaves, while all the legitimate children of the republic became soldiers. When the Romans thought themselves injured by any nation, they sent one of the *Feciales** to demand redress. If it was not immediately granted, 33 days were permitted to elapse, and then the priest went again to the confines of the nation, threw a bloody spear upon the ground, and formally declared war. Every citizen was considered a soldier from the age of sixteen to that of forty-six; nor could any person hold an office in the city who had not served ten campaigns. The soldiers were formed into legions. Each legion was divided into ten cohorts, each cohort into three bands, each band into two centuries, or hundreds: to complete the legion, 300 horse were added. They fought with slings, spears, javelins, and swords. The standard of the legion displayed an *eagle*, with the letters "S. P. Q. R.," Senate, People, and Quirites of Rome.

15. The load which a Roman soldier carried was enough to break down a common man. Provisions for fifteen days, a saw, a basket, a mattock, an ax, a hook, a leathern thong, a chain, a pot, &c., &c., amounting in all to 60 lbs. weight, besides his armor, which was not unfrequently made of brass plates, or rings, impenetrable to the spear. When a general, after consulting the auspices, had determined to attack the enemy, a red flag was hoisted on the point of a spear from the top of his tent. Then the trumpet sounded, the soldiers cried out "to arms," and, pulling up their standards, rushed on to battle. After a victory the general assembled his troops, and bestowed rewards on those who merited them. The pay of a soldier amounted only to about five cents a day besides his food, which he dressed himself. After a successful campaign the senate granted a triumph to the general, a festivity in which all the army were allowed to participate.

16. Funeral Ceremonies.—The Romans, for the same reasons that influenced the Greeks, paid the greatest attention to funeral rites. When any one was dying, his nearest relative endeavored to catch his last breath with his mouth, under the impression that in that the soul took its departure. The eyes and mouth of the deceased were immediately closed, those present repeating his name several times,

* A class of priests.

Questions.—14, 15. What is said of the occupations of the Romans? Of their equipments for fighting? Of their fighting? Of their pay? 16. Of their funeral ceremonies?

and calling out *Vale*, "farewell." The corpse, having been bathed, and dressed in its richest robes, was laid on a couch in the vestibule, and a small coin for the fee of Charon was put into its hand. The funeral was solemnized in the night, with torches, the order of the procession being regulated by law. A mingled train of musicians, hired mourners, players, and buffoons, freedmen, friends, and relatives attended the body to the place of burning or burial.

17. Fabulous History.—The first pages of Roman history, like those of the nations we have already considered, are but the intricate fables of a dark age, embellished by the fancy of the poet. At what point these mythic legends assume the form and substance of probability and truth we shall not attempt to decide. We strongly suspect that if the renowned Romulus were stripped of the drapery which the glory of *Rome* throws around him, he would appear in the form of a barbarous robber, or melt away into one of those fictitious heroes whose exploits serve only "to point a moral or adorn a tale." Virgil, the Homer of Rome, has given in his Æneid an account of the distinguished individual claimed by the Romans as their great progenitor. From this poem we learn that Æneas, son of Venus and Anchises, having escaped from the plains of Troy, after many romantic adventures landed in Italy, where the Latins then lived in all their savage simplicity. The chief of the Latins received him kindly, and gave him his daughter Lavinia in marriage. The descendants of Eneas and Lavinia were called kings of Alba, and continued to sit upon the throne of that country for a space of 400 years, which brings us to the century distinguished by the founding of that city, afterwards the acknowledged Queen of the World.

18. B. C. 753. Rome Founded by Romulus.—The fourteenth descendant of Æneas left two sons, Numitor and Amulius. To the eldest the kingdom was bequeathed, while the youngest received the treasures remaining of those brought from Troy. Amulius, not satisfied with his portion, conspired against his brother, and succeeded in depriving him of his throne. To remove all apprehensions of being one day disturbed in his ill-gotten power, he put his brother's sons to death, and caused Rhea Silvia, their sister, to take the vow of a vestal. His precautions were vain. Rhea Silvia and (as it was affirmed) Mars, the god of war, were the parents of two boys, who were no sooner born than devoted by the tyrant to destruction. The mother was buried alive, and the cradle containing the helpless babes

---

Questions.—17. Of the fabulous history of Rome? 18. Who were Numitor and Amulius? Give the history of Numitor. Of Amulius.

was thrown into the Tiber; but the river having overflowed its banks, the frail bark drifted along the margin of the stream till it became entangled in the roots of a wild vine, at the foot of the Palatine hill. Faustulus, the king's shepherd, found the children, and carried them home to his wife, who named them Romulus and Remus, and brought them up as her own sons.

19. The youths, ignorant of their real ancestry, grew to manhood among the wilds of Alba, sharing the toils and perils of their foster-father. The noble bearing and daring courage with which nature had endowed them, early gave them the pre-eminence in the little world to which they were confined, and they were soon honored as leaders of the youthful herdsmen who banded together to resist the aggression of robbers or rivals. In a quarrel which arose between the servants of Amulius and Numitor, Remus was taken prisoner and carried before his grandfather. While Numitor hesitated what punishment to inflict, Faustulus and Romulus hastened to the place of trial, and stopped all further proceedings by revealing the real origin of the delinquent. The aged Numitor was rejoiced to believe that the two noble youths who stood before him were the destined avengers of his wrongs, and hastily acquiesced in their proposal to expel Amulius, and restore the throne of Alba to its rightful possessor. Romulus, followed by the young men who had so long acknowledged him their leader, besieged the castle of Amulius, and in the confusion that ensued the usurper was slain.

20. Numitor being thus reinstated in the sovereignty of Alba, the two brothers requested permission to build a city of their own, upon the spot where their lives had been so miraculously preserved. The shepherds who had hitherto assisted them joined in this enterprise with alacrity, and soon men enough were collected to commence the work. A dispute then arose between the brothers about the precise location of the future city, and finally it was agreed to refer the matter to an augury from the flight of birds. Remus took his station upon Mount Aventine, and Romulus sat down upon the Palatine hill. At sunrise Remus saw *six* vultures, and soon after Romulus saw *twelve.* The partisans of Remus contended for him, as having seen the first good omen, while the followers of Romulus insisted that his omen was most complete. Romulus prevailed; and proceeded to mark out the boundaries of the intended city.

Questions.—18, 19, 20. Of Remus. Of Romulus. What circumstance made Romulus and Remus acquainted with their origin? What fate awaited the usurper and murderer of Amulius? What dispute is mentioned? How was it decided?

21. THE CITY.—Persons skilled in sacred mysteries were called to direct as to the manner in which every thing should be done. First, a circular ditch was dug, into which each deputy cast a handful of earth which he had brought from his own country. About three furlongs from this point the city walls were marked out in a square, including the Palatine hill, and a portion of land at its base. Romulus, having fitted a brazen plowshare to a plow, drew a furrow around the boundaries, his attendants following, and carefully turning every clod inwards. Four times he took up the plow and carried it a short distance, and in these places were built the gates.* This took place on the 21st of April, B. C. 753. While the wall was beginning to rise above the surface, Remus leaped over it, saying contemptuously, "Shall such a wall as this keep your city?" Upon which Romulus struck him dead with the implement he had in his hand, exclaiming, "So perish whosoever shall hereafter overleap these ramparts." The work then went on without interruption; and in a short time the walls were raised to a suitable height, and a thousand thatched cottages were built.

22. To increase as rapidly as possible the population of his new city, Romulus set apart a grove as a sanctuary for malefactors and run-away slaves; "every one that was in distress, and every one that was in debt," flocked thither also; those who were pleased with novelty, and those who were fond of adventure, contributed likewise to the number of inhabitants; so that Romulus soon found himself at the head of a people willing to drop all former distinctions for the yet untarnished appellation of *Romans*. To introduce order and sobriety among such a mixed multitude, some kind of government was necessary. Accordingly, Romulus was unanimously elected chief of their religion, sovereign magistrate of Rome, and general of the army. He was preceded wherever he went by twelve lictors, armed with axes tied up in bundles of rods. One hundred old men were selected to transact the business of the state. They were called *fathers*, and their descendants, *patricians*. By decrees of the senate, and authority of the people, laws were made for the regulation of public affairs, and the interests of religion were carefully guarded.

23. UNION WITH THE SABINES.—It will be readily imagined that the character and prospects of the individuals composing the body politic

* Called *portes*, from *porter*, to carry.

Questions.—21. Give the particulars of the beginning of the city. Where were the gates placed? When was that done? How did Remus lose his life? 22. How was the city peopled? In what manner did Romulus govern his city? From what is the word patrician derived? *Ans.* Pater, meaning father.

were not such as to invite the alliance of the surrounding tribes; the proposals of marriage which the Roman youth made to several aristocratic neighbors were rejected with scorn, and after striving in vain to make their persons and their homes more agreeable to the fair daughters of the Sabines, it was decided, in the fourth month after the building of the city, to obtain by force what was denied to entreaty. Public shows and games were proclaimed, and persons came from all parts, bringing their wives and children to witness the prowess of the competitors. While every eye was intent upon the scene, the Roman youth rushed in among the crowd, and, seizing the most beautiful girls they could find, carried them off. The Sabines remonstrated in vain. The Romans, having secured their wives, treated them with the utmost kindness and attention; and the women, won by the unexpected tenderness of their captors, consented to "forsake their fathers and mothers and cleave unto their husbands."

24. The fathers and mothers were not, however, so easily satisfied. As the Romans obstinately refused to restore their daughters, Tatius, the Sabine king, led an army of 25,000 men to the very gates of Rome. The Romans, unable to meet so strong an army in the field, having placed their flocks upon the Capitoline hill, and strongly fortified it, withdrew within their walls. Tarpeia, daughter of the commander of that fortress, going to a neighboring spring for water, was seized by the Sabines, and entreated to betray one of the gates to them. She agreed to do so for what the soldiers wore upon their arms, meaning their bracelets; but no sooner had she opened the gate than they threw their bucklers upon her, and crushed her to death. From her the cliff of the Capitoline hill was called the Tarpeian rock. The Romans rushed out of their city to regain possession of this important point, and soon a fierce engagement ensued in the valley between the Capitoline and Quirinal hills.

25. In the midst of the conflict, the attention of the combatants was diverted by loud cries and lamentations. While they paused in astonishment, the Sabine women rushed in between the two armies, entreating their husbands to spare their fathers, and their fathers to spare their husbands. The fierce warriors listened, and suffered their weapons to fall from their hands. Affection finally mastered resentment, and by the mediation of these amiable females a peace was concluded, on condition that the two nations should be united in one, and Romulus and Tatius reign jointly in Rome. The new citizens were called *Quirites*,

Questions.—23. Describe the manner in which the Romans secured wives for themselves. 24, 25. Who was the Sabine king? In what expedition was he engaged? Give an account of the expedition and its results.

whence the initial "Q." in the royal standard. One hundred Sabines were added to the senate, and the number of men in the legion was also doubled. Thus every event, however adverse, served to advance the interests of the new city, and Romulus had the happiness of seeing a hostile army converted into peaceful citizens in the course of a few hours.

26. The death of Tatius, about five years after, left Romulus again sole monarch of Rome. He conquered Fidenæ, and, engaging in a war with the Veians, compelled them to give up their salt-pits near the Tiber. One day, while he was reviewing his army, a dreadful thunder-storm arose. The people fled in different directions to seek for shelter, and when the tempest passed over Romulus was nowhere to be found. It was conjectured that he had been carried to heaven by his father, the god Mars, a supposition that was confirmed by one Proculus, who declared that as he was returning by night from Alba to Rome, Romulus appeared to him in a form of more than mortal majesty, and bade him tell the Romans "that Rome was destined to be the chief city of the world; that human power should never be able to withstand her people; and that he himself would be their guardian god Quirinus."

27. U. C.* 37.—B. C. 716. After the death of Romulus, the senate undertook to govern the city by each member's acting the part of king for five days in succession. The people submitted to this changing government for a year, till, finding in it the authority of a monarch without his paternal care, they insisted upon the election of a king. They accordingly fixed upon Numa Pompilius, a citizen of Cures, who, though married to the daughter of Tatius, had always lived in retirement. Numa was born the very day Rome was founded, and was consequently in his fortieth year when embassadors came to beg his acceptance of the crown. He left the sacred groves, where he had spent the best part of his life, with unfeigned reluctance, and prefaced his departure with many sacrifices. The senate and people met him on the way, and the women welcomed him into the city with blessings and shouts of joy. Attended by the priests and augurs, he went

* *Urba Condita*, "after the building of the city."

Questions.—25. How did the initial "Q." get into the royal standard? What further is stated of the Sabines? 26. What event made Romulus sole monarch of Rome a second time? What successes in war did he have? What was the fabled account of the death of Romulus? What of the prophecy? 27. How was Rome governed during the next year? What did the people desire? Who was chosen to wear the crown? How old then was Numa? What account can you give of his life up to that time? How was Numa met at Rome? What were the qualifications for the throne?

to the top of the Tarpeian rock, where the chief augur laid his hand upon his head, and, turning his face to the south, waited in silence till several birds flew by, on his right hand. Then being invested with the royal robe, Numa went down to the people and was hailed as their king.

28. No monarch could have been more suitable than Numa, for a multitude whose opinions, tastes, and habits were unsettled. The inhabitants of various petty states, lately subdued and but ill united, needed a master who could soften their fierce dispositions, and introduce among them the love of religion and virtue. Numa had superstition enough to awaken their reverence, and policy enough to turn his power to good account. By the instruction of the goddess Egeria, he founded the whole system of the Roman religion, he increased the number of augurs, regulated the duties of the pontiffs, and instituted several new orders of priests.

29. Tullius.—Ancus.—Tarquin.—B. C. **700.** Numa also divided among his subjects the lands which Romulus had conquered in war, and set landmarks, consecrated to the god Terminus, upon every portion. He abolished the distinction between Romans and Sabines, by dividing the artisans according to their trades, and compelling all those of the same profession to dwell together. He built the temple of Janus, to be shut in the time of peace, and open in time of war; and so profound was the quiet he had produced, that though this temple was erected in the first year of his reign, it continued shut till his death, which happened in his 83d year.

30. U. C. 82.—B. C. 671. Tullius Hostilius.—After the death of Numa, the senate again tried the experiment of carrying on the government themselves, till at length Tullius Hostilius, a man of Latin extraction, was elected monarch. His talents and inclinations differed entirely from those of his predecessor. He was more inclined to war than even Romulus had been, and only waited a plausible pretext for seizing upon the territories of his neighbors. An incursion of the Alban shepherds gave him an opportunity to demand redress, and he took care to do it in such a manner as to insure a refusal. War being thus made necessary, the two armies were drawn out in battle array, five miles from Rome. Just as they were about to engage, the Alban general proposed that the matter should be referred to three champions, chosen from each side.

Questions.—28. Why was the selection of Numa for king a good one? 29. What policy did Numa adopt in relation to conquered lands, landmarks, &c.? What distinction did he abolish? What temple found? In what respects was he a good king? 30. Who succeeded Numa? What was the character of Tullius. Hostilius? What pretext did he find to gratify his warlike propensity? Where was Alba? (See map No. 4.)

31. The offer was accepted. Three Horatii were chosen for the Romans, and three Curatii for the Albans. The mother of the Horatii was sister to the mother of the Curatii; and all six of the young men were distinguished for courage, strength, and activity. When every thing was arranged, the champions were led forth amid encouraging shouts, and then both sides rested upon their arms, and gazed with breathless anxiety upon the scene. Victory at first inclined to the Albans. Two of the Horatii lay dead upon the field, and the third seemed to fly, while the Curatii, all wounded, feebly pursued him. The Romans were ready to give up in despair, when suddenly Horatius, having separated his antagonists, turned and slew them, one after another, sacrificing, as he said, "two to the manes of his brothers," and offering "the third to his country's honor." The Albans threw down their arms and submitted to the Romans; and Horatius, having stripped his cousins of their armor, returned in triumph to Rome.

32. Not long after, the Albans having engaged in a conspiracy against the Romans, a decree was passed that Alba should be razed to the ground, and the whole Alban people removed to Rome. The walls of the city and every human habitation were totally demolished, and new dwellings assigned to the houseless tribe, upon the Celian hill. Thus another nation was incorporated within the limits of the Roman state. Hostilius contributed to the comfort of the citizens by inclosing an open space for the meetings of the *Comitia*, or assembly of the people, and the building of a senate-house. Toward the close of his reign his mind was affected with superstitious fears, and to avert the anger of the gods, he had recourse to the sacred rites formerly practiced by Numa. His invocations had, however, a contrary effect. His palace was struck by lightning, and himself, with all his family, perished in the flames.

33. U. C. 115.—B. C. 638. ANCUS MARTIUS.—After an interregnum, as in the former case, Ancus Martius, grandson of Numa, was elected king. He strove to imitate the virtues of his grandfather, and carry out his maxims of government. He increased the number of his subjects, by bringing several thousand Latins to Rome, and settling them on Mount Aventine. He constructed the first bridge over the Tiber; he extended his dominions on both sides of the river to the seacoast, and built the harbor of Ostia, thus securing the trade of the Tiber and the salt-pits adjacent. He encouraged strangers to settle in the city; and

Questions.—31. Recite the story of the champions. Which way was Alba from Rome? (See map No. 4.) 32. Give the further history of Alba. What good things did Hostilius do for Rome? Give the closing history of him. 33. Who succeeded Hostilius? What benefits did Ancus Martius seek for his country? What did he accomplish?

one of these, an opulent Greek, having gained his peculiar favor, was appointed guardian of his children.

34. U. C. 138.—B. C. 615. Lucius Tarquinius Priscus.—A merchant of Corinth, having amassed considerable wealth in trade, emigrated to Tarquinia, a city of Italy. Dying, he left all his wealth to his only son, Lucius. This Lucius married Tanaquil, a lady of high birth in Tarquinia, and was by her persuaded to remove to Rome, then the center of attraction for all adventurers. As they approached the city, an eagle stooping from above took off his hat, and, flying round his chariot for some time, with much noise put it on again. This his wife interpreted as a presage that he should one day wear the crown, and they both spared no pains to bring about the accomplishment of the prophecy. This was the Greek who paid his court so effectually to Ancus as to be appointed guardian of his children. When the Romans met to elect a new king, he made a set speech to them, urged the friendship he felt for them, and the fortune he had expended in their service. The people acknowledged the justice of his claims, and he was soon invested with the royal robes. To reward his partisans, who were chiefly plebeians, he added 100 of them to the senate, thus making that body 300.

35. He laid the foundations of the great circus, or amphitheater, where gladiatorial shows were afterwards exhibited. The Latin states having made incursions upon his territories, he engaged in a war with them, during which he took and plundered nine towns. Tarquin also overcame the Etruscans in several engagements, and received from them a golden crown, an ivory throne and scepter, a purple tunic, and a robe embroidered with gold. Such were the military exploits ascribed to Tarquin; but his lasting fame was inlaid with the very foundations of the city. The forum, with its rows of shops and ornamental porticoes, was marked out by his order, and a wall around the city, of massy stones, commenced.

36. He built the *cloaca maxima*, or great sewers, to drain off the water from between the Palatine and Capitoline hills. "This vast drain was constructed of huge blocks of hewn stone, triply arched, and of such dimensions that a barge could float along in it beneath the very streets of the city. Earthquakes have shaken the city and the adjacent hills, but the *cloaca maxima* remains to this day unimpaired, an enduring monument of the power and skill of the people and the

Questions.—34, 35, 36. Who was Lucius Tarquinius Priscus? Relate the story of the eagle. Why did that event prove important? How did Tarquin reward his partisans? In what successful wars did he engage? What did his military exploits gain for him and Rome? What monuments of his power and skill remain?

king by whom it was constructed." The augurs, under the patronage of Tanaquil, came into great reputation; and such was the ascendency which they finally gained over the mind of Tarquin, that no battle was fought, no army levied, no assembly dismissed, nor peace proclaimed, without due reference to the chirping and flying of birds.

37. SERVIUS.—TARQUIN II.—CONSULS.—B. C. **600.** Tarquin, in the Sabine war, had vowed to build a temple to the three great deities, Jupiter, Juno, and Minerva, and preparations were going forward for this magnificent work when the hand of the assassin dismissed him from all public employments. The sons of Ancus Martius, impatient to enjoy a throne which Tarquin had made so desirable, hired two countrymen to murder the king. The ruffians entered the palace as if to bring a cause before Tarquin, and struck him dead with an ax. The lictors immediately seized them, and put them to death; but the sons of Ancus made their escape. The rumor of the death of Tarquin filled the city with confusion. The citizens ran in crowds to the palace to learn the truth of the report. Tanaquil, who had her own purpose to serve, assured them that her husband was only stunned by the blow, and that he had deputed the government to his son-in-law, Servius Tullius, till his recovery.

38. B. C. 577. SERVIUS TULLIUS.—Servius comes before us arrayed in the garb of fable, like his predecessors. He was said to have been the son of a bond-woman. While an infant in the cradle a lambent flame played around his head, which, as an omen of his future greatness, secured for him the patronage of Tanaquil. Receiving him into her family, she gave him an education suited to the high station he was destined to fill, and married him to her daughter. Upon the death of Tarquin he issued from the palace, clothed with the ensigns of power, and proceeded to administer the government, as he said, by directions of his father-in-law. When he had thus made good his party, the body of the murdered monarch was brought out and buried, and Servius was proclaimed king.

39. The government of Servius Tullius paved the way for the republic. He divided the lands among the citizens, and built dwellings for the poor; he was the friend of the people, and chose his habitation in the plebeian quarter of the city. He ordained that once in five years every man should resort to the Campus Martius,* clad in complete

* A large plain without the walls of the city, where the Roman youth performed their gymnastic exercises. It is the principal situation of modern Rome.

Questions.—37. What vow had Tarquin made? What prevented its accomplishment? How did Servius secure the throne? 38. Relate the fable, also the history of Servius until he was crowned king. 39. In what ways did he show himself to be a friend of the people?

armor, and there make oath to an exact account of his family and fortune. This census was closed by a feast, called a *lustrum*. Servius steadily carried forward the building of the Capitol, begun by his predecessor; and inclosed the Viminal and Esquiline hills also within the walls of the city. This king is said to have engaged in war with three of the neighboring states, which continued twenty years, and resulted in an acknowledgment of the supremacy of Rome.

40. To secure the crown to his family, Servius, it is related, had married his two daughters to the two brothers of his wife, Aruns and Tarquin; and as both the women and men differed greatly in disposition, he sought to correct their tempers by marrying the imperious Tullia to the gentle Aruns, and the ambitious Tarquin to her milder sister. This very measure defeated his design. The *imperious* and *ambitious* broke through the feeble bonds which their meek companions imposed, and, having both murdered their consorts, were soon united to each other. The first crime made way for the second, and the second was but a preparation for the third. Tarquin and Tullia saw a crown before them, and no remorse of patriotism or filial affection could prevent their grasping it. They encouraged every murmur of discontent which reached their ears, and made a strong party among the patricians by spreading a rumor that Servius intended to abolish the regal form of government, and give to the plebeians equal weight in the commonwealth with the more aristocratic part of the community.

41. Having thus every thing prepared, Tarquin went to the senate-house, seated himself on the royal chair, and summoned the senators to meet king Tarquinius. While he was speaking Servius entered, and, accusing Tarquin of treason, offered to push him from his seat; but the usurper seized the old man, dragged him to the door, and threw him down the steps. A body of assassins followed the wounded king as he was feebly making his way to the palace, and, having put an end to his life, left his body bleeding and mangled in the street. Tullia, meanwhile, mounted her chariot and drove to the senate-house. After saluting her guilty husband as king, she set out on her return, and the charioteer, by her direction, drove over the body of the murdered Servius. The blood of her father stained her chariot wheels, and sprinkled the robe in which she had arrayed herself to be hailed a queen.

42. B. C. 533. LUCIUS TARQUINIUS SUPERBUS.—Tarquin the Proud,

Questions.—40, 41. By what means did Servius endeavor to perpetuate the crown in his own family? Describe the tragedy that followed the ambitious father's folly. 42. What character is given of Tarquin the Proud?

having thus seized upon the throne as a right, refused to submit to a vote of the people, and every other act of his administration showed the same disposition to make himself absolute, in defiance of all law or religion. He surrounded himself with a body-guard, and either banished or put to death all whom attachment to the late king or love of justice inclined to criticise his measures. The Latins and the Volscii felt the power of Rome, and every fresh acquisition made Tarquin more imperious and tyrannical. The capitol, upon which his predecessors had labored so diligently, employed him four years; and an occurrence which he reported contributed not a little to the zeal with which the people wrought in the work.

43. One day a Sibyl* came to the palace of Tarquin with nine books, which she said were of her own composing, but she asked so high a price for the mysterious volumes that Tarquin refused to purchase them. She went away, burned three of them, and returned, demanding the same price for the remaining six. Again the king refused to buy, and again she went away and burned three of her precious works; but when she came into his presence the third time, and insisted upon his taking the three books, without any abatement of price, his curiosity was so excited that he sent for the augurs. By their advice the volumes were purchased, and deposited in stone chests, in the vault of the new capitol. Proper persons, called the quindecemviri, were appointed to take charge of them; and thus the sibylline leaves became the oracles of the nation. Tarquin also finished the cloaca maxima, and reduced the city of Gabii by the stratagem† of his son Sextus.

44. The tyrant father and dissolute son had filled Rome with mourning; and Sextus, having crowned his enormities by violating the honor of a noble Roman lady, precipitated the doom which had so long been hanging over the devoted house of Tarquinii. This lady was Lucretia, wife of Collatinus, a descendant of the first Tarquin.

* The Sibyllæ were certain females who lived in different parts of the world, and were thought to possess the power of foretelling future events.

† The stratagem was this. Sextus counterfeited desertion, and was kindly received at Gabii. Being apparently successful in his engagements with the Romans, the simple Gabians made him general of their army. He then sent to his father for instructions. Tarquin made the messenger no answer, but, taking him into the garden, silently cut down the tallest poppies. Sextus took the hint; and, under various pretexts, put to death or banished the most distinguished Gabians, till the people, finding themselves completely in his hands, submitted to his father without striking a blow.

Questions.—42. To what regulations did he refuse to submit? How did he treat the friends of the murdered king? 43. Give the story of the Sibylline books. 44. Relate the circumstances preceding the banishment of Tarquin.

Unable to pardon herself for the crime of another, she sent for her husband and father, entreating them to come to her immediately, as an indelible disgrace had befallen the family. They obeyed her summons, bringing with them Valerius, a kinsman, and Junius Brutus, whose father Tarquin had put to death. In brief terms she related what had befallen her, and, having required a pledge that they would avenge her injuries, she drew a knife from under her robe and stabbed herself to the heart.

45. While the rest stood motionless and silent with grief and consternation, Brutus, the pretended idiot, drew the bloody poniard from the reeking wound, and, holding it up to the assembly, exclaimed: "I swear by this blood, which was once so pure, and which nothing but the detestable villainy of Tarquin could have polluted, that I will pursue Lucius Tarquinius the Proud, his wicked wife, and their children, with fire and sword; nor will I suffer any of that family, or any other whatsoever, to reign at Rome. Ye gods! I call ye to witness this my oath." Then, presenting the dagger to Collatinus, Lucretius, Valerius, and the rest of the company, he engaged them to take the same oath. That the man who had so long been kept as an idiot in the king's house, to make sport for his children, should thus stand forth the friend of justice and the assertor of Roman liberty, was a miracle that roused the feelings of the people no less than the wrongs of the virtuous Lucretia.

46. The citizens came together in crowds, the gates of the city were shut, and the senate decreed that Tarquin and his family should be forever banished from Rome, and that to plead for, or attempt his return, shovld be a capital crime. Tarquin, who was absent with the army, hearing of these commotions, hastened to Rome without delay. He found the gates barred against him, and the walls filled with armed men. Disappointed and enraged, he turned again to join his army; but Brutus, taking another route, had reached the camp before him, acquainted the soldiers with what had taken place, and enlisted their feelings in the cause of justice. Thus this proud monarch, who had reigned 25 years, being expelled from his kingdom, was forced to take refuge in a little city of Etruria, and thus ended, with him, the regal state of Rome, after it had continued 245 years.

47. Consuls.—The regal power being thus overthrown, Rome became a republic, and two magistrates called Consuls were annually

---

Questions.—45, 46. What course did Brutus take? How far was he successful? How long did the regal state of Rome continue? 47. After the overthrow of regal power what did Rome become? By whom were the affairs of government administered?

chosen to administer the affairs of government. No one could be consul who had not before been quæstor, ædile, and prætor. The consuls had all the badges of kings, except the crown; every one went out of the way, uncovered his head, dismounted from his horse, or rose up when these officers passed. Brutus and Collatinus were chosen first consuls of Rome. Hardly was this new order of things established, when embassadors came from Tarquin to say that he would peaceably relinquish the kingdom if the Romans would send him his treasures and effects. These embassadors had another object in view, which they proceeded to unfold while the senate debated upon Tarquin's proposition.

48. They took up their residence in the house of the Aquilii, nephews of Collatinus, and by their aid collecting such young men as had been brought up in idle attendance upon the king, formed a conspiracy to restore monarchy. Even the sons of Brutus, displeased with the stern frugality of their father, entered into the scheme, and all together bound themselves not to betray the plot, by the horrid ceremony of drinking the blood of a man sacrificed for the purpose. A slave, however, discovered the whole affair, and hastened to the upright Valerius with the startling intelligence. Valerius, with a sufficient force, proceeded immediately to the place, found the papers, and, seizing the conspirators, twisted their gowns about their necks, and dragged them into the forum. The consuls, hearing the tumult, repaired to the spot, and silence being gained, the accusation was entered and proved. The young men pleaded nothing for themselves, but with conscious guilt awaited their sentence in silent agony.

49. A melancholy stillness reigned; the tears of Collatinus and the irrepressible emotions of Valerius stimulated some of the most compassionate to speak of banishment; but Brutus alone, seeming to have lost all the softness of humanity, called upon each of his sons: "You, Titus, and you, Tiberius, why do you not make your defense against this charge?" This question he repeated three times, in a stern voice, but receiving no answer, he turned to the lictors, and saying, "Yours is the part that remains," resumed his seat, and with an air of determined majesty beheld his sons stripped, scourged, and beheaded. Collatinus, not equally firm, was just going to grant his nephews a reprieve, when Valerius interposed, and the people voted that they should receive the punishment they so well merited. This conduct

Questions.—47, 48, 49. What qualifications were required for the office of consul? What badges of distinction belonged to them? Who were the first consuls? What embassadors were sent from Tarquin? What proved to be the real object of these embassadors? Relate the story of the conspiracy, with its heart-rending consequences.

of Collatinus rendered him suspected by the citizens; he was deposed from the consulship and banished, and Valerius, surnamed Publicola, "the people's most respectful friend," was elected in his room.

50. Tarquin now enlisted the Veians, and advanced with a considerable army toward Rome. Valerius Publicola and Brutus, having made suitable preparations, went out to meet him on the Roman borders. Aruns, son of Tarquin, seeing his despised playfellow at the head of the Roman armies, spurred on to meet him; and Brutus, equally enraged, rode out of the ranks, and engaged with him in single combat. Nerved by the deadliest hate, neither thought of defending himself, and both fell dead upon the field. The battle, whose onset was so dreadful, had not a milder conclusion. The carnage was terrible, and continued till the armies were separated by a storm. On numbering the dead, it was found the Veians had lost one man more than the Romans, and they accordingly confessed defeat. Tarquin fled to Clusium, and engaged Porsenna, one of the most powerful princes of Italy, to undertake his cause. By his army the Roman commonwealth was reduced to the very brink of destruction. The consuls were wounded in the field, and forced to retire.

51. Rome was besieged, and the inhabitants were wasting under the influence of famine, when the city was saved by an act of heroism superior to any before related. A young man named Mutius, disguised like an Etrurian peasant, entered the camp of Porsenna and slew the king's secretary, mistaking him for the king himself. Upon his arrest he declared unreservedly who he was, informed the king of his country and design, and added, that three hundred Roman youth were equally resolved to destroy their enemy, or perish in the attempt; then, thrusting his hand into a fire burning upon an altar, he held it there with the utmost composure until it dropped off, saying: "You see the Romans know how to suffer, as well as how to act." Porsenna, charmed with his noble spirit, ordered him to be safely conducted back to Rome, and offered the besieged honorable conditions of peace.*

52. DICTATORS.—TRIBUNES.—DECEMVIRS.—B. C. **500.** Tarquin,

* It is said that the Romans actually submitted, and only recovered their city and territory on condition of giving up the use of iron, except for implements for husbandry.

Questions.—49. Who was chosen consul in place of Collatinus? 50. What steps were then taken by Tarquin? Where did the armies meet? How did the noble Brutus fall? How did the battle terminate? By whose assistance did Tarquin once more wage destructive war upon Rome? 51. During the siege, what was the condition of the Romans? Give the story of the heroic young man, Mutius. How did his conduct affect the mind of Porsenna? Who was Porsenna? Which way from Rome was Clusium? (See map No. 4.)

though often disappointed, was still unsubdued. He stirred up the Latins to hostilities, united twenty-four towns in a confederacy, and secretly worked by his agents within the very walls of Rome. The Romans under their kings had only two ways of subsisting, by agriculture and by plunder. After the extinction of royalty, the senators appropriated the conquered lands to themselves, and thus the soldier, who left his family to enlarge the dominions of Rome, had neither farm nor money for reward; besides, if the poor man fell in debt, the rich creditor might sell him for a slave until the sum was paid. This complication of evils filled the city with discontent and murmuring; and when the consuls came to levy men in order to oppose Tarquin, all the poor refused to enlist, declaring they would not go to war till their debts were canceled by a decree of the senate. The number of the malcontents increased every hour, and the senate, who saw the commonwealth upon the brink of ruin, had recourse to an expedient, which in the lapse of ages proved fatal to the republic.

53. Dictators.—Unable to raise an army to meet the threatened invasion, they proposed to the people to elect a temporary magistrate, who should have absolute power, not only over patricians, plebeians, and magistrates, but over the laws themselves. The people complied, and Lartius was created the first Dictator of Rome. He entered upon his office surrounded with all the ensigns of royalty; and the people, awed by his display of power, obeyed implicitly all his directions. Before his six months were expired the Latins were conquered, the murmurs appeased, and at the end of his time he laid down his authority, with the reputation of having exercised it with blameless lenity.

54. Tribunes.—When the term of his office expired, matters were in no better state than before, and at last the great body of the plebeians resolved to quit the city which gave them no shelter from oppression. They therefore formed themselves under their respective ensigns, chose new commanders, and retired to Mons Sacer, a mountain about three miles from Rome, saying, as they went along, that "Italy would anywhere supply them with air and water, and a place of burial; and that Rome, if they stayed in it, would do no more." Message after message was sent to them in vain; the discontented in the city scaled the walls to join them, and the senate was divided in

---

Questions.—52, 53. What machinations was Tarquin still employing to destroy Rome? What was the condition of the Roman people at that time? What difficulties did they encounter in raising men to oppose Tarquin? What expedient was adopted by the senate? What power was delegated to the dictator? Who first filled the office? How far was success attained? 54. After the office of dictator expired, what new discontent arose?

opinion as to the course to be taken. Finally, a deputation of the most respectable persons in the city went to them, and one, by birth a plebeian, related to them the celebrated fable of "the Body and the Members."

55. This fable had an instantaneous effect upon the people; they began to talk of an accommodation, and at length concluded to go back, upon condition that five new officers should be created from their own body, called TRIBUNES *of the People*, who should have the power of annulling such decrees as bore hard on the plebeians. The senate also agreed to abolish all debts; and things being thus adjusted, the multitude returned in triumph to Rome. The new officers were then appointed. They had their seats placed before the doors of the senate-house, and, examining every statute, annulled it by the word *Veto*, "I forbid it," or signed it with T., which gave it validity. Seed-time passed while the people were on the mountain; the fields produced no harvest the ensuing year, and famine began again to excite those murmurs which the concessions of the senate had appeased.

56. A fleet came laden with corn from Sicily, and the starving multitude waited impatiently while the senate were deliberating upon its distribution. Coriolanus, a general distinguished in the Volscian wars, insisted that the senate should take this opportunity to secure their former power. He had been seventeen years a warrior, and was greatly beloved by the people till he began to oppose their aggressions. Now, when he took so decided a stand against the distribution act, they accused him of converting the spoils of the enemy to his own use. He was consequently sentenced to banishment. He returned to his house, embraced his mother, wife, and children, passed out of the city gates, and took his solitary way, no one knew whither. Having after some time matured a plan for humbling his enemies, he proceeded to the country of the Volscians, over whom he had gained so many victories. Finding out the house of Tullus, his most implacable enemy, he entered, walked directly up to the fireplace, and seated himself among the household gods, without saying a word. Tullus rose from supper, and demanded, in astonishment, who he was, and upon what business he had come. Coriolanus, still retaining his seat in the sacred place, related the particulars of his exile, and laid before him his desires of vengeance. The noble Volscian instantly gave him the hand of friendship, and espoused his quarrel.

Questions.—54. In what manner was it reconciled? 55. What were the new officers called? How was the veto power first used? 56. What relief came to the starving people of Rome? State the circumstances attending the banishment of Coriolanus. What measures did he take to humble his enemies?

57. It was not difficult to find a pretext for war, and the Volscians, headed by Tullus and Coriolanus, invaded the Roman territories, ravaging all the lands belonging to the plebeians, but leaving those of the patricians untouched. The levies in Rome went on but slowly; and the consuls feared, with a reluctant army, to meet the renowned Coriolanus in the field. One town after another submitted to the Volscians, and the injured exile finally pitched his camp within five miles of Rome. The city, so lately the scene of turbulence and animosity, was now filled with timidity and despair. The people, who had clamored for the banishment of Coriolanus, begged the senate to recall the edict. The senate obstinately refused. However, when the Volscians came up to the very walls and demanded the freedom of Roman citizens, both senate and people unanimously agreed to send deputies to Coriolanus, with proposals of restoration if he would draw off his army.

58. The indignant general received the embassadors at the head of his officers, informed them that, as commander of the Volscians, he had only their interest to consider, and that if the Romans wished for peace, they must conclude within thirty days to restore all the towns originally belonging to Volscii. This deputation returned to Rome, and another was immediately sent to entreat Coriolanus not to exact of his country any thing improper for Romans to grant. He treated these envoys with great severity, and only allowed the senate *three* days for deliberation. A more dignified embassy was then prepared, to move the heart of the stern general. The pontiffs, priests, and augurs, clothed in sacred vestments, issued from the city, and, entering the camp of the conqueror with imposing solemnity, conjured him by the fear of the gods to give peace to his country. He treated them with respect, but dismissed them without lessening his demands.

59. When the people saw the ministers of religion repulsed, they gave up the commonwealth for lost. While all ranks were filling the temples with despairing cries, the aged sister of Publicola suddenly rose from before the altar, and, calling upon the matrons of Rome to attend her, proceeded to the house of Veturia, mother of Coriolanus. Actuated, as she said, by a divine impulse, she had come to beseech her to go with them, and make one more effort to save Rome. Veturia obeyed the heavenly call, and, accompanied by Volumnia, wife of

---

Questions.—57. Give an account of the success of Coriolanus. 58. How did he receive the message sent by the citizens and senate of Rome? In what manner did he receive and treat the second envoys? What term of time did he allow for deliberation? By what circumstances did they dignify the third embassy? State the result. 59. What then were the feelings of the people? Give the interesting particulars that brought safety to Rome.

Coriolanus, his two children, and the principal ladies of Rome, took her way to the camp of her son.

60. Coriolanus saw the mournful train from a distance, and determining to deny their request, sent for the Volscian officers to witness his resolution; but when his little ones clasped his knees, and his wife hung upon his neck in tender entreaty; when his aged mother fell at his feet, and mingled the tears of an afflicted parent with the lofty remonstrances of a Roman matron, his inflexible spirit gave way. He raised her in his arms, and gazing upon her venerable countenance with melancholy forebodings, exclaimed, "Ah, my mother, thou hast saved Rome, but thou hast lost thy son." The victorious deputation returned with a truce to the city; and Coriolanus, pretending that Rome was too strong to be taken, drew off his army. Tullus, who had long envied the great popularity of Coriolanus, represented this as an act of treachery to the Volscians, and the noble Roman was soon after slain.

61. Agrarian Law.—The people, thus delivered from threatened destruction, and encouraged by the concessions already made, clamored for the passage of the Agrarian law; but the senators steadily resisted the demand. Thus matters grew worse and worse. The Equii and Volscii continually made incursions upon the Roman territories without, and the plebeians as constantly made encroachments upon the privileges of the patricians within. One consul was killed in battle; the other, intimidated by the aspect of affairs, said he could do nothing alone, and must have a colleague. The senate fixed upon Quintius Cincinnatus for this office. He was a man of unblemished integrity, who, though a patrician and a soldier, had given up all ambitious thoughts, and retired to a small farm beyond the Tiber. The deputies found him in the field, diligently following the plow.

62. He appeared little elated with the ensigns of power they brought him, or the pompous ceremony with which they addressed him, but instantly responded to the call of the senate, saying with regret to his wife, as he changed the homely garb of a husbandman for the purple robe of a consul, "I fear, my Atilla, that for this year our fields must remain unsown." His skill, moderation, and humanity reconciled the contending factions; the tribunes ceased to urge the passage of the obnoxious law, and the senators adopted more conciliatory manners. Scarcely had Cincinnatus retired from his office, when the Equii and

Questions.—60. What was the fate of Coriolanus? 61, 62. What new internal commotions distracted the commonwealth? What was the agrarian law? *Ans.* A law to divide all the lands equally among the people. By whom were the difficulties reconciled? What was the enviable character of Cincinnatus?

Volscii made new inroads into the territories of Rome. The general sent to repel them, through want of skill or want of courage, suffered his troops to be driven into a defile between two mountains, where the enemy blockaded them, presenting the three terrible alternatives, submission, famine, or death. A few knights escaped, and carried the news to Rome. Consternation seized all ranks of people, and again Cincinnatus was summoned from his cheerful labors to assume the unlimited power of dictator, B. C. 458.

63. On entering the city, he gave orders that every person capable of bearing arms should repair before sunset to the Campus Martius, with necessary equipments and provisions for five days. At the head of this force he commenced his march that night, and before daybreak arrived in sight of the enemy. Coming up in the rear of the Volscian army, his soldiers set up a loud shout, which was gladly echoed by the Romans within the defile. The Volscii, amazed to find themselves between two enemies, commenced the attack, but were entirely beaten, and compelled to beg a cessation of arms. Cincinnatus gave them their lives, but obliged them to pass under the yoke, in token of servitude. Thus, having rescued a Roman army, defeated a powerful enemy, and gained an immense amount of spoil, he returned to Rome and resigned his dictatorship, after enjoying it four days.

64. The next year, however, all the tribunes joined together, and required that Mount Aventine should be given to the plebeians; this was ceded, but the people were not satisfied. The Agrarian law was constantly agitated, and disputes upon the subject often ended in blows. A day was finally fixed for the public discussion of this important measure; and to this meeting came one Siccius Dentatus, a well-known patriot. He had served his country in wars 40 years; had been an officer 30, first a centurion, then a tribune; he had fought 120 battles; had gained 14 civic,* 3 mural, and 8 golden crowns, besides 83 chains, 60 bracelets, 18 gilt spears, and 23 horse-trappings; he had received 45 wounds, the scars of which he exhibited; yet he had never obtained possession of any of those lands which his courage had won

* A civic crown, made of oak-leaves, was given to him who had saved the life of a citizen. A mural crown was awarded to him who first scaled the walls of a city, and a golden crown was the tribute to the brave soldier who first mounted the rampart in the face of the enemy.

Questions.—62. What troubles recalled Cincinnatus? What power was given him? When did that occur? 63. What commands did Cincinnatus issue? What march commence? What army conquer? What enemy subjugate? What spoils accumulate? How was the yoke made? *Ans.* By setting two spears upright and placing another across the top of them. How long was Cincinnatus dictator? By what act did he cease to be such? 64. What troubles followed during the next year? What is said of Dentatus?

and his valor defended. His had been a life of poverty and contempt, while others enjoyed in indolent security the fruit of *his* labors. The wrongs of Dentatus created such a clamor as drowned the voices of those senators who wished to speak against the law. Reason could no longer be heard; and the young patricians, seeing the people about to vote, ran in among the throng, broke the balloting-urns, and dispersed the crowd. This, for the time being, put off the hated law.

65. Solon's Laws brought to Rome.—The commonwealth of Rome had been for 60 years fluctuating between the contending orders which composed it, and each side began to wish for something more settled and definite than decrees of the senate and votes of the people. They therefore agreed to send embassadors to Athens, to bring home such laws as by experience had been found best adapted to the purposes of a republic. Three senators were chosen for this solemn deputation, and three galleys were fitted out to convoy them to Greece in a manner suitable to the majesty of the Roman people. In about a year they returned, bringing a digest of Solon's laws, and a collection of the principal civil codes of Greece and Italy. The tribunes then required that a body of men should be appointed to put their new laws into proper form, and enforce their execution. After long debates, ten of the principal senators were elected, whose power, continuing one year, should be equal to that of kings and consuls, without any appeal. Thus the whole constitution took at once a new form, and all magistrates resigned their authority.

66. Decemviri.—These officers agreed among themselves to reign in succession, one day at a time, the ruler of the day only bearing the ensigns of power. By the help of an interpreter they formed a body of laws from those brought from Greece, submitted them to the approbation of the people, and then, causing them to be engraven on plates of brass, hung them up in the most conspicuous part of the forum. The people supposed that they would lay down their power at the end of the year, but, pretending that something still remained to the completion of their purpose, they retained their office another term; and the third year they seized upon the administration of government, in defiance of senate and people, and ruled without control. The tyranny of the decemviri, however, like that of Tarquin, was overthrown by the virtue of a Roman female.

67. Story of Virginia.—Appius, sitting one day upon his tribunal,

---

Questions.—64. What circumstance put off the hated law? 65. What new form of government did they then seek? What instructions in government did they get from abroad? 66. What is said of the decemviri?

saw a maiden of exquisite beauty, passing to one of the public schools, attended by a matron, her nurse. The next day, she passed again; her loveliness attracted his attention, and awakened his curiosity. He made inquiries concerning her name and parentage, and finding that her father was a centurion in the army, he gave up all thoughts of marriage; for the very laws he had been so industriously preparing, forbade the intermarriage of patricians with plebeians. After vainly endeavoring to corrupt the fidelity of her nurse, he had recourse to an expedient still more criminal. One Claudius was instructed to claim her as a slave, and refer the cause to the tribunal of the decemvir. Claudius accordingly entered the school where Virginia was playing among her companions, and seizing upon her as his property, was about to drag her away by force, when he was stopped by the crowd drawn together by her cries. At length he prevailed so far as to be permitted to lead the weeping girl to the tribunal of Appius, where he stated that she was the daughter of his female slave, who, having been sold, and adopted in infancy by the wife of Virginius, had been educated as the child of the centurion. He begged time to collect his witnesses of these facts, and insisted on retaining possession of the maiden, as her lawful master.

68. Appius, with the air of an impartial judge, decided this to be a just demand; and Claudius was taking her away, when Icilius, her lover, seconded by the multitude, raised such a commotion that Appius, fearing an insurrection, thought proper to suspend his judgment till Virginius could return from the army, then about eleven miles from Rome. The day following was fixed for the trial, and Appius, in the mean time, sent letters to the generals to confine Virginius, as his arrival in town might excite sedition. These letters were intercepted by the centurion's friends, who gave him a full relation of the affair. Virginius immediately obtained permission to leave the camp, and flew to the protection of his child. At the appointed hour, to the astonishment of Appius, he appeared before the tribunal, leading his lovely daughter by the hand, both habited in the deepest mourning. Claudius was there also, attended by a female slave, who swore positively that she had sold Virginia to the wife of her reputed father.

69. Virginius then introduced the most unanswerable proofs of his paternity, and was proceeding to make an appeal to the people, when Appius interrupted him, by saying that he was sufficiently instructed in the merits of the case. "Yes," said he, "my conscience compels

---

Questions.—67, 68, 69, 70, 71. Relate the story of Virginia, and the merited vengeance of the suffering father.

me to declare, that I myself am a witness to the truth of the deposition of Claudius. Most of this assembly know that I was left guardian to this youth, and I was very early apprised of his right to this young woman; but the affairs of the public, and the dissensions of the people, then prevented my doing him justice. However, it is not now too late, and by the power vested in me for the public good, I adjudge Virginia to be the property of Claudius, the plaintiff. Go, therefore, lictors, disperse the multitude, and make room for a master to repossess himself of his slave."

70. The lictors, in obedience to this command, drove off the crowd, and, seizing upon Virginia, were delivering her up to Claudius, when Virginius, seeming to acquiesce in the sentence, mildly entreated Appius to be permitted to take a last farewell of one whom he had so long considered as his child. With this the decemvir complied, upon condition that their endearments should pass in his presence. Virginius took his almost expiring daughter in his arms, supported her head upon his breast, and wiped away the tears that rolled down her cheeks; then, gently drawing her near the shops that surrounded the forum, he snatched up a knife that lay upon the shambles, and crying out, "My dearest, lost child, this alone can preserve your honor and your freedom," buried the weapon in her breast! Then holding it up, reeking with her blood, "Appius," he exclaimed, "by this blood of innocence, I devote thy head to the infernal gods."

71. Appius ordered him to be seized, but in vain. As if maddened by the dreadful deed, Virginius, with the bloody knife still in his hand, ran through the streets of the city, calling upon the people to strike for freedom; nor did he stop till he had reached the camp, and displayed before the soldiers the terrible instrument which had taken away the sweet Virginia's life. He asked their pardon, and the pardon of the gods, for the rash act he had committed, but ascribed it to the dreadful necessity of the times, and conjured them, by that blood which he held dearer than his own, to redeem their sinking country from the hands of its tyrants. One thrilling sentiment of sympathizing indignation filled every bosom; the soldiers called to arms, plucked up their standards, and, marching to Rome, seized upon Mount Aventine. The feelings of the senate corresponded to those of the army. The former government was restored; Appius and Oppius died by their own hands in prison; the other eight decemvirs went into voluntary banishment; and Claudius was driven out after them.

72. Military Tribunes.—Quiet was scarcely restored, when the

Questions.—71. What became of Appius and Oppius? Of the other offenders?

tribunes proposed two laws: one to sanction the intermarriage of plebeians with patricians, and the other to admit the plebeians also to the consulship. The senate, with great reluctance, granted the first, with the limitation, that a woman marrying a plebeian should lose all her patrician rights; and evaded the second, by proposing that six governors should be elected, called MILITARY TRIBUNES, with *consular authority divided among them all;* and at the end of a year, it could be determined whether these tribunes, or consuls, should administer the government. The people eagerly embraced the proposals. Both patricians and plebeians put on the white robes of candidates, and begged the votes of the comitia; but so fickle were the multitude, that all the new officers were chosen from among the patricians. Their power was, however, of short duration. The augurs found something amiss in the ceremonies of the election, and in about three months they were compelled to resign to the consuls.

73. CENSORS.—B. C. 437.—To lighten the weight of the consular duties, two new officers, called CENSORS, were chosen to take an account of the citizens. Seated in their curule chairs, the censors reviewed the senate, deposed those proven unworthy of their high office, dismounted such knights as did not merit their spurs, and required of every citizen an exact account of his family and fortune. This calm was broken by a famine. At the next election the tribunes insisted upon having military tribunes instead of consuls, and during the succeeding twenty years the government changed from tribunes to consuls, and from consuls to tribunes, four times; besides which, dictators were chosen upon several occasions.

74. Things continued in this state of commotion for a long period, factions becoming every day stronger, and government weaker. The barbarous neighbors of the Romans seized every opportunity to encroach upon their territories, and whenever levies were to be raised, the tribunes of the people vetoed the decree, until some concession was made increasing the authority of the lower orders. The citizens were at the same time husbandmen and soldiers; the hands that drew the sword in one season, held the plow in another, and every man was obliged to furnish his own arms and provisions during a campaign. The hopes of plunder, and the honors of returning in triumph, were the chief incentives to enlist. But it often happened that the campaigns lasted through seed-time and harvest, and then debts were con-

Questions.—72. What is said of the military tribunes that followed? How long were they in power? 73. What new officers were then chosen? What duties did the censors perform? What was the condition of the government for the next twenty years? 74. What revolution finally took place and changed that mode of warfare?

tracted which led to a train of extortions and exactions, which kept the plebeians constantly irritated against the patricians, and covetous of power for themselves. To remove these constant sources of disquiet, the senate laid a tax upon every citizen, and from this fund paid a regular sum of money to every soldier. Thus the whole method of warfare was changed, and regular lengthened campaigns took the place of mere predatory excursions.

75. VEII TAKEN.—ROME BURNED BY THE GAULS.—SAMNITE WAR. B. C. **400.**—The city of Veii had maintained with Rome many gallant disputes for glory and power. The senate, now reconciled to the people, and masters of an army that they could keep in the field as long as they thought proper, determined that, cost what it might, Veii should fall; and the Romans in consequence encamped before the place, prepared for a long and obstinate resistance. The soldiers had been accustomed to make a summer campaign, and return home to winter, but now they were obliged to stay year after year in the enemy's country, living in tents made of the skins of beasts, and suffering, as might be supposed, every hardship from the sallies of the besieged and the inclemencies of the weather. The length and expense of the war excited murmurs and discontent, both in the camp and at home; and in the tenth year, *tribunes* and *consuls* having been alike unsuccessful, the senate appointed Fabius Camillus *dictator.*

76. This officer soon changed the aspect of affairs. Keeping up the regular attacks, to amuse the enemy, he employed a great part of his soldiers in digging a mine beneath the walls. The work was pursued with vigor, and the subterranean passage was finally terminated directly beneath the temple of Juno, in the citadel. An assault was then made without, to call the Veians to the walls, while a select band, marching underground to the temple, removed the pavement over their heads, and suddenly appeared to priests before the altar. They fled in dismay. Fresh bodies of Romans poured in, and the city was taken after a short but ineffectual resistance. Thus, like a second Troy, Veii fell, after a ten years' siege. The army returned home greatly enriched by the spoils, and Camillus triumphed with excessive pomp, painting his face with vermilion, and riding through the city in a chariot drawn by four milk-white horses, a distinction which displeased most of the spectators, and excited that envy which afterwards wrought his ruin.

77. EXILE OF CAMILLUS.—Not long after, the tribunes proposed

Questions.—75, 76. Describe the siege and taking of Veii. What circumstance of folly destroyed Camillus? Why did Camillus act thus? *Ans.* In imitation of the gods.

that the senate and the people should be divided into two equal parts, and that one part should remain in Rome, while the other settled in Veii. Camillus opposed this measure, and invented delays of various kinds, to keep it from being brought before the comitia. The tribunes, in revenge, accused him of converting two brazen gates, taken from Veii, to his own use. He was cited to appear before the people. The proud spirit of Camillus could not brook the infamy of a public trial. After embracing his wife and children, he departed from Rome. As he passed the gates, he turned his face to the capitol, and, lifting his hands to heaven, entreated the gods, that "if he were driven out without any fault of his own, the Romans might quickly repent their envy and injustice, and express to the world their want of Camillus."

78. About two centuries before this time, the Gauls had sent out vast numbers of emigrants in search of more fruitful lands than the frozen shores of the Baltic. A band of them settled in the northern part of Italy, took eighteen cities from the Tuscans, and, invited by the softness of the climate, but more especially by the softness of the wines, spread themselves still farther to the south. Hordes of these barbarians, wild from their original deserts, were now besieging Clusium, under the command of Brennus, their king. The inhabitants of Clusium entreated the assistance of the Romans. The senate, who had long made it a maxim never to refuse succor to the distressed, sent embassadors to the Gauls, to inquire what offense the citizens of Clusium had given them.

79. Brennus received the deputies with great complaisance, listened to what they had to say with due respect, and replied with becoming gravity: "The injury the Clusians do us, is their keeping to themselves a large tract of ground while they can only cultivate a small one, and refusing to give a part to us, who are numerous and poor. We follow, like the Romans, the most ancient law, which directs the weak to obey the strong; cease then to commiserate the Clusians, lest you teach the Gauls to pity those who have been oppressed by your own people." The Roman embassadors, instead of returning home with this cutting answer, entered the city, and, forgetful of their sacred characters, headed a sally of the besieged, and one of them was surprised in an attempt to strip a Gaul whom he had just slain. Brennus, calling the gods to witness that against all the sacred laws of

Questions.—77. What accusations were brought against Camillus to effect his banishment? What did Camillus do? 78. What is said of the movement of the Gauls? Where was Clusium? (See map No. 4.) What assistance did the Clusians ask for? How did the Romans respond? 79. What reply did Brennus make? What then did the embassadors do? To what did their conduct lead?

nations an embassador had acted as an enemy, immediately led off his army toward Rome.

80. Rome Burned by the Gauls.—The prodigious numbers of the Gauls, their glittering arms, their fury and impetuosity, struck terror wherever they came; Brennus, however, neither pillaged the fields nor insulted the cities, but passed on as rapidly as possible, crying out that he was at war with the Romans only, and considered all others as his friends. Six military tribunes at that time commanded the Roman army. They met the Gauls on the banks of the river Allia, about eleven miles from the city. The Romans engaged in a disorderly manner, were shamefully beaten, and put to flight. Some escaped to Rome, and some to Veii. The account of the fugitives filled all ranks of people with terror. The Gauls, however, not knowing the extent of their victory, continued two days feasting upon the field of battle. In this time all the Romans capable of bearing arms retired to the capitol, which they fortified with strong ramparts and provided well with arms. The Vestal Virgins took up the Sacred Fire and holy relics, and fled away with them to the little city of Cære.

81. The priests and most ancient of the senators could not think of leaving the city. Therefore, clothing themselves in their holy vestments and robes of state, in a form dictated by the pontifex maximus, they devoted themselves for their country, and, seating themselves in their ivory chairs, in the most conspicuous part of the forum, calmly awaited their fate. The rest of the people, a poor, helpless multitude of old men, women, and children, sought shelter in the neighboring towns, or shut themselves up in their houses, to end their lives with the ruin of Rome. On the third day, Brennus appeared with all his forces before the city. None disputed his approach; the walls were undefended; the gates stood wide open to receive him, so that at first he suspected some stratagem; but, finding that the people had really given up to despair, he entered by the Colline gate, set a strong guard before the capitol, and went on to the forum.

82. There he beheld the undaunted senators sitting in their order, leaning upon their staves, in the most profound silence. The splendid habits, the majestic gravity, and the venerable looks of these old men, awed the barbarians into reverence; they took them for the tutelar deities of the place, and commenced a species of adoration, till one,

Questions.—80. What further can you state of the conduct of Brennus? Where did the Romans meet the Gauls? What was the result? What then followed? 81. Give an account of the course taken by the priests, senators, and other people of Rome. Of the taking of Rome by Brennus.

more forward than the rest, stretched out his hand, and stroked the long white beard of Papyrius, the former dictator. The indignant senator, lifting his ivory scepter, struck the savage to the ground. The Gaul returned the blow with his sword; a general slaughter ensued, and every one of the devoted band poured out his blood upon the spot where he had dedicated himself to the infernal gods. Nor did the carnage stop here. The savages continued the slaughter three days, sparing neither sex nor age, and then, setting fire to the city, burned every house to the ground.

83. The capitol alone resisted all their efforts. Every thing without that fortress was an extensive scene of misery and desolation—every thing within showed that resolution which springs from despair. Those magnificent buildings which were once the pride of Rome were a heap of shapeless ruin. All the neighboring towns shared a similar fate; for Brennus, taking up his quarters in Rome, sent out foraging parties, who ravaged the country with fire and sword. It happened that a body of the barbarians strayed into the neighborhood of Ardea, where Camillus, since his exile, had lived in absolute retirement. The noble-minded Roman, having engaged the youth of Ardea in his service, was waiting an opportunity to strike a blow for his country. The Gauls, loaded with plunder, encamped upon the plains in a disorderly manner, and night found them intoxicated with wine, and overcome with sleep. Camillus attacked them about midnight; the sounding of the trumpets aroused the Gauls in such haste and confusion, that they were incapable of concerted action. A few, whom fear made sober, snatched up their arms and fell fighting; but the greater part of them, buried in sleep and wine, were surprised, and easily dispatched.

84. The fame of this action reached the neighboring cities, and drew crowds to Camillus. The Romans who had fled to Veii flocked to his standard, and urged him to take the title of dictator, and lead them to the relief of the city, but he refused to do so till legally appointed by the Romans in the capitol. It seemed impossible for a messenger to pass into the citadel, surrounded as it was by enemies. However, a young man named Pontius Cominius readily undertook the fearful task. Having dressed himself in mean attire, under which he concealed large pieces of cork, he traveled all day, and reached the Tiber about dusk. There he took off his clothes, wrapped them around his

Questions.—82. Of the slaughter of the senators. Of the further carnage. What else did the Gauls do? 83. In what effort were the Gauls foiled? Describe the then condition of Rome. In this emergency what was the conduct of Camillus? 84. Who was Pontius Cominius? Describe the part he took in the drama.

head, laid himself down upon his cork buoys, and easily swam across to the city.

85. The siege had now lasted more than six months; the provisions of the garrison were almost exhausted; the soldiers dispirited with continual fatigue; and the sentinel, as he walked his weary round, saw nothing within but haggard, despairing countenances, and nothing without but the ruins of his loved city. Suddenly his attention was arrested by the sight of a man climbing up the steep rock, and making his way directly toward him. He hailed the strange intruder, and received a reply in the native Latin. This was Pontius Cominius, bringing tidings to the besieged. The old and the young gathered around with tearful interest while he told them of the efforts their brethren were making for their relief, and assured them that the generous Camillus was levying an army, and only waited for the order of the senate to enter the field and give the barbarians battle. The small portion of the senate that remained immediately issued a decree, by which Camillus was made dictator; and the messenger, having received assurance that they would sustain the siege to the last extremity, returned the way he came, and, escaping all the dangers of his perilous route, arrived at Veii in safety.

86. A few days after, Brennus discovered the tracks which Cominius had made in climbing to the citadel. In the evening he assembled the lightest and most active of his troops, and offered the highest rewards to those who would reach the top by the same path. A number readily undertook the dangerous enterprise, and before midnight a band of the bravest had scaled the precipitous steep, and stood upon the very wall. The sentinel was fast asleep; the dogs within gave no signal, and the enemy stealthily advanced to the surprise, when the Romans were awakened by the gabbling of some sacred geese kept in the temple of Juno. The besieged awoke at once to a sense of their danger, and each, snatching the weapon he could most readily find, ran to oppose the assailants. Manlius, a patrician, was the first who inspired courage by his dauntless bravery. He encountered two Gauls at once, killed one with his sword, and dashed the other down the precipice; then, standing upon the rampart, he shouted to his fellows, and soon the summit was cleared of the enemy. Having thus escaped this imminent danger, they threw the sleepy sentinel down the rock after the vanquished foe, and decreed to Manlius all they had to bestow

Questions.—85. How were the tidings of Pontius Cominius received? What afflictions were still pressing upon the besieged? What action was taken by the portion of the Roman senate remaining in the capitol? 86. What discovery did Brennus make? What offer did he make? How was it responded to? Give an account of what followed.

—the allowance of each man for one day—which was only a half a pound of bread and a small draught of water.

87. From this time the Gauls began to lose courage. Provisions were scarce; they could not forage for fear of Camillus; and the besieged, though starving, threw over several loaves into their camp, to convince them that they had no fear of famine. Sickness, too, which took its rise from the unhealthiness of an atmosphere filled with ashes, and corrupted by the effluvia of dead bodies, destroyed many of their bravest men, and depressed the spirits of the remainder. The Romans, equally in want, and unable to hear any thing of Camillus, began to incline toward a treaty. The advanced guards commenced conversation, and proposals of accommodation soon passed between them. It was agreed that the Romans should pay the Gauls one thousand pounds of gold ($225,000), and that the Gauls should immediately quit the city and its territories. The conditions having been confirmed by an oath on each side, the gold was brought out, but while they were weighing it, the Gauls kicked the beam. The Romans expressing their resentment, Brennus, in a contemptuous manner, threw his sword, belt and all, into the scale, and when one inquired what that meant, "What should it mean," said he, "but woe to the conquered?"

88. Some of the Romans were highly incensed, and talked of taking away their gold; others contended that the indignity lay not in paying more than was due, but in paying any thing. The dispute was rapidly progressing to blows, when a new speaker suddenly appeared upon the stage. This was Camillus. At the head of a large army, he had silently entered the gates, and sending the main body through the principal streets, marched rapidly himself, with a select band, to the scene of debate. The Romans instantly gave way, and received the dictator with respect and silence. He took the gold out of the scales, and giving it to the lictors, with an air of authority, ordered the Gauls to be gone, telling them "it was the custom of the Romans to ransom their country, not with gold, but with iron;" adding, "It is I, only, that can make peace, as the dictator of Rome, and my sword alone shall purchase it."* A skirmish ensued, but the Gauls retreated to their camp, and in the night Brennus drew his forces out of the city,

* Many contend that the Gauls kept their gold, and left Rome voluntarily.

Questions.—87. How were the Gauls affected? What sufferings did they undergo? What accommodations were prepared? In what manner was the pledge rejected? 88. In this crisis who came to the relief of the Romans? State how. Give an account of the skirmish and battle that followed. What took place in process of time?

and pitched his tent eight miles distant, on the Gabian road. Here a battle was fought, in which the Gauls were completely routed; and in process of time the Roman territories were entirely cleared of the formidable invaders, who had occupied them from the ides of July to the ides of February.

89. Rome Rebuilt.—The refugees returned with their wives and children; the famishing denizens of the capitol met them with tears of joy; and the priests and vestals brought back the holy things into the city. But there were no houses for the people to dwell in, no temples to receive the venerated images; the tribunes, who maintained a respectful demeanor while the Gauls were in sight, began again to urge the removal to Veii; and so fearful were the senate of this event, that they would not permit Camillus to lay down the office of dictator, though no person had ever before held it more than six months. The people, affected by a heartless despondency, urged that they had no materials for building, and no means of purchasing any; that their bodies were weak, and their strength insufficient to patch up the ruins of a deserted city, while Veii stood entire, and ready to receive them.

90. The senate, on their part, showed them the monuments and tombs of their ancestors, and begged them to remember the holy places consecrated by Romulus and Numa. They reminded them of the predictions that Rome was to be the head of Italy, and they urged the disgrace it would be, to extinguish again the sacred fire which the vestals had lighted since the war. Camillus, after exerting all his eloquence in favor of his native country, called upon the oldest senator to give his opinion. Just then a centurion, passing the house with the day-guard, called out to the ensign "to stop, and set up his standard there, for that was the best place to stay in." The senator, who had opened his mouth to speak, thanked the gods for this seasonable omen; and the others, equally affected by superstition, decided that Rome should be their future residence. The people acquiesced, and all hands were speedily united in the work of rebuilding walls, temples, and dwellings.

91. B. C. 384.—The bravery of Manlius in defending the capitol did not go unrewarded. The Romans erected a house for him near the place where he so distinguished himself, and appointed him a public fund for his support. But his ambition was only increased by an

---

Questions.—89. What difficulties attended the rebuilding of Rome? 90. What did the senate do on their part? What Camillus? What happened just then? What was the effect? 91. How was Manlius rewarded? How did he then act?

acknowledgment of his merits. He labored to ingratiate himself with the populace, paid their debts, and railed at the patricians. He talked about a division of land among the people; insinuated that there should be no distinction of rank in the state, and was always attended by a crowd, whom he had made his very dear friends by repeated gifts. To counteract the effect of his seditious speeches, the senate proposed Camillus for military tribune; and no sooner was he installed in office, than he appointed Manlius a day to answer for his crime. Manlius made no defense, but pointed silently to the capitol, as if to remind the people of his contest with the Gauls. Camillus, perceiving the effect of this upon the multitude, had him taken to the Peteline grove, and there, being out of sight of the scene of his exploits, the people condemned him to be thrown from the Tarpeian rock.

92. THE LICINIAN LAW.—But this sacrifice did not give quiet to Rome. Many of the plebeians, during the distresses of their country, had acquired large fortunes, and were desirous to add to them a share of the honors of Rome. Fabius Ambustus had married his eldest daughter to Sulpicius, a rich patrician, and the youngest to an ambitious plebeian, named Licinius Stolo. It happened one day, when the wife of Stolo was visiting at the house of her sister, that Sulpicius came home from the forum, and his lictors with the staves of their fasces thundered at the door. She was greatly frightened, but her sister laughed at her as one lamentably ignorant of high life. This ridicule she could not endure, and from mortification and envy fell into a settled melancholy. The father and husband, having been made acquainted with the cause of her distress, assured her that her state should soon be made equal to that of her sister; and from that time Ambustus and Stolo exerted themselves in putting forward a plebeian for consul. To give popularity to the proposal, they coupled with it the Agrarian law.

93. The contests which those hated measures excited were so great, that for five years no supreme magistrates were chosen, the tribunes and ædiles administering the government with as much moderation as the anarchy of the times would permit. Then they chose military tribunes two years; then made Camillus dictator; but this excellent man, finding the people resolved upon a plebeian consul, soon resigned his office; the senate created another, but he did nothing more remarkable than making Stolo master of the horse, an office which no plebeian

---

Questions.—91. What ambitious views destroyed him? What was done to counteract the effect of his speeches? What then followed to Manlius? 92, 93, 94. Relate the story of Stolo's wife and her sister. What first gave existence to the Licinian law? Relate the story of Stolo's success.

had before held. Stolo also gained another point, which, though it did not bring his wife into the higher ranks, had a tendency to bring the higher ranks down to her. He secured the passage of a law* forbidding any person to own more than 500 acres of land; but, unfortunately, having afterwards possessed himself of 1,000, he was punished by his own edict. In this manner the flame of contention continued to burn, till it threatened to destroy all the virtue and patriotism of Rome; and so far was the impudence of the people carried, that, on one occasion, the tribunes sent lictors to take Camillus off the public tribunal, where he sat dispensing justice, and carry him to prison.

94. The patricians who stood around boldly repulsed the lictors, but the plebeians cried out, "Down with him, down with him." Camillus, perceiving that the people were determined upon having a consul, called the senators into a neighboring temple, and entreated them to give peace to the city by their compliance; then, turning his face to the capitol, he vowed to build a temple to Concord in case he saw tranquillity restored. In consequence of his advice, a law was passed that one of the consuls should be a patrician and one a plebeian; and Licinius Stolo having been duly elected to this office, his wife enjoyed the supreme felicity of hearing her husband's lictors thunder at the door. Thus Camillus, having spent a long life in the service of his country (being now above eighty), laid down his dictatorship, and commenced the more peaceful occupation of superintending the erection of the temple of Concord, built by a vote of the people, on a spot in the forum, fronting the place of assembly. He was five times dictator, five times military tribune, had the honor of four triumphs, and was styled "The second founder of Rome." He died the next year, of pestilence, which carried off a prodigious number of the inhabitants,† B. C. 361.

95. Samnite War.—The Romans having triumphed over the Sabines, the Etrurians, the Latins, the Equii, and Volscii, began to look for greater conquests. About one hundred miles east of their city lived the Samnites, a hardy nation, descended from the Sabines, who possessed a large tract of country, were strong in numbers and discipline,

* This law was called the Licinian law, from *Licinius* Stolo.

† About this time a gulf was opened in the forum, which the augurs declared would never close till the most precious things in Rome were thrown into it. Quintius Curtius, a young Roman of great bravery, declaring that nothing was more truly valuable than patriotism and military virtue, leaped into it, horse and all; upon which, says the historian, the gulf closed immediately, and Curtius was never seen again.

Questions.—94. What temple was built by Camillus? What was he called? Why was he so called? In what year did he die? How old was he then? 95. What success led the Romans to desire greater conquest?

and linked with confederated states. Some incursions upon the Campanians offered a pretext for a war, which lasted 71 years, and involved the Romans, finally, with the Grecian states. The Latins also revolted, and engaged with the Samnites. As the Romans were originally descended from this people, spoke the same language, and wore a similar dress, great care was necessary to prevent confusion in the battle; and Manlius Torquatus issued orders that no Roman should leave the ranks upon any provocation, under penalty of certain death. With these injunctions both armies were drawn out in array, and ready to begin, when the general of the Latin cavalry pushed out from his lines, and challenged any knight in the Roman army to single combat.

96. There was a general pause, no soldier daring to disobey orders, till Titus Manlius, the consul's own son, burning with shame to see the whole Roman army standing as if intimidated, rode out into the open space, encountered the challenger, killed him, stripped him of his armor, and returned amid the shouts of his companions. Yet, doubtful of his reception from his father, he advanced with a modest air, and laid the spoils at his feet. He was made sensible of his error when the stern general, turning away, ordered him to be led forth in presence of the whole army. Then, addressing him with a firm voice, though the tears streamed down his cheeks, "Titus Manlius," said the afflicted parent, "as thou hast regarded neither the dignity of the consulship nor the command of thy father, as thou hast destroyed military discipline and set a pattern of disobedience by thy example, thou hast reduced me to the deplorable extremity of sacrificing my son or my country. But let us not hesitate in this dreadful alternative. Thou thyself wilt not refuse to die, when thy country is to reap the reward of thy sufferings. Go, lictor, bind him, and let his death be our future example."

97. The whole army remained silent with horror while the inflexible father pronounced this sentence; but when they saw the head of their young champion rolling in the dust, their execrations and groans filled the air. Their indignation found vent upon the enemy; the battle was joined with inconceivable fury, and victory seemed equally balanced for a long time. The augurs had declared that if any part of the Roman army should be distressed, the commander of that portion must devote himself to his country. Manlius commanded the right wing, and Decius the left. The latter, finding his men overborne

Questions.—95, 96. What pretext for war was given them? What melancholy story is related of Titus Manlius? 97. How was the father's sentence received by the soldiers? What circumstance finally gave victory to Rome?

by numbers, clothed himself in a long robe, covered his head, stretched forward his arms, and, standing upon a javelin, devoted himself to the celestial and infernal gods for the safety of Rome. Then, arming himself and mounting on horseback, he drove furiously into the enemy, carrying terror and consternation wherever he went, till he fell, covered with wounds. The Romans considered his death a certain presage of victory; and the Latins, equally superstitious, fled in dismay.

98. This was the last battle of consequence that the Latins ever fought with the Romans. They concluded a peace upon the hardest conditions, and were brought into entire submission. The remainder of this century was spent in the Samnite war. Each party suffered severe defeats; several truces were made and broken, and many brave men were killed in battle. At one time a whole Roman army was taken prisoners at the Caudine Forks, and compelled to pass under the yoke, a disgrace which was inflicted in turn upon the Samnites.

99. PYRRHUS DEFEATED.—FIRST AND SECOND PUNIC WARS.—B. C. **300.**—The Samnites alone could not have sustained so long a contest with the Roman power. The neighboring states assisted with all their forces. Among others, the Tarentines entered the lists, but, finding in the sequel that they had drawn an implacable enemy upon themselves, they sent messengers across the narrow sea which separated them from Epirus, to entreat the assistance of Pyrrhus, then the most renowned warrior of Greece.

100. B. C. 280.—Pyrrhus, who had always been ambitious to rival Alexander in the extent of his conquests, gladly accepted the call. He left the shores of Epirus with 20,000 foot, 3,000 horse, and 20 elephants. A great tempest agitated the Ionian Sea during his passage. The wind, as if in league with the Romans, drove a great part of his vessels a wreck, and prevented his landing, till at last he was compelled to leap into the sea and swim ashore. He found the Tarentines occupied with the pleasures of bathing, feasting, and dancing, quite willing that he should fight their battles and earn the fame he had come so far to gain. The measures he took to inspire a more warlike spirit were not the most agreeable to them, and many left the city, as they said, to escape slavery.

101. In the midst of these *flattering* prospects, he received intelligence that the Roman consul, Lævinus, was coming against him with

Questions.—98. How was the remainder of the century employed? What was going on in Greece at that time? 99. What difficulties commenced with the third century B. C.? 100. What call did Pyrrhus accept? How large was the force which he had? State the difficulties he encountered.

a great army. Though all the Samnite cities had not yet joined his standard, nor all his own forces arrived, yet, looking upon it as a disgrace to sit still, he took the field with what troops he had, first sending proposals to the Romans to act as umpire between them and the Tarentines. To this message Lævinus answered, "That the Romans neither accepted Pyrrhus as a mediator, nor feared him as an enemy." War being thus determined, both armies pitched their tents in sight of each other upon the opposite banks of the river Lyris. The Roman consul, with the impetuosity of inexperience, gave orders for fording the river; and the Grecian, as might be expected, stationed his troops in such a manner as to oppose the attempt. In spite of the efforts of the Thessalian cavalry and Epirean foot, the Roman legions effected their purpose, gained the southern bank of the river, and formed in good order in face of the enemy.

102. The engagement then became general, and victory was long in suspense. The Romans had seven times repulsed the enemy, and had been seven times themselves driven back, when Pyrrhus sent his elephants into the midst of the battle. The Romans, who had never before seen creatures of such magnitude, were terrified by their fierceness, and by the castles upon their backs, filled with armed men. The horses shared in the general consternation, and, throwing their riders, fled snorting from the scene of terror. The rout became general. A dreadful slaughter of the Romans ensued; 15,000 were killed, and 1,800 taken prisoners.

103. The conquerors were also severe sufferers, and Pyrrhus was heard to remark, "One such victory more, and I am undone." Next day he entered the deserted Roman camp. As he gazed upon the bodies of the dead, and marked the noble resolution still visible upon their countenances, he exclaimed, "O, with what ease could I conquer the world, had I the Romans for soldiers, or had they me for their king." The Samnites and Lucanians joined him after this battle, so that with a recruited army he advanced within thirty-seven miles of Rome. But the Romans, though defeated, were still unconquered. They used all diligence in levying forces and forming alliances, and never was there a time when their military and patriotic virtues shone with clearer luster.

104. THE ORATOR'S SUCCESS.—Pyrrhus, who boasted that he had won more cities by the eloquence of Cineas than by the force of arms,

---

Questions.—101. Give the preliminaries of the first battle between Pyrrhus and the Romans. 102. Give an account of the battle. 103. What were the fruits of such a victory? What then was the condition of Rome? What efforts did the Romans make?

sent his famous orator to negotiate a peace. The crafty Grecian, accustomed to the corrupt bribery which had wrought so many revolutions in his own country, took with him splendid presents, not only for the senators, but for their wives. The Roman matrons, however, refused his gifts, saying *they would accept his presents when the senate had decided to accept his friendship.* A public audience was granted, and the disciple of Demosthenes used all his eloquence to persuade the Romans to enter into a treaty with Pyrrhus, which should secure safety for the Tarentines. Some inclined to peace, urging that they had lost one great battle, and had still greater disasters to expect. An illustrious Roman, named Appius Claudius, who, on account of his great age and the loss of his sight, had retired from public business, ordered his servants to carry him in his chair to the senate-house. A respectful silence ensued upon his appearance, and all listened with the deepest interest, while he delivered his sentiments in the following terms:—

105. "Hitherto, I have regarded my blindness as a misfortune, but now, Romans, I wish I had been as *deaf* as I am *blind*, for then I should not have heard of your shameful counsels, so ruinous to the glory of Rome. Where now are your speeches, so much echoed about the world, that if Alexander the Great had come into Italy when we were young, and our fathers in the vigor of their age, he would not now be celebrated as invincible, but, either by his flight or his fall, would have added to the glory of Rome. You now show the vanity and folly of that boast, while you dread that very people who were ever a prey to the Macedonians, and tremble at the name of Pyrrhus, who has all his life been paying his court to one of the guards of that Alexander. Do not expect to get rid of him by making an alliance with him. That step will only open a door to many invaders, for who is there that will not despise you, and think you an easy conquest, if Pyrrhus not only escapes unpunished for his insolence, but gains the Tarentines and Samnites, as a reward for insulting the Romans?"

106. As soon as Appius had done speaking, the senate voted unanimously for the war, and dismissed Cineas with this answer: "That when Pyrrhus had quitted Italy, they would enter upon a treaty of friendship and alliance with him, if he desired it; but while he continued there in a hostile manner, they would prosecute the war against him with all their force, though he should have defeated a thousand

Questions.—104, 105, 106. By what means did Pyrrhus undertake to negotiate a peace? How were his gifts received by the Roman matrons? Who was Appius Claudius? What order did he give? Who decided the question of peace or war? What were the arguments of Appius Claudius? With what answer was Cineas dismissed?

Lævinuses." Cineas made a faithful report of all he saw in Rome to Pyrrhus. He said, that "the senate appeared to him like an assembly of kings; and as to the people, he was afraid that he had to do with a Lernæan hydra." But the character of the Romans was exhibited in a position still more elevated when Fabricius, an ancient senator, a pattern of cheerful poverty and virtue (who, though formerly a consul, had no plate in his house but a silver cup, the bottom of which was horn), came to treat with Pyrrhus upon exchange of prisoners.

107. Pyrrhus received him with great distinction, and privately begged him to accept of a large sum in gold, as a pledge of friendship and hospitality. Fabricius refused the presents. Pyrrhus pressed him no further, but the next day he ordered an elephant to be armed, and placed behind a curtain. Upon a concerted signal the huge animal raised his trunk over the venerable warrior's head, and used all his arts to intimidate him. Fabricius, without being the least discomposed, said to Pyrrhus, smiling, "Neither your gold yesterday, nor your beast to-day, has made any impression upon me." Pyrrhus, charmed with the equanimity of a barbarian who had never learned philosophy, granted him all the prisoners without ransom, on the assurance of Fabricius that they should be returned in case of a renewal of the war.

108. The Second Battle.—B. C. 279.—By this time, the Romans were ready again to take the field against the Grecians. Both armies met near Asculum, being about 40,000 strong. The Romans fought with more than common valor, but the Grecian phalanx stood immovable amidst the desperate slaughter; and the elephants, pressing into the midst of the legion, again decided the victory in favor of the king. The Romans left 6,000 men dead upon the field, nor had Pyrrhus great reason to boast of his triumph; 4,000 of his soldiers were slain, including officers, and friends who had followed him from Greece; so that when one congratulated him upon his victory, he exclaimed again, "One such triumph more, and I am undone." This battle finished the campaign, and both parties retired into winter quarters. The next spring, Pyrrhus having received new supplies from home, and the Romans having made Fabricius consul, two armies, equal to those formerly victors and vanquished, were led into the field.

109. While they were approaching, a letter was brought to Fabricius from the king's physician, in which the writer offered, for a suit-

---

Questions.—106, 107. What report did Cineas make? What purity of patriotism was exhibited by Fabricius? What was its effect upon Pyrrhus? 108. Describe the second battle. In what condition did the armies meet the following spring?

able reward, to take his master off by poison, and thus rid the Romans of their most powerful enemy. Fabricius, indignant at the base proposal, sent the letter to Pyrrhus, telling him that he had chosen men of virtue and honor for enemies, and knaves and villains for friends. "Admirable Fabricius," cried Pyrrhus, at this new proof of his magnanimity, "it would be as easy to turn the sun from its course, as thee from the paths of honor." He punished the physician as he deserved, returned all his prisoners without ransom, and again desired peace.

110. The senate, not to be outdone, sent back the same number of captive Samnites and Tarentines, but refused peace, except on the former condition. Pyrrhus was divided between shame and necessity. He was ashamed to leave the war unfinished, and he saw how hopeless was the prospect of subduing the Romans. An entreaty of the Sicilians for assistance against the Carthaginians relieved his embarrassment. He placed a garrison in Tarentum, and embarked with all his forces for that island; and the Romans, profiting by his absence, carried on the war with vigor for two years. At the end of this time Pyrrhus returned, and another battle with the Romans ensued.

111. The Third Battle.—Pyrrhus, finding the balance turning against him, had recourse once more to his elephants. But for these the Romans were now prepared. Having ascertained that fire was the most effectual weapon against the huge creatures, they threw burning balls of flax and rosin against them, and drove them, mad with terror, back upon their own ranks. Pyrrhus in vain attempted to stop the flight and slaughter of his men; the panic was general. He lost in that disastrous affair 23,000 of his best troops, and his camp was also taken. This last conquest was of the greatest service to the Romans. The Grecian method of encampment became thenceforth their own, and many of their succeeding victories were the direct result of the lessons they had learned of the unfortunate Epirots.

112. Pyrrhus returned to Tarentum. Finding it impossible to raise another army among the disheartened Samnites, he privately embarked, and returned to Epirus with the remains of his shattered forces, leaving a garrison in Tarentum, merely to save appearances. This garrison lorded it so inhumanly over the poor luxurious Tarentines that they surrendered; and thus ended the Samnite war, after continuing

---

Questions.—109. How did Fabricius treat the offer of the king's physician? What exclamation burst from the lips of Pyrrhus? 110. How did Fabricius's conduct influence his actions? How long before another battle was fought with Pyrrhus? 111. Describe the third battle. Of what service was the conquest to the Romans? 112. What movements did Pyrrhus then make? By what act did the Samnite war end? How long had it continued?

71 years. The Roman commonwealth was at this time rich. There were 200,000 citizens capable of bearing arms; and such was their renown abroad, that Ptolemy Philadelphus sent embassadors to congratulate them upon their success, and entreat their alliance.

113. First Punic* War.—We come now to consider Rome in a most interesting period of her history; when, venturing beyond the bounds of Italy, she stretched her arms across the sea, and began the conquest of other lands. About 100 years before the foundation of Rome, Dido, sister of Pygmalion, king of Tyre, fled from the tyranny of her brother, with a select band of followers, and landed in Africa, near the spot where Tunis now stands. There a city was founded, which extended its commerce along the shores of the Mediterranean, and became one of the richest and most powerful cities in the world. Carthage also possessed, in the opinion of Aristotle, one of the most perfect governments of antiquity. At the time of the Punic wars she had under her dominion 300 of the smaller cities of Africa, with their territories. The expulsion of Pyrrhus from Italy—the subjugation of the Samnites and Tarentines—had made the Romans masters of the garden of Europe. Sicily was their granary, but, not content with the supplies of corn annually received, they secretly desired to possess the island itself, the more, perhaps, because Carthage claimed some of its cities, and sent her fleets unquestioned into the bay of Tarentum and up the Adriatic.

114. A trifle could serve as a pretext for declaring war when both parties were predisposed for the contest, and *that* trifle was found in Sicily. Hiero, king of Syracuse, making war upon the Mamertines, entreated the aid of Carthage; and the Mamertines, to escape impending ruin, threw themselves upon the protection of the Romans. The Romans came to the point at once, and boldly declared war against Carthage. But a serious difficulty presented itself in the outset. The Carthaginians were the greatest mariners in the world. The Romans had never been out of sight of land. The genius of Rome, however, patiently leveled every obstacle in its way to empire. A Carthaginian vessel was driven ashore upon the coast of Italy. The Romans immediately set about imitating this ship, and in two months had 120 galleys ready for sea. Men long accustomed to husbandry alone now

* Called "Punic," from Phenicia, the parent state.

Questions.—112. What then was the condition of the Roman commonwealth? Who sent embassadors? To whom were they sent? For what purpose were they sent? 113, 114. What war do we next come to? What was the origin of Carthage? What is said of its government? What gave rise to the first Punic war? What difficulty was overcome by a seeming accident?

became sailors, and committed themselves to the sea in their clumsy fleet.

115. The consul Duillius, though ignorant of maritime affairs, invented an instrument which, upon an impulse of two ships, kept them grappled together, so that by this means the Romans had an opportunity of engaging their enemies hand to hand. When the rival fleets met, he gained the victory by the superior courage of his soldiers, and took fifty of the enemy's ships. This unexpected success so gratified the senate that they decreed Duillius a signal triumph, and ordered that whenever he went out to supper a band of music should attend him. The contest went on by land in Sicily, in the mean time, with varying success; victory sometimes declaring for the Carthaginians, and sometimes for the Romans. The latter took Agrigentum in Sicily, Alberia in Corsica, and the islands of Lipari and Malta.

116. Expedition to Africa.—But these trifling successes could not satisfy the ambition of the Romans. The conquest of Sicily they saw was only to be obtained by humbling the power of Carthage at home. They decided, therefore, to carry the war into Africa. A fleet of 300 sail was fitted out, manned with 140,000 men, and Regulus and Manlius were created consuls to conduct the expedition. This armament, the greatest that had ever left an Italian port, was met by the Carthaginians with a fleet as powerful, manned by *sailors* rather than soldiers. The Carthaginians managed their vessels with the greatest skill, and seemed at first to have the advantage; but when the ships came in close contact the Romans prevailed; the enemy's fleet was dispersed, and 54 ships were taken. No further obstacle intervening, the consuls made a descent upon the coast of Africa, captured a Carthaginian city, and took 20,000 prisoners. Soon after, Manlius was recalled to superintend the Sicilian war, and Regulus directed to continue his conquests in Africa, and as his term was nearly expired he was made general, with the title of *Proconsul.*

117. At first, Regulus was successful in his contests with the Carthaginians. He defeated them in a pitched battle, and filled the land with such terror of the Roman name, that 80 towns submitted to his arms. The Numidians united with him, and ravaged the lands of Carthage; the peasants fled on every side to the city, and filled it with

Questions.—115. Who was Duillius? What instrument did he invent to aid the Romans? Give an account of the naval contest. How was Duillius rewarded? What towns and islands did the Romans afterward take? 116. In what manner did these trifling successes affect the Romans? What did they consider necessary in order to humble Carthage? What expedition was sent? Give an account of the naval battle that occurred. What further success did the Romans have? Why was Manlius recalled? To what position was Regulus appointed? 117. Give an account of the successes of Regulus.

despairing cries for bread. The Carthaginians, as a last resort, sent to the Lacedemonians for help, offering to give their general the command of the army. To provide also for the worst, they dispatched some of their principal men to Regulus, to beg a peace. This noble old general had long wished to return to his native country. He had heard that his steward was dead; that his servant had stolen all his instruments of husbandry; that his farm of seven acres lay uncultivated; and that his children were in danger of suffering actual want. All his personal feelings were therefore in favor of peace; yet, considering the duty he owed his country as paramount to all others, he dictated such terms as he knew the Carthaginians would refuse.

118. The treaty was consequently broken off, and both parties prepared for another engagement. Xanthippus, the Lacedemonian general, arrived in due season; and by a skillful disposition of his forces, and the aid of his elephants, succeeded in defeating the enemies of Carthage. The Roman army was almost entirely destroyed, and *Regulus was taken prisoner.** Nor was the defeat of their army, and the capture of Regulus, the only misfortune that befell the Romans. They lost Agrigentum; their whole fleet perished in a storm; they built another, which shared the same fate; they built yet another, which the mariners drove upon quicksands; and, finally, they gave up for a time all hopes of rivaling Carthage by sea. They however continued their efforts by land, till they gained the greater part of Sicily.

119. Regulus.—The Carthaginians, exhausted by the length of the war, determined to send embassadors to Rome, to negotiate a peace, accompanied by Regulus, whom they had now kept in prison four years. A promise was exacted from him, that he would return in case the senate did not accept of their offers, and he was given to understand that his life depended upon the success of his mission. When the venerable general approached the city, his friends came out to meet and conduct him home; but Regulus refused, with settled melancholy, to enter the gates, saying that he was but a slave to the Carthaginians, and unfit to partake in the liberal honors of his country. The senate assembled without the walls, to give audience to the em-

* Roman historians say that the Carthaginians attempted to assassinate Xanthippus, that he might not take the honor of this victory away from them.

Questions.—117. What aid did the Carthaginians solicit? What private feelings did Regulus surrender to his patriotism? 118. Who aided to defeat the Romans? Give an account of the battle that then occurred. What is said of Regulus? What evils to the Romans followed in rapid succession? What advantage did they gain in Sicily? 119. Why did the Carthaginians again make offers of peace? To what place did they send embassadors? Who accompanied the embassadors? Under what conditions was Regulus sent? In what manner were they received by the Roman senate?

bassadors, and Regulus opened his commission, as directed by the Carthaginians. The senate, wearied with an eight years' war, were willing to accede to almost any proposals which would terminate it with honor; nor was it a slight consideration with them, that peace would liberate a brave old general, whom all the people revered and loved.

120. Regulus, as one of the senate, had also the privilege of giving his opinion. When he came to speak, to the surprise of all, he insisted upon continuing the war. He assured the Romans that the Carthaginians could not hold out much longer; he said the people were harassed out with fatigues, and the nobles with contention; and he supported his opinion by the consideration so weighty with the Romans, that their ancestors had never made peace till they were victorious. Advice so unexpected and magnanimous filled every one with admiration. The senate could not deny the justice of his remarks; every feeling of patriotism enforced the counsels of Regulus; and every sentiment of humanity cried out against consigning the noble captive to torture and death. But Regulus himself relieved their embarrassment by breaking off the treaty, and rising to return to his bonds.

121. It was in vain that the senate and all his dearest friends entreated him to stay; in vain his wife and children begged permission once more to embrace him; he persisted in keeping his promise; nor would he see his friends, lest their despair should move his resolution. Without taking leave of those he should never again behold, he departed with the embassadors for Africa. Nothing could equal the disappointment and fury of the Carthaginians when informed by their deputies of the part Regulus had taken, and the influence he had exerted against them. The utmost ingenuity of savage cruelty was exerted to torture him. In the darkness of his prison, his eyelids were cut off, and then he was brought out and exposed to the burning rays of a tropical sun. Finally, he was put into a barrel stuck full of nails, that pointed inwards, and left to die of agony.

122. THE TREATY.—Both sides now took up arms with more than former animosity. The Romans, though so often wrecked, once more fitted out a fleet to dispute with Carthage the empire of the sea. In this effort they were again unsuccessful, and finally became so discouraged by the disasters they suffered from winds and waves, that for seven years they abstained from all naval expeditions. But their

Questions.—120, 121. What was the advice of Regulus? What course did he then take? What is said of the consequent disappointment and fury of the Carthaginians? What was the fate of Regulus? 122. How was the war then prosecuted? What is said of the next contest on the sea? Of its effects upon the Romans?

inflexible spirits could not be broken. In seven years the boys had become men, and the memory of storms and tempests had ceased to intimidate the former mariners. Another fleet was constructed, and by two splendid victories their fortunes were retrieved, and the power of Carthage so humbled at sea, that she was forced to conclude a peace on the very terms which she had before refused to Regulus. These were, that the Carthaginians should lay down 1,000 talents of silver to defray the expense of the war; that they should pay 2,200 more in ten years' time; that they should quit Sicily and the adjacent islands; that they should never make war against the allies of Rome, or come with any vessels of war within the Roman dominions; and that all Roman prisoners and deserters should be delivered up without ransom. To these hard conditions the Carthaginians subscribed; and thus ended the first Punic war, which had lasted 24 years.

123. Peace.—War with the Gauls.—This war being closed, a profound peace ensued, in which the temple of Janus was shut for the second time since the foundation of the city. The Romans now turned their thoughts to domestic improvement. They began to have a relish for poetry. Dramas were acted upon the Grecian model; elegiac, pastoral, and didactic compositions assumed new beauties in the Latin tongue, and satire was invented by Lucilius. The Gauls, having again crossed the Apeninnes, entered Etruria, and wasted all with fire and sword, till they came within about three days' journey of Rome.* The celebrated Marcellus, afterwards called "The *Sword* of Rome," was appointed to lead forth the army against these invaders.

124. Viridomarus, king of the Gauls, clothed in armor set off with gold and silver, rode out on horseback, and challenged the Roman general to single combat. Marcellus, who never refused a challenge, nor ever failed of killing the challenger, spurred on his horse to the contest, vowing to consecrate the armor of the barbarian to Jupiter. With a mighty stroke of his spear he pierced the breastplate of the Gaul, and with two or three more blows dispatched him. The two

* The Romans, who still retained the remembrance of the sufferings of their city from these barbarians, made extraordinary preparations to meet them. They applied to the sibyls' books for counsel, and, in compliance with the oracles, buried alive two Greeks (a man and a woman), and two Gauls also, in the beast market.

Questions.—122. Of the two victories gained by the Romans? Of the terms of peace exacted by Rome? How many years had the Punic war lasted? 123, 124. During the peace that followed, what advancements were made in literature and science? What difficulty with the Gauls diverted the attention of the Romans? Who was appointed to lead the Roman army? Who was king of the Gauls? Describe the encounter between the two personages.

armies then met, and a prodigious slaughter of the Gauls ensued; till, entirely beaten, they sued for peace. The triumph of Marcellus was one of the most splendid ever seen. The general, having cut the trunk of an oak into the form of a trophy, adorned it with the glittering armor of Viridomarus, and, setting it upon his shoulder, rode through the city in a chariot drawn by four horses, while the army followed, singing songs and odes made for the occasion, and displaying the spoils they had taken from the enemy.

125. SECOND PUNIC WAR.—B. C. 217.—The peace between Rome and Carthage had now continued 23 years. During this time, a man had grown up in the latter city to whom historians give the highest place as a general and a warrior. This was HANNIBAL, the son of Hamilcar, former general of Carthage. When his son was only nine years old, Hamilcar took him to the altar, and, laying his hand upon the victim about to be sacrificed, made him swear that he would never be in friendship with the Romans, nor desist from opposing their power, till he or they should be no more. This hatred, so early implanted, and so sedulously cultivated in the breast of Hannibal, had grown with his growth and strengthened with his strength; and now, in the prime of life, he prepared himself to try whether Rome or he should fall.*

126. The Carthaginians, who made peace only because they were no longer able to continue the war, having now recovered from their embarrassments, were excited by Hannibal to throw off their burdensome tribute, and attempt to regain the cities they had lost. To open the campaign, Hannibal crossed into Spain with a considerable body of forces, and laid siege to Saguntum, a city in alliance with the Romans. As soon as news of this affair reached Rome, embassadors

* The testimony of the historian may aid us in forming an idea of this extraordinary man. "He was possessed of the greatest courage in opposing danger, and the greatest presence of mind in retiring from it. No fatigue was able to subdue his body; no misfortune could break his spirit. He was equally patient of heat and cold; and he was frequently found stretched upon the ground among his sentinels, covered only with his watch-coat. He was the best horseman and the swiftest runner of his time. He was experienced, sagacious, provident, bold, prudent in carrying out the most extensive designs, and fertile in expedients to perplex his enemies." In consequence of his history having been written by those in Roman interest, the cruelty, faithlessness, and hypocrisy ascribed to him have found no friendly hand to palliate their enormity, and the failure of his mighty plans to redeem his country left him without a panegyrist; so that, great as he unquestionably was, and wonderful as were his exploits, his character stands before us in a position which obscures its splendor and represses our admiration.

Questions.—124. The battle that followed. Marcellus's manifestations of triumph. 125. For what period of time did peace continue between Carthage and Rome? Give the early history of Hannibal, with his father's consecration and vow. 126. To what did Hannibal incite the Carthaginians? Where did he open the campaign?

were sent to Carthage to complain of the infraction of the treaty, and to require that Hannibal should be given up. This demand was refused. The principal embassador, perceiving the state of feeling among the Carthaginian ministry, held out the skirt of his robe, saying, that "he brought them peace or war, and they might choose between them." They desired him to deliver which he thought proper. "Then let it be war," said the indignant Roman, and immediately took his departure.

127. War being thus declared, nothing was left but again to build fleets, levy armies, raise supplies, and in every possible way prepare for conflict. Saguntum surrendered, and Hannibal soon overran all Spain with his victorious troops. Then, having collected a large army of all languages and nations, he resolved to carry the war into Italy itself, as the Romans had before carried it into the dominions of Carthage. With 50,000 foot and 9,000 horse, he passed the Pyrenees into Gaul, traversed the vast forests, defeated the savage enemies, and crossed the rapid rivers which opposed his march, and in ten days arrived at the foot of the Alps, over which he had determined to explore a new passage into Italy.

128. Passage of the Alps.—It was midwinter when this astonishing project was undertaken. The mighty glaciers which had been accumulating for ages frowned upon him from above, and vast caverns, through which the mountain torrents roared fearfully along, yawned from below; the rude cottages which seemed to hang upon the sides of the precipices offered no friendly shelter; and bands of people, barbarous and fierce, dressed in skins covered with long, shaggy hair, rendered the prospect more forbidding, and the wilderness more terrible. But nothing could subdue the courage of Hannibal. Assuring his followers that they were now scaling, not the walls of Italy, but of Rome, he led them up the sides of the mountains, along the dizzy heights, over the icy paths; and, driving back the barbarians, after nine days of incredible fatigue, gained a summit whence his soldiers could descry the fertile vales of Italy, spread out in beauty beneath the warm rays of the sun.

129. After two days' rest, they prepared for the descent—a work more perilous than even the ascent had been. Prodigious quantities of snow had fallen, in which multitudes were buried; every new advance seemed to increase the danger, till, at last, they came to the

Questions.—126. In this crisis, of what did the Romans complain? What did they require? In what manner was war finally declared? 127. What success attended Hannibal? 128, 129. Describe the passage over the Alps. Where was Ticinium? Trebia river? (Map No. 4.)

verge of a rock above 300 yards perpendicular, which seemed utterly impassable. Despair appeared in every face but Hannibal's. He could not go round it; he would not turn back. He therefore made preparations to *level* the obstruction. Great numbers of trees were felled, piled against it, and set on fire. "The rock, being thus heated," says Livy, "was softened by vinegar, and a way opened through which the whole army might safely pass." Then, as they descended, the valleys became more fertile, the cattle found pasture, and at the end of fifteen days Hannibal found himself upon the plains of Italy with about half his army—the rest having fallen victims to the inclemency of the weather, or the hostility of the natives.

130. BATTLES OF TICINIUM AND TREBIA. B. C. 218.—The senate, during all this time, had not been idle. The army, headed by Scipio, had been ordered into the field to intercept the course of the invader; and before the Carthaginians had recovered from their fatigues, they were attacked by the Romans near Ticinium. The consul was wounded in the beginning of the fight, and would have been slain, had not his son Scipio (afterward Africanus) saved his father's life at the hazard of his own. The engagement was for some time carried on with equal valor on both sides, till a party of Numidian horse, making a circuit, attacked the Romans in flank, and routed them with considerable loss.

131. The Gauls, having been treated with great respect by the Carthaginians, joined the army of Hannibal. Sempronius, the other consul, resolving to repair the injury sustained by his colleague, gave battle again upon the banks of the river Trebia. Hannibal, aware of Roman impetuosity, sent off a body of 1,000 horsemen, each with a foot-soldier behind him, to ravage the country, and provoke the enemy to engage. The Romans drove them back, and they, seeming to be defeated, took to the river. The consul pressed on after them, and not till he had reached the opposite bank did he perceive that the day was lost; for his men, fatigued with wading the river, and benumbed with the coldness of the water, which reached their armpits, could not withstand the tremendous charge of the Carthaginians, and 26,000 were either killed or drowned in the river.

132. The loss of these two battles did not intimidate the Romans, nor lull Hannibal into false security. Preparations for the ensuing campaign were carried on with the greatest vigor on both sides. The Carthaginian general approached Rome by way of Etruria, through the

Questions.—130. Where did the enemies meet for the first battle? What service did Scipio render his father? What circumstance decided the fate of the battle? 131. What new force joined Hannibal? By what stratagem did Hannibal provoke a second battle? Give an account of it. 132. Give a further account of Hannibal's march toward Rome.

marshes of the river Arno. All the former fatigues of his army were nothing in comparison with what they suffered here. For three days and three nights successively, they marched up to the knees in water, without sleep or rest; the hoofs of the horses came off, and multitudes of the baggage beasts were left dead in the mud.

133. Hannibal himself rode upon an elephant, the only one he had left, and, in addition to the feelings occasioned by the complicated distress of his army, suffered so much from an inflammation in his eyes that he lost one of them entirely. Hearing that Flaminius, with his army, lay in the direct road toward Rome, he turned aside, as if desirous of avoiding him, and ravaged the country with fire and sword. This had the desired effect. The consul could not bear to wait quietly for a re-enforcement, while the enemy was thus laying every thing waste around him, and, contrary to the advice of his friends, determined to risk an engagement.

134. BATTLE OF THRASYMENUS. FABIUS.—Hannibal took a position with his army near Lake Thrasymenus, upon a chain of mountains, between which and the lake was a narrow passage, leading to a valley embosomed in hills. Into this valley Flaminius led his men to the attack. A mist rising from the lake obscured the sight of the Romans, so that they could not perceive the number or position of their enemies. They were accordingly defeated without having been able to do any thing worthy of the Roman name.* 15,000 fell in the valley, and 6,000 surrendered prisoners of war. Flaminius did every thing that valor could do to rally his forces, and finally died fighting alone in the midst of the enemy.

135. When this news reached Rome, the prætor assembled the people, and made the following proclamation: "Romans, we have lost a great battle; our army is cut to pieces, and Flaminius is slain; think, therefore, what is to be done for your safety." After the first consternation had subsided, they unanimously agreed to elect Fabius Maximus dictator; a man whose spirit and dignity admirably fitted him for the office. His house was one of the most illustrious in Rome, for the Fabian family once undertook alone to cope with the power of Veii, and 306 of them perished in one expedition. It was

* While the battle lasted, an earthquake overturned whole cities, changed the course of rivers, and tore off the tops of mountains; yet so desperate was the fight, that neither party perceived the violent motion.

Questions.—133. By what means did he hasten another battle? 134. Where did the two armies meet? What gave the advantage to the Carthaginians? With what success was it followed? What was the fate of Flaminius? 135. At this crisis, who was made dictator of Rome? What was the character of Fabius? What is related of his house?

the policy of Fabius* to *harass*, rather than *fight*, the Carthaginians. He always encamped on the high grounds, out of the way of the enemy's cavalry. When they sat still, he did the same; when they moved, he showed himself upon the hills, as if preparing for action; he straitened their quarters, cut off their provisions, and kept them in constant fear of surprise.

136. Hannibal, finding it impossible to bring on a general engagement, used all his arts to make Fabius appear the coward, rather than the skillful general. This impression actually pervaded the Roman camp, and some of the officers called Fabius the pedagogue† of Hannibal; and his general of horse sneeringly inquired "if he intended to take his army up into heaven, or to screen them from the enemy with clouds and fogs." Fabius bore all their taunts with the greatest equanimity; nor would he change his tactics, though he witnessed the ravaging of Samnium, and the plunder of many flourishing cities. At last, Hannibal determined to make use of a stronger bait, to draw the dictator from his impregnable station. For this purpose, he ordered his guides to conduct him to the plains of *Casinum;* but they, mistaking the word, through his barbarous pronunciation, led him to *Casilinum*, a valley stretching out to the sea.

137. As soon as he had entered, Fabius seized the narrow outlet, and there held him in a most disadvantageous position, without any place of egress. Hannibal crucified his guides for their mistake, and set his African cunning at work to devise some means of escape. The plan he adopted was this. One dark night, he ordered lighted fagots to be tied to the horns of 2,000 oxen. The creatures were then driven slowly toward the pass, like an army marching with torches. The Romans took them for what they appeared; but when the fire burnt to the quick, and the animals, mad with pain, ran up the hills with their foreheads flaming, and filling the air with unearthly sounds, the detachment set to guard the outlet, expecting they knew not what, fled to the main body. The Carthaginians seized the pass, and Hannibal escaped through the defile to Apulia.

138. The Romans now murmured more than ever against Fabius, and his office soon after expiring, a violent contest arose about the

* Washington has been called the American Fabius.

† The office of a pedagogue was to attend children, to carry them about, and conduct them home.

Questions.—136, 137. By what policy did he thwart the wishes of Hannibal? Into what strait was Hannibal by mistake driven? How did he free himself from the threatened danger? Where was Lake Thrasymenus? Casinum? Casilinum? (Map No. 4.)

election of consuls. The citizens at length chose Varro, a man sprung from the dregs of the people, rash and self-confident, and joined with him Emilius Paulus, father of that Paulus Emilius who so distinguished himself afterwards in Greece, and father-in-law of Scipio the Great. Fabius, who saw the danger that threatened the state from two such ill-matched commanders, entreated Emilius to guard against the devices of Hannibal and the rashness of Varro. Emilius promised to heed his caution, and set forth with his plebeian colleague at the head of 90,000 men, the flower of Italy. Hannibal, who had only about two-thirds as many troops, was encamped upon the plains of Cannæ, in such a position that the south wind, which raised clouds of sand from the dry plains, would drive directly in the faces of an approaching enemy.

139. BATTLE OF CANNÆ.—On the first day of their arrival it was Emilius's turn to command, and though Hannibal did all in his power to bring him to battle, yet he declined fighting under circumstances so disadvantageous. The next day, Varro, without waiting for the concurrence of Emilius, hung out the scarlet mantle, and, leading his troops across the river Aufidus, set the battle in array. Hannibal, who had been from daybreak marshaling his forces, disposed them in such a manner, that when the main body should give way before the impetuosity of the Roman charge, the wings should surround the enemy, and thus engage on all sides at once. This was the principal cause of the carnage that followed. The Romans, penetrating the center, were completely embosomed; and Hannibal's army, taking the form of a crescent, closed in behind them, and suffered none to escape.

140. Varro fled with a few horse, and Emilius, covered with darts, which stuck in his wounds, sat down in anguish and despair, waiting for the enemy to dispatch him. His head and face were so disfigured with dust and blood, that many of his friends passed by without knowing him. At last Lentulus, a tribune, flying on horseback, came up to the spot, and recognizing him, dismounted; "Emilius," cried he, "you at least are guiltless of this day's slaughter; take my horse, while you have any strength remaining; I will assist you, and will defend you with my life."—"I thank thee, Lentulus," cried the dying consul, "but go, I command thee, and tell the senate to fortify Rome against the conqueror. Tell Fabius, also, that Emilius followed his

Questions.—138. Who was chosen in place of Fabius to lead the Roman army? Why was not Fabius rechosen? What is said of Varro? Who was Emilius Paulus? What advice did Hannibal give to Emilius? 139, 140. Why did Emilius decline to give battle? What course did Varro pursue? Describe the battle that followed. Relate the conversation between Emilius and Lentulus. By what name is that battle known?

directions to the last, but was first overcome by Varro, and then by Hannibal." While he was yet speaking the enemy approached, and Lentulus, before he was out of sight, saw the consul expire, feebly fighting in the midst of hundreds.

141. In this battle the Romans lost 53,000 men, several officers, and so many knights, that it is said Hannibal sent three bushels of gold rings to Carthage, which those of this order had worn upon their fingers. Hannibal's friends advised him to follow the fugitives immediately to Rome, assuring him that in five days he might sup in the capitol; but he did not think proper to attempt the siege of a city sheltered by walls and ramparts till he had formed alliances with the neighboring states. The battle of Cannæ so changed the face of affairs, that the Carthaginians, who had been obliged to move from place to place, like a great band of robbers, now saw the best provinces of Italy in their power; and Capua, the most considerable city, open to receive them.

142. At Rome, nothing was heard but shrieks and lamentations; one-third of the senators were slain; one-half the city were in mourning for their dearest friends; and an enemy, whose vindictive cruelty had been fully proved, was daily expected at their gates. Fabius alone walked about the city with an unruffled countenance, encouraging the magistrates, placing the guards, and adopting suitable precautions for the safety of the commonwealth. The people found in his judgment their temple, their altar, and their hope; and from his calm demeanor seemed to gather new resolution and confidence. When Varro arrived, the senate, instead of reprimanding him for his rashness, went out to meet him, and returned him thanks that he had not despaired of the safety of Rome. Hannibal did not come on as they had expected; and inspired with fresh courage, they enlisted slaves, and made all possible preparations for another campaign.

143. Fabius the *shield*, and Marcellus the *sword*, of Rome, were appointed to lead her armies; and though Hannibal offered peace it was refused, but upon condition that he should quit Italy. This general took up his winter quarters in Campania. In the fertile vales of that state a new scene of pleasure opened to his soldiers, which served to destroy the energies of barbarians unaccustomed to any lux-

---

Questions.—140. What became of Emilius? 141. How many did the Romans lose in this engagement? How many gold rings were sent to Carthage? To what did Hannibal's friends advise him? Why did he not act as advised? 142. What then was the condition of Rome? In the emergency, who alone was found able to advise? How was Varro received by the Romans? 143. Who were appointed to lead the Romans in the next campaign? Who made proposals of peace? Where was Campania? (Map No. 4.)

ury. Though Rome had lost *four* important battles, she could yet bring into the field four times as many men as Hannibal. Marcellus, who often engaged in skirmishes, gained frequent advantages, while Fabius straitened the movements of the Carthaginian general, and, like a constant stream, undermined all his defenses.

144. The Romans, however, do not deserve all the credit of the ruin of Hannibal. He received his first fatal blow from his friends. His glory had made enemies for him in the councils of Carthage; the men he required were not sent; and the supplies that he demanded did not arrive. For years he carried on the unequal conflict, sometimes advancing, sometimes retreating, frequently destitute of money and provisions, and feeling that the desperate game which he was playing must finally turn against him, through the envy and ingratitude of his countrymen. After the Romans had gained the city of Tarentum, he acknowledged to his friends that he had always thought it difficult, and now saw it impossible, with the forces he had, to conquer Italy.

145. The senate of Carthage at length came to the resolution of sending his brother, Asdrubal, to his assistance with a body of forces. Asdrubal landed in Italy without accident; but the Romans surrounded him in a defile, into which he had been led by the treachery of his guides, and cut his whole army into pieces. Hannibal had long waited for these succors with great impatience; he was assured that his brother was on his way, and the very night that he expected to embrace him with renewed hope, Asdrubal's head was thrown into his camp by the Romans! He saw in the bloody relic the downfall of Carthage, and observed with a sigh to those around him, "Fortune seems fatigued with granting her favors."

146. Siege of Syracuse.—But it was not in Italy alone that fortune frowned upon the Carthaginians. The unconquerable Romans, though surrounded with enemies at home, and still bleeding from their defeat at Cannæ, sent legions into Spain, Sardinia, and Sicily, and undertook a new war against Philip, king of Macedon, for having made a league with Hannibal. Marcellus, who had charge of the war in Sicily, led his forces against Syracuse. There, for a long time, he found all his efforts baffled by the arts of one man. This man was Archimedes, the great mathematician. He was the kinsman of Hiero,

---

Questions.—143. What successes did Marcellus and Fabius gain? 144. From whom did Hannibal receive his first fatal blow? Give an account of Hannibal's "ups and downs." 145. Who at last was sent to the aid of Hannibal? Give an account of Asdrubal's misfortune. What was done with his head? 146. Where, beside Italy, did fortune frown upon the Carthaginians? Against what place did Marcellus lead his forces? Who, for a time, baffled him? Give an account of Archimedes.

the king of whom we have spoken as giving occasion to the first Punic war, and in conversation had assured his royal patron, that *with a fulcrum and lever he could move the world.** To prove so startling an assertion, he drew upon land the king's loaded galleys by a machine turned with one hand.

147. Hiero, astonished at the force of his art, prevailed upon Archimedes to make for him all sorts of engines which could be used in a siege, for attack or defense. These machines, which had lain inactive during the life of Hiero, were now brought out, and employed with great effect by the inventor. When Archimedes began to play his engines, the Romans stood aghast with terror. All sorts of missile weapons, and stones of an enormous size, were sent forth with such noise and rapidity that nothing could stand before them. Huge beams were on a sudden projected over the walls, which, striking the galleys, sunk them at once; sometimes burning glasses lighted mysterious flames in the sails; and sometimes a sort of iron crow with two claws, let down by a lever, caught hold of the ships, drew them towards the walls, whirled them about, and dashed them against the rocks; so that the fear of this one man haunted them continually. Finally, the Romans were so terrified, that if they saw a stick put over the walls, they cried out that Archimedes was leveling some machine at them, and fled in dismay.

148. Marcellus desisted for a time from his efforts against Syracuse, but employed himself, meanwhile, in overrunning the island, and subduing smaller cities. Then returning, he seized the town by surprise one night, when the citizens had drunk to intoxication in honor of Diana. Archimedes was in his study, absorbed in his scientific researches, when the Romans entered; nor did he perceive that the city was taken till a soldier entered his room, and commanded him to follow him into the presence of Marcellus. Archimedes requested him to wait till he had finished his problem, upon which the soldier

* So engaged was Archimedes with mathematics, that he neglected his meat and drink. He was often carried by force to the bath, and, when there, amused himself with drawing geometrical figures in the ashes, or marking lines with his fingers upon his body when it was anointed. A jeweler had made a crown for Hiero; but the king, suspecting that it had been fraudulently alloyed with silver, set Archimedes to examine into the affair. Archimedes thought upon the subject a long time in vain. One day in the bath, perceiving that his body displaced a quantity of water equal to its bulk, the doctrine of *specific gravity* unfolded at once before his mind. Transported with joy, he ran out into the street, crying out *Eureka! Eureka!* "I have found it! I have found it!" Then, by comparing the specific gravities of gold and silver, he detected the cheat of the jeweler.

Questions.—146, 147, 148. What assurance did he give to Hiero? What means did the people of Syracuse use for defense? What is said of the fear produced among the Romans? By what surprise was the city finally taken? What caused the death of Archimedes?

drew his sword and killed him. Marcellus, much grieved, ordered his body to be honorably buried, and a tomb erected to his memory. This monument has ages since mingled with the dust, but the simple instrument, *Archimedes's screw*, still survives, and interests every philosophical student in the history of its great inventor. Marcellus, on his return, was made consul a fifth time, and again went to fight with Hannibal. With a small detachment, he fell into an ambuscade and was slain.

149. Scipio Africanus.—The Romans also suffered some severe reverses in Spain. Two of the Scipios were slain, but that youth who saved his father's life at the Ticinium, being appointed to the proconsulship in that country, though but twenty-four years old, soon retrieved these losses. He was superior to Hannibal in tenderness and generosity, and won the hearts of as many by his affability and justice as by force of arms. Spain and Sicily were subdued, but Hannibal still maintained his ground in Italy, unsupported at home, and but little aided by the alliances he had formed. For fourteen years he had sustained himself by the most skillful management, and the most judicious plans. He had never lost a battle, and his terror was upon his enemies; but his old army was worn out; and while the Roman youth were growing up, eager to distinguish themselves against the Carthaginians, his friends and followers were dying about him of fatigue or excess.

150. In this posture of affairs Publius Scipio returned from the conquest of Spain, and was made consul at the age of 29. With the foresight of an older person, he determined to carry the war into Africa, and make the Carthaginians tremble for their own city. Scipio had not been long in Africa, when accounts were brought to Rome of his glorious and wonderful achievements. A Numidian king was taken prisoner, and two camps were burned and destroyed. Rich spoils confirmed these cheering reports. The Carthaginians were so terrified by these repeated defeats, that they sent a positive command to Hannibal, their great champion, to return and defend Carthage. He obeyed the mandate with a sad foreboding of calamity, and took leave of Italy with tears, after having kept possession of its most beautiful portions more than fifteen years. In that country he had lost his two

Questions.—148. By whom was he mourned? What still survives to tell the philosophical student that Archimedes lived? What became of Marcellus? 149. What losses did the Romans suffer in Spain? What is said of Scipio Africanus? Of Hannibal's long success in Italy? Of his decreasing army? 150. How old was Publius Scipio when he was made consul? What success had he previously attained? What resolution as regards Africa did he determine upon? What success did he have in Africa? Why was Hannibal recalled home? What were his feelings upon leaving Italy?

brothers, his bravest generals, and most of those soldiers who had shared his toils and dangers from earliest youth.

151. After a melancholy passage he arrived in Africa, and marched toward Zama, a city within five days' journey of Carthage. Scipio led his army on to meet him; and to show how much he felt his superiority, sent back the spies of Hannibal, with a full account of all his preparations. Unwilling to risk every thing upon a single battle, Hannibal invited Scipio to an interview. It was in an extensive plain between the armies that the two greatest generals in the world met, and silently regarded each other for a time with mutual reverence. Hannibal, dark, swarthy, one-eyed, with the sternness of the old warrior upon his features; Scipio, in the prime of life, with all the energy and vigor of the Roman beaming in every look. The arguments which Hannibal adduced in favor of a peace, Scipio said he would have regarded had they been proposed in Italy; and both, parting dissatisfied, prepared to decide the controversy by the sword.

152. Battle of Zama. B. C. 202.—The battle of Zama was one of the bloodiest recorded in history. Hannibal conducted the charge with the greatest skill; but Scipio's army, composed of the flower of Roman youth, was far superior in numbers and discipline to the worn-out Carthaginians and their allies. The Romans were victorious, and Hannibal fled. The conquerors dictated the terms of peace, as sovereigns. The Carthaginians were to pay 10,000 talents; to give hostages for the delivery of their ships and elephants; to restore to Masinissa, the Numidian king, all his territories; and they were not to make war, even in Africa, without permission of the Romans.

153. B. C. **200.** Spain, Africa, Macedonia, and Greece, made Roman Provinces.—Philip, king of Macedon, had attempted to make an alliance with Hannibal while he was in Italy. The war which resulted in Greece was still going on, and in the beginning of this century the Macedonian monarch was defeated several times by Galba, the Roman consul. He was compelled to raise the siege of Athens; was driven from the straits of Thermopylæ by Flaminius; was again defeated at Cynocephale, and forced to conclude an inglorious peace. Ten commissioners, with Flaminius at their head, attended the Isthmian games, and gave to each Grecian state the power of making its own laws.

Questions.—151. Where did Hannibal and Scipio meet? In what way did Scipio show his feeling of superiority? Give an account of the conference. 152. When was the battle of Zama fought? Give an account of it. What terms of peace were dictated? 153. Who attempted to make an alliance with Hannibal while in Italy? What defeats did the Macedonian monarch experience? What was he at last compelled to do? What power was given by the ten commissioners to the Grecian states?

154. The next enemy of consequence who interfered with the Romans was Antiochus the Great. Against him Scipio, brother of the famous Africanus, was sent with the Roman legions. The ill-concerted manner in which Antiochus conducted his expedition has been already described. Scipio drove him out of Europe, defeated him in Asia, and obtained from his success the surname of Asiaticus. The proud successor of Alexander was glad to procure peace of the Romans, on condition of paying 15,000 talents; giving hostages of fidelity; and surrendering Hannibal,* who had been some time a resident at his court.

155. In the third year after the war with Antiochus, the tribunes of the people accused Scipio Africanus of defrauding the treasury, and set a day for his trial. Scipio came at the appointed time, and listened to the charges with a serene air. Instead, however, of attempting a defense, he reminded his countrymen that on that very day, 15 years before, he had won the battle of Zama. The assembly rose at once, left the tribunes in the forum, and attended Scipio to the capitol, to return their annual thanks to the gods for this victory. Scipio afterwards retired to Campania, and spent the short remnant of his days in peace and privacy—testifying his displeasure against his countrymen only by this epitaph, which he ordered to be engraved upon his tomb: "Ungrateful country—my very bones shall not rest among you." Hannibal, Philopœmen, and Scipio died the same year, B. C. 182. The Second Macedonian war next engaged the Roman arms. Emilius overthrew Perseus, and carried him in triumph to Rome, to

* The misfortunes of this illustrious man now drew to their tragical close. All that could be done for Carthage he had done, even after the battle of Zama. His ungrateful countrymen, hating any check upon their vices, accused him to the Romans of intriguing to renew the war. To escape the fate of a captive he left Carthage, and began his voluntary exile. He sailed to Tyre, and thence found his way to the Syrian court, where he was kindly received, and made admiral of the fleet. Here his skill and sagacity were exercised to destroy the Romans; but when fortune turned against his patron, and he found his name in the articles of treaty, he fled again to the king of Bithynia. He lived with Prusias five years; the Romans, however, having sent a demand for him, he again became a wanderer. Finding that the envoys of Rome were ever on his track, he desired one of his followers to bring him poison, saying, "Let us rid the Romans of their terrors, since they are unwilling to wait for the death of an old man like me." The poison operated speedily, and Rome was freed from the fear of her greatest enemy.

Questions.—154. Who was the next enemy that interfered with the Romans? Who was sent against him? What success attended Scipio? To what terms of peace did the successor of Alexander submit? What interesting account is related of Hannibal in the note? 155. What accusation was brought against Scipio? By whom were the charges made? How were they punished for their ingratitude? Where did Scipio die? What was his epitaph? In what year did he die? When did Hannibal die? What war next engaged the Roman arms? Who overthrew Perseus? To what was Perseus subject?

walk before his chariot. These conquests brought immense riches into the Roman treasury, and *Macedon became a Roman province.*

156. B. C. 149. THIRD PUNIC WAR.—About this time, Masinissa, king of Numidia, made some incursions upon the territory claimed by the Carthaginians. This people, having recovered in some measure from the effects of their wars, repelled the invasion. Cato the Censor, then nearly 90, was sent into Africa to inquire into the cause of the infraction of the treaty. When he arrived at Carthage, he found that city not in the exhausted and humbled condition which the Romans imagined, but full of men fit to bear arms; well supplied with money and warlike stores, and in a fair way to regain all its former greatness. Having made these observations he returned home, and represented to the senate the necessity of humbling a power which might once more involve Rome in a long and dangerous contest for empire. So fixed was this persuasion in his mind, that he never gave his opinion in the senate, upon any point whatever, without adding, "And my opinion is that Carthage should be destroyed;" so that "*Carthago delenda est*" passed into a proverb. Moved by his representations, the senate ordered war to be proclaimed, and the consuls set out with a resolution to destroy the ancient rival of Rome.

157. The Carthaginians too late perceived the wisdom of Hannibal in insisting upon *public measures*, rather than *private interest.* Now alarmed by the Roman preparations, they punished those who had quarreled with Masinissa, and most humbly offered satisfaction. The senate demanded 300 hostages within 30 days. To their surprise and regret, the Carthaginians sent their children within the given time; and soon after the consuls landed at Utica, deputies waited upon them to know what further the senate might require. The consuls, who had express directions to destroy Carthage, were not a little perplexed at this ready submission. They now, however, demanded the arms of the Carthaginians. These also were delivered up. The Carthaginians were then ordered to leave their city, and build another in any part of their territories within ten miles of the sea. The deputies employed tears and lamentations to gain a respite from so hard a sentence; the consuls were inexorable; and with heavy hearts they departed, to bear the gloomy tidings to their countrymen.

158. The unfortunate Carthaginians, finding that the conquerors

Questions.—155. How did these conquests affect Rome and Macedon? 156. Who at that time encroached upon the Carthaginian territory? How did the Numidian king fare? What report did the aged Cato bring from Africa? What was his advice to the Romans? Was the advice taken? 157. What demands did the Carthaginians comply with? What movement, at last, were the Carthaginians ordered to make?

would not desist from making demands while they had any thing left to supply, prepared to resist with all the energy of despair. Those vessels of gold and silver which ministered to their pride were converted into arms. The women parted with their ornaments for this sacred purpose, and even cut off their hair to make bow-strings. A general whom they had a short time before condemned for opposing the Romans was taken from prison to lead their army; every thing was done which prudence could suggest or ingenuity devise; so that when the consuls arrived before the city, which they expected to find an easy conquest, they met with such resistance as quite dispirited their forces. Several engagements were fought before the walls, in which the assailants were repulsed; and the Romans would have been compelled to retreat, with loss and dishonor, but for the gallant conduct of the son of Emilius (adopted son of Scipio Africanus). By his skill in drawing off his forces after a defeat, and his talent at inspiring new hopes, he quieted the murmurs which had arisen in the camp.

159. Pharneas, master of the Carthaginian horse, thinking his country absolutely ruined, deserted to the Romans; and Scipio cut off all supplies by land at the same time that he blockaded the harbor and stopped all relief by sea. He soon after killed 70,000 men and took 10,000 prisoners, and, having forced one of the gates, advanced to the forum. Great numbers fled to the citadel, and Scipio took possession of a city filled with heaps of dead and dying. Famine compelled the refugees in the citadel to surrender; the Carthaginian general gave himself up; but a few of the most resolute perished in the flames of the temple. This magnificent city, 24 miles in compass, was then set on fire by the merciless conquerors, and continued burning 17 days.* The walls were demolished; the lands given to the friends of the Romans; the slaves prepared for the market; and the consuls, having completed their work of destruction, struck their tents, and returned home in triumph, B. C. 146.

160. In the same year, Corinth, one of the cities of the Achæan League, having made war upon the Lacedemonians, was sentenced to the same fate. So rich were its temples and dwellings, that it is said

* Though Scipio was obliged by the orders of the senate to demolish the walls of Carthage, yet he wept bitterly over the tragical scene, expressing his fears that Rome would at some future day perish in a similar conflagration.

Questions.—158. What course did they then determine upon? What preparations were made? Give an account of the siege. 159. Who deserted to the Romans? Give the particulars of Scipio's successes. Of the result of the siege. In what year was Carthage destroyed? Where was Carthage? (See map No. 1.) 160. In what year was Corinth destroyed? Who destroyed it? What is said of the richness of Corinth?

Corinthian brass became additionally precious from quantities of silver and gold melted down with it. Spain was soon after entirely subdued, and the Romans from this time began to look upon the world as their own, and to treat all who withstood their arms as revolters. The triumphs and spoils of Greece, Syria, Spain, and Africa introduced a taste for splendid expense; the ancient modesty, plainness, and severity of the Romans were exchanged for avarice, luxury, and ostentation; and corruption commenced its work in the commonwealth.

161. THE GRACCHII.—Cornelia, daughter of Scipio Africanus, and wife of Tiberius Gracchus, was left a widow with twelve children, all of whom died young except three. To these children she devoted herself with so much parental affection and greatness of mind, that though her sons were gifted above all their Roman contemporaries, education was said to have contributed more to their perfections than nature. A lady who once visited her, having displayed her jewels, desired to see Cornelia's. She evaded the request till the return of her children from school, and then presenting Tiberius and Caius to her visitor, exclaimed, "These are my jewels." And well did her children reward her care. Her daughter was married to Scipio the Younger, of whom we have already spoken; and her sons, beautiful, wise, eloquent, and virtuous, sacrificed their lives in attempting to stem the corruptions of the state, and preserve to Rome the freedom and simplicity which had given the world to her arms. Indeed, Cornelia is blamed for the untimely fate of her sons, because she fostered their ambition. Plutarch says, that she used to reproach her sons that she was called the mother-in-law of Scipio, rather than *the mother of the Gracchii.*

162. The first public act of Tiberius was an attempt to revive the Licinian law, which forbade any person to possess more than 500 acres of land. The distinctions, *patrician* and *plebeian*, had faded away into the still more obnoxious classification, *rich* and *poor.* The poor, who perceived at once the benefit to themselves of this law, sustained Tiberius, and inflamed his spirit by acclamations and blessings; the rich, who were thus called upon to surrender a part of their ill-gotten gains, opposed him, and represented that he desired to overthrow the constitution. But the eloquent Tiberius easily silenced their invectives. The people gathered about him when he ascended the rostrum, and

Questions.—160. What country next fell under the power of Rome? What change took place in the taste, habits, and honesty of the Romans? 161. Relate the story of Cornelia. 162. What was the first public act of Tiberius? What distinctions had faded away? Into what were they merged? What course did Tiberius pursue?

pleaded for the poor in language such as this: "The wild beasts of Italy have their caves to retire to, but the brave men who spill their blood in her cause have nothing left but air and light. Without any settled habitations, they wander from place to place with their wives and children; and their generals do but mock them when, at the head of their armies, they exhort them to fight for their sepulchers and domestic gods; for, among such numbers, there is not perhaps a Roman who has an altar that belonged to his ancestors, nor a sepulcher in which their ashes rest."

163. By these speeches were the minds of the poor inflamed; debate ripened into enmity, and enmity into sedition. The law was passed; but Gracchus had made himself too conspicuous to escape the malice of the rich. Attalus, king of Pergamus, dying, made the Roman people his heirs. Tiberius found here another opportunity to gratify his followers. He proposed that the money so left should be distributed among the poor for the purchase of farming utensils. This bill produced greater disturbances than the other. Tiberius spoke eloquently in its favor, but the patricians excited a mob, and one of the tribunes struck the orator dead with a piece of a seat. Not less than 300 of his followers shared a similar fate; many were banished; some put to death by the public execution; and all who supported his measures were found guilty of sedition.

164. Caius Gracchus.—Caius, the other son of Cornelia, who was but twenty-one at the time of his brother's death, refrained from all interference in political affairs for many years. During this time he filled the office of quæstor in Sardinia, and discharged his duties with such ability that the king of Numidia, sending a present of corn to the Romans, ordered his embassadors to say that it was a tribute to the virtues of Caius Gracchus. The senate treated the embassy with contempt; and Gracchus, stung by the indignity, returned from the army and offered himself for tribune. The *rich* united their forces to oppose him, but crowds came from all parts of Italy to support his election; and the Campus Martius not being large enough to contain them, they gave their votes from the tops of houses. Being elected by a very large majority, he prepared to avenge the death of Tiberius, and carry out those reforms which would throw the weight of government into the popular scale.

165. He procured the banishment of Pompilius, one of the murder-

Questions.—162. What arguments did he use? 163. Give a history of events until the death of Tiberius. How was he killed? What then followed? 164. What was the name of the remaining son of Cornelia? What is said of the present of corn? Why did Caius offer himself for tribune? Give an account of his election. 165. What measures did he then take?

ers of his brother; he secured the passage of an edict by which the price of corn was fixed at a moderate standard, and monthly distributions made to the poor—a measure which brought all the paupers in Italy to Rome. With his associate tribunes, he then proceeded to inspect the corruptions of the senate; and that body being found guilty of bribery, extortion, and the sale of offices, the power of judging magistrates was transferred to *three hundred knights*, chosen for the purpose. The senators now hated him more than ever; and Scipio the Younger, who had opposed the measures of Gracchus, being found dead in his bed, it was whispered about that Gracchus had murdered his own brother-in-law. To escape the odium thus heaped upon him, Gracchus procured a decree for rebuilding Carthage, and went himself with 6,000 families to Africa. Several unfavorable omens, however, dampened the zeal of the adventurers, and he returned to Italy within seventy days. Here he joined the party of Flaccus, in an attempt to pass the Agrarian law, and went with an armed crowd to the capitol. High words and blows ensued, and a lictor was slain.

166. Flaccus and Gracchus were summoned to appear before the senate and answer for the murder. Instead of obeying the citation, they took possession of Mount Aventine, with a body of adherents, and proclaimed liberty to all the slaves who would join their party. This was considered open rebellion, and the consul immediately surrounded the place with his forces. Flaccus was taken prisoner and dragged to execution, while Gracchus made his escape across the Tiber. He took refuge in a grove dedicated to the Furies, where he prevailed upon a slave to dispatch him.* Thus died Caius Gracchus, about ten years after his brother Tiberius; and thus by ambitious lives and untimely deaths did the children of Cornelia so distinguish themselves, that to this day she is styled "the mother of the Gracchii."

167. JUGURTHINE WAR.—Micipsa, king of Numidia, an ally of the Romans, had brought up his nephew, Jugurtha, with his own sons, Hiempsal and Adherbal. At his death he divided the kingdom equally among the three boys. Jugurtha murdered Hiempsal, and was preparing to seize Adherbal, when the young prince escaped to Rome,

* The consul had offered its weight in gold for the head of Gracchus. The soldier who found his body cut off his head, carefully abstracted the brains, filled the cavity with lead, and received seventeen lbs. of gold for it.

Questions.—165, 166. What is stated of Scipio the Younger? Give an account of the enterprise Gracchus then undertook. Of his connection with Flaccus. Of his death. How is Cornelia still styled? 167. Who was Micipsa? How was the Jugurthine war commenced? Where was Numidia? (See map No. 4.)

and laid his cause before the senate. Jugurtha, however, by rich bribes, turned aside the sword of justice, so that the successors of those men who would not *look* upon the presents of Pyrrhus, *pocketed* the gold of the wily African, and sent over commissioners to divide Numidia between him and the surviving son of Micipsa. Emboldened in crime, Jugurtha made war upon Adherbal as soon as he was established in his government, took him prisoner, and put him to death. The homicide was summoned to Rome to stand a trial. His gold enabled him to elude his fate, and as he left the city he exclaimed, "O Rome! how readily wouldst thou sell *thyself* couldst thou find a man rich enough to purchase thee."

168. Another act of treachery on the part of Jugurtha engaged the senate in a war with him, which lasted five years. The glory of terminating it fell to Caius Marius,* who fought a battle with the usurper, and took him prisoner. Jugurtha followed in the triumph of Marius, and was afterwards starved to death in a dungeon. Thus ended the Jugurthine war, B. C. 106. POMPEY and CICERO were born the same year.

169. MARIUS AND SYLLA.—B. C. **100.** In the year 90 B. C., the states of Italy, having waited long in vain for the promised title and privileges of Roman citizens, united in an attempt to throw off their allegiance to Rome. This contest was marked by frequent and bloody battles; and during its progress Rome lost 300,000 lives. Marius and Sylla† were both officers in the army, but, while the former daily lost popularity, the latter, by his free and easy manners, was gaining authority and friends. The Social War, as it was called, was finally terminated by concessions on the part of the Romans, which satisfied the allies.

170. MITHRIDATIC WAR.—Mithridates, king of Pontus, was one of the most formidable enemies Rome ever encountered. He was distin-

* Caius Marius was the son of poor parents in Arpi. He was a man of gigantic stature, great strength, and undaunted bravery. He was an enemy of the patricians, and consequently the idol of the people. In his first consulship he defeated Jugurtha; in his second, he enjoyed a triumph for having closed the war in Africa; and in four succeeding consulships distinguished himself by his bravery and cruelty.

† Sylla was the son of a poor patrician, but gifted and ambitious. He took Jugurtha captive, and contended for the honor of terminating the war in Africa. For this Marius became his implacable enemy. Sylla espoused the patrician cause, and opposed the measures of Marius with success.

Questions.—167, 168. Give an account of its progress and end. When did it end? Who were born that year? 169. What disturbances occurred in Italy about that time? Mention some particulars. How did the Social War terminate? 170. What is said of Mithridates? For what was he distinguished? Where was Pontus? (Map No. 3.)

guished in his early youth by his bodily strength and daring spirit; and in riper years by the sagacity of a statesman and the dignity of a monarch. He was also the greatest scholar of his time, being able to converse in twenty-two different languages. The Romans, in their wars with Antiochus and his successors, had overrun a great part of the east, and stationed troops in various parts. Mithridates, as sovereign of Asia, commanded all the Roman legions to leave his dominions; but, before they had time to do so, a dreadful massacre was commenced, in which 80,000 perished. The islands of the Egean, with Athens, and several other cities of Greece, joined the standard of revolt.

171. To avenge the blood of her slaughtered citizens, to humble the power of Mithridates, and to bring back her provinces to their allegiance, now occupied the attention of Rome. Sylla was consul, but, being absent from the city, Marius secured the appointment of commander in Asia. Sylla immediately marched to Rome with his army, crushed the opposite faction, drove Marius into banishment, restored the authority of the senate, and departed with his army for the east.

172. MARIUS.—Marius, at the age of seventy, having been declared a public enemy, escaped from his pursuers in the meanest disguise. Being driven into the marshes, he spent one night up to his chin in a quagmire. The next day he was taken and thrown into a prison. The governor of the place sent a Cambrian slave to dispatch him. As the assassin approached, Marius cried out in a stern voice, "Darest thou kill Caius Marius?" The barbarian threw down his sword, and, rushing out of the dungeon, declared he could not kill him! The governor, thinking this an omen in the unhappy exile's favor, set him at liberty. After many toils and dangers, Marius landed in Africa, and, musing on the instability of earthly grandeur, went and seated himself among the ruins of Carthage.

173. After wandering about for several months, like a wild beast hunted from his thicket, he heard that Cinna, the consul, had overcome the Syllian faction, upon which he sailed for Italy. Retaining the miserable robe which he had worn during his misfortunes, with untrimmed beard and solemn countenance, he went round among the smaller states, and having collected a horde of robbers and semi-barbarians, approached Rome. The defenseless senate sent out embassadors to beg that matters might be accommodated in a peaceable man-

Questions.—170, 171. Give the origin of the Mithridatic war. Give an account of it. In what did it result? 172. What is said of Marius at the age of seventy? Give an account of him until he arrived at Carthage. 173, 174. Give a further account, including of his death. What is said of him by an historian?

ner. Marius seemed willing to grant their request, but said, that having been banished by a public decree, he could not enter the gates till it was revoked. The frightened citizens undertook to authorize his return, but scarcely had they begun to vote when he marched into the city, sword in hand, and massacred without remorse or pity all who had ever been obnoxious to him. His barbarians, infuriated by the sight of blood, rushed on like wolves to the carnage, sparing neither age, sex, nor rank.

174. For five days and nights the slaughter was continued; the streets of Rome were deluged with blood, and the grim monster, enjoying the miseries of his country, gazed with savage delight upon the heads which were ranged in the forum for his special gratification. When his vengeance was thus fully satisfied, he made himself consul for the seventh time, without the formalities of a public assembly. He, however, enjoyed the power he had enslaved his country to gain only seventeen days. Worn out with wars and excesses, his faculties began to fail; and the intelligence that Sylla was returning with a victorious army, filled his mind with inquietude. "He died," says the historian, "with the chagrin of an unfortunate wretch who had not obtained what he wanted."

175. Sylla.—When Sylla passed through Greece, on his way to meet Mithridates, every city except Athens sent tokens of submission. To this place, therefore, the Roman advanced with his troops. His impatience to return led him to push the siege with the greatest vigor. He used a multitude of warlike engines, and when wood failed, the sacred groves of the Academy and Lyceum fell beneath the soldier's ax. To supply his troops with money, he sent for the treasures of Delphi and Olympia, which the Amphictyons, with many tears, surrendered. Poor Athens, who had suffered so much from wars, tyrannies, and seditions, was now seized with her last agonies. Within was famine, without was the sword. The city was finally taken by a night assault. No computation can be made of the number of the slain; but ancient writers tell us that the blood flowed through the gates, and overspread the suburbs. Sylla at length gave orders to stop the carnage, saying, that he "forgave the living for the sake of the dead."

176. In Beotia, Sylla defeated the general of Mithridates, and, having concluded a peace with that renowned king, hastened home to meet again the Marian faction. No sooner had he landed in Italy, than

Questions.—175. What is said of Sylla's march through Greece? Describe the fate of unfortunate Athens. 176. What followed until Sylla entered Rome a conqueror?

the shattered remains of his party flocked to his standard; Crassus and Pompey threw their influence upon his side, while Scipio and young Marius took the field against him. In a great battle that ensued, Marius was entirely defeated. The contest lasted till late at night, and the morning sun arose upon more than 50,000 bodies of victors and vanquished, promiscuously heaped in death. Sylla entered Rome like a conqueror, at the head of his army. Immediately after, he caused 8,000 of those he esteemed his enemies to be shut up in a large house and massacred, while he was addressing the people; and when the senate, amazed at the horrid outcries of the victims, inquired if the city was given up to plunder, the vindictive consul informed them, with an unembarrassed air, that the sounds they heard were only the shrieks of some criminals who were punished by his order.

177. The next day he proscribed forty senators and 1,600 knights; and so, day after day, the work of death went forward; a public list of the doomed being made out, and a reward offered for the heads of those who succeeded for a time in eluding their pursuers. Sylla next depopulated those Italian states which had joined the Marian faction, and parceled out their lands among his veteran troops. The office of dictator, which had not been conferred upon any individual for 120 years, he now assumed without limit as to time; and thus the government of Rome, having passed through the various forms of monarchy, aristocracy, and democracy, seemed settled at last in despotism. Crassus employed himself in buying up the effects of the proscribed; Pompey put away his wife, to marry the dictator's step-daughter; and Julius Cæsar, to evade a similar requisition, exiled himself from the city. Sylla spared his life, but remarked, " there are many Mariuses in Julius Cæsar."

178. How great was the surprise in Rome, when one day the sanguinary dictator appeared before the people, resigned his power, divested himself of his official robes, offered himself for public trial, and, sending away his lictors, continued to walk in the forum unattended and alone. At the approach of evening he retired to his house, the people following him in respectful silence. Of all that great multitude whom he had robbed of relatives and friends, not one was found hardy enough to reproach or accuse him; his act of abdication having, as it were, thrown a vail over the enormity of his crimes. He died not long after, at his country-seat, leaving the following

Questions.—176. Give an account of the massacre of the 8,000. 177. Give a further description of Sylla's path to power. How did Crassus employ himself? What wrong did Pompey commit? What movement did Julius Cæsar make? 178. What event crowned the public life of Sylla? Give the particulars.

inscription for his tomb: "Here lies Sylla, who was never outdone in good offices by a friend, nor in acts of hostility by his enemy."

179. POMPEY'S EXPLOITS.—After the death of Sylla, several years of faction and animosity ensued, till finally the question of "who should be greatest" seemed to settle upon Crassus and Pompey; the former,* celebrated for his vast wealth, which he employed in feasting the multitude at public tables, and buying comforts for the poor; the latter, distinguished by his splendid victories in Spain, by his address in terminating the Servile War,† and by his success in overcoming the Illyrian pirates. The consul Lucullus, the personal friend of Sylla, had been carrying on the war in Asia during eight years. Such was his vigor and ability, that Mithridates, after repeated defeats, was compelled to fly to his son-in-law, Tigranes, king of Armenia. Lucullus pursued him into that country, and gained two victories; but the mutinous disposition of his soldiers embarrassed his efforts, and his enemies at home persuaded the people that he protracted the war on account of the wealth to be gained from it, and he was consequently recalled.‡

180. At this juncture the friends of Pompey proposed a law, "That all the armies of the empire, with the government of all Asia, and the management of the war against Mithridates, should be committed to him alone." The question was warmly discussed, and the motion would have been lost but for the eloquence of Cicero. The law was passed by all the tribes, and Pompey departed for Asia, B. C. 67. When the Roman general arrived at the seat of war, he found that Mithridates had retrieved his losses, and secured the various passes and strongholds of the country. Pompey's first measure was to drive the enemy out of Asia Minor, by garrisoning all the maritime towns from Tyre to Byzantium. He then advanced to attack the camp of

* Crassus had increased a small estate to the value of $7,500,000.

† A company of gladiators broke away from their fencing-school, and, enlisting fugitive slaves, kept all Italy in alarm three years. This was called the "Servile War." Both Crassus and Pompey claimed the glory of terminating it.

‡ The account of the wealth brought home by Lucullus seems almost incredible. He exhibited in his triumph a statue of Mithridates in massy gold; and mules, loaded with ingots, followed his car. He took no part in public affairs after his return, but devoted himself to the adorning of his villas with all the curious works of science and art which he had collected in the east. It was nothing uncommon for him to spend $6,000 on one supper.

Questions.—178. What inscription did he leave for his tomb? 179. Name the exploits of Pompey. Who was his rival? For what was Crassus noted? What is said of Lucullus in connection with the wars in Asia? 180. In what year did Pompey depart for Asia? Give the circumstances preceding his going. Follow him until Mithridates effects his escape after the siege.

Mithridates in Armenia. The Pontian king stood a siege of forty-five days, and then effected a retreat.

181. Pompey overtook him again near the Euphrates. An engagement ensued by night. The Romans were victorious. Mithridates escaped with 800 horse, but no sooner did he reach the open plain, than even this small remnant fled, leaving him with only three attendants. At the castle of Inora the wretched fugitives stopped, and there Mithridates bestowed his treasures upon all who joined him, taking care to furnish each of his friends with a quantity of poison, that they need not fall alive into the hands of the enemy. The unfortunate monarch, hearing that his son-in-law had made alliance with the Romans, directed his flight to Colchis; Pompey pursued him; and the king, finding everywhere the terror of the Roman name, sought shelter among the barbarous Scythians.

182. After two years' war with these savage tribes, without gaining any tidings of his enemy, Pompey turned his face to the south, animated, like Alexander, with the hope of extending his conquests to the ocean which surrounds the world. Having subdued Syria, he entered Judea. Aristobulus, the usurping priest, converted the venerable temple at Jerusalem into a citadel for his soldiers, and resisted the power of the Romans three months: 12,000 Jews were slain, and the place was finally taken. Pompey entered the sanctuary with mingled curiosity and reverence; he even ventured into the Holy of Holies, and gazed upon those sacred mysteries which none but the high-priests were ever permitted to behold. Respecting, however, the feelings of the Jews, he left the holy things unprofaned; and having restored Hyrcanius to the priesthood, pursued his way to Arabia Petræa. In the course of his march he had received the submission of twelve kings.

183. B. C. 63.—CATILINE'S CONSPIRACY.—While Pompey was thus extending the empire of Rome over all the eastern world, the commonwealth had been brought to the brink of ruin by the machinations of a few dissolute noblemen, who, having "wasted their fortunes with riotous living," were determined to revolutionize the government, seize the lucrative offices, and reign together, each a Sylla. At the head of the conspiracy was Lucius Catiline, a patrician of the most fascinating manners, the most daring courage, and the most diabolical

Questions.—181. Give an account of the defeat and escape of Mithridates. Of his escape to the Scythians. 182. With what ambition was Pompey animated? What success did he have in Syria? What in Judea? How many kings had submitted to him? 183. How, meanwhile, had Rome been brought to the brink of ruin? Who was at the head of the conspiracy?

cruelty. In the bloody scenes of his youth he took an active part; having been quæstor to Sylla, to please whom he murdered his own brother. Associated with him were many persons of rank and fortune. Lentulus and Cethegus, members of distinguished families; the two Syllas, nephews of the dictator; and others, of equal celebrity, were leaders of the plot.

184. It was proposed to enlist the veterans of Sylla, and the fragments of his party about Italy; to kill the whole senate, and set the city on fire in a hundred places at once; while Catiline, coming down from Etruria with his army, should subdue the minor towns, and take military possession of Italy. As a preparatory measure, Cicero, the consul, was to be assassinated in his bed. Scarcely, however, was this plan of action settled by the conspirators, when every particular was related to Cicero by a woman who had persuaded her lover to reveal the secret. The consul immediately convened the senate, and warned them of the impending danger. Catiline also took his accustomed seat with that august body, and, asserting his innocence, offered securities for his good behavior.

185. Cicero, however, assailed him with a torrent of invective; and the guilty Catiline, after vainly endeavoring to counteract the effect of the orator's eloquence, rushed out of the senate-house, threatening destruction to all that opposed him. He left the city that night to bring his army to the gates of Rome. Cicero secured the other conspirators, and, having obtained sentence against them, caused them to be strangled in prison. Catiline, hearing that his accomplices were no more, attempted to fly, but, finding that the passes were all secured, he turned like a lion at bay upon his pursuers. A fierce battle was fought in Etruria. Catiline died sword in hand, and most of his followers imitated his example. The praises of Cicero were now the theme of every panegyrist, and, by the advice of Cato, he was styled the "Father of his Country."

186. Pompey's Triumph.—To return to Pompey. Scarcely had he pitched his camp in Petræa, when he received the following letter from Asia Minor: "Mithridates is dead. He killed himself upon the revolt of his son, Pharnaces. Pharnaces has seized all that belonged to his father, which he declares he has done for himself and

---

Questions.—183. What is said of the deeds of his youth? Who were associated with Catiline in the conspiracy? 184. In what way was it proposed to carry out the conspiracy? What proposition is mentioned as a preparatory measure? How was the plot discovered? What steps were immediately taken? What course did Catiline take? 185. Give an account of the overthrow of the conspiracy. By what title was Cicero afterward known? 186. What put an end to the war in Asia?

the Romans."* The campaign being thus terminated, the soldiers gave loose to their joy, and Pompey made arrangements for settling immediately the affairs of Asia, and returning home with the laurels of a conqueror.

187. Rome had scarcely recovered from the distress into which the conspiracy of Catiline had thrown her, when she was again agitated by the intelligence that Pompey, like Sylla, was returning at the head of his victorious legions. The alarm of the senate was, however, changed to admiration when the conqueror of Mithridates arrived at Brundusium, and, disbanding his army, journeyed to Rome in the humble garb of a private individual. The whole city met him with acclamations; a triumph was immediately decreed, and never had Rome witnessed such grandeur and magnificence as were then displayed. Captive princes walked in his train; treasures and trophies adorned his chariot; and a sum of money equal to $18,000,000 was deposited in the treasury of the commonwealth.

188. He soon after erected a temple to Minerva, with an inscription containing a summary of his deeds. He said that "he had finished a war of thirty years; had vanquished, slain, and taken 2,183,000 men; sunk or taken 846 ships; reduced 1,538 towns and fortresses, and subdued all the countries between Lake Mœris and the Red Sea." He had before extended his conquests in Africa to the Great Sea, and stretched the Roman dominions in Spain to the Atlantic; his first triumph had been for Africa, his second for Europe, and now his third was for Asia; so that when he threw aside his armor, and clothed himself in the unostentatious robe of a Roman citizen, he deserved, both for his achievements and his moderation, the title of POMPEY THE GREAT.

189. FIRST TRIUMVIRATE.—B. C. 59. Pompey was the most powerful man in Rome, and the idol of the army. Crassus was the richest man in the state, and a favorite of the senate. Both were candidates

* After Pompey's departure, Mithridates returned to Pontus, and made himself master of several places; Pharnaces, however, rebelled against him, in favor of the Romans. The unhappy king sent to his son, offering to resign the crown if he would aid him in making his escape. The unnatural son bade the slave to tell his father that death was now all that remained for him. Thus cut off from every hope, the wretched monarch assembled his wives, and, presenting a cup of poison, bade them choose between death and captivity. Together they drank the fatal draught, and together they died in the palace of the Pontian kings.

Questions.—187. What intelligence distressed the Romans? How was the distress changed to admiration? Give an account of Pompey's reception. 188. What temple is spoken of? What inscription? What deeds were enumerated? What further is stated of Pompey? 189. Who then was the most powerful man in Rome? Who the richest? In what year was the first triumvirate established?

for the highest offices of the republic. At this juncture, when the suffrages of the Roman people seemed vibrating between the two strong attractions of *gold* and *glory*, Julius Cæsar* returned from his prætorship in Spain. It was the time for electing consuls, and, perceiving that if he gained the influence of one of these great men, he made the other his enemy of course, he set about reconciling them. Having procured an interview between the rivals, he showed them the benefit of a union of interests, and finally engaged them in a combination, by which it was agreed that *nothing should be done in the commonwealth without their mutual concurrence and approbation.* This was called the First Triumvirate.†

190. To cement this union, Cæsar gave his daughter Julia in marriage to Pompey, though she had long been affianced to Marcus Brutus; and both Crassus and Pompey sustained the nomination of Cæsar for the consulship. He was successful, and then they ratified all his acts. The triumvirate next agreed to share the world between them. Pompey chose Spain and Italy; for, being already at the pinnacle of military fame, he wished to remain in Rome. Crassus selected Syria and the East, because those provinces generally enriched their governors; and to Cæsar were left the unconquered territories of the Gallic tribes; but as these promised little more than a harvest of danger, his command was granted for five years.

191. The obedient senate and the misguided people sanctioned all these arrangements, and Cæsar soon after marched to the north with six legions. During the summer, he pushed his conquests among the barbarous tribes inhabiting Gaul, Britain, and Germany; and every winter he returned to Cisalpine Gaul, and passed the season very agreeably with friends who came from Rome to see him. At one time there were in his camp 120 lictors waiting upon their masters, and 200 senators honoring him with their assiduities. At the end of five years Crassus and Pompey visited him, and agreed to get his

* This extraordinary man belonged to one of the most ancient and honorable families in Rome. His aunt, Julia, was the wife of Marius, and he himself married the daughter of Cinna. He was of a fair complexion, and delicate constitution; but ambition and early exposure enabled him to endure great fatigue. Such was his capacity for business, that he could dictate four letters at the same time.

† Soon after the triumvirate was formed, Cicero was driven into exile for having put Catiline's accomplices to death, and Cato was sent on an expedition to Cyprus.

Questions.—189. What claims had the rival candidates for the suffrages of the people? Who acted as conciliator? What combination was formed? 190. By what acts was the union cemented? What division of the world did the three aspirants make? Why was Cæsar's portion the least enviable? What object had Crassus in going east? Why did Pompey choose Spain and Italy? 191. What did the senate and people do? What conquests did Cæsar make? How did he secure his re-election?

command continued five years longer, while he sent money to Rome to buy votes for their election to the consulship.

192. B. C. 54. This year Crassus departed for the east. The people, who understood that he intended to make war upon their allies, the Parthians, were very much displeased; and when he went out of the city one of the tribunes devoted him, and all who should follow him, to the infernal gods. Undismayed, however, by this dreadful denunciation, Crassus continued his course, and, landing in Asia Minor, soon overran all Mesopotamia. He plundered the temple at Jerusalem, and took up his winter quarters in Syria. The next spring he set out for Parthia, but, trusting an Arabian chief for guide, his forces were led over dry and sandy plains, where neither stream, nor plant, nor tree appeared; and finally, surrounded by an active enemy in the midst of a hostile country, they all perished except Caius Cassius, and a band of 500 horse. The head and right hand of Crassus were cut off, and sent to the Parthian king.

193. Cæsar extended the power of Rome far to the north. It would be tedious to enumerate all his exploits. Suffice it to say, that "in less than ten years he took 800 cities, conquered 300 nations, fought 1,000 battles, killed 1,000,000 of men, took as many more prisoners, crossed over to Britain twice, and subdued all the tribes from the Mediterranean Sea to the German Ocean." The laurels of Miltiades would not allow Themistocles to sleep; and the praises of Cæsar had a similar effect upon Pompey. By the death of Crassus they were left the sole competitors for supreme authority; and the decease of Julia broke the tender tie which had bound them together. Pompey effected the recall of Cicero, gained the favor of the stern Cato, and, seeming to feel a deep anxiety for the welfare of the commonwealth, proposed that Cæsar should be required to disband his army.

194. Cæsar's friends urged that the republic had more to fear from the unlimited authority of *one*, than from the conflicting interests of *two*, and therefore insisted that the rivals should both *resign*, or both *retain* their power; but Pompey, who was enjoying the dignity of sole consul, would not agree to this proposition. The senate, who were in Pompey's interest, passed a decree requiring Cæsar to lay down his military power within a given time, under penalty of being declared an enemy to his country. *Antony and Cassius vetoed the bill.* The

Questions.—192. When did Crassus depart for the east? Give an account of his exploits and death. 193. What was Cæsar doing in Gaul at that time? Name some of his exploits. How was the triple chain broken? What followed? 194. What did Cæsar's friends urge upon him? Why would not Pompey consent? What decree did the senate pass? Why was the decree not carried out?

senate then had recourse to their highest prerogative, and directed the consuls "to provide for the safety of the commonwealth." Pompey was appointed commander-in-chief of the armies of the republic. Antony and Cassius, thinking their lives in danger, fled to the camp of Cæsar.

195. CÆSAR PASSES THE RUBICON.—That general, perceiving that the time had come to decide whether he should submit to Pompey or Pompey to him, immediately broke up his camp in Cisalpine Gaul and marched toward Rome. He paused upon the banks of the Rubicon,* as if impressed with terror at the greatness of his enterprise. "If I pass this river," said he, "what miseries shall I bring upon my *country!* but if I now stop short, *I* am undone." At last, with an air of stern resolve, he plunged into the water, exclaiming, "The die is cast!" and was promptly followed by his soldiers. "On his march," says Plutarch, "as if war had opened wide its gates, not *individuals* were seen, as on other occasions, wandering about Italy, but whole *cities*, broken up and seeking refuge by flight."

196. Most of the tumultuous tide flowed toward Rome; and that city was so filled with agitation and alarm, that the consuls were unable to discharge the solemn trust of their office. Pompey, who had all along assured the senate that "he could raise an army with the stamp of the foot," was now overwhelmed by censures from every side. He could gain no certain intelligence of Cæsar's movements, but was continually embarrassed by terrifying reports. After vacillating some time between hopes and fears, the conqueror of Mithridates left Rome for Capua, where two legions, formerly in Cæsar's service, were stationed. The greater part of the senate and his own private friends and dependents accompanied him; and all ranks of people followed him some distance, with outcries and good wishes.

197. Cæsar, knowing that Rome would fall to the conqueror, did not take that city in his way, but pursued Pompey to Capua. Pompey retired to Brundusium, and embarked for Greece. Cæsar, being

* This was a little river which the Romans had ever considered the sacred boundary of their domestic empire. The senate had caused to be engraven on stone, and set up by the side of the stream, an edict, devoting to the infernal gods, and branding with the crime of sacrilege and parricide, any person who should presume to pass the Rubicon with an army, a legion, or even a single cohort.

Questions.—194. What then followed? What appointment was given to Pompey? What course did Antony and Cassius then take? 195. What, finally, did Cæsar perceive? How is the Rubicon situated? (Map No. 4.) What is stated in the note about the Rubicon? How did Cæsar reason about crossing the Rubicon? Give the statement made by Plutarch. 196. What was the condition of Rome at that time? Give an account of Pompey's movements. 197. Give a further account of his movements. Where was Capua? (Map No. 4.)

unable to follow him for want of shipping, returned to Rome, with the glory of having reduced Italy in sixty days without spilling a drop of blood. He treated all who surrendered with the greatest kindness, telling them that he came not to destroy the liberties of his country, but to restore them.

198. Cæsar goes to Spain.—Securing the treasures of Rome, he now determined to deprive Pompey of the assistance he expected from Spain. Accordingly, having refreshed his men, he led them once more a long and fatiguing march across the Alps, through dense forests and over rapid rivers, into Spain; and when we consider that every soldier carried 60 lbs. weight of armor and ten days' provision, we must admire the address of a man who could, under such circumstances, retain the allegiance of his army. Cæsar's success equaled his expectations. In forty days he subdued all Spain, and dismissed his vanquished adversaries the richer and the happier for having been conquered. When the victor arrived at Rome he was received with demonstrations of joy, and created dictator and consul.

199. Dyrrachium.—While Cæsar was thus employed, Pompey was equally active in Greece. All the monarchs of the east declared in his favor; crowds came from Italy to join his army; and Cicero and Cato, the known advocates of freedom, secured for his cause the sanction of the good throughout the world. Cæsar, resolving to terminate the conflict as soon as possible, after much difficulty and danger, succeeded in transporting his troops to Epirus. A battle was fought at Dyrrachium, in which Pompey had the advantage; but, neglecting to make his success complete by seizing the camp, Cæsar remarked, "This day the victory had been the enemy's had their general known how to conquer."

200. The scarcity of provisions soon after compelled Cæsar to remove to Thessaly. Pompey's soldiers immediately cried out with one voice, "Cæsar is fled." Some called upon their general to pursue; others advocated his return to Italy; others sent their servants to Rome to hire houses near the forum; and not a few went over to Lesbos to congratulate Cornelia, the wife of Pompey, on the conclusion of the war. Pompey, however, thought it best to pursue Cæsar, and wear him out with famine; but when he overtook his rival upon the plains of Pharsalia he suffered himself to be overruled, and orders were consequently given to prepare for battle.

Questions.—197. What is said of Cæsar upon his return to Rome? 198. In what way did he "head off" Pompey? What honors did he receive in Rome? 199. How was Pompey meanwhile employed? Give an account of his successful preparations. Of the battle of Dyrrachium. Where was Dyrrachium? (Map No. 2.) 200. What step was Cæsar compelled to make? What then did the soldiers of Pompey do? What did Pompey think it best to do? Where did he overtake Cæsar? What change of purpose was then made?

201. Battle of Pharsalia.—B. C. 48. Cæsar, who had in vain used every art to bring on an engagement, was preparing early in the morning to break up his camp, when his scouts brought intelligence that the enemy were handling arms, as if getting ready for an attack. Upon this news Cæsar joyfully exclaimed, "The long-wished-for day is come when we shall fight with men, and not with famine." The red mantle was immediately displayed before his pavilion, and the soldiers, with the greatest alacrity, harnessed for the battle. Cæsar, to obviate his want of cavalry, had trained six cohorts to fight between the files of horsemen, not by discharging their javelins, according to the usual custom, but by aiming directly at the visages of the enemy; "For those fair young dancers," said he, "will fly to save their handsome faces." The plain of Pharsalia was now covered with men, and horses, and arms; and the two generals walked from rank to rank, animating their soldiers with prospects of victory.

202. It was a fearful sight to see the same arms on both sides, troops marshaled in the same manner, the same standards, the same fierce Roman countenances; in short, the flower and strength of the same city turned upon itself. On one side, Pompey prepared to do battle against the man whom he had raised to power; on the other, Cæsar stood ready to tear the laurel from the brow of the husband whom his departed darling Julia had loved better than life. The word on Pompey's side was "Hercules the Invincible;" that on Cæsar's, "Venus the Victorious." Cæsar's soldiers rushed on with their usual impetuosity, but, perceiving the enemy standing motionless, they stopped short in the midst of their career. A terrible pause ensued, in which both sides, being near enough to recognize the countenances of their assailants, continued to gaze upon each other with dreadful serenity; at length Cæsar's men, having taken breath, ran furiously forward, first discharging their javelins, and then drawing their swords. Pompey's infantry sustained the attack with great resolution, and his cavalry charging at the same time, Cæsar's men began to give ground.

203. At this moment Cæsar's six cohorts advanced, and the cavalry, just spurring on to victory, received an immediate check. The unusual method of fighting pursued by the cohorts, their aiming at the faces of the enemy, and the horrible disfiguring wounds they made, stopped the career of the "handsome dancers," and caused them to fly in great disorder. The cohorts then attacked the infantry in flank,

---

Questions.—201. When was the battle of Pharsalia fought? Give an account of the manner in which it was brought about. 202, 203. Give an account of the battle. To what was Cæsar indebted for victory? Where was Pharsalia? (See Map No. 2.)

and fresh troops coming up in front, that body also began to waver, upon which Cæsar called out, "Pursue the strangers, but spare the Romans." The fight had continued from break of day till noon; the soldiers were faint and weary; but Cæsar, thinking his victory not complete, summoned his men from the pursuit of the fugitives to storm the camp.

204. POMPEY'S FLIGHT.—As for Pompey, no sooner had he seen the fate of his cavalry than he quitted the ranks like one distracted, and, without considering that he was Pompey the Great, or making any effort to rally his men, retired, step by step, to his tent, where he sat down without saying a word. He was aroused by intelligence that the enemy had commenced the work of plunder. "What," cried he, "into my very camp, too?" No time was to be lost. Silencing his vain regrets, and hastily exchanging his armor for a disguise more suitable to his present circumstances, he took his solitary way through the delicious vale of Tempe, wrapped up in such thoughts as a man might be supposed to have who had been accustomed for thirty-four years to conquer, and now felt for the first time the mortification of defeat; as one who had lately seen himself guarded by fleets and armies, and now was so meanly attired that his enemies passed him by as of no consequence. He threw himself upon the ground, took his evening draught from the river Peneus, and passed the night in the hut of a poor fisherman.

205. The next morning he embarked in a small ship and sailed for Lesbos, where Cornelia was waiting till he should come and take her in triumph to Rome. When a messenger told Cornelia that her husband had arrived with only one ship, and that not his own, she ran down to the shore with tears and lamentations, and fell fainting into his arms. A few friends speedily assembled, and embarked with the fugitive pair for Asia Minor. They coasted along for several days, uncertain where to land, and fearing lest every ally should prove an enemy; finally, Pompey, who had been a benefactor to Ptolemy Auletes, decided on going to Egypt. The vessel came to anchor off the coast, while Pompey sent a message to the young king, imploring protection. The corrupt ministers of the Egyptian court, thinking it equally unsafe to receive or refuse him, proposed that he should be invited on shore and slain.

206. END OF POMPEY THE GREAT.—In pursuance of this treacher-

Questions.—204. How did Pompey behave directly after the battle? How, after the enemy had commenced plundering his camp? Where did he pass the night? 205. For what place did he sail next morning? Where was the island of Lesbos? (See Map No. 2.) Give an account of his flight to the time of his reaching Egypt.

ous design, Septimius, formerly a centurion in Pompey's army, and Achillas, master of the Egyptian horse, embarked in a small galley and rowed off toward the ship. The meanness of the preparations excited the suspicions of the Romans; but Achillas coming up, welcomed Pompey to Egypt with great cordiality, and apologized for his little boat, by saying that the shallows prevented the sailing of a larger one. After tenderly embracing Cornelia, Pompey stepped into the galley with only two attendants. The most profound silence reigned, till Pompey, recollecting the face of Septimius, remarked, "Methinks, friend, you and I were once fellow-soldiers together." Septimius nodded his head without saying a word.

207. In this manner they neared the shore; and Cornelia, who had never lost sight of the bark and its precious freight, began to breathe more freely when she saw the people crowding down to the beach, as if anxious to welcome her husband's arrival; but the instant Pompey rose Septimius stabbed him in his back, and Achillas immediately seconded the blow. At this horrid sight, Cornelia shrieked so loud as to be heard from the shore; but the danger she herself was in did not allow the mariners time to look on; and, a favorable wind springing up, they escaped the pursuit of the Egyptian galleys. Pompey's murderers, having cut off his head, caused it to be embalmed as a present for Cæsar; his body was thrown naked on the strand, a spectacle for the idle or curious; his faithful freedman, however, kept near it, and, when the crowd had dispersed, washed it in the sea. Then, gathering the wrecks of a fishing-boat, he composed a pile and prepared to burn it.

208. While thus piously employed he was joined by an old Roman soldier, who begged for "the last sad comfort of assisting at the funeral of the bravest general Rome ever produced." Together they stood on that inhospitable shore, watching the flame till it died away; and then, collecting the ashes of their beloved master, scraped with their hands a little mound of earth over them, where afterward this inscription was placed: "He whose merits deserve a temple can now scarce find a tomb." Such was the end and such the funeral of POMPEY THE GREAT—a man who preserved a spotless character in the midst of associates plunged in rapine and massacre; whose virtues were obscured by the faults of the triumvirate, but whose melancholy and undeserved fate converts all censure of his weaknesses into compassion for his misfortunes.

Questions.—206, 207, 208. Of his inglorious death. What is said of Cornelia? Of the disposition made of Pompey's body? Where did the scene take place?

209. Cæsar again.—Cæsar gave liberty to the Thessalians, in gratitude for the victory at Pharsalia, and then pursued Pompey to Egypt. He landed at Alexandria with a select body of troops, and, soon after, the young king's preceptors brought him the head and ring of Pompey. He turned away with horror from the ghastly countenance of his rival, but he took his signet and wept over it. On the spot where his humble grave had been made he ordered a magnificent tomb to be erected, and treated every friend of Pompey with peculiar kindness. The attempts of Cæsar to settle the succession to the throne of Egypt in favor of Cleopatra involved him in a difficult and dangerous war with the Egyptians. He first suffered from an attack in the palace; next, his enemies stopped the aqueducts which supplied him with water; then he was forced to burn his own ships to prevent their being taken; and again he was near losing his life in a sea-fight, when, leaping into the water, he swam from one vessel to another, holding his Commentaries in one hand and his coat of mail in his teeth. A re-enforcement arriving not long after, and Ptolemy being drowned, Cæsar was enabled to establish Cleopatra upon the throne.

210. The Egyptians submitted peaceably to her dominion, and Cæsar himself was completely captivated by her charms. Week after week, and month after month, he lingered in Alexandria, till the brave veterans who had followed his fortunes boldly rebuked his conduct, and refused to accompany him in his excursions with the Egyptian queen. From this inglorious ease Cæsar was aroused by intelligence that Pharnaces, son of Mithridates, had seized upon Armenia and Colchis. He immediately marched against the rebel, and reduced him with such ease, that he wrote to Rome a letter containing only three words, "*Veni, vidi, vici*" (I came, I saw, I conquered). Having settled affairs in this part of the empire, gathered the revenues, and bestowed provinces upon his followers, Cæsar returned to Italy. During his absence he had been created consul for five years, dictator for one year, and tribune for life.

211. End of Cato.—Pompey's party had, meantime, rallied in Africa, under Scipio, Cato, and Juba (king of Mauritania). Scarcely, therefore, had Cæsar laid aside his armor, when he was forced again to buckle it on and embark for Africa. In the great battle of Thapsus he totally defeated his antagonists. Juba and his general killed

Questions.—209. How did Cæsar treat the Thessalians? How did he act with reference to the head and friends of Pompey? How did he involve himself in a war with Egypt? How did he establish Cleopatra upon the throne of Egypt? 210. What influence did Cleopatra exert upon Cæsar? Upon what occasion did Cæsar write his celebrated laconic letter? Give the words of that letter, with their meaning. In what direction did Cæsar next go? 211. What account can you give of the battle of Thapsus? What became of Juba?

each other in despair; Scipio was drowned in an attempt to escape by sea; so that of all the leaders of that unfortunate party, Cato alone survived. After the battle of Pharsalia this extraordinary man had led the wretched remnants of Pompey's army through burning deserts, infested by fiery serpents, to the city of Utica, where he formed the principal persons into a senate, and established a government according to his ideas of liberty.

212. This city he attempted to defend against the whole force of Cæsar, but, finding that the inhabitants were intimidated by the greatness of the undertaking, he resolved no longer to force them to be free. Having, accordingly, made arrangements for some of his friends to save themselves by sea, and directed others to rely upon Cæsar's clemency, he retired to his room, observing, "that as to himself, he was at last victorious." He read in Plato's Dialogue concerning the soul till past midnight, when he fell into a profound sleep. Upon awaking, and learning that his friends had embarked, he ordered his attendants to leave the room, and, drawing his sword, gave himself a mortal wound. As he fell upon the bed, he overturned a stand upon which he had been drawing some geometrical figures; his family, hearing the noise, rushed in, and found him in the agonies of death. "Cato," said Cæsar, when he heard of it, "I envy thee thy death."

213. Cæsar Dictator.—The war in Africa being thus terminated, Cæsar returned to Rome. He had conquered more countries than any of his predecessors, and his triumph was proportionably splendid. It lasted four days. The first was for Gaul; the second, for Egypt; the third, for Asia; and the fourth, for the conquest over Juba in Africa. His veteran soldiers, who had followed him from the frozen shores of the Baltic to the burning sands of Africa; who had shared his toils and dangers 13 years, now, all scarred with wounds, received their honorable discharge, and accompanied him, crowned with laurel, to the capitol. To every soldier he gave a sum equal to $700; double that sum to a centurion; and four times as much to the superior officers. To every citizen he gave ten bushels of corn, ten pounds of oil, and about $5 in money. He feasted the people at 20,000 tables, and treated them to such games and shows of gladiators as drew immense crowds into the city.

214. The Romans, charmed with his munificence, seemed eager to find new methods of doing homage to their benefactor. He was

Questions.—211. Of Scipio? Where was Thapsus? (See Map No. 1.) What had Cato accomplished since the battle of Pharsalia? 212. Give the particulars preceding the death of Cato. Also, of his death. 213. The war in Africa being ended, what did Cæsar then do? How did he reward his soldiers? What did he give to each citizen? What else did he do?

created Magister Morum;* he received the titles of Emperor, and Father of his country; his person was declared sacred, and his statue was placed by the side of that of Jupiter in the capitol. While matters were going on thus prosperously at home, the sons of Pompey again renewed the war in Spain. It took Cæsar nine months to quell this revolt, and his danger was so great in one battle, that he observed, "he had often fought for *victory*, but this was the first time he ever fought for *life*." One of the sons of Pompey was slain; the other collected a fleet, and made his home upon the sea.†

215. Cæsar, by this last blow, subdued all his avowed enemies. He returned to Rome, to beautify and adorn it with all the works which art could furnish, and all the treasures which different climes could bestow. Like Alexander, he conceived the project of consolidating all governments into one great empire. It was his intention to visit Parthia, avenge the death of Crassus, pass through Hyrcania, enter Scythia along the banks of the Caspian, cut his way through the untrodden forests of Germany into Gaul, and so return to Italy. The senate, with an adulation that marked the degeneracy of the times, continued to load him with fresh honors. They called the month *Quintilis* "July," after his name; they stamped money with his image;‡ they instituted sacrifices on his birthday, and talked of enrolling him among the gods.

216. One title, and one only, they denied him, and this title, above all others, Cæsar coveted. It was KING. The crimes which the conduct of the Tarquinii had attached to that name, the hatred of it which had consequently been cherished in every Roman breast, made it more odious than all other names beside. Old men who had hailed Sylla *perpetual dictator* with joy; veterans who had saluted Pompey *imperator*, with enthusiastic acclamations; and young men who called Cæsar *emperor*, *father*, *god*, were equally shocked with the thought of his being KING.

217. END OF CÆSAR.—Antony, at one of the public festivals, offered Cæsar a diadem; the multitude looked on in dejected silence; but when Cæsar refused the bauble, they rent the air with shouts. A few

* Master of the morals of the people.

† Antony had taken possession of Pompey's house in Rome.

‡ See Mark xii. 13—17.

Questions.—214. What follies did the Romans commit in doing homage to their benefactor? What happened in Spain? What became of Pompey's sons? 215. After this victory, what was the pursuit of Cæsar? What ambitious views were burning in his heart? Of what adulation were the Roman senate guilty? 216. What is said of Cæsar in connection with the title of king? 217. How did Cæsar receive the offer of a diadem?

days after, Cæsar's statues were seen adorned with crowns. Two of the tribunes went and tore them off, and the people applauded the deed, styling the independent magistrates Brutuses; but Cæsar called them *brutes*, and deposed them from their offices. These, and similar acts, gave rise to a conspiracy, of which Caius Cassius was the head. Marcus Brutus, the son-in-law of Cato, and about sixty senators, were engaged in the plot. Brutus was descended from that Brutus who first gave liberty to Rome. He fought on Pompey's side in the battle of Pharsalia, but Cæsar pardoned him, and loaded him with favors.

218. It was agreed to carry the plot into execution on the *ides of March*, a day on which Cæsar's friends proposed to invest him with the title of *king of all the conquered countries*, while he should still be styled dictator in Italy. The augurs had warned him to beware of the ides of March; and as his wife, the night before, dreamed he was assassinated in her arms, Cæsar had determined not to go to the senate-house that day. One of the conspirators, however, came in, and, assuring him that the senate were waiting, prevailed upon him to change his resolution. As he went along, a Greek philosopher handed him a paper containing the particulars of the plot, but Cæsar gave it to his secretary without reading. As he entered the senate-house, he met the augur: "Well, Spurina," said he, "the 'ides of March' are come."—"Yes," replied the augur, "but not gone."

219. No sooner had the dictator taken his seat, than the conspirators crowded around him; and one, on pretense of presenting a petition, knelt down and took hold of the bottom of his robe. Upon this signal Casca stabbed him in the shoulder. Cæsar instantly turned, and wounded the traitor with his stylus. All the conspirators now drew their swords, and surrounded him in such a manner, that whichever way he turned he saw nothing but steel gleaming in his face, and met nothing but wounds. Still he defended himself, pushing back one enemy, throwing down a second, and wounding a third, till Brutus, coming up, thrust his dagger into his thigh. As if heart-broken with the cruel wound, the dying Cæsar exclaimed, "*et tu Brute*," (and *thou*, too, Brutus); and, disposing his robe so as to fall with decency, sank down at the foot of Pompey's statue, the base of which was all dyed with his blood.

220. Measures of the Conspirators.—There the mangled body lay, while Brutus, raising his gory dagger, called on Cicero to rejoice in his country's liberty, and, ascending the tribunal, began to harangue

---

Questions.—217, 218, 219. What conspiracy followed soon after? Describe the tragedy in the senate-house. 220. What was the course of Brutus? Of Antony?

the senators; they all fled, however, in such haste and dismay, that their lives were endangered in the throng. Brutus and the rest of the conspirators marched to the capitol, and garrisoned the place with a band of gladiators. Next day Brutus made a speech to the people, and congratulated them upon their freedom; while Antony and Lepidus, taking possession of the forum, convened the senate, to decide whether Cæsar had been a lawful magistrate or a tyrannical usurper. To stop commotions, to save confiscations and executions, this august body *approved all the acts of Cæsar*, and yet *granted a general pardon to his murderers.*

221. Antony, however, being determined to ride into power on the waves of popular commotion, brought out the body of Cæsar for burial; and having read the dictator's will, in which every citizen was munificently remembered, he so excited the minds of the people, that they tore up the benches, and burned the body in the forum. Then snatching flaming brands from the pile, they ran to set fire to the houses of the conspirators, who fled from the city. The dead Cæsar was proclaimed a god, divine honors were paid to his memory, and an altar was erected on the spot where his body was burned. While Antony was thus clothing himself with popular favor, the individual before whose genius "the star of his destiny turned pale" appeared in Rome. This was Octavius Cæsar, grand-nephew of the late dictator. He had been in Athens at school, but, hearing of his uncle's death, hastened over to Italy to claim his inheritance, and bestow legacies upon his friends. Antony, who was using this money to forward his own plans, was little pleased to be called to an account; and when the senate set up the young Octavius for his rival, his rage knew no bounds.

222. Cicero joined the party of Octavius; and the senate passed a decree that Antony should resign his government of Cisalpine Gaul, and await their pleasure upon the banks of the Rubicon. Antony indignantly refused to obey. The senate declared him an enemy to Rome, and sent Octavius against him. A battle was fought, in which Antony was entirely defeated, and compelled to fly to Lepidus, in Farther Gaul. This victory made Octavius too powerful. The senate refused him a triumph and the consulship. Perceiving that it was their intention to play him off against Antony, Octavius signified to that general and Lepidus his desire of an accommodation. The place

Questions.—221, 222. What further is said of Antony's course? Who was Octavius? What was his business in Rome? What troubles portended? What battle was fought? Why did the senate refuse Octavius a triumph and the consulship? What course did Octavius then decide upon? Where is the town of Bologna? (See modern map.)

appointed for the meeting was a little island in the Rhine, not far from the present town of Bologna. They met as friends, and seated themselves in that isolated spot to settle a plan of operations which should give to them sovereign power, and enable them to triumph over their enemies.

223. Second Triumvirate.—B. C. 43. During the fatal three days which the conference lasted, a *Second* Triumvirate was formed by Lepidus, Antony, and Octavius; and there, with the world spread before them as a map, they divided kingdoms, deposed governors, and proscribed their fellow-citizens, with the utmost composure. Antony was to have Gaul; Lepidus, Spain; and Octavius, Africa and the islands of the Mediterranean. Italy and the eastern provinces were to remain in common till the conspirators were subdued. The last article of this agreement made Rome weep tears of blood. Each one presented a list of his enemies for proscription. Lepidus gave up his brother; Antony, his uncle; and Octavius consented to sacrifice the immortal Cicero to the vengeance of Antony; besides which 200 senators and 2,000 knights were doomed to death. That was a dreadful day for Rome, when the triumvirs, strong in their union, and strong in the allegiance of the army, sent forth their assassins to seal with the blood of her citizens the horrid compact made in the solitude of a desert island in Gaul. Nothing but cries and lamentations were to be heard within the walls, scarce a house escaping without a murder.

224. Cicero evaded his pursuers for some time, and put off to sea, but soon landed again, declaring that "he would die in the country he had so often saved." The assassins of Antony found him, cut off his head and right hand, and placed them over that rostrum where he had so often declaimed upon the rights and privileges of Roman citizens. Thus the proscription went on; many escaped to Macedonia, where Brutus and Cassius were raising an army to restore the ancient liberties of the republic; and some fled to Sextus Pompey, who covered the Mediterranean with his ships. At last the vengeance of the triumviri seemed fully satisfied, and the executions being at an end, Octavius and Antony marched with their army to oppose the conspirators, leaving Lepidus to manage affairs in their absence.

225. Battle of Philippi.—B. C. 43. Brutus and Cassius had, meantime, persuaded the Roman students in Athens to arm in the

---

Questions.—222. What is said of the meeting? 223, 224. By what means were Antony and Octavius made friends? What object had they in common with each other? Who constituted the second triumvirate? Give an account of their proceedings. Of their proscriptions, &c. 225. In what year did the battle of Philippi take place? Where was Philippi? (See Map No. 2.) Who commanded the Roman youth?

cause of freedom ; auxiliaries also flocked to them from Macedonia and Asia Minor, so that their army numbered twelve legions, and they could count upon supplies for protracting the war to any length of time. Antony and Octavius encountered them at Philippi. The first engagement was indecisive. Brutus put the troops of Octavius to flight, but Cassius was defeated and slain. Twenty days after, Brutus was compelled again to give battle. His spirits were very much depressed, and a sad foreboding of his fate diminished his natural ardor.* He, however, led forward his troops and attacked the enemy with great fury. As before, he was successful where he commanded in person, but the troops of Cassius, remembering their former defeat, fled before the impetuous charge of Antony, and victory soon declared in favor of the triumvirs.

226. Brutus, surrounded by his most valiant officers, fought for a long time with amazing valor, and not till the son of Cato and the brother of Cassius had fallen by his side could he be persuaded to leave the field. With much difficulty he escaped from his pursuers, and concealed himself under the shadow of a bending rock. A few friends gathered round, with whom he conversed for a time, upon the adversity which virtue suffers at the hand of fortune. He then retired to a little distance, and having persuaded Strato, his master in oratory, to hold his sword, threw himself upon it and expired.† Antony treated the body of Brutus with great respect, threw his own robe over it, and caused it to receive funeral honors.

227. Dissolution of the Triumvirate.—After the victories at Philippi, Antony passed through Greece and Asia Minor, settling the revenues of the provinces, and calling governors to account with the air of a sovereign.‡ But when the beautiful Cleopatra, queen of Egypt, came to Tarsus to answer for having furnished supplies for the con-

* When Brutus was in Sardis he was in the habit of waking at midnight and studying till morning. "One night," says Plutarch, "when the whole army lay in sleep and silence, Brutus, turning toward the door, saw a horrible specter standing silently by his side. 'Art thou God or man?' said the intrepid general. 'I am thy evil genius, Brutus,' replied the phantom; 'thou wilt see me at Philippi.' When the apparition was gone, Brutus called his servants, but, finding they had seen nothing, resumed his studies. The night preceding this second battle of Philippi it is said the specter came again and warned him of his doom."

† It is observed, that of all those who had a hand in the murder of Cæsar, not one died a natural death. Porcia, Cato's daughter (the wife of Brutus), killed herself by swallowing burning coals.

‡ He established Herod in the kingdom of Judea, and supported him against every opposer.

Questions.—225. What auxiliaries flocked to their standard? What is said of the first engagement? Of the second? Who were the victors? 226. What was the fate of Brutus? 227. After the victories of Philippi what did Antony do? What is said of him and Cleopatra?

spirators, the conqueror became a captive, and was led off to Egypt in her chains. Octavius returned to Rome, where he commenced a train of operations which finally put him in possession of absolute power. He dispossessed the peaceful inhabitants of the fertile vales of Italy, and established his veteran soldiers in their habitations. The poet Virgil alone, of all the people of Mantua, was permitted to retain his patrimonial farm. A civil war, excited by Fulvia, wife of Antony, next distracted the Roman state. Fulvia, being conquered, went to Greece and died there. Antony, roused by the trump of war, hastened to Italy to fight with Octavius. They met at Brundusium; a reconciliation took place, and Antony married Octavia, sister of his brother triumvir. Though this was a political union, yet the virtue and beauty of Octavia exercised a beneficial influence upon Antony, and for four years he remained with her, in harmony with Octavius and Lepidus.

228. A new division of the empire was made, by which Antony received the east; Octavius, the west; Lepidus, Africa; and Sextus Pompey, the islands of the sea. Antony undertook an expedition into Parthia, but returned after an inglorious campaign to Cleopatra. Octavius quarreled with Pompey, and drove him from one place to another, till he was put to death by Antony's lieutenant. He then commenced a war with Lepidus for the island of Sicily, and having secured the person of his opponent, banished him. Antony was now the sole obstacle of his ambition, and Octavius began his machinations against him by rendering his character as contemptible as possible at Rome. In this he was very successful, for Antony's mismanagement in the Parthian expedition, his neglect of the injured Octavia, his all-absorbing devotion to Cleopatra, and his display of power in giving away crowns and thrones, irritated the people, and disposed them to take up arms against him.

229. BATTLE OF ACTIUM, B. C. 31. War between the rivals was finally declared in due form. Octavius approached from Italy with all the forces of the west, and Antony came on from the east with an overwhelming army. The bay of Actium, on the coast of Epirus, was the *Pharsalia* of these two triumvirs; and here again a decisive battle sent the one a fugitive to Egypt, and gave to the other the empire of

---

Questions.—227. What did Octavius do? What is said of Fulvia? What induced Antony to hasten to Italy? Where did he meet Octavius? In what manner did they become reconciled? 228. What new division of the empire was made? In what was Antony unsuccessful? What became of Pompey? Of Lepidus? What machinations did Octavius instigate against Antony? How far was he successful? 229. Where was Actium? (See Map No. 2.) When was the battle of Actium fought? Give an account of it.

the world. After having spent two years in the east, arranging the affairs of Egypt, Greece, Syria, and Asia Minor, Octavius returned to Rome. He had now no rivals and no avowed enemies. The laws of the triumvirate were abolished, and after his seventh consulship he resigned his power. The senate, however, besought him to retain it; and with apparent reluctance he continued to do so, under the title of PRINCE OF THE SENATE. By degrees all offices of trust and dignity were united in his person. He was styled *imperator*, or commander-in-chief by sea and land; he was elected *proconsul* of all the provinces; *perpetual tribune* of the people; *censor*, and *pontifex maximus;* the laws were made subject to him, and the observance of them depended upon his will.

230. Thus secure in power, he laid aside the vices which had deformed his character, and strove to make the people forget in the beneficent rule of the EMPEROR AUGUSTUS the tyranny of the triumvir Octavius. The wars which he carried on in Spain, Germany, and other countries, were all terminated in favor of the Roman arms; a treaty was concluded with the Parthians, by which they gave up Armenia, and restored the eagles taken from Crassus and Antony; and thus completing the victories of his predecessors, and awing the nations into peace, he made Rome the mistress of the world!* The little city founded by Romulus 750 years before, now contained within its massy walls 4,000,000 of souls, and held in subjection all nations from the Euphrates to the Atlantic; from the Scandinavian wilds to the immense deserts of Africa and the cataracts of the Nile.

* Tacitus thus sums up the causes which conspired to place Augustus in the position he occupied: "The fate of Brutus and Cassius being decided, the commonwealth had no longer an army engaged in the cause of liberty. The younger Pompey received a total overthrow on the coast of Sicily; Lepidus was deprived of his legions, and Mark Antony fell on his own sword. In that situation the partisans of Julius Cæsar had no leader but Octavius, who laid aside the invidious title of triumvir, content with the more popular name of consul, and with the tribunitian power which he professed to assume for the protection of the people. In a little time, when he had allured to his interest the soldiery by a profusion of largesses, the people by distributions of corn, and the minds of men in general by the sweets of peace, his views grew more aspiring. By degrees and almost imperceptibly he drew into his own hands the authority of the senate, the functions of the magistrates, and the administration of the laws. To these encroachments no opposition was made. The true republican had perished either in the field of battle or by the rigor of proscriptions; of the remaining nobility, the leading men were raised to wealth and honors in proportion as they courted the yoke; and all who, in the distraction of the times, had risen to affluence, preferred immediate ease and safety to the danger of contending for ancient freedom."

Questions.—229, 230. How did Octavius spend the next two years? Relate the history of Octavius until the Christian Era. Bound the Roman Empire on Map No. 1.

THE CHRISTIAN ERA.

SECTION VIII.

1. A. D. **100.** AUGUSTUS* was now emperor of the world. For 26 years he had reigned without a rival. A perfect calm prevailed at Rome. The younger part of the community were born since the battle of Actium, and the old during the civil wars. Augustus, in the vigor of health, maintained at once his own dignity, the honor of his house, and the public tranquillity. The temple of Janus was closed for the third time; and the bloody trade of war was exchanged for the quiet pursuits of the husbandman and artisan.

2. "In those days, when Herod was king in Judea, and Cyrenius was governor of Syria, there went out a decree from Cæsar Augustus, that all the world should be taxed." Joseph and Mary, of the house and lineage of David, in consequence of this decree, were called to the little town of Bethlehem, and there was born the "Saviour, who is Christ the Lord." Angels published his advent; shepherds worshiped around the holy babe; and wise men, guided by his star, came from the east and presented to him gifts—gold, frankincense, and myrrh; but Augustus sat upon his gilded throne, in the palace of the Cæsars, unconscious that in the far-off province of Judea, in the humble village of Bethlehem, the *Prince of Peace* had appeared to purchase and establish a kingdom, before which "the gold, the silver, the brass, and the *iron*" of all former dominions "should become as the chaff of the summer threshing-floor."

3. Augustus lived fourteen years after this event, every year increasing his fame by acts of beneficence, and by the splendid works with

* Augustus was something below the middle size, but well proportioned. His hair was of a yellowish brown, and inclined to curl; his eyes were bright and lively; but the general expression of his countenance was remarkably calm and mild.

THE CHRISTIAN ERA.—Section VIII.—*Questions.*—1. At this epoch who was emperor of the world? How many years did he reign without a rival? 2. Give an account of the birth and lineage of our Saviour. 3. How many years did Augustus live after this event?

which he adorned his native city;* and every year receiving new honors from the senate, and increased homage from the people. Altars were erected to him, and the month *Sextilius* was named "August" in his honor. He had divorced his third wife to marry Livia, the wife of Tiberius, an unprincipled woman, who in his old age completely ruled him. He had also many domestic troubles. His daughter Julia he was forced to banish for her bad conduct; her sons, whom he had appointed his successors, died young; Tiberius, the eldest son of Livia, he had sent into exile; and Drusus, the youngest son, whom he tenderly loved, fell a victim to disease on his return from Germany. These afflictions, and the infirmities of age, disposed him to seek the quiet of the country. He died at Nola, in Campania, A. D. 14, in the 76th year of his age, and the 45th of his reign.

4. TIBERIUS.—Tiberius, the son of Livia, was immediately acknowledged his successor. The time had not yet come when an aspirant could assume the purple as an hereditary right. Tiberius, therefore, affected to decline the homage of the senate, and to distrust his own ability to sustain the weight of the empire. He proceeded, however, to deliver the royal standard to the prætorian guards, and to secure their attendance upon his person; while he put to death Agrippa, the last grandson of Augustus, as he said, by command of the late emperor. These acts were but the commencement of the dark, crooked, and sanguinary policy which marked his administration. Those whom he hated, those whom he feared, and those whom he ought to have loved, were alike suspected, watched, and destroyed. A gloomy jealousy kept him constantly alive to the reports of spies and informers. The law of violated majesty† became the occasion of numerous executions and confiscations.

5. Germanicus, the son of his brother Drusus, quelled a dangerous revolt in Germany, and refused the title of emperor which the legions insisted upon his assuming; but this display of virtue only roused the suspicions of Tiberius. Germanicus was recalled, ostensibly to enjoy

* He beautified Rome so much that it was truly said of him: "He found it of brick and left it of marble."

† By a law of the Twelve Tables libels were strictly prohibited. Sylla construed all aspersions upon his character into violations of the majesty of the Roman people; and many persons in consequence suffered under the penalty of this law. Augustus revived it, and Tiberius made it a permanent law of the empire. Whoever was obnoxious to the prince or his favorites was brought within the law of majesty. Every thing was a state crime, and the trade of a public accuser became one of the most lucrative in the city.

Questions.—3. What were his domestic troubles? In what year did he die? At what place? (See Map No. 4.) 4. Who was Tiberius? What deeds of cruelty characterized his reign? 5. What is said of Germanicus? Of his fate?

a triumph, and fill the office of consul. The noble general entered Rome seated in a lofty triumphal car, with his five children, while his followers displayed the spoils of the conquered, with various pictures of battles, mountains, and rivers, or led in chains the captive barbarians. The people rent the air with acclamations; and Tiberius, seeming to share in the general joy, distributed money to the multitude in the name of his nephew. Not long after, Tiberius laid the condition of the eastern provinces before the senate, representing to the fathers that he was now in the vale of years, and his son Drusus yet a youth. His conclusion was, that to settle the troubles in Syria and Armenia, recourse must be had to the wisdom of Germanicus. The new consul was accordingly sent thither, accompanied by Piso, a man capable of any crime. He never returned. His widow, Agrippina, brought home his ashes in an urn, and demanded justice upon the murderer of her husband. Tiberius gave up Piso to the senate. The wretched man, not daring to accuse the emperor, escaped the ignominy of a public execution by suicide.

6. A vicious Volscian, Sejanus, had ingrafted himself into the affections of Tiberius. During the eight years which this unworthy favorite retained his influence over the emperor, Drusus, the only son of Tiberius, was poisoned; the two oldest sons of Germanicus were put to death, and Agrippina was banished. By his persuasions the emperor left Rome in the twelfth year of his reign, and took up his residence upon the little island of Capræa. The impure orgies with which this retreat was disgraced cannot be recounted here. Tiberius, who was almost always intoxicated, gave up all the cares of state to Sejanus; and the servile senate bestowed upon him honors second only to those of the emperor.

7. The law of violated majesty was strictly enforced by the sanguinary minister. The rich and noble, objects of suspicion to a jealous tyrant, and obstacles in the path of an ambitious favorite, were daily sacrificed to quiet the apprehensions of the one or the other; till finally, the heirs of the imperial family being destroyed, the power of the great enfeebled, and the prætorian bands gained over to his interest, Sejanus thought the empire within his grasp. The plot was detected, and Antonia,* the mother of Germanicus, accused him to the emperor. Sejanus was strangled by the executioner. His death was almost immediately followed by that of his royal master. The sick-bed of the emperor was attended by Caligula, only son of Germanicus,

* This Antonia was the daughter of Antony and Octavia.

Questions.—6, 7. What of Sejanus? Of the law of violated majesty?

who, having waited some time in vain for the last breath of the tyrant, pressed a pillow upon his mouth, and avenged, though late, the wrongs of his parents and brothers. The news of Tiberius's death was received at Rome with cries of "Tiberius to the Tiber." His body was, however, carried to the city by the soldiers, and buried with funeral honors, A. D. 31, aged 78.

8. In the eighteenth year of Tiberius's reign, Jesus Christ was crucified. Shortly after, Pontius Pilate wrote to Tiberius an account of his miracles and resurrection, upon which the emperor made a report of the whole to the senate, requesting that Christ might be acknowledged a god by the Romans. The fathers, however pliant upon other subjects, were obstinate upon this, and, under plea of an ancient law, refused the emperor's demand, and ordered all Christians to quit the city.

9. CALIGULA.—Caius Cæsar spent the early years of his life in the camp in Germany. He was a great favorite with the legions, and was surnamed by them "Caligula" from his wearing a little pair of shoes (caligæ), such as covered the feet of the common soldiers. After his father's death and his mother's banishment, he lived with his great-grandmother Livia; when she died, he removed to the family of his grandmother Antonia. In his twentieth year Tiberius invited the young Cæsar to take up his abode with him upon the island, where he displayed such wanton cruelty that the emperor predicted that "Caius would prove a serpent to swallow Rome, and a phæton to set the world on fire." Caligula, however, was no sooner possessed of sovereign power than he assumed an appearance of great virtue and moderation. The authority of the magistrates was restored; the will of Tiberius faithfully executed; and all prosecutions for treason were forbidden.

10. This delightful state of things lasted eight months, when the emperor fell dangerously sick, in consequence, it was supposed, of a love-potion given him by his mistress. When he recovered, either deranged by disease or wearied of dissimulation, he began his course of cruelty and crime. In a short reign of four years, he so distinguished himself by every species of wickedness that "the tyranny of Tiberius was forgotten in the enormities of Caligula." With him, prodigality and avarice went hand in hand. He dissipated the treasures which Tiberius had collected in the most foolish and expensive works, and found occasions against noble and wealthy people to get

Questions.—8. In whose reign was Christ crucified? In what year did it occur? 9. Who was Caius Cæsar? Why was he called Caligula? What was the prophecy of Tiberius concerning him? How did Caligula at first reign? 10. Give an account of his subsequent reign. How did he proclaim his poverty?

possession of their estates. He sold all the property of his sisters, the furniture of the old court, the clothes of Augustus and Tiberius, and, having a daughter born, he proclaimed his poverty, and stood in his vestibule to receive presents of all who came to congratulate him.

11. He made an expedition into Gaul, and even set sail for Britain; but soon ordered his troops to draw back to the shore, and fill their helmets with sea-shells. "This booty," cried he, "ravished from the sea, is worthy my palace and the capitol." His horse seemed to have a peculiar claim upon his affections. It was kept in a stable of marble, and fed from a manger of ivory. Sometimes it was invited to the table of the emperor, and presented with gilt oats, and wine in a golden cup. The wanton murders and confiscations with which Rome was filled had caused several conspiracies against Caligula, which, being discovered, brought the usual train of impeachments and executions. Cherea, a tribune of the prætorian bands,* at last delivered the empire from the tyrant, A. D. 41.

12. CLAUDIUS.—No sooner was the death of Caligula known, than the royal guards began to wreak their vengeance upon all those whom they supposed concerned in his murder. As they were hurrying through the palace in their work of death, they found Claudius, uncle of the late king, hiding in an obscure corner, and immediately proclaimed him emperor, assigning as their reason, "his relationship to the whole family of the Cæsars."† Claudius was now fifty years old; he had been a rickety child, and disease, together with severe treatment, had perpetuated the timidity and indolence of childhood. Though styled "the silly emperor," his imbecilities were to be attributed rather to his vices than to his want of abilities. He embellished Rome with many magnificent works, and went in person to the war in Britain; but, suffering himself to be ruled by women of the most abandoned character, he was induced to put to death many of the nobles of Rome upon false charges of conspiracy, and to bestow their estates upon his unworthy favorites.

13. Claudius married Agrippina, daughter of Germanicus, his niece. She prevailed on him to set aside his own Britannicus, and adopt

* In every Roman camp the general's tent was called the PRÆTORIUM. The soldiers who formed the emperor's body-guard were called the *prætorian cohorts.* These soldiers were quartered at Rome, till Sejanus, in order to forward his own dark designs, persuaded Tiberius to form a prætorian camp without the city.

† He was the brother of Germanicus, and consequently the nephew of Tiberius.

Questions.—11. What further account can you give of him? How many years did he reign? What was the cause of his death? 12. Relate how Claudius was made emperor. How old was he then? What was his character? 13. Whom did he marry?

Nero, her child by a former husband. The weak father having afterwards shown a disposition to change the succession, Agrippina prepared for him a dish of mushrooms, spiced with poison. It was nothing uncommon for the emperor to eat and drink till he was perfectly stupid; when, therefore, he was carried from the table to bed after this fatal repast, no surprise was excited; and Nero, under the guidance of his mother, had time to secure the guards and take possession of the imperial authority before the death of Claudius was generally known. He reigned almost 14 years.

14. Nero.—A. D. 54. Nero, the fifth in descent from Antony, though but seventeen years old, was hailed as emperor with joy by the Roman populace, and with all due professions of respect by the obsequious senate. He had been carefully educated by Seneca the philosopher, and the first five years of his reign were distinguished by justice and clemency. Agrippina, who had gone to such lengths in crime to secure the throne for her son, was ambitious to share his power. When, however, he rejected her counsels, and gave his confidence to Acte, a female slave, the indignant queen broke out into open reproaches, and threatened to inform the soldiers of the means by which Britannicus had been set aside. The death of Britannicus at a banquet was the consequence of this threat. The funeral took place the same night, and Nero followed the atrocious act by a proclamation calling upon the Roman people to support him, "now the only branch of a family born to rule the world." This murder forms the commencement of Nero's series of cruelties. He divorced his wife Octavia to marry Poppæa, whom he had taken from her husband Otho. This beautiful but unprincipled woman led him on to still greater crimes. Agrippina continued her struggles for power; and Nero, wearied of the contentions between her and Poppæa, caused his mother to be assassinated.

15. In the year A. D. 64, a fire broke out in the circus at Rome, which raged about ten days with the greatest fury. It was believed that these flames were kindled by Nero's order, and a report was circulated that during the conflagration he went to the theater and sung some verses upon the burning of Troy. Wishing, however, to escape popular indignation, Nero threw the odium of the act upon the Christians, of whom there were great numbers in Rome, and the most ter-

Questions.—13. Give the closing account of him. 14. Who was Nero? When did he become emperor? By whom had he been educated? What is said of the first five years of his reign? What is said of Britannicus? What crimes followed? 15. What fire occurred? What belief prevailed in connection with the fire? Give an account of the persecution of the Christians.

rible persecutions of these peaceable citizens consequently ensued. "Some were covered with the skins of wild beasts, and left to be devoured by dogs; some were crucified; great numbers were beheaded; and many, covered over with inflammable matter, were lighted up when the day declined, to serve as torches during the night."*

16. For the convenience of seeing this tragic spectacle, Nero lent his own gardens, and varied the entertainments by driving round in his curricle and engaging in the sports of the circus. Nero caused the city and his own house to be rebuilt with ruinous splendor. The rubbish was removed to the marshes of Ostia; the streets were made wide and long; the houses were carried up to a specific height, and adorned with areas and porticos in front. In the same year the Jews, roused to fury by the cruelty and impiety of Florus, their procurator, took up arms to resist the Roman power; and such was the desperation with which they fought, that Nero, with ill-concealed terror, ordered Vespasian, an officer who had distinguished himself in Britain, to repair immediately to the east. A conspiracy against the emperor was discovered, and followed by the usual train of judicial murders. Many innocent persons were put to death upon false accusations, among whom were Seneca and the poet Lucan.

17. About the same time, Poppæa died in consequence of a kick received from her brutal husband. Childishness and cruelty at length became the principal characteristics of the emperor. His voice was weak and unpleasant, but, fancying himself a splendid singer, he determined to exhibit in the theater. No person was allowed to leave the house while he was performing; soldiers were stationed in different places to see that the audience bestowed the proper quantity of applause, and one old senator, having unfortunately dropped to sleep, came very near losing his life.

18. Wearied at last with the commendations of his countrymen, he resolved to display his talents to the refined Grecians. Messengers were sent before the monarch, to require the celebration of all the games in one year. At Olympia he undertook to drive ten horses around the Stadium, and though he was thrown from his seat, yet the obsequious judges bestowed upon him the victor's wreath. The Greeks, indeed, spared no pains to win his favor. *They conferred upon him* 1,800 *crowns!* Nero entered Rome upon his return seated in the chariot of Augustus, with his wild olive garland around his

* In this persecution St. Paul was beheaded and St. Peter crucified?

Questions.—16. What is said of the rebuilding of Rome? Of the war with the Jews? Of Seneca and Lucan? 17. Of Nero as a singer? 18. Of Nero in Greece?

head, the Pythian bay in his hand, and his 1,800 laurels by his side. The whole city was illuminated; incense was burned in the streets; the pavements were strewed with saffron, and flowers were showered upon him from the windows. The detestable acts of Nero and his predecessors had filled the provinces with discontent, and a general revolt was the consequence. Galba, the prætor of Spain, was proclaimed emperor by the legions, and immediately began his march to Rome.

19. Nero heard this intelligence while he was at supper. He overturned the table with his foot; fell into a swoon; then into a violent fit of rage, threatening to poison the senate, and turn the wild beasts loose upon the people; then talked of taking refuge in Parthia, and finally gave orders for packing his musical instruments, and preparing his women for departure. The prætorian guards, meantime, declared for Galba, and the citizens of Rome, rejoiced at the prospect of a change in the administration, joined in the revolt. His friends deserted him; his domestics plundered his house and fled; and the senate condemned him to death. The unhappy tyrant made his escape to the house of his freedman, where, after several ineffectual attempts, he succeeded in giving himself a mortal wound, in the 32d year of his age, and 14th of his reign. The race of Cæsar ended with Nero. He was the last and the worst of that illustrious house, which held the sway in Rome for more than one century.

20. Galba.—A. D. 68. The united reigns of the three monarchs, Galba, Otho, and Vitellius, did not amount to two years. Galba was 72 years of age when he returned from Spain to ascend the throne of the Cæsars. He was rigidly attached to the ancient discipline, and immediately made preparations to reform the state. The army, however, clamored loudly against his efforts, and the various favorites who surrounded his person artfully increased the dissatisfaction. One ridiculed his simplicity, another exclaimed against his cruelty. Otho, the husband of Poppæa, having bribed two officers of the prætorian bands, gained that whole body over to his interest, and was proclaimed emperor. Galba caused himself to be carried out in a litter to suppress the mutiny, but the tumultuous shouts of Otho's partisans so frightened the litter-bearers, that they threw the old man down and ran away. Galba, seeing the soldiers coming up, bent his head forward and bade them strike it off, if it were for the good of the people.

Questions.—18. Of Galba? 19. Of the end of Nero? What race ended with him? 20. In what year did Galba ascend the throne? How old was he then? By what obstacles was he opposed? How was he killed?

They took him at his word, and the bloody head of the emperor was soon after exposed upon a lance to the sneers of the multitude. He reigned seven months.

21. Otho.—A. D. 68.—The early life of Otho was disgraced by licentiousness and crime; his brief enjoyment of power was marked by moderation and clemency. Vitellius had been proclaimed emperor by the legions in Germany, before the death of Galba; and scarcely was Otho seated upon the throne, when he was summoned to lead the prætorian cohorts against their veteran brethren. He was defeated in battle, and fell on his own sword, after a reign of ninety-five days.

22. Vitellius.—A. D. 69.—Vitellius had been long accustomed to the atmosphere of the court. He ministered to the pleasures of Tiberius in Capræa; he drove a chariot for Caligula; he gamed with Claudius; and he praised the singing of Nero. In all the corruptions, crimes, and prodigalities of the age, he excelled his masters. His soldiers, in their march southward, committed every species of excess; and when he reached Rome, he made the whole city his camp, and filled all the houses with armed men. The miseries which the empire suffered at the hands of Vitellius were fortunately soon terminated. The legions in the east had scarcely acknowledged Galba, when they were called upon to ratify the usurpation of Otho. Now, when the cruel and voluptuous glutton, Vitellius, claimed their allegiance, they openly revolted, and proclaimed Vespasian, their own general, emperor. Vitellius attempted to make good his claims by the sword, but the lieutenant of Vespasian, while his master was arranging the affairs of the east, stormed the camp of the guards, took Vitellius prisoner, dragged him through the streets, and cast his mangled body into the Tiber.

23. Vespasian.—A. D. 69. During five years Vespasian had pushed the Jewish war with vigor. The maritime towns of the Mediterranean had submitted; all Galilee* was subdued, and the general was just preparing for the siege of Jerusalem when the revolutions in the empire changed the course of his destiny and recalled him to Rome.

* At the city of Jotapata, in Galilee, he took Josephus prisoner. The captive, being brought into his presence, thus addressed him: "I come to thee, O Vespasian, as the messenger of great tidings. Dost thou send me to Nero? *Thou*, O Vespasian, art Cæsar and emperor, thou and this thy son." The Roman general did not then believe him; but after the prophecy was fulfilled he released Josephus from his bonds and treated him with great favor. Josephus remained with Titus, and witnessed the destruction of Jerusalem.

Questions.—21. Who next ascended the throne? What caused his death? How long had he reigned? 22. By whom was he succeeded? When did Vitellius commence his reign? Who was proclaimed emperor by the people? To what miserable death was Vitellius doomed? 23. When did Vespasian succeed him? In what wars did Vespasian engage? What occurred to recall him to Rome?

Leaving then the Jewish war in the hands of his son Titus, he returned to Italy by way of Egypt, and, having overcome his enemies, was acknowledged emperor by the senate and people.

24. Jerusalem was built upon two mountains, and surrounded by three walls on every side, except where the rocks rose so precipitously as to be a natural defense. Mount Sion, the loftiest summit, was fortified by three towers, the most impregnable and beautiful of which was Antonia. A deep valley, through which flowed the sweet waters of Siloam, separated it from Mount Acra, which bent toward it in the shape of the moon when it is horned. A third part of the city was Bezetha, separated likewise from Acra by a valley partly filled up, and defended by the outermost wall. The lofty towers which ran along the steep brow of Sion were built of white marble, cut in large blocks, joined so perfectly as to seem hewn out of the solid rock.

25. "High above the city rose the temple, uniting the commanding strength of a citadel with the splendor of a sacred edifice. It covered a space of a furlong on each side, and the precipitous sides of the rock were faced up to it on the east with huge blocks of stone. Passing the marble columns of dazzling whiteness which supported the splendid porticos of the outer court, the eye rested upon a lofty arch, covered with gold, through which glittered the gate of the temple, sheeted with the same precious metal. Within, the golden candlestick spread out its flowering branches; the golden table supported the shew-bread, and the altar of incense flamed with its costly perfume." The roof of the temple was set all over with sharp glittering spikes; the marble turrets reflected the beams of the sun with dazzling radiance, and at a distance "the whole temple looked literally like a mount of snow fretted with golden pinnacles."

26. This beautiful but guilty city was occupied by three factions. Eleazar, with a party called the zealots, kept possession of the temple; John, who had been driven from Gischala, fortified himself in the lower town; and Simon, with his followers, defended Bezetha. Such was the city, such were its fortifications, and such its defenders, when Titus, in the spring of A. D. 70, at the time of the general assembly of the Jews to celebrate the feast of the passover, approached the devoted place and pitched his camp east of the vale of Cedron, upon the Mount of Olives. The efforts of the Jews to compel the Romans to raise the siege were almost incredible. They burned the engines of the enemy,

Questions.—23. To whom did he commit the command of the Jewish war? By what authority was he then acknowledged emperor? 24, 25. Describe Jerusalem. 26. What factions existed there? Give their names and locations. In what year was the city besieged by Titus? Where did he encamp with his army?

and attacked the legions with such fury that Titus, quite dispirited, gave up the idea of taking the place by storm, and employed his soldiers in constructing a wall which would prevent all egress from the gates.

27. No sooner were the operations of the Romans intermitted than the factions in the city raged with tenfold fury; battles were fought within the walls; a company of assassins entered the temple and cut off Eleazar and his party in one general massacre; conflagrations destroyed great quantities of corn; so that when the day had come to Jerusalem that "her enemies cast a trench about her and kept her in on every side," her own sons were lying like murdered victims upon her altars, and her little ones were perishing in the streets with famine. Portents and prodigies announced the coming doom. Swords glittered in the air; embattled armies seemed hurrying to combat in the sky; the portal of the temple flew open, and a voice from the excellent glory pronounced, in no mortal tones, "Let us depart!" A terrific sound, as of a multitude rushing forth, was heard, and then an appalling silence reigned throughout the holy courts.

28. The Jews converted these fearful admonitions into omens of speedy deliverance, and, disregarding the dreadful ravages of famine and pestilence, obstinately refused the offers of accommodation which Titus repeatedly made by the mouth of Josephus. The Romans, wrought to fury by the desperation of the Jews, made incessant attacks upon the walls, and finally gained possession of Antonia. At length the day approached in the revolution of ages, the tenth of August—the anniversary of that fatal day in which Nebuchadnezzar burned the temple of Solomon. The daily sacrifice had failed for want of men to offer it; and the Romans, having overturned the foundations of Antonia, began to ply their battering-rams upon the sacred walls of the temple. A Roman soldier in the tumult, actuated as by a divine fury, seized a smoking brand, and, climbing to the top of the portico, threw it into one of the courts; and soon the whole building was wrapped in flames.

29. The wail of agony which the despairing Jews sent forth upon seeing the destruction of their temple, could not move the hearts of the infuriated Romans. Titus, unable to make himself heard in the uproar, withdrew to the fort of Antonia, and, gazing upon the conflagration, exclaimed, with a sigh, "The God of the Jews has fought against them; to Him we owe our victory." The numbers who perished amounted to 1,000,000; the captives to 100,000. John and

---

Questions.—27, 28, 29. Give a detailed account of the taking of Jerusalem.

Simon were taken. The former was imprisoned for life; the latter was "conveyed to Rome, to clank his chains at the chariot wheels of the conqueror."

30. When Titus returned with his victorious army, the senate decreed a triumph to him and his father. Vespasian and his son entered Rome in the same triumphal car. Upon the standards and ensigns were painted all the events of the Jewish war. The green vales of Galilee, the vine-clad hills of Judea, and the blue waters of lake Gennesareth, encompassed and crossed by the Roman legions, were depicted in the liveliest colors; while from the spreading canvas fair Salem's towers and bulwarks displayed the Roman eagle; and the golden gates and pinnacles of the temple glowed in the ruddy flames which terminated the tedious and bloody siege. The spoils of the conquered nation gave magnificence to the scene; and the Book of the Law, wrapped in a rich golden tissue, was exposed to the curious eyes of the people.

31. The venal inmates of the palace found, upon the accession of Vespasian, that truth and virtue were once more in fashion. Cruelties and crimes were discountenanced; industry was encouraged; and he was said to have founded and established the government of one thousand nations. Julius Agricola subdued the Britons, and a profound peace ensuing, the temple of Janus was closed for the fourth time. In the civil war with Vitellius, the capitol was burned. It was now rebuilt with the greatest magnificence. Vespasian loved a joke, and was exceedingly fond of money. On one occasion, the inhabitants of a city proposed to raise a statue in his honor. He held out his hand and said, with a smile, "Let this be the base of your statue; place your money here." He was the second emperor that died a natural death, and the first that was succeeded by his son. He reigned ten years.

32. Titus.—A. D. 79. Though Titus, whom Tacitus calls "the delight of mankind," was a wise and beneficent sovereign, yet his short reign was filled with a series of disasters. In the first year occurred that dreadful eruption of Vesuvius, by which Herculaneum and Pompeii were destroyed.* The miserable fugitives who made

* After an interval of extreme drought, the whole plain around Vesuvius was shaken as if by an earthquake. A column of black ashes arose into the air, hovered a few moments over the devoted cities, and fell, burying the inhabitants in their dwellings, the priests at

Questions.—30. What triumph and honors awaited Titus and his father? What is said of the Book of the Law? 31. Give an account of the reign of Vespasian. How many years did he reign? By whom was he succeeded? 32. When did Titus become emperor? What is said of him? What series of disasters occurred in his reign?

their escape, found an asylum in Rome; but a pestilence soon after appeared, in which 10,000 died daily for a considerable period. A fire succeeded, which raged till a great number of buildings were destroyed. Titus gave liberally of the sums laid up by his father to the relief of the sufferers, and rebuilt the edifices which had been consumed, with increased magnificence. The famous Colosseum, begun by his father, was completed by his care. The sports of the dedication lasted 100 days. On the last day of the games, the emperor appeared dejected, and even shed tears. A fever ensued, which was rendered fatal by the immoderate use of the bath. He died in the same house where his father expired, after a reign of little more than two years.

33. DOMITIAN.—A. D. 81. Titus had named his brother, Domitian, as his heir, and both the senate and the army hailed his accession to the throne with the greatest joy. They soon, however, had cause to repent of their raptures. In the character of Domitian, the gloomy dissimulation of Tiberius seemed combined with the ridiculous assumptions of Caligula, and the cruel levities of Nero. The usual train of accusations, proscriptions, and executions kept the best families of Rome in constant mourning; while the author of their calamities demanded golden statues, and the worship of the gods. The Roman arms, too, were unsuccessful in the north, and several disgraceful treaties were concluded with the barbarians.

34. These were his public acts: in private, he varied the disgusting round of his pleasures by catching flies, and nailing them to the wall with bodkins. The empire, after suffering in all its departments for fifteen years, was at length relieved of this monster by the hand of the assassin. The senate decreed that his statues should be taken down, his name erased from the *annals*, and his funeral omitted. He was the last of the twelve Cæsars. NERVA.—A. D. 96.—The first of the five good emperors of Rome was a pattern of justice and clemency. He reigned, however, not quite two years, during which time no important events occurred.

35. A. D. **200.** THE FIVE *good* EMPERORS.—TACITUS AND PLUTARCH.—The life of Nerva, as it occurred, has also been given in the

their altars, and the flying multitudes in their fields. Darkness sank down upon the plains, and for three days no light was visible but the lurid flames of the volcano.

Questions.—32. What acts of liberality distinguished him? How long did he reign? What caused his death? 33, 34. Who was his successor? When did Domitian become emperor? Give his character. What was the condition of Rome during his reign? How long did he reign? What was the decree of the senate respecting him? Who succeeded him? In what year was that? What is said of the reign of Nerva?

preceding chapter. Before his death, he caused Trajan to be acknowledged Cæsar* by the army and senate. Trajan was with the army in Germany at the time of his adopted father's decease, but immediately marched to Rome, where he was received with the usual congratulations. Plutarch,† his tutor, wrote him a letter, entreating him to follow the counsels he had received in early youth. The emperor did not, like Nero, disgrace the name of his preceptor. "He was equally great as a ruler, a general, and a man. He conquered the warlike Dacians, and, to facilitate his entrance into their country, built a stupendous bridge across the Danube, the ruins of which continue to this day. The dominions of the empire were thus extended beyond the bounds of any of the former great monarchies.

36. The rejoicings at Rome upon the return of the victorious emperor lasted four months, during which no less than 10,000 gladiators fought in the amphitheater for the amusement of the multitude. The Pillar of Trajan, which may yet be seen in the grass-grown Forum, was erected in commemoration of this event. After adorning Rome with many public buildings, Trajan turned his arms against the Armenians and Parthians. He overran the greater part of what had been the Assyrian empire, and, throwing a bridge across the Tigris, followed the track of Alexander to the Persian Gulf. Regretting that his age forbade the thought of his invading India, he left the care of the army to Adrian, his nephew, and returned to Syria. He died in Cilicia, after a reign of nearly twenty years.

37. ADRIAN.—A. D. 117. The first care of Adrian was to conclude a peace with the Persians, making the Euphrates the boundary of the empire on the east. On his return to Rome, the senate decreed him a triumph; he refused the honor for himself, but caused the statue of

* The *emperor* was styled "Augustus;" the *heir expectant* was dignified with the title of "Cæsar."

† Plutarch was a native of Beotia. He was a student at Delphi, when Nero went to Greece to display his wonderful skill in horsemanship and music, A. D. 66; he must at this time, therefore, have been an old man. He visited Italy when quite young, and probably remained there till Domitian, by a public decree, banished all philosophers from the country. He wrote many works, some of which are lost, but his "Parallel Lives" still exist, as models of biography. Tacitus published his history some time in Trajan's reign. It began with the accession of Galba, and continued to the death of Domitian, comprising a period of 27 years, full of important events and sudden revolutions. It was written in 36 books, only five of which are now extant. His Annals are recommended to the attention of every student. Tacitus was the son-in-law of Agricola, and the friend of the younger Pliny.

Questions.—35. Whom did Nerva pronounce Cæsar before his death? What events occurred in the reign of Trajan? 36. What rejoicings at Rome took place? What successful wars did Trajan undertake? Where did he die? How long had he reigned? 37. By whom was he succeeded? When did that event occur? What was the first act of Adrian?

Trajan to be carried in the pompous procession of the victorious army. Adrian was remarkable for every manly and scientific accomplishment. He was equally skillful in the war or the chase; he was well versed in mathematics and medicine; he wrote beautifully both in prose and verse; he was a proficient in drawing and painting; he was an elegant orator; a *better singer than Nero;* and his moral qualities were equal to his accomplishments, if we except the envy and vainglory which his rare endowments and the adulation of the people were calculated to excite.

38. It was his maxim that an emperor ought to imitate the sun, by dispensing favors to all parts of the earth. Accordingly, he spent thirteen years in traversing his dominions. Finding that the bridge of Trajan proved as great a convenience to the barbarous tribes as to the armies of the empire, he caused it to be broken down; passing from Dacia through Germany and Holland, he sailed to Britain, where he ordered a wall to be erected for the protection of his subjects from the Scots; thence he journeyed south through Gaul and Spain, and thence to Rome. He visited Asia Minor; wintered at Athens; sailed for Sicily; examined Mount Etna, and directed his course to Africa, where he rebuilt the city of Carthage, and called it Adrianople. When he returned to Rome to take up his abode, the joy of the people knew no bounds.

39. During his reign, an impostor, called the "Son of a Star," claiming to be the Messiah, persuaded the Jews to revolt. Three years were employed in bringing them again into subjection. As a punishment, every sacred place was studiously profaned. A temple was built to Jupiter on Mount Sion; a statue of Venus set up in the place of crucifixion; and the grotto of Bethlehem consecrated to Adonis. The Jews were forbidden the sight of Jerusalem, and no descendant of Abraham was permitted to enter the city, except upon the memorable tenth of August, the anniversary of its destruction. Adrian died of a dropsy, after a reign of twenty-one years.

40. Antoninus.—A. D. 139. Antoninus, surnamed the *Pious*, had been made Cæsar by the late emperor, and now peaceably ascended the throne. His long and quiet reign allowed almost one generation of Romans to pass away without the experience of distressing wars abroad, and arbitrary executions at home. Even the Christians, whose resolute refusals to worship idols kept the Romans constantly

---

Questions.—37, 38, 39. Give a description of his character? What events distinguished his reign? When did he die? How long had he reigned? 40. Who was made Cæsar before his death? Give an account of the reign of Antoninus Pius.

irritated, came in for a share in the clemency of this excellent monarch, who proclaimed religious toleration by a letter from his own pen. Such was his reputation for wisdom and virtue, that princes came from beyond the bounds of the Roman empire to make him the arbiter of their differences. He reigned twenty-two years.

41. MARCUS AURELIUS.—A. D. 161. Aurelius, the son-in-law of Antoninus, claimed his descent from Numa. He was a stoic philosopher, and a wise and virtuous monarch. He took for his colleague Lucius Verus, a man whose vices served to show in stronger relief the perfections of Aurelius. The two emperors were scarcely seated upon the throne when the empire was attacked on every side by its barbarous neighbors. Verus went to the east to repel the Parthians, but stopped at Antioch while the war was carried on by his lieutenants. They were successful, and Verus returned in triumph. Rome had, however, little cause to rejoice. She was visited successively by a vicious, cruel emperor; a raging pestilence; clouds of devouring locusts; dreadful earthquakes; distressing inundations; and a wasting famine.

42. The priests, to avert the anger of the gods, offered the most costly sacrifices in vain, till finally the Romans, attributing all their calamities to the impieties of the Christians, commenced a dreadful persecution, in which Justin Martyr and the venerable Polycarp, bishop of Smyrna, fell victims to superstitious fury. Aurelius marched to the north to repel the invasions of the Vandals and others, who constantly harassed the frontiers. A. D. 180. He died of the plague at Vienna, expressing with his last breath his solicitude for the future welfare of his country and of his son. He reigned almost nineteen years.

43. FIVE *bad* EMPERORS.—During the last twenty years of this century five emperors assumed the imperial purple: Commodus, Pertinax, Severus, Niger, and Albinus. Commodus* had accompanied Aurelius on his expedition against the northern tribes, but no sooner was his

* With the reign of Commodus properly commenced the *Decline of the Roman Empire.* The remaining events of its history are so exceedingly complex that it is impossible to condense them into the brief limits of this work without creating confusion in the mind of the pupil. For a true picture of the times the reader is referred to "Gibbon's History of the Decline and Fall of the Roman Empire."

Questions.—40. What particular letter did he write? How long did he reign? 41. In what year did Marcus Aurelius ascend the throne? What was his character? Whom did he take for a colleague? What distresses did Rome suffer? 42. To what cause did the priests attribute the wars and judgments that were visited upon Rome? Who became martyrs to this superstition? What caused the death of Aurelius? How many years did he reign? In what year did he die? 43. How many emperors assumed the purple during the last twenty years of this century? What century is meant? Name the five emperors.

father dead, than, impatient to revel in the pleasures of the capital, he concluded a disgraceful peace with the barbarians, and hastened to Rome. The senate, army, and people acknowledged him as emperor and Augustus, in consideration of his father's virtues. He soon proved that he had no merit of his own, being extremely ignorant of every thing a monarch ought to know, and exceedingly indifferent to the duties of an emperor, at the same time that he was eminently skillful in useless accomplishments, and exceedingly fond of low company and sensual pleasures.

44. He drew the bow and threw the javelin with wonderful address, always killing the animal at which he aimed, though running at full speed; he cut off the heads of an hundred ostriches in their swiftest motions, with arrows headed in the shape of a half moon; a bird upon the wing could not escape his unerring aim; and he came off victorious in 735 gladiatorial combats. At first he left the administration of affairs to the præfect of the prætorian guards; and after this monster was slain by his own soldiers, a Phrygian slave held the reins of the government, while the monarch became himself a slave to the worst passions of human nature, and distinguished himself by overcoming wild beasts in the amphitheater. The senate showed their degradation by styling him the Hercules of Rome, and offering to change the name of the eternal city to *Colonia Commodiana.* These were his public acts.

45. In the sacred hours of retirement he indulged in all the gluttony, sensuality, and frivolity that disgraced Domitian, so that in one may be seen the counterpart of the other. He kept a list of such persons as he designed for destruction; and his favorite mistress, Marcia, having found her name among the proscribed, administered poison, and thus the Roman world was delivered from its odious master, after submitting to his cruelties twelve years. The friends and assistants of Marcia wrapped up the body of Commodus as a bale of useless furniture and carried it out through the drunken guards, who were first made acquainted with the murder of their monarch by the shouts which hailed his successor.

46. PERTINAX.—A. D. 193. This prince forms an exception among the five bad emperors. His reign, however, was so very brief that his character as a sovereign was not fully developed. The sudden and striking changes that took place in his life gave him the surname of

---

Questions.—43, 44, 45. Give a general outline of the character of Commodus. What was his fate? 46. Who was his successor? In what year did Pertinax succeed him? What account can you give of Pertinax?

"*The Tennis Ball of Fortune.*" His father was a dealer in charcoal; he himself had been a schoolmaster, a lawyer, a soldier, a captain, a consul, the commander of a legion, and præfect of the city. When the conspirators came to his house in the night, after the murder of Commodus, he supposed they were sent by the tyrant to put him to death, and cheerfully prepared for execution; and it was not without reluctance that he suffered the prætorian guards to clothe him in the purple: but the obedient senate sanctioning his election, he was proclaimed emperor on the night before the first of January, A. D. 193. A few days of severe discipline, however, displeased the *emperor-makers*, and, disdaining any secret conspiracies or private contrivances, they marched into the palace three hundred strong, slew their monarch, cut off his head, and carried it back to the camp. He reigned not quite three months.

47. THE ROMAN EMPIRE SOLD.—The prætorians then offered the empire to the highest bidder. The father-in-law of Pertinax, and Didius, the foster-brother of Marcus Aurelius, were the only competitors. The former made magnificent promises; the latter bestowed substantial presents. The guards accordingly proclaimed Didius emperor, and accompanied him in a body to the senate-house, where he made a very short and comprehensive speech: "*Fathers, you want an emperor, and I am the fittest person you can choose.*" The senators, convinced by the eloquence of Didius or the menacing looks of his guards, acquiesced in this sentiment, but the people cursed him as he passed the streets.

48. The legions of Syria, Illyria, and Britain refused to confirm the election of the prætorians. Each party chose its own monarch. Niger was acknowledged by all the Romans and tributary princes of Asia; Albinus was proclaimed in Britain, and Severus marched from Illyria directly to Rome. All the towns and garrisons declared for him; the prætorian guards forsook their wealthy prince to join his standard; and the senate decreed that Didius should be slain, and Severus reign in his stead. He reigned 66 days. The executioners led the unfortunate monarch into one of the secret baths and struck off his head; and Severus took peaceable possession of the palace of the Cæsars.

49. SEVERUS.—The first act of Severus was to banish the prætorian auctioneers one hundred miles from Rome. Then, having promised

---

Questions.—46. How long had he reigned? 47. How then was the Roman empire disposed of? Give an account of Didius. 48. After his death, who took possession of the palace of the Cæsars? 49. What was the first act of Severus?

the senate to rule with clemency and justice, he seized the children of the officers in the east as hostages, and marched against Niger. The battle between these two rivals was fought upon the plains of Issus, on the very spot where Alexander and Darius met, more than 500 years before. Niger was defeated and slain. Severus then returned to settle the contest with Albinus. A tremendous battle was fought near the present city of Lyons, and Albinus, being taken prisoner, soon followed his colored brother, Niger, to the land of shades!

50. A. D. **300.** TWELVE EMPERORS.—THIRTY TYRANTS.—Many nobles of Spain and Gaul were put to death for having taken the part of Albinus; and 29 senators also fell victims to his sanguinary orders. Severus was a great warrior. The Parthians, who continued hostilities in the east, suffered a severe defeat at his hand, and Seleucia and Babylon were taken. His next foreign war was in Britain. The Picts and Scots were driven back into their mountain fastnesses, and a wall twelve feet high was built across the island, to prevent their future incursions. Severus died at York, heart-broken by the quarrels of his children. He reigned nearly eighteen years.

51. CARACALLA AND GETA.—A. D. 211. The two sons of Severus succeeded him. The first act of Caracalla was to assassinate Geta in his mother's arms, and every subsequent exercise of power showed the same sanguinary spirit. All who had been connected with Geta shared his fate, till the number of victims amounted to 20,000. The people were forced to suffer in silence, for Caracalla, like Sylla, attached the soldiers to his interest by the most liberal donations. He professed to admire the character of Alexander the Great, and with ridiculous affectation inclined his head to one side in imitation of that monarch. He made an expedition into Asia, where he visited the grave of Achilles, and sacrificed one of his freedmen, to imitate the grief of Homer's hero over Patroclus.

52. Having treacherously seized the king of Armenia, he was involved in a war with that people, in which he suffered defeat. After this he went to Alexandria, where he made an offering of his ornaments at the tomb of Alexander, and consecrated the dagger with which he had slain Geta in the temple of Serapis. His reign lasted more than six years, during which he did every thing to degrade the throne of the Cæsars, and many things to increase the magnificence of

Questions.—49. What war was waged? Where was a battle fought? What was the fate of Niger? Where was the next battle fought? What was the end of Albinus? 50. In what character was Severus distinguished? What wars were successfully prosecuted by him? How many years did he reign? 51, 52. Who succeeded him? What was the character of Caracalla? Give an account of his crimes. How did he secure the soldiers to his interest?

Rome. Some of the most splendid structures that graced the capitol were raised by his order. MACRINUS.—A. D. 217. Macrinus, the præfect of the prætorians, who murdered Caracalla, was made emperor by the army, and reigned little more than a year. He was succeeded by the son of Caracalla.

53. HELIOGABALUS.—A. D. 218. Heliogabalus, the son of Caracalla, though only fourteen years old, was, by the intrigues of his mother, proclaimed emperor in the east. He was a vicious boy; a disgusting glutton; and an odious sovereign. His actions were whimsical and cruel. He gave a supper to eight blind men, eight lame men, eight deaf men, eight black men, and eight men so fat that they could hardly sit in their chairs. Sometimes he smothered his guests with roses, and sometimes let wild beasts loose upon them. Sometimes his chariot was drawn by elephants, sometimes by lions, sometimes by dogs, and sometimes by *women*. The soldiers finally revolted to his cousin, Alexander, and Heliogabalus was thrown into the Tiber. He reigned little more than three years.

54. ALEXANDER.—A. D. 222. Alexander was an excellent monarch, but the eternal city had already passed the crisis of her fate, and nothing could stop her decline. The Persians revolted in the east, and, having overthrown the Parthian dynasty of Arsacidæ, defied the power of the Romans. The northern nations began to pour down upon the more fertile portions of the empire. Alexander defeated the Persians, and then marched into Germany, where his attempts to restore discipline occasioned a mutiny in which he was slain, after a short but glorious reign of thirteen years.

55. The army then elected Maximin, a Thracian giant, who became the most cruel tyrant upon earth. During the next five years, five emperors rose by treason and fell by conspiracy, while the empire was assailed by the Persians, and enfeebled by seditions and civil wars. The power of the senate was gone; the virtue of the people had been buried in the grave of their patriotism; the army alone possessed any authority, and this was seldom exercised for the good of the body politic. About the middle of this century, the Goths commenced their devastations in Thrace, and spread ruin on every side.

Questions.—52. How long did his reign continue? What account is given of Macrinus? How long did he reign? Who succeeded him? 53. Who was Heliogabalus? How old was he when proclaimed emperor in the east? Give an account of him. What was his fate? Who succeeded him? 54. When did Alexander become monarch? What is said of him? What counteracted the healthful influence of his reign? How long did he wear the ensigns of royalty? 55. Who was elected by the army? What followed during the next five years? What were the Goths then doing in Thrace?

56. THIRTY TYRANTS USURP THE THRONE.—From the resemblance between the miseries of this period and those which Athens suffered under the dominion of Sparta, it has been said that thirty tyrants assumed the imperial purple; this exact number, however, cannot be traced; and among the emperors who swayed the Roman scepter, from A. D. 250 to 300 must be reckoned the good Valerian, the valiant Aurelian, the venerable Tacitus, and the upright Probus. It would be tedious to relate or read all the conspiracies, cruelties, and crimes which raised, disgraced, and dethroned the thirty monarchs. Only a few of the most worthy will be mentioned, in whose reigns important events occurred.

57. The good Valerian was made emperor by the army in A. D. 253. In his reign the empire was attacked on all sides. The Franks, the Goths, the Alemanni, and the Persians vexed the frontiers with continual incursions, and Valerian was compelled to commit Europe to the care of his vicious son, Gallienus, while he marched into Asia to oppose Sapor, king of Persia. He was defeated, and taken prisoner by his enemies. "For seven years the Roman emperor bowed himself down, that his body might serve as a stepping-stone to the Persian king when he mounted on horseback; he was at last flayed alive; and his skin, stuffed in the form of a human figure, and dyed with scarlet, was preserved in a temple in Persia." The wicked Gallienus made no effort to free his father from captivity, nor to avenge his death.

58. AURELIAN.—When Aurelian ascended the throne, A. D. 270, barbarians, famine, pestilence, conspiracies, and proscriptions had swept from the empire *one-half of its inhabitants;* the western provinces were in a state of revolt, and the eastern had been brought under the dominion of the celebrated ZENOBIA, queen of Palmyra.* She was the widow of Odenatus, a prince who strove to deliver Valerian from Sapor, and had received from the Romans the title of Augustus. After his death, Zenobia, like Semiramis, assumed the command of his dominions, and by her surpassing attractions and uncommon abilities held beneath her sway the voluptuous Syrians, and the fierce Arabs of the desert.

* Palmyra, or "Tadmor in the wilderness," was built by Solomon in an oasis of the Syrian desert, 140 miles east of Damascus. Situated as it was in a green and fertile spot, sheltered by high mountains, on the great route from India, Persia, and Mesopotamia to Syria, it became the resting-place of caravans, and was soon enriched with all the treasures of the east.

Questions.—56. What is said about the thirty tyrants? 57. In what year was the good Valerian made emperor? What difficulties menaced his reign? To whom did he commit the care of Europe? What indignities and cruelties did he suffer seven years? 58. When did Aurelian ascend the throne? What then was the condition of Rome? Who was Zenobia?

59. Aurelian, determining to humble her power, marched with his army into Asia. He found the city of Palmyra defended by warlike engines of great power, and when he summoned the queen to surrender, he received a reply so spirited that all his anger was roused. He surrounded the city, cut off her supplies, and defeated three armies which were marching to her relief. Finally, Zenobia attempted to fly upon her dromedaries, but was taken prisoner at the fords of the Euphrates. She was carried to Rome, and walked in the triumph of the conqueror, loaded with chains of gold and costly jewels. Her sons married distinguished Roman ladies, and she lived in splendor the remainder of her life.

60. The characters of the Roman emperors seemed to exercise no control over the decrees of fate. The purple was but the passport to the poniard; the good and the bad, when clothed with authority, were alike exposed to the assassin's knife. Aurelian fell by the hand of a general whom he had always loved and trusted; and the army, with a respect which had long been unknown among the legions, wrote to the senate, begging the *fathers* to place the emperor among the number of the gods, and appoint a successor. For eight months, the empire was quiet without an emperor. Finally, Tacitus, a senator descended from the eminent historian, was persuaded to assume the diadem of the Cæsars. He reigned, however, only two hundred days.

61. THE TWO AUGUSTII AND THE TWO CÆSARS.—The next emperor we shall notice is Dioclesian, who, having been elected by the soldiers, chose Maximian, a brave and uncultivated officer, for his colleague. Finding, after the lapse of a few years, that the empire needed a sovereign in every part, these two monarchs adopted each a soldier as his successor. Galerius married the daughter of Dioclesian, and Constantius married the daughter of Maximian. The two emperors were called Augustii; the two heirs-expectant, Cæsars. The empire was then parceled out to the monarchs. Dioclesian and his son-in-law took that portion east of the Adriatic, while Maximian and his Cæsar shared the west. The barbarians were thus kept in awe, and the empire was for a time prosperous and happy. Dioclesian defeated the Persians, and forced them to conclude a treaty, by which they resigned all the country west of the Tigris.

Questions.—59. Upon what did Aurelian determine? Give an account of his measures and success. What further is stated of Zenobia? 60. By whose hand did Aurelian fall? What state of things followed? Who succeeded Aurelian? How long did Tacitus reign? 61. To what position was Dioclesian raised? Who was Maximian? What compact was made? How was it strengthened? What were the two emperors called? What name was given to the two heirs-expectant? How was the empire divided?

62. A. D. **400.** CONSTANTINE THE GREAT REMOVES THE SEAT OF GOVERNMENT TO CONSTANTINOPLE.—THEODOSIUS DIVIDES THE EMPIRE.—Notwithstanding the nine bloody persecutions which successive generations of Christians had endured, the leaven of the Gospel had been constantly at work in the empire, and many persons of rank and consequence professed the doctrines of the cross. In the year A. D. 303, Dioclesian issued an edict against the Christians, in consequence of which the most dreadful persecution raged for ten years. The churches were pulled down; the Scriptures were burned; and such numbers of people perished, that at last the murderers declared that the Christian name and superstition were rooted out of the empire. This was the last persecution of the Christians by the Romans. In the midst of these scenes of slaughter, Dioclesian and Maximian triumphed at Rome, and once more regaled the multitude with the combats of gladiators and wild beasts.

63. This was the last triumph the imperial city ever saw. Her days of victory were nearly passed, the weakness of age had come upon her, and the hour of her dissolution was rapidly approaching. Not long after, Dioclesian *resigned his authority*, and required Maximian to do the same. Dioclesian retired to the southern part of Austria, and Maximian to the southern part of Italy. Constantius and Galerius having thus become the Augustii, two new Cæsars were chosen. Constantius, however, died at York, in Britain, within two years after his accession to power, and the army immediately saluted his son, Constantine, as emperor. Galerius and the two Cæsars refused to ratify the act; and Maxentius, son of Maximian, being invested by the *senate* with the imperial dignity, called his father from retirement to give weight to his authority.

64. There were thus *six* competitors for the empire; and a scene of contention followed, scarcely paralleled in the annals of Rome. Maximian quarreled with his son, and was put to death. Galerius died not long after, which reduced the number of aspirants to *four*. Maxentius speedily commenced open hostilities, and Constantine, at the head of a powerful army, marched toward Rome. During this journey, that famous change took place in his religion or politics, which resulted in the overthrow of paganism, and the establishment of Christianity as the religion of the empire. One evening, while employed in medita-

---

Questions.—62. Give an account of the progress of Christianity. In what year did Dioclesian issue an edict against Christianity? Give a history of the persecution. 63. What is further stated of Dioclesian? Of Maximian? What is said of Constantius? Of Galerius? 64. What scene of contention is depicted? What caused the overthrow of paganism?

tion upon the conflicting opinions which agitated mankind, he sent up his ejaculations to Heaven for divine direction. As if in answer to his prayer, a luminous cross suddenly appeared above the declining sun, bearing the inscription, "IN THIS, OVERCOME." The same night a vision confirmed the miracle, and Constantine became a convert to Christianity. A royal standard was made to resemble that seen in the sky, and carried before him as an ensign of victory and celestial protection. Maxentius was defeated, and drowned in the Tiber. The competitors were thus reduced to *three.*

65. Constantine entered Rome, and, disclaiming the adulation which the servile Romans offered, set up a cross at the right hand of his statues, declaring that he owed all his success to a superior power. He restored the authority of the senate, reformed abuses, *and banished the prætorian guards.* He then marched to Milan, where he formed an alliance with one of the Cæsars, and gave him his sister in marriage; the other Cæsar was overthrown and slain, so that only two rivals remained of the six. In the year 323,* a battle was fought between these *two.* Constantine was victorious, and became sole monarch of the empire, after eighteen years of contention and civil war. Being now possessed of unlimited power, he issued an edict that in all the provinces of the empire the orders of the bishops should be obeyed; and a general council, assembled at his request, condemned the "Arian heresy." Perceiving the necessity of fixing his residence in the center of his dominions, or wishing to rival the fame of Romulus, Constantine formed the design of removing the seat of government to the spot where the "*Golden Horn*" of the Bosphorus encircled the oft-conquered and reconquered Byzantium.

66. With the wealth of the world at his command, nothing of course was neglected which could contribute to the splendor of the new capital. Magnificent churches, palaces, and private dwellings sprang up with almost magical rapidity; while baths and gardens, parks and private walks, exhibited all the refinements of eastern luxury. The court followed the monarch to the rising city of *Constantinople;* and Rome, who had suffered so much from a multitude of emperors, now saw herself deserted by the *one* who had concentrated all authority in himself. These were the principal events of the reign of Constantine. In his old age he was guilty of great cruelty, and his conduct during

* Alexander became monarch of the world, 323 B. C. Constantine sole emperor, 323 A. D.

Questions.—64. What evidence, if any, did Constantine give of Christianity? 65. How did he become sole monarch of the empire? What edict did he issue? What induced him to change the seat of government? 66. What is said of the building and growth of Constantinople? What is said of Constantine in his old age? What further is said of his conduct?

his whole life stamps him as a political rather than a pious advocate of Christianity.

67. CONSTANTINE, CONSTANS, AND CONSTANTIUS.—A. D. 337.—On the death of Constantine, his dominions were divided between his three sons, youths, who, without inheriting the virtues of their father, imitated his relentless cruelty, and added to it the vices of a voluptuous court. With the exception of two cousins, these princes destroyed all the male members of the Constantine family, and then turned their arms upon one another. Constantine was dethroned and slain within three years after the death of his father, by his brother Constans, who, ten years later, suffered a similar fate from the hand of his own general. Constantius, being thus left sole emperor, called his cousin, Julian, to a share of power. To escape the jealous fury which destroyed all his relations, Julian had buried himself in study and retirement, but upon being clothed with the title and power of a Cæsar, he showed himself an able and valiant general. His success in a war with the Sarmatians roused the latent envy of Constantius, and the legions of the west having proclaimed him emperor, the nations beheld again with terror the marshaling of armies for a civil war. The death of Constantius averted the threatened danger, and Julian peaceably ascended the throne.

68. JULIAN THE APOSTATE.—A. D. 361. The new Augustus had little reason to love a religion which the children of Constantine had professed, and his hatred of Christianity was immediately shown by his attempt to re-establish paganism. To disprove the prophecy of Christ, he attempted to rebuild the temple at Jerusalem. His impious design was frustrated by the hand of Providence. "Horrible balls of fire breaking out from the foundation, with frequent and reiterated attacks, rendered the place inaccessible to the workmen; the victorious element continuing in this manner, seemed obstinately bent to drive them to a distance, and the hopeless attempt was abandoned."

69. Julian was killed in battle with the Persians, after a reign of 16 months. Jovian, one of his domestics, was proclaimed emperor by the soldiers. He gave up the cities which had been taken from the Persians, and conducted the Romans in safety back to Antioch, where he had only time to revoke the decrees against the Christians, when he also died. Valentinian, commander of his body-guard, was proclaimed

Questions.—67. When did he die? What division took place after his death? Give the character of the three brothers. Who was Julian? How was he called to govern? 68. What did Julian undertake to do? How did he attempt to disprove the words of Christ? What was the result? 69. By whom was Julian killed? Who succeeded him? Give an account of Jovian's course. Who became his successor?

his successor. He divided the empire, giving to his brother, Valens, the dominion of the east, while he took up his residence at Milan, as monarch of the west. Wars with the northern tribes occupied the time of both emperors. After a reign of twelve years, Valentinian died, leaving the scepter to his son, Gratian, then a youth of 17. THE HUNS now came forth from the wilds of Scythia, upon their work of destruction.*

70. The Goths, intimidated by the invasion of a nation more barbarous than themselves, entreated the emperor, Valens, to grant them lands on the southern side of the Danube. The request was acceded to, on certain conditions; and a million of savages were thus settled in Thrace. The treachery of a Roman governor excited them to revolt, and Valens fell a victim to their vengeance. Two-thirds of his army perished in battle, and the country was ravaged to the very gates of Constantinople. The young Gratian advanced from the west too late to save the life of his uncle, but in season to rescue the capital from the invaders. Feeling his inability to sustain the weight of an empire tottering to its fall, he called in Theodosius, a native of Spain, to his assistance, and gave to him the empire of the east.

71. In four years, Theodosius, by his wisdom and firmness, subdued the Goths, and received great numbers of them into the Roman armies. After the death of Gratian, Theodosius married Galla, the beautiful daughter of the deceased emperor, and became *the last sole monarch of the empire.* He visited Italy. The idols which had so long been worshiped in the imperial city were thrown down; the images were defaced, and the temples deserted, to give place to the less imposing forms of Christian worship. Before his death, Theodosius divided the empire between his two sons, Arcadius and Honorius.† It was never after re-united, and the subsequent pages will be devoted to the history of the Western Empire.

72. Theodosius died in the month of January, A. D. 395, and before the opening of spring, the Gothic nation was in arms. The barriers of the Danube were opened, and the savage warriors of Scythia

* See map No. 1.

† Rufinus, a Gaul, governed the councils of Arcadius; while Stilicho, a Vandal, directed the administration of Honorius.

Questions.—69. With whom did Valentinian divide the empire? What is said of Valentinian? To whom did he leave his scepter? What then did the Huns begin? 70. What request did the Goths make? With what success? Why did the Goths revolt? What became of Valens? What then took place? Why did Gratian associate Theodosius with him? 71. Did Theodosius succeed against the Goths? How and when? After the death of Gratian what did Theodosius do? How did he divide his empire? 72. When did he die? What destruction came after?

"rolled their ponderous wagons over the broad and icy back of the indignant river." The fertile fields of Greece were covered with a deluge of barbarians, who massacred the men, and drove away the beautiful females, with the cattle of the flaming villages.

73. A. D. **500.** ITALY PLUNDERED BY GOTH, VANDAL, AND HUN.—AUGUSTULUS, LAST EMPEROR.—ALARIC'S THREE INVASIONS.—Between the years 400 and 403, Alaric, at the head of his savage legions, invaded Italy. Stilicho, the able and faithful general of Honorius, defeated him, and finally hired him to enter the service of the Romans. In 408, Alaric, not having received the stipulated sums, again led his army into the garden of Europe. The queen of the world purchased her safety with the treasures of the capitol. During a period of 619 years, the seat of the empire had never been violated by the presence of a foreign enemy; but when, in 409, the king of the Goths crossed the Po, spread hi armys along the banks of the Tiber, seized the port of Ostia, and threatened to destroy the magazines of corn, the terror of famine overcame the pride of the senate, and they assented to Alaric's proposal of placing a new emperor upon the throne of the unworthy Honorius. The gates of the city were thrown open, and Attalus, the man whom Alaric had selected, was clothed in the purple of the Cæsars, and conducted by Gothic guards to the palace of Augustus and Trajan.

74. But Attalus wanted the spirit to command, and the docility to obey. Alaric became tired of his puppet-king, and the next year stripped him of his royal robes, and sent them to Honorius, who had shut himself up in Ravenna. The king of the Goths, no longer dissembling his appetite for plunder and revenge, now appeared in arms under the walls of the capital; the senate were unable to guard against the treachery of their domestics; a gate was silently opened, and the inhabitants were roused from their slumbers by the tremendous sound of the Gothic trumpet. 1163 years after the founding of Rome, the "eternal city" was sacked and plundered by the savage tribes of Germany and Scythia. The gold and jewels of the nobles were first secured; the massy furniture and silken wardrobes of the great were piled upon wagons; exquisite works of art, once the pride of Athens, Corinth, or the splendid cities of the east, were shivered in pieces; and vases of the most beautiful workmanship were divided by the stroke of the battle-ax and distributed among the rapacious soldiers.

Questions.—73. Give an account of the invasions of Alaric. What revolution was produced in Rome? Who was selected for the palace of Augustus? 74. When weary of Attalus, where did Alaric send him? Describe the plundering of the city that followed.

75. The Goths evacuated the city on the sixth day. At the head of an army encumbered with rich and weighty spoils, Alaric advanced along the Appian way to the southern point of Italy. There the fertile island of Sicily attracted his attention, and his active mind immediately formed the design of preparing a fleet which should transport his followers across the narrow strait of Messina, and waft them to the shores of Africa. The winds and waves, more potent than the Roman arms, sunk or scattered his ill-constructed galleys; and death, the conqueror of kings, soon after fixed the fatal term of his conquests. His soldiers, with true barbaric grief, turned the course of the little river Busentinus, and constructed his splendid sepulchre in its ancient bed; the waters were then restored to their natural channel; and thus have they flowed, age after age, over the tomb of *Alaric the Visigoth.*

76. Adolphus, the brother-in-law of Alaric, succeeded to the sovereignty of the Gothic people. In the sack of Rome they had taken captive the beautiful Placidia, daughter of Theodosius; and the noble barbarian, won by her charms, now offered peace to Honorius on condition of receiving the hand of his sister in marriage. The fair Placidia consented, and the union was consummated before the Goths left Italy. The bride, adorned like an empress, was placed upon a throne of state, while her husband, clothed in the Roman toga, occupied a less elevated seat at her side. Fifty beautiful slaves, dressed in silken robes, presented her with fifty basins of gold, and fifty basins of gems; yet even this extraordinary nuptial gift formed but a small part of the rare and magnificent spoils of her country.

77. Adolphus retired with his bride and his people into Gaul, and thence into Spain, where *he founded the kingdom of the Visigoths.* In the year 415, Adolphus was assassinated by one of his domestics, and Wallia, his successor to the sovereignty of the Gothic nation, led his followers in the track of Alaric to the southern shore of Italy. The tempestuous sea again prevented the projected expedition to Africa; and Constantius, the brave general of Honorius, forced the barbarians to conclude a peace, and exchange the unfortunate Placidia for 6,000 measures of wheat. The hand of the widow of Adolphus was the

---

Questions.—75. When did the Goths evacuate Rome? What did Alaric do? How did he lose his life? Where was he buried? 76. Who succeeded to the sovereignty of the Goths? How was peace consummated between Rome and Adolphus? Describe the ceremonious splendor of the marriage. 77. What kingdom did Adolphus found? What was the fate of Adolphus? Who was his successor? How was the expedition to Africa prevented? Who effected a peace for Honorius? What became of the unfortunate Placidia? What was the reward of Constantius?

reward of Constantius, and the care of her children, Valentinian and Honoria, thenceforth occupied her attention.

78. THE VANDALS.—At the very time that the Goths were engaged in the plunder of Italy, a similar devastation was going on in Spain. The Suevi, the Vandals, and the Alani forced the passes of the Pyrenees, establishing themselves in the most fertile portions of that country, and enslaved the original inhabitants. In the year 429, Genseric led the Vandals across the strait of Gibraltar, and, re-enforcing his army by enlisting the Moors, proceeded to *wrest from the Romans all their possessions in Africa.* On a sudden, the seven fruitful provinces from Tangier to Tripoli were overwhelmed by the bloody tide of war. During eight years, the Vandals spread themselves like locusts over the land, and completed their conquests by once more destroying Carthage, the capital of the African world. About the same time, *the Goths, the Burgundians, and the Franks obtained a permanent seat in the provinces of Gaul.*

79. As early as the time of Cicero, it was the opinion of the augurs that the *twelve vultures* which Romulus had seen represented the *twelve centuries* assigned for the fatal period of his city. Now, when the loss of the provinces beyond the Alps impaired the glory and greatness of Rome; when her internal prosperity was irretrievably destroyed by the separation of Africa; and when the twelfth century, clouded with disgrace and misfortune, was almost elapsed, the people remembered the fearful omen, and looked forward with gloomy foreboding to the accomplishment of the prophecy. After a disgraceful reign of twenty-eight years, Honorius died of a dropsy, and the scepter of the Western Empire descended to the feeble hands of Valentinian III., the infant son of Constantius; Placidia being declared regent. At a suitable age, he was married to his cousin, Eudoxia; but his mother still retained her influence, and ruled in his name for twenty-five years.

80. ATTILA.—The Goths and the Vandals, from whom the imperial city suffered so much, fled before the Huns; but in the year 433 the Huns themselves marched southward to the Danube, and under Attila. surnamed the "Scourge of God," became the terror of the world, From the banks of the Volga to the banks of the Rhine, the savage

Questions.—78. What was going on in Spain at that time? Who forced the passes of the Pyrenees? What was their object? Who led the Vandals across the strait of Gibraltar? What possessions did they wrest from the Romans? What further conquests attended them? 79. What became a proverb in the time of Cicero? To what were the people of Rome then looking? What was the condition of Rome after the death of Honorius? 80. By whom were the Goths and Vandals routed? What mention is next made of the Huns? Describe the ravages of the chieftain Attila.

chieftain extended his fearful sway, and, disdaining to dismount from his horse, dictated to embassadors from Constantinople the terms of a peace, each condition of which was an insult to the Roman name. The treaty was soon broken, and the whole breadth of Europe was invaded, occupied, and desolated by the myriads of barbarians whom Attila led into the field. In the year 452 he passed the Alps, subdued Italy, and took Aquileia, Milan, and Pavia.

81. It is a saying worthy of the ferocious pride of the Hunnic chief, that the grass never grew on the spot where his horse had trod. Yet this savage destroyer undesignedly laid the foundation of a city, which for a long time sheltered and nourished the sciences and arts. Before this irruption, fifty Venetian cities clustered around Aquileia, and, supported by commerce and manufactures, gradually accumulated extraordinary wealth. The peaceful inhabitants of these cities, scattered like wild-fowl before the storm of war, found a safe but obscure resting-place in the neighboring islands; and there, nestling as it were upon the bosom of the waves, where the swell of the Adriatic feebly imitates the tides of the ocean, they reared the amphibious city of Venice, which, in the middle ages, was the great commercial emporium of Europe.

82. Valentinian fled from Ravenna to Rome, and his ministers purchased the safety of Italy by paying to the barbarian the immense dowry of the princess Honoria, and consenting to add the granddaughter of Theodosius to the list of his innumerable wives, within a stipulated time. The king of the Huns then drew off his myriads, and retired to his wooden palace beyond the Danube, where death found him in the arms of sleep, and silenced forever his claims upon the empire of Rome. His remains were inclosed in three coffins, of gold, of silver, and of iron; and in the darkness of night committed to the earth, together with the spoils of nations and the bodies of slaughtered captives.

83. A. D. 455. The death of Attila broke the power of the Huns, but the next year Valentinian was assassinated by Maximus, a senator of illustrious birth, who was proclaimed emperor by the senate and people, while the bleeding corpse of his rightful sovereign lay at his feet. This was the last day of his happiness; his hours were disturbed by remorse or terror; and his throne was shaken by the seditions of

---

Questions.—81. In what manner did he give existence to Venice? 82. To what place did Valentinian flee? How was the safety of Italy purchased? What is said of the death of Attila? What disposition was made of his remains? 83. What became of Valentinian? Who then was proclaimed emperor? How were the hours of the new emperor disturbed?

the soldiers, the people, and the confederate barbarians. Eudoxia, the widow of Valentinian, had been compelled to violate her mourning to appear as the bride of the usurper. From the east she could expect no assistance; the scepter of Constantinople was in the hands of a stranger; and, despairing of aid from her own people, she turned her eyes to Africa, and begged the aid of *Genseric*, the king of the Vandals. The royal barbarian had already a powerful fleet in the ports of the Mediterranean; and six hundred years after the total defeat of the naval power of Carthage by the Romans, the ships of Genseric, manned by a motley crew of Vandals, Moors, and Africans, issued from the harbors of the city of Dido, to take vengeance upon Imperial Rome.

84. When the Vandals disembarked at Ostia, Maximus prepared for instant flight; but no sooner did he appear in the streets than the infuriated populace assaulted him with a shower of stones, and his mangled body at length found its grave in the Tiber. Rome and its inhabitants were delivered to the violence of the Vandals and Moors. The pillage lasted fourteen days and nights. The spoils of pagan temples and of Christian churches, the holy instruments of Jewish worship which had been displayed in the triumph of Titus, the gilded roof of the capitol (which cost not less than $10,000,000), the imperial ornaments of the palace, and the magnificent furniture of private dwellings, were carefully collected and laboriously removed to the fleet.

85. Eudoxia herself, who advanced to meet her deliverer, was rudely stripped of her jewels, and with her two daughters, the only surviving remains of the great Theodosius, was compelled, as a captive, to follow the haughty Vandal to Africa. Her elder daughter, Eudocia, became the reluctant bride of Hunneric, the eldest son of Genseric; and the queen, with her younger daughter, after several years of captivity, was honorably restored to the eastern emperor. The shores of Italy, Spain, and Greece were afflicted by the incessant depredations of the Vandal pirates. In the spring of each year they sailed from the ports of Carthage, and Genseric, remarking that "the winds would transport them to the guilty coasts, whose inhabitants had provoked divine justice," suffered his ships to float at ease upon the bosom of the Mediterranean, till the sight of some wealthy city tempted him to land. He continued thus the tyrant of the sea to an

Questions.—83. What was Eudoxia compelled to do? What afterward did she do. Was she successful? 84. At what place in Italy did the Vandals disembark? Relate the fate of Maximus. What then followed? What is said of the pillage and spoils? 85. What treatment did Eudoxia receive? What is related of the depredations of the Vandal pirates?

advanced age, and lived to witness the final extinction of the Empire of the West.

86. In the space of twenty years after the death of Valentinian, nine emperors successively disappeared from the Roman stage, and the last would be least entitled to the notice of posterity, if his reign, which was marked by the fall of the Western Empire, did not leave a memorable era in the history of mankind. In these times of confusion and discord, when Italy (now all that was left to Rome) was alternately defended and ravaged by the barbarians who ranged themselves under the banners of the sinking empire, Orestes, a Pannonian chief, having gained the favor of the troops, invested his son, *Romulus Augustus* * with the imperial purple, and seated him upon the throne of the Cæsars. The youth who was thus made the instrument of his father's ambition was distinguished only by his beauty and misfortunes. The troops who had assisted in his elevation claimed one-third of the lands of Italy as their reward; this insolent demand was denied, and Odoacer, chief of the Heruli, roused them to revolt from their inoffensive monarch.

87. Pavia was taken by storm; Orestes executed, and the helpless Augustus, who could no longer command the respect, was reduced to implore the clemency of Odoacer. The barbarian spared his life, and the "last emperor of Rome," having signed his abdication in due form, was permitted to retire to the splendid castle of Lucullus, upon the shores of Campania. Odoacer, despising the empty title of Augustus and Cæsar, caused himself to be proclaimed *King of Italy;* and the senate, mindful of their ancient dignity in the last hour of their authority, addressed an epistle to the eastern emperor, solemnly disclaiming the necessity or even the wish of continuing any longer the imperial succession in Italy, and consenting to receive the administration of justice from the hand of Odoacer.

Thus ended the empire of Rome, A. D. 476, 1,229 years after the foundation of the city by Romulus.

* Romulus was corrupted into *Momyllus* by the Greeks, and Augustus changed by the Latins into the contemptible diminutive, *Augustulus*, "little Augustus."

Questions.—86, 87. What further is stated of the final overthrow of the Roman empire? By what means did Odoacer obtain power? In what year did the empire of Rome end? How many years had it existed?

REVIEW QUESTIONS.

		PAGE
1.	Give an account of the building of Rome	314, 315
2.	What can you state of the inhabitants?	315, 316
3.	Of the religion of the Romans?	316, 317
4.	Of marriages among the Romans?	317
5.	Of the government of Rome?	317, 318
6.	How were trials among the Romans conducted?	318
7.	What can you state of the occupations of the Romans?	319
8.	Of their preparations for battle?	319
9.	Of their funeral ceremonies?	319, 320
10.	Of the fabulous history of Rome?	320
11.	Give the early history of Rome	320, 321, 322
12.	The history as connected with that of the Sabines	322–324
13.	Now give the biography of Romulus	314–324
14.	Give the biography of Numa Pompilius	324, 325
15.	Give an account of the reign of Tullius Hostilius	325, 326
16.	Of the reign of Ancus Martius	326, 327
17.	Of the reign of Lucius Tarquinius Priscus	327, 328
18.	Of the reign of Servius Tullius	328, 329
19.	Of the reign of Lucius Tarquinius Superbus	329–331
20.	What change in the government then took place?	331, 332
21.	What efforts did Tarquin make to recover power?	332–334
22.	How was the conspiracy attempt frustrated?	332, 333
23.	How, the one to capture Rome by siege?	333
24.	The one in which twenty-four towns were confederated?	334
25.	Give the origin of the "veto" power	335
26.	Why was Coriolanus banished from Rome?	335
27.	What then was his plan for vengeance?	335
28.	Give the particulars of his movements	336
29.	How, at last, was he influenced in favor of Rome?	336, 337
30.	What further can you state of Coriolanus?	337
31.	Give the story of Cincinnatus	337, 338
32.	Of Siccius Dentatus	338, 339
33.	What change then took place in the government of Rome?	339
34.	Relate the story of Virginia	339–341
35.	What changes, proposed by the tribunes, were adopted?	342
36.	What other changes afterward occurred?	342, 343
37.	Give an account of the taking of Veii	343
38.	Of Camillus till he departed from Rome	343, 344

PAGE

39. Who was Brennus? 344
40. Why did Brennus attack Rome? 344, 345
41. Give an account of his successes 345, 346
42. Give an account of the success of Camillus 346
43. Of the success of Pontius Cominius 346, 347
44. Of the success of Manlius 347, 348
45. What agreement was made between the Romans and Gauls? ... 348
46. Why was it not carried out 348
47. What further is stated of the Gauls? 348, 349
48. What arguments were used against rebuilding Rome? 349
49. Why was it determined to rebuild the city? 349
50. Give an account of Manlius 347–350
51. Of Licinius Stolo 350, 351
52. Who were the Samnites? 351
53. With whom were they engaged in war? 351, 352
54. Who was Manlius Torquatus? 352
55. Relate the story of Titus Manlius 352
56. Give an account of the battle 352, 353
57. How did Pyrrhus get involved in the Roman war? 353
58. Give an account of the movements of Pyrrhus 353, 354
59. Of his first victory over the Romans 354
60. Of his conduct after the battle 354
61. Of his failure to negotiate a peace 354–356
62. State how Fabricius gained his point 356
63. Give an account of Pyrrhus's second victory 356
64. What further can you state of Fabricius? 356, 357
65. Give an account of Pyrrhus's defeat 357
66. What movements did he afterward make? 357
67. Give the early history of Carthage 358
68. What was the origin of the first Punic war? 358
69. How were the Romans enabled to cope with Carthage on the sea? 358
70. Give an account of their first success on the sea 359
71. What successes did they have in Africa? 359
72. What were the successes of Regulus? 359, 360
73. What misfortunes befell him? 360, 361
74. What failure next awaited the Romans? 361
75. What success at last did they have? 362
76. How did the Romans use the peace that followed? 362
77. In what war were they next engaged? 362
78. Who was Viridomarus? 362
79. What challenge did he put forth? 362
80. State what followed 362, 363
81. What time elapsed between the first and second Punic wars.... 363

PAGE
82. Who was Hannibal?.. 363
83. Give the origin of the second Punic war.,.................. 363, 364
84. Of Hannibal's success in Spain............................. 364
85. Of his passage of the Alps................................. 364, 365
86. Of his first two battles with the Romans................... 365
87. Of Hannibal's suosequent movements......................... 365, 366
88. Of the battle of Thrasymenus............................... 366
89. Of Fabius and his policy................................... 366–370
90. Of Varro and his defeat at Cannæ........................... 368
91. What were the consequences of that defeat?................. 369
92. What misfortunes attended Hannibal?........................ 370–372
93. Give an account of the siege of Syracuse................... 370, 371
94. What successes did Scipio Africanus gain?.................. 372
95. Give an account of the battle of Zama...................... 373
96. What were the occurrences in Greece?....................... 373–375
97. What successes did the Romans gain over Antiochus?......... 374
98. Give the account of Scipio Africanus's closing career...... 374
99. How did the third Punic war originate?..................... 375
100. What misfortunes befell the Carthaginians?................ 375
101. Describe what followed till Carthage was destroyed........ 376
102. What added to the growing importance of Rome?............. 376, 377
103. What is said of Cornelia Gracchus?........................ 377
104. Give an account of Tiberius Gracchus...................... 377, 378
105. Of Caius Gracchus and Flaccus............................. 378, 379
106. Of the Jugurthine war..................................... 379, 380
107. Give an account of Caius Marius........................... 380, 382
108. What can you state of the early career of Sylla?.......... 380
109. How was the Mithridatic war commenced?.................... 381, 382
110. Give an account of its progress........................... 381, 382
111. Of the great victory gained by Scylla in Italy............ 382, 383
112. Of his subsequent career of crime......................... 383
113. Give the closing account of his deeds and death........... 383, 384
114. Give some account of Crassus.............................. 383–388
115. What were Lucullus's successes in Asia?................... 384
116. How came Pompey to supersede Lucullus?.................... 384
117. Give the closing account of the Mithridatic war?.......... 384–386
118. Give an account of Catiline's conspiracy.................. 385, 386
119. Of Pompey's return to Rome................................ 386, 387
120. How was the first triumvirate effected?................... 387, 388
121. What division did the triumvirs agree on?................. 388
122. What successes did Cæsar gain?............................ 388, 389
123. What career did Crassus run?.............................. 389
124. Name the events preceding the passing of the Rubicon...... 389, 390

PAGE

125. Give the particulars of that event.......................... 390
126. What flight and pursuit then followed?...................... 390
127. Give an account of Cæsar's next success..................... 391
128. Of the battle fought at Dyracchium.......................... 391
129. Of the next battle, that of Pharsalia....................... 391–393
130. What further account can you give of Pompey?............... 393, 394
131. Why did Cæsar go to Egypt?.................................. 395
132. What did he accomplish in Egypt?............................ 395
133. What in Africa, west of Egypt?.............................. 395, 396
134. What other successes did Cæsar gain?....................... 396, 397
135. Give an account of the end of Cæsar........................ 397, 398
136. Describe what followed...................................... 398–400
137. How was the second triumvirate brought about?............. 400, 401
138. What were the terms agreed upon by the triumvirs?.......... 400
139. How was the "proscription" carried out?.................... 400
140. State what took place in Greece............................. 400, 401
141. Give an account of Antony's next movements................ 401, 402
142. Of the aims and movements of Octavius....................... 402
143. What new division of power was made?....................... 402
144. What became of Pompey and Lepidus?.......................... 402
145. Give the particulars of what followed....................... 402
146. Of the battle of Actium and its consequences............... 402, 403
147. Give the particulars of Octavius's successes............... 403
148. What is stated of the reign of Augustus?................... 404
149. Give an account of his family affairs and death............ 405
150. What can you state of the reign of Tiberius?............... 405
151. Of Germanicus and his career?............................... 405, 406
152. Of Sejanus and his career?.................................. 406
153. Of the close of Tiberius's reign, and of his death?........ 406, 407
154. Of Caligula, his career and death?.......................... 407, 408
155. Of Claudius, his career and death?.......................... 408, 409
156. Of Nero, his career and death?.............................. 409–411
157. Of Galba, his career and death?............................. 411, 412
158. Of Otho, his career and death?.............................. 412
159. Of Vitellius, his career and death?......................... 412
160. Of Vespasian, and what he and Titus accomplished?.......... 412–415
161. Of Titus, his career and death?............................. 413–416
162. Of Domitian, his career and death?.......................... 416
163. Of Trajan, his career and death?............................ 416, 417
164. Of Adrian, his reign and death?............................. 417, 418
165. Of Antoninus, his reign and death?.......................... 418, 419
166. Of Marcus Aurelius, his reign and death?................... 419
167. Of Pertinax, his reign and death?........................... 420, 421

PAGE

168. What events followed the death of Pertinax?................ 421
169. What were the events of Servius's reign?.................. 421, 422
170. What the events during the next eighteen years?............ 422
171. Give an account of the career of Caracalla.................. 422, 423
172. Of Heliogabalus, his acts and death 423
173. Give the events during the next eighteen years............... 424
174. What is stated in relation to the thirty tyrants?............. 425
175. In relation to Valerian, his acts and death?................. 424
176. In relation to Aurelian, his acts and death?................. 424, 425
177. Name the closing events of the century...................... 425
178. What is stated of the ten persecutions?...................... 426
179. Give the particulars of Constantine's accession to power...... 426, 427
180. Of his important acts and death.............................. 427, 428
181. Name the events of the next twenty-four years................ 428
182. Give the account of Julian and Jovian........................ 428
183. Of Valentinian.. 428, 429
184. Of Gratian and Theodosius..................................... 429
185. Give the particulars of Alaric's invasion..................... 429, 430
186. Of his subsequent acts, movements, and death................. 430, 431
187. Give the story of Placidia.................................... 431, 432
188. What misfortunes did the Vandals inflict?.................... 432
189. What other misfortunes befell Rome?......................... 432
190. What conquests were made by Attila?......................... 432, 433
191. Give the account of Maximus.................................. 433, 434
192. Of Eudoxia.. 433, 434
193. What did Rome suffer from the Vandals and Moors?............ 434
194. Give the particulars of Genseric's career.................... 434, 435
195. Give the account of Romulus Augustus......................... 435
196. Give the account of Odoacer.................................. 435
197. When was the Roman empire brought to an end?................ 435

INDEX

AND

RULES FOR PRONUNCIATION.

EVERY accented vowel, ending a syllable, has its long sound, as C*a*-to, the accent being designated by an *italic* letter. Every accented vowel, not ending a syllable, has its short sound, as M*a*n-lius. The diphthongs, *æ* and *œ*, are pronounced exactly like our English *e; ei*, like our *i; eu* is generally a part of two syllables, as, I-dom-e-n*e*-us; *e*, final, always forms a distinct syllable, as, Pe-n*e*l-o-pe. *C* and *g* are hard before *a*, *o*, and *u*; and soft before *e*, *i*, and *y*; before *ia*, and like terminations, they assume *sh*, as Ac-ci-us, Ca-d*u*-ceus; *Ch* has always the sound of *k*, as Co*l*-chis; *M*, like other consonants, is silent before *n*, as Mn*e*-mon; *P* is silent before *s* and *t*, as Psamme*t*ichus, Pto*l*emy.

The rules for *accent* will be best expressed by the following verse:—

"Each monosyllable has stress, of course;
Words of two syllables the first enforce:
A syllable that 's long, and last but one,
Must have the accent upon that or none;
But if this syllable be short, the stress
Must on the last but two its force express."

The pupils, in writing the biographies of the *individuals* here mentioned, will read the pages specified, and such other authorities as may be found in the School Libraries, being careful to designate the time *when*, and the place *where*, the person lived.

In describing a *people*, let the migrations, settlements, and political changes be carefully noted.

In writing the history of a *city*, let all the remarkable events of which it was the scene become the subject of thought, in chronological order.

This method will cultivate a taste for reading and a habit of research, at the same time that it teaches composition and classification of ideas.

A-be*d*-ne-go..............12
Ab-ra-d*a*-tes....43, 46, 47, 48
A-b*y*-dos......67, 71, 187, 194
Abys-si*n*-i-a..........16, 417
Ac-a-d*e*-mus........196, 221
A-chæ*m*-e-nes.........71, 72
A-ch*æ*-us.................98
A-ch*a*-i-a........215, 243–287
A-chi*l*-las...............394
A-chi*l*-les....... 94, 100, 227
A*c*-ti-um............309, 402
A-cra....................413
Ad-he*r*-bal...............379
Ad-m*e*-tus...............155
A-do*l*-phus..............431
A-d*o*-nis.................418
A dri-an...........417, 418
A-dri-an-*o*-ple...........418
A-dri-a*t*-ic..........425, 433
Ag-a-me*m*-non...........243
Ag-a-ri*s*-te..............160
A-gat*h*-o-cles........289, 298
A-ges-i-l*a*-us....126, 202–219
A-ge-si*p*-o-lis.......126, 209
A-gis...........126, 185–280
A-g*o*-ra..................150
Ag-ri-ge*n*-tum.......359, 360
A-gri*p*-pa................405
Ag-rip-p*i*-na.........406, 408
A*l*-a-ric.............430, 431
Al-b*i*-nus..............419–422
Al-ci-b*i*-a-des........175–198
Alc-m*œ*-on..........113–124
Al-e-ma*n*-ni..............424
Al-ex-a*n*-der........237–270
A*l*-li-a...................345
A-m*a*-sis......12, 13, 29–53
A-me*n*-o-phis..............21
Am-phi*c*-ty-on........98–382
Am-phi*p*-o-lis...174, 224–274
Am-phi*s*-sa..........234, 235
Am-phi-tr*i*te..............93
A-m*y*-it...................13
A-m*u*-li-us..........320, 321
A-my*n*-tas.......73, 208, 223
An-a-cy*n*-dar-ax-es......246
An-ax-a*g*-o-ras...........160
An-ch*i*-a-lus.............246
A*n*-cus..............325–328
An-c*y*-ra.................246
A*n*-dros............191, 192
An-ta*l*-ci-das..........82, 207
A*n*-ti-och...........419, 428
An-ti*g*-o-nus.....271, 272-274
An-t*i*-o-chus....191, 284–374
An-ti*p*-a-ter.....242, 270–276
An-t*o*-ni-a...........413, 414
An-to-n*i*-us..........418, 419
A*n*-to-ny....303–311, 389–402
A-n*y*-sis..................25
A-pis........13, 17, 55, 56, 84
A-po*l*-lo.............118, 122
A*p*-pi-us........339–341, 355
A-pri-es........13, 29, 30, 31
A-p*u*-li-a................367
Aq-ui-l*e*-i-a..............533
A-r*a*-bi-a.......13, 20, 22, 46
A-ra*s*-pes..........40, 43, 45
Ar-*a*-tus............278–282
Ar-b*a*-ces...........9–11, 35
Ar-b*e*-la..........84. 251–254
Ar-c*a*-di-a...110–136, 191–241
Ar-c*a*-di-us...........88, 429
Ar-che-l*a*-us.........104, 223
A*r*-chi-as........209, 210, 211

Ar-chi-da-mus..127, 159, 170
Ar-chi-me-des..........370
Ar-e-op-a-gus........120, 160
Ar-gi-a................104
Ar-gi-nu-sæ.....192, 193, 198
Ar-gi-ves...........191, 277
Ar-gæ-us................224
Ar-gos.....110, 158, 196, 283
Ar-go-lis................89
Ar-i-dæ-us.......223, 270–273
A-ri-ma-ni-us............34
A-ri-æ-us..........77, 78, 79
Ar-is-tag-o-ras.....62, 63, 124
A-ris-to-bu-lus............385
A-ris-to-de-mus..........104
Ar-is-to-gi-ton.......122, 258
Ar-is-tom-e-nes..110-113, 159
Ar-is-ton-i-a..............58
Ar-is-tot-le..14, 231, 237, 238
Ar-is-ti-des.128, 132, 143–175
Ar-me-ni-a........7, 395, 403
Ar-ta-ba-nus..........70, 71
Ar-ta-ba-zus.....72, 148, 149
Ar-ta-pher-nes.62, 63, 123–127
Ar-ta-xerx-es......71–85, 155
Ar-te-mis-i-a............245
Ar-sa-ces.............74, 292
Ar-sin-o-e...........289, 305
As-dru-bal..............370
Ash-dod...................27
As-pa-si-a...............175
As-pen-dus...............245
Ass-hur..........7, 13, 14, 35
As-syr-i-a........7–15, 26–39
As-ty-a-ges.........37–40, 85
As-y-chis..................25
Ath-ens...........36, 62–430
At-ta-lus............378, 430
At-ti-la.........337, 432, 433
At-tos-sa..........56, 57, 64
At-ro-pos..................93
Au-gus-tu-lus............430
Au-gus-tus......310, 399–404
Au-le-tes........297, 303, 304
Au-re-lius............419, 421
Au-ro-ra...................92
A-zo-tus..................27

Ba-bel.................7, 19
Bab-y-lon........8–15, 28–59
Bac-chus............260, 306
Bac-tri-a...........8, 72–267
Ba-go-as................83, 84
Bel-e-sis...............9, 10
Bel-shaz-zar.........14, 15, 49
Be-lus..............247, 258
Ber-e-ni-ce......291, 297–303
Bes-sus.............254–258
Bez-e-ta..................413
Bi-thyn-i-a..........184, 198
Bœ-o-tia.......70, 75, 89–218
Bo-re-as............187, 139
Bos-pho-rus.....60, 189, 427
Bras-i-das.......... 173, 174
Bren-nus............344–347
Brit-ain........ 418, 421, 426
Bri-tan-ni-cus...........408
Brun-du-si-um......390, 402
Bru-tus.....331–332, 388–401
Bu-ceph-a-lus...238, 252, 261
Bu-sen-ti-nus............431
Bu-si-ris.................20

By-zan-ti-um..80, 81, 153–427

Cad-me-ia........98, 209, 211
Cæ-sar......304–312, 388–398
C-æsar (Octavius)....399–405
Cai-ro..............19, 24, 81
Ca-lig-u-la..........407–416
Ca-lis-the-nes............259
Cal-lic-rat-i-das......192, 193
Cam-by-ses............30–85
Cam-pa-ni-a.....369, 374, 435
Ca-naan.....................7
Can-næ....................368
Cap-i-to-line.........314, 323
Cap-ræ-a..................412
Cap-u-a...................390
Car-a-cal-la..........422, 423
Car-thage............53–434
Cas-i-li-num.............367
Ca-si-num................367
Cas-san-der.........272–275
Cas-si-us............389–401
Cat-i-line................385
Cat-a-na.........177–179, 182
Ca-to.......285, 375, 389–396
Ce-dron...................413
Ce-phren-i-us..............24
Ce-rau-nus..........289, 290
Cer-be-rus.............93, 95
Ce-the-gus................386
Chal-ce-don......188–195, 207
Chal-chis.................284
Chal-cid-i-ce.........63, 208
Chal-de-a...............12–29
Cham-pol-lion.........20, 21
Char-i-de-mus...225, 242, 247
Char-i-la-us.............104, 105
Char-mi-on................312
Cha-ron..93, 95, 210, 211, 320
Cher-o-ne-a.......89, 205–241
Cher-so-ne-sus 61, 100,127–276
Chi-os..........184, 185, 191
Chit-tim..................301
Christ...............404, 428
Chry-sos..................118
Cic-e-ro.........386–400, 432
Ci-li-ci-a............9, 44, 76
Ci-mon..............153–162
Cin-cin-na-tus.......337, 338
Cin-e-as.........354, 355, 356
Cin-na....................381
Cir-rha..........118, 196–227
Ci-thæ-on............146, 147
Clau-di-us...........408, 409
Cle-ar-chus....75, 76, 78, 201
Cle-om-bro-tus......126, 209
Cle-om-e-nes........123–282
Cle-on..............172–175
Cle-o-pa-tra.........304–401
Clis-the-nes........123, 160
Cli-tus..............244, 258
Clo-tho....................99
Cly-tem-nes-tra.......99–104
Co-drus.........102, 109–114
Col-chis...........23, 99, 395
Col-la-ti-nus.........330–333
Col-os-se-um..............416
Com-mo-dus...............419
Co-non...............192–208
Con-stan-tine........426–428
Con-stan-ti-no-ple....426–434
Con-stan-ti-us.......425–432

Cor-cy-ra............155–171
Cor-inth............70–164
Co-ri-o-la-nus.......335–337
Cor-ne-lia.......302, 377–394
Co-ræ-bus.................108
Cras-sus............383–389
Cre-te.......90, 100, 105, 116
Cris-sa..............117-118
Crit-i-as............198–200
Crœ-sus...........14–48, 244
Cu-nax-a.............81, 201
Cu-ra-ti-i................326
Cur-ti-us.................351
Cy-ax-a-res......11, 37–51, 85
Cy-lon.............113, 166
Cyn-o-ceph-a-le......282, 373
Cyn-o-sar-ges.......130, 150
Cy-re-ni-us...............404
Cy-rus.......14, 15, 29, 34–50

Da-ci-a..............417, 418
Da-mas-cus................10
Dan-iel.......12–15, 250, 275
Dar-da-nus...............100
Da-ri-us I.............57–64
Da-ri-us II........73, 74, 185
Da-ri-us III..........84, 243
Da-tis...........63, 127, 130
Da-vid.....................12
De-ci-us..................352
De-jo-ces...........35, 36, 85
De-los..149, 161, 163, 168, 201
Del-phi........30, 69, 88–160
Dem-a-ra-tus....68, 125, 126
De-me-tri-us....282, 285, 286
De-me-tri-us I.......272–276
De-me-tri-us II.290, 294, 302
De-mos-the-nes I.172, 180–183
De-mos-the-nes II...225–270
Den-ta-tus..........338, 339
Deu-ca-li-on...............98
Di-a-na.................. 371
Did-i-us..................421
Di-do...............358, 434
Di-o-cle-si-an........425, 426
Di-og-e-nes...............234
Di-o-do-rus....20, 21, 73, 219
Di-o-nys-i-us....221, 297, 304
Di-o-me-des................92
Do-do-na..............96, 97
Do-mi-ti-an.........416, 420
Do-ri-ans........102, 159–223
Do-rus...............98, 101
Dra-co.............114, 115
Dru-sus................. 405
Du-il-li-us...............359
Dyr-rach-i-um..........391

Ec-ba-ta-na..... 35, 204, 254
E-ge-an.......58–67, 100–187
E-gi-na.........70, 136–169
E-gypt....................297
E-lam.....................35
E-la-te-a.................235
E-le-a-zar...........413, 414
E-lis...............215, 216
E-mil-i-us.......368, 374, 376
E-o-li-a............207, 267
E-o-lus..................94, 98
E-pam-in-on-das.....211–220
Ep-i-dam-nus........163, 164
Eph-e-sus........... 23–292

Ep*h*-o-ri....154, 188, 204–280
E-pip*h*-a-nes.........290–301
E-p*i*p-o-læ...........180–182
E-p*i*-rus..........88, 227–357
E-r*e*-tria................128
E-sar-ha*d*-don...........11
E-thi-*o*-pi-a 9–26, 53–55
E-to*l*-i-an...........281–292
E-tr*u*-ri-a...........331–362
Eu-b*œ*-a............225, 284
Eu-cl*i*-des................199
Eu-d*o*-cia.................434
Eu-d*ox*-i-a..........432, 434
Eu-er-ge-tes.........291–30
Eu-me-nes.........272–274
Eu-pa-tor...........290, 294
Eu-phr*a*-tes....7–66, 201–247
Eu-ri*p*-i-des.........183, 259
Eu-r*o*-tas..................214
Eu-ry-b*i*-a-des..141, 142, 143
Eu-ry*m*-e-don.......157–245
Eu-ry*s*-the-nes..104, 125, 126
Euxine (Yu*x*-in).........207
E-va*g*-o-ras...... ...195, 206
E-vil Mer-*o*-dach...14, 15, 39

F*a*-bi-us Ca-mi*l*-lus 343
F*a*-bi-us Ma*x*-i-mus......366
Fa-br*i*-ci-us.........356, 357
Fau*s*-tu-lus..............321
Flac-cus...................379
Fla-mi*n*-i-us.....283, 284, 373
Fl*o*-rus...................410
Franks.................424, 432
Fu*l*-vi-a.........306, 307, 402

Ga*l*-ba..........373, 411, 412
Ga-d*a*-tes 43, 49
Ga-le-ri-us 425, 426
Ga*l*-i-lee...........412, 415
Ga*l*-la....................429
Gal-li-*e*-nus...............424
Gaul........418, 422, 431, 432
G*a*-za.....................250
Ge-ne*s*-a-reth............415
Ge*n*-se-ric...........432, 434
Ge*r*-ma-ny......417, 423, 430
Ger-ma*n*-i-cus.......405, 406
G*e*-ta......................422
Go-bry-as..........43–58, 73
Go-mo*r*-rah................35
Go-n*a*-tus 277
Go*r*-di-um................245
Go*r*-di-us............ ...245
Goths.......... ...423–432
Grac-chus.......377, 378, 379
Gra*n*-i-cus.......84, 243, 258
Gr*a*-tian ... .429
Greece 87
Gry*l*-lus.................
Gy-li*p*-pus 179–184
Gis-ch*a*-la...............413

Hal-i-car-na*s*-sus.........245
Ham 7, 8, 19
Ha-mi*l*-car 363
Ha*n*-ni-bal 292, 363, 374
Har-m*o*-dius.........122, 253
He*c*-tor 101
He*l*-en..............99, 100
He*l*-i-con 88, 102
He-li-o-ga*b*-a-lus..........423
He-li-o*p*-o-lis......21, 23, 250
He*l*-len........24, 97, 98, 103
He*l*-le......................99
He*l*-las...........89, 215–273
Hel-les-pon*t*......... 60–191
H*e*-lot 108–111, 136–173
Her-a-cl*i*-dæ.........102, 280
He*r*-a-cli-dæ........102, 104
Her-cu-l*a*-ne-um... 415
He*r*-cu-les...28–110, 176–264
He*r*-od....................404
He-r*o*d-o-tus......16–73, 137
He*s*-i-od 90
Hez-e-k*i*-ah..........10, 11
H*i*-e-ro.............358, 370
Hi-em*p*-sal...............379
Hi*p*-p*a*r-chus........122, 127
Hi*p*-pi-as......62–64, 122–130
Hip-poc-ra-tes...........160
His-t*i*-æ-us........ 61, 62, 63
Ho*l*-land..................418
H*o*-mer...........24, 95–105
Ho-n*o*-ri-a...........432, 433
Ho-n*o*-ri-us.........429–432
Huns...................429–435
Hy-das-pes......260, 261, 263
Hyr-c*a*-ni-an.......42, 44, 73
Hy-pe*r*-bo-lus.............175
Hyr-c*a*-nius...............385
Hys-ta*s*-pes.....57, 58, 71, 72

I-do*m*-e-neus............100
I-lus, or I*l*-i-um.......67, 99
Il-ly*r*-i-a.........88, 224–240
I*n*-a-chus..................97
I*n*-a-rus..............72, 161
I*n*-di-a.........9–44, 251–267
I*n*-dus.........38–58, 61, 260
I-*o*-ni-a..............98–206
Ip*h*-i-tus...........102, 103
I*p*-sus......274–276, 289, 291
I*s*-ra-el.........10, 11, 26, 27
I-sis. 310
I-s*o*c-ra-tes...............221
I*s*-sus...............251, 252
I*t*-a-ly...............176–430
It*h*-a-ca....................100
I-tho-me....................214

J*a*-nus......325, 362, 404, 415
Jap*h*-eth................7, 97
J*a*-van..................7, 97
Ja*x*-ar-thes........... 257
J*u*-ba..................395, 396
J*u*-dah..............10, 25, 29
Ju-d*e*-a........10, 58, 293, 415
Ju-gu*r*-tha..........379, 380
J*u*-lia..................388, 389
J*u*-li-an....................428
J*u*-no........91, 103, 278–347
J*u*-pi-ter A*m*-mon.....9–108
J*u*-piter...................418
Je-h*o*-a-haz................28
Je-h*o*i-a-kim..........12–28
Jer-o-b*o*-am..............
Je-r*u*-sa-lem..........413, 428
Job...........................44
John..................413, 414
J*o*-nah........................9
J*o*-seph......................21
Jo-s*e*-phus........51, 249, 414
J*o*-vi-an....................428
La-bor-a*s*-oar-chod.....14–44
Lac*h*-e-sis....................93
La-c*o*-ni-a....... ...105–284
Lac-e-d*e*-mon 104–130
L*a*-gus......................298
La*m*-a-chus...............175
La*m*p-sa-cus..........194, 195
La-o*d*-i-ce.............. 291
Lat*h*-y-rus......297, 302, 303
Le*n*-tu-lus...............368, 386
Le-o*n*-i-das I.....68–125–151
Le-o*n*-idas II....... 280
Le-o-tyc*h*-i-das..125–149, 202
Le-on-*a*-tus................237
Le*p*-i-dus.......399, 400–402
Le*s*-bos.....184–207, 391, 393
Le-uc*t*-ra......... 89, 218–280
Li-ci*n*-i-an..................350
Li*v*-i-a.......................407
Li*v*-y..........................73
Lu-cr*e*-ti-a..........330, 331
Lu-cu*l*-lus............384, 435
Lu*x*-or........................21
Ly*b*-i-a...................22–72
Ly*c*-i-a.................245–293
Ly cu*r*-gus......104–121, 190
Ly*d*-i-a...........14, 37–267
Ly-sa*n*-der.......74, 190–205
Lys-a*n*-dra 289
Ly-si*m*-a-chus...272, 275, 289
L*o*-cris 186, 216, 274

Mac-e-d*o*-ni-a.....71, 131–229
Ma-cr*i*-nus..................423
Ma-na*s*-seh....................11
Man-d*a*ne..............38, 39
Ma*n*-li-us..............347–359
Man-ti-n*e*-a...........216–223
Ma*r*-a-thon 64–202
Mar-ce*l*-lus 362–369
Mar-d*o*-ni-us...........70–223
Ma*r*-cus 419
M*a*-ri-us 380
Mas-i-ni*s*-sa..................375
Ma*r*-ci-a......................419
Ma*x*-i-mus..............433, 434
M*e*-di-a................. 13–84
Medes..............11, 14, 33–51
Meg-a-b*y*-sus 59, 72, 161
Me*g*-a-cles..............113–166
Me*g*-a-ra....167, 169, 209, 273
Me*l*-i-tus......................200
M*e*-lon 210–211
Me*m*-phis......17–30, 52–251
Me*m*-non..................... 21
Men-e-l*a*-us.........24, 99, 100
M*e*-nes.....................17, 19
Me*n*-tor 83
Me*r*-cu-ry......................91
Me-sa*b*-a-tes 77, 81
Mes-s*e*-ni-a..........109–219
M*e*-shach......................12
Mes-o-po-t*a*-mi-a.267, 291, 389
Me-th*o*-ne 225–231
Mi-ci*p*-sa....................279
Mi-l*e*-tus......61–75, 124–245
Mil-t*i*-a-des......61, 127–160
Mi-ne*r*-va.............92–287
M*i*-nos.................94, 105
Mi*s*-ra-im.................7, 19
Mith-ri-d*a*-tes.........81, 380
Mn*e*-non..............74, 201

Mœ-ris 20, 26, 387
Mo-los-sus 155
Moors....................434
Mount Si-on.........413, 418
Mount A-cra............. 413
Mount of Ol-ives........ 413
Mount Et-na.............418
Mum-mi-us...............286
Mu-ti-us.................333
Myc-a-le,........132, 149, 150
My-cé-nae................136
Myn-da-rus...........187, 188

Na-bis..............283, 284
Na-bo-po-las-sar.11, 15, 28, 38
Na-hum 38
Ne-ar-chus......264, 265, 268
Neb-u-chad-nez-zar.....11-37
Ne-bros...................118
Ne-cho.........12, 28-31, 264
Ner-e-glis-sar..........14, 15
Nep-tune....92, 103, 149, 287
Ne-ro.......409-411, 412-418
Ner-va.................. 416
Ni-ca-tor.............290, 291
Nic-i-as..............172-188
Ni-ger..........419, 421, 422
Nim-rod...................8, 10
Nin-e-veh........7-14, 35-48
Ni-nus...........8, 9, 10, 247
Nin-y-as.......................9
No-ah......................7, 19
No-la......................495
No-thus......................74
Nu-bi-a............16, 19, 22
Nu-ma......324-326, 349-419
Nu-mi-tor 320, 321

Oc-ta-via.......306, 307, 402
Oc-ta-vius................399
O-chus..........73, 83, 84, 85
Od-e-na-tus 424
Od-o-a-cer 435
O-lym-pi-as..95-109, 134-273
O-lym-pus... 88-91, 102-231
O-lyn-thus..173-210, 223-232
O-res-tes 104-435
Or-phe-us 94
On-o-mar-chus......... .229
Op-pi-as 341
Os-sa.................88, 135
O-si-ris.........16, 17, 19, 25
Os-ti-a..............410, 434
Os-y-man-di-as........20, 54
O-ta-nes...............56, 57
O-tho...............409, 412
Ox-y-ar-tes 258

Pac-to-lus 48
Pal-la-dium............. 92
Pal-es-tine....12-28, 249-321
Pal-my-ra...........424, 425
Pam-phyl-i-a........157, 245
Pan-do-ra...................92
Pan-the-a..........43, 46, 48
Pan-the-on............. 90
Pan-ti-tes 140
Paph-la-go-ni-an.........246
Pa-ris............24, 99, 100
Par-nas-sian...88-91, 118, 140
Par-thi-a....292, 306, 397, 402
Par-thi-ans..........417-422
Par-y-sa-tis 78-41
Pa-ros 181
Par-a-lus....... 171, 195, 251
Par-e-to-ni-um...........250
Par-me-ni-o............231-259
Pat-ro-clus 422
Pau-lus..............286, 368
Pau-sa-ni-as.........126-155
Pa-vi-a............ 433, 435
Pe-las-gi....................97
Pe-li-on...............88, 139
Pe-lop-i-das..........210-224
Pe-lops...........98, 99, 101
Pel-o-pon-ne-sus 89-159
Pe-lu-si-um...21-52, 250, 310
Per-dic-cas...........223-275
Per-i-cles.......160-188, 228
Per-ga-mus.................378
Per-sep-o-lis....253, 264, 265
Per-se-us...........286, 374
Per-si-ans...............417-428
Per-ti-nax......419, 420, 421
Pe-træ-a....................386
Phal-e-rum........70, 130-152
Pha-ra-oh.............19, 25
Phar-na-ba-ces............74
Pha-ros....................299
Phar-na-ces........ 386, 395
Phar-ne-as.................376
Phar-sa-lia......391, 392, 395
Pha-yl-lus 229, 230
Phe-ni-ci-a........7, 12, 29-61
Phil-a-del-phus.......291-298
Phi-le-mon.................298
Phil-ip..............223-227
Phil-lip-pi...........226, 400
Phil-o-me-ter........297, 301
Phil-o-me-lus........228, 229
Phi-lo-pœ-men..282-285, 374
Phi-lop-a-ter.........290-300
Phi-lo-tas...........255, 256
Phli-us................ 136
Pho-cis.............88, 205, 266
Pho-ci-on...137-191, 227-230
Phy-li-das...........210, 211
Phœ-bi-das..........209, 227
Phra-or-tes........... 36, 85
Phryg-i-an 98-246
Phryx-us.....................99
Phys-con........297, 301, 302
Pi-ræ-us.............150-189
Pi-sid-i-an....................75
Pi-sis-tra-ti-dæ..121, 123, 160
Pi-sis-tra-tus.........120-127
Pi-so........................406
Pi-thom.......................21
Pla-cid-i-a............431, 432
Pla-te-a.......88, 89, 129-153
Pla-to............198, 220, 221
Plau-cus....................306
Plis-tar-chus 126
Plis-the-nes 99
Plis-to-nax................ 145
Plu-tarch...136, 219, 390-417
Plu-to..............93-95, 138
Po-li-or-ce-tes 275
Pol-lux..................99, 259
Pol-y-carp 419
Po..........................430
Po-lyb-i-us.................285
Po-lys-per-chon.....272-274
Pom-pe-ii 415
Pom-pey........384, 388-394
Pom-pey (Sextus)........402
Pom-pil-i-us 378
Pon-ti-us....................346
Pop-pæ-a.............409, 410
Por-sen-na 333
Po-rus..........260, 261, 263
Pot-i-dæ-a.......165-174, 209
Po-tiph-e-ra 21
Prex-as-pes........55, 56, 57
Pri-am..............100, 101
Pro-bus 424
Præ-tors.....................318
Pro-cles.........104, 125, 126
Pro-me-the-us 92
Pro-pon-tis......... 153, 243
Prop-y-læ-a................150
Pro-te-us 24
Prox-e-nus..................201
Pryt-a-nes 235
Psam-me-ni-tus.30, 31, 52, 53
Psam-met-i-chus...27, 28, 31
Psam-mis.................29, 31
Ptol-e-my.............271-298
Pub-lic-o-la.............333, 336
Pul.............................9
Pyd-na..........155, 225-273
Pyr-e-nees 432
Pyth-i-a....118, 124, 133, 135
Pyr-rhus....276-278, 353-355
Py-thag-o-ras..............124
Py-thon......................91
Py-thon-ess...........69, 96

Quæs-tors 318
Quin-de-cem-vi-ri.........316
Quin-ti-us......282, 283, 337
Qui-ri-tes...........319, 323

Rav-en-na...........430, 433
Ra-ma-ses................ 21
Reg-u-lus 359-362
Re-ho-bo-am.................25
Re-mus 321-322
Rhad-a-man-thus.........94
Rhe-a Sil-vi-a..............320
Rhe-gi-um......112, 176, 214
Rhine........................432
Rho-di-an....83, 113, 252, 282
Rome 314
Rom-u-lus...314-349, 427-435
Rox-a-na...223, 258, 269, 270, 271, 273, 274
Ru-bi-con 390

Sab-a-chus 25
Sa-gun-tum 363
Said 20
Sal-a-mis 70, 114-146
Sal-ma-nas-er...............10
Sa-lem.......................415
Sa-ma-ri-a 10
Sam-ni-tes............351-358
Sa-mos.........191, 192, 197
Sa-por........................424
Sar-dan-a-pa-lus.9, 10, 11, 246
Sar-a-cus..............11, 38
Sa-ron-ic....................142
Scip-i-o..............365, 395
Scy-lax.......................61
Scyth-i-a..............37-430
Se-ja-nus 406

Se-leu-ci-dæ.....275, 290, 291
Se-leu-cus..........272–303
Sel-eu-ci-a..............422
Se-mir-a-mis.....8, 9, 13, 424
Sen-e-ca 410
Sen-na-che-rib......10, 11, 26
Sep-tim-i-us............394
Se-ra-pis...............422
Ser-vi-us...........328, 329
Se-sos-tris.........21, 22, 23
Ses-tos.................194
Se-ve-rus........419, 421, 422
Sex-tus.................330
Shad-rach.................12
Shem.....................7, 35
Shi-shak..................25
Sic-il-y............418, 431
Si-don..........29, 248, 249
Sic-y-on......89, 97, 278, 307
Sic-ci-us...............338
Si-lo-am 413
Si-mon.............413, 415
Si-on 413
Sis-y-gam-bis........255, 269
Smer-dis....55, 56, 57, 58, 85
Soc-ra-tes....79, 175, 193–221
Sod-om....................30
Sog-di-a-na....73, 85, 254–258
Sol-o-mon........12, 25, 414
So-lon.......30, 199, 220, 339
Soph-ro-nis-cus..........200
Spain........94, 178, 363–432
Spar-ta 64–123
Spho-dri-as..............212
Spi-tam-e-nes........... 258
Sta-gi-ra 237
Sta-ti-ra I..........75, 81, 82
Sta-ti-ra II......265, 269, 271
Stry-mon............71, 149
Su-sa....................267
Su-ni-um 70
Su-si-a-na 43, 44, 292
Syl-la..............380, 422
Syr-a-cuse 358
Syr-i-a..............10–424

Tac-i-tus.........73, 415–425
Tan-a-quil...........327–329

Tan-gier.................432
Tan-ta-lus.................99
Tar-quin I............325-327
Tar-quin II...........328–339
Ta-ren-tum.....357, 358, 370
Tar-sus.........246, 305, 401
Tar-ta-rus.................90
Ta-ti-us 323, 324
Ta-yg-e-tus..............158
Te-ge-ans................149
Tel-lus.................. 119
Tem-pe..............88, 135
Ter-mi-nus...............325
Thap-sa-cus 251
Thap-sus.................395
Theb-a-is.................19
The-bes 19–209
The-mis-to-cles.......70–188
The-o-do-si-us.......426–434
Ther-am-e-nes.......193–198
Ther-mop-y-læ.68–98,126–205
The-se-us..................95
Thes-pi-ans.....136, 138, 241
Thes-sa-ly.....70–98, 100–217
Thes-sa-lo-ni-ca......271–275
Thrace 289
Thra-ci-ans..........28–230
Thras-y-bu-lus.......192–207
Thras-y-me-nus 366
Thym-bria............44–45
Thu-cyd-i-des.......122–183
Ti-ber 423–434
Ti-be-ri-us 405–407
Ti-cin-i-um..............372
Ti-gra-nes 384
Ti-gris 8, 38, 267, 417
Ti-man-dra 198
Tis-sa-pher-nes74–82, 184–202
Tir-i-ba-zus.........207, 208
Ti-thraus-tes.............205
Ti-tus..............282–434
To-ro-ne............209, 224
Tra-jan.........417, 418, 430
Trip-o-li.................432
Tro-pho-ni-us..............96
Troy 92–101, 243–343
Tul-lia...................329
Tul-li-us............325, 328

Tul-lus..............335–337
Tyn-da-rus...........99, 100
Ty-re......12, 58, 61, 248–358

U-cho-re-us................20
U-lys-ses.........92, 94, 100

Va-le-ri-an..............424
Va-le-ri-us 331, 332, 333
Va-lens 429
Van-dals........419, 430–434
Var-ro 368
Ve-i-ans.........324, 333, 343
Ve-i-i.............. 343–349
Ve-nus............24, 92, 95
Ven-ice..................433
Ves-pa-si-an.........412–415
Ve-su-vi-us..............415
Ve-tu-ri-a...............336
Vi-en-na 419
Vir-gin-i-a..........340, 341
Vir-gin-i-us.............340
Vi-tel-li-us......411, 412, 415
Vol-sci-i............330–338
Vul-can............26, 27, 92

Wallia...................431

Xan-thip-pus....131, 149–160
Xan-tip-pe...............200
Xerxes I.........64, 71, 131
Xerxes II..................78
Xen-o-phon...48–81, 198–218
Xu-ther 98

York...............422, 426

Za-cyn-thus..............172
Za-ma 378
Zan-cle..................112
Zech-a-ri-ah...............58
Zed-e-ki-ah...........12, 29
Ze-no-bi-a...........424, 425
Zeph-y-rus 92
Ze-rah 251
Zop-y-rus.............59, 72
Zor-o-as-ter...........82, 84
Zo-ro-ba-bel...............51

www.ingramcontent.com/pod-product-compliance
Lightning Source LLC
LaVergne TN
LVHW021130110826
845150LV00005B/984
9781425549893